Generativity and Adult Development

Generativity and Adult Development

How and Why We Care for the Next Generation

Edited by

Dan P. McAdams
Ed de St. Aubin

American Psychological Association
Washington, DC

Published by
American Psychological Association
750 First Street, NE
Washington, DC 20002

Copies may be ordered from
APA Order Department
P.O. Box 92984
Washington, DC 20090-2984

In the UK and Europe, copies may be ordered from
American Psychological Association
3 Henrietta Street
Covent Garden, London
WC2E 8LU England

Typeset in Goudy by EPS Group Inc., Easton, MD

Printer: Data Reproductions Corporation, Auburn Hills, MI
Cover Designer: Minker Design, Bethesda, MD
Technical/Production Editor: Catherine R. W. Hudson

Library of Congress Cataloging-in-Publication Data
Generativity and adult development : how and why we care for the next generation
  / edited by Dan P. McAdams and Ed de St. Aubin.—1st ed.
     p.   cm.
     Includes bibliographical references and indexes.
     ISBN 1-55798-470-0 (acid-free paper)
     1. Adulthood—Psychological aspects.   2. Children and adults.   3. Social psy-
chology.   I. McAdams, Dan P.   II. de St. Aubin, Ed
BF724.5.G46   1998
155.6—dc21   97-32831
                                                                                          CIP

British Library Cataloguing-in-Publication Data
A CIP record is available from the British Library.

Printed in the United States of America
First Edition

For Ruth, Amanda, and Shawn Laree

CONTENTS

CONTRIBUTORS

Andrew M. Boxer is director and co-founder of the Evelyn Hooker Center for Gay and Lesbian Mental Health, and he is assistant professor in the Department of Psychiatry at the University of Chicago. His current research includes a program of study on psychosocial development across the life course of gay men and lesbians. He is co-author (with Gilbert Herdt) of *Children of Horizons: How Gay and Lesbian Teens Are Leading a New Way out of the Closet* (1996).

Peter Yuichi Clark is a doctoral candidate in religion at Emory University in Atlanta and is chaplain at Emory University Hospital. An ordained minister in the American Baptist Churches (U.S.A.), he has written for *Pastoral Psychology*, *The Journal of Pastoral Care*, *Religion and the Arts*, and *The American National Biography* (Oxford University Press, in press). His research focuses on the connections among aging, ethnicity, and spirituality among Asian Americans and the interreligious dialogue between Buddhists and Christians.

Bertram J. Cohler is the William Rainey Harper Professor in the College of the University of Chicago and professor in the departments of psychology (Committee on Human Development) and psychiatry. He has written widely in the areas of adult development and the life course. His present work focuses on the ways in which people make sense of adversity across the course of life and the impact of misfortune on the life story.

Lee Ann De Reus is assistant professor in the Department of Human Development and Family Studies at the Pennsylvania State University, Altoona. Her research interests include women's adult development, family stress and coping, and family poverty.

Ed de St. Aubin is assistant professor of human development and psychology at the University of Wisconsin, Green Bay. His research interests are in the area of life-span developmental psychology, with a particular focus on generativity, life narrative, and the development of personal ideology.

David C. Dollahite is associate professor of family sciences at Brigham Young University and a clinical member of the American Association for Marriage and Family Therapy. He has published widely in the areas of family therapy and fathering. He is co-editor of *Generative Fathering: Beyond Deficit Perspectives* and a co-producer of the award-winning web site *Fatherwork: Stories, Ideas, and Activities to Encourage Generative Fathering* (http://fatherwork.byu.edu).

Carol E. Franz is the research coordinator at the Center for Health Services Research in Primary Care at the University of California Davis Medical Center. Her primary interests and publications are in life-course development and midlife adulthood, viewed from the perspectives of both qualitative and quantitative assessment approaches. She is co-editor (with Abigail J. Stewart) of a book of case studies on women's lives: *Women Creating Lives: Identities, Resilience, and Resistance* (Westview Press, 1994).

Holly M. Hart is currently a postdoctoral fellow at the Foley Center for the Study of Lives, Northwestern University. Her research interests are in adult development and aging, with a focus on generativity and wisdom.

Alan J. Hawkins is an associate professor of family sciences and director of the Center for Studies of the Family at Brigham Young University. He has published widely on the topic of father involvement and generativity. He is co-author of *Generative Fathering: Beyond Deficit Perspectives* and co-producer of the award-winning web site *Fatherwork: Stories, Ideas, and Activities to Encourage Generative Fathering* (http://fatherwork.byu.edu).

Andrew J. Hostetler is a doctoral student in the Committee on Human Development at the University of Chicago. His research interests include studies of gay and lesbian lives, particularly across the second half of life.

Avi Kay is an assistant professor in the Department of Psychology, Touro College, Jerusalem. His research interests are in adult development, generativity, and the lives of Holocaust survivors.

Corey Lee M. Keyes is assistant professor in the Department of Sociology and the Rollins School of Public Health, Emory University.

Dr. Keyes is a social psychologist and an associate of the John D. and Catherine T. MacArthur Foundation Research Network on Successful Midlife Development. His research focuses on the self-concept, aging, and mental health and well-being.

John Kotre is professor of psychology at the University of Michigan, Dearborn. He is creator of the Public Broadcasting System series *Seasons of Life* and author of six books on life-historical subjects. Two of his books—*Outliving the Self: How We Live on in Future Generations* and *White Gloves: How We Create Ourselves through Memory*—have recently been issued in paperback by Norton.

Kathy B. Kotre is a doctoral candidate in psychology and social work at the University of Michigan and a therapist in private practice in Ann Arbor. Along with John Kotre, she is the recipient of the 1991 American Psychological Association National Award for Excellence in Media (Radio).

Susan A. Lee is professor in the School of Speech at Northwestern University with a joint appointment in the School of Education and Social Policy. She is also founding director of the Center for Interdisciplinary Research in the Arts and of the dance program in the theater department at Northwestern. Dr. Lee has published extensively in the areas of psychology and dance, artists' lives, and women in authority.

Shelley M. MacDermid is associate professor and director of the Center for Families in the School of Consumer and Family Sciences at Purdue University. Her research interests focus on relationships between work conditions and family life (particularly in small workplaces) and on adult development during midlife. The Groves Conference on Marriage and Family recently honored Dr. MacDermid with its Feldman Award for work pertaining to families in the field of sex roles.

Shadd Maruna is a doctoral candidate in human development and social policy at Northwestern University and a fellow of the University of Chicago/Northwestern University Poverty Institute. A recent recipient of both a Fulbright Grant and a Guggenheim Fellowship, Mr. Maruna has been working in Liverpool, England, on a project examining how and why chronic juvenile delinquents are able to break away from criminal behavior.

Dan P. McAdams is the Charles Deering McCormick Professor of Teaching Excellence and professor of human development and psychology at Northwestern University. His research interests are in adult personality development, with a focus on generativity and adult identity as a life story. He is the author of *Power, Intimacy, and the Life Story* (1985), *The Stories We Live By* (1993), and *The Person: An Introduction to Personality Psychology* (1994).

Gerald F. Moran is professor of history in the Department of Social Sciences at the University of Michigan, Dearborn. His areas of scholarly interest are early American social and religious history and the history of the family, education, childhood, and youth. Dr. Moran's most recent publications include a book, co-authored with Maris Vinovskis, titled *Religion, Family, and the Life Course: Explorations in the Social History of Early America* (University of Michigan Press).

Bill E. Peterson is assistant professor of psychology at Smith College. He has also worked as a faculty member at the University of New Hampshire and Pomona College. Dr. Peterson's research interests and recent publications focus on adult personality development, generativity, and the psychology of authoritarianism.

Carol D. Ryff is a professor in the Department of Psychology and Interim Director of the Institute on Aging in Adult Life at the University of Wisconsin, Madison. She has published widely in the areas of adult personality and conceptions of psychological adaptation and well-being.

Brent D. Slife is professor of psychology at Brigham Young University, where he holds joint appointments in the theoretical psychology and clinical psychology programs. He is editor of the *Journal of Theoretical and Philosophical Psychology*. Dr. Slife's most recent books include *Time and Psychological Explanation* (SUNY Press, 1993) and *What's Behind Research? Discovering Hidden Assumptions in the Behavioral Sciences* (Sage, 1995).

John Snarey is professor of human development and ethics at Emory University (Atlanta) and the author of *How Fathers Care for the Next Generation* (Harvard University Press, 1993). He has been the recipient of the James D. Moran Award for Exceptional Research in Family Relations and Child Development from the American Association of Family and Consumer Sciences and of the Outstanding Human Development Research Award from the American Educational Research Association. His theoretical interests center on the works of Lawrence Kohlberg and Carol Gilligan, Erik Erikson and Bernice Neugarten, and William James. His current research focuses on sociomoral and psychosocial development during adulthood.

Abigail J. Stewart is professor of psychology and women's studies and director of the Institute for Research on Women and Gender at the University of Michigan. She was awarded the Distinguished Faculty Achievement Award there and the Henry A. Murray Award from the American Psychological Association for research in personality and the study of lives. Her primary research interests are personality development and psychological responses to change, especially social change.

Elizabeth A. Vandewater is currently a postdoctoral fellow at the Program in Social Research on Aging at the University of Michigan. She is the author of several articles on women's adult development and aging, including examinations of social role commitments, role quality, personality, and well-being.

Jerome C. Wakefield is professor in the School of Social Work and in the Institute for Health, Health Care Policy, and Aging Research, both at Rutgers University. He is also lecturer in the Department of Psychiatry, College of Physicians and Surgeons of Columbia University. Dr. Wakefield writes about the conceptual foundations of the mental health professions. His recent work has focused on the validity of *DSM-IV* diagnostic criteria and especially the problem of distinguishing normal suffering from mental disorder in clinical diagnosis and epidemiological surveys.

FOREWORD

ROBERT COLES

During the middle and late 1960s I taught in Erik Erikson's under-graduate course and took a graduate seminar he gave. I was in my 30s, a child psychiatrist who had gone astray, as it were. I had happened upon the civil rights struggle in the South and become a participant in it as well as a worker in the field, making home and school visits to learn how desegregation affected the Black and White children caught in its midst. It was Erikson, actually, who helped me come back to the psychoanalytic psychiatry in which I had been trained—we corresponded and we met, and then we worked together. Eventually, I would be asked to write a profile of him for *The New Yorker*, and that effort enabled me to have many conversations with this much-revered psychoanalytic theorist, who had the knack of connecting his ideas to the concrete particulars of everyday life, and who, as well, wrote with clarity and eloquence.

As I read the various chapters that make up this book—in their sum, a salute to Erikson, the developmental psychologist—I remembered a con-versation Erikson and I had about the very subject matter examined so carefully and thoroughly in the pages ahead. I was sitting in Erikson's study in his summer home, at Cotuit, on Cape Cod, and he spoke of the "psy-chology of creativity" with a good deal of obvious interest and no small amount of intellectual passion:

> Some of us who have spent our lives tracing things back in the lives of our patients have forgotten to look at what they've accomplished in life, no matter the odds against them, and [have also forgotten to look at] what we ourselves are doing in the daily course of our work. After all, many people who go into analysis—as future analysts or as troubled patients—have managed to be rather worthwhile individuals, maybe even quite creative and productive. Yes, we all have our problems—but it is not very accurate for us to emphasize psychopa-thology to the exclusion of the truth that stares you in in the face:

what people have managed to accomplish in their personal or profes-sional lives, sometimes an enormous amount, for all their worries and fears and difficulties.

He stopped, and I asked him when he first began to think in the way he had just spoken. He smiled, then offered this:

> It's almost common sense (it *is* common sense)—what I just said. But sometimes we lose track of that. We get all caught up in something important, but we allow ourselves to forget the proverbial "larger pic-ture." Anna Freud [his analyst and teacher] once told me how impor-tant it is to go back and forth, back and forth, between the contem-porary life of an analysand and his or her past life. She was anxious for us to make connections between the two. But it's important that we know what we're connecting—so we have to study "adulthood" as well as childhood, and be as serious with our examination of "gener-ativity" as we are with those earlier [developmental] stages.

Soon enough, he was being "serious"—expanding on what *generativity* meant to him, to all of us as men and women who try to find some meaning in this life and try to affirm what we have discovered through our deeds. In so doing, I noticed, he emphasized not only what takes place in our minds, but the impact of the world around us on our thinking, the coming together of place and time and individual experience: all of us creatures alive at a particular moment, immersed in a particular society in a partic-ular way (class and race as ever so significant) and possessed of a particular life's memories and shaping encounters (the family as the first society we get to know). Moreover, he was at pains then to mention certain men and women whose lives clearly exemplify the generativity he was postulating —and not only artists or well-known political figures. For him generativity was by no means a synonym for creativity, an assumption all too readily made by some of us who reside in the upper precincts of the bourgeoisie. I had told Erikson some stories of civil rights activitists I had met in the rural South, many of them middle-aged men and women who had dared risk their quite vulnerable lives in order to stand up against sheriffs by no means reluctant to club and shoot those Blacks arrogant enough (*crazy* enough) to claim the right to vote. "Generativity can be found in an artist's studio, a writer's study," Erikson observed, "or on the steps of a county courthouse in the rural South." Many of us, then, trying to connect our experiences in that rural South with our knowledge of psychoanalytic the-ory, were grateful for such an observation—itself an aspect of a most thoughtful analyst's generativity.

This book also shines with Erikson's generativity. The chapters reflect and illustrate and attest to his ideas in all their suggestive, compelling authority. In his own way, he rescued psychoanalysis from the reductionist folly, enabled many of us to understand our progress through life as something more than the endlessly repetitive enactments of childhood memories and events. Moreover, in his own work (the biographical studies of Luther and Gandhi) he showed how each of us can hand one another along. Those studies harken back respectfully to Freud, yet give his ideas a new amplification and language and provide another way of seeing things. Now, the psychologists who appear in this book do likewise. They call on Erikson, yet extend his vision by bringing it into new territory and building on its insights. Both are measures of gratitude and respect; surely sentiments that those who read the pages ahead will also feel toward both Erikson and these psychological heirs of his.

INTRODUCTION

Adulthood teaches that although people do not live forever, we do live on through others. A signal realization of middle age, wrote Erik Erikson, is that "I am what survives me" (1968, p. 141). There is a continuity to human life and identity that is both biological and cultural. Human beings reproduce. In a literal sense, offspring carry forward the substance of their progenitors, and in a rich variety of cultural forms, human beings create, care for, and contribute people, ideas, traditions, products, and outcomes that outlive the self to become legacies for generations to come.

I am what survives me. I am my children, in their manifold incarnations: my sons and daughters, students, and protégés; the babies I care for in the nursery where I work; the kids on the Little League team I coach; the parishioners in the church I serve; but also the business I started, the neighbors I helped (and hurt), the institutions I influenced (for good and for ill), the organizations for which I volunteered, the poems I wrote, the quilt I made, the jokes I told, the words of advice I gave, the examples I set for others, my reputations, how others think of me, how others will remember me. As adults, we all *generate* legacies, even unwittingly so. We all find ourselves caring for and contributing to the next *generation*, even if the contributions are tiny, indirect, or negative, and even though we never know, and can never know, what impact our efforts will have in the long time that is ahead of us. As adults, we all come to know the challenges, rewards, and frustrations of *generativity*.

This book is about generativity and its central place in adult lives. Over 40 years ago, Erikson (1950) introduced the concept of generativity in his landmark theory of the human life cycle. According to Erikson, "generativity vs. stagnation" is the psychosocial centerpiece of the seventh of eight stages of human life—the stage loosely associated with the middle-adult years. Generativity vs. stagnation follows the early-adult stages of "identity vs. role confusion" (Stage 5) and "intimacy vs. isolation" (Stage

6). As Erikson taught, once the adult has consolidated a sense of who he or she is (identity) and established long-term bonds of intimacy through marriage, friendships, or both, he or she is psychosocially ready to make a commitment to the larger sphere of society as a whole and its continuation, even improvement, through the next generation.

From Erikson's point of view, generativity may be expressed in bearing and raising children. Many adults find their most rewarding, as well as most frustrating, expressions of generativity in their efforts to conceive children to begin with and to feed, clothe, protect, provide for, nurture, guide, discipline, educate, advise, and eventually "let go of" their own children. Indeed there may be no more important expression of generativity than that which is directed at one's own children. However, the concept of generativity is not limited to parenthood. One may be generative in a wide variety of life pursuits and in a vast array of life settings, as in work life and professional activities, volunteer endeavors, participation in religious and political organizations, neighborhood and community activism, friendships, and even leisure-time pursuits. Indeed, generativity shares meanings with concepts like "creativity" and "leadership." Some of Erikson's most compelling examples of generativity appear in his psychobiographical explorations of the lives of such creative leaders as Martin Luther (Erikson, 1958) and Mahatma Gandhi (Erikson, 1969), both of whom appear to have been their most generative in the bright light of public action rather than in the private realm of friends and family.

At its core, *generativity* is the concern for and commitment to promoting the next generation, through parenting, teaching, mentoring, and generating products and outcomes that aim to benefit youth and foster the development and well-being of individuals and social systems that will outlive the self. In their roles as parents, teachers, coaches, mentors, leaders, helpers, and volunteers, generative adults serve as norm bearers and destiny shapers in families, schools, churches, neighborhoods, and the workplace. From a *psychological* standpoint, generativity is experienced as both an inner desire and an age-appropriate demand whose successful engagement or resolution may enhance the generative adult's well-being and adaptation. From the standpoint of *society and culture*, generativity is a critical resource that may undergird social institutions, encourage citizens' contributions and commitments to the public good, motivate efforts to sustain continuity from one generation to the next, and initiate social change.

In both its private and public manifestations, generativity draws adults out of their self-preoccupations and connects them to other people, institutions, and even societal and global concerns that are deemed worthy of one's care, investment, and contribution. Not only adults themselves—individuals who may or may not seek to be generative in their daily lives —but institutions, too, and communities and even societies writ large may be understood with respect to their collective generativity. In *The Good Society*, sociologist Robert Bellah and his colleagues argued that contemporary society in the United States may be experiencing something of a crisis with respect to

> what the psychologist Erik Erikson called "generativity," the care that one generation gives the next. Generativity is the virtue that Erikson initially situates in the concern of parents for children, but he extends it far beyond the family so that it becomes the virtue by means of which we care for all persons and things we have been entrusted with. What kind of society will we endow our children and our children's children, what kind of world, what kind of natural environment? By focusing on our immediate well-being (are you better off than you were four years ago?), and by being obsessively concerned with improving our relative income and consumption, we have forgotten that the meaning of life derives not so much from what we have as from what kind of person we are and how we have shaped our lives toward future ends that are good in themselves. (Bellah, Madsen, Sullivan, Swidler, & Tipton, 1991, p. 274)

Bellah calls on U.S. citizens and their leaders to embrace a "politics of generativity," through which we may be able to "anchor our economic and political institutions firmly in the moral discourse of citizens concerned about the common good and the long run" (p. 279). Although they may find it difficult to express clearly their feelings, many people in the United States are indeed concerned about the common good and the long run, Bellah maintains. Their desires, concerns, beliefs, and commitments to and about generativity can still be heard, even amidst the cacophony of individualism and consumerism decried by so many observers of contemporary society.

Both as a psychological phenomenon and as a societal concern, generativity is a rich and multifaceted idea that appears to have profound implications for adult development, mental health and well-being, counseling and psychotherapy, the functioning of the family, education, religious belief and worship, political involvement, volunteerism, and citizenship. Despite its theoretical richness and pervasive psychosocial relevance, however, generativity has not been the subject of much social–scientific attention until quite recently. It is true that a handful of scholars such as Bernice Neugarten (1968), Daniel Levinson (1978), and George Vaillant (1977) used Erikson's concept of generativity in their influential expositions of adult development. However, it has only been within the past 10 years or so that researchers and theorists have begun to examine closely the meanings and manifestations of generativity. One of the first to do so was John Kotre (1984), whose book *Outliving the Self* was perhaps the first to extend and modify the line of theorizing begun by Erikson and explicitly illustrate the workings and the dilemmas of generativity in intensive case studies of adult lives. Since then, a number of researchers have launched important empirical investigations of generativity from both psychological and sociological perspectives. Theorists have begun to elaborate the construct further, revealing a host of interesting conceptual dilemmas that may not be apparent from a first reading of Erikson, and clinicians, counselors, and social workers have begun to import the concept of generativity into their work.

The central aim of our volume is to bring together the most creative thinking and the most informative research being done today on the psychological, social, and cultural aspects of generativity in adult lives. The contributors are theorists, researchers, and practitioners who are currently making the most significant impact on the understanding of generativity. Our distinguished list draws from the fields of developmental and life-span psychology, personality and social psychology, clinical and counseling psychology, sociology, history, philosophy, and the arts. This interdisciplinary volume includes an unusually large and varied assortment of social-scientific discourses. We include reports of recent empirical research, theoretical expositions, case studies, psychobiographical explorations of successes and failings in generativity, discussions of generativity in counseling and therapy, and a historical analysis of generativity in U.S. society.

We have grouped the chapters into three large sections. The first includes theory and research focused primarily on the psychology of generativity, with particular focus on developmental issues. The volume's second section includes chapters that more explicitly consider generativity in the broad contexts of society, culture, and history. The third section groups together innovative applications of the concept of generativity in case biographies and in counseling and psychotherapy. Taken together, the chapters in this volume attest to the rising ferment of scholarly activity that has surrounded the concept of generativity in recent years, yielding striking empirical findings concerning the developmental course of generativity and its role in mental health and well-being; providing fresh theoretical insights about the many different facets and permutations of generativity in adult lives and explaining how generativity is contoured through culture and history; and raising difficult new questions about conflict, narcissism, ambivalence, and cost in generativity and adult development.

Generativity and Adult Development is a book for psychologists of many stripes, including researchers, theorists, and clinicians. It is a book that should appeal, as well, to sociologists, anthropologists, and other social scientists interested in the nature of the human life cycle, in the relation between adult lives and social institutions, and in such topics as volunteerism, political and religious participation, and citizenship. It is also a book for those many adults in the "helping professions"—ministers, rabbis, social workers, teachers, and counselors—whose daily efforts to intervene in the lives of others in a beneficial way are prime examples of the drive to generativity. Most generally this is a book for the many people who have ever worried about or struggled with their own efforts to care for and contribute to the next generation, in ways both small and large. As editors, we like to think of this volume itself in generative terms, hoping that it will touch others in meaningful ways and make some modest and positive contribution to the confusing world wherein we all live. Indeed, we have found our collaboration on this book about generativity to be extraordinarily rewarding from the beginning, and we think that this is partly due to the nature of the topic we have chosen.

We, the editors, owe a great debt of thanks to each of the distinguished and highly generative scholars who contributed chapters to this volume. It is perhaps a testament to the old adage that social scientists often study themselves that we found working with this group of generativity experts so satisfying. We wonder if editors of books on "sociopathy" and "paranoid delusions" enjoy their collaborations so much! In addition, we would like to thank all the people who served as chapter reviewers and who provided other substantive commentary for the volume as a whole for their generative efforts. They are Pamela Adelmann, Jim Anderson, Ted Baroody, Alan Elms, Ravenna Helson, Ruthellen Josselson, Gary Kenyon, Eric Knowles, Richard Logan, Dan Mroczek, Barbara Newman, Alice Rossi, Mac Runyan, Peggy Schlegel, Jefferson Singer, Avril Thorne, and Paul Wink. We offer special thank-yous to our wives, Rebecca Pallmeyer and Shawn Laree de St. Aubin, for their emotional support and patience throughout. We thank the Spencer Foundation, whose grant to Dan P. McAdams helped support the preparation of this volume. Finally, we are pleased to thank the Foley Family Foundation and Dr. Jeanne M. Foley for their dissertation award to Ed de St. Aubin and for their continued support of research on generativity and adult development through the establishment of the Foley Center for the Study of Lives at Northwestern University.

DAN P. MCADAMS
Northwestern University

ED DE ST. AUBIN
University of Wisconsin, Green Bay

REFERENCES

Bellah, R. N., Madsen, R., Sullivan, W. M., Swidler, A., & Tipton, S. M. (1991). *The good society*. New York: Knopf.

Erikson, E. H. (1950). *Childhood and society*. New York: Norton.

Erikson, E. H. (1958). *Young man Luther: A study in psychoanalysis and history*. New York: Norton.

Erikson, E. H. (1968). *Identity: Youth and crisis*. New York: Norton.

Erikson, E. H. (1969). *Gandhi's truth: On the origins of militant nonviolence*. New York: Norton.

Kotre, J. (1984). *Outliving the self: Generativity and the interpretation of lives*. Baltimore: Johns Hopkins University Press.

Levinson, D. J. (1978). *The seasons of a man's life*. New York: Knopf.

Neugarten, B. L. (Ed.). (1968). *Middle age and aging*. Chicago: University of Chicago Press.

Vaillant, G. E. (1977). *Adaptation to life*. Boston: Little, Brown.

I

THE PSYCHOLOGY OF GENERATIVITY: THEORY AND RESEARCH

INTRODUCTION

Each of the five chapters that compose Part 1 of this book focuses on the *generative individual* as he or she moves through the adult years. The authors present theory and research addressing the psychology of generativity in human lives. They provide conceptual clarification and empirical evidence for the existence of several facets of individual generativity and for the changing composition of one's generativity over time. These investigations into the nature and vicissitudes of generativity at the level of the individual human being lay the foundation for the chapters in Part 2 (Generativity in Society, Culture, and History), which examine the embeddedness of generativity within the sociohistorical context, and for those in Part 3 (Applications: Generativity in Biography and Therapy), which explore the manifestations, transformations, and rehabilitations of generativity in particular lives experienced within specific contexts.

In "The Anatomy of Generativity" (chapter 1), Dan McAdams, Holly Hart, and Shadd Maruna draw from the theory-based and multimethod research agenda that McAdams and his colleagues have been conducting over the past decade. These authors anatomize the concept of generativity to investigate its several components. The result of this concept dissection is a seven-faceted model of generativity that has generated several empirical investigations by McAdams's Northwestern University research cadre and others. This model of generativity, which serves as the cornerstone of chapter 1, captures the motivational sources, cognitive aspects, and behavioral manifestations of generativity as well as the meaning that generativity provides to one's narrative understanding of self. McAdams, Hart, and Maruna present an extensive theory of generativity, yet the chapter is empirically grounded in that the authors outline research that quantifies individual differences in several aspects of generativity, that examines the age–cohort developmental trends of generativity, and that relates genera-

3

tivity to behavioral patterns (social involvements and parenting styles) and other aspects of personality (traits, motives, and well-being). The significance that generativity plays in one's self-defining life story is captured in discussions of the "commitment" stories that characterize the narrative identities of highly generative individuals and the generative "stories of reform" related by ex-criminals. Narrative is employed as both a theoretical construct and a methodological technique. Generativity narration, the meaning one gives to generativity in one's life story of personal identity, is one of the seven features of the model, and the content analysis of life stories and biographies is described as an empirical method of quantifying this phenomenon.

Narrative plays a central part in John Snarey and Peter Yuichi Clark's "A Generative Drama: Scenes From a Father–Son Relationship" (chapter 2) as well, but in a different way. This chapter is structured around a father–son "story" related in dialogue and soliloquy scenes. The story that the authors tell highlights the dynamics of fatherhood as grounded in Erikson's psychosocial writings concerning generativity and as investigated through the intergenerational and longitudinal data originally collected by Sheldon and Eleanor Glueck in 1939. The sample of 240 fathers has produced extremely rich data, which the authors harvest well (the nomothetic examination of generative fatherhood within this sample is more extensively reported in Snarey's 1993 *How Fathers Care for the Next Generation: A Four-Decade Study*). In the present chapter, Snarey and Clark summarize this empirical evidence for the predictors (boyhood precursors and concurrent variables) and results (midlife consequences and outcomes measured in one's child) of different types of adult male generativity. The father–son case illuminates these findings and assists the authors in expressing theoretical extensions of Erikson's generativity scholarship. This theory elaboration includes the introduction of terms such as *generativity chill* and *generative ethics*. Generativity chill describes the anxiety caused by a threatened loss of one's child or generative product. Generative ethics refers to a moral stance predicated on the principle of caring for the next generation. One of the several strengths of this chapter is its use and reporting of longitudinal data, an essential but seldom-used method of investigating inherently developmental phenomena such as generativity.

Abigail Stewart and Elizabeth Vandewater also employ longitudinal methods in their investigation reported in "The Course of Generativity" (chapter 3). Noting several ambiguities in Erikson's conceptualization of the temporal pattern of generativity—observing that generativity may be the predominant psychosocial crisis for several decades of an individual's life—these authors review the scholarship addressing the change and movement of generativity over time. The generativity of a typical 35-year-old is surely not identical to that of a 60-year-old. One would expect the complex and dynamic generativity to change in form and manifestation through the adult years. On the basis of longitudinal data from two cohorts of college-educated women (drawn from the Radcliffe College class of 1964 and the University of Michigan class of 1967), Stewart and Vandewater outline a developmental pattern of generativity whereby generative *desire* surfaces in young adulthood, the *capacity* for generativity emerges in middle adulthood, and generativity is *accomplished* in late adulthood. The authors discuss the significance of gender and cohort as each applies to this course of generativity and to the relation between generativity and well-being.

Bill Peterson also draws his data from the responses of women in the Radcliffe class of 1964 in his "Case Studies of Midlife Generativity: Analyzing Motivation and Realization" (chapter 4). Peterson clusters the Radcliffe sample into four groups on the basis of scores (high or low) of generativity *motivation* (assessed through the Thematic Apperception Test) and generativity *realization* (measured through a Q sort) and then provides case studies of three women from each of the resulting four groups. Both the TAT and the Q-sort methods of quantifying generativity that were created by Peterson and his colleagues are described in this chapter. Focusing on the women's generativity in occupation and family roles, this idiographic exploration offers 12 portraits of generativity within lives. Furthermore, the author examines differences among the four groups, which leads to important insights regarding conceptualizations of generativity and the impact that generativity has on individual lives. For instance, Peterson notes the stressful life circumstances surrounding educated women who are relatively low in both generativity motivation and realization. He also finds that the lives of women who are low in generativity realization yet high in the motivation to be generative are characterized by frustrations and disappointments in generativity goals. Although his analysis examines individual lives, Peterson ends his chapter with a plea that scholars also investigate "global generativity" as a possible avenue to understanding the dynamics of environmental destruction and potential nuclear devastation.

Although each chapter in this section is unique, Jerome Wakefield's "Immortality and the Externalization of the Self: Plato's Unrecognized Theory of Generativity" (chapter 5) stands apart in that it is purely philosophical and is based on neither empirical data nor individual lives. Wakefield hopes his philosophical approach will agitate generativity scholarship, for he laments the "paucity of theoretical conflict in the generativity field." He compares Erikson's writings on generativity (and love) to Plato's discussions of "love" and "desire for immortality" in the *Symposium*, arguing convincingly that Plato should be credited as the original generativity theorist. However, this argument is peripheral. Wakefield's engrossing comparison of Erikson to Plato serves a higher goal: It enriches our understanding of generativity as a concept and as a developmental phenomenon. For example, the author's examination of the relation between love and immortality as expressed by Plato and Erikson elucidates the way that Erikson's sixth stage (Intimacy vs. Isolation) prepares one for the realization of generativity by promoting capacities such as ego loss and commitment that are integral yet external components of generativity.

1

THE ANATOMY OF GENERATIVITY

DAN P. McADAMS, HOLLY M. HART, AND SHADD MARUNA

It requires only a passing familiarity with the popular writings of Erik Erikson to have an inkling of what the concept of *generativity* is all about. It is about the next generation, about bearing, raising, caring for children —one's own and others. It is about assuming the role of responsible parent, mentor, shepherd, guardian, guide, and so on, vis-à-vis those whose development and well-being benefit from the care that role provides. It is even about assuming such a role vis-à-vis society writ large, about being a responsible citizen, a contributing member of a community, a leader, a mover, and a shaker. In addition, it is about *generating*: creating and producing things, people, and outcomes that are aimed at benefiting, in some sense, the next generation, and even the next. Generativity is clearly *about* many things. In Erikson's writings, furthermore, one finds reference to generativity as an instinctive "drive," a "need," a "motive," a psychosocial "issue," a "trait" on which people differ, a "stage" in development, and a criterion of psychological "adaptation" and "maturity." There are generative people, generative situations, and generative societies.

We thank Ed de St. Aubin, Ravenna Helson, and Barbara Newman for their comments on early drafts of this manuscript. Preparation of the manuscript was aided by two grants to Dan McAdams from the Spencer Foundation and by support for Dan McAdams and Holly Hart from the Foley Family Foundation.

Generativity, therefore, appears to be a multifaceted psychosocial construct that exists in many different forms, that connects to many different activities and outcomes, and that manifests both individual and societal features. This chapter moves beyond the passing familiarity with the concept of generativity that is readily gleaned from popular writings to articulate a clearer and more precise understanding of just what generativity is about. We seek to take the concept of generativity apart, to examine its anatomy. Our exercise is more than conceptual, however, for we also show how a differentiated heuristic model for the concept of generativity has generated a research program that itself has provided important insights into the role of generativity in adult lives.

We begin this chapter with a brief overview of our conceptual model for generativity. The model specifies how generativity exists as a cluster of seven features, or components, that constellate the general psychosocial goal of providing for the well-being and development of the next generation. We then circle back to consider each of the seven features in some detail, reviewing recent research findings and introducing some new inquiries that address each. Conceptually these studies cover a wide range of topics including age–cohort differences in generativity and the relations between generativity on the one hand and mental health, societal involvements, parenting styles, personality traits and motives, and life stories on the other. Methodologically the studies employ traditional self-report surveys and questionnaires, content analysis of open-ended responses from written materials and interviews, and the analysis of published autobiographies. We conclude the chapter with suggestions for future research and further theoretical articulation.

A MODEL OF GENERATIVITY

Adapted from McAdams and de St. Aubin (1992), Figure 1 provides a schematic representation of a model for generativity that incorporates seven different features of this complex psychosocial construct. According to the model, (a) *inner desire* for agentic immortality and communal nurturance combine with (b) age-graded societal norms experienced as a *cultural demand* to produce in the adult years an increasing and more or less conscious (c) *concern* for the next generation. Ideally reinforced by a (d) *belief* in the goodness or worthwhileness of the human enterprise, generative concern leads to (e) generative *commitment*, which, in turn, may produce (f) generative *action*. Generative acts may take the form of creating, maintaining, or offering that which has been created or maintained to a community. Finally, the adult apprehends his or her own generative efforts—giving meaning to the unique pattern of inner desire, cultural demand, generative concern, belief, commitment, and generative action in

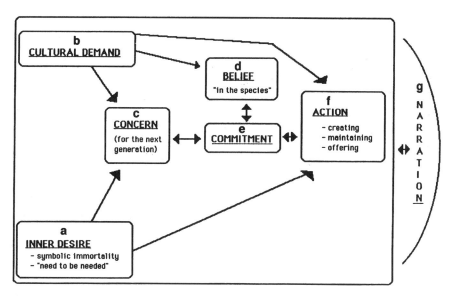

Figure 1. Seven features of generativity.

his or her own life—by constructing a (g) *narration* of generativity, which becomes part of the larger life narration, or life story, that makes up a person's identity (McAdams, 1985). A person's life story can itself be a kind of generative legacy, for the story itself is psychosocially created and maintained and sometimes offered to others (e.g., one's children or others who may benefit from knowing about one's life) as a lesson or gift (Maruna, 1997; McAdams, 1993). All seven features of generativity are oriented around the overall goal—a goal that (ideally) the individual and society share—of *providing for the next generation*. Thus, generativity consists of a constellation of inner desire, cultural demand, conscious concern, belief, commitment, action, and narration revolving around and ultimately justified in terms of the overall psychosocial goal of providing for the survival, well-being, and development of human life in succeeding generations.

As people move into and through adulthood, they typically desire to be generative in various ways, and this desire is stimulated and encouraged by many forces in the social environment. When one seeks to know, therefore, where generativity ultimately comes from, one needs to look both within the person and into the person's social and cultural environment. In terms of the model in Figure 1, then, the ultimate motivational wellsprings for generativity lie in both (a) *inner desire* and (b) *cultural demand*.

Erikson (1963) and others (e.g., Browning, 1975; Kotre, 1984) have described generativity as an inner drive, need, or motive that is experienced in adulthood as an especially compelling desire or want; however, the desire appears to come in two different forms. First, theorists such as Kotre (1984) and McAdams (1985) have suggested that generativity stems in part from a desire for symbolic immortality. According to Kotre (1984), generativity is the "desire to invest one's substance in forms of life and work that will outlive the self" (p. 10). McAdams (1985) invokes Becker's (1973) concept of heroism in describing generativity as partly the creation of a self-defining legacy that may be offered to society and to succeeding generations as a gift. As such, adults desire to defy death by constructing legacies that live on. Second, theorists have also described generativity in terms of a "need to be needed" (Stewart, Franz, & Layton, 1988, p. 56): a desire to nurture, assist, or be of some importance to other people. These two contrasting forms of generative desire mirror two general motivational tendencies in human lives, described first by Bakan (1966) and later by many others (e.g., Helgeson, 1994; McAdams, 1988; Wiggins & Trapnell, 1996) as *agency* and *communion*. The desire for immortality appears to be one manifestation of agency, a tendency to assert, expand, and develop the self in a powerful and independent way. The desire to nurture others appears to be one expression of communion, the general tendency to relate to others in loving, caring, and intimate ways, even to be at one with others.

Although generativity stems partly from inner desire, it is just as strongly determined by cultural demand. One of the reasons that generativity emerges as a psychosocial issue in the *adult* years is that society comes to demand that adults take responsibility for the next generation, in their roles as parents, teachers, mentors, leaders, organizers, "creative ritualizers" (Browning, 1975), and "keepers of the meaning" (Vaillant & Milofsky, 1980). Generativity, then, is prompted by developmental expectations encoded in cultural demand. The demand is normative and age-graded. As adults move into their 30s and 40s, those who are unable or unwilling to contribute to and assume responsibility for the next generation, usually through family or work, are considered to be "off time" (Neugarten & Hagestad, 1976) and at odds with the "social clock" (Helson, Mitchell, & Moane, 1984).

In addition to expectations about the timing of the life cycle, society also presents economic, ideological, and occupational opportunities and constraints that fundamentally shape the expression of generativity. For example, middle-class American women in the 1950s tended to conceive of their generative efforts as limited to the domain of home and child rearing. Being a good homemaker and mother were simpatico with postwar cultural demand. The women's movement of the 1970s, however, broadened generativity options for many U.S. women by encouraging them to seek opportunities for productivity and leadership in the paid workforce. Another example of the effect of cultural demand on how adults think about their own generativity comes from recent news reports from China. The Chinese national policy of limiting family size has dramatically altered the social construction of generativity in the world's most populous nation. According to one recent report, many contemporary Chinese parents dote on their one offspring to an extent unprecedented in Chinese history, leading some educators to worry that they are raising a pampered generation of "little emperors" (Tyler, 1996).

In terms of Figure 1, (a) inner desire and (b) cultural demand combine to promote in adulthood a conscious (c) *concern* for the next generation. Inner desires for agentic immortality and communal nurturance come together with developmental expectations about making a contribution to the next generation in adulthood to promote the extent to which the person cares for and about the development of the next generation. Erikson wrote that "care" is "the widening *concern* for what has been generated by love, necessity, or accident" (1964, p. 131, italics added). With respect to Figure 1 again, adults may translate their (c) generative concern into (e) generative *commitment*, taking responsibility for the next generation by making decisions and establishing goals for generative behavior. Moving, then, from (c) concern for the next generation to (e) making a commitment to act on that concern, the adult begins to establish, organize, and work on strivings (Emmons, 1986), personal projects (Little, 1989), life tasks (Cantor & Zirkel, 1990), and goals (Pervin, 1989) that seek to put generativity into action. The move from concern to commitment may be enhanced or undermined by (d) *belief*. In discussing why some parents do not behave in especially generative ways, Erikson (1963) suggested that they may lack the requisite "*belief* in the species" to support their generative efforts. Erikson was referring to a basic and general belief in the fundamental goodness and worthwhileness of human life specifically as envisioned for the future. To believe in the (human) species is to place hope in the advancement and betterment of human life in succeeding generations, even in the face of strong evidence of human destructiveness, deprivation, and depravity (Van de Water & McAdams, 1989). When such a belief is lacking, the adult may find it difficult to articulate goals and strivings about generativity because it may appear that a generative effort may not be useful. By contrast, a strong belief in the species can keep adults focused on generative goals during difficult times, enabling them to engage in (f) generative *action*. Ideally, then, generative action is guided by commitment, which itself is a product of desire, demand, concern, and belief.

When it comes to generativity, action is not the end, as Figure 1 suggests. Generative acts are given meaning in (g) *narration*, and these meanings feed back to inform inner desire, cultural demand, conscious concern, belief, commitment, and later generative acts. We conceive of generativity in terms of McAdams's (1985, 1993, 1996a, 1996b) life-story theory of adult identity. According to this view, the modern adult defines himself or herself in society by fashioning an internalized and dynamic life story, or personal myth, that provides life with unity, purpose, and meaning. The process of identity development in adulthood, therefore, is the gradual construction and successive reconstruction of a narrative integrating one's perceived past and present and anticipated future while specifying ways in which the individual fits into and distinguishes himself or herself in the social world. Rather than viewing identity as part of a psychosocial stage for late adolescence and young adulthood (e.g., Erikson, 1963), McAdams has suggested that identity development is the major psychosocial issue for the preponderance of one's adult life and that generativity is incorporated within it as one of many different and important aspects.

In the context of an evolving life story, an adult constructs and seeks to live out a generativity script, specifying what he or she plans to do in the future to leave a legacy of the self for future generations. The generativity script is an inner *narration* of the adult's awareness of where efforts to be generative fit into his or her own personal history and into contemporary society and the social world he or she inhabits. The generativity script, which may change markedly over the life course, addresses the narrative need in identity for a "sense of an ending" (Charme, 1984; Ricoeur, 1984), a satisfying vision or plan concerning how, even though one's life will eventually end, some aspect of the self will live on through one's generative efforts. The generativity script enables the person's life story to assume the form of "giving birth to." As Erikson wrote, in midlife and after, the adult is increasingly likely to define himself or herself as "I am what survives me" (1968, p. 141).

Therefore, generativity takes on personal meaning in an adult's life as the adult incorporates his or her own generative efforts into a self-defining life story. The narrativization of generativity is strongly influenced by the cultural stories that are generated and valued by societies, communities, churches, schools, and families (Bellah, Madsen, Sullivan, Swidler, & Tipton, 1991). In ways both small and large, culture teaches adults not only how to be generative but also, of equal importance, how to think about—how to make narrative sense of—generativity. As generativity becomes a more dominant feature of an adult's life story (an adult's identity), the story comes to emphasize the extent to which the adult has "given birth to" things, people, and outcomes that may "outlive the self" (Kotre, 1984). Because all good stories anticipate an ending (Charme, 1984), the narration of generativity in one's life may help to confer on a life story a sense of an ending that is *good* and justified, an ending that, by virtue of its thematic emphasis on "giving birth to," may engender new beginnings.

MOTIVATIONAL SOURCES: INNER DESIRE AND CULTURAL DEMAND

Desire: Human Needs for Agency and Communion

As a psychological construct, generativity is similar to the concept of caregiver–infant *attachment* (Bowlby, 1969) in that both generativity and attachment are multifaceted psychosocial phenomena whose origins are likely traceable to the instinctive patternings of human nature. In the case of attachment, Bowlby proposed that infants and caregivers seek physical proximity in accord with an evolutionarily adaptive (but culturally flexible) plan that functions to maximize protection of the infant from predators and other dangers. The attachment system works because both partners (caregiver and infant) *desire* to be in physical proximity to each other. Phenomenologically, the desire feels natural, for indeed it *is* natural. In a similar vein, generativity may spring from inner desires that feel natural because they have proved adaptive over the course of human evolution. As the prototype for generativity, bearing and raising children are species-typical tasks of ultimate significance in human evolution, and thus human beings are strongly and naturally predisposed to accomplish these tasks with some felicity (Buss, 1991).

There is more to generativity than bearing and raising children, however. Forms of generativity that go beyond one's kin may represent expansions or generalizations of the instinctive patternings associated with reproduction and care of offspring, and they may also tap more generally into other, related evolutionary tasks and mandates. Hogan (1987) identified status ("getting ahead") and acceptance ("getting along") as the two fundamental social tasks that have faced human beings over the course of evolution. Hogan's two tasks map nicely onto Bakan's more general dichotomy of agency and communion, raising the possibility that human beings have evolved to be especially sensitive to opportunities and incentives centered more generally on agentic and communal domains. We suggest that generativity draws much of its compelling *desire* from agency and communion, more specifically from the agentic desire to expand the self infinitely in time (i.e., immortality) and the communal desire to care for that which one has created, to nurture and sustain it until it is ready to be on its own. Indeed, *the narrow but evolutionarily crucial task of successful biological reproduction is a primal microcosm of an agency–communion dynamic that is at the heart of all generative expressions.* Fundamentally, the organism reproduces itself (agency) and then cares and provides for the offspring (communion) until the offspring can ultimately do the same. Overdetermined and multiply expressed, generativity in its manifold forms may owe its evolutionary pedigree both to the adaptive challenge of self-reproduction and (relatedly) to the expression of fundamental desires concerning agency and communion.

If generativity draws some of its motivational impetus from certain recurrent desires associated with agency and communion, one might expect that adults with especially heightened agentic and communal desires would show higher levels of generativity. To test this hypothesis, McAdams, Ruetzel, and Foley (1986) administered the Thematic Apperception Test (TAT) and life-story interviews to 50 midlife adults, ranging in age from 35 to 49 years. They scored TAT protocols for power and intimacy motivation, two well-validated personality constructs that tap into important aspects of agentic and communal desires, respectively. The power motive (need for power) is a recurrent preference for experiences of *feeling strong* and *having impact* in the world (Winter, 1973). The intimacy motive (need for intimacy) is a recurrent preference for experiences of *feeling close to others* and engaging in *warm and communicative interpersonal interaction* (McAdams, 1980). The researchers assessed generativity as expressed in the adults' personal plans for the future. The results showed that adults scoring high on *both* power and intimacy motivation articulated plans for the future emphasizing generativity. In addition, intimacy motivation alone predicted generativity scores at modestly significant levels, whereas power motivation scores alone were positively but nonsignificantly related to generativity.

Additional support for the link between agency and communion desires and expressions of generativity comes from two studies conducted by Peterson and Stewart. In the first (Peterson & Stewart, 1993), TAT measures of the agentic motives of power and achievement and of the communal motives of intimacy and affiliation were positively associated with expressions of generative concerns and behaviors among women in their late 20s, but not among men. In the second (Peterson & Stewart, 1996), the combination of agentic (power and achievement) and communal (affiliation) motives assessed in adolescence significantly predicted (a) Q-sort ratings of generativity at midlife and (b) a thematic measure of generativity motivation in a longitudinal sample of well-educated women. Finally, de St. Aubin and McAdams (1995) showed that self-report measures of the agentic needs for dominance and achievement and communal needs for affiliation and nurturance were significantly positively correlated with a self-report measure of concern for the next generation in a sample (N = 152) of young (age 22–27), midlife (37–42), and older (67–72) community adults.

Overall, therefore, studies have provided empirical support for a positive correlation between individual differences in agentic (power, dominance, achievement) and communal (intimacy, affiliation, nurturance) needs on the one hand and expressions of generative concern and behavior on the other, although the results are somewhat stronger for women than men and for the communal as against the agentic motives. Data from the agency domain are especially ambiguous in that needs for power, dominance, and achievement are inadequate proxies for the hypothesized agentic desire for symbolic immortality (Kotre, 1984; McAdams, 1985). Indeed, no study has sought to measure directly such a desire. Nonetheless, the available correlational data are consistent in a general way with the proposition that generativity draws some of its motivational resources from recurrent desires associated with agency and communion.

Demand: Cultural Conceptions of Timing and Role

If generativity's internal origins lie in desire, cultural demand may be seen as its external motivational source. Culture strongly influences both the form and the timing of generative expression (see chapter 9, this volume, for a historical perspective on the issue; see also chapter 8). All societies require that adults care and provide for the next generation. The continuity of a society's traditions, values, and practices depends on adults' involvement in activities that affirm and transmit those aspects of culture that are deemed worthy of affirmation and transmission. In a certain sense, then, the generative adult must identify with some aspect of what society offers. To some minimal extent, the generative adult must work within the economic and ideological frameworks made available by society if he or she is to assume such generative roles as teacher, mentor, healer, arbiter, advocate, leader, activist, organizer, and citizen. The generative adult who rejects dominant values and norms offered within a society will of necessity adopt some available alternative framework that provides him or her with the material, social, psychological, and ideological resources out of which generative expressions are formed. Without some kind of cultural setting, there can be no generativity.

In a fundamental sense, generativity is tied up with a society's overall conception of *time*. In that generativity refers to the creation (generation) of new forms that will outlive the self, generativity points to the future. In that generativity also refers to the maintenance, preservation, and passing on of that which has been valued in a given social context, it points to the past. In its linking of generations, generativity links past and future time. The linkage is not without tension, however, for the demands of the future may be seen as undercutting the verities and virtues of the past. Such a tension may be especially salient in modern societies, in which the struggle between tradition (past) and progress (future) can undermine community and even tear families apart. Amidst the dizzying cultural change experienced in many modern societies, for example, youth may no longer value the wisdom of their elders, for that wisdom may be seen as specific to a bygone world. An older generation may seek to be generative through passing on traditional values and ways of life, but the targets of those efforts—the younger generation—may want and need guidance and resources that better address new challenges in the future. Parents are not always able to give children what they need, and children do not always value what parents have to offer. Although generativity mismatches are surely as old as human civilization, they appear to take on added salience under conditions of rapid social change, as is often witnessed in modern societies.

Overall, modernity affirms a progressive and developmental understanding of time as it demythologizes the authority of the past (Giddens, 1991; Habermas, 1987). From the modern point of view, economic growth promotes the advance of society; medical research lengthens the expected life span and improves the quality of life; science and technology lead to progress in society; and political systems promise a better world in the future. Notions such as growth, advancement, improvement, and progress strike the modern ear as especially generative ideas. However, such generative notions become highly problematic when modern worldviews (a) threaten to destroy those things most cherished in the past or (b) fail to deliver on their promises for a better world in the future. What some scholars describe as the contemporary turn toward cultural postmodernism represents, in part, a rejection of the modern faith in progressive time (Gergen, 1992; Sloan, 1996). If it is true that modern men and women have typically imported the language of progress into their attempts to make sense of their generative efforts, one wonders what mental forms generativity will take when people lose faith in the idea that the future can be better than the past. In its deepest sense, probably experienced unconsciously, an adult's orientation toward time is bound to the religious and spiritual dimensions of life, touching on apprehensions of life-in-time, immortality, death, and ultimate meaning. However, these deep sources for time orientation are selective internalizations of what culture has to offer, traceable even to early-childhood experience in the family, school, neighborhood, and church. The multiply layered relation between generative expression on the one hand and adults' culturally mediated understanding of time on the other appears to be a ripe area for creative research, both cross-cultural studies and empirical explorations within any single complex modern society.

Cultural assumptions and expectations about time are tied to generativity in a second sense, the sense of being "on time" in the life span (see especially chapter 8, this volume). Erikson situated generativity within the *middle time* of the human life cycle. The seventh of eight developmental stages, "generativity vs. stagnation" defines the central psychosocial issue for adults during that long and variously defined time in the life cycle that is called "midlife." Different societies and different groupings within a society offer significantly different timetables for assuming generative roles. Becoming a parent at age 16 is generally considered "off time" in middle-class American society, despite the fact that teenaged pregnancy may be biologically routine. The healthy 45-year-old man who feels he is "not ready yet" to invest time and energy in any kind of nurturing relationship with others is viewed by others as especially immature or perhaps narcissistic. If he were 25 years old, society might be more forgiving, but 20 years later the timing seems off. One manifestation of cultural demand, therefore, is general developmental expectations or assumptions about the timing of generative roles in the life cycle. These culturally constructed developmental guidelines may be fairly elastic in some societies, but there are always limits—biological and cultural—beyond which the guidelines cannot readily be stretched.

Rather than viewing generativity as a discrete developmental stage in the life cycle, we prefer to conceive of it as subject to developmental expectations and assumptions about time and timing that vary somewhat from one society to the next. We believe that the traditional reading of Erikson's stage conception implies much more structural change in adult personality development than most contemporary experts and virtually all data support (cf. Flavell, 1982; McCrae & Costa, 1990; Peterson & Stewart, 1990). Psychosocial issues do not follow one another in the kind of lockstep order that strong stage models imply. Furthermore, the construct of generativity is too multifaceted to be considered a single thing that develops in a single way. Thus, in a given life, generativity may ebb and flow as a function of life circumstances, and different domains of generativity (e.g., parenting and volunteer work) may follow their own more or less autonomous developmental paths, strongly influenced by cultural roles (see chapter 6, this volume). Nonetheless, we believe that Erikson was right in situating generativity, in a general fashion, in the middle of the human life span. At least within U.S. society, cultural demand urges adults to assume generative roles as they move into their 30s and 40s, and those who do not do so are considered to be off time.

What does empirical research say about the timing of generativity in the United States? Surprisingly few studies have addressed this question (cf. Ryff & Heincke, 1983; Vaillant & Milofsky, 1980; chapter 3, this volume). In a direct test of the relationship, McAdams, de St. Aubin, and Logan (1993) administered four different measures of generativity to groups of young (age 22–27), midlife (age 37–42), and older (age 67–72) adults. The 152 men and women in this cross-sectional study constituted a stratified random sampling of citizens living in Evanston, Illinois, a mostly middle-class city of approximately 80,000 inhabitants. Generativity indexes included self-report and open-ended measures tapping into generative concern, commitment, action, and themes in life narrative (Features 3, 5, 6, and 7, respectively, in the model displayed in Figure 1). Aggregating across the four generativity measures, the results showed a significant quadratic

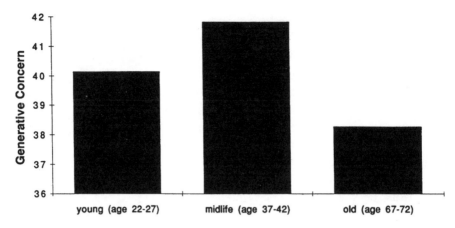

Figure 2. Generative concern by age-cohort.

effect for age-cohort: *Midlife adults scored higher on generativity measures overall compared with both younger and older adults.*

Figures 2 through 5 display the results for each of the four indexes of generativity. The advantage for the midlife cohort is clearest for the measures of generative actions (an act-frequency list asking people to check off generative behaviors performed in the previous two months) and generative concern (a self-report questionnaire, the Loyola Generativity Scale [LGS]). However, the open-ended measure of generativity themes in life narrative showed a moderately high mean score for older adults (though still lower than the mean for midlife adults), and the measure of generative commitment (generativity coded in open-ended accounts of daily goals and strivings) revealed equally high mean scores for older and midlife adults.

Overall, then, the midlife cohort (baby boomers, born after the end

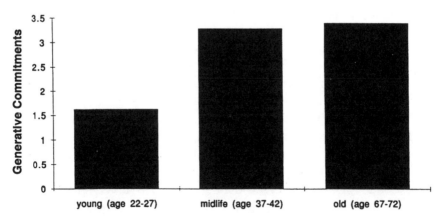

Figure 3. Generative commitments by age-cohort.

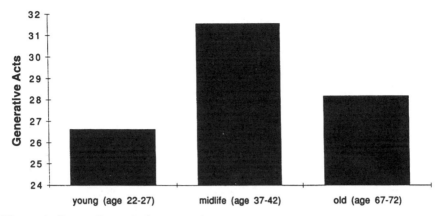

Figure 4. Generative acts by age-cohort.

of World War II) showed higher levels of generativity, especially with respect to concern for the next generation and generative behaviors, than did the young-adult cohort (born in the mid-1960s) and an older cohort (born in the early 1920s). Whether these results are due to developmental or historical cohort effects cannot, of course, be determined from this cross-sectional study. Still, the results are consistent with the general developmental expectation concerning the timing of generativity in the life span —that, in keeping with cultural demand, generativity among American adults should be especially salient in the midlife years.

PERFORMANCE SEQUENCES: CONCERN, BELIEF, COMMITMENT, AND ACTION

Generativity begins with inner desire and cultural demand. Desire and demand motivate adults to begin the performance of generativity. Per-

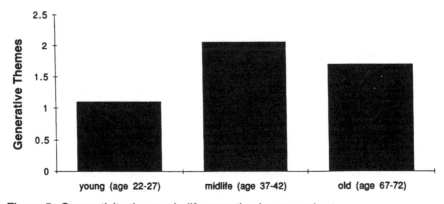

Figure 5. Generativity themes in life narrative by age-cohort.

forming generativity involves a sequence of psychological moves beginning with concern for the next generation and moving through belief in the species, generative commitment, and finally generative action. The sequence is fluid and recursive. Concern for the next generation can combine with belief in the species to move the adult to make a commitment to generative goals, which can lead to generative action. Results of the action, then, can feed back to modify goals, increase or decrease belief, change the nature of overall concern, and so on. Concern, belief, commitment, and action represent an idealized sequence in generative performance. Because human lives often deviate from the idealized, however, generative action can ensue in the absence of generative goals, concern need not lead to commitment or action of any kind, people can be highly generative in their behavior even when they are unable to summon up optimistic belief in the species, and so on. Nevertheless, we find the proposed performance sequence heuristically useful and instructive as a differentiated model for a full and prototypical expression of generativity in an individual life.

Concern for the Next Generation

The most global feature of the performance sequence is the adult's concern for the next generation. To what extent is the adult concerned about and invested in caring for the next generation? To what extent is the adult interested in (and able to begin) the process of making a generative contribution of some kind? Concern for the next generation refers to an overall orientation or attitude regarding generativity in one's life and social world. Adults would be expected to show wide individual differences with respect to this global feature of generativity. Whereas some adults may reveal an intense concern for and interest in promoting the next generation in one way or another, other adults may express little concern and interest, bordering on indifference.

McAdams and de St. Aubin (1992) constructed and validated a 20-item self-report questionnaire, the LGS, to measure individual differences in overall generative concern. It can be seen in Exhibit 1 that LGS items tap into many of the main content domains highlighted in the generativity literature, such as the ideas of teaching and passing on knowledge, making positive contributions to society, caring for and taking responsibility for others, being creative and productive, and leaving an enduring legacy. The measure has high internal consistency and short-term test–retest reliability, and it shows low correlations with indexes of social desirability. Overall, no significant sex differences have been shown for LGS scores in adult samples, although among college students women score significantly higher than men (McAdams &

EXHIBIT 1
Items From the Loyola Generativity Scale

1. I try to pass along the knowledge I have gained through my experiences.
2. I do not feel that other people need me.
3. I think I would like the work of a teacher.
4. I feel as though I have made a difference to many people.
5. I do not volunteer to work for a charity.
6. I have made and created things that have had an impact on other people.
7. I try to be creative in most things that I do.
8. I think that I will be remembered for a long time after I die.
9. I believe that society cannot be responsible for providing food and shelter for all homeless people.
10. Others would say that I have made unique contributions to society.
11. If I were unable to have children of my own, I would like to adopt children.
12. I have important skills that I try to teach others.
13. I feel that I have done nothing that will survive after I die.
14. In general, my actions do not have a positive effect on other people.
15. I feel as though I have done nothing of worth to contribute to others.
16. I have made many commitments to many different kinds of people, groups, and activities in my life.
17. Other people say that I am a very productive person.
18. I have a responsibility to improve the neighborhood in which I live.
19. People come to me for advice.
20. I feel as though my contributions will exist after I die.

de St. Aubin, 1992). Adults score significantly higher on the LGS than college students, and as documented previously, midlife adults score significantly higher than both young adults (age 22–27) and older adults (age 67–72).

What is the relation between parenting and generative concern? One might expect that, all other things being equal, parents would express higher levels of generative concern, as assessed on the LGS, compared to nonparents. In addition, one might expect that generative concern would be associated with effectiveness in parenting or perhaps some index of parental investment. McAdams and de St. Aubin (1992) found that, controlling for age differences, parenting was associated with generative concern, but only among men. Fathers scored significantly higher on the LGS compared to men who reported they had never been fathers. Among women, however, generativity scores were not a direct function of motherhood. This admittedly isolated, correlational finding raises the intriguing possibility that fatherhood may have a dramatic impact on men's generativity, considerably increasing their concern for the next generation, a concern that may remain relatively low until they actually become fathers (see chapter 2, this volume, for an extended discussion of generativity and fatherhood). Men who have never been fathers score significantly lower on the LGS than fathers and women overall. It is also possible that having a strong generative concern to begin with predisposes a man to become more interested in being a father. With respect to parenting itself, Nakagawa (1991) found that parents of children enrolled in Chicago schools were more invested in their children's education if they scored high in generative concern. When socioeconomic and other demographic factors were controlled for, LGS scores predicted the extent to which mothers and fathers helped their children with their homework, attended parent–teacher meetings, participated in the local school council, and involved themselves in activities at their children's schools.

If parenting within the family is seen as the most private and local realm of generative expression, social involvements among one's peers, at work, in churches, and in the community offer opportunities for a more public expression of generativity. Hart (1997) examined the relations between generative concern and social involvements in a community sample of African American and White adults ranging in age from 35 to 65 years. Adults high in generative concern reported more extensive networks of friends and social support in the community and greater levels of satisfaction with social relationships compared with adults scoring low in generative concern. Among White adults, generative concern was positively associated with church attendance. Among Black adults, those scoring high on the LGS were significantly more likely than those scoring lower to have voted in the last presidential election, to have worked for a political party or campaigned for a candidate, and to have called or written to a public official about a social concern or problem. In a broader study of political participation, Cole and Stewart (1996) found that generative concern, assessed with a short form of the LGS, correlated highly with measures of sense of community and political efficacy, suggesting that adults with strong generative concerns also tended to express strong feelings of attachment and belongingness to their communities and tended to view themselves as effective agents in the political process. In this study, generative concern, sense of community, and political efficacy all loaded on a general factor of Social Responsibility.

On a more personal level, Erikson suggested that generativity is a mark of psychosocial maturity in the middle adult years and that it should be associated with overall psychological adjustment. With respect to the relation between generative concern and maturity, however, de St. Aubin and McAdams (1995) found that LGS scores in adulthood were not related to stages of ego development (Loevinger, 1976). Thus, adults exhibiting the complex and autonomous cognitive frameworks typically associated with high stages of ego development in Loevinger's scheme were no higher on generative concern than adults showing more-conventional and less-complex ego frameworks for making meaning in their lives. In this study, however, few adults scored especially low in ego development. At Loevinger's lowest ("pre-conformist") stages (at which individuals are expected to manifest an especially egocentric stance in the world), one might expect to see low levels of generative concern. It should be noted, furthermore, that Loevinger's model of ego development emphasizes cognitive differentiation and psychological sophistication, neither of which may be a prerequisite for exhibiting a strong concern for the next generation.

De St. Aubin and McAdams (1995) found significant positive correlations between generative concern and self-ratings of satisfaction with life in two different samples. The positive relation between LGS scores and life satisfaction was especially strong among adults scoring high in a test of Loevinger's concept of ego development, as evidenced by a significant Ego Stage × Generative Concern interaction effect. In other words, LGS scores were an especially strong predictor of life satisfaction among adults at high levels of ego development but a rather weak predictor of life satisfaction among adults at low (conformist) ego stages. Loevinger's measure of ego maturity, therefore, may function as a moderator variable for the relation between generative concern and life satisfaction, implying that generative concern is an especially important ingredient of well-being for men and women with relatively mature (highly differentiated) ego frameworks but perhaps less closely tied to well-being among adults at lower ego states.

McAdams and Azarow (1996) examined relations between generative concern and a host of measures assessing overall well-being in middle-aged White and African American adults. The results showed generative concern to be significantly associated with self-report indices of life satisfaction, happiness, self-esteem, goal stability, and sense of coherence in life and negatively associated with depression. In general, the patterns of correlations are similar for Whites and African Americans and for women and men. Generative concern is also associated with some measures of physical well-being, such as self-ratings of health satisfaction and (negatively) number of physical symptoms reported. Finally, positive associations have been documented between generative concern and measures of stable personality traits as displayed in the five-factor model of traits (McCrae & Costa, 1990). LGS scores are significantly and positively associated with overall trait measures of agreeableness, extraversion, and openness to experience and negatively associated with neuroticism (Auge, 1996; de St. Aubin & McAdams, 1995).

Belief, Commitment, and Action

In the idealized generativity performance sequence, a general *concern* for the next generation combines with a *belief* in the worthwhileness of the human enterprise to produce generative *commitments*, as evidenced in life goals, plans, projects, and strategies centered on generativity. From generative commitments spring generative actions. We first discuss the measurement of commitment and action and then return to belief to address the extent to which belief supports generative commitments and acts.

McAdams et al. (1993) developed a method for assessing generative commitments by adopting Emmons's (1986) procedure for collecting *personal strivings*. A personal striving refers to any objective or goal that a person is trying to accomplish in daily life. In an open-ended written procedure, individuals are asked to list 10 particular strivings that they are currently "working on." Reported strivings ranged widely from the most mundane maintenance goals—"I am trying to stop biting my nails"—to the grandest and most abstract life projects—"I am training to be a concert pianist" and "I am trying to figure out the meaning of my life and my place in the world." To code strivings for generative commitments, the scorer looks for three different generativity ideas in each response: (a) involvement with the next generation, as in strivings concerning children, young people, or subordinates; (b) providing care, help, assistance, instruction, guidance, comfort, and so on or attempting to promote or establish a positive outcome in another person's life; and (c) making a creative contribution to others or society in general.

As reported previously, McAdams et al. (1993) found that midlife (age 37–42) and older (age 67–72) adults showed significantly higher levels of generative commitment, as assessed from personal strivings, than did young adults (age 22–27). Indeed, relative to the midlife and older adults, the young adults in that study showed remarkably depressed scores on generative commitment, rarely reporting that the things they were trying to accomplish on a daily basis involved such potentially generative goals as becoming involved with younger people, caring for others, or making creative contributions to others. By way of illustration, consider the personal strivings reported by three women in the study, ages 26, 40, and 68 years, respectively. The young woman reported that she is typically trying to "make my job more interesting than it really is," "be more open to others," "figure out what I want to do with my life," "be a good person," "enjoy life," "avoid uncomfortable situations," "keep up with current events," "be well-liked," "make my life more interesting and exciting," and "make others believe that I am completely confident and secure." Her strivings appear to revolve around social acceptance and the maintenance of daily well-being. There is no generative content, although she wishes to "be a good person." By contrast, the midlife woman described 4 out of 10 strivings in generative terms. She is trying to "be a positive role model for young people," "explain teenage experiences to my son and help him work through difficult situations," "provide for my mother to the best of my ability," and "be helpful to those who are in need of help." Similarly, the older woman reported that she is trying to "counsel a daughter who was recently let go from a job due to cutbacks," "help another daughter with her sick child," "help as a volunteer at a nonprofit organization," "assist a candidate running for election," and "offer financial aid to someone close (friend or relative) if needed."

Personal strivings tap into goals and plans about behavior. McAdams and de St. Aubin (1992) developed the Generative Behavior Checklist (GBC) to assess what a person actually does. Generative action can be measured using an act-frequency method that asks how many times in the past 2 months a person has performed each of 50 different acts, 40 of which are suggestive of generativity. Examples of purported generative acts include "taught somebody a skill," "read a story to a child," "attended a neighborhood or community meeting," "donated blood," and "produced a piece of art or craft." The generative acts cover a wide spectrum and include some behaviors that have a very low base rate, such as "invented something" and "became a parent." It must be conceded that the GBC is a rather crude measure in that no single behavior divorced from context can truly be said to entail generativity. For example, one may read a story to a child to manipulate that child in a negative way; one may attend a neighborhood or community meeting to attack enemies verbally. Similarly, ostensibly nongenerative acts, such as "attending a dinner party," may take on a generative meaning, as would be the case if the dinner party provided opportunities to create an intergenerational community. With these limitations, the GBC lists discrete acts that seem to have reasonable potential to be considered to be performed in the service of generativity.

By and large, each act in the GBC corresponds to one of three different kinds of behavior suggested by the construct of generativity: *creating, maintaining,* and *offering.* One meaning of generative behavior is to generate things and people; to be creative, productive, and fruitful; to give birth to, both figuratively and literally. Indeed, Stewart et al. (1988) identified productivity as one of four main themes in generative content of personal documents, and McAdams (1985) emphasized that generativity, unlike simple altruism or general prosocial behavior, involves the creation of a product or legacy in one's own image, a powerful extension of the self. Equally generative is behavior that involves the conservation, restoration, preservation, cultivation, nurturance, or maintenance of that which is deemed worthy of such behavior, as in nurturing children, preserving good traditions, protecting the environment, and enacting rituals (in the school, home, or church) that link generations and ensure continuity over time. Third, generative behavior sometimes involves the seemingly selfless offering of that which has been created or maintained, passing something or someone on to the next generation as a gift, and granting the gift its own autonomy and freedom (Becker, 1973; McAdams, 1985). For example, the truly generative father is both a self-aggrandizing creator and a self-sacrificing giver. Biologically and socially, he creates a child in his own image, working hard and long to promote the development of that child and to nurture all that is good and desirable in the child. However, he must eventually grant the child his or her own autonomy, letting go when the time is right. He must let the child develop his or her own identity, make his or her own decisions and commitments so that the child may ultimately create those offerings of generativity that will distinguish that child as one who was given birth to in order to give birth to.

We propose that generative commitment and generative action are supported by what Erikson (1963) called a "belief in the species." In speculating on the antecedents of adult *failure* in generativity, Erikson wrote that "the reasons are often found in early childhood impressions; in excessive self-love based on a too strenuously self-made personality; and finally (and here we return to the beginnings) in the lack of some faith, some 'belief in the species,' which would make a child appear to be a welcome trust of the community" (1963, p. 267). In other words, generative commitment and generative action are founded on a basic belief or faith in the goodness and worthwhileness of human life, specifically as envisioned for the future. To believe in the (human) species is to place hope and trust in the future of the human enterprise. Generativity requires a fundamental faith in humankind and hope for the future. On the basis of writings on cultural modernity (e.g., Giddens, 1991; McAdams, 1996b), one might expect that in a modern society the most generative adults would hold a strong belief in human progress.

Van de Water and McAdams (1989) examined the relation between belief in the species and generative commitments among 70 adults ranging in age from 22 to 72 years (mean age = 43 years). As a rough empirical approximation of Erikson's concept of belief in the species, the authors employed three self-report scales, one each assessing faith in people (Tipton, Harrison, & Mahoney, 1980), trust (Ochse & Plug, 1986), and hope for the future (Nuttin, 1985). The participants were asked to describe in detail the four most important commitments of their lives. The open-ended commitment responses were coded for themes of generativity, such as showing awareness of responsibility to younger people, leadership, and a broad societal perspective. The results showed that scores on hope for the future were positively and significantly associated with generativity in life commitments; a positive nonsignificant trend was shown for the trust scale; and faith in people showed no relationship to generativity. The study, therefore, provided mixed support for the hypothesis that belief in the species enhances generative commitment. Adults who expressed high levels of hope for the future tended to construe their major life commitments in generative terms, but measures of trust and faith in people, which seemed to capture part of Erikson's notion of belief in the species, were not significantly associated with generative commitments in this study.

Summary and Interrelations

Empirical research concerning the performance sequence of generativity has suggested that generative concern, as operationalized on the LGS, is associated with being a father among men and with investment of time and effort in their children's education among parents of schoolchildren. Adults with strong generative concern reported that they are more meaningfully and satisfactorily involved in social relationships, feel stronger attachments to their community, participate to a greater extent in the political process, and view themselves as effective political agents. Generative concern is also positively associated with a number of measures of psychological well-being and with the personality traits of extraversion, agreeableness, openness to experience, and emotional stability (low neuroticism). In accord with developmental expectations, midlife adults tend to score higher than younger and older adults on both generative concern and generative action. Midlife and older adults score higher than young adults on generative commitments. Research has supplied modest support

TABLE 1

Intercorrelations Among Measures of Generative Concern,
Commitment, Action, and Narration (Generativity Themes)
in Three Different Samples

	Concern	Commitment	Action	Narration
Concern (LGS)	—			
Commitment (strivings)	.23**[b] .24**[c]	—		
Action (GBC)	.59***[a] .53***[b] .46***[c]	.20*[b] .25***[c]	—	
Narration (themes)	.40**[a] .47***[b] .26***[c]	.42***[b] .29***[c]	.45***[a] .39***[b] .33***[c]	—

Note. LGS = Loyola Generativity Scale; GBC = Generative Behavior Checklist.
[a]$N = 79$ adults, ranging in age from 25 to 74 years. From "A Theory of Generativity and Its Assessment Through Self-Report, Behavioral Acts, and Narrative Themes in Autobiography," by D. P. McAdams and E. de St. Aubin, 1992, *Journal of Personality and Social Psychology, 62,* p. 1011. Reprinted with permission. The measure of generative commitments (personal strivings) was not employed in this study.
[b]$N = 152$ adults in three age cohorts: young (age 22–27), midlife (age 37–42), and older (age 67–72). From "Generativity Among Young, Midlife, and Older Adults," by D. P. McAdams, E. de St. Aubin, and R. L. Logan, 1993, *Psychology and Aging, 8,* p. 221–230. Reprinted with permission.
[c]$N = 213$ adults, ranging in age from 35 to 65 years; approximately one third of the sample is made up of African American adults and two thirds is White. From *Generativity in Black and White: Relations Among Generativity, Race, and Well-Being,* by D. P. McAdams and J. Azarow, August 1996, paper presented at the convention of the American Psychological Association, Toronto, Canada.
*$p < .05.$ **$p < .01.$ ***$p < .001.$

for the hypothesis that a strong belief in the species, as operationalized on a scale measuring hope for the future, supports generativity in life commitments.

Table 1 shows intercorrelations of generative concern, commitment, and action, as well as a fourth measure—generativity themes in autobiographical narratives—as assessed in three different samples of adults (McAdams & Azarow, 1996; McAdams & de St. Aubin, 1992; McAdams et al., 1993). The four different measures of generativity are positively and significantly associated with one another in all three samples. The strongest relations are between generative concern (on the LGS) and generative action (on the GBC), with correlations ranging from .46 to .59. By contrast, commitment scores, determined from content analysis of personal strivings, tend to be only modestly related to concern and action, with correlations ranging from .20 to .25. Across the board, the intercorrelations for concern, commitment, action, and generativity themes are consistently significant but not so high as to suggest that the different measures are assessing precisely the same thing. The measures appear instead to be tapping into related features of a multifaceted construct.

STORIED MEANINGS: CONSTRUCTING THE GENERATIVE LIFE

A number of theorists in psychology and sociology have recently observed that contemporary U.S. adults make sense of their sometimes scattered lives by fashioning and internalizing stories that integrate their reconstructed past, perceived present, and anticipated future (e.g., Cohler, 1982; Hermans & Kempen, 1993; Howard, 1991; Kenyon, 1996; Singer & Salovey, 1993). With his life-story theory of identity, McAdams (1984, 1985, 1996a, 1996b) has argued that, beginning in late adolescence and young adulthood, men and women living in modern societies seek to construct more or less integrative narratives of the self to provide their lives with a semblance of unity and purpose. Because stories are the traditional vehicle of choice for conveying how human beings make sense of intentional action organized in time (Bruner, 1990; Ricoeur, 1984), they are ideally suited for making sense of one's own life in time (McAdams, 1993; Polkinghorne, 1988). Identity, therefore, may itself be viewed as an internalized and evolving life story, a way of *telling* the self, to the self and to others, through a story or set of stories complete with settings, scenes, characters, plots, and themes.

Constructing a meaningful and coherent self through narrative may be a psychosocial challenge that is especially characteristic of modern Western societies (McAdams, 1996b). According to Giddens (1991), modernity brings with it the problem of exploring, controlling, developing, and crafting a self as a reflexive project that the Western man or woman works on. Increasingly since about 1800, Western adults have faced the challenge of fashioning a modern self that affirms both similarity to others and individual uniqueness, finding a niche within society that can be individualized so that it becomes one's own (Baumeister, 1986; Langbaum, 1982). As modern men and women fashioning individual selves, they draw on the established literary traditions of the culture, rendering life stories that contain, for example, origin myths set in early family experience, turning points in which the protagonist gains new insights, heroes who support the protagonist's strivings and villains who stand in the way, and endings that resolve conflict and bring events to a satisfying conclusion (Denzin, 1989). Within modernity, therefore, "a person's identity is not to be found in behavior, nor—important though this is—in the reactions of others, but in the capacity to *keep a particular narrative going*" (Giddens, 1991, p. 54).

It is not uncommon for modern adults to leave considerable space in their life stories for generativity (McAdams, 1985). Generative *narration* (see Figure 1) refers to the characteristic way in which a man or woman makes narrative sense of his or her generative efforts and projects in the context of his or her self-defining life story. For many adults, generativity is narrated to produce a meaningful ending for the life story, envisioned for the future, through which one's products and outcomes outlive the self as self-extending legacies that suggest a way in which endings, in a sense, give birth to new beginnings (Becker, 1973; McAdams, 1985). However, generativity is not an equally salient feature of all adult life stories. Developmental theory (Erikson, 1963) and some research (McAdams et al., 1993) suggest that its salience may increase into and through middle adulthood. Furthermore, within a given age grouping, adults show considerable individual differences with respect to generative narration.

From the standpoint of research, individual differences in generative narration can be addressed in two different ways. First, one can compare and contrast different life stories with respect to how much generativity is in the story. This is essentially the intent behind the coding of generativity themes in autobiographical accounts, as described by McAdams et al. (1993). Whereas some people reveal many generativity themes in their accounts of such key life-story scenes as peak experiences and turning points in their lives, others narrate key life events in different terms. More globally, one 55-year-old woman may construct a self-narrative that is laden with themes and images having to do with caring for the next generation, giving birth to products and outcomes, establishing an enduring legacy, and so on. Another 55-year-old woman may leave little room in her self-defining story for generative themes and generative imagery. The two women, therefore, would manifest starkly different identities (that is, life stories) with respect to the extent to which their stories were organized along the lines of generative narration.

A second approach to research involves comparing and contrasting the life stories of adults who differ with respect to *aspects of generativity assessed outside the life story*. For example, in what ways might the life story of a man showing high levels of concern for the next generation and generative action, as assessed through quantitative measures such as the LGS and GBC, differ from the life story of a man showing low levels of concern and action? The obvious prediction would be that the former would exhibit more generativity themes in his life story compared to the latter. Beyond the obvious, how might the two stories differ further? How do adults who exhibit high levels of generative concern and behavior in their daily lives make sense of their lives—and perhaps justify their significant generative investments—in terms of their overall life stories? How do they reconstruct childhood? In what ways do they anticipate the future? How do their life stories differ from the stories constructed by less generative adults?

Life Stories of Highly Generative Adults

In an intensive interview study, McAdams and his colleagues contrasted the life stories of 40 highly generative adults to those of a matched group of 30 less generative adults. Chosen for the high-generativity group were school teachers and community volunteers who scored high on measures of generative concern (LGS) and generative action (GBC). The contrasting group consisted of 30 adults with similar demographic backgrounds who were not involved in either teaching or community work and who, in general, scored relatively low on the LGS and GBC. Each participant was interviewed according to McAdams's (1985, 1993) life-story method. In the 2-hour interview the participant is asked to outline the major "chapters" in his or her life story, to describe in detail eight significant scenes in the story (including a high point, or "peak" experience; a low point, or "nadir" experience; a "turning-point" experience; and an earliest memory), to describe four important people in the story, to anticipate what the future chapters of the story may bring, to articulate one's basic values and beliefs about one's own life and life in general, and to identify a major "life theme." Interviews were tape-recorded and transcribed, yielding over 2,100 pages of single-spaced typed text. The transcriptions were then coded in a number of different ways according to highly reliable content-analysis procedures.

Mansfield and McAdams (1996) coded all the accounts of key scenes in the interviews for themes of agency and communion according to a coding system developed by McAdams, Hoffman, Mansfield, and Day (1996). They found that the highly generative adults tended to include more themes of communion in their stories compared to the less generative adults. Thus, accounts of high points, turning points, and earliest memories in the life stories of highly generative adults emphasized themes of love and friendship, dialogue and communication, caring for others, and feelings of community. The highly generative adults did not differ from the less generative adults, however, with respect to themes of agency in their accounts of life-story scenes. The two groups did not differ on agentic themes of self-mastery, status, achievement, and empowerment. Adopting a psychodynamic frame, Shlaes (1995) scored the same data for quality of object relations, using a complex coding system developed by Westen (1991). The highly generative adults showed significantly higher levels of object relations, as indexed by descriptions of story characters in warmer tones and more complex terms, compared to their less generative counterparts.

The most extensive examination of the interviews was completed by McAdams, Diamond, de St. Aubin, and Mansfield (1997). The authors found that, although each life-story interview provided a unique account of a life in time, the life stories constructed by the highly generative adults as a group differed in significant ways from the stories constructed by their less generative peers. The differences began in accounts of childhood. The highly generative adults were significantly more likely to identify a way in which they *were singled out in childhood with a special advantage*. One protagonist was "the teacher's favorite"; another was blessed with musical talent; another was given a cherished family name; yet another was "lucky" because "we were the only Jewish family in that small provincial town, so I learned to be an individual and stand up for my beliefs." At the same time, the highly generative adults reported that they were more sensitive to the *suffering of others* at an early age. They described incidents from childhood in which they witnessed pain, injustice, discrimination, or the cruel indignities of the playground. "We had a retarded kid on our street; I always felt sorry for him." Thus, in their reconstruction of the past, the highly generative adults set up a narrative contrast between their own blessing and the suffering of others: I was lucky; others were not. As a result, I came to believe that I was *called* to service in some manner, that it is my destiny or obligation to be of some use to other people in life.

Analysis of the interviews indicated further that, as the protagonists in the life stories constructed by highly generative adults moved through adolescence and into adulthood, they were guided by a clearly articulated and strongly held ideology that remained steadfast over time. This *moral steadfastness* survived questioning and doubt and suggested that for all the changes that the protagonist went through in life, his or her basic values and beliefs did not change much. Thus, the hero or heroine in these life stories is not the Sartrean quester filled with existential angst. With respect to personal ideology, periods of psychosocial moratorium (Erikson, 1963) are, as the story tells it, surprisingly rare. A 50-year-old church minister was once a girl scout den mother, then a prostitute, and later a con artist,

EXHIBIT 2
Examples of Redemption Sequences: Condensed Accounts

Sacrifice
  pain of delivery → birth of "beautiful baby"
  difficult years working in "service club" → S sets a positive example for
    others
  S leaves husband because he wants her to have abortion; poverty → joy of
    loving son
Recovery
  bout of severe depression → regained positive mood for good
  near-fatal injuries → surprising recovery
  severe anorexia → therapist "saved my life"
Growth
  death of father → brings family closer together
  loneliness of childhood → "made me resilient" as an adult
  failed love affair → S becomes more assertive and confident
  mother's death → S experiences enhanced power and now feels closer to her
  episode of anger and crying about father's death → S no longer stutters,
    decreased anxiety
  got fired from job → S comes to see self as "whole person"
  divorce → S develops better relationship with son
  husband has sexual affair → S experiences enhanced "strength of ego"
  seizure disorder → S experiences enhanced courage and independence
  drugs, dereliction → S moves to new place, changes name, "got my life
    together"
Learning
  exhausting workload → S realizes that life needs more balance
  family poverty means S cannot go to prom → learns lessons about honesty,
    money
  severe criticism from co-worker → S becomes better employee
  tough neighborhood fights → "but I learned a lot"
  mother-in-law hates S → S learns how to be a good mother-in-law herself
Improvement
  period of chaos → happiest time in life
  very bad marriage → very good marriage
  bad year of teaching → S moves to new school where she finds success,
    affirmation
  traffic accident → "all of a sudden it started to become a cool experience"
  divorce, anger → S becomes successful in order to prove self to ex-spouse
  terrible first semester in college → S ends up getting all As

Note. From "Stories of Commitment: The Psychosocial Construction of Generative Lives," by D. P. McAdams, A. Diamond, E. de St. Aubin, and E. D. Mansfield, 1997, *Journal of Personality and Social Psychology, 72*, p. 694. Reprinted with permission.

and she spent two terms in a federal prison. Her life-story account is filled with tumult and transformation from beginning to end, but throughout it all "I was always doing ministry." She insists that her most basic beliefs and values never wavered since her teen-aged years.

The emotional tone of the stories constructed by the highly generative adults was no more optimistic or pessimistic than that of those constructed by the contrasting sample. The two groups did not differ with respect to the narrative elaboration of such basic positive emotions as joy and excitement and such negative emotions as anger, fear, and sadness. However, the highly generative adults were more likely to articulate key scenes in their stories in which bad events and negative emotions are immediately followed by good events and positive emotions. In such *redemption sequences*, bad scenes are redeemed or salvaged through good outcomes, even if the outcomes spring from blind chance. A woman's husband has a sexual affair (bad), which leads her to take control of her own life (good). A girl's brother is killed in a traffic accident (bad), but the insurance money enables her to go to college (good). Redemption sequences may be further classified into episodes of sacrifice, recovery, growth, learning, and improvement. Exhibit 2 displays examples of each type of redemption sequence, taken from McAdams et al. (1997).

Whereas a redemption sequence involves a move from bad to good, the opposite move can be narrated in a *contamination sequence*. In a contamination sequence, a good event is ruined or spoiled by a bad, negative turn. Here are some examples from the data: A young man is winning a race (good), and then his body gives out and he falls to the ground (bad). A boy builds the perfect model airplane, and then a class bully breaks the plane at school. A girl enjoys a sexual experience with her boyfriend, and then her father breaks into the room and beats the boy up. A woman loses weight, but then she gets anxious because boorish men now find her attractive. An assistant professor eagerly anticipates a reunion with his graduate school mentor, but then the mentor is killed in a car accident on the way to the reunion. The highly generative adults were less likely than the less generative adults to construe their life stories in terms of contamination sequences. The authors coded narrative accounts of life-story low points (nadir experiences) and turning-point experiences for both redemption and contamination sequences and identified the number of redemption and contamination scenes spontaneously narrated in the opening life chapters section of the interview. Figure 6 shows the statistically significant group differences on redemption and contamination sequences.

Finally, in imagining the future chapters in their life story, highly generative adults articulated a greater number of prosocial goals aimed at benefiting society at large. By contrast, the less generative adults articulated a greater number of personal goals aimed at benefiting themselves. The two groups did not differ on the number of family goals articulated. Thus, highly generative adults articulated stories in which protagonists made commitments to the betterment of society in the future, underscoring the possibilities of human development and societal progress over time and from one generation to the next.

In summary, although every life-story account collected in the study had its own unique features, the themes differentiating the stories produced by highly generative from those by less generative adults converged on a particular patterning of narrative that the authors termed a *commitment story*.

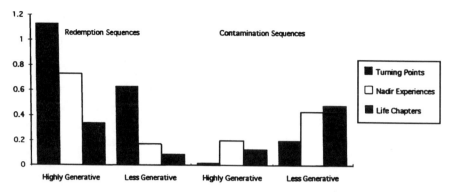

Figure 6. Redemption and contamination sequences for highly generative and less generative adults.

The commitment story bears strong resemblance to Tomkins's (1987) model of a commitment *script* (see Carlson, 1988) and shares similarities with what Colby and Damon (1992) observed in their case-study interviews of men and women who had been nominated as "moral exemplars" in their local communities. In the prototypical commitment story, the protagonist comes to believe early on that he or she has a special advantage (family blessing) that contrasts markedly with the pain and misfortune suffered by many others (suffering of others). Experiencing the world as a place where people need to care for others, the protagonist commits the self to living in accord with a set of clear and enduring values and personal beliefs that continue to guide behavior throughout the life span (moral steadfastness). Moving ahead with the confidence of early blessing and steadfast belief, the protagonist encounters an expectable share of personal misfortune, disappointment, and even tragedy in life, but these bad events often become transformed or redeemed into good outcomes (redemption sequences), sometimes because of the protagonist's own efforts and sometimes by chance or external design. Thus, bad things happen, but they often turn into good things, whereas when good things happen they rarely turn bad. Looking to the future with an expanded radius of care, the protagonist sets goals that aim to benefit others, especially those of the next generation, and to contribute to the progressive development of society as a whole and to its more worthy institutions.

The commitment story appears to be one highly effective life-narrative form for supporting an adult's generative efforts, an efficacious matchup of identity and generative behavior. The adult who works hard to guide and foster the next generation may make sense of his or her strong commitment in terms of a story that suggests that he or she has been called or summoned to do good things for others and that the calling is deeply rooted in childhood, reinforced by a precocious sensitivity to the suffering of others, and bolstered by a clear and convincing ideology that remains steadfast over time. Perceiving one's own life in terms of redemption sequences, furthermore, provides the hope that hard work today will yield dividends for the future, a hope that may sustain generative efforts as private as raising one's own child (Kotre, 1984) and as public as committing oneself to the advancement of one's own society or even one's own people (Erikson, 1969). A commitment story provides a language or discourse for the self that supports a caring, compassionate, and responsible approach to social life. In *Acts of Compassion*, a study of volunteerism in the United States, Wuthnow (1991, p. 45) wrote that: "the possibility of compassion depends as much on having an appropriate discourse to interpret it as it does on having a free afternoon to do it. To ask whether compassion is possible, therefore, is to ask about the language in which its very conceivability depends."

Generativity in Stories of Reform

The language of generativity is a powerful force in many different kinds of life stories. Maruna (1997) identified generativity as a central theme in the narrative accounts provided by men and women who have "gone straight" after a life of crime. As part of his ongoing research on desistance from criminal behavior, Maruna analyzed 20 published autobiographies written by successfully reintegrated ex-convicts in terms of theme, plot structure, and character. He identified a prototypical *reform story* with which virtually all of the accounts shared remarkable similarities. It is a story that gives generativity a key role.

The plot of the prototypical reform story begins with a long period of passive victimization in childhood. This leads to an ill-fated search for agentic and communal fulfillment, often identified as "respect" and "family," within delinquent subcultures. As the young protagonists move deeper and deeper into criminal activity, they may encounter dramatic moments or scenes that reveal the striking disparity between what they believe to be good and right on the one hand and their behavior on the other. Over time, the scenes may become progressively more dramatic, frightening, or tragic, foreshadowing an eventual epiphany. Finally, the protagonist experiences a "moment of clarity," a turning point that typically follows immediately either from an especially tragic episode or from the sagelike advice offered by a trusted friend. As a result, the protagonist decides to desist from criminal behavior or at least seriously questions life's direction. But these protagonists subsequently experience societal or psychological "roadblocks" that prevent them from going straight. It is not until they are able to experience successful agency, communion, or both from outside the criminal subculture that they are finally able to make the break from crime and live out the truth revealed in the moment of clarity. Typically, then, narrators credit this redemption to the enormous generosity of others (and frequently a higher power) who are willing to reach out and give them a chance to succeed.

The final chapter of the reform story is the establishment of a life plan for the future designed to "give something back" and help out others in similar circumstances who may not have been as lucky. The narrator explicitly advertises this new, prosocial self to secure others' trust and atone for previous crimes. He or she comes to see the formulation and the telling of such a life story as a quintessentially generative project: the discovery and the passing on of a life story that begins with childhood victimization and ends with a thank you to the world for offering the protagonist a second chance to succeed. The recipients of the ex-convict's story are often young people who are in situations similar to those the protagonist faced. One ex-offender wrote, "Because of my past life and conversion, I have a special burden in my heart for prison inmates." Another, who works as a youth counselor, said the following:

> I was confident my own life was ruined beyond repair, but I found I could derive a certain vicarious satisfaction by becoming concerned with the future of the younger inmates—kids who had gotten into trouble once or twice, but who still had a useful life ahead of them if they could be straightened out in time.

Many of the ex-offenders suggested that they were publishing their narratives to leave a lesson for younger generations, so they do not repeat the mistakes the narrators made. This narrative move may be a variation on what Kotre and Kotre (chapter 11, this volume) describe as the commitment to be generative by terminating a negative legacy and proclaiming that "the damage stops here." One former gang member and drug dealer concluded his autobiography by saying, "I hope that some of the young people who read this book will learn from what they read about me." Another ex-convict wrote, "My burning hope for the remainder of my life will be to share my criminal and prison experiences with young people everywhere in the hope that they can get some insights into their own feelings." In Maruna's sample of 20 stories, it seems that constructing the autobiography itself was an important element in sustaining significant behavioral reform. The development of a coherent story of reform that integrates past faults into a generativity script for the future may reinforce the narrator's desistance from crime while serving as a generative offering for readers whose life stories could follow similar lines.

CONCLUSION

Our model of generativity begins with (a) inner desires for agentic immortality and communal care and (b) cultural demands concerning the timing and form of adult lives, and it ends with the life stories adults elaborate to make sense of past generative efforts and to articulate generative futures for themselves and their communities. In the middle is the generative performance sequence: Adults become concerned about the next generation; reinforced by a belief in the species, they translate their concern into generative commitments, which in turn lead to generative acts of creating, maintaining, and offering up. The full expression of generativity integrates inner desire, cultural demand, concern for the next generation, belief in the species, generative commitment, generative action, and the narration of adult lives around the individual and societal goal of providing for the survival, well-being, and development of human life into succeeding generations.

The research generated by our model has tended to emphasize individual differences in various features of generativity. We find, for example, that people who have strong inner desires concerning agency and communion tend to manifest stronger and more elaborate generative commitments; that individual differences in generative concern predict generative acts as well as psychological well-being and societal involvements; that midlife adults tend to show higher levels of generative concern and action compared to younger and older adults; and that men and women who have distinguished themselves in their communities for their generative behaviors tend to construct life narratives organized by themes of childhood blessing, affective redemption, moral steadfastness, and the integration of societal goals. Our research on generativity is, nonetheless, still in its infancy. As the field of generativity studies matures, the theoretical model we offer could potentially stimulate many different kinds of empirical inquiries. In conclusion, we envision three different kinds of research programs that might follow the model's lead.

The first is essentially a continuation of what we have begun: a broad-based inquiry into each of the seven features of the model, emphasizing individual differences and guided by the kinds of questions that are typically posed by personality psychologists and some life-span developmentalists. From this perspective, we still do not know much about each of the model's seven features. Indeed, each of the seven could conceivably be the focus of its own research program. What is the nature of the inner desires that give rise to generative inclinations? Is the desire for symbolic immortality as important in motivating generativity as our theory suggests? What are the different ways in which cultural demand influences the timing and the form of generative expression? What are the personality and mental health correlates of generative concern? How important is a belief in the species for sustaining generative commitments? What happens when commitments are not translated into actions? The area of generative narration appears to offer especially exciting research opportunities. We have identified one particular life-narrative form—the commitment story—that seems to structure identity for some highly generative adults. However, generativity can surely be sustained by many different kinds of life stories. What other forms might be identified? Do highly generative men construct different kinds of life stories than do highly generative women? How do race, ethnicity, and class impact the narrative construction of the generative life?

A second approach might seek to contextualize further the constructs identified in the model, adopting perspectives from social ecology and life-span developmental approaches emphasizing social context. MacDermid, Franz, and De Reus (chapter 6, this volume) and Peterson and Stewart (1993) have shown that generativity can be construed in role-specific terms. One person may express generativity in multiple roles whereas another person may channel generativity into one. A person may be generative in the parenting role but not as a co-worker. Roles shift over the course of development, and generativity may move around from one role to another as life circumstances change. To the extent, then, that generativity is role- or domain-specific, *each role or domain may specify a particular patterning of inner desire, cultural demand, concern, belief, commitment, action, and narration.* Some personality psychologists might be especially interested in the extent to which patternings are integrated across roles, whereas other investigators more attuned to the social ecology of development might focus their inquiries on the multiplicity of roles and expressions in generativity and how patternings shift over time and across circumstances.

A third program for research might focus on process and contingencies, perhaps borrowing familiar research paradigms from social and cognitive psychology. How are cultural demands about generativity represented in social cognition? Under what conditions are such demands activated in thought? Precisely how does generative concern lead to generative commitment? In what situations does a belief in the species support generative goals and plans? What are the cognitive and situational determinants of generative acts having to do with creating, maintaining, and offering? When do people fail to be generative? What are they thinking about when they fail? Can we predict generative behavior in a particular situation or under particular conditions? These kinds of questions deemphasize individual differences in persons and focus instead on the overall process of generative expression among all people and the particular cognitive and situational contingencies that influence such expression.

Our anatomy of generativity brings together many traditional and contemporary sources in personality, developmental, and life-span psychology and in psychoanalytic thought to articulate some key conceptual distinctions and offer some important categories for construing generativity. We believe that generativity is a broad and multifaceted construct; however, generativity does not encompass everything of import in adult development. The construct has boundaries that can be sketched and an inner structure that can be delineated with some precision. We have yet to be as precise as we should eventually be. We hope, therefore, that our model will help to generate research aimed at elaborating further the anatomy we have proposed and drawing on the insights provided to understand better the structure, functions, meanings, and manifestations of generativity in adult development.

REFERENCES

Auge, S. (1996). *The Big Five as they relate to generativity*. Unpublished senior thesis, Northwestern University, Evanston, IL.

Bakan, D. (1966). *The duality of human existence: Isolation and communion in Western man*. Boston: Beacon Press.

Baumeister, R. F. (1986). *Identity: Cultural change and the struggle for self*. New York: Oxford University Press.

Becker, E. (1976). *The denial of death*. New York: Free Press.

Bellah, R. N., Madsen, R., Sullivan, W. M., Swidler, A., & Tipton, S. M. (1991). *The good society*. New York: Knopf.

Bowlby, J. (1969). *Attachment*. New York: Basic Books.

Browning, D. (1975). *Generative man*. New York: Dell.

Bruner, J. (1990). *Acts of meaning*. Cambridge, MA: Harvard University Press.

Buss, D. M. (1991). Evolutionary personality psychology. In M. R. Rosenzweig & L. W. Porter (Eds.), *Annual review of psychology* (Vol. 42, pp. 459–491). Palo Alto, CA: Annual Reviews.

Cantor, N., & Zirkel, S. (1990). Personality, cognition, and purposive behavior. In L. Pervin (Ed.), *Handbook of personality theory and research* (pp. 135–164). New York: Guilford Press.

Carlson, R. (1988). Exemplary lives: The uses of psychobiography for theory development. *Journal of Personality, 56,* 105–138.

Charme, S. T. (1984). *Meaning and myth in the study of lives: A Sartrean perspective*. Philadelphia: University of Pennsylvania Press.

Cohler, B. J. (1982). Personal narrative and the life course. In P. Baltes & O. G. Brim (Eds.), *Live span development and behavior* (Vol. 4, pp. 205–241). New York: Academic Press.

Colby, A., & Damon, W. (1992). *Some do care: Contemporary lives of moral commitment*. New York: Free Press.

Cole, E. R., & Stewart, A. J. (1996). Meanings of political participation among Black and White women: Political identity and social responsibility. *Journal of Personality and Social Psychology, 71,* 130–140.

de St. Aubin, E., & McAdams, D. P. (1995). The relations of generative concern and generative action to personality traits, satisfaction/happiness with life, and ego development. *Journal of Adult Development, 2,* 99–112.

Denzin, N. K. (1989). *Interpretive biography*. Newbury Park, CA: Sage.

Emmons, R. A. (1986). Personal strivings: An approach to personality and subjective well-being. *Journal of Personality and Social Psychology, 51*, 1058–1068.

Erikson, E. H. (1963). *Childhood and society* (2nd ed.). New York: Norton.

Erikson, E. H. (1964). *Insight and responsibility*. New York: Norton.

Erikson, E. H. (1968). *Identity: Youth and crisis*. New York: Norton.

Erikson, E. H. (1969). *Gandhi's truth: On the origins of militant nonviolence*. New York: Norton.

Flavell, J. H. (1982). Structures, stages, and sequences in cognitive development. In W. A. Collins (Ed.), *The concept of development* (pp. 1–28). Hillsdale, NJ: Erlbaum.

Gergen, K. J. (1992). *The saturated self: Dilemmas of identity in contemporary life*. New York: Basic Books.

Giddens, A. (1991). *Modernity and self-identity: Self and society in the late modern age*. Stanford, CA: Stanford University Press.

Habermas, J. (1987). *The philosophical discourse of modernity*. Cambridge, MA: MIT Press.

Hart, H. M. (1997). *Generativity and social involvements among African-American and White adults*. Unpublished doctoral dissertation, Department of Human Development and Social Policy, Northwestern University, Evanston, IL.

Helgeson, V. S. (1994). Relation of agency and communion to well-being: Evidence and potential explanations. *Psychological Bulletin, 116*, 412–428.

Helson, R., Mitchell, V., & Moane, G. (1984). Personality and patterns of adherence to the social clock. *Journal of Personality and Social Psychology, 46*, 1079–1096.

Hermans, H. J. M., & Kempen, H. J. G. (1993). *The dialogical self: Meaning as movement*. New York: Academic Press.

Hogan, R. (1987). Personality psychology: Back to basics. In J. Aronoff, A. I. Rabin, & R. A. Zucker (Eds.), *The emergence of personality* (pp. 79–104). New York: Springer.

Howard, G. S. (1991). Culture tales: A narrative approach to thinking, cross-cultural psychology, and psychotherapy. *American Psychologist, 46*, 187–197.

Kenyon, G. M. (1996). The meaning/value of personal storytelling. In J. Birren, G. M. Kenyon, J. E. Ruth, J. J. F. Shroots, & J. Svendson (Eds.), *Aging and biography: Explorations in adult development* (pp. 21–38). New York: Springer.

Kotre, J. (1984). *Outliving the self: Generativity and the interpretation of lives*. Baltimore: The Johns Hopkins University Press.

Langbaum, R. (1982). *The mysteries of identity: A theme in modern literature*. Chicago: University of Chicago Press.

Little, B. R. (1989). Personal projects analysis: Trivial pursuits, magnificent obsessions, and the search for coherence. In D. M. Buss & N. Cantor (Eds.), *Personality psychology: Recent trends and emerging directions* (pp. 15–31). New York: Springer-Verlag.

Loevinger, J. (1976). *Ego development*. San Francisco: Jossey-Bass.

Mansfield, E. D., & McAdams, D. P. (1996). Generativity and themes of agency and communion in adult autobiography. *Personality and Social Psychology Bulletin, 22,* 721–731.

Maruna, S. (1997). Going straight: Desistance from crime and life narratives of reform. In R. Josselson & A. Lieblich (Eds.), *The narrative study of lives* (Vol. 5). Newbury Park, CA: Sage.

McAdams, D. P. (1980). A thematic coding system for the intimacy motive. *Journal of Research in Personality, 14,* 413–432.

McAdams, D. P. (1984). Love, power, and images of the self. In C. Z. Malatesta & C. E. Izard (Eds.), *Emotion in adult development* (pp. 159–174). Beverly Hills, CA: Sage.

McAdams, D. P. (1985). *Power, intimacy, and the life story: Personological inquiries into identity.* New York: Guilford Press.

McAdams, D. P. (1988). Personal needs and personal relationships. In S. W. Duck (Ed.), *Handbook of personal relationships* (pp. 7–22). London: Wiley.

McAdams, D. P. (1993). *The stories we live by: Personal myths and the making of the self.* New York: Morrow.

McAdams, D. P. (1996a). Narrating the self in adulthood. In J. E. Birren, G. M. Kenyon, J-E Ruth, J. J. F. Schroots, & T. Svensson (Eds.), *Aging and biography: Explorations in adult development* (pp. 131–148). New York: Springer.

McAdams, D. P. (1996b). Personality, modernity, and the storied self: A contemporary framework for studying persons. *Psychological Inquiry, 7,* 295–321.

McAdams, D. P., & Azarow, J. (1996, August). *Generativity in black and white: Relations among generativity, race, and well-being.* Paper presented at the convention of the American Psychological Association, Toronto, Canada.

McAdams, D. P., & de St. Aubin, E. (1992). A theory of generativity and its assessment through self-report, behavioral acts, and narrative themes in autobiography. *Journal of Personality and Social Psychology, 62,* 1003–1015.

McAdams, D. P., de St. Aubin, E., & Logan, R. L. (1993). Generativity among young, midlife, and older adults. *Psychology and Aging, 8,* 221–230.

McAdams, D. P., Diamond, A., de St. Aubin, E., & Mansfield, E. D. (1997). Stories of commitment: The psychosocial construction of generative lives. *Journal of Personality and Social Psychology, 72,* 678–694.

McAdams, D. P., Hoffman, B. J., Mansfield, E. D., & Day, R. (1996). Themes of agency and communion in significant autobiographical scenes. *Journal of Personality, 64,* 339–377.

McAdams, D. P., Ruetzel, K., & Foley, J. M. (1986). Complexity and generativity at midlife: Relations among social motives, ego development, and adults' plans for the future. *Journal of Personality and Social Psychology, 50,* 800–807.

McCrae, R. R., & Costa, P. T., Jr. (1990). *Personality in adulthood.* New York: Guilford Press.

Nakagawa, K. (1991). *Explorations into the correlates of public school reform and pa-*

rental involvement. Unpublished doctoral dissertation, Department of Human Development and Social Policy, Northwestern University, Evanston, IL.

Neugarten, B. L., & Hagestad, G. O. (1976). Age and the life course. In R. H. Binstock & E. Shanas (Eds.), *Handbook of aging and the social sciences* (pp. 35–55). New York: Van Nostrand Reinhold.

Nuttin, J. (1985). *Future time perspective and motivation.* Hillsdale, NJ: Erlbaum.

Ochse, R., & Plug, C. (1986). Cross-cultural investigation of the validity of Erikson's theory of personality development. *Journal of Personality and Social Psychology, 50,* 1240–1252.

Pervin, L. A. (Ed.). (1989). *Goal concepts in personality and social psychology.* Hillsdale, NJ: Erlbaum.

Peterson, B. E., & Stewart, A. J. (1990). Using personal and fictional documents to assess psychosocial development: A case study of Vera Brittain's generativity. *Psychology and Aging, 5,* 400–411.

Peterson, B. E., & Stewart, A. J. (1993). Generativity and social motives in young adults. *Journal of Personality and Social Psychology, 65,* 186–198.

Peterson, B. E., & Stewart, A. J. (1996). Antecedents and contexts of generativity motivation at midlife. *Psychology and Aging, 11,* 21–33.

Polkinghorne, D. (1988). *Narrative knowing and the human sciences.* Albany: State University of New York Press.

Ricoeur, P. (1984). *Time and narrative.* Chicago: University of Chicago Press.

Ryff, C. D., & Heincke, S. G. (1983). Subjective organization of personality in adulthood and aging. *Journal of Personality and Social Psychology, 44,* 807–816.

Shlaes, J. (1995). *Generativity and object relations.* Unpublished doctoral dissertation, Department of Counseling Psychology, Northwestern University, Evanston, IL.

Singer, J., & Salovey, P. (1993). *The remembered self: Emotion and memory in personality.* New York: Free Press.

Sloan, T. (1996). *Damaged life: The crisis of the modern psyche.* London: Routledge & Kegan Paul.

Stewart, A. J., Franz, E., & Layton, L. (1988). The changing self: Using personal documents to study lives. *Journal of Personality, 56,* 41–74.

Tipton, R. M., Harrison, B. M., & Mahoney, J. (1980). Faith and locus of control. *Psychological Reports, 46,* 1151–1154.

Tomkins, S. S. (1987). Script theory. In J. Aronoff, A. I. Rabin, & R. A. Zucker (Eds.), *The emergence of personality* (pp. 147–216). New York: Springer.

Tyler, P. E. (1996, June 25). As a pampered generation grows up, Chinese worry. *The New York Times,* pp. A-1, A-6.

Vaillant, G. E., & Milofsky, E. (1980). The natural history of male psychological health: IX. Empirical evidence for Erikson's model of the life cycle. *American Journal of Psychiatry, 137,* 1348–1359.

Van de Water, D., & McAdams, D. P. (1989). Generativity and Erikson's "belief in the species." *Journal of Research in Personality, 23,* 435–449.

Westen, D. (1991). Clinical assessment of object relations using the TAT. *Journal of Personality Assessment, 56,* 56–74.

Wiggins, J. S., & Trapnell, P. D. (1996). A dyadic-interactional perspective on the five-factor model. In J. S. Wiggins (Ed.), *The five-factor model of personality: Theoretical perspectives* (pp. 88–162). New York: Guilford Press.

Winter, D. G. (1973). *The power motive.* New York: Free Press.

Wuthnow, R. (1991). *Acts of compassion: Caring for others and helping ourselves.* Princeton, NJ: Princeton University Press.

2

A GENERATIVE DRAMA: SCENES FROM A FATHER–SON RELATIONSHIP

JOHN SNAREY AND PETER YUICHI CLARK

PROLOGUE

In Shakespeare's comedy *As You Like It*, the character Jaques compares the life of a human being to a theatrical performance, a genre the Bard knew well: "All the world's a stage, And all the men and women merely players: They have their exits and their entrances; And one man in his time plays many parts, His acts being seven ages ..." (Act 2, Scene 7). Two aspects of this familiar metaphor intrigue us. First is the awareness that life has a dramaturgical flavor. Second is the surprising fact that none of Shakespeare's "seven ages" of life addresses parenting or, more specifically, fathering.[1] With this chapter, we hope to claim the gift that Shakespeare has given us—the metaphor of a drama to speak about human

We gratefully acknowledge helpful suggestions received from Ed de St. Aubin, Robin Ficklin-Alred, Rodney J. Hunter, Dan P. McAdams, Christy L. McGuire, William McKinley Runyan, and Mark B. Tappan.

[1] The seven ages mentioned by Jaques are infant, schoolboy, lover, soldier, justice (in the sense of a respectable middle-aged man), Pantaloon (a character in *commedia dell'arte*, usually a slim, older fool; Jaques seems to mean "early old age" here), and "second childishness," which appears to indicate extreme old age marked by frailty and dementia. Whether Jaques's opinion is shared by Shakespeare is, of course, open to debate.

life—and also to correct an oversight that the Bard committed, by bringing the richness of his metaphor to bear on fatherhood.

In recent years, there has been a resurgence of interest among academics, helping professionals, and parents in the importance of the roles that fathers play in family life and the larger society. This chapter offers a perspective on the subject of fatherhood that is informed both by Erik H. Erikson's psychosocial developmental theory, especially his understanding of generativity, and by the results of the most extensive longitudinal investigation of fathers to date. Specifically, we explore several scenes—both dramatic dialogues and soliloquies—between a father and a son, and we place these scenes in the context of Eriksonian theory and of the findings originally reported in *How Fathers Care for the Next Generation: A Four-Decade Study* (Snarey, 1993). In this chapter, we construct what Dan McAdams has called a "generativity script," or narration, to illustrate related dimensions of Erikson's theory and Snarey's research. (See McAdams & de St. Aubin, 1992, and chapter 1, this volume.)

At the outset we acknowledge our own investment in this issue. We are a father raising his biracial family in the Quaker tradition (J.S.) and a father of Japanese ancestry steeped in the Baptist faith (P.Y.C.); our perspectives on the work and joy of caring for children were not reached in a vacuum. We also share a moral agenda that states that research on fathers and families should contribute to a practical knowledge that both professionals and fathers will find useful in fostering healthy family relationships and thereby encourages human communities to move toward what Robert Bellah and his colleagues (Bellah, Madsen, Sullivan, Swidler, & Tipton, 1991) termed the "good society."

THE STUDY'S SETS AND PROPS

Theoretical Underpinnings

Erikson's concept of generativity formed the foundation for Snarey's study of how fathers care for the next generation. Erikson coined the term to denote the primary developmental task of middle adulthood, which involves caring for and contributing to the life of future generations. According to Erikson, social, psychological, and biological processes interact throughout the human life cycle to produce a series of vital psychosocial developmental tasks that intensify to a crisis or turning point in an eight-stage sequence. In this model, the psychosocial task of Stage 7 is the attainment of a favorable balance between generativity and stagnation. The fundamental challenge is to realize an excess of procreativity, productivity, and creativity over a pervading mood of personal inertia or self-absorption. Such a realization results in the growth of the ego strength of *care*, defined as "the widening concern for what has been generated by love, necessity, or accident; it overcomes the ambivalence adhering to irreversible obligation" (Erikson, 1964, p. 131). As we humans learn to care more broadly and deeply, we link our lives with the lives of others present and future, exercising and reprising the hope we discovered in our infant years (Browning, 1973; Clark, 1995). The converse of care is *rejectivity*, a kind of indifference that Erikson (1982) defined as "the unwillingness to include specified persons or groups in one's generative concern—one does not care to care for them" (p. 69). However, "one cannot ever be generative and careful without being selective to the point of some distinct rejectivity" (p. 68). Thus, the continual struggle of adult human beings, from an Eriksonian perspective, is to enlarge the circle of persons, products, and ideas one cares for while also adequately caring for oneself (cf. Gilligan, 1982; Hawkins & Dollahite, 1997; Skoe, Pratt, Matthews, & Curror, 1996).

Generativity is more complex, multifaceted, and differentiated than any other stage in Erikson's model, in part because it spans a greater number of years than the other stages. Erikson drew implicit distinctions among three types of generativity: (a) biological procreation, (b) parenthood, and (c) societal productivity or creativity. When speaking of generative fathers, therefore, it is possible to distinguish between the ways men contribute to and renew the ongoing cycle of the generations through the care they provide as (a) birth fathers (biological generativity), (b) child-rearing fathers (parental generativity), and (c) cultural fathers (societal generativity; Snarey, 1993; see Kotre, 1984, for a further distinction between two types of societal generativity, technical and cultural). These different types of generativity are interrelated. Biological generativity ideally links intimacy (Stage 6) to parental generativity as a couple expands their mutual interests and invests themselves "in that which is being generated and cared for together" (Erikson, 1982, p. 67). Parental generativity, in turn, is a tendon connecting biological and societal generativity. Generative parents interact with their children and thereby offer important support for their children's development. Concurrently, however, children interact with their parents and create (or make them aware of) opportunities that will help the parents develop their competencies to care for the wider community.

The Sample

Although *How Fathers Care* applies Erikson's concept of generativity to fathers, the nature of the research itself is intergenerational. The sample of 240 fathers was drawn from a group of men who were originally participants in a longitudinal study begun in Boston in 1939 by Sheldon and Eleanor Glueck of the Harvard University Law School. The fathers were part of a group of 500 boys selected by the Gluecks as controls for comparison to a second group of 500 boys who were persistent delinquents.

Original control group members were White men between the ages of 10 and 17; chosen from the Boston public schools; designated as "nondelinquent" by parents, teachers, social workers, police officers, and the boys themselves; and matched with the 500 delinquents on age, ethnicity, neighborhood of residence, and IQ (Glueck & Glueck, 1950; Sampson & Laub, 1993). Eventually 19% of the control group spent some time in jail, which suggests that the original control group is only modestly biased toward good behavior. In their initial research, the Gluecks interviewed the boys, their parents, and their teachers. In the second and third phases of the study, 456 of the nondelinquent boys were reinterviewed when they were young adults (at age 25 and again at age 31). During a fourth phase of the study, conducted by George E. Vaillant and his colleagues at Harvard University's Health Services, 392 of the men were again interviewed as men at midlife (average age = 47 years) and have since completed periodic questionnaires (Snarey & Vaillant, 1985; Vaillant & Vaillant, 1981). Of the 456 men who were reinterviewed, 240 met the requirements of the fatherhood investigation and were included in the "father sample" (Snarey, 1993).

Overall, about one third of the 240 men could be characterized as fathers who were "uncaring, unconnected, or uninvolved"; their longitudinal interviews showed that they were not significantly or positively involved in their children's lives. A little more than one third of the men were "good enough fathers" who were significantly and adequately supportive of their children's development. Finally, a little under one third of the men were clearly "good fathers"; they were highly and wisely involved in their children's lives through the supportive care they provided for their children's growth and development. To supplement the empirical data on these men and to provide a rating reliability sample, a subgroup of fathers and their oldest children were selected for extended tape-recorded interviews, which included individual, private segments and a lengthier joint father–son or father–daughter conversation (for further details, see Snarey, 1993, pp. 29–31, 44). The vignettes, or "scenes," that are presented in this chapter come from the 26,000-word transcript of one such interview with a "good father" (Gordon Sr.) and his son (Gordon Jr.). We selected an example of a good father for presentation because we agree with those who claim that family life scholars, practitioners, and fathers themselves stand to learn the most from "concrete images of fathers caring for and connecting to their children" (Dollahite, Hawkins, & Brotherson, 1996, p. 333; cf. Hawkins & Dollahite, 1997). We also had to be selective in terms of the scenes presented from the case; for each one presented, numerous equivalent or similar scenes were left waiting in the wings. Our selection was guided by the criteria that the overall constellation of scenes included should be representative of the participants' typical experiences and that each scene should be understandable without extensive background information.

Finally, before we introduce the "players" in our drama, we offer two qualifications. The first is that historical events place obvious limits on the generalization of our findings: Because we are dealing with a unique data set, there are limits to how much one may generalize to historically different cohorts. Of course, specificity also offers a definite advantage. Being part of the postwar baby boom and growing up in the 1950s, 1960s, and 1970s are circumstances consistent with the experience of many of today's fathers.

The second qualification is that, although the sample population is ethnically diverse, it is not representative in terms of racial or socioeconomic backgrounds. There were no African Americans or Asian Americans in the sample, and nearly all of the fathers were born into the urban working class. Although one fourth of them entered the middle class during early adulthood, this sort of mobility is not equally accessible for all groups, especially for people who are considered members of marginalized populations. This is a significant limitation on the generalizability of the research results. The fact that the sample is predominantly of the working class, however, is also an asset to the study because these men represent one of the largest and most "typical" segments of the U.S. population. Our findings about working-class child-rearing fathers help confirm the idea that generative fathering transcends class boundaries: It is not a phenomenon confined to socioeconomically advantaged classes.

With these qualifications, we present our play, hoping it will demonstrate how fathers care for the next generation.

DRAMATIS PERSONAE: FATHER AND SON

Gordon Sr., one of the Gluecks' original nondelinquent boys, is 59 years old at the time of this interview. He is of average height and build, but looks vitally healthy and has salt-and-pepper hair and gray-green eyes. His own father, "the first Gordon," was a railroad laborer, and his mother, Mary, worked in a candy factory; both of his parents' schooling ended after the seventh grade.

Gordon Sr. attended high school for a year and then joined his brothers doing carpentry work, which he continued throughout his first two decades of child rearing. At midlife, he changed jobs and became a supervisor for the U.S. Postal Service, where he guides and coordinates the activities of other workers. He also has served as an officer for a local community organization and as the vice president of his local labor union. Gordon Sr. has been married for about 40 years; he and his wife, Bernice, raised two sons and one daughter.

Gordon Sr.'s oldest son, Gordon Jr., is 39 years old. He has his father's eyes and soon will have the same color hair as his father. He graduated from high school, attended college for a year, and has taken several evening courses in business administration over the years. He and his business partner own and operate a highly profitable commercial enterprise. Gordon Jr. has been married to Donna for over 15 years, and they are the parents of two children. The family configuration at the time of this conversation is pictured as a genogram in Figure 1.

The sociohistorical context in which Gordon Sr. and Gordon Jr. have lived is one shaped by the Great Depression and the baby boom in the United States. Gordon Sr., like many of the boys in the Gluecks' study, was born between the time that the Wall Street stock market crashed (1929) and Adolf Hitler rose to the chancellorship of Germany (1933). During this period, the average annual income for U.S. families fell by nearly 40%, forcing many parents to struggle for their household's economic survival. Gordon vividly remembered that his father worked long hours and that he had to adjust to his father's absences from the home. The economic realities of that time also limited Gordon Sr.'s education; he did not graduate from high school (only about 38% of the 240 men in this study did graduate, on par with the national average before World War II, according to the U.S. Bureau of the Census). However, the rising post-

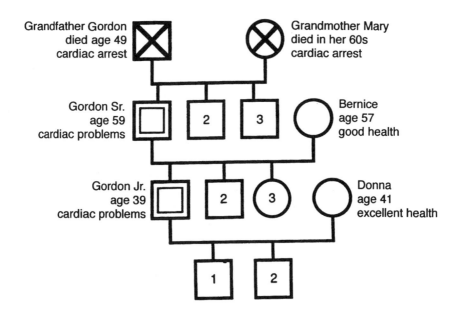

Figure 1. Genogram of Gordon Sr. and Gordon Jr.'s Family. All names and some details have been modified to protect confidentiality.

war economy, combined with the resiliency of his generation, helped Gordon Sr. experience some occupational mobility.

Like many members of his cohort, Gordon Sr. married young (age 19), and he and his wife (who also left high school in the 10th grade) both worked outside the home to make ends meet. They also began having children immediately, but Gordon's participation in child care was moderated to some degree by the expectations of U.S. society of that era. He recalled that Bernice gave birth to Gordon Jr. while he was at work, yet he had to finish his job before his employer would allow him to go to the hospital; when he did arrive at the hospital, he was taken aback by his son's appearance: "She [Bernice] says, 'He's beautiful, huh?' I said, 'Yeah . . . but how come he looks pink and his head is flat?'" The nurse then said, "Oh, you fool, that's how babies look." The expectation that Gordon lacked knowledge about babies and the enforced prioritizing of work over family were common experiences of his peers as they fathered a boom in the number of babies born between 1946 and 1964.

It has been argued that Gordon Sr. and his contemporaries were caught in a cultural contradiction:

> Becoming a new father increased one's dependence on the very [child development] experts who had first mapped this new parental terrain; moreover, men's responsibilities as breadwinners coupled with the ironies of parent education, children's attachment to their mothers, changes in the nature of breadwinning, and the emergence of a distinctive, school-centered peer culture worked to make outsiders of men. (Griswold, 1993, p. 120)

Although Gordon Sr. was affected by cultural factors, such as the delegating of child care tasks along a traditional sexual division of labor, Gordon's interaction with his children was not consistent with broad conclusions about being an "outsider." Indeed, as we contend later, the research in *How Fathers Care* documents a highly involved style of fathering that was fairly common among working-class men.

Gordon Jr., like most of the study's 240 children, was born during the placid, prosperous 1950s, the "middle years" of the boomer cohort. Gordon Sr. tried to ensure that his son would experience a better economic milieu than he himself had: "I bought him things that I never had when I was a kid growing up. . . . When new things would come out, we'd always make sure they had them." Often he would do this despite his own financial uncertainty; he recalled not being able to work during the winter (when he was involved in construction) and wondering where he would find the money for Christmas presents. Gordon Jr., nevertheless, benefited from his working-class parents' economic progress, and he was the first in his family to graduate from high school. As Gordon Jr. came of age, though, the United States was becoming more enmeshed in the Vietnam conflict, and like many of his generation, he began to question the values of his parents. His Eriksonian search for identity took the form of long hair, drug use, and an ironic attempt to enlist in the Navy that his father discouraged, as had Gordon Sr.'s father before him (Gordon Jr. did not enlist; Gordon Sr. had served in the Army). For Gordon Jr., the path toward identity wound through both rebellion and conformity toward parental authority and institutional structures.

The sheer number of middle baby boomers like Gordon Jr. made personal occupational success a slower proposition than it had been for the earliest born members of the baby boom and for their parents. However, Gordon Jr. identified a business opportunity for which his extraverted and altruistic personality was an important asset. He successfully built a strong company that made him fairly wealthy. Now a parent, Gordon Jr. is "juggling" the challenges of managing his business in an uncertain economic climate and spending time with his children so that they can experience the same sort of care that he enjoyed from his own father. (For a fuller description of the sociohistorical context in which Depression-era fathers and their baby boom offspring came of age, see Snarey, 1993, pp. 2–13).

In the following sections, we hear from Gordon Sr. and Gordon Jr., speaking in their own words in a series of six scenes.

Scene 1: Adventures in Active Child Rearing

The first scene possesses a sense of action and adventure. The anecdote revolves around Gordon Jr.'s participation in a youth football league called Pop Warner Football, named after Hall of Fame coach Glenn "Pop" Warner (1871–1954), who, having no children of his own, took a fatherly interest in all of his players (Warner, 1934). The scene also reveals a watershed event in the lives of both father and son.

> Father: Then he played football. He was a good football player, too.
> Son: We played on Saturday, so he never saw any of my [complete] football games—he would sneak down for an hour, but then he went back to his work. He'd come down, and no sooner did he get there, and I saw him and I ran and got a touchdown. He was all excited because that happened, and he had been there with his brothers and some other friends, and it was, "Look! I just got here, and he got the touchdown!" That and my schoolwork. He was proud of that. [When I was younger], he even coached my team. I must have been about 10 or so, I guess, when you coached that team?
> Father: Oh, the [youth] football team? Yeah. That was Pop Warner.
> Son: That was funny. We had a whole team together, and somebody's father or friend was supposed to coach the team, but he skipped town. So I said to my father, "Geez, we don't have a coach. We all had to pay some money for uniforms, we lost five games, and then [the coach] took off with the money." [laughter]

Father: He did, he took off.

Son: We were stuck without our money, without uniforms, without a coach, and we couldn't win a game to save our lives.... We each had a helmet and shoulder pads, but that was it. Dad took over the team, and we used to practice. I remember the nights he'd come home from work (he'd still have his work clothes on) and we'd be down [on] the field. He says, "Okay, here's the ball, run! Okay, everybody go get 'em." It was a game called Suicide. But we loved it, and we did that until it got dark. We'd go on and on for hours. What you do is you just run with the ball, everybody would tackle you, throw the ball up in the air, the next guy grabs it, and he runs. So he was building up our skills in tackling.

Father: I was picking out people that way. I'd have them run around the park. Then I'd be watching to see who had the best speed. See, they were all playing the wrong positions, and that's why they lost all their games. I had to reposition everybody. I had to see who was aggressive and who was not aggressive. When you play the game of Suicide, you'd find out the aggressive person, because he would hold onto the ball and get tackled. The other one would throw it away. So it was simple. You didn't embarrass anybody in that sense. So then I rearranged the whole team, and they came up with a pretty good team. I think they won the rest of the year.

Son: Oh, yeah, we were winning *everything* after that.

This scene shows Gordon Sr.'s presence in his son's life and the impact of Gordon Sr.'s willingness to "step in" as a presence in his son's peers' lives. It was not simply his being there that counted, although that was important; it was also what he did with his son and how he did it.

Evaluating the care that fathers like Gordon Sr. provided for their children was a major impetus of the study described in *How Fathers Care*. Fathers' participation in specific activities and assumption of responsibilities were categorized and then grouped by the time of occurrence (whether in childhood or adolescence). This method allowed each of the 240 men's longitudinal interviews to be rated on six areas of paternal support: (a) social–emotional development in childhood, (b) intellectual–academic development in childhood, (c) physical–athletic development in childhood, (d) social–emotional development in adolescence, (e) intellectual–academic development in adolescence, and (f) physical–athletic development in adolescence. (Examples from Gordon Sr.'s child-rearing narrative are listed in Exhibit 1.)

On average, 9.3 child-rearing activities were noted in the fathers' two combined child-rearing assessments. Thirty-five percent of the fathers in the Gluecks' sample (85 men) participated in 6 or fewer child-rearing activities (on average, not very involved). Another 41% (98 men) participated in 7 to 12 activities (significantly involved), and 57 fathers (24% of the sample) were involved in 13 to 24 or more activities (highly involved).

EXHIBIT 1
Examples of Generative Fathering in Gordon Sr.'s Story

Childhood Decade

Social–emotional support
- Played guitar for Gordon Jr. and his neighborhood friends to sing along.
- Encouraged and worked with children as they performed Tuesday night "talent shows."
- Coached Gordon Jr.'s football team in such a way as not to embarrass any individual player.

Intellectual–academic support
- Supported his son when he got his first "B" on a report card (Gordon Jr. had been a straight "A" student to that point).
- Helped Gordon Jr. with his homework.
- Allowed his son to try music lessons with various instruments (clarinet, accordion, classical guitar) so he could find "his instrument."

Physical–athletic support
- Wrestled and ran races with Gordon Jr. and his neighborhood friends.
- Praised his son for signing himself up for the Babe Ruth baseball league.
- Coached his son's Pop Warner football team and successfully taught the members how to improve their skills.

Adolescent Decade

Social–emotional support
- Allowed his son to bring his girlfriend on a family trip (as long as they slept in separate rooms).
- Played social games and practical jokes with his son.
- Empathized with his son's rebellious nature while not compromising his own values.

Intellectual–academic support
- Foiled, with good humor, his son's attempt to cut catechism classes.
- Praised his son for receiving his high school diploma and encouraged him to continue his education.
- Supported his son's participation in an Upward Bound college preparatory program.

Physical–athletic support
- Took his son to the children's hospital for heart monitoring.
- Supported his son in his sport endeavors while redirecting him toward sports that were not contraindicated for his son's heart condition.
- Enrolled in aikido classes with his son.

Gordon Sr. was in the "highly involved" group. Gordon's involvement with his son was higher in his son's adolescence than childhood; he showed an increase in his support of social–emotional, intellectual, and physical growth during adolescence. What is remarkable here is that this pattern of involvement is an exception to the general pattern reported in *How Fathers Care.* The study found that total father participation was, on average, higher during the childhood decade than during the adolescent decade. For both decades, fathers gave more support for children's social–emotional development than the other categories, although there was a decline after the first decade. Physical–athletic development was notably encouraged in childhood, but this support declined in adolescence, whereas support for intellectual–academic development slightly increased during adolescence.

The general patterns of association among the types of parental generativity were informative. In the childhood decade, no significant correlations were found among any of the three types of child care; that is, fathers who gave especially strong child-rearing support in one area were not necessarily more inclined than others to offer support in other areas. In the adolescent decade, however, all three types were significantly and positively intercorrelated; fathers active in one area of child rearing tended to be active in all three areas (suggesting that fathers may pursue a more integrated approach to promoting their children's development by the time their children reach adolescence). Furthermore, if a father actively provided support in a particular area in the childhood decade, he tended to support that same area actively in the adolescent decade. Finally, fathers who were highly supportive of their offspring's physical–athletic development in childhood also tended to shift gears and encourage intellectual–academic development during adolescence. The pattern of continuities and discontinuities in paternal child care suggests an evolving relationship between parent and child in which each adapts to the other's competence and experience.

In Scene 1 Gordon Sr.'s volunteer work as a coach demonstrated his high level and personal style of parental generativity. The scene also hints, however, at how children and child rearing affect fathers themselves, including the core areas of their existence: work life, family life, and the life of the self. In *How Fathers Care,* an assessment of the impact of children on parents was formulated as three research questions: (a) Does a father's parental generativity predict the state of his occupational career at midlife? (b) Does a father's parental generativity predict the state of his marriage at midlife? and (c) Does a father's parental generativity predict his psychosocial maturity at midlife?

To answer these questions, the researchers used hierarchical multiple regression analysis to account for variance in three midlife outcomes: marital success, occupational mobility, and societal generativity. The control variables included the background characteristics of the participants' boypants' boyhood family of origin and the current characteristics of their adulthood family of procreation. The six parental generativity variables listed previously served as predictor variables of the outcomes (for a detailed description of this procedure see Snarey, 1993, pp. 96–105).

On average, the study fathers were upwardly mobile, advancing one occupational level above that of their parents. The hierarchical regression model explained over a third of the variance in the fathers' occupational mobility. After controlling for all other variables, the total contribution made by child rearing to fathers' occupational mobility was 6% beyond that explained by the background variables, and the contribution was both positive and significant. One specific domain of child-rearing activity— fathers' care for their teens' social and emotional maturation—made a significant individual contribution to fathers' work mobility. Despite the work trade-offs, role conflicts, and reframing of career goals that fathers endure, the fathers' child rearing did not appear to have a measurable long-term negative impact on occupational mobility. Contrary to common expectations, in fact, child-rearing activity modestly predicted career mobility in the study. It could well be that child-rearing participation and occupational success are reciprocally related to a modest degree. (See chapter 7, this volume, which focuses on the coordinates of social stratification.) We emphasize, however, that this association of work mobility and parental generativity does not necessarily mean that the latter caused the former. We also point out that this finding is specific to a cohort in which women did the lion's share of housework.

As for fathers' marital success, about 3 out of every 10 men showed clear marital enjoyment at midlife, another 5 out of 10 remained married but their marital enjoyment was unclear or absent, and 2 out of every 10 men's marriages ended in divorce. After all other variables were controlled for, the total contribution made by child rearing to the explained variance in fathers' marital outcomes was 21% beyond that explained by the background variables. Of that 21%, 12% could be attributed to fathers' child rearing in the first decade, particularly their nurturing of social–emotional growth. Another 9% of the variance came from fathers' child rearing during the adolescent decade, with support of social–emotional development and intellectual–academic development each providing significant contributions. Simply put, fathers who cared for their children's emotional development during childhood and adolescence and who cared for their children's school success during the teen years were men who had greater marital stability and happiness at midlife.

This outcome was certainly true for Gordon Sr. In another part of his interview, for instance, Gordon Sr. described taking his family to visit New York City and stay at the hotel where he and Bernice had spent their honeymoon. Gordon Jr. wanted to invite his girlfriend (now wife), Donna, to come along, and his father allowed her to go with them, with one ground rule: "You, me, and your brother will sleep in one room, and your mother, sister, and Donna can sleep in another room." What we found interesting about this incident was Gordon Sr.'s linking of his life as a father to his relationship with his wife. Both he and Bernice seemed to have no thought of going alone, or any resentment at having their three children and son's girlfriend join them. From this welcoming atmosphere, humor and good vacation memories followed. For Gordon Sr., it seems clear, marital intimacy and parental generativity were linked in a vital—and mutually reinforcing—way.

Societal generativity, or "cultural fatherhood," was clearly evidenced at midlife by 2 out of every 10 men, whereas some degree of societal generativity was shown by another 2 out of 10 men; no evidence of societal generativity was exhibited by the remaining 6 out of every 10 men. A hierarchical regression model accounted for 22% of this variance in societal generativity: Fathers' child-rearing activities contributed 14%, and background variables contributed 8%. As with marital success, fathers who cared for their children's social–emotional growth in both decades and for their children's intellectual–academic maturation in adolescence were notably more likely to have become generative beyond the family sphere.

These findings suggest, in summary, that the supportive care fathers offer to their children's social–emotional and intellectual–academic development makes a significant contribution to fathers' own ability to be happy in their marriage and to nurture citizens of the larger community. There was no evidence that parental generativity has a significant negative influence on men's occupational mobility.

Gordon Sr.'s life also appears to confirm these conclusions. He was assessed as experiencing some upward vocational movement, as being married with clear marital enjoyment, and as having demonstrated clear societal generativity. Gordon Sr.'s coaching of his son's football team especially illuminates his psychosocial development as a father and his emerging societal generativity. Acting without formal coaching experience but with sound psychological intuition, he found a way of working with the children on the team so that they retained their enthusiasm and will to play—a way of moving players around without humiliating them. In Gordon Sr.'s case, moreover, the coaching tale shows not only his characteristic flexibility in being willing to become a coach on the spur of the moment but also his embrace of a broader vision of fathering. By caring for and nurturing the development of the other children on the team, Gordon Sr. learned that fathering also functions to bond a father to the larger community and, thereby, to allow parental generativity to begin to evolve into societal generativity.

Scene 2: Humor, Autonomy, and Mobility

The following vignette has some of the flavor of a comic romp. However, like much good comedy, there is significant truth hidden amidst the laughter, in this case, a family interactional style and a father's nurturing of his son's later achievements:

> Father: Tuesday nights we'd have family night, "talent night," at our house. These guys were funny!
>
> Son: They would sit here, and we would go in the other room, and put on a different outfit or act in a different way or come out and sing, or just do something funny. Then he'd contribute because he was always playing the piano, and we'd sing, or his brothers would come down, and they'd play their instruments, and we'd have singalongs, and just do kind of crazy things.
>
> Father: That was great, though. The kids would always come up with something. They'd try to outdo each other. That was the funny part of everything. They were all good, but trying to outdo each other was the funniest.
>
> Son: This was ad lib, just off the cuff. We'd just make Dad and Mom laugh. Pretty much every Tuesday night. Of course, we didn't always come up with a new act. Sometimes it was the same act, but polished up a little more. They'd still laugh.

In addition to showing creative flexibility, this story illustrates that humor is another family *legacy*, something handed down from generation to generation. In their stories about themselves and their fathers, both Gordon Sr. and Gordon Jr. highlighted the centrality of humor to their way of being in the world. Also in this interview, for instance, Gordon Sr. related that, as a boy, he had cut the legs off his father's favorite chair to make it into a rocking chair and that his father reacted not angrily but with easygoing humor. He and Gordon Jr. recalled that when Gordon Jr. was skipping his Catholic catechism meetings, Gordon Sr. arranged for the priest to be waiting at the house when Gordon Jr. came home. Gordon Jr. was quite surprised, as intended, and Gordon Sr. and the priest savored the ironic comedy resulting from their cooperative efforts to hold Gordy accountable. The ubiquitous humor also makes us wonder if it is a pressure valve that allows for the reduction of conflict and hence protects and preserves the family's stability. Humor, as Hampes (1993) observed, both reduces stress and facilitates creativity and generativity. Perhaps Gordon Sr. and Gordon Jr., men who grew up in less than optimal economic circumstances, were embodying with their *joie de vivre* what Mark Twain once said: "Against the assault of laughter nothing can stand" (1922, p. 132).

Beyond humor and creativity, this anecdote reiterates the father's role in nurturing his son's psychosocial growth. When Gordon Sr. encouraged

Gordon Jr. and his other children to create these "talent nights," he was providing opportunities for the children to exercise their initiative and industry, both critical Eriksonian developmental tasks. Evolving from these talent nights was Gordon Jr.'s interest in learning to play a musical instrument. Patiently and with good humor, Gordon Sr. allowed his son to try several in succession, paying for lessons and other incidentals, until Gordon Jr. found an instrument he liked and wanted to play. These paternal qualities enhanced Gordon Jr.'s sense of autonomy and may have been formative in his ability to explore educational and vocational opportunities. These observations lead to the question of how fathers' child rearing affects their children's educational and occupational success.

How Fathers Care addresses two structurally similar research questions: (a) Does extent of fathers' child rearing predict daughters' educational and occupational mobility? and (b) Does paternal generativity predict sons' mobility? To answer these questions, the researchers rated the children on two early-adulthood outcomes: educational mobility and occupational mobility. Control variables addressed the family's background and context (e.g., the father's occupational and educational levels, his wife's occupational and educational levels, the father's marital affinity or commitment, his wife's employment outside the home, the age of the child, and the number of children in the family). The predictor variables, as before, were the six parental generativity variables (Snarey, 1993, pp. 164–167).

The children, on average, exhibited upward mobility by achieving one educational level above that of their parents. Gordon Jr., whose father and mother had finished the 10th grade, graduated from high school and then attended but did not graduate from college. Gordon Jr. was like 47% of the firstborn children in that respect; of the others, 23% earned bachelor's degrees, about 10% obtained further professional training, and 5% earned graduate degrees.

How Fathers Care examines the educational mobility of both daughters and sons. For daughters, after background variables were controlled for, the fathers' child-rearing generativity accounted for 16% of the variance in educational mobility. The strongest contributor was fathers' high levels of care for physical–athletic development during the childhood decade and high levels of support for both physical–athletic development and social–emotional development during the adolescent decade. For sons, again after background variables were controlled for, the fathers' child-rearing participation accounted for 11% of the predicted variance in sons' educational mobility. The major contributing forms of child care were support of intellectual–academic and social–emotional development during childhood and support of intellectual–academic development again during adolescence.

Occupationally, the children were also, on average, upwardly mobile by approximately one occupational level above that of their parents. This frequently meant that children whose parents held semiskilled or skilled blue collar jobs became owners of small businesses, technicians, or semiprofessionals. During early adulthood, 15% of the firstborn children entered major professions (e.g., becoming accountants, educators, lawyers, architects, and members of the clergy), 21% became semiprofessionals (e.g., becoming business managers, dental hygienists, and court reporters), 36% became technicians or small business owners, 19% entered the skilled trades, and 9% were semiskilled or unskilled workers.

Evaluating the predictors of occupational mobility meant again distinguishing between daughters and sons to detect differences. For daughters, after background variables were controlled for, fathers' care contributed an additional 8% to the explained variance, with high levels of support for physical–athletic and social–emotional development during adolescence making significant individual contributions. For sons, again after background variables were controlled for, fathers' care during the childhood decade contributed an additional 6% to the explained variance, with the strongest contributing factor being support of physical–athletic development.

In summary, daughters' mobility was measurably higher when their fathers supported their physical–athletic development during the childhood decade and when their fathers supported both their social–emotional and their physical–athletic development during adolescence. In contrast, sons were more upwardly mobile when their fathers supported their social–emotional, intellectual–academic, and physical–athletic development during the childhood decade but benefited from their fathers' support of only their intellectual–academic development during the adolescent decade. The results support an Eriksonian view that daughters and sons need different types of paternal help during different decades of growth: for sons, identification with fathers in childhood and differentiation from them in the teen years, and for daughters, provision of opportunities for initiative in childhood and encouragement to differentiate from their mothers and establish autonomous identities in adolescence. Moreover, it would seem that forms of child rearing that are less stereotyped about gender roles tend to be beneficial for children of both sexes because those forms give children the broadening life experience that they might not receive elsewhere. (Our finding that paternal support is vital to children's occupational and educational development seems to be confirmed by Franz, McClelland, & Weinberger, 1991, whose study demonstrated a connection between father warmth and children's conventional social accomplishment.)

Scene 2 addressed how children are affected by their fathers' parenting. We now consider how fathers themselves can be powerfully influenced by their children through a phenomenon called *generativity chill.*

Scene 3: The Heart of Generativity Chill

The modern French philosopher Paul Ricoeur (1965) contended that people experience their human existence as a continuous tension between anxiety and hope and that these seemingly contradictory moods are actually two ways of experiencing the same reality. This assertion is perhaps no more true than in the face of a potential tragedy. In the following anecdote, Gordon Sr. and Jr. speak of such an occurrence involving a medical condition, but for them it is an event in which hope endures amidst profound anxiety:

Father: His health gave us some concern during his teen years. I took him over to the children's hospital twice a week for monitoring. He was on medication; he had to take it three times daily or whatever, and the doctors looked at him twice a week. [*Turns to son*] It all started when you were about 11 years old?

Son: Yeah, about 11 or 12, because I found out when I went up to the Boys Club to take a routine physical. The doctor there said, "Geez, you'd better get your mom to take you to a doctor to have your heart checked." Naturally, as a kid, I panicked! They took me up to the local clinic, to our family doctor, and he sent us over to the children's hospital. They ran all their tests and then told me, "You can't do this, you can't do that. . . ."

Father: I was worried that he would still do these things anyway. Because, see, that happened to me when I was a kid. In fact, I lost a year of school because of it. I had a bad heart, so no contact sports; I wasn't supposed to swim, and I wasn't supposed to do this or that. Yet I did everything! So I thought he was going to be doing the same thing; that's what used to worry me. . . . I was thinking, "I know when my mother told me I couldn't do this and I couldn't do that, I still went and did it." So I figure he's going to be doing the same thing. I was worried.

Son: They knew more about it than I did. All I know is, no one ever told me anything. They said, "You have a heart murmur." I didn't know how severe it was. I didn't realize until later in life that I had a valve problem. Then all I thought was I had a murmur. I didn't know how bad. So I just dismissed it, "Hey, it's not bad"; no one told me it was bad.

Father: He had a bad heart; he wasn't supposed to play any contact sports, and it kind of shook us up there a bit, but sports don't matter really, in life. It's life that matters in life. The doctor said it would be all right if he runs, so we got him interested in other things, and he excelled in track. I was always proud of him, no matter what he did. He was one of those kids that you're proud of all the time.

Son: No matter what sport I did, he was always, "Good job," very supportive. The heart problem went on for quite a while, and then I still had to go back every 2 or 3 months for visits. That was during the day, and my mother took me for that. I had to get out of school. But when I was going back and forth at nights and late afternoons, my dad was taking me over there. At the time, I just thought he didn't want us taking the subway, knowing how bad it was. He never really let me know how worried he was. He always let me know he was concerned, but I could never see that he was quite worried.

I still have it. I still go every 3 or 4 months to the doctor. They monitor it still, but it's a lot less severe, I think, than they thought back then.

This exchange between father and son highlights the idea of generativity chill, an extension Snarey (1993) made of Erikson's theory. Generativity chill refers to a type of ego anxiety (an awareness of the self as finite and bounded) that results from a specific type of existential imperilment (the threatened loss of one's child, creation, or creativity). (We note that the situation described in this scene is only one type of generativity chill; *How Fathers Care* describes other types of this phenomenon.) In this context, generativity chill arises when an adult faces the possibility of losing one's child—psychologically, socially, or physically (cf. Hawkins & Dollahite, 1997). Whatever the potential threat, its entrance and the chill that follows underscore the circularity between generativity and death: Awareness of death progressively prompts biological, parental, and societal generativity, and in turn, all three types of generativity progressively assuage the fear of death through a maturing love of life. When generativity is endangered, the fear of death may be reactivated, and then Kierkegaard's maxim may ring all too true: "The sickness unto death is despair" (1849/1980, p. 11).

For Gordon Sr., generativity chill came with the discovery of his son's heart murmur. The depth of Gordon Sr.'s experience of generativity chill becomes obvious, however, in his candid flashback:

Father: I wish I'd got to know [my own dad] better, as a man. My memory of him hasn't changed since then. I still have the same feelings. I understand more about him now, of course, than I did before, but I still have the same feelings.

[In September of 1950], when I was going to get married, [Bernice and I] went in town to get our marriage license. My dad came with us in case we had any problems, my being 19 years old—you needed your parents' consent. (I was in the service then and came home on a weekend pass and filled out the marriage forms and so forth.) The fellow behind the counter said, "That'll be $2.08." I looked at him. I didn't have no money [*laughs*]. Dad jokes to my wife, Bernice, "Boy, are you off to a bad start—he's broke already!" [*Laughter*] So he paid for the license. . . . Then he took us out to have something to eat. He was always a fine man. . . .

He got sick that Christmas. I was home, and he wasn't feeling good, and I kept saying, "Pa, why don't I get the doctor?" He said, "No, that's all right, I'll be all right." So I went back to camp, and he did get sicker. They rushed him to the hospital with a bad heart attack. Fluid and so forth. Then I got a call at camp, and they told me that my father had passed away. That was it, for my father.

I'm being monitored, too [*laughter*]. I had extensive bypass surgery done a few years ago.

Cardiac disorders caused Gordon Sr.'s father's premature death and, more than a decade later, also claimed his mother. Because of this family's shared genetic predisposition to heart problems, it is little wonder that Gordon Sr. was so concerned about Gordon Jr.'s health and that he stated, "It's life that matters in life." Like humor and creativity, generativity chill apparently is a legacy that this family passed from one generation to the next.

His inheritance seemed to spur more intentionality in Gordon Sr.'s parenting. This phenomenon is not unusual. As *How Fathers Care* reports, the total quantity of all types of parental generativity combined was significantly higher among fathers who had experienced generativity chill than among fathers who had no such experience. It appears that generativity chill intensified the parental generativity of the men in the sample who experienced it because it forced them to become reflective and tenacious in their desire to be fathers.

Gordon Sr.'s final comments about his father were that "my memory of him hasn't changed since then. I still have the same feelings. I understand more about him now, of course, than I did before, but I still have the same feelings." Here we have a foreshadowing of scenes to come.

Scene 4: Intergenerational Conflict

Thus far the portrait we have painted of this father and son has been one colored by legacies of flexibility, humor, and anxiety. Their relationship—and this drama—probably seem rather idyllic. Ever since Aristotle wrote his classic exposition on comedy and tragedy in the *Poetics*, however, Westerners have affirmed that dramatic works derive their force from portraying the complications and tensions that emerge when human characters interact. Every human story involves some conflict, and the tale of the two Gordons is no exception. We hear of one such incident in their conjoint interview.

Son: I was a little more trouble in high school than I was in elementary and junior high school.... Not real bad stuff, but still, for me, it was more trouble. We had a separation period, in my later teens, during the late '60s. I was going through a thing where I had long hair, and I was taking drugs.

Father: Yeah. I was like, "I understand what you're doing, but it's not right." We kind of separated a little bit there.

Son: We never really were distant, but there was a time when we didn't see eye to eye.

Father: It was more serious than some of the other stuff, but we could still sit down and talk about it.

Son: Yeah, long talks. He always said, "Sit down with me and explain," and the closing line was, "And if you ever do it again. . ." This is like a warning, "You do it again and I'll. . . ." The fear of just him yelling was enough to scare me.

This is a fascinating exchange because it describes an experience of conflict without stimulating an affect of further conflict. To be precise, the potential for conflict was reduced by the son in the past and is again in the present. In the past, as he admits, "the fear of just him [Gordon Sr.] yelling was enough to scare me"; apparently, Gordon Jr. did what he could to avoid facing his father's anger even when he rebelled. In the present, it is reduced by the son's acknowledgment of his past actions; he openly confesses to contributing to the alienation felt between father and son in Gordon Jr.'s teenage years, an assessment with which Gordon Sr. concurs. Intriguingly, Gordon Sr. evidently feels no need to admit that his own actions may have contributed to not being able to see "eye to eye" with his son.

Because the emotive energy of this conflictual interaction lies somewhere other than with the narrative itself, we are left to speculate about what is happening in the interview. Two possibilities come to mind. One is that the conflictual energy is being channeled in such a way as to maintain the homeostasis of the family relationship. If so, the avoidance of overt conflict has a use for the two Gordons similar to the use of humor, which we mentioned earlier. This avoidance of overt tension may be exacerbated by the artificial nature of an interview. One hears a self-report given to a relative stranger (although the father should be accustomed to this sort of scrutiny because he has been part of a 40-year longitudinal study). Consequently, there may be some felt pressure to paint the best possible picture for the researcher and keep signs of conflict "offstage," in Goffman's (1959) sense of the term.

The second and perhaps more compelling possibility arises from a secret carried by the father during the interviews. In neither the individual nor the conjoint interview does the father reveal what he disclosed on his medical history questionnaire: Gordon Sr. has abused prescription medicines. This problem occurred in the past, and it was not a problem for Gordon Sr. when he was interviewed; yet he was not willing to talk freely about it. It appears that Gordon Sr. had won his battle with prescription drugs not long before Gordon Jr. began taking nonprescription drugs. If this is correct, two other implications come into play. The first is that Gordon Sr., because of his own past experience with drugs, was more sensitive to Gordon Jr.'s situation; he knew that it was more complicated than telling his son to "just say no." However, it was also clear to him that he had to be forceful: Gordon Jr. had to stop using controlled substances before they ruined his life. The incident illustrates another kind of generativity chill, affecting Gordon Sr. in a dual-pronged dilemma. If he did not control his own drug use, he would shorten his life span (and the amount of time he would have to be generative); if his son did not stop taking drugs, there was the the possibility that his son might die as a consequence. Much was at stake for the elder Gordon. The other implication at work here is that Gordon Sr.'s situation—he "hides" his past experience while drawing on it to advise his child—parallels the dilemma that Gordon Jr. and his contemporaries currently face with their adolescent children. Amidst a rising trend in teenagers' drug use in the United States, do their parents admit their own drug use ("yes, I inhaled"), and will that admission erode their moral capital in exhorting their children not to experiment with drugs?

This situation, if we have interpreted it correctly, highlights what Kotre (1984) called the "dark side" of generativity: its vulnerability to becoming distorted (p. 9). The legacies we pass on to our children can be morally ambiguous and even dangerous. Whereas we have focused on the ways in which Gordon Sr.'s fathering has conveyed positive legacies to Gordon Jr., we must not lose sight of the fact that generativity can be distorted so that it propagates harm as well as good, curse as well as blessing. The two Gordons are fortunate; their legacies have been genuinely generous and life affirming. Those legacies did not come prepackaged, however; they were adapted and transformed as the two Gordons discovered and used them. It is this process, a rhythm of modeling and reworking what one has received, to which we turn in the scene to follow.

Scene 5: The Cogwheeling of Modeling and Reworking

In this scene, as in the previous scenes, the father and son reminisce and evaluate their life, tasks that often accompany the transition into older adulthood (cf. Butler, 1963; Cohler, 1982; Erikson, Erikson, & Kivnick, 1986). Gordon Sr. in this scene (and Gordon Jr. in the next scene), however, shows that such remembrance and self-examination are not just the province of the elderly (cf. Neugarten, 1969):

> Father: My dad influenced the way I raised my own children, I would say. When my son was born, I was a little more active than my dad was. Because you do things and you don't even realize it. My children also had to get home at a certain time. As my sons got older, I gave them a dime, and I'd say, "Hey, listen, take this dime, put it in your pocket, if you ever have any problems, you call the house. Never come home late." They never had an excuse to be late, because they had a dime [laughs]. They respected us for that, my kids, I think; they all came home when they were supposed to.
>
> I look back, it was like I was the threat. Bernice would say to the kids, "When your father gets home tonight. . . ." I never chastised them

that much, I just more or less always was there, too. Maybe once in a while I gave them a crack when they needed it, but nothing to scar them for life. I don't take off the strap, of course, but we all do basically a lot of the same things as our own parents; we kid around the same way, so you can see it's like a hand-me-down sort of thing. My brother raises his daughter that way, and my other brother raised his children that way, and if you looked at all of our children, you could see that we all came from one mold, one time or another. If he [Gordon Sr.'s father] were here today, I think he'd say he was proud of me. He'd probably talk about how I went to the post office and became a supervisor over there. I had dropped out of school, but I still accomplished these things. He'd be proud that my wife also worked hard, and we got our own house. He'd be proud that my wife and I raised our children the way we did. Gordy has accomplished a tremendous amount. Oh, my father would have been so proud of him. He'd be proud of all three of my children. We all know how to work when you work and how to be happy when you're happy.

Gordon Sr. is speaking here, during his individual interview, about his relationship with his own father. His comments lead to the question of how one might explain a father's child care behavior and involvement. This problem, in the *How Fathers Care* study, became two research questions: (a) Does the fathering that men received during their own boyhood years predict their subsequent parental generativity as adults? (b) Among concurrent variables, would the characteristics of the fathers themselves or of their children or of their wives be the best predictors of the fathers' parental generativity? To answer these questions, a multivariate analysis was conducted that included 23 different predictor variables. These included five indices of the fathers' boyhood personal characteristics, five boyhood assessments of their fathers' background and child-rearing style, and five boyhood assessments of their mothers' characteristics. Also included were eight concurrent predictor variables based on the simultaneous characteristics of the men's children, their wives, and themselves. The outcomes being predicted were the same six parental generativity variables mentioned earlier.

What the research uncovered was that concurrent variables were the best predictors of men's global, or total, quantity of child-rearing activity but that boyhood variables were the most consistent predictors of the six specific types of parental generativity. Regarding the overall quantity of parental generativity, regression analyses accounted for 27% of the variance, with the men's boyhood IQ, marital affinity, the wives' educational level and work outside the home, the men's mothers' level of education, and generativity chill all making significant contributions to the explained variance.

In terms of predicting specific styles of paternal generativity, two variables predicted fathers' activity in social–emotional development during childhood: the men's fathers' level of education and their own current marital affinity, which together accounted for 13% of the variance. Fathers who became highly and positively involved in promoting their children's social–emotional development during adolescence tended to be men whose own fathers had been distant or nonnurturant but had shown a significant degree of occupational achievement and had otherwise provided them with a positive home environment (as was the experience of Gordon Sr.). This finding suggests that the men's own style of fathering was based on a blend of modeling and reworking of their own experience of being fathered. These men also tended to have clear and positive marital commitments and to have experienced generativity chill with their adolescent children (all of which were true of Gordon Sr.). Together, these variables accounted for 26% of the variance in fathers' child-rearing support of adolescent social–emotional development.

In the area of intellectual–academic development, fathers' activity in the first decade was predicted by their boyhood IQ and their children's ages, explaining 6% of the variance. During adolescence, five variables— generativity chill, fathers' poor relationship with their fathers, boyhood IQ, wives' educational level, and (as a negative incentive) the men's mothers' level of education—contributed 12% to the explained variance. Boyhood IQ was the only variable that was predictive for both decades.

Concerning physical–athletic development in the childhood decade, two variables (unsuitable supervision by the men's fathers and generativity chill with their own children) explained 5% of the variance. This result suggests that fathers were attempting to rectify their own boyhood experience of their fathers' erratic or extreme supervision and to cope with their existential anxiety over a threatened loss by becoming more involved in their children's physical maturation. Men tended to become more highly and positively active in their adolescents' athletic development when their children were younger teens, when their own fathers had used or threatened physical punishment to control them as boys, when they had felt a threat to their biological generativity, and when their wives worked outside of the home and were better educated than wives of other men in the study. Together, these variables explained 22% of the variance in the fathers' support of their adolescents' physical–athletic development. The experience of generativity chill was the only variable that was predictive for both decades.

From these findings, two broad conclusions can be drawn: First, in terms of men's total or overall level of child-rearing involvement, the characteristics of the women in the men's lives generally accounted for the largest amount of unique variance. A wife's working outside of the home, for instance, often provided an immediate incentive for fathers to increase their level of child care. Second, once the father was involved, the characteristics of the fathers' own fathers generally accounted for the greatest amount of unique variance in each of the *specific* types of child care (i.e., support of social–emotional, intellectual–academic, or physical–athletic development). The fathers did not randomly select the specific types of care they tended to emphasize in their child-rearing activities. Rather, the findings support the Eriksonian idea that the fathers used child rearing to replicate the specific positive fathering they had received as boys and to rework or rectify the specific unsatisfactory fathering they had received. Each man faces the challenge of crafting a fathering style with the materials he has available; what happens, as Neugarten aptly declared in another context, is that as a man and a father "he *invents* his future self" (1969, p. 123; cf. Pruett, 1989).

In Gordon Sr.'s case, of course, it is important to note another incentive: He and Bernice started their own family almost immediately after his own father's death, and Gordon Jr. was named after both his father and his deceased grandfather. In the interview excerpt, Gordon Sr. portrayed himself as being a father in the same manner as his own father. He admitted to using corporal punishment on occasion, as his father had; he also reported "always watching" his children and stressing their compliance, as his story about giving a dime—and taking away an excuse for violating curfew—illustrates. However, he was very much unlike his father in being more physically and emotionally accessible to his children. In fact, Gordon Sr. illustrates the pattern for both modeling and reworking: Gordon Sr.'s parents provided a cohesive boyhood home atmosphere, and later he himself worked to provide his children with social–emotional support in their adolescence (one of the modeling trends); his focus on his teenagers' social–emotional and intellectual–academic growth is predicted by his own father's distant or nonnurturant behavior (one of the reworking patterns). Hence Gordon Sr.'s fathering style evolved out of both modeling and reworking the fathering he had received.

In Gordon Sr.'s reminiscence about his own father, we find two other dimensions that are important for our understanding of fathering. The first, and perhaps most obvious, is that the father spoke with great pride of his son, even imagining that his own father would be happy to know of his grandson's success. Connected with that is Gordon Sr.'s expressed desire that his father be proud of him, too. This appears to be an example of *adaptive grandiosity*: "The projection of the father's special, ideal self onto his child is part of [the] fatherly love and glue that preserves family love and solidarity" (Wolson, 1995, p. 286). Healthy fathers identify with their children's achievements and seek also to maintain their empathic sensitivity to their children as separate individuals. In this light, Gordon Sr. expressed clear adaptive grandiosity toward his son, and then he projected onto his own father a similar grandiosity toward both his son and himself. Such a move is itself akin to the reevaluation of the self that occurs as a parent becomes a grandparent and his or her care expands to the level of grand-generativity. As Erikson also observed, "Elders consider their children's parenting as a supplementary way to review their own active parenting of an earlier decade. . . . Our informants find it important to view themselves as having been good parents—as having provided their children the wherewithal to succeed professionally, to raise and guide yet another generation, and to surmount with integrity whatever adversity they may confront" (Erikson et al., 1986, pp. 76–77). Gordon Sr. assessed his own hope that he had been a good parent by looking at himself through his father's eyes.

This discussion leads to the other noteworthy feature of Gordon Sr.'s story, which was foreshadowed at the end of Scene 3. Gordon Sr.'s discussion of his father, as we mentioned before, clarifies for us the ambivalence in many sons' relationship with their father that leads to a combination of modeling and reworking in the sons' parenting style. It also is indicative of some affective work in Gordon Sr.'s life because he alluded to his father's absence: "I was a little more active than my dad was." He also knew why his father was not available more often and that his situation was not unique: "Right after the Depression, times were tough for everyone." By allowing for his own father's extenuating circumstances, Gordon Sr. reconciled himself with his father, aware that his own father had usually done his best, and he certainly no longer believed that his own father should have been perfect. Now he has reworked the shortcomings in the fathering he received by becoming the kind of father to his children that he wished his own father had been, thus transforming his anger into something productive for future generations. Gordon Sr. healed his woundedness through "a new and different love of [his] parents, free of the wish that they should have been different" (Erikson, 1968, p. 139; cf. Pleck, 1995). Even the best fathers leave their children with something to rework as well as to replicate. In one sense, then, Gordon Sr.'s reconciliation with his father becomes part of the cycle of generations that Gordon Jr. will continue in his recollection.

Scene 6: Generative Ethics

In this final scene, Gordon Jr. speaks during his individual interview to the ethical meanings of men's lives. The scene highlights the fact that fathers sustain a developing ethical relationship with their children and generally illustrates the application of Eriksonian *generative ethics*, an ethical position that begins with thoughts of the next generation (Hawkins & Dollahite, 1997). It is this "ethical orientation," according to Erikson (1975), that "makes the difference between adulthood and adolescence" (p. 207) and, we might add, between good and inadequate fathering.

> Son: I know my father is pleased with me. He tells me that quite a
> bit. Probably the main way he has influenced me has been through his

personality. His attitudes. I think he was always the first to say, "Don't lie. Tell the truth. If you've come home and you've done something wrong, don't lie about it, because if you lie, you'll be more punished than you will if I ask you and you tell me the truth." So he taught me that and, "If you're going to do a job, do it. Stay involved with it, don't quit. . . ."

I think my father was more involved with us than most fathers just because he got a lot of enjoyment out of seeing us having fun. It was his way of relaxing. He was always ready to have a good time with his kids. My mother always says to him, "You're a good-time Charlie." I think he hoped I would achieve more in life than he did. Although I wanted to work with him, he just said, "This isn't the type of work you want. You are a lot smarter. You can go on to college and do a lot better things." I think he just wanted me to be happy and be successful.

I don't know how to explain why I have done well, really. I think a lot of the upbringing that I had: Respect people, do your work, work hard, be kind to people, treat everybody like you'd like to be treated. A lot of that in my upbringing I think had to do with where I am today. I think I see him the most clearly in me in the way I am towards my kids, involved with my family.

Becoming a father has been a great, great experience for me. It's in that respect that I see a lot of my father in me. As much as I think I'm like my mother, personality-wise, I think I'm a lot more like my father with my son. Like he was with me. Always have a good time, and I try to pass on the same things to my son in terms of treating people well, and attitudes. I see a lot of that being passed on. My son is also a lot like my father. Very musical. A jokester. Rather spend his time in a joke shop and a music shop than anywhere else. The two of them are unbelievably alike. . . .

I do basically the same type of things with my kids that he was doing with us: the family things, the family get-togethers, and I have my kids doing different chores now and then so that it doesn't seem that they're getting all this for nothing. I think I'll continue to do the same things.

I think it's important for a son to show his father that whatever influence that he's instilled on you, works. That all of his years of upbringing, bringing you up and spending time with you, that it worked well, and that I'm a better person for it. Of course, my relationship with my father has changed a little since I've become a father myself. Like we mentioned, we kind of separated a little bit there in my later teens. Then I got married and had kids. Now we're more buddies.

Gordon Jr., in reflecting on his father and his own fathering, definitely reprises the themes of reconciling with his father. However, his tone is much less ambivalent than Gordon Sr.'s tone in speaking of his father. Throughout his individual interview, Gordon Jr. strongly affirmed his father's care of him as being of great formative value. In his own parenting,

Gordon Jr. saw characteristics of his father in his children—that the legacy of humor had been received by the next generation—and he saw traits of his father in his own style of child rearing. Primarily Gordon Jr. saw himself as modeling his father's way of parenting, especially in the way that Gordon Sr. enjoyed being with his children, with the major difference that he has experienced more difficulty in expressing his anger with his children in a way that they will take seriously.

The legacy that Gordon Jr. seemed to emphasize centers around values and a life ethic. The ethic that Gordon Jr. received and has tried to communicate to his children includes respect for other people (his variation of the Golden Rule), persistence in work, and a kind of playful love and love of play, with the goal of being happy and successful in life. Although moral formation has been creatively approached from an Eriksonian perspective (Capps, 1993; Nunley, 1993), attention here is drawn to the fact that these ethical ideas of Gordon Jr.'s owe much of their origin to his relationship with his father (Rutter, 1983). This fact argues compellingly that parenting is a serious moral endeavor that calls on parents to be involved for the welfare of their children and for future generations; thus parents discover a generative ethic as part of their own psychosocial development (Hawkins & Dollahite, 1997). The challenge of giving one's children the best care that one can, in effect, ideally summons forth the ethic that sustains continued work on their behalf. Such an ethic yields— and also depends on—an intentionality to parent that stands on the shoulders of an instinctual empathic responsiveness that Benedek (1970) called "genuine fatherliness." This parental intentionality, as both seed and fruit of a generative ethic, is perhaps what William Wordsworth had in mind when he wrote in the poem "My Heart Leaps Up" that "the child is father of the man."

Since Gordon Jr. has become an adult and has tasted the joys and responsibilities of being an adult and a father, he has come to a different sort of relationship with Gordon Sr. As Rubin (1982) stated in a discussion of fathers and sons, for their "relationship to get better—or for it to remain good—it must change. A central challenge for both . . . is to transform a childhood relationship marked by the father's authority and the [child's] dependence to an adult relationship between two autonomous people" (p. 28). The conclusion of our drama finds these two men not just father and son but close friends as well.

EPILOGUE

Since the beginning of theater, many playwrights and actors have relied on the device of a chorus to help shape the telling of the dramatic narrative. A chorus (which can be composed of several actors or only one) sometimes sings, sometimes dances, and usually offers its comments, but when present, the chorus always advances and interprets the story. We have served as the chorus for the generative drama of Gordon Sr. and Gordon Jr. As we have examined the characteristics of fathers in the Gluecks' sample, however, another chorus has been at work. That chorus is the voice of Erik Erikson, insisting that parenting helps the next generation and, at the same time, helps parents themselves to grow and mature. Growth and maturity, however, require time and patience and the realization that one does not become a mature parent overnight but slowly, gradually—and sometimes painfully—over a lifelong journey.

Because we have focused our attention on dramatic scenes as a way of envisioning fathering, it seems appropriate to close with a brief scene from the EMI-Universal film *Tender Mercies*, directed by Bruce Beresford and written by Horton Foote. In this scene Mac Sledge (played by Robert Duvall), a country-and-western singer and recovering alcoholic, is driving his truck home from church with his new wife, Rosa Lee, and his stepson, Sonny, beside him:

> Sonny: Well, we've done it, Mac. We're baptized.
> Mac: Yeah, we are.
> Sonny: Everybody said I was going to feel like a changed person. I guess I do feel a little different, but I don't feel a whole lot different. Do you?
> Mac: Not yet.
> Sonny: You don't look any different. [*Sits up to look at himself in the driving mirror*] Do you think I look any different?
> Mac: Not yet. (Foote, 1989, p. 134)

In the film Mac's baptism symbolizes not only his rebirth as a "new creation" through faith in a heavenly Father but also his rebirth as a singer, a husband, and a *father*. Because of his alcoholism he failed once, but he is now willing to try again both with his new wife and stepson and with his ex-wife and estranged daughter. Besides being born and having to grow as a father, Mac is also learning that few mistakes are irredeemable. Although he is unable to save his daughter from her self-destructive lifestyle, he does manage to renew his ties with her, and the painful awareness that he was not a good father for her becomes contrasted with the companionship and care that he provides for Sonny. When asked by Sonny if he feels any different now that he has been baptized, Mac replies, "Not yet"; those words should be heard not as an expression of disappointment but rather as a voice of hope. As one biblical writer said, "What we will be has not yet been revealed" (1 John 3:2, NRSV). Mac realizes that he is changing but that it is happening slowly.

Mac and Gordon Sr. both provide good examples of what we learned from the Gluecks' sample of 240 fathers, a lesson aptly stated by George and Caroline Vaillant (1981): "The things that go right in our lives do predict future successes and the events that go wrong in our lives do not forever damn us" (p. 1438). Generative parenting is a lifelong process with many chances for mistakes and, fortunately, many opportunities for repair. If fathers can approach it expectantly, as an opportunity for their children's and their own growth, they are likely to find what has not yet been revealed.

REFERENCES

Bellah, R. N., Madsen, R., Sullivan, W. M., Swidler, A., & Tipton, S. M. (1991). *The good society*. New York: Knopf.

Benedek, T. (1970). Fatherhood and providing. In E. J. Anthony & T. Benedek (Eds.), *Parenthood* (pp. 167–183). Boston: Little, Brown.

Browning, D. S. (1973). *Generative man*. Philadelphia: Westminster Press.

Butler, R. N. (1963). The life review: An interpretation of reminiscence in the aged. *Psychiatry, 26*, 65–76.

Capps, D. (1993). *The depleted self*. Minneapolis, MN: Fortress.

Clark, P. Y. (1995). The "cogwheeling" of Don Browning: Examining his Eriksonian perspective. *Pastoral Psychology, 43*, 141–161.

Cohler, B. J. (1982). Personal narrative and the life course. In P. Baltes & O. G. Brim (Eds.), *Life span development and behavior* (Vol. 4, pp. 205–241). San Diego, CA: Academic Press.

Dollahite, D. C., Hawkins A. J., & Brotherson, S. (1996). Narrative accounts, generative fathering, and family life education. *Marriage and Family Review, 24*, 333–352.

Erikson, E. H. (1964). *Insight and responsibility*. New York: Norton.

Erikson, E. H. (1968). *Identity: Youth and crisis*. New York: Norton.

Erikson, E. H. (1975). *Life history and the historical moment*. New York: Norton.

Erikson, E. H. (1982). *The life cycle completed*. New York: Norton.

Erikson, E. H., Erikson, J. M., & Kivnick, H. Q. (1986). *Vital involvement in old age*. New York: Norton.

Foote, H. (1989). *To Kill a Mockingbird; Tender Mercies; and The Trip to Bountiful: Three screenplays*. New York: Grove Press.

Franz, C. E., McClelland, D. C., & Weinberger, J. (1991). Childhood antecedents of conventional social accomplishment in midlife adults: A 36-year prospective study. *Journal of Personality and Social Psychology, 60*, 586–595.

Gilligan, C. (1982). *In a different voice*. Cambridge, MA: Harvard University Press.

Glueck, S., & Glueck, E. (1950). *Unraveling juvenile delinquency*. New York: Commonwealth Fund.

Goffman, E. (1959). *The presentation of self in everyday life*. New York: Doubleday.

Griswold, R. L. (1993). *Fatherhood in America*. New York: Basic Books.

Hampes, W. P. (1993). Relation between humor and generativity. *Psychological Reports, 73,* 131–136.

Hawkins, A. J., & Dollahite, D. C. (Eds.). (1997). *Generative fathering: Beyond deficit perspectives.* Newbury Park, CA: Sage.

Kierkegaard, S. (1980). *The sickness unto death.* Princeton, NJ: Princeton University Press. (Original work published 1849)

Kotre, J. (1984). *Outliving the self: Generativity and the interpretation of lives.* Baltimore: The Johns Hopkins University Press.

Kotre, J. (1995). Generative outcome. *Journal of Aging Studies, 9,* 33–41.

McAdams, D. P., & de St. Aubin, E. (1992). A theory of generativity and its assessment through self-report, behavioral acts, and narrative themes in autobiography. *Journal of Personality and Social Psychology, 62,* 1003–1015.

Neugarten, B. L. (1969). Continuities and discontinuities of psychological issues into adult life. *Human Development, 12,* 121–130.

Nunley, T. W. (1993). *Erikson's value orientation stages.* Unpublished honors thesis, Department of Psychology, Emory University, Atlanta, GA.

Pleck, J. H. (1995). The father wound. In J. L. Shapiro, M. J. Diamond, & M. Greenberg (Eds.), *Becoming a father* (pp. 210–223). New York: Springer.

Pruett, K. D. (1989). The nurturing male: A longitudinal study of primary nurturing fathers. In S. H. Cath, A. Gurwitt, & L. Gunsberg (Eds.), *Fathers and their families* (pp. 389–405). Hillsdale, NJ: Analytic Press.

Ricoeur, P. (1965). *Fallible man.* Chicago: Regnery.

Rubin, Z. (1982, June). Fathers and sons: The search for reunion. *Psychology Today, 16,* 23–33.

Rutter, M. (1983). *A measure of our values: Goals and dilemmas in the upbringing of children.* London: Friends House.

Sampson, R. J., & Laub, J. H. (1993). *Crime in the making: Pathways and turning points through life.* Cambridge, MA: Harvard University Press.

Skoe, E. E., Pratt, M. W., Matthews, M., & Curror, S. E. (1996). The ethic of care: Stability over time, gender differences, and correlates in mid- to late adulthood. *Psychology and Aging, 11,* 180–192.

Snarey, J. (1993). *How fathers care for the next generation: A four-decade study.* Cambridge, MA: Harvard University Press.

Snarey, J., & Vaillant, G. E. (1985). How lower and working class youth become middle class adults. *Child Development, 56,* 899–910.

Twain, M. (1922). *The mysterious stranger, and other stories.* New York: Harper & Brothers.

Vaillant, G. E., & Vaillant, C. O. (1981). Natural history of male psychological health: X. Work as a predictor of positive mental health. *American Journal of Psychiatry, 138,* 1433–1440.

Warner, G. S. (1934). *"Pop" Warner's book for boys.* New York: Robert M. McBride.

Wolson, P. (1995). Some reflections on adaptive grandiosity in fatherhood. In J. L. Shapiro, M. J. Diamond, & M. Greenberg (Eds.), *Becoming a father* (pp. 286–292). New York: Springer.

3

THE COURSE OF GENERATIVITY

ABIGAIL J. STEWART AND ELIZABETH A. VANDEWATER

It is inevitable that a theory as rich and fertile as Erikson's includes some contradictions and puzzles. In this chapter we explore three apparent contradictions in his writing, one running throughout his developmental theory, and two more specific to generativity. We propose that these contradictions can be resolved by elaborating a developmental theory of generativity covering the course of adulthood. In making this proposal, we note that one source of confusion lies in the many different elements sub-

Author Note: The research reported here depends on data collected with support from Boston University Graduate School, National Science Foundation Visiting Professorships for women, the Society for the Psychological Study of Social Issues, the MacArthur Foundation Network for Research on Successful Midlife Development, Radcliffe Research Support and Midlife Program Grants from the Henry A. Murray Research Center, the University of Michigan Horace H. Rackham Graduate School, and National Institute of Mental Health subgrants under prime grants 1-RO1-MH43948 and 1-RO1-MH47408. Computer-accessible data and copies of some of the raw data for several waves of both of the studies have been archived at the Henry A. Murray Research Center, Radcliffe College.

We are grateful to the participants for their contribution of time and reflections over many years and to Sandra Tangri for her generous collaboration in the Michigan sample follow-up. We are also grateful to Ravenna Helson, Joan Ostrove, Bill E. Peterson, and David G. Winter for many stimulating and clarifying discussions of Erikson's theory and midlife psychological development and to Avril Thorne for her thoughtful feedback on this chapter. We are particularly grateful to the editors for providing this opportunity to think about the course of generativity, for their own generative work in this area, and for their helpful comments on a previous version of this chapter.

sumed within Erikson's broad concept of generativity, whereas another lies in the notion that these different elements all peak in middle age. In contrast, we propose that the *desire* to be generative emerges by early adulthood, although only in late adulthood can generativity be *accomplished*. In the intervening years, the *capacity* for generativity gathers force. From this perspective, middle age seems uniquely characterized by generativity because it is then that the capacity is greatest, the desire is still present, and accomplishment is becoming visible.

We examine our proposed developmental model in two longitudinal studies of women studied in early and middle adulthood. In both samples we have found evidence to support the notion that the desire for generativity characterizes early adulthood more than middle adulthood. Equally, we have found evidence that the desire for generativity in early adulthood is associated with midlife well-being and generativity accomplishment, whereas the desire for generativity in midlife is not. We conclude by considering the role of generativity development in successful aging, as well as the importance of gender and generation in an expanded developmental theory of generativity.

THE COURSE OF GENERATIVITY

Some Theoretical Puzzles

In laying out his epigenetic theory, Erikson suggested that psychosocial development occurs in a sequence of "steps predetermined in the growing person's readiness to be driven toward, to be aware of, and to interact with, a widening social radius" (Erikson, 1950, p. 270; see Erikson, 1982, p. 28, for a later statement of the same point). Furthermore, Erikson argued that "epigenesis . . . also determines certain laws in the fundamental relations of the growing parts to each other . . ." (1982, p. 28). In fact, the relationship of these parts is such that "the whole ensemble depends on the proper development in the proper sequence of each item" (1982, p. 29). It is clear, then, that Erikson viewed the stages as occurring in a specific order, with each stage's resolution affecting the next stage's shape.

Despite this hypothesized dependence of each stage on the preceding stages, Erikson also argued that "all of them exist in the beginning in some form" (1959/1980, p. 56). The first tension we note in the theory, then, is that Erikson locates each stage at a particular point in the sequence of stages and tries to establish fairly clear normative ages associated with them, while at the same time he suggests that the preoccupations of all stages are always present.

This theoretical puzzle produces two further dilemmas in the particular case of generativity, the stage Erikson viewed as following the establishment of a socially confirmed identity and an intimate partnership. The first dilemma concerns the core activities characteristic of generative individuals; the second concerns the dependence of generativity on identity and intimacy. Both of these dilemmas emerged within Erikson's writings directly and in connection with his thoughts about how gender plays a role in psychosocial development.

In outlining his theory of generativity, Erikson stressed the role generativity plays in giving meaning to adult activities of love and work. Emerging after the resolution of the crisis associated with both identity formation and intimate commitment, generativity reflects, in his view, the fact that the adult human "needs to be needed" and feels "love for his works and ideas as well as for his children" (see, e.g., Erikson, 1964, p. 132). This focus on parenting and work as domains of generativity ensures both that much of adult life falls within the generative period and that it is specifically the aspects most subject to powerful gender norms that are included.

Even in 1950, when Erikson's vision was first articulated, adulthood was likely to last for many years; as the 20th century draws to an end, it can be expected to last for several decades. Yet generativity is a single stage preoccupation that is expected to fill most of those years—at least the ones following the establishment of a social identity and a committed, intimate partnership. As Erikson put it, "the stage of generativity . . . encompasses a long period of responsibilities demanding stamina and dedication" (Erikson, Erikson, & Kivnick, 1986, p. 285). In 1980, writing about the Freud–Jung correspondence, Erikson pointed out that "I have committed myself to ascribing to middle adulthood a crisis of generativity which includes procreativity as well as productivity and creativity" (p. 45), but he worried about the fact that this led him to place both Jung at age 30 and Freud at age 50 in the same psychosocial stage. This problem was inevitable, given Erikson's commitment both to the notion that generativity is "primarily the concern in establishing and guiding the next generation"— most often a task begun in early adulthood—and to the notion that generativity "is meant to include such more popular synonyms as *productivity* and *creativity*" (Erikson, 1950, p. 267).

Although the tasks of parenting, at least young children, most often arise in early adulthood, the labor of "maintenance of the world" is more associated with later middle age (one of Erikson's favored descriptions of this stage; see, e.g., Erikson, Erikson, & Kivnick, 1986, p. 50). Moreover, these tasks have been carried out in very different ways by men and women, although Erikson viewed these gendered and temporally distinct tasks as equally encompassed by generativity. We propose that one way to clarify the confusion in this area is to posit a developmental course to generativity in adulthood. In fact, Erikson himself suggested that there might be a developmental course within stages. He pointed out that the preoccupations associated with each stage are present "in the beginning" but that "Each comes to its ascendance, meets its crisis, and finds its lasting solution ... toward the end of the stages mentioned" (1959/1980, p. 56). In the relatively brief childhood stages ascendance, crisis, and finding of solutions may all occur in a relatively undifferentiated timespan. Even the stages involving identity and intimacy may be short enough that a single period describes these different processes. But the separate phases within the long generativity stage may be predictable and psychologically distinct.

Finally, there is the question of the dependence of generativity on the resolution of the identity and intimacy stages. Here Erikson was faced squarely with the problem that the social demands for identity were experienced quite differently by men and women when he introduced his theory during the late 1940s and early 1950s. As Franz and White (1985) pointed out, this problem reflects a larger tension in Erikson's theory: his ambivalence about whether the stages of psychosocial development are essentially the same for men and women or whether they are profoundly different. In the specific case of generativity, gender seems to matter mostly because of the ways in which it was hypothesized to be affected by identity resolution. According to Erikson, women often deferred identity formation "until they knew their man" (Evans, 1967, p. 49). Moreover, Erikson suggested that motherhood is a central aspect of women's identity (though he made no parallel claim about fatherhood for men; see Erikson, 1968, pp. 290–291). It is, then, conceivable to Erikson that generativity (in the form of concern about "establishing and guiding the next generation") could emerge for a woman before she established her identity. Here Erikson may well have been responding to the social realities of his time, rather than articulating a developmental difference that transcended social history; he pointed out (Erikson, 1974) that women's identity formation had—to that point—taken place in the context of social exploitation and prejudice and that it might look different in different times. Therefore, it is critical to consider how the larger social context, which may support or undermine generativity, may affect different generations of women—and men. Potential effects might include not only the way that a preoccupation (like generativity) might be expressed (e.g., more in parenthood or in work productivity) but also its position in the sequence of other psychosocial stages.

These are, then, three dilemmas in Erikson's theory that underly our examination of the empirical literature and our own longitudinal data. The first is Erikson's simultaneous claims that each stage has a time of unique importance and that each stage is present at all ages. The second is the paradoxical assertion that generativity is most strongly defined by procreativity, which ordinarily takes place (particularly for women) in early adulthood, *and* that it is equally well-defined in terms of productivity and creativity, which extend throughout most of adulthood. This dilemma is best evaluated in the context of his frequent identification of generativity with the entire span of "middle age." Finally, we consider the question of the alleged dependence of generativity on identity and intimacy along with the recognition that for women intimacy and parenthood (and thereby generativity) may actually predate identity formation.

Theorizing Generativity: A Developmental Course

One resolution to these complexities might be to expand Erikson's account of generativity to specify different phases within this unusually long stage. In the first phase (which might coincide with exploration of identity or intimacy), the individual may experience a longing or desire to be generative, whereas in later ones (which may depend more on the resolution of identity) the individual may experience something more like an awareness of a capacity for successful generativity and finally, perhaps, a sense of having accomplished it.

GENERATIVITY AND THE COURSE OF ADULTHOOD: EMPIRICAL EVIDENCE

Although there is a growing literature on the correlates of generativity, particularly in midlife adults (see, e.g., Cole & Stewart, 1996; DeHaan & MacDermid, in press; MacDermid & Crouter, 1994; MacDermid, Heilbrun, & Gillespie, in press; McAdams & de St. Aubin, 1992; McAdams, Ruetzel, & Foley, 1986; Peterson & Klohnen, 1995; Peterson & Stewart, 1993, 1996; Snarey, Son, Kuehne, Hauser, & Vaillant, 1987; Vaillant, 1977; Vaillant & Milofsky, 1980; Van de Water & McAdams, 1989), there are relatively few empirical studies that address the possibility of a "course" of generativity in adulthood. Three kinds of studies could provide useful evidence: cross-sectional comparisons of adults of different ages, case studies following a single individual over an extended period of adulthood, and longitudinal studies following entire samples over an extended period that assess generativity at several points. Studies that also address the presence or absence of other stage-related concerns (particularly identity and intimacy) are particularly pertinent to addressing the questions of simultaneity and sequence in stage preoccupations.

Cross-Sectional Studies of Generativity in Adulthood

As part of the large series of studies of Kansas City middle-aged and older adults conducted by a team of researchers headed by Robert Havighurst in the 1950s (see Neugarten et al, 1964 for a description), Gruen (1964) assessed age, gender, and social class differences in all eight of

Erikson's stages in a stratified sample of adults ranging in age from 40 to 65. Stage scores were based on global ratings of the detailed notes of 2-hour interviews. The rater judged the degree to which the individual had achieved positive resolution of the relevant stage (thus, in the case of generativity, avoidance of self-absorption and stagnation plus positive evidence of generative activities and orientation). Interrater reliability of these ratings was reasonably high (.72 for generativity). Gruen found no social class, gender, or age effects on this measure, although he pointed out that the age range was quite narrow. In a commentary on this and other studies, Neugarten (1964) suggested that "socioadaptational" measures (ones oriented toward "the adaptive, goal-directed and purposive qualities of personality," p. 192) tended generally not to show age effects in middle and older adulthood, whereas measures focused more on the "intrapsychic" ("the processes of the personality that are not readily available to awareness or to conscious control and which do not have direct expression in overt patterns of social behavior," p. 192) did show such effects.

In a much later study, Ryff and Heincke (1983) assessed perceived, recalled, and projected generativity (using a 25-item measure designed to assess Erikson's construct) in adults of three widely differing ages: young (average age about 21 years), middle-aged (average age about 48 years) and older (average age about 69 years). They found that the young adults actually scored highest in generativity ratings across the three ages assessed (current and prospective middle and old age). However, they also found that young, middle-aged, and older adults all rated themselves as higher on generativity in middle age than in youth or old age. Thus, the "course of generativity" implied by the cross-sectional comparison of scores (highest in young adults, and then declining) was quite different from the raters' self-perception of actual or anticipated change over adulthood (increasing from youth to middle age, then declining). Results in this study are reported for the 25-item scale as a whole. The description of the measure includes features of parental generativity ("expresses concern in establishing and guiding the next generation; possesses awareness of responsibilities to children," p. 809) as well as productivity ("views self as a norm-bearer and decision maker; shows awareness of leadership role and has a sense of maximal influence capacity," p. 809). It is impossible to tell whether some items on this scale account for the high ratings of young adults (relative to the other groups) and different items account for the high ratings of themselves by all groups in middle age as compared with their young or older selves.

In a related study, Ryff and Migdal (1984) found that middle-aged women graduate students (40 to 55 years old) rated themselves as more generative in the present than in the past; however, young women college students (18 to 30 years old) also rated themselves higher in the present than in the future (in middle age). Thus the anticipated and retrospective life courses were different for the young and middle-aged women; moreover, the young adult and middle-aged women rated themselves in the present at about the same level. In this study, the fact that the women were drawn from different birth cohorts may be important. The indirect measures of generativity employed in this study assessed breadth of interest, dominance, and innovation. Perhaps the changes in women's roles and opportunities between these two generations of women resulted in a higher level of these measures at a younger age.

Using a 10-item rationally derived measure of generativity (with items based on direct quotations from Erikson's writings), Ochse and Plug (1986) assessed age differences in four cohorts of White and Black South Africans: 15- to 19-year-olds, 20- to 24-year-olds, 25- to 39-year-olds, and 40- to 60-year-olds. They found a significant main effect for age, with the oldest (middle-aged) group scoring highest on generativity. No details were provided about which groups differed significantly from one another. Again, it is difficult to judge the degree to which cohort (rather than age) may affect these results. Moreover, it is difficult to know whether there are cultural differences in generativity norms or scores on this measure that might produce different results with U.S. samples.

Finally, McAdams, de St. Aubin, and Logan (1993; see also McAdams, Hart, and Maruna, chapter 1, this volume) assessed four aspects of generativity in three age groups: young (22 to 27 years old), middle-aged (37 to 42 years old), and old (67 to 72 years old). They examined conscious generativity concerns, generative commitments (current daily goals or objectives), generative actions or behaviors, and generative narration or self-representations in autobiographical recollections. They found that the open-ended measures (generative commitments and generative narration) showed a clear age effect, with midlife adults scoring higher than young adults in both cases, and older adults scoring higher than young adults in the case of generative narration. Although the measure of generative concerns (a closed-ended measure quite similar to the other self-report measures used by Ochse & Plug, 1986, and by Ryff & colleagues, 1983, 1984) showed a nearly significant effect, this was due to the fact that midlife adults scored higher than older adults but not higher than young adults. McAdams, de St. Aubin, and Logan point out that this kind of measure is "a test of self-perceptions assessing how strong one believes one's own generative concerns to be," given that those concerns focus on a general "preoccupation with having a positive and enduring impact on the next generation" (p. 227). Their different results for current commitments and autobiographical recollections suggest that, although preoccupation or concerns with generativity may emerge quite early, spontaneously reported daily goals and projects, as well as self-representations, peak in middle age but persist for a long time.

These cross-sectional studies provide a rather confusing picture of the course of generativity in adulthood. The early Gruen study (1964) found no age differences, but the age range was restricted. The two Ryff studies suggested that generativity is high in middle age but that it may also sometimes be high in young adults. Ochse and Plug (1986) reported that among South African adults generativity "goes up" in middle age, but their youngest groups are much younger than those in other studies, and they do not report where the significant differences lie. Moreover, they had no older comparison group to assess post-middle-age declines in generativity. Finally, McAdams, de St. Aubin, and Logan (1993) reported the expected increase in middle age for two of their measures and no decline in older age. They pointed out that their older group is only 67 to 72 years old and may not view themselves as past middle age—or at least not past generativity. In addition, on the generative concerns measure—most similar to those measures employed in the other studies—they too found that young adults score as high as the middle-aged. Overall, then, there is some support for the notion that middle-aged people are especially preoccupied with generativity, but there is also considerable evidence that young adults are too and that the decline in the preoccupation may happen both gradually and fairly late.

There are other methodological issues that make interpretation of these studies tricky. They differ in the precise ages of the samples studied, in the measures employed, and in other characteristics (age, ethnicity, culture) of the samples. In addition, even a consistent picture would be difficult to interpret because they all inevitably confound age and cohort.

Case Studies of Generativity in Adulthood

Kotre (1984) provided several powerful case studies in generativity; however, his data were all collected from individuals who were middle-aged at the time (thus, these are *generative narrations* in the terms of McAdams, de St. Aubin, and Logan, 1993). Although individuals provided some information about their past lives and personalities, the accounts were based on narratives collected at only one point in time. Peterson (chapter 4, this volume) analyzed the lives of 12 midlife women who differed in their profile of generativity scores. He examined their life courses but not changes in generativity itself over time. Erikson (1969) himself provided an extended case study of Gandhi and thought of his account as a study of generativity. He pointed out that Gandhi "emerged as the father of his country" when he was 49 years old, suggesting that this fact "lends greater importance to the fact that the middle span of life is under the dominance of the universal human need and strength which I have come to subsume under the term *generativity*" (p. 395). Although Erikson developed a rich account of the precursors of Gandhi's middle-aged ideology and political strategy, he did not make any attempt systematically to consider change over time in Gandhi's adult generativity.

There are, however, some systematic content analyses of generativity over time. For example, Espin, Stewart, and Gomez (1990) assessed identity, intimacy, and generativity themes in the letters of an adolescent girl who eventually emigrated from her nation of origin. In these letters, generativity themes increased significantly between the age of 13 and the age of 22, when she became a mother, although overall identity themes continued to predominate in that period. These results suggest that generativity preoccupations were indeed present in early adulthood for this young woman but were vastly outnumbered by identity and intimacy themes. These data did not extend, however, into middle age.

In a study of Vera Brittain's personality, Stewart, Franz, and Layton (1988) assessed identity, intimacy and generativity concerns both as expressed in Brittain's diary in early adulthood and as retrospectively described in her autobiography, from the vantage point of middle age. As in Espin, Stewart, and Gomez's (1990) study, they found that Brittain's identity concerns vastly outweighed the intimacy and generativity themes in the period during and immediately following World War I, when she was a young woman. In this case, however, midlife data are available. Peterson and Stewart (1990) assessed Brittain's personality in her fiction and diaries in her young adulthood (1914 to 1916, during World War I; she was 21 years old in 1914), early middle age (1932 to 1937 between the wars; she was 39 years old in 1932), and later middle age (1939 to 1944 during World War II; she was 46 years old in 1939). They found that there was a clear decrease in identity and intimacy concerns and a clear increase in generative concerns. However, although they did confirm that intimacy preoccupations outweighed generativity preoccupations in early adulthood and generativity concerns outweighed intimacy concerns in middle age, identity concerns predominated at all times. They speculated that self-reflective documents and novels may tend to encourage expressions of identity themes and that perhaps Brittain was unusually preoccupied with identity issues. Finally, in an analysis of the particular themes that dominated Brittain's expressions of generativity, they found that in early middle age she was mainly preoccupied with issues of productivity, whereas in the later period (which coincided both with World War II and her separation from her children), expressions of the theme of caring dominated.

Overall, these findings suggest that generativity concerns may increase in middle age and that they may take new or different forms in different phases of middle age. The findings also suggest that generativity preoccupations are sometimes present in early adulthood, at the same time that identity concerns are dominant. However, these case studies are based on data provided by particular individuals, whose personalities and life situations were no doubt unique; it is difficult, therefore, to generalize from these data.

Longitudinal Studies of Aging Samples

Although a few longitudinal studies have reported on predictors of midlife generativity (e.g., Peterson & Klohnen, 1995; Peterson & Stewart, 1996; Snarey, 1993; Vaillant, 1977; Vaillant & Milofsky, 1980), very few indeed discuss changes in generativity over time. Vaillant (1993) reports on the percentage of men in the "college men" or Grant Study sample who achieved generativity. Raters assessed interview protocols collected in alternate years to identify the age at which they believed each man had attained the generativity stage, with ages ranging from 25 to 60 years old. The percentage increased in a nearly linear fashion, from nearly 0% at age 25 to 83% at age 60 (e.g., with about 50% at age 40).

Whitbourne, Zuschlag, Elliot, and Waterman (1992) employed a sequential design covering the ages 20 through 42 years old to study all eight of Erikson's stages. Using Constantinople's (1969) measure, as adapted and extended by Waterman and Whitbourne (1981), they assessed each of the eight stages with five close-ended items. They tested three age-cohorts: one at age 20 in 1966 (although generativity scores were not available at that time), at age 31 in 1977, and at age 42 in 1988; a second at age 20 in 1977 and again at age 31 in 1988; and a third only at age 20 in 1988. Longitudinal analyses did not show significant change over time from ages 31 to 42 for Cohort 1 or from ages 20 to 31 for Cohort 2. Although these results do suggest that generativity was present at about equal levels in the time span from age 20 to 42, the truly longitudinal data addressed only two separate and much more limited age spans (31 to 42 years and 20 to 31 years). In addition, cohort differences were identified, with the older cohort scoring higher overall than the younger one. This may indicate either that there is a developmental trend in the data (because only Cohort 1 reached middle age within this study) or that there are enduring cohort differences between these two generations. Only a further follow-up (e.g., when Cohort 2 is age 42 and Cohort 1 is age 53) could settle this question.

There are, in addition, some longitudinal studies that assessed constructs related to generativity. Howard and Bray (1988), in a study of male managerial candidates at AT&T, found that men did not appear to increase in generativity in the relational sphere at all; in fact, the need for friendships and for the understanding of others actually decreased over time, while hostility increased. They also found, in less relational areas, that ambition declined in adulthood, but autonomy increased. Howard and Bray suggested that these men's work lives had toughened them and increased their capacity to take on responsibilities independently; this stance was, however, associated with maintenance of a certain distance from relationships at work. They concluded that "If Erikson's (1950) conceptualization of generativity ... were to be applied, it would more likely be realized in productive work than in nurturing the young" (p. 411).

In an analysis of personality change over 30 years and 40 years in the longitudinal Oakland Growth and Berkeley Guidance Studies, Jones and Meredith (1996) reported that there were increases in self-confidence and outgoingness at age 40 in their longitudinal data, whereas increases in cognitive commitment (which includes intelligence, intellectual interests, and introspection) and dependability (which includes calm productivity) emerged at around age 30 and remained stable and high through age 50. MacDermid, Franz, and De Reus (in press, see also chapter 6, this volume) found some evidence of overall change in a Q-sort measure of generativity realization in the Berkeley sample between the thirties and fifties, but no change in the Oakland sample. Schuster, Langland, and Smith (1993) reported that female participants in a University of California; Los Angeles study of gifted students described themselves as having become more socially comfortable and more self-confident by midlife. Similarly, Helson and Moane (1987) found that women in the Mills Longitudinal Study scored higher in confidence, dominance, and coping skills when in their forties than they scored when in college. These women were also found to have increased confidence, autonomy, and adherence to their own ideals and values from their 40s to their 50s (see Helson & Wink, 1992; Mitchell & Helson, 1990). In a more impressionistic way, Brown and Pacini (1993) summarized their findings about the Vassar graduates of the classes of 1957 and 1958 (who were in their mid-50s) as indicating that they "exude confidence about themselves" (p. 188) and are "clearly involved in a generative phase" (p. 187).

Overall, then, there is general support from cross-sectional, case study, and aggregate longitudinal data that middle age involves an increase in some of the characteristics associated with generativity. However, the evidence is strongest for an increased sense of confidence or efficacy than for any other feature of generativity. In addition, there is some evidence that some forms of generativity may actually be fairly high in early adulthood, at least for some cohorts, as well as in middle age. It is clear that additional longitudinal evidence about generativity, ideally from more than one cohort and assessed in more than one way, is sorely needed.

LONGITUDINAL DATA FROM TWO COHORTS OF COLLEGE-EDUCATED WOMEN

We used data from two longitudinal cohorts of educated women to examine the course of generativity: (a) the Radcliffe Longitudinal Study of the class of 1964 (see Stewart & Vandewater, 1993, for an overview), and (b) Tangri's longitudinal study of a stratified random sample of the women of the University of Michigan class of 1967 (see Tangri & Jenkins, 1993, for an overview). The two samples were similar in age and graduated from college in a similar time period. However, in contrast with the Radcliffe cohort, the Michigan cohort attended a coeducational state university, which was somewhat selective but drew fairly broadly from the college-bound population in the state.

Material for these analyses was mainly drawn, for the Radcliffe sample, from data collected from the women in 1974 (when they were 31 years old), in 1979 (when they were 36 years old), and in 1986 (when they were 43 years old). A few measures were obtained in 1990 (when they were 48 years old). Because all women did not participate in every wave, analyses for this study focused on the 49 women with complete data who participated in the crucial three waves (1974, 1979, and 1986) coded for generativity. Analyses aimed at assessing potential bias in the sample were conducted on all available variables (including demographic, well-being, and personality variables). These analyses did not reveal systematic differences among the participants selected for this study and those omitted because of missing data.

For our analyses of the Michigan cohort, we examined data collected in 1967, 1970, 1981, and 1992, when the women were ages 21, 24, 31, and 47. Our analyses focused on the 64 women with complete data who participated in all four waves. Jenkins (1989, 1994) reported that sample attrition from 1967 to 1981 did not systematically bias the follow-up sample. Similarly, Cole and Stewart (1996) reported no detectable bias in the 1992 wave.

Measuring Generativity in the Two Cohorts

We did not have a measure of the felt capacity for generativity, so we limited this investigation to aspects of *generativity desires* and *generativity accomplishment*; these were assessed in different ways in the two cohorts (Figure 1). Generativity desires were assessed in terms of women's expressed goals for the future (the next 10 years) at each wave of data collection (ages 31, 36, and 43 for Radcliffe; ages 21, 24, 31, and 47 for Michigan) using the coding system originally developed by Stewart, Franz, and Layton (1988; see also, Peterson & Stewart, 1990). This allowed us to examine change in generativity desires over time. A second measure of generativity desires was obtained using Peterson and Stewart's (1996) Thematic Apperception Test (TAT)-based measures because TATs had been administered to both samples in the last wave (age 43 for Radcliffe; age 47 for Michigan).

A subjective sense of generativity accomplishment in both samples (age 43 for Radcliffe; age 47 for Michigan) was assessed on the basis of

	Radcliffe	Michigan
Generativity Desire	Future Goals (next 10 years) Motivation (TAT)	Future Goals (next 10 years) Motivation (TAT)
Generativity Accomplishment	Realization (Q sort) High Points (past 5–10 years)	Realization (Q sort) High Points (past 5–10 years) Loyola Generativity Scale (LGS)

Figure 1. Overview of generativity measures in the Radcliffe and Michigan cohorts. *Note:* For Radcliffe, Future Goals assessed at ages 31, 37, and 43. Motivation assessed at age 48. Realization and High Points assessed at age 43. For Michigan, Future Goals assessed at ages 21, 35, and 47. Motivation, Realization, and High Points assessed at age 47.

women's expressed "high points" in the past 5 or 10 years (also coded according to Stewart et al., 1988). A second (observer-based) measure of generativity accomplishment was Peterson and Klohnen's (1995) Q-sort measure of generativity realization (also at age 43 for Radcliffe; age 47 for Michigan). Finally, for the Michigan sample only, a short form of the McAdams and de St. Aubin (1992) Loyola Generativity Scale (LGS; probably best considered a self-report measure) was administered at age 47.

Coding Generativity in High Points and Future Goals

In both samples, the women's open-ended responses to the questions about high points ("Looking back over the last 10 years, what do you consider major high points, or the most satisfying activities?") and future goals ("If you could do anything you wanted in the next 10 years, what would you do?") were coded according to the scoring system developed by Stewart, Franz, and Layton (1988). This coding system was based on Erikson's writings and includes the components of generativity he described. Responses are coded into five categories: general concerns; parental generativity, or concerns about children; generative caring for people other than children; productivity; and the need to be needed. Statements scored for general generative concerns included expressions of concerns about making a lasting contribution to, or caring for, future generations or the world at large (for example, "I'm concerned about the future of the planet" or "I'd like to see world peace"). Statements scored for parental generativity included expressions of desires to have children or raise a family. Statements scored for generative caring expressed concern about the capacity to care for others (not children), including specific acts of kindness, caregiving, and help (e.g., "helped a Russian emigre family adjust to life in a small town"). Statements scored for productivity included descriptions of work on products that are intended to make a lasting contribution ("finish my book as well as I'd like" or "write a major piece of nonfiction"). Statements scored for the need to be needed expressed concern about being needed by others, such as aging parents or grown children (e.g., "It's nice to discover that my kids still come to me for advice and help").

Statements were coded without knowledge of the participant's age at the time of the follow-up to a high standard of interrater reliability (category agreement was maintained above 85% throughout the coding process for both samples). Scores for all open-ended statements were corrected for modest, but generally significant, correlations with verbal fluency (total word counts), according to the standard regression procedure described in Smith, Feld, and Franz (1992).

Generativity Desires over Time

Figure 2 depicts the course of generativity responses to the goals question for the Radcliffe sample. These expressions of a desire for generativity were at their highest point when the women were age 31, declined at age 37, and declined again to age 43. Repeated measures ANOVAs revealed that desire for generativity significantly decreased over time ($F[2, 96] = 7.41$, $p < .001$), and that desire for generativity was significantly higher at age 31 ($M = .90$, $SD = .97$) than it was at either age 37 ($M = .44$, $SD = .74$) or age 43 ($M = .32$, $SD = .69$).

Figure 3 depicts the course of generativity responses for the Michigan sample. For these women, expressions of generativity desire were high at age 21, increased somewhat to age 24, then declined to age 35, and

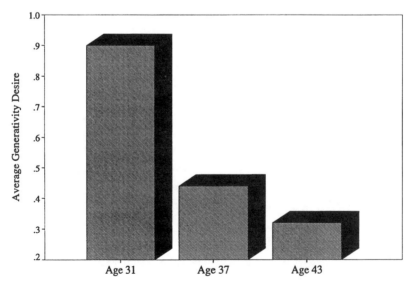

Figure 2. Generativity desire over time in Radcliffe sample: future goals.

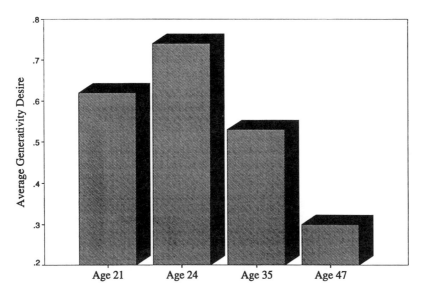

Figure 3. Generativity desire over time in Michigan sample: future goals.

declined again to age 46. As with the Radcliffe sample, repeated measures ANOVAs indicated that desire for generativity changed significantly over time ($F[3, 189] = 8.46$, $p < .001$), with the overall trend showing a decrease in generative desire. Specifically, desire for generativity significantly decreased from ages 21 ($M = .62$, $SD = .53$), 24 ($M = .74$, $SD = .38$), and 35 ($M = .53$, $SD = .54$) to age 46 ($M = .30$, $SD = .63$). Additionally, there was a significant decrease in desire from age 24 to age 35 (thus, these women's generativity desire peaked in early adulthood).

In both of these samples, then, generativity desires were most prominent features of early adulthood and declined over the course of adulthood. By middle age (middle or late 40s), generativity desires were significantly lower than they had been in early adulthood.

GENERATIVITY DESIRES AND ACCOMPLISHMENT: ARE THEY REALLY DIFFERENT?

We have argued that generativity desires and generativity accomplishment are conceptually distinct, but can the differences between them be demonstrated empirically? Peterson (chapter 4, this volume) provides evidence differentiating generativity desires and generativity accomplishment in a detailed study of 12 women who scored high or low on one, the other, or both. Using aggregate data, we anticipated that different measures of motivation or desire and of generativity accomplishment should be correlated among themselves but that measures of desire and accomplishment should be largely independent. In addition, we anticipated that measures of generativity accomplishment (because they suggest some level of resolution) should be positively correlated with indicators of well-being, but measures of generativity motivation should be independent of, or negatively correlated with, well-being.

In the Michigan (but not the Radcliffe) sample it was possible to correlate the measure of conscious generativity desire (in the form of future goals) with three other measures of generativity at the same time: generativity desire assessed on the TAT (Peterson & Stewart, 1996), generativity accomplishment assessed using the Q-sort realization measure on the basis of midlife questionnaire data (Peterson & Klohnen, 1995) and the LGS. In fact, the measure of generativity desire was significantly correlated with the TAT measure of generativity motivation ($r = .63$, $p < .001$), and not with either the Q-sort measure of realization ($r = .11$, ns) or the LGS ($r = -.05$, ns), which were in turn significantly correlated ($r = .28$, $p < .01$) with each other.

It was possible in both samples to assess the relationships between midlife generativity desire and accomplishment and midlife well-being (life and family satisfaction items, an overall health item, anxiety, and depression, and overall adjustment). Midlife generativity desires were either uncorrelated with well-being (true of the TAT measure of generativity motivation in both samples) or were associated with negative outcomes (see Table 1; desires for productivity were correlated with greater anxiety and lesser family satisfaction for Radcliffe women and lesser life and family satisfaction and health for Michigan women). Accomplishment indicators, in contrast, were associated with positive well-being in both samples. Specifically, observer report of generativity accomplishment (Q-sort realization) was associated with higher levels of family and life satisfaction, lower levels of anxiety and depression, and higher scores on CPI Realization in both samples. Additionally, among Radcliffe women, accomplishment as measured by parental high points was associated with higher levels of health and lower levels of depression. Among Michigan women, accomplishment as measured by the LGS was associated with higher levels of family satisfaction and health, lower levels of anxiety and depression, and higher CPI Realization scores. These results echo those reported in Peterson's case studies (chapter 4, this volume).

We have evidence, then, to support the notion that midlife generativity desire is in fact distinct from accomplishment of generativity. Moreover, our evidence suggests that by middle age desires for generativity may not be normative because they are associated with poorer well-being. In contrast, generativity accomplishment—spontaneously reported in high points, self-reported on the LGS, or assessed in observer ratings on the Q sort—is associated with midlife well-being (see McAdams & Azarow, 1996,

TABLE 1
Correlations Between Generativity Desire and Accomplishment and Midlife Well-Being in the Radcliffe and Michigan Cohorts

	Life Satisfaction	Family Satisfaction	Overall Health	Anxiety[1]	Depression[2]	Realization[3]
Radcliffe at age 43:						
Desire for Generative Productivity (Future Goals)	.12	−.23*	−.12	.30*	−.01	.06
Generativity Accomplishment (Q-sort Realization)	.19†	.27*	.19†	−.19†	−.38***	.28**
Generativity Accomplishment (Parental High Points)	.17	.05	.25*	−.13	−.21*	−.01
Michigan at age 47:						
Desire for Generative Productivity (Future Goals)	−.22*	−.21*	−.22*	.17†	.02	.11
Generativity Accomplishment (Q-sort Realization)	.33***	.36***	.01	−.21*	−.22*	.29*
Generativity Accomplishment (LGS)	.09	.34***	.35***	−.21*	−.36***	.29*

†$p < .10$.   *$p < .05$.   **$p < .01$.   ***$p < .001$.
[1]Profile of Mood States (McNair, Lorr, & Droppleman, 1971) for Radcliffe; Zung (1971) Self-Rating Anxiety Scale for Michigan.
[2]Profile of Mood States for Radcliffe; Zung (1965) Self-Rating Depression Scale for Michigan.
[3]California Psychological Inventory (Gough, 1987).
Note. Radcliffe well-being variables were measured at age 43 (anxiety, depression) and age 48 (life satisfaction, family satisfaction, health, realization); Michigan well-being variables were measured at age 47.

EXHIBIT 1
Relationships Among Generativity Desires, Accomplishment, and Well-Being in Early and Middle Adulthood

Generativity desire in early adult-hood	Higher generativity accomplishment Unrelated to well-being
Generativity desire in middle adulthood	Unrelated to generativity accomplishment Lower well-being
Generativity accomplishment in middle adulthood	Higher well-being

and McAdams, Hart, & Maruna, chapter 1, this volume, for similar findings using the Loyola Generativity Scale in other samples).

We can also demonstrate that early adult generativity desire does not have the same implications as does midlife generativity desire. We have no measures of early adult well-being in the Michigan sample, but we do have data for early adult generativity desire—that is, from age 24. These scores are significantly positively correlated with midlife generativity accomplishment ($r = .23$ with the Q-sort measure, $p < .05$; $r = .21$ with the LGS, $p < .05$), but uncorrelated with midlife well-being. In the Radcliffe sample, we do not have scores from a comparably early age, but we do have early adult generativity scores from 1974, or at age 31. These scores were not correlated with midlife generativity accomplishment (assessed with the Q-sort measure) or with measures of well-being obtained at age 33 (depression and anxiety scales; Zung, 1965, 1971). Thus, although early adult generativity desires may facilitate midlife generativity accomplishment (as they do in the Michigan sample), they have no relationship to early or midlife well-being. In contrast, midlife generativity desires are unrelated to midlife generativity accomplishment and are negatively correlated with midlife well-being. Finally, midlife generativity accomplishment is positively correlated with midlife well-being.

Taken together, these findings suggest that healthy early adult generativity may be reflected in the formulation of generativity desires or goals, whereas healthy midlife generativity is instead reflected in generativity accomplishment. (Exhibit 1 summarizes the relationships we have found.) Much of the association of generativity accomplishment and midlife well-being may come from the sense of efficacy that is part of felt generativity.

Midlife Phenomenology: Differentiating Efficacy, Generative Capacity, and Generative Accomplishment

So far we have only been able to separate generativity desires from generativity accomplishment in these empirical analyses; we have suggested, however, that there may be a third element, a felt capacity for generativity. This form of generativity may in fact be the closest to the sense of efficacy that is so salient in studies of the phenomenology of middle age. In recent research, Stewart, Ostrove, and Helson (1997; see also Stewart, 1995, 1996) developed four scales to assess aspects of the subjective experience of aging in middle-aged adults. These four scales assess an inner sense of certainty about one's identity, preoccupation with aging and growing closer to death, feelings of confident power, and feelings of *generativity capacity*, which include feelings of productivity, influence, and vision. Items associated with each scale are indicated in Exhibit 2. Interestingly, Stewart, Ostrove, and Helson reported that both of the measures that get at features of generativity—confident power and felt capacity for generativity—produced higher scores than identity-certainty and age-preoccupation in three middle-aged samples of college-educated women; and both confident power and capacity for generativity were felt to increase from the 30s to the 40s, and from the 40s to the 50s (Mills classes of 1958 and 1960; Michigan class of 1967; and Smith College class of 1964). However, reports of confident power were associated only with midlife well-being. The measure of felt capacity for generativity was unrelated to midlife well-being in all three samples but was positively related to a sense that aging involved increased insight and self-knowledge.

These results suggest that, although midlife generativity may include a sense of personal efficacy (or accomplishment) that is a source of midlife well-being, it also includes a vision of the self as operating in a broader field that is not associated with midlife well-being (perhaps because the potential for successful efficacy is lower when the aspirations are larger— as in making changes in the community or society). However, this willingness to imagine the self as an actor on a larger stage probably underlies

EXHIBIT 2
Subjective Experience of Aging in Middle Adulthood

I. Identity-Certainty
   A sense of being my own person
   Feeling secure and committed
   (Not) searching for a sense of who I am
II. Generativity Capacity
   Influence in my community or area of interest
   A new level of productivity or effectiveness
   Having a wider perspective
III. Confident Power
   Feeling more confident
   Feeling more powerful
IV. Age-Preoccupation
   Looking old
   Thinking a lot about death

the possibility of midlife adults actually taking responsibility for "mainte-nance of the world" (in Erikson's terms). We suspect that measures of generativity acts and generative strivings, or daily preoccupations, are re-flections of this broad sense of generative capacity (see McAdams, de St. Aubin, & Logan, 1993; McAdams, Hart, & Maruna, chapter 1, this vol-ume). As the formulation of generativity goals in early adulthood may support later development of a generative capacity, the felt capacity for generativity may well set the stage for development of a firm late life sense of generative accomplishment. Equally, both the felt generative capacity at midlife and the generativity accomplishment may help clear the way for the kind of personality development that Erikson depicted as taking place at the end of life (that is, the development of a sense of integrity and the avoidance of despair).

CONCLUSION

The human impulses to create and to preserve what has been created are grouped by Erikson under the rubric of generativity and are attributed to the long period of mature adulthood. We agree with McAdams and de St. Aubin (1992) that this broad rubric can be usefully separated into different elements and we further propose that different elements dominate in different periods of adulthood. Specifically, we propose that healthy early adulthood includes the formulation of generativity goals or desires, while healthy midlife includes the subjective experience of the capacity to be generative as well as the beginning of a sense of satis-faction in generative accomplishment. Thus, the midlife experience of ge-nerativity may be usefully differentiated as including both an increased sense of efficacy and a vision of oneself as having made contributions to a wider community. The former facilitates a sense of well-being in midlife, but the latter may both support the hardworking middle-aged person's ef-forts to take responsibility in a new sense and pave the way for later life wisdom and acceptance of "one's one and only life cycle" (Erikson, 1950, p. 268).

Further research can illuminate this course of generativity by employ-ing different measures of generativity like those discussed here and assessing individuals throughout the course of adulthood. We need, then, measures of generativity desire (using Peterson & Stewart's, 1996, TAT measure of motivation or the goals measure employed here), subjective experiences of generative capacity (using scales assessing subjective experience like those developed by Stewart, Ostrove, & Helson, 1997), as well as generativity accomplishment (e.g., as assessed in Peterson & Klohnen's, 1995, Q-sort measure of generativity realization). Only with studies extending over time and employing all three kinds of assessments can we establish whether the

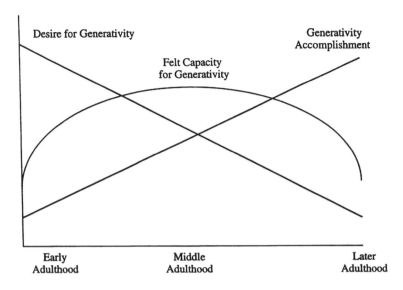

Desire for Generativity

Felt Capacity
for Generativity

Generativity
Accomplishment

| Early Adulthood | Middle Adulthood | Later Adulthood |

Figure 4. Hypothesized model of the course of generativity in adulthood.

course of generativity fits the model illustrated in Figure 4, with early adult formulation of generativity desire, a midlife peak in confidence and capacity for generativity, and actualization or accomplishment of generativity increasing in middle and later years. Longitudinal studies would also allow us to assess whether generative accomplishment in turn facilitates the sense of personal integrity Erikson recommends in old age.

Separating the elements of generativity in this way would address all three of the theoretical dilemmas we outlined earlier in this chapter. First, it would suggest that although generativity may have its period of "ascendance" in middle age in the form of a felt capacity, it is vitally present in the form of desire in early adulthood and of equally crucial importance as an accomplishment in old age. Second, there may be shifts over time in the narrowness of focus of generativity. Perhaps individuals develop generative desires first in relatively narrow, even gendered, domains (e.g., parenting or work), but over time those desires, and individuals' efforts and felt capacity, may broaden to encompass both private and public spheres. Finally, the problem of sequence recedes in importance if the early phase of generativity is conceived as the development of generative desire because this desire is perfectly compatible with simultaneous preoccupation with attainment of identity, intimacy, or both. Later stages of generativity (felt capacity and accomplishment) may depend much more on a solidly established sense of personal identity, and thus may elude groups (e.g., women of some generations) blocked from developing firm identities (see the high motivation–low accomplishment group described by Peterson, chapter 4, this volume). A theory of generativity development, then, allows us both to address these tensions in Erikson's account and to enrich our understanding of the course of adulthood.

Empirical examination of the proposed theory of generativity development must also address issues of gender and generation. We are mindful of the fact that all of the data we have examined come from women in a single, broadly defined generation. Both gender and generation may contribute to the patterns we have observed, particularly because the women in our two samples are members of a generation of educated American women with an unusually high degree of variability in adult life patterning of parenting and work activities. Men and generations of women with more powerful normative patterns (including gender-based norms) of generativity-relevant activities may look different from these samples. However, we note that, despite the high degree of variability in the sequencing and combining of career and family activities in our closely related cohorts of women, we identified a fairly consistent and uniform pattern of age-related change in generativity desire. Moreover, the relationships between generative desires and accomplishment and well-being were consistent in these two samples and among women with different life patterns within each sample. This consistency in the context of variability supports the developmental hypothesis we have advanced, but we need more data from other groups to confirm it.

Finally, there may be subtler differences in generativity between this generation and others or between men and women. For example, Mac-Dermid, Franz, and De Reus (in press; see also chapter 6, this volume) found that communal forms of generativity realization were higher in women than in men, that men declined in communal generativity realization over middle age, and that the younger Berkeley cohort showed more change in generativity realization overall than the older Oakland cohort. The generation we have studied was one in which political activism or social protest was a prominent feature of late adolescence and early adulthood. Perhaps generations with less socially preoccupied, activist youths form generative desires later or more consistently in the private sphere. Similarly, perhaps men and women differ in the sequencing or timing of the development of generative desires, capacity, or accomplishment in public versus private spheres. For example, perhaps men develop a sense of their capacity for generativity earlier than women do, given social support—or demand—for efficacy and confidence in men. To assess generational or gender differences in the course of generativity in these more complex terms, we will need to separate the elements of generativity even further and examine data from longitudinal studies of multiple cohorts and of both men and women. We hope future research will not only assess the usefulness of the developmental model of generativity offered here but also expand and refine it further.

REFERENCES

Brown, D. R., & Pacini, R. (1993). The Vassar classes of 1929–1935: Personality patterns in college and adult life. In K. D. Hulbert & D. T. Schuster (Eds.), *Women's lives through time* (pp. 93–116). San Francisco: Jossey-Bass.

Cole, E. R., & Stewart, A. J. (1996). Black and White women's political activism: Personality development, political identity and social responsibility. *Journal of Personality and Social Psychology, 71,* 130–140.

Constantinople, A. (1969). An Eriksonian measure of personality development in college students. *Developmental Psychology, 1,* 357–372.

Erikson, E. H. (1950). *Childhood and society.* New York: Norton.

Erikson, E. H. (1964). *Insight and responsibility.* New York: Norton.

Erikson, E. H. (1968). *Identity: Youth and crisis.* New York: Norton.

Erikson, E. H. (1969). *Gandhi's truth.* New York: Norton.

Erikson, E. H. (1974). Once more the inner space: Letter to former student. In J. Strouse (Ed.), *Women and analysis: Dialogues on psychoanalytic views of femininity* (pp. 365–387). New York: Dell.

Erikson, E. H. (1980). *Identity and the life cycle.* New York: Norton. (Original work published 1959)

Erikson, E. H. (1980). Themes of adulthood in the Freud-Jung correspondence. In N. J. Smelser & E. H. Erikson (Eds.), *Themes of work and love in adulthood* (pp. 43–74). Cambridge, MA: Harvard University Press.

Erikson, E. H. (1982). *The life cycle completed: A review.* New York: Norton.

Erikson, E. H., Erikson, J. M., & Kivnick, H. Q. (1986). *Vital involvement in old age.* New York: Norton.

Espin, O., Stewart, A. J., & Gomez, C. A. (1990). Letters from V: Adolescent personality development in sociohistorical context. *Journal of Personality, 58,* 347–364.

Evans, R. (1967). *Dialogue with Erik Erikson.* New York: Harper & Row.

Franz, C. E., & White, K. M. (1985). Individuation and attachment in personality development: Extending Erikson's theory. *Journal of Personality, 53,* 136–168.

Gough, H. G. (1987). *California psychological inventory administrator's guide.* Palo Alto, CA: Consulting Psychologists Press.

Gruen, W. (1964). Adult personality: An empirical study of Erikson's theory of ego development. In B. L. Neugarten, *Personality in middle and late life: Empirical studies* (pp. 1–14). New York: Atherton.

Helson, R., & Moane, G. (1987). Personality change in women from college to midlife. *Journal of Personality and Social Psychology, 53,* 176–186.

Helson, R., & Wink, P. (1992). Personality change in women from the early forties to the early fifties. *Journal of Personality and Social Psychology, 7,* 46–55.

Howard, A., & Bray, D. (1988). *Managerial lives in transition: Advancing age and changing times.* New York: Guilford.

Jenkins, S. R. (1989). Longitudinal prediction of women's careers: Psychological, behavioral, and social-structural effects. *Journal of Vocational Behavior, 34,* 204–235.

Jenkins, S. R. (1994). Need for power and women's careers over 14 years: Structural power, job satisfaction, and motive change. *Journal of Personality and Social Psychology, 66,* 155–165.

Jones, C. J., & Meredith, W. (1996). Patterns of personality change across the life span. *Psychology and Aging, 11,* 57–65.

Kotre, J. (1984). *Outliving the self: Generativity and the interpretation of lives.* Baltimore: The Johns Hopkins University Press.

MacDermid, S., & Crouter, A. C. (1995). Midlife, adolescence and parental employment in family systems. *Journal of Youth and Adolescence, 24,* 29–54.

MacDermid, S. M., Franz, C. E., & De Reus, L. A. (in press). Adult character: Agency, communion, insight, and the expression of generativity in midlife adults. In J. B. James (Ed.), volume for Character and Competence Research Program, Murray Research Center, Cambridge, MA.

McAdams, D. P., & Azarow, J. (1996, August). *Generativity in black and white: Relations among generativity, race, and well-being.* Paper presented at the American Psychological Association Convention, Toronto, Ontario, Canada.

McAdams, D. P., & de St. Aubin, E. (1992). A theory of generativity and its assessment through self-report, behavioral acts, and narrative themes in autobiography. *Journal of Personality and Social Psychology, 62,* 1003–1015.

McAdams, D. P., de St. Aubin, E., & Logan, R. L. (1993). Generativity among young, midlife, and older adults. *Psychology and Aging, 8,* 221–230.

McAdams, D. P., Ruetzel, K., & Foley, J. M. (1986). Complexity and generativity at midlife: Relations among social motives, ego development, and adults' plans for the future. *Journal of Personality and Social Psychology, 50,* 800–807.

McNair, D., Lorr, M., & Droppleman, L. (1971). Profile of mood states. San Diego, CA: Educational and Industrial Testing Service.

Neugarten, B. L. (1964). Summary and implications. In B. L. Neugarten, *Personality in middle and late life: Empirical studies* (pp. 188–200). New York: Atherton.

Neugarten, B. L. and others (1964). *Personality in middle and late life: Empirical studies.* New York: Atherton.

Mitchell, V., & Helson, R. (1990). Women's prime of life: Is it the fifties? *Psychology of Women Quarterly, 14,* 451–470.

Ochse, R., & Plug, C. (1986). Cross-cultural investigations of the validity of Erikson's theory of personality development. *Journal of Personality and Social Psychology, 50,* 1240–1252.

Peterson, B. E., & Klohnen, E. C. (1995). Realization of generativity in two samples of women at midlife. *Psychology and Aging, 10,* 20–29.

Peterson, B. E., & Stewart, A. J. (1990). Using personal and fictional documents to assess psychosocial development: A case study of Vera Brittain's generativity. *Psychology and Aging, 5,* 400–411.

Peterson, B. E., & Stewart, A. J. (1993). Generativity and social motives in young adults. *Journal of Personality and Social Psychology, 65,* 186–198.

Peterson, B. E., & Stewart, A. J. (1996). Antecedents and contexts of generativity motivation at midlife. *Psychology and Aging, 11,* 21–33.

Ryff, C. D., & Heincke, S. G. (1983). Subjective organization of personality in adulthood and aging. *Journal of Personality and Social Psychology, 44,* 807–816

Ryff, C. D., & Migdal, S. (1984). Intimacy and generativity: Self-perceived transitions. *Signs, 9,* 470–481.

Schuster, D. T., Langland, L., & Smith, D. G. (1993). The UCLA gifted women, class of 1961: Living up to potential. In K. D. Hulbert & D. T. Schuster (Eds.), *Women's lives through time* (pp. 211–231). San Francisco: Jossey-Bass.

Smith, C. P., Feld, S. C., & Franz, C. E. (1992). Methodological considerations: Steps in research employing content analysis systems. In C. P. Smith (Ed.), *Motivation and personality: Handbook of thematic content analysis* (pp. 515–536). New York: Cambridge University Press.

Snarey, J. (1993). *How fathers care for the next generation.* Cambridge, MA: Harvard University Press.

Snarey, J., Son, L., Kuehne, V. S., Hauser, S., & Vaillant, G. (1987). The role of parenting in men's psychosocial development: A longitudinal study of early adulthood infertility and midlife generativity. *Developmental Psychology, 23,* 593–603.

Stewart, A. J. (1995, April). *Rethinking middle age: Learning from women's lives.* Invited address, Eastern Psychological Association, Boston, MA.

Stewart, A. J. (1996, August). *Personality in middle age: Gender, history and midcourse corrections.* Invited address, American Psychological Association, Toronto, Ontario, Canada.

Stewart, A. J., Franz, C. E., & Layton, L. (1988). The changing self: Using personal documents to study lives. *Journal of Personality, 56,* 41–74.

Stewart, A. J., Ostrove, J., & Helson, R. (1997). Middle-aging in women: Patterns of personality change from the 30s to the 50s. Manuscript under review.

Stewart, A. J., & Vandewater, E. A. (1993). The Radcliffe class of 1964: Career and family social clock projects in a transitional cohort. In K. D. Hulbert & D. T. Schuster (Eds.), *Women's lives through time* (pp. 235–258). San Francisco: Jossey-Bass.

Tangri, S., & Jenkins, S. (1993). The University of Michigan class of 1967: The women's life paths study. In K. D. Hulbert & D. T. Schuster (Eds.), *Women's lives through time* (pp. 259–281). San Francisco: Jossey-Bass.

Vaillant, G. E. (1977). *Adaptation to life.* Boston: Little, Brown.

Vaillant, G. E. (1993). *The wisdom of the ego.* Cambridge, MA: Harvard University Press.

Vaillant, G. E., & Milofsky, E. S. (1980). Natural history of male psychological health: 9. Empirical evidence for Erikson's model of the life cycle. *American Journal of Psychiatry, 138,* 1433–1440.

Van De Water, D. A., & McAdams, D. P. (1989). Generativity and Erikson's "belief in the species." *Journal of Research in Personality, 23,* 435–449.

Waterman, A. S., & Whitbourne, S. K. (1981). The inventory of psychosocial development. *JSAS Catalog of Selected Documents in Psychology, 11,* 5. (Ms. No. 2179).

Whitbourne, S. K., Zuschlag, M. K., Elliot, L. B., & Waterman, A. S. (1992). Psychosocial development in adulthood: A 22-year sequential study. *Journal of Personality and Social Psychology, 63,* 260–271.

Zung, W. K. (1965). A self-rating depression scale. *Archives of General Psychiatry, 12,* 63–70.

Zung, W. K. (1971). A rating instrument for anxiety disorders. *Psychosomatics, 12,* 371–379.

4

CASE STUDIES OF MIDLIFE GENERATIVITY: ANALYZING MOTIVATION AND REALIZATION

BILL E. PETERSON

Almost 50 years ago Erikson (1950/1963) introduced the concept of midlife generativity. According to Erikson, generative individuals express themselves by working to maintain the structure of their society and by nurturing the people around them. His ideas were based on an intuitive understanding of generational interdependence and on observations and case studies of individuals within the context of their cultures (e.g., Erikson, 1969). In this chapter I build on Erikson's ideas by using multiple case study methodology. After discussing attempts by psychologists to operationalize the construct of generativity, I use two measures to select highly generative and less generative adults for more textured, idiographic analyses.

Although introduced within the context of a larger model of human

I thank Abigail J. Stewart for providing me with access to the Radcliffe longitudinal case files. Dr. Stewart was kind enough to read several of the cases, and our subsequent discussions helped to clarify important aspects of this chapter. I also thank Lauren E. Duncan, Dan P. McAdams, Ed de St. Aubin, Elizabeth A. Vandewater, and Paul Wink for thoughtful readings of prior drafts.

development, the concept of generativity in particular has received increasing attention in the psychology literature. For example, McAdams (1985) and colleagues expanded on Erikson's ideas by elaborating a multidimensional model of generativity (de St. Aubin & McAdams, 1995; Mansfield & McAdams, 1996; McAdams & de St. Aubin, 1992; McAdams, de St. Aubin, & Logan, 1993). In the course of their investigations (including work appearing in this volume), they argued that generativity was best understood from multiple vantage points, each vantage point assessed through the use of different methodological techniques. Thus, generativity *concerns* were measured through the use of the self-report Loyola Generativity Scale (LGS), whereas generative *activity* was assessed through the Generative Behavior Checklist. These tests, developed on the basis of theory, represent advancements in the assessment technology used to measure generativity. Earlier empirical efforts relied on proxy measures, labor-intensive coding schemes, and simplified definitions of the construct (e.g., Peterson & Stewart, 1993; Ryff & Heincke, 1983; Stewart, Franz, & Layton, 1988; Vaillant & Milofsky, 1980).

In an empirical discipline like psychology, it is no surprise that researchers have tried to establish valid and reliable measures of generativity. Indeed, my colleagues and I have also been concerned with issues of assessment. In the words of Kotre (1992), we have been working on ways to "spot the generative individual." On the basis of the theoretical writings of Erikson (1950/1963), Kotre (1984), and McAdams (1985), we have developed two different ways to identify the generative person. The first relies on Block's (1961/1978) California Q sort (Peterson & Klohnen, 1995), and the second relies on Thematic Apperception Test (TAT) techniques (Peterson & Stewart, 1996).

These two measures tap different manifestations of generativity. More specifically, the Q sort assesses the *realization* of generative potential, whereas the TAT assesses generativity *motivation*. Our reasoning for this categorization is based on the pattern of life correlates associated with the two measures and on the nature of the Q sort and TAT as measurement techniques. By using Stewart and Vandewater's (see chapter 3, this volume) distinction, Q-sort generativity could be considered an aspect of generative accomplishments, whereas TAT generativity could be considered an aspect of generative desires.

THE Q SORT AS A MEASURE OF GENERATIVITY REALIZATION

The California Q sort consists of 100 personality, behavioral, and physical descriptors written out on 100 cards (Block 1961, 1978). Researchers use the Q sort to describe an individual by reading each card and placing it on a continuum from 1 (*extremely uncharacteristic*) to 9 (*extremely characteristic*) for the individual being rated. Examples of items include "feels a lack of personal meaning in life" and "values own independence and autonomy." The method limits the number of items that can be placed into each of the 9 points of the distribution in such a way that the resulting Q-sort profile is based on an approximately normal distribution. Therefore, five cards are placed at the extremely characteristic end and five cards are placed at the extremely uncharacteristic end. Eighteen cards, on the other hand, are placed in the middle (as being relatively unimportant for describing the individual being assessed). The generativity index was constructed by using 13 of the Q-sort items as indicators of generativity (e.g., "behaves in a giving way toward others" and "is productive, gets things done"). Peterson and Klohnen (1995) argued that participants rated highly on these 13 items have achieved high levels of generativity (see Exhibit 1 for the item content of the index).

Q-sort generativity index scores were validated on two samples of educated women at midlife (Peterson & Klohnen, 1995). The investigators generated Q-sort-based descriptions of these women (using all 100 items) by reading extensive questionnaire material provided by each woman at age 43. At least three different psychologists read through over 200 case files to generate Q-sort descriptions. The Q sort summarized in a convenient and fairly comprehensive way all the attitudinal and life-outcome data collected at age 43. As such, my colleagues and I argued that scores on the 13-item Q-sort generativity index could best be thought of as representing the extent to which participants had realized their generative potential or accomplished generative goals (at least in the eyes of an outside observer). The life-outcome and personality correlates associated with this new measure provided further evidence for this claim. Women who scored high on Q-sort generativity were likely to be parents and to indicate that they were competent in the parental role. They possessed positive personality characteristics (e.g., responsibility and empathy) and were more interested in work that allowed them to help others. They wrote accounts of many generative experiences they had had throughout their life and scored high on measures of psychological adjustment.

THE TAT AS A MEASURE OF GENERATIVITY MOTIVATION

In contrast, the TAT seemed to assess generativity *motivation* rather than *realization*. As a measurement strategy, the use of the TAT goes back to the pioneering work of Morgan and Murray (1935). Building on classic psychoanalytic techniques of dream interpretation and free association, Murray (1938) used the spontaneous stories produced by participants in response to TAT picture cues as a measure of nonconscious, internally based motivational needs. According to McClelland and his colleagues

EXHIBIT 1
Components of the Q-Sort and TAT Measures of Generativity

Q-Sort Items (Generative Realization)	TAT Scoring Categories (Generativity Motivation)
Behaves in a giving way toward others	Parental Generativity
Behaves in a considerate or sympathetic manner	Parental concern toward own or other children
Is protective of those close to him	Focus on child's future
Has warmth; has the capacity for close relationships; is compassionate	Tension about child's independence
Is turned to for advice and reassurance	Caring
Is a genuinely dependable and responsible person	Teaching or advising others
Is productive; gets things done	Concern for others
Behaves in an ethically consistent manner; is consistent with own personal standards	Broad societal concern
Tends to proffer advice	Productivity
Has a wide range of interests	Personal productivity
Is socially perceptive of a wide range of social cues	Current feelings of stagnation (scored in negative direction)
Able to see to the heart of important problems	Insight
Is concerned with philosophical problems	Tolerance of conflicts
	Layers of meaning

Note. More complete information can be found in articles by Peterson and Klohnen (1995) for the Q sort and by Peterson and Stewart (1996) for the TAT. TAT = Thematic Apperception Test.

(McClelland, 1980; McClelland, Koestner, & Weinberger, 1989; Weinberger & McClelland, 1990), the TAT, as an indirect measure of nonconscious motivation, is currently the only viable method psychologists have for assessing affectively based implicit motives. Although research using the TAT has focused primarily on the motives for achievement, affiliation, intimacy, and power, other motivational constructs can be assessed as well.

Peterson and Stewart (1996) developed a measure of generativity based on the TAT. Categories for scoring generative imagery in any sort of open-ended text were developed after a thorough review of Erikson's writings (e.g., 1950/1963, 1985). Four types of general imagery were scored for evidence of generativity motivation: themes of *caring*, *productivity*, *insight*, and *parenting*. For example, parental generativity would be scored if someone wrote in a TAT story that a character was building a treehouse for his daughter's (or other young person's) enjoyment. Exhibit 1 lists the four coding categories and the subcategories of the scoring system. The TAT measure was validated on one of the two samples of educated woman used to validate the Q-sort measure. At age 48, more than 100 women in this sample completed four TAT protocols that were scored for images of generativity. We assumed that women who expressed generative imagery in their stories were motivated to become generative in their lives, and the pattern of correlates for the TAT measure supported this claim. In this longitudinal study, women who wrote generative stories at age 48 expressed many different kinds of generative wishes but not experiences. Women who scored high on generativity motivation were also more likely to express gratitude toward a special mentor who helped them through crises or supported their bids for autonomy and excellence. TAT generativity was correlated with a past history of political involvement. Women who wrote generative stories were informed about past and contemporary politics; in fact, many of the women expressed anger concerning the lack of caring and responsibility that they perceived from those in power. Women involved in careers who scored high on the TAT expressed emotional satisfaction at self-mastery and caring for others through their work. For women who did not have careers, generativity motivation was related to the enjoyment of parenting. On the basis of these findings, Peterson and Stewart (1996) concluded that the TAT tapped an *affectively* based motive to act in generative ways. Stewart and Vandewater (chapter 3, this volume) discuss further evidence supporting the view that the TAT captures generativity motivation (or desire), whereas the Q sort assesses generativity realization.

THE RELATIONSHIP BETWEEN Q-SORT GENERATIVITY AND TAT GENERATIVITY

In the sample of educated women from whom we collected both measures, scores on the Q sort and TAT were moderately correlated ($r = .30$,

$p < .01$). This indicates that Q-sort and TAT generativity share conceptual space, but the lack of complete overlap suggests that the two measures assess slightly different aspects of the construct. In other words, generativity motivation has only a moderate degree of bearing on generativity realization. The strength of this correlation between the Q sort and TAT is consistent with the argument of McClelland et al. (1989) concerning implicit and self-report variables. McClelland and his colleagues argued that there are at least two different motivational systems involved in human behavior: affectively based implicit motives (best tapped by the TAT) and cognitively based self-attributed motives (best tapped by self-report). Implicit motives were hypothesized to be built on early affective experiences, to predict long-term behavioral trends, and to interact with intrinsic activity incentives to affect behavior. Self-attributed motives, on the other hand, were hypothesized to develop later in life when people have more elaborated cognitive schemas about the world and themselves, to predict short-term behavior, and to interact with social incentives to affect behavior. McClelland and his colleagues have argued that standard self-report and TAT-based measures of similar constructs (such as self-report and TAT motives for achievement) are seldom related statistically and display different, although relevant, behavioral correlates. Although Q-sort generativity is scored from self-report material, it is also based on observer judgments of how successfully an individual has accomplished her generative projects. Scores on generativity realization as assessed by the Q sort, therefore, should correlate positively with generativity motivation as assessed by the TAT; however, the relationship between motivation and realization should not be too high because the Q sort also involves self-reports (which McClelland has shown correlate at approximately zero with TAT measures). The TAT and Q-sort measures, therefore, do not represent overlapping assessment techniques. In fact, the following case studies of people who scored differentially high on these two measures will further clarify the general differences between the TAT and Q sort (i.e., as measures of motivation and realization, respectively).

The correlation of .30 between motivation and realization is also consistent with Erikson's (1950/1963) emphasis on the struggle between generativity and stagnation. In Erikson's formulation, generativity is not achieved once and for all at midlife; rather, individuals constantly rework aspects of generativity to maintain a balance of psychosocial strengths. Because generativity is hypothesized to be a pervasive midlife phenomenon that touches many aspects of human existence (e.g., parenting, work and psychological health), it is unrealistic to expect individuals to achieve optimal experiences in all of these disparate domains at the same time. Hence, motivational desires to be generative may not always be in synchrony with realization of generative goals. In fact, Stewart and Vandewater (chapter 3, this volume) postulate that different types of generativity may get expressed at different points in the life cycle. According to their argument, generativity motivation may be important for young adult development, whereas generativity realization may be more important at midlife.

USING NOMOTHETIC METHODS IN IDIOGRAPHIC RESEARCH

Researchers often use assessment devices like the Q sort and TAT to investigate the psychology of human experience. However, in addition to using standardized testing procedures to conduct nomothetic, variable-centered research, it is important to conduct idiographic, person-centered research as well (e.g., Carlson, 1971; Franz & Stewart, 1994; McAdams & Ochberg, 1988; Runyan, 1982). Idiographic research shifts attention away from abstract psychological variables (like generativity motivation) and reorients it toward the lives of individuals. Idiographic methods allow researchers to examine complex intrapsychic and interpersonal patterns within one person's life.

As suggested by Newton (1995), idiographic research in the form of case studies serves a heuristic function by helping psychologists to generate hypotheses that can be tested once again at the variable level. One way to conduct a case study is to use scores on nomothetic measures to choose people to study in depth using idiographic methods (e.g., Healy & Stewart, 1991; Helson, Mitchell, & Hart, 1985). In this chapter, I describe research that combines the variable-centered and person-centered methods by using the Q sort and TAT to select individuals for multiple case study. I compared people who scored extremely high on generativity motivation and realization with people who scored extremely low on these measures. These in-depth analyses highlight the importance for personality psychologists of distinguishing between motivation and realization.

MULTIPLE CASE STUDIES

Participants

Participants were selected from a longitudinal study of women who graduated from Radcliffe College in the mid-1960s. Stewart (1978, 1980; Stewart & Vandewater, 1993) collected extensive open-ended and closed-ended questionnaire data from these women at ages 18, 31, 37, 43, and 48. Two hundred forty-four women took part in the survey at age 18, and approximately 100 women participated in each subsequent follow-up. Although there were exceptions, Ostrove and Stewart (1994) reported that most of the women came from middle- to upper-middle-class backgrounds. In terms of educational attainment, 77% of the women received degrees beyond their bachelor's degree, forming an educationally elite group. Because they were not, in general, suffering from economic hardship, they were positioned well to realize their aspirations. As such, the goal of this chapter is not to generalize from Radcliffe women's lives but to examine how people free from economic constraints might express generativity motivation and realization.

Twelve women were selected for case study on the basis of their midlife scores on the generativity motivation and realization measures. These women were divided into four groups: (a) those who scored high on both measures, (b) those who scored high on the TAT and low on the Q sort, (c) those who scored low on the TAT and high on the Q sort, and (d) those who scored low on both measures. This strategy allowed for a comparison between women who valued and achieved generative goals (Group A) with women who did not value or achieve generative goals (Group D). In addition, the strategy allowed a discussion of generativity motivation in the absence of realization (Group B) and generativity realization in the absence of motivation (Group C). To select the cases, a scatterplot of standardized Q-sort (x axis) and TAT (y axis) scores was created ($M = 50$, $SD = 10$). In Figure 1, the horizontal line through the scatterplot depicts the median score for the TAT, and the vertical line represents the median score for the Q-sort measure. The 12 points that are circled represent the women selected for case study. These women were chosen on the basis of

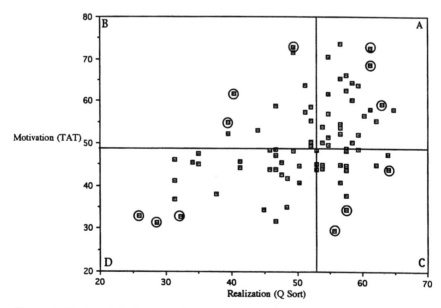

Figure 1. Scatterplot of scores for generativity realization and motivation. Generativity scores of participants selected for case study have been circled. TAT = thematic apperception test.

the extremity of their scores on the two measures of generativity. To be-selected, each woman had to have participated in at least three out of the four follow-up assessments at ages 31, 37, 43, and 48. For example, the participant who scored highest on the TAT measure of generativity (and high on the Q-sort measure) was *not* included as a case in Group A because she did not return surveys at ages 31 and 37.

To protect the privacy of the women in each category, we discuss their lives only in general terms and we use pseudonyms. In some instances, details are left intentionally vague to guard further against detection; I hoped that the lack of particulars for any one individual would be balanced by the presentation of multiple cases within each of the four groups. To prepare the cases for study, copies of all questionnaire material were made for each of the 12 women. These complete case files typically consisted of about 50 pages of written material consisting of answers to numerous open-ended questions (e.g., about marriage, parenting, careers, life wishes and daily activities). I read each woman's file once to develop a basic under-standing of her life trajectory. After a second reading, I wrote a two-page statement for each woman summarizing her major generativity concerns. Four one-page statements compared each of the women with the others in her group. In making interpretations I referred back to case files for clari-fication.

Exhibit 2 provides some basic information about each woman at the time of the 1990 (age 48) assessment. All of the women who scored high on both measures of generativity (Group A) were major professionals (e.g., physician, lawyer or professor). They each had at least two children, and two have been married for many years to the same person. The women in Group B (high motivation, low realization) had more varied life situations: One was a major professional, one was a minor professional (e.g., social worker or junior college teacher), and the third held various jobs. One woman had been married for many years with children, one was divorced with children, and one had never married or had children. Of the women in Group C (low motivation, high realization), one was a major profes-sional, one was a minor professional, and one had never worked for pay. They each had at least two children, and two of the women have been married to the same person for many years. The women in Group D (low on both measures) were all working for pay; two of the women were minor professionals, and the third was a major professional. Two were divorced with children, while the third was married without children.

In these case studies, I focus on the women's sense of generativity in the areas of occupation and family life. Both of these areas were important to all 12 women. However, generative motivations or realizations not re-lated to career or family are discussed for each individual when important. (See MacDermid, De Haan, & Heilbrun, 1996, for recent research that investigated the usefulness of examining generativity in multiple roles.)

EXHIBIT 2

Basic Demographic Information About the 12 Women Selected for Case Study

Group A (high on both measures)
Amanda: Major professional; married with children
Alex: Major professional; married with children
Anne: Major professional; divorced with children

Group B (high on motivation, low on realization)
Barbara: Various jobs; never married, no children
Bobby: Minor professional; married with children
Beth: Major professional; divorced with child

Group C (low on motivation, high on realization)
Carmela: Not working for pay; married with children
Cary: Minor professional; married with children
Claire: Major professional; divorced, remarried with children

Group D (low on both measures)
Deborah: Minor professional; divorced with children
Darcy: Major professional; married with no children
Dee: Minor professional; divorced with children

Note. This information comes from the age 48 assessment.

Women Who Scored High on Generativity Motivation and Realization

Individual Cases

Together, the women in Group A scored over 1 standard deviation above the mean on both measures of generativity: 61.72 on the Q sort and 66.86 on the TAT. Befitting the high scores, these women demonstrated quite a bit of generative activity in their lives. Both Alex and Amanda skillfully blended career and family responsibilities. Amanda was a professional who took pride in "helping families with problems." Amanda's decision to pursue an advanced degree emerged early in life: "My father is so happy in his work . . . that I followed him into [his career] in spite of his recommendation against it. He would come home from work really excited about something he had seen or learned—no one else's parents did that. . . . And I feel the same way. In spite of really resenting [the late work hours], I would not pick another career for myself." Amanda's choice of a career mirrors a root metaphor of generativity: She followed in her father's footsteps.

In terms of her own parenting, Amanda wrote that she was "anxious about her latchkey kids" when she started work full time, but this seemed not to have created many problems. At age 43 she wrote that she felt "very positive about motherhood" and considered parenting one of the major high points of the past 10 years. Her marriage was also a source of pleasure; she wrote that she and her husband shared domestic work pretty fairly and that she was gratified with the intellectual equality of her marriage. Amanda expressed the view that her marriage was "going quite well, unlike [the marriages of] most of my friends!" In summary, Amanda has carved out a comfortable lifestyle for herself that enables her to actualize generative aspirations by helping others at work and raising children within an egalitarian partnership.

Although her personal life was going well, Amanda expressed frustration and dissatisfaction with the political climate of the United States. In 1986 Amanda wrote that a low point of the past 10 years was contemporary politics and what it "represents in a turning away from social responsibility by the entire privileged portion of the country." She was "appalled and ashamed" at the leadership provided by national figures. If she could have any wish, she would "negotiate enough super-power cooperation and trust to establish a nuclear freeze and disarmament" and "use all that money for public health world wide." Her resentment of the current political milieu led her to channel energy into active commitments; she became involved in politics at a local level and is a member of several national political organizations. Thus, despite the generative realizations in her work and family life, Amanda was motivated to extend her generative influence by alleviating social problems that she perceives harm this country.

The second case, Alex, also successfully negotiated career and family responsibilities. Like Amanda, Alex mentioned several role models who led her to pursue her research interests. For example, Alex discussed the influence of a grade school science teacher: "I admired her very much and decided I wanted to be a scientist like her." Alex was self-effacing; in response to a question about her strongest points as a person, she wrote that she had "some scientific ability." Her career realizations, however, indicated more than a little skill in these areas. In fact, Alex had the skill and ability to start her own business. This move followed Alex's quitting her old job on specific moral grounds.

Although Alex reported that she loves her husband, she was somewhat resentful that he and she do not share domestic chores equally. However, she tempered this with the statement that "I am reluctant to let him get involved and interfere with what I regard as my domain." As a parent, Alex enjoyed time with her children and was proud of their accomplishments. She articulated a complex understanding of her children's needs; she wrote that one of the best things about having children is "watching unique individuals develop. One tries to provide guidance, but I am left with the feeling that they are their own people." She seems engaged in a reciprocally rewarding relationship with her kids: "Having children totally dependent on [me], gives [me] a chance to rise to the challenge. Having children question one's values provides many opportunities to reconsider what is important." In a sentence filled with generative symbolism, Alex, at age 43, wrote that a high point of the past 10 years occurred during a family vacation in the wilds: "an afternoon when my kids and I watched a goose egg hatching."

Like Amanda, Alex had a successful marriage and accomplished generative goals through career pursuits and parenting. Unlike Amanda, however, Alex did not seem to channel generativity motivation into political involvement. Alex's motives for generativity were manifest currently in her career decision to start a new company; maintaining the viability of her fledgling organization required daily effort. Such a generative commitment indicates a concern with extending the self through important productive efforts. In this sense, Alex and our third case, Anne, shared generative aspirations to express the self through work.

Anne had entered into a career track at midlife; she only recently received an advanced degree and began work as an assistant professor. This choice of an academic career was not surprising given Anne's lifelong commitment to teaching. Because of her husband's job requirements, Anne spent many years abroad. While there, she not only taught her own children for several years but also started a nursery school for neighborhood children. In 1974 Anne wrote the following as a high point: "Teaching [these] children who have been my friends, giving them experiences which I feel sure will be the greatest help to them when they have to go to school, has been extremely rewarding." Indeed, one of her wishes at this time was to "begin whatever preparations turn out to be necessary for a career in the area of helping children."

After her divorce, Anne's goals were modest. She simply wanted to earn a certificate to teach elementary school. At this time, Anne worked with children in a variety of formats (e.g., day care provider, board member of a local school, girl scout leader, and elementary school teacher). These job activities, however, were only a prelude to greater challenges. An important figure in Anne's life encouraged her to pursue a graduate degree. When Anne returned to a university setting, she found that the intellectual challenges thrilled her, and she began work toward her doctorate. She has since achieved her goal of publishing her research and teaching as an assistant professor.

Throughout her educational pursuits, Anne remained devoted to her children. At midlife she wrote that children were a "permanent commitment—takes time and energy and you always have to consider them, [but] they give you an intense joy I've never yet found in another context." She seemed genuinely happy as a single mother with a career.

To use McAdams's (1985) terminology, Anne exemplified the *imago* of a teacher. Her generativity was expressed through her love of working with young people in a variety of contexts. She actualized her goal of earning a doctoral degree and maintained a commitment to children in her ongoing research. Anne took logical steps to advance her latent career interests; it was a long climb with many twists and turns, but once she set her goals of obtaining an advanced degree, she pursued it with tenacity. Although she has begun to actualize generative goals through career productivity, she has a lot of ground to make up. For this reason, it may not be surprising that her motives for generativity remain high.

Summary of Group A

Exhibit 3 provides brief psychological sketches of all three women. Amanda and Alex were similar in that they skillfully blended stable marriages with children and careers. They achieved a sense of generativity in their domestic and occupational lives. Both women also had directed their generative motives toward a specific target. Amanda was quite concerned about a destructive political environment. She spent a lot of time volunteering with political organizations trying to correct the political imbalances that she saw. In response to a harsh corporate climate, Alex found it necessary to start her own company. No doubt a lot of generative energy was directed toward the continued success of her new venture. Anne makes an interesting contrast to Alex and Amanda. She did not have a long history of working in a career track. Although currently a major professional, the route Anne took to her career was circuitous. She did not

EXHIBIT 3
Summary Table of Group A: Women High on Generativity Realization and Motivation

Overall Finding: Women in Group A had realized generative goals in their family and career life. However, their generativity motivation remained high. The reason for this seemed to be tension or frustration in an area important for their sense of continued generative accomplishment. These specific frustrations are listed below.

Amanda:
Realization: Happy in her career choice—she followed in her father's footsteps. Amanda was also happy as a spouse and parent.
Motivations: Amanda was unhappy with the contemporary political landscape. She felt responsible for doing what she could to improve the welfare of children at a national level.

Alex:
Realization: Alex was generally happy as a spouse and parent. Her career was important to her; she was currently trying to be productively self-employed in her field of expertise.
Motivations: During the midlife assessments, Alex was experiencing great career uncertainty. She was investing time and energy to make her new business intellectually stimulating and financially successful.

Anne:
Realization: Anne represented a teacher imago (McAdams, 1985). She has taught a variety of students from varied backgrounds and educational levels. Although divorced, Anne found that the role of parent provided her with tremendous joy.
Motivations: At the time of the midlife assessment, Anne had just started on her most challenging teaching role yet. She was working hard to be a successful college professor.

possess decades of career success but was clearly motivated toward a new sense of productivity at midlife. Anne, as an excellent example of a teacher imago, is someone quite interested in caring for and instructing the next generation.

It is interesting to note that all three of these women acknowledged the role that a special mentor played in their career aspirations (e.g., parent, teacher or important friend). This generative role model, or source of wise counsel, was inspirational in helping them to attain high levels of productivity and career satisfaction. At the point of the last questionnaire, these women were continuing to struggle with specific generativity issues even as they lived generative lives.

Women Who Scored High on Motivation and Low on Realization

Individual Cases

On average, the three women in Group B expressed a high degree of generativity motivation (M = 63.18 on the TAT) and moderate levels of generativity realization (M = 43.04 on the Q sort). In reading through these case files, I noted that Barbara and Bobby seemed frustrated in their attempts to realize generative goals, whereas the life of Beth illustrates the importance of defining clearly what it means to act in a generative way.

For over a decade, Barbara worked in various clerical, administrative, and teaching jobs while pursuing an advanced degree. Like Anne, Barbara recently received her degree; however, the length of time it took Barbara to complete requirements left her with a history of temporary and part-time jobs. There are many indications that she has not accomplished as much as she would like in a career. In fact, in 1986 Barbara indicated that her one regret was that "I wanted to be a [medical] doctor."

In addition, Barbara has not attained high levels of intimacy in her life. For example, she never married and has no children. This is somewhat surprising given her 1974 wish that in the next 10 years she would "get married and have two kids [and] live in a white cottage with a flower garden in front and a vegetable garden in the rear." Although the image of a white cottage (with picket fence) is a cliche, there was no reason to doubt the sincerity of this statement. In 1986 Barbara wrote that she liked children. She has thought of adopting or having kids but decided not to for financial reasons and because she does "not feel [she] can take on the responsibility." She also considered marriage to a particular individual but ultimately rejected the idea because of "incompatibility of lifestyles."

In both her career aspirations and relationships, therefore, Barbara has been frustrated. These frustrations make it difficult to realize a sense of generative productivity or caring. This is not to say that Barbara is incapable of expressing generativity. In fact, throughout her life Barbara has found ways to help others, such as serving in the Peace Corps, providing transportation services to the needy, and volunteering time in the churches that she attended. There is, however, a sense of diffusion in her commitment to so many activities. For example, in the span of 3 years, Barbara was attending several churches, traveling extensively, participating in many clubs and historical groups, and working on a variety of new hobbies. From an Eriksonian perspective, it may be that Barbara continues to negotiate aspects of psychosocial identity. Although she expresses generative strivings, she had yet to find a way to actualize these desires in a consistent manner.

Bobby has had similar frustrations. Although she obtained a doctorate, her work situation has been less than ideal. For years Bobby struggled with the tension between teaching at a less than satisfying school to maintain a certain lifestyle and wanting to work in a more demanding university setting. In 1979 she wrote, "I haven't done much research. . . . I like spending time with the family, as these part-time and temporary jobs allow." Although she subsequently had a spate of research productivity, Bobby continued to work at the same college. The lifestyle that she and her husband created for themselves and their children prevented her from seeking better employment opportunities. Under career regrets, Bobby wrote that there were many "jobs in urban centers for which [she] did not apply." Under low points she reiterated this theme: "My career getting stuck— overworked, underpaid at a stifling college." To compensate for the lack of intellectual challenge in her career, Bobby turned to writing short stories and investing much time and effort in a specialized hobby.

Bobby cares a lot about her children as individuals. In 1986 she wrote that the best things about having children were "watching them evolve. Teaching them important things—about love, sex, peace." She wrote that a woman's life is changed by having children because one "feels a connection to past and future generations. Even more than after marriage, realization that she cannot make choices just for *self*." Although she and her husband went through hard times, they seem to have patched up differences. During our last assessment, Bobby and her entire family spent an enjoyable year abroad while she taught.

Like Barbara, Bobby was motivated to act in generative ways. For example, Bobby demonstrated a genuine concern for her students: "Teaching can be exhilarating when I present material well, when students are involved, [and] when I get to know them as people." Like Amanda, Bobby also had a heightened political consciousness. She wrote about the impact that the Civil Rights Movement had on her; she learned that "our lives didn't have to be limited, restricted—prejudice could be fought!" In fact, her decisions about career and lifestyle seemed based, in part, on her beliefs about the dangers of capitalist consumption. These examples illustrate Bobby's commitment to act in generative ways; however, she has yet to overcome specific frustrations in her career productivity.

Beth, the third person in Group B, also has earned an advanced degree. Unlike Bobby and Barbara, however, Beth has maintained a highly productive career at a research-oriented university. She wrote that work was her "identity and the center of her life." In her research, she makes an active effort to combine political theory with social policy, and she broke at least one barrier to advance women's rights. It is clear that Beth cares about her work and uses her intellectual prowess to articulate the subtle and not so subtle oppression that women face. Her motivation to improve women's lives was steadfast, and she realized many of her generative goals at a broad societal level. Despite this creative productivity, however, Beth was rated as relatively low on the measure of generativity realization, probably the result of her choice to live a life of relative isolation from others.

Although she had been married, Beth and her husband divorced over "his expectations of an attractive home and [her expectation of] his equal participation in housework and child-care." Beth came to the conclusion that marriage "mobilizes and reveals latent sex-role expectations." In her questionnaire responses, Beth did not discuss children very much (although it was clear Beth took parenting duties seriously), but in 1986 she fantasized about having two more children and a "househusband" to take care of them. In terms of friendships, Beth seemed uninterested in indulging the concerns of others. As examples, the least gratifying aspect of work for Beth was "being confronted with too many people who want something from me, if only my attention." After receiving a large research grant, Beth hired a friend and rapidly lost the friendship because "she couldn't cope with being my employee." Finally, Beth discussed a research project "with a colleague/friend with whom I then broke." Although she is an articulate and intelligent scholar, Beth acknowledged difficulty in maintaining intimate relationships with others. In 1986 she wrote that she would like to become "more flexible and relaxed about emotional and physical intimacy/openness in casual or every-day relationships."

Beth is an extremely productive academic who successfully applied research and theory to advance the status of women in society. Although these efforts indicate the successful realization of a creative form of generativity, Beth was rated relatively low on the Q-sort (realization) measure. Such a situation suggests a possible refinement of the Q-sort measure of generativity realization: dividing the measure into subscales of productivity and caring. Clearly, in the case of Beth, what is important for assessing generativity are the agentically oriented items (e.g., is productive, gets things done, is a genuinely dependable and responsible person), and not the communal items (e.g., has warmth, has the capacity for close relationships). Kotre (1984) warned, however, that agency untempered by communion can lead to generative failures. Similarly, McAdams, Hart, and Maruna (chapter 1, this volume) argue that both agentic and communal desires are important for the expression of generative concerns and actions. Future empirical work will be needed to explore the communal and agentic aspects of generativity realization.

Summary of Group B

Exhibit 4 provides brief sketches of the women in Group B. Barbara and Bobby were similar in that they experienced specific frustrations related to their career expectations. Bobby went to great lengths to accommodate her family's lifestyle; the physical location of her home precluded the possibility of employment in a more fulfilling job. Barbara, on the other hand, spent years working on a degree that has yet to pay off in terms of scholarly productivity. Barbara also expressed frustration that she never married and had no children. She was very giving but diffused her energy into a variety of causes, which contributed to problematic relational and career commitments. Both women were motivated to behave in generative ways but have yet to find clear avenues for the expression of productive generativity. Beth,

EXHIBIT 4
Summary Table of Group B: Women Low on Generativity Realization and High on Motivation

Overall Finding: Women in Group B experienced specific frustrations in their careers or family life. However, they were actively concerned with resolving these tensions.

Barbara:
   Realization: Barbara seemed dissatisfied with the absence of intimate relationships in her life. She has an advanced degree but was underemployed.
   Motivations: In her early surveys, Barbara expressed a desire for intimate relationships and children. These generative goals have yet to be realized. Barbara has also not been able to sustain a solid career trajectory.

Bobby:
   Realization: Bobby was married with children and working in a career. Her family life and career choices, however, were in constant tension.
   Motivations: Bobby seemed extremely frustrated that career goals could not be actualized owing to commitments made to family and lifestyle.

Beth:
   Realization: Beth was happy and productive in her career. However, she admitted discontent in her intimate relationships.
   Motivations: Beth would like to become less guarded about personal relationships.

---

on the other hand, was a high-powered academic finding little fulfillment in the realms of marriage and friendship. She devoted a great deal of motivational energy toward the improvement of women's lives, which paid off in high levels of occupational productivity. However, her scores on generativity realization remained low because the Q-sort measure, as it stands, weighs communal generativity as equally important to agentic productivity.

Consistent with the contention of Stewart and Vandewater (chapter 3, this volume), it may be that generativity motivation is ideally expressed during *young adulthood*, when identity and intimacy issues are normatively resolved and when generative goals might first be formulated. At midlife, on the other hand, the expression of high levels of generativity motivation may indicate problematic resolution of personally important aspects of generativity. Perhaps issues of social clock timing (e.g., Helson, Mitchell, & Moane, 1984) were involved in setting up expectations of generative realizations that were frustrated for this group of women.

Women Who Scored Low on Motivation and High on Realization

Individual Cases

The average scores for Group C were 58.70 for generativity realization and 35.91 for generativity motivation. Reflecting their high Q-sort scores, this group of women manifested key aspects of generativity, but unlike the women of Group B, they did not seem to be struggling with generative frustrations.

Carmela illustrates this pattern nicely. After graduation she served in the Peace Corps for a few years. She wrote that she was motivated to join by former president Kennedy and the impact of his assassination. When she returned to the United States she worked to put her husband through graduate school, but she gave up paid employment to take care of her child. Throughout her surveys, Carmela seemed happy as a stay-at-home parent. Running an efficient household gave her pride, and she enjoyed the "flexibility to participate in volunteer activities of [her] choice." Indeed, at one point she was spending over 15 hours a week in volunteer work and meetings with various clubs and societies. In discussing how a woman's life is changed by having children, Carmela wrote that one "becomes less self-centered, more caring, [putting] the welfare of the family unit over personal interests or pleasures, perhaps only temporarily." Carmela recognized that this kind of lifestyle is not for everyone. However, in her family, both her mother and her grandmother did not work after their children were born; "it was more the tradition to do volunteer work, help children's organizations, garden, or just cope with the domestic scene. I've never seriously thought of doing otherwise and luckily have not needed to financially." Carmela took seriously a responsibility to contribute to her community and maintain a comfortable home for her family. In 1990 she listed her employment as "homemaker/volunteer."

There are some signs of role strain in her life that, perhaps not surprisingly, revolved around the very things that gave her pleasure. For example, Carmela wrote that she would like to "have the time and energy to do more than be a housewife and mother—learn to play [a sport] well, return to [my major] field, travel again, generally get involved in 'adult' activities again!" But she handles these desires with patience and equanimity. Consistent with recent findings about educated midlife women (Mitchell & Helson, 1990), Carmela does not seem to dread the impending empty nest. In fact, she recently became involved in field work as a research assistant and would like to "commit regular blocks of time to it when my family is more on its own."

Carmela has successfully adopted the role of a traditional homemaker. She expressed generativity by caring for her family and participating in volunteer activities. Although she acknowledged that she wanted more out of life, this issue did not seem to eat away at her; rather, she implied that she would make changes in her life when time (and the empty nest) allowed.

In some ways, Cary's life paralleled Carmela's. While her children were young, Cary stayed at home to care for them. She occasionally worked part-time, but her husband's occupation kept them moving so she could never maintain consistent employment. No matter where they were living, Cary made sure that her children were happy while she took advantage of opportunities to study the local culture, art, and language. For example, in one survey entry she wrote that she was "becoming fluent in [a foreign language and] helping at daughter's nursery school." As her children continued to grow more independent, Cary began serious work toward a professional degree. By the 1990 survey she had received a master's degree in a helping profession and has been applying her skills in paid employment.

Like Anne (who was high on generativity motivation and realization), Cary took strides toward a new career at midlife. Unlike Anne, however, Cary did not score high on generativity motivation. Her low motivation score indicates that she was not preoccupied with generative desires, perhaps because she carefully scripted her life to include a fulfilling midlife career. In 1974 she wrote that "I do not resent giving up a few years to the raising of my family, but I do want to do something more with my life once they are less dependent on me." At midlife, as she planned, her time had come. In her later surveys, there was evidence that Cary and her husband were experiencing a role crossover at midlife (e.g., Gutmann, 1987; Wink & Helson, 1993). Cary wrote that her wishes were to "get a degree and continue working [on my career], travel with husband, [and] settle somewhere where he could retire and I could work."

Claire offers an interesting contrast to Cary and Carmela. Claire pursued an advanced degree a few years after graduating from college. She married and divorced early in life, and this problematic marriage delayed her entrance into graduate school. However, she quickly made up for lost time and now works as a successful academic. Claire is close to her children: "They helped me have a sense of family during the [years] I was single. Were very important to me then. People admired me for managing to do what I did and raise them all by myself. . . . I love them. I am proud of them now—their abilities, their character." In fact, she and her second husband went on a "very fun" and extensive trip abroad with their adult children.

As a scholar, Claire has achieved high levels of productivity. She continues to publish books and articles at a steady pace. She does not, however, care for the teaching aspect of her job: "The struggle to communicate with ill-prepared undergraduate students has made a large portion of my job and career worse than unattractive." Clearly Claire does not express generativity through teaching; rather, she seems to have realized generative productivity through her scholarly output.

At this point, Claire has found a satisfying equilibrium in two important aspects of her life: family and scholarly career. She accomplished a generative stance in these two domains and works to maintain her status quo. She would like to teach "better, smarter, more cultivated students," but this concern has not led her to take active steps to actualize this possibility. Claire was productive and caring, but like Carmela and Cary, she had no pressing agenda that characterized her as high in generativity motivation. She enjoyed interacting with her family and liked living the life of an active scholar whose work permits (and requires) much travel abroad.

Summary of Group C

Exhibit 5 provides summary descriptions of the women in Group C. Carmela and Cary stayed at home to raise children while supporting their husband's work life. Carmela never expressed a desire for a paid career, whereas Cary clearly subordinated professional goals during this time. However, Cary scripted her life well; now that her children are independent, she has taken steps to reclaim her latent career interests. After a false start, the third woman in this group, Claire, has maintained an active scholarly presence in her field of study and seems to enjoy the company of her family.

These women scored high on generativity realization because they were productive and nurturing in particular ways. Despite some evidence of role strain in all of their lives, Claire, Cary, and Carmela have succeeded and were generative in the life domains that they chose. Only rarely did

EXHIBIT 5
Summary Table of Group C: Women High on Generativity Realization and Low on Motivation

Overall Finding: Women in Group C seemed generally content with their expressions of generativity. Unlike the women in Group A, they did not mention any pressing agendas that would impact one way or another on their sense of generative realization.

Carmela:
   Realization: Carmela seemed content in her role as a stay-at-home parent and spouse.
   Motivations: Carmela did not articulate any pressing psychosocial agenda, although she seemed to be anticipating the increased freedom that the impending empty nest would provide.

Cary:
   Realization: Cary was content in her role as parent and spouse.
   Motivations: At the time of the midlife assessments, Cary was just beginning a career. However, unlike some of the women in Groups A and B, Cary's career move was long anticipated and completely in keeping with her expectations.

Claire:
   Realization: Claire was content in her role as an academician. She was also happy with her children and in her marriage.
   Motivations: Claire did not articulate any pressing psychosocial agenda, although she mentioned that she wished she had higher quality students to teach.

these women articulate concerns that they were not as generative as they could be. As a group, the life vignettes of these women were consistent with Stewart and Vandewater's (chapter 3, this volume) argument that midlife generativity realization is related to psychological well-being. In this sense Group C differed from Groups A and B: The women in Group C did not have major frustrations or struggles with expressing higher degrees of generativity. It seemed that women who scored high on generativity motivation (TAT) were currently dissatisfied with generative aspects of their lives (e.g., Bobby and Barbara) or were in the midst of pursuing new ventures that require generative commitment (e.g., Alex and Anne).

Women Who Scored Low on Generativity Motivation and Realization

Individual Cases

The woman in Group D scored about 2 standard deviations below the mean on both measures of generativity: 28.88 on the Q sort and 32.29 on the TAT. This does not signify that these women were antigenerative; rather, the scores indicate that generativity did not occupy a central focus in these women's lives.

Deborah has certain aspects in common with both Dee and Darcy, so we begin with an analysis of her life. Like many of the women in Group C, Deborah got married early to a husband whose job required a lot of movement. This early lifestyle of constant disruption serves as an appropriate metaphor for Deborah's lack of commitment to her own identity and generativity. In response to the 1974 question about wishes, Deborah wrote, "To my disgust, I don't know [what I want]. . . . I do want desperately to do something on my own, something physical and positive. But I have to be where I can get off my tail and find the job that needs doing." In response to the same question in 1986, she wrote, "I have yet to think this one out fully. What I would like to do, and what I may be able to achieve, are two totally different things. . . . Luck has always played a major role in my life, though—so who says it won't continue?" This lack of emotional investment in goals seemed to extend to a lack of investment in her children as well. In reference to the birth of her first child, Deborah wrote, "All actions automatic. No emotional involvement with anything, totally self-preserving, but very unpleasant." She enjoyed her children more as they grew older, but her relationship with them does not seem warm. This reflected her own lack of connection to her father, of whom Deborah said that all human emotions were absent.

After many years of marriage, Deborah underwent a difficult divorce. She began work in "a blur of meaningless jobs while slowly proceeding with the overdue process of growing up." At this point in her life, Deborah had no energy to devote to generative activity. Although Deborah voiced generative sentiments in several places, they were always in the context of fantasy projects or in areas that she admitted she could not control. For example, "I could dream of great power positions [where I could solve problems with] world population control, and management of international rain forests. Foresight is one of my strong points—except when it deals with my personal life—and I do firmly believe that not enough decision-makers are projecting themselves beyond immediate political goals into the future." The words embody generativity, but at this time Deborah was in no position to accomplish these goals or devote motivational energy to them. From an Eriksonian perspective, she was focusing energy on reworking aspects of identity and intimacy rather than generativity.

Like Deborah, Darcy had problematic relations with her parents. At many points, Darcy remarked how different she was from her mother. For example, "My mother thought [children] were wonderful—I didn't." My "mother is very sentimental—made me the reverse." In reference to her father, she simply stated "never marry a man who has less education, status, etc. . . . ." Darcy followed her own advice; both she and her husband were highly paid professionals. However, her demanding occupation did not dispel a sense of boredom and stagnation. In 1986 she remarked that low points were the "increasing dissatisfaction with old job, boredom of doing the same thing for so long—there was always so much change when I was younger." Darcy knew that she wanted "more challenge—[but] don't even know what kind." According to her reports, relationships with others did not provide her with much satisfaction either: "Tired of [people] my own age. All caught up in trying to succeed, full of ego/identity problems." It may be that this pervading sense of ennui is part and parcel of living at midlife with few outlets for the realization of generativity.

Her occupation, for example, does not deal with the welfare of people directly; she deals daily with objects and faceless units. Her family life also was quite limited. By choice, she had no children: "I don't think I'd be a good mother. I don't want them enough to make the effort it takes and I don't have any self image as a mother because I have such a bad relationship with my own." The lack of parental role modeling notwithstanding, Darcy understood the importance of generativity and legacy. For example, she wrote, "What the modern woman needs is a few role models on which to pattern herself. Probably only the passage of time will give her this by creating a generation of such women passing down what they know to the next generation." Such sentiments embrace the essence of Erikson's formulation of generativity; however, at this point in time, Darcy expressed a pervading sense of life stagnation. At present, this stagnation remains untempered with any clear motivation for generativity expression.

The final woman in Group D, Dee, also seemed to be experiencing stagnation. Dee has a master's degree and was married for a long time before divorcing her husband. She concluded that "marriage is disastrous for women, especially the traditional marriage of the type I was involved in." After her divorce, Dee moved to a large city where she took her first job. This decision to move to a large urban area was somewhat unexpected given Dee's strong preferences for a rural lifestyle. In 1974 she wrote that she would like to "build a cabin . . . and sit and watch and maybe write about the woods or go off and become a wildlife biologist." She then quoted from the Audubon group: "In wilderness is the preservation of the world; and in the next generation is the preservation of the wilderness." In other places she also wrote about someday becoming a naturalist; her decision to move to a city may be attributed to the availability of jobs, but symbolic in this move was the loss of a dream. In regard to her current job in the city, Dee wrote that she would like "less public contact, more creativity, more control, and more money!"

At this point in her life, Dee remained bitter about her marriage. According to Dee, little good came of her marriage other than her children. She wrote that they provided a "sense of continuity, visible immortality, sense of realization, sense of having produced and helped create good human beings." By the time she moved to the city, however, her children were old enough to live on their own. Like Deborah, Dee had no motivational energy to devote to generative activity. At this point, she was regaining equilibrium to stay afloat in difficult life circumstances.

Summary of Group D

Exhibit 6 provides brief descriptions of the three women in Group D. These three women were quite different from the other women in that they showed no evidence of becoming or desire to become generative. All three women were facing issues of stagnation. Although Darcy was wealthy and had remained married, the other two were just putting careers together after unhappy relationships. These women were quite intelligent and candid in their responses, and they all expressed some vivid generative imagery. It may be that once these women resolve issues of boredom, stagnation, intimacy, and identity dissolution, they will have more freedom to express generativity in vital and creative ways. At the very least, their quotations reveal that Dee, Darcy, and Deborah understand the metaphors of legacy and caring. In the terms of McAdams, Diamond, de St. Aubin, and Mansfield (1997), the women in Group D have yet to formulate a *redemption sequence*, whereby bad life events are psychologically or physically transformed into something positive and ego affirming.

General Discussion

Although presented in brief, these case studies enhance the understanding of generativity as a theoretical construct. Women scoring high on

EXHIBIT 6
Summary Table of Group D: Women Low on Generativity Realization and Motivation

Overall Finding: Women in Group D seemed to be experiencing current dissatisfaction with their career, family life, or both. These experiences were associated with feelings of stagnation that seemed to interfere with active attempts to resolve their dissatisfaction.

Deborah:
   Realization: Deborah was unhappy in her job and dissatisfied with the state of her intimate relationships.
   Motivations: Deborah seemed focused on reworking aspects of psychosocial identity and intimacy.

Darcy:
   Realization: Darcy was a successful professional, although she was unhappy with her current occupation.
   Motivations: At the time of the midlife assessments, Darcy expressed a pervading sense of stagnation concerning her career and friendships; she had not yet articulated a clear solution to her discontent.

Dee:
   Realization: Dee was unhappy in her job. She mentioned that her children provided her with satisfaction but that they had moved away to start their own lives.
   Motivations: Like Deborah, Dee seemed focused on reworking aspects of psychosocial identity and intimacy.

generativity motivation (Groups A and B) were experiencing ongoing concerns with generative issues. The women in Group A were preoccupied with generative concerns directly related to their careers or to political involvement. For example, Anne and Alex were dealing with major career changes at midlife. Alex worked hard to maintain the viability of her new company, and Anne began work as an assistant professor. Amanda was frustrated with the perceived lack of caring by politicians, so she became heavily involved with national and local politics to redress injustices.

The women in Group B, on the other hand, although as motivated with generative concerns as the women in Group A, seemed frustrated in their pursuit of generative goals. For example, Barbara experienced disappointment in her career and her lack of children, and Bobby faced a tension between college teaching and favoring a particular lifestyle with her family. Beth, on the other hand, seemed to lack an intimate support group, although she was an extremely productive academic. The presence of ongoing concerns with generativity motivation seems to have different effects depending on whether avenues for the realization of generativity are open or blocked. That is, the women in Group A were able to voice generative concerns and then act to resolve them. The women in Group B, on the other hand, seemed frustrated in their expression of generativity, whether because of choice or chance. It is quite likely that other personality variables (such as optimism or locus of control) moderate the expression of generativity motivation and affect whether generative goals are accomplished.

The women in Group C were not preoccupied with generative concerns. Perhaps this was because they had accomplished generative goals and, unlike Group A, were not in the midst of situations demanding a lot of generative energy. Carmela and Cary found generative outlets through stay-at-home parenting, whereas Claire enjoyed the challenge of maintaining her position as a high-profile scholar while caring for her children. Perhaps if these women began work on difficult generative tasks they would experience higher levels of generativity motivation. Or it may be that elevated levels of motivation are necessary to provide impetus to engage in difficult generativity goals at midlife. These questions of temporal sequence cannot be answered with the data available because TAT generativity was assessed only at one point in time (at age 48). It may well be that the women in Group C expressed high levels of generativity motivation earlier in life, and having actualized their generative goals, they now scored higher on realization and lower on motivation.

Supporting Erikson's notion that generativity is important for midlife well-being, the women in Group D (low scores on both measures of generativity) were currently facing the most distressful life circumstances of all the participants. Why should their lack of generativity realization be associated with feelings of stagnation and ennui? After all, these women did not seem to care about generativity; at least they expressed low levels of generativity motivation in their TATs. The answer to this question may involve societal expectations and cultural mandates to behave in generative ways (see chapter 1, this volume). Societal pressures to act generatively may make it impossible for individuals to absolve themselves of generative activity without experiencing dissatisfaction with self.

Finally, in addition to sharpening the conceptual understanding of the TAT and Q-sort measure of generativity, these case studies suggest other issues that need investigation. For example, the importance of mentors arose in 6 of the 12 cases. Amanda, Anne, Alex, and Carmela stressed the importance in their lives of parents and other role models. These four women scored high on generativity realization. Deborah and Darcy specifically mentioned the lack of generative parenting that they received, and both of these women scored low on the two generativity measures. These cases provide specific examples of Peterson and Stewart's (1996, p. 29) claim that "generative ideals are passed on through positive role models." It should be a priority in future research to untangle the role of mere parenting from that of generative parenting (e.g., Snarey, 1993) in producing psychosocially generative children.

It is also important for researchers to document the diverse ways that people can express generativity; these 12 well-educated women graduated into a historical time period and cultural context that permitted occupational and family responsibilities for both men and women (Stewart & Vandewater, 1993). It is no surprise, therefore, that these case studies focused mostly on careers and parenting; these two domains were important for most of these women, and they wrote a lot about them. However, there are other ways to express generativity, including artistic productivity, religious expression, and political service. For example, 3 of the 12 women discussed in detail the political commitments they had made to improve the world. Their comments support the emerging research linking generativity with political involvement (Cole & Stewart, 1996; Peterson, Smirles, & Wentworth, 1997; Stewart & Gold-Steinberg, 1990). Some of the other ways that people express generativity are examined in this edited volume, but at this point in time, the understanding of generativity and its implications for adult development remain nascent.

POSTSCRIPT

In 1983, 33 years after the publication of *Childhood and Society*, Erikson (1983) hinted that the scope of generative concerns must broaden from the nuclear family to account for the effects of the nuclear age:

> The nuclear situation . . . exposes in an almost incomprehensible way the fact that (yes, ingenious) technology is about to eradicate (or already has) all the relative safety zones associated with the existing territories on earth. No matter how many children can be brought up in what territorial areas and with whose humanitarian help, only [human]kind as a whole can assure their survival and their future. (p. 12)

Erikson's sentiment was clear; once humans had split the atom, individual forms of generativity (such as raising one's own children or living a productive life) became insufficient manifestations of care and concern. In this passage, Erikson hinted that people must expand generative horizons to encompass a larger worldview. Expressions of such global generativity may be important for the survival of present and subsequent generations of humans.

The kinds of generativity motivation and realization discussed in this chapter revolved around personal and familial responsibilities. Another form of generativity shifts the level of analysis from the psychological realm of personality to the political domain of global consequences. Techniques for assessing generativity at a collective level could be developed to provide a fuller understanding of the sociological concomitants of generativity expression. Such an analysis may help psychologists to facilitate individual manifestations of generativity, thus supporting, in turn, structural forms of generative behaviors at national levels. On the other hand, given that immediate benefits for national expressions of generativity are unclear at best, prejudice in the form of ethnic rivalries and national boundaries may make it difficult for generative sentiments to exist between nations. The attitude that the world is a zero-sum game seems antithetical to the demonstration of care for humanity's future that is at the heart of Erikson's (1950/1963) theory. Nonetheless, research that examines how generativity manifests in global contexts is important for understanding the full range of generativity expression.

In addition to increasing the understanding of individual forms of generativity, therefore, psychologists might do well to consider societal expressions of the construct. This is important because at least two global threats have emerged during the final half of the 20th century: the possibility of nuclear devastation and the destruction of the environment. Although the recent breakup of the Soviet Union has decreased the chances of a thermonuclear exchange between military superpowers, the spread of cold war technology and bombs to "nonnuclear" countries serves as a ghastly reminder that the future of humankind remains at risk. In addition to the threat of nuclear war, there is a growing awareness across the globe of problems associated with environmental destruction. As the population of this planet grows at a geometric rate and people use more and more natural resources, the ecosystem becomes increasingly unbalanced causing unexpected (and expected) repercussions for human existence, such as the threat of global warming owing to massive deforestation.

The threat of extinction has co-occurred (in industrialized countries) with dramatic increases in length of life. Because of improvements in nutrition and sanitation, the average newborn in the United States can expect to live about 75 years. In 1900, by contrast, the typical newborn had a life expectancy of 47 years. As pointed out by Kotre and Hall (1990), this increase of more than 25 years means that more and more generations of family members are alive at the same time; it is not unusual for a child to know his or her great-grandparents. As population demographics change and people grow older, it is becoming important for psychologists to understand in greater detail human propensities for the development, maintenance, and care of objects and people belonging to younger generations. Fostering such commitments seems vitally important in a society that can entertain the possibilities of global extinction.

REFERENCES

Block, J. (1978). *The Q-sort method in personality assessment and psychiatric research.* Springfield, IL: Charles C Thomas. (Original work published 1961)

Carlson, R. (1971). Where is the person in personality research? *Psychological Bulletin, 75*, 203–219.

Cole, E. R., & Stewart, A. J. (1996). Meanings of political participation among black and white women: Political identity and social responsibility. *Journal of Personality and Social Psychology, 71*, 130–140.

de St. Aubin, E., & McAdams, D. P. (1995). The relation of generative concern and generative action to personality traits, satisfaction/happiness with life and ego development. *Journal of Adult Development, 2*, 99–112.

Erikson, E. H. (1963). *Childhood and society*. New York: Norton. (Original work published 1950)

Erikson, E. H. (1969). *Gandhi's truth*. New York: Norton.

Erikson, E. H. (1983). Reflecting. *Adolescent Psychiatry, 11*, 9–13.

Erikson, E. H. (1985). *The life cycle completed*. New York: Norton.

Franz, C. E., & Stewart, A. J. (Eds.). (1994). *Women creating lives: Identities, resilience, & resistance*. Boulder, CO: Westview Press.

Gutmann, D. (1987). *Reclaimed powers: Toward a new psychology of men and women in later life*. New York: Basic Books.

Healy, J. M., Jr., & Stewart, A. J. (1991). On the compatibility of quantitative and qualitative methods for studying lives. In A. J. Stewart, J. M. Healy, Jr., & D. Ozer (Eds.), *Perspectives in personality* (Vol. 3B, pp. 35–57). London: Kingsley.

Helson, R., Mitchell, V., & Hart, B. (1985). Lives of women who became autonomous. *Journal of Personality, 53*, 257–285.

Helson, R., Mitchell, V., & Moane, G. (1984). Personality and patterns of adherence and nonadherence to the social clock. *Journal of Personality and Social Psychology, 46*, 1079–1096.

Kotre, J. (1984). *Outliving the self: Generativity and the interpretation of lives*. Baltimore: The Johns Hopkins University Press.

Kotre, J. (1992, May). Generative outcome. In E. de St. Aubin (Chair), *Emerging perspectives in adult personality development: Research concerning generativity*. Symposium conducted at the annual meeting of the Midwestern Psychological Association, Chicago.

Kotre, J., & Hall, E. (1990). *Seasons of life: Our dramatic journey from birth to death*. Boston: Little, Brown.

MacDermid, S. M., De Haan, L. G., & Heilbrun, G. (1996). Generativity in multiple roles. *Journal of Adult Development, 3*, 145–158.

Mansfield, E. D., & McAdams, D. P. (1996). Generativity and themes of agency and communion in adult autobiography. *Personality and Social Psychology Bulletin, 22*, 721–731.

McAdams, D. P. (1985). *Power, intimacy, and the life story: Personological inquiries into identity*. New York: Guilford Press.

McAdams, D. P., & de St. Aubin, E. (1992). A theory of generativity and its assessment through self-report, behavioral acts, and narrative themes in autobiography. *Journal of Personality and Social Psychology, 62,* 1003–1015.

McAdams, D. P., de St. Aubin, E., & Logan, R. (1993). Generativity among young, midlife, and older adults. *Psychology and Aging, 8,* 221–230.

McAdams, D. P., Diamond, A., de St. Aubin, E., & Mansfield, E. D. (1997). Stories of commitment: The psychosocial construction of generative lives. *Journal of Personality and Social Psychology, 72,* 678–694.

McAdams, D. P., & Ochberg, R. L. (Eds.). (1988). Psychobiography and life narratives [Special issue]. *Journal of Personality, 56.*

McClelland, D. C. (1980). Motive dispositions: The merits of operant and respondent measures. In L. Wheeler (Ed.), *Review of personality and social psychology* (Vol. 1, pp. 10–41). Beverly Hills, CA: Sage.

McClelland, D. C., Koestner, R., & Weinberger, J. (1989). How do self-attributed and implicit motives differ? *Psychological Review, 96,* 690–702.

Mitchell, V., & Helson, R. (1990). Women's prime in life: Is it the fifties? *Psychology of Women Quarterly, 14,* 451–470.

Morgan, C. D., & Murray, H. A. (1935). A method for investigating fantasies. *Archives of Neurology and Psychiatry, 34,* 289–306.

Murray, H. A. (1938). *Explorations in personality.* New York: Oxford University Press.

Newton, P. M. (1995). Some suggestions for the conduct of biographical research. *Journal of Adult Development, 2,* 147–158.

Ostrove, J. M., & Stewart, A. J. (1994). Meanings and uses of marginal identities: Social class at Radcliffe in the 1960s. In C. E. Franz & A. J. Stewart (Eds.), *Women creating lives: Identities, resilience, & resistance* (pp. 289–308). Boulder, CO: Westview Press.

Peterson, B. E., & Klohnen, E. C. (1995). Realization of generativity in two samples of women at midlife. *Psychology and Aging, 10,* 20–29.

Peterson, B. E., Smirles, K. A., & Wentworth, P. A. (1997). Generativity and authoritarianism: Implications for personality, political involvement, and parenting. *Journal of Personality and Social Psychology, 72,* 1202–1216.

Peterson, B. E., & Stewart, A. J. (1993). Generativity and social motives in young adults. *Journal of Personality and Social Psychology, 65,* 186–198.

Peterson, B. E., & Stewart, A. J. (1996). Antecedents and contexts of generativity motivation at midlife. *Psychology and Aging, 11,* 21–33.

Runyan, W. M. (1982). *Life histories and psychobiography: Explorations in theory and method.* New York: Oxford University Press.

Ryff, C. D., & Heincke, S. G. (1983). Subjective organization of personality in adulthood and aging. *Journal of Personality and Social Psychology, 44,* 807–816.

Snarey, J. (1993). *How fathers care for the next generation: A four-decade study.* Cambridge, MA: Harvard University Press.

Stewart, A. J. (1978). A longitudinal study of coping styles in self-defining and socially defined women. *Journal of Consulting and Clinical Psychology, 46,* 1079–1084.

Stewart, A. J. (1980). Personality and situation in the prediction of women's life patterns. *Psychology of Women Quarterly, 5,* 195–206.

Stewart, A. J., Franz, C. E., & Layton, L. (1988). The changing self: Using personal documents to study lives. *Journal of Personality, 56,* 41–74.

Stewart, A. J., & Gold-Steinberg, S. (1990). Midlife women's political consciousness: Case studies of psychosocial development and political commitment. *Psychology of Women Quarterly, 14,* 543–566.

Stewart, A. J., & Vandewater, E. A. (1993). The Radcliffe class of 1964: Career and family social clock projects in a transitional cohort. In K. D. Hulbert & D. Tickton Schuster (Eds.), *Women's lives through time: Educated American women of the twentieth century* (pp. 235–258). San Francisco: Jossey-Bass.

Vaillant, G. E., & Milofsky, E. (1980). Natural history of male psychological health: IX. Empirical evidence for Erikson's model of the life cycle. *American Journal of Psychiatry, 137,* 1348–1359.

Weinberger, J., & McClelland, D. C. (1990). Cognitive versus traditional motivational models: Irreconcilable or complementary? In E. T. Higgins & R. M. Sorrentino (Eds.), *Handbook of motivation and cognition* (Vol. 2, pp. 562–597). New York: Free Press.

Wink, P., & Helson, R. (1993). Personality change in women and their partners. *Journal of Personality and Social Psychology, 65,* 597–605.

5

IMMORTALITY AND THE EXTERNALIZATION OF THE SELF: PLATO'S UNRECOGNIZED THEORY OF GENERATIVITY

JEROME C. WAKEFIELD

Generativity consists of motives that are directed at creating and caring for children, things, or ideas that last beyond one's own life span and play a role in the perpetuation of society. The concept of generativity is firmly associated with Erik Erikson's (1963) epigenetic theory of adult development, and it is commonly believed that Erikson was the first theoretician to put forward a systematic account of generativity.

This common belief is in error. Another "grand theory" of generativity that is every bit as sophisticated as Erikson's—indeed, that is in some ways more precisely elaborated than Erikson's—was put forward by Plato in his dialogue *Symposium* about 2,500 years before Erikson wrote. As far as I know, Plato's theory of generativity has not been recognized for what it is, for a variety of reasons. One reason is that Plato did not coin a special term corresponding to Erikson's *generativity*; it would not have occurred to him that a special term was needed because, according to his theory, existing concepts such as "love" or "desire for immortality" are sufficient to identify generative motives. A second reason is that Plato's theory of generativity is obscured by the much broader discussion of love within which it is embedded. Consequently, philosophers have taken the *Symposium* to be exclusively about love. They do not make the connection to Erikson, and they focus on the dialogue's implications for more traditional philosophical issues.

Nevertheless, the theory of love discussed in the *Symposium* does contain within it an ambitious and quite explicit theory of generativity. Plato's theory contains many novel hypotheses and at the same time addresses an issue that is at the center of contemporary generativity theory, namely, the role of the desire for symbolic immortality in motivating generativity (e.g., Kotre, 1984; McAdams, 1985; McAdams & de St. Aubin, 1992; also see chapter 1, this volume). This chapter is devoted to excavating Plato's theory of generativity, to pondering some of the questions it raises, and to formulating tentatively some related hypotheses of my own. I also compare Plato's theory to Erikson's, offer some comments on the conceptual limitations of the two theories, and attempt in my own account of "externalization" to integrate aspects of the two theories. My main goal, however, is simply to present Plato's theory—often initially in his own words, through extended quotes—and to interpret and reflect on crucial Platonic passages with respect to their implications for generativity theory.

Aside from its intrinsic intellectual and scholarly interest, there are other reasons that an explication of Plato's theory is worthwhile. U.S. culture seems to be in the midst of a generativity crisis manifested in areas as diverse as the distribution of social resources among the young and the old, protection of the environment, public debt, and maintenance of society's physical infrastructure. Improving our understanding of generativity should thus be a high priority for psychology. Attention to generativity theory may be encouraged by linking contemporary thought to its rightful roots in classical philosophical theories of motivation. Also, for a subject dealing with such momentous topics, there is a surprising paucity of theoretical conflict in the field, and presentation of an additional theoretical perspective might help to stimulate clarification of concepts and elaboration of hypotheses.

Moreover, despite the considerable amount of interesting empirical research and theoretical writing on generativity that has appeared since Erikson's time (e.g., Browning, 1975; de St. Aubin & McAdams, 1995; Kotre, 1984; MacDermid & Gillespie, 1992; Mansfield & McAdams, 1996; McAdams, 1985; McAdams & de St. Aubin, 1992; McAdams, de St. Aubin, & Logan; 1993; Peterson & Stewart, 1993; Snarey, 1993; Stewart, Franz, & Layton, 1988; Vaillant, 1977), Erikson's framework continues to dominate the field, and the perceived limitations of his theory tend to be seen as the field's limitations. For example, Erikson claimed that generativity is a naturally selected instinctual impulse, but he did not pay careful attention to the justification of such evolutionary claims. There is also a fuzziness to Erikson's generativity construct that continues to plague the field. In addition, Erikson's conception of generativity as caring or nurturance comes close to altruism, a perspective partially retained by more recent theoreticians in the form of a hypothesized "communal" component in generative motivation (e.g., Kotre, 1984; see also chapter 1, this volume), whereas social science in the United States is heavily biased against altruistic theories of motivation (Wakefield, 1993). A fresh look at generativity from Plato's perspective, which is thoroughly egoistic, noninstinctual, conceptually precise, and in other ways non-Eriksonian, might help to open discussion in the field. Even when Plato is wrong, his provocative theory may prompt the asking of fruitful new questions that are not addressed by other accounts. At the least, the pedigree of generativity theory will be radically altered.

Because this chapter crosses disciplinary boundaries, a few caveats are appropriate: (a) I focus on the *Symposium* and ignore accounts of love presented elsewhere in Plato's works. (b) I assume that the doctrines expressed in the dialogue by the characters Socrates and Diotima (a priestess with whom Socrates constructs an imaginary interchange) are the views of Plato, although this is still a topic of scholarly debate. (c) I retain in my commentary some of the philosophical language of the *Symposium* rather than always translating it into more modulated psychological terminology. For example, I use the standard translation "soul" rather than "mind," without any religious connotation intended. (d) Extracting as unencumbered and relevant a theory of generativity as possible from Plato's dialogue necessitates some scholarly compromises. For example, in some passages, Plato emphasized the generative development of men who engage in homosexual sex, whereas I focus on what the theory says that is of universal relevance.

As I have noted previously, there have been many important contributors to generativity theory since Erikson, a number of whom are represented in this volume. However, because Erikson remains the preeminent theoretician of generativity, in this initial consideration of Plato's theory I focus my comparative comments primarily on Erikson. Unless otherwise noted, quotations from Plato are from Jowett's (1956) widely available translation of the *Symposium*.

ERIKSON ON GENERATIVITY AND LOVE

In this section, for purposes of comparison to the analysis of Plato's theory that follows, I briefly present some aspects of Erikson's account of generativity and its relationship to love. The centrality of generativity to Erikson's overall theory and to the logic of his developmental scheme is often not adequately appreciated. Indeed, Erikson noted in his original discussion of adult developmental stages by noting that, if it were not for the fact that he was focusing on childhood stages, "the section on generativity would of necessity be the central one" (1963, p. 266). Erikson believed that generativity is the central element around which all the other life stages are naturally and teleologically ordered; earlier stages, such as those concerning trust and identity, derive their significance from their contribution to making generativity possible, and the one later stage, integrity, is essentially a reaction to the success or failure of the generative urge.

The importance of generativity derives from its role in the perpetuation of culture. Cultures can exist continuously for thousands of years, yet they consist of no more than a series of groups of individual human beings. For cultures to exist over enormous periods of time in a stable fashion, there must be a way that the generations of people that compose them are linked to ensure stability of social structures. Each generation, having been nurtured in its childhood by the past generation, must create and nurture the next generation, and in this act of cultural reproduction the next generation must be given the emotional, cognitive, and psychosocial skills and the cultural infrastructure and symbols to be capable of reproducing itself and maintaining social structures for the following generation. According to Erikson, generativity is the stage in instinctual development at which this nurturing of the next generation becomes life's primary task. Inadequacies in generative commitment can produce problems in the next generation, from mistrust and emotional turmoil to lack of socialization and inadequate skills, which, through that next generation's resultant generative failure, can resonate down through the generations. For human cultures to exist and thrive, there must be something about the nature of human motivation that ensures that proper generative nurturing generally tends to occur. Such instinctual motives constitute generativity, as conceived by Erikson.

Erikson's hypothesis that generativity is the teleological end of psychosocial development may be considered the psychosocial analogue of the evolutionary hypothesis that reproductive fitness is the teleological end (i.e., naturally selected function) of all biological mechanisms. Just as biological structures come to exist in the current population by influencing reproductive success and thus being passed down through the generations, so psychosocial traits exist in current cultures because they are the ones that influenced generative success and thus were passed down through the generations. Generativity thus ultimately explains the continued existence both of the societies that form the necessary medium for human psychosocial structures and of the psychosocial structures themselves in generation after generation.

It is only the stage of generativity that justifies Erikson's basic idea of a "life cycle" or "epigenetic" developmental account, which provides the framework for his overall theory:

> The experiences of caring, nurturing, and maintaining—which are the essence of generativity—make of the stages of a life *cycle*, re-creating the beginning of the cycle in each newborn. These same experiences make of the sequence of life cycles a *generational* cycle, irrevocably binding each generation to those that gave it life and to those for whose life it is responsible. (Erikson, Erikson, & Kivnick, 1986, p. 73)

Within Erikson's developmental scheme, individual lives by themselves are not cyclical, except in the superficial sense that individuals may return to a dependent and thus in certain respects childlike condition in old age. Rather, the cyclical nature of the life cycle derives from the relations that individuals have to the lives and developmental trajectories of preceding and subsequent generations. Each individual is nurtured by the previous generation in a way that allows the individual ultimately to nurture the next generation in a way that allows that generation to go on and nurture the following generation. The generative strivings of one generation match the needs for nurturance of the next and result from the generative nurturance of which they themselves were the recipients earlier in their lives. The repetition of the generations, the dovetailing developmental histories of the generations, and in particular, the movement from passive recipient to active provider of generative nurturance constitute the cycle.

Because generativity has the function of cultural reproduction and maintenance rather than individual biological reproduction, it extends beyond childbearing and child raising to encompass artistic and intellectual creativity, productivity, and devotion to long-term social change. However, because societies necessarily consist of human beings, it remains true that the bearing, raising, and guiding of children is perhaps the most fundamental generative activity:

> Generativity, then, is primarily the concern in establishing and guiding the next generation, although there are individuals who, through misfortune or because of special and genuine gifts in other directions, do not apply this drive to their own offspring. And indeed, the concept generativity is meant to include such more popular synonyms as *productivity* and *creativity*, which, however, cannot replace it. (Erikson, 1963, p. 267)

However, procreation, creativity, and productivity in themselves may or may not express generative motives. Their generativity depends on how their products are cared for, nurtured, and offered to society-at-large. Thus, generativity primarily consists not of generative products but of generative attitudes, which Erikson, Erikson, and Kivnick characterized as: "The experiences of caring, nurturing, and maintaining" (1986, p. 73).

It is clear, then, that Erikson and his colleagues delineated what they considered to be a motivational variable rather than one that refers in the first instance to behaviors, products, or outcomes. For example, Erikson described generativity as a "drive" (1963, p. 287), a "concern in establishing and guiding the next generation" (1963, p. 267), and "a strong wish to take care" (1986, p. 245), which are motivational descriptions. Of course, such motives would be expected to yield generative behaviors, products, and outcomes under standard conditions.

Erikson was never precise about the exact aim of the instinctual motive he postulated. From various passages, one might get the impression that people are motivated to care, to nurture, to maintain society, to perpetuate society by establishing and guiding the next generation, to be productive, to participate in social institutions, and to immortalize ourselves. These aims are conceptually different and often diverge (e.g., caring is not always aimed at perpetuating society). Erikson offered no systematic account that sorted out these different aims and identified the basic generative instinct and its relationship to other motives.

The stage immediately preceding generativity in Erikson's developmental scheme is that of love, and in the remainder of this section I consider what I call Erikson's *externalist* account of the relation between love and generativity. Erikson claimed that successful development of love relations is essential for the later development of generativity. From Erikson's viewpoint as an evolutionary psychosocial developmentalist who thought that generativity was the teleological end of development, the consummation of love, pleasant and procreative as it may be, is not a self-explanatory end in itself. The psychosocial developmental question is, What is love for? What is its role in the development of generative capacities? Within Erikson's epigenetic framework, success at each stage is a "demonstrable necessity" (1985, p. 61) for proper development of the remaining stages. This means that Erikson must explain love's "evolutionary rationale" (1964, p. 127); that is, he must explain why love exists by showing how love contributes necessary elements to performing the ultimate psychosocial task of generativity.

Of course, love is commonly assumed to have the evolutionary functions of bringing people together to procreate and of keeping them together long enough to bear and raise children, functions that are broadly generative in their impact. However, Erikson's concerns went beyond these obvious points. He asked how the experience of love changes the ego so that new psychosocial capacities come to exist that cultivate generative motives and enable the ego to succeed in generative tasks.

The overall answer is that Erikson saw love as the pivotal point in the transition from being primarily a recipient of care to being primarily a caregiver: "Love in the evolutionary and generational sense is, I believe, the transformation of the love received throughout the preadolescent stage of life into the care given to others during adult life" (1964, pp. 127–128).

Erikson elevated into a developmental stage only one form of love, the intimate sexual love that typically occurs in young adulthood and leads to marriage and family. However, the term *love* clearly encompasses much more and cuts across developmental stages, as Erikson noted: "Does not love bind together every stage? There are, to be sure, many forms of love, from the infant's comfortable and anxious attachment to his mother to the adolescent's passionate and desperate infatuation" (1964, p. 127). Thus, Erikson must explain "why love is here assigned to a particular stage and a particular crisis in the unfolding human life cycle" (1964, p. 127).

The answer, according to Erikson, is that the features of intimate sexual love of early adulthood, which occurs after adolescent identity formation and simultaneously with the formation of fidelity to people and ideals, allow for the formation of the specific psychological capacities and social structures that make generativity possible:

> Love in its truest sense presupposes both identity and fidelity. While many forms of love can be shown to be at work in the formation of the various virtues, it is important to realize that only graduation from adolescence permits the development of that intimacy, the selflessness of joined devotion, which anchors love in a mutual commitment. Intimate love thus . . . binds into a "way of life" the affiliations of procreation and of production. (Erikson, 1964, p. 128)

For Erikson, love was in effect a psychological laboratory for the development of psychological capacities critical to generativity. The development of these capacities constitutes the psychosocial function of love. These capacities include (a) *egoloss*: a sense of identification with the other and a selflessness that allow for a diminution in the focus on one's own ego; (b) *caring*: development of the ability to care about and for another individual; (c) *commitment*: development of a pattern of devotion that transcends immediate personal needs and lasts through difficulties and sacrifices and therefore has an ethical dimension; and (d) *division of labor*: acceptance of one distinct role within a complementary relational "social structure" (e.g., the couple) in which different patterns of life are subsumed within a broader framework that allows for different productive contributions from each individual. Of these features, Erikson made the commitment (or "fidelity") to caring for the beloved the centerpiece of his account of love and saw the broadening of such commitment as the path to generativity: "The new 'virtue' emerging from this antithesis, namely, Care, is a widening commitment to take care of the persons, the products, and the ideas one has learned to care for" (1985, p. 67).

Although Erikson claimed that erotic love is necessary to the development of generativity, all of the developmental functions of love that he identified are logically "external" to generativity in the sense that they are not generative in themselves. Rather, they are capacities that develop in the course of loving that are later exploited or built on in realizing the generative impulse. For Erikson, then, love was not intrinsically directed at generativity. This proves to be a critical point of divergence between Erikson and Plato.

LOVE AND THE DESIRE FOR IMMORTALITY

In this section, I consider the theory of love that forms the backdrop for Plato's theory of generativity. The theory of generativity proper is examined in the next section. This division is to some degree arbitrary because the two theories are so completely intertwined.

Unlike Erikson, Plato saw love as intrinsically and intimately tied to generativity, so much so that Plato's theory of generativity essentially consists of his theory of love. The point might be put this way: In casting about for an ordinary term that best approximates the theoretical notion of a generative impulse, Erikson settled on *caring*; the corresponding term that most closely captured the generative motive for Plato is *love*.

Plato was deeply impressed by the obvious relationship between erotic love and procreation. On the basis of the model of procreation resulting from erotic passion, Plato argued that we value love (all love, not just erotic love) because love has the ability to bring out what is good within us and to perpetuate that goodness outside of ourselves, providing a form of immortality. For Plato, generativity is motivated by the desire for immortality, especially in the form of a good reputation that will live on after one is dead. Plato thus built a desire for immortality through generativity directly into the internal structure of love's longings, in contrast to Erikson's "externalist" account of the relationship between love and generativity. Vlastos (1981a) characterized the resulting account of love as follows:

> Plato is the first Western man to realize how intense and passionate may be our attachment to objects as abstract as social reform, poetry, art, the sciences, and philosophy—an attachment that has more in common with erotic fixation than one would have suspected on a pre-Freudian view of man. . . . He discerns, as the link between such disparate involvements, the sense of beauty. . . . And, instead of undertaking, as did Freud, to explain the attractiveness of beauty in all its diverse manifestations as due to the excitation of lust, open or disguised, Plato invokes another drive, the hunger to create, and argues that this is what we all seek to appease in every activity propelled by beauty. (pp. 27–28)

Plato attempted to connect love to generativity by offering a series of three arguments, considered in the following sections, regarding what is essential about love. These arguments progressively shift the focus of theoretical attention from love itself to love's generative products: (a) The first argument shifts the focus from the beauty and desirability of love itself to the beauty and desirability of the object at which love is immediately directed; (b) the second shift of focus is from love's immediate object, the beautiful person or thing that is loved, to love's ultimate usefulness in achieving happiness; and (c) finally, there is a shift from love's usefulness in bringing happiness to the specific way that love's object brings happiness, namely, by ensuring immortality through generativity.

Love is a complex phenomenon with many facets. Plato's theory that love is essentially directed at generativity seems easily refutable if one takes it to be an exhaustive account of love rather than an attempt to capture one important strand of the truth. Vlastos (1981a) put the point well: "That Plato's explanation is onesided does not damn it. So is Freud's. Where comprehensive insight is denied us even partial glimpses of the truth are precious" (p. 28).

Love as Desire to Possess the Beautiful

The *Symposium* is set at a dinner party hosted by Agathon and attended by Socrates, at which the guests decide to take turns making speeches in praise of love. The characters wax eloquent about the beauty, goodness, and desirability of love. Plato thought that such praise of love reveals a fundamental conceptual error. He aimed to show that in itself "love is neither fair nor beautiful" (p. 43). This is a first step in his overall argument that love is important not for itself but because it is a means to generative ends.

Plato began his account of love with an argument about desire. He noted that love, like all intentional states, is directed at an object: "Love is of something" (p. 40), but what exactly is the psychological attitude that the lover directs at the beloved object? Plato asserted as a second fundamental premise that love is not just a sense of happiness, satisfaction, commitment, or caring, but at least in part a *desire* for the object of the love. When one feels love, according to Plato, one desires or longs for whatever is loved; "Love desires that of which love is" (p. 40). "Desire" is here taken to imply a longing for possession of the object. A third preliminary point is that every desire must by its nature be a desire to possess something that one lacks; one cannot desire to possess something that one already fully possesses: "He who desires something is in want of something" (p. 41). Consequently, desire reveals something unsatisfying about one's situation.

In summary, Plato claimed that (a) love is directed at an object; (b) love is a desire for the object at which it is directed; and (c) a desire is always directed at the possession of something one lacks.

After just these three observations, Plato's argument already seems to be in trouble! The three claims together lead to the assertion that love is a desire to possess something that one does not currently possess, but this assertion seems to fly in the face of the commonsense observation that a lover sometimes continues to love a beloved object even after the object is "possessed" in the sense relevant to erotic fulfillment. If love is indeed a form of desire, then it appears that one can continue to desire what one already possesses, contrary to Plato's third claim.

Plato, aware that his claims seemed problematic, offered a persuasive explanation of why his claims were in fact consistent with everyday statements that one loves or desires what one has:

> When a person says, I am well and wish to be well, or I am rich and wish to be rich, and I desire simply to have what I have—to him we shall reply: 'You, my friend, having wealth and health and strength, want to have the continuance of them; for at this moment, whether you choose or not, you have them.' . . . He desires that what he has at present may be preserved to him in the future, which is equivalent to saying that he desires something which is nonexistent to him, and which as yet he has not got. (pp. 41–42)

Plato's explanation is that the desire for a beloved whom one already possesses anticipates the possibility of losing the beloved; one desires to continue possessing the beloved. The future possession of the desired object, Plato noted, is something one does not possess at the time one has the desire to continue possessing it, and so it is a desire for something that is lacking.

To say that love is directed at an object is rather vague. What, more precisely, is love a desire for? Not everything about a beloved is the object of the love. If love is a kind of desire, one may ask, at which aspects or properties of the beloved is this desire aimed? There are many different people and things that are loved, but to the extent that love is a specific form of desire, there should be some common property of all these beloveds that triggers love. (Analogously, although people desire to eat many different things, one can give a general account of the properties of things that trigger hunger, such as taste and nutritive value.) Note that the phrase "object of love" is used here in two senses. The first refers to the individual who is loved, and the second, on which I now focus, refers to the beloved features or aspects of the individual.

Taking his inspiration from the model of erotic attraction, Plato concluded that love is a desire to possess what the lover finds beautiful about the beloved: "Love is the love of beauty" (p. 42). Therefore, the "object" of love consists of the perceived beauty of the beloved object. Plato thus suggested a simple theory of love object choice; love is proportional to perceived beauty. Vlastos (1981a) noted that, in arguing that love is directed at certain aspects of the beloved and that it is these aspects alone that people truly love, Plato rejects the common notion that one loves an individual as a whole person.

A longing for what one lacks can hardly be considered intrinsically beautiful. Thus, the points made so far are enough to allow Plato to reject the claim that "love is beautiful" and to emphasize instead that it is the beloved object that is beautiful. Because people tend to associate love with the beauty of the objects with which they fall in love, they tend to think of love itself as beautiful, but that is not really so, as anyone suffering from unrequited love can attest. Plato concluded, contrary to the praise lavished on love by Socrates' dinner companions, that it is the beloved, not love, that is beautiful and that it is possession of the beloved, not the experience of love, that is desirable and brings happiness:

> The error in your conception of love was very natural and, as I imagine from what you say, has arisen out of a confusion of love and the beloved, which made you think that love was all beautiful. For the beloved is the truly beautiful and delicate and perfect and blessed; but the principle of love is of another nature, and is such as I have described. (p. 45)

Plato made clear that the fact that love is not intrinsically good or beautiful does not imply that it is bad or ugly. Love, like all desire, is an intermediary state, not good in itself but a means by which people are led to the good. Greek culture, like our own, tended to deify love as an intrinsic good. Plato's argument places love in a radically different moral framework in which what is important is not love but loving the right objects.

Why did Plato care so much about this point? In rejecting the reflexive praise of love, he attempted to open his interlocutors' minds to his coming argument that love is not an end in itself but merely a means directed at the satisfaction of a further end, namely, immortality through generativity.

Love as an Instance of the Generic Desire for Happiness

Plato next argued for a link between love and the broader desire for happiness. Love is often thought of as the prototypically irrational emotion, not subject to the dictates of reason or usefulness. However, in the discussion of love in the *Symposium*, Plato accepted a distinctive Socratic doctrine, namely, that all desire is ultimately aimed at achieving personal happiness by possessing good things, and he interpreted love through the lens of this rationalistic Socratic view. "Good things" here must be taken in the broadest sense, as including anything, from money to virtue, that helps one lead a happy life. This doctrine, applied to love, leads to a conclusion directly opposite to the irrationality view, namely, that love, being a desire to possess beauty, must depend on a belief that possession of beauty is a means to possessing good things and, ultimately, happiness. Within this framework, the interesting question about love concerns what it contributes to attaining happiness. By attempting to understand the special role that love plays in the quest for happiness, Plato hoped to illuminate the nature of love itself.

This instrumental approach to love, which is the rationalistic analogue of Erikson's evolutionary account of love's developmental purpose, emerges in a question Socrates poses to Diotima: "Assuming love to be such as you say, what is the use of him to men?" (p. 45). Diotima notes that they agree that love is desire for the possession of beauty, and she rephrases Socrates's question as follows: "What is given by the possession of beauty?" (p. 46). Diotima notes that people love to possess good things because such things lead to happiness ("the happy are made happy by the acquisition of good things" [p. 46]) and that happiness is the ultimate goal of all desire. Diotima then asks, "And is this wish and this desire common to all, and do all men always desire their own good, or only some men?— what say you?" and Socrates answers, "All men; the desire is common to all" (p. 46).

Plato thus argued that all desire is ultimately motivated by a desire for the good and for happiness; given that love is a form of desire, love must be in part merely one more instrumental desire aimed at the common goal of happiness. However, if love has the same ultimate goal as other desires, then there is a sense in which all intense desire can be considered love. Plato assumed here the Socratic doctrine that desires for different means to the same end must be considered essentially the same desire; for example, Plato argued in the dialogue *Gorgias* that patients who take medicine desire not to swallow unpleasant medicine but to possess the health that the medicine brings and that merchants who go on dangerous sea voyages desire not to risk their lives at sea but to possess the riches they believe the voyage will bring them. If desire is always for the ultimate end and not for the means, then love, which is ultimately aimed at happiness, is not fundamentally different from other forms of intense desire. To this extent, it is arbitrary that other pursuits are not called "love":

> "You may say generally that all desire of good and happiness is only the great and subtle power of love; but they who are drawn toward him by any other path, whether the path of money-making or gymnastics or philosophy, are not called lovers—the name of the whole is appropriated to those whose affections take one form only—they alone are said to love, or to be lovers." (pp. 46–47)

The examples of alternative paths to happiness that people may "love"— money making, gymnastics, and philosophy—represent a common Greek division between external goods, bodily goods, and goods of the soul, and they illustrate the broad conception of love to which Plato subscribes.

There is a remarkable affinity between Plato's generic conception of love as all desire for happiness and Freud's pansexualist conception of sexual libido, or love, as the motivation behind all striving for pleasure. Indeed, Freud (1921/1955) himself noted the relationship: "In its origin, function, and relation to sexual love, the 'Eros' of the philosopher Plato coincides exactly with the love-force, the libido of psychoanalysis" (pp. 90–91). Freud observed that it is not inconsistent with ordinary language to use the word *love* as a label for all desire; we often say that we "love" ideas, food, money, literature, work, exercise, art, and anything else that brings us happiness. (See Santas, 1988, for a discussion of the relationship between Freud's and Plato's concepts of love.)

Plato offered a dramatic example to drive home his counterintuitive point that love is subservient to happiness and is just a desire for the good conferred by the object. He observed that, despite the fact that people love their own bodies, they will undergo amputation of a limb if they think it will make them happier: "And they will cut off their own hands and feet and cast them away if they are evil, for there is nothing that men love but the good" (p. 47). Plato thus argued that one certainly loves one's own hand but that when it is gangrenous and therefore a threat, one is willing to cut it off; asserted that this principle applies to all loves. Although Plato's argument is not airtight or conclusive (many people fail to "cut off" a relationship that they know is bad for them), it does seem true that people often fall in love at least partly because of the good they believe the beloved will bring out in them and that to some extent love wanes if they find they are mistaken.

To gain something from Plato's argument, one need not fully accept Plato's instrumental account of love. One need accept only that this instrumental approach captures something that is true about love as a pursuit of what one finds beautiful, namely, that the pursuit is seen as a means to happiness and that the perception of whether love will be good for the lover does often affect his or her propensity to love. This instrumental notion is not unique to Plato; even so astute an observer of love as Stendahl expressed it in his aphorism "beauty is the promise of happiness." If love is to some extent regulated in its intensity or expression by broader considerations of happiness, this is a sufficient basis for Plato's subsequent arguments.

Love and the Desire for Immortality

After arguing that love is a desire for the good things that bring happiness, (the desire is pursued in a distinctive way that has yet to be specified), Plato next provided a critical and striking addition to his account of desire for the good. This addition occurs in a sequence of claims made by Diotima, each of which is agreed to by Socrates:

> Then, the simple truth is that men love the good.... To which must be added that they love the possession of the good?... And not only

the possession, but the everlasting possession of the good? ... Then love may be described generally as the love of the everlasting possession of the good? ... And if, as has been already admitted, love is of the everlasting possession of the good, all men will necessarily desire immortality together with the good—wherefore love is of immortality. (pp. 47, 48)

This is a pivotal moment in the dialogue. Up until now, Plato had been considering either erotic love or generic human desire, neither of which had yet been connected to generativity. The introduction of immortality as a general human goal that is part of love and indeed part of all pursuits of good things forges the potential link to generativity.

There seem to be two unexplained leaps in this argument. First, how did Plato get from the claim that people love the good to the claim that people desire the everlasting possession of the good? Plato implicitly relied here on his earlier analysis of the situation in which one possesses something but still says that one desires it. Recall that Plato argued that such desires are really for the continued possession of the desired good into the future. The examples he presented (e.g., strength, swiftness, health, and wealth) were prototypical cases of good things that bring happiness and thus suggested that people desire to continue to possess good things. Therefore, Plato considered himself to have already established that people want the possession of good things to go on indefinitely, or at least as lastingly as possible, and this conclusion seems true enough.

Second, how did Plato move from the premise that people desire to possess the good everlastingly to the conclusion that people desire immortality? Plato presented evidence that humans aspire to immortality, and specifically strive for immortal reputation, in subsequent passages in the dialogue, with examples ranging from inexplicably intense personal ambition to acts of self-sacrifice. Of course, no argument is needed to show that most people would like to live forever, or at least for a very long time, assuming that their life is a good one; however, Plato claimed that the desire for immortality is an integral part of the desire to possess good things lastingly that motivates all human action. His argument is simply that if one wants to possess something indefinitely, then of necessity one wants to exist indefinitely. That is, an integral part of the desire to go on possessing the good indefinitely is a desire to go on with one's existence indefinitely *to the degree that that existence is good and that it is a necessary precondition of possessing the good things*. Plato does not say that the desire to possess goods forever encompasses two separable desires, the desire for the good and the desire to live forever; immortality, for Plato, is a means to continue to possess good things, not an end in itself. Life itself, without good things, is neither desired nor desirable.

At this point in his argument, Plato had argued that love is a desire to possess beauty as a means to happiness and presented a framework for linking love to generativity through the desire for immortality. It remained for Plato to explain exactly how love plays a role in achieving immortality and hence generativity. If the goal of love is the same as that of all desire, then love must be distinguished by the means used to approach this goal. To provide an account of love, Plato had to turn from his exploration of what love shares with all desire to his original concern with what is special about erotic love.

THEORY OF GENERATIVITY: BIRTH IN BEAUTY AS THE MEANS TO IMMORTALITY

Birth in Beauty: Procreation as the Model for Generativity

Plato now turned to the critical question: What is special about the manner in which the erotic lover attempts to pursue eternal possession of the good? That is, what is the distinctive "instrumental use" of love in the pursuit of happiness? The answer, argued Plato, is that erotic love has a more direct relationship to immortality than other desires. Diotima's description of this relationship brings the reader to the heart of Plato's account of the generativity motive:

> Then if this be the nature of love, can you tell me further what is the manner of the pursuit? What are they doing who show all this eagerness and heat which is called love, and what is the object which they have in view? . . . Well, I will teach you—the object which they have in view is birth in beauty, whether of body or of soul. . . . I mean to say, that all men are bringing to the birth in their bodies and in their souls. There is a certain age at which human nature is desirous of procreation—procreation which must be in beauty and not in deformity; and this procreation is a union of man and woman, and is a divine thing; for conception and generation are an immortal principle in the mortal creature. . . . Beauty, then, is the destiny or goddess of parturition who presides at birth, and therefore, when approaching beauty, the conceiving power is propitious, and diffusive, and benign, and begets and bears fruit; at the sight of ugliness she frowns and contracts and has a sense of pain, and turns away, and shrivels up, and not without a pang refrains from conception. And this is the reason why, when the hour of conception arrives, and the teeming nature is full, there is such a flutter and ecstasy about beauty, whose approach is the alleviation of the pain of travail. For love, Socrates, is not, as you imagine, the love of the beautiful only. . . . It is the love of generation and of birth in beauty. . . . Because to the mortal creature generation is a sort of eternity and immortality, and if, as has been already admitted, love is of the everlasting possession of the good, all men will

necessarily desire immortality together with good—wherefore love is of immortality. (pp. 47–48)

This passage deserves careful scrutiny because it presents a procreative model that sets the framework for the theory of generativity to come. Plato wanted to establish the "manner of the pursuit" of happiness by the erotic lover and to know "what they are doing," that is, what end they have in mind when they act so passionately desirous. Plato's answer—and his central thesis—is that love is aimed at "birth in beauty, whether of body or of soul." That is, love is a desire to possess the other person's beauty with the hope that it will inspire one to bring forth something good out of oneself, whether physical, such as a child, or mental, such as a theory or work of art. In the case of erotic love, if one is a male and one's beloved is a female, and if one's generativity is expressed through procreation, then what comes out of oneself is literally "born in beauty," that is, the child that is partially the product of one's semen literally gestates within the beloved and emerges from her. The lover's mental products may be "born" in the beloved, as well (see the following). "Birth in beauty," however, also has the more general meaning of being born in the presence of and through the inspiration of beauty, and this more general scheme encompasses the great variety of generative relationships allowed by Plato's theory.

Plato asserted that all people are "pregnant" with physical or mental generative products and that erotic love intrinsically inspires one to bring forth such products. The anticipation (or perhaps just the dim awareness) of this prospect is what gives love its intense "eagerness and heat," for bringing forth long-lasting products is the best way to satisfy the urgent desire for immortality. In summary, erotic love is a special form of desire that aims to possess beauty as a means of generating products with which one is "pregnant" that will live on after one is gone. Thus, according to Plato, erotic desire itself is partly aimed at generativity and immortality.

Elaborating on the procreational model of the link between love and generativity, Plato indicated that the desire to bring forth or "give birth" to what is inside of one's body is an innate natural urge (it is derived from "human nature") that occurs spontaneously at a "certain age" (presumably, he refers to young adulthood). He implied that similar natural urges apply to the desire to bring forth what is in one's mind. However, what is inside will emerge only if one is inspired by a relationship with someone or something that one perceives to be beautiful. Beauty is thus "the goddess of parturition who presides at birth," and it is in search of such a midwife to what lies within us that we seek out beauty. The postulation of this aesthetic dimension to the defining goals of generative striving is distinctive of Plato's account.

Plato used the vivid metaphor of male sexual arousal and ejaculation to describe how the internal structure that one is "bringing forth" in the procreative or creative process is encouraged and inspired by beauty but "contracts" and "shrivels up" at the sight of ugliness. These sexual references may be intended as more than an amusing metaphor. Plato likely believed that semen contains elements of a human embryo and is secreted during sexual orgasm by both male and female and ejaculated together into the womb to grow to birth. This would imply that there is a sense in which both sexes generate offspring in sexual intercourse, so that sex itself is generative. Birth would be yet another point of generation.

Like Erikson, Plato saw more than just an analogy between procreation on the one hand and creativity and productivity on the other. He saw all these processes as manifestations of the same ultimate desire for immortality. However, Plato did not see other creative goals merely as sublimations of procreative impulses, as did Erikson (1985, p. 53). Plato saw these as separable and independent aspirations (one may be pregnant in body, in soul, or both), and one simply chooses the means that are best for oneself in the overall pursuit of immortality. In considering the different forms of generativity merely as different means to the same end, Plato adhered to a strong form of what might be called the "substitutability thesis," namely, that generative products can substitute for one another because what counts is the end and not the means.

Generativity as a Triadic Relationship

A unique feature of Plato's theory of generativity, derived from the procreative model, is that it defines generativity as a triadic rather than dyadic relationship. For Erikson, generativity was essentially a dyadic relationship between an individual who is generative and a product that the person creates or nurtures. For Plato, however, generativity was essentially a triadic relationship among the generative individual, a generative love object that serves as a catalyst for the creation and nurturance of the generated product, and a generative product that is brought forth because of the relationship to the love object. (Actually, there is a fourth—or in Erikson's case, a third—component to the generative impulse, namely, the generative aim, which for Erikson is care and for Plato is birth in beauty.)

Although the preceding passage focuses on procreative generativity and describes the generative love object as a human individual, the passage hints at another possible kind of generative love object, namely, beautiful instances of art, mathematics, science, literature, social institutions, laws, virtue, and other such abstract objects. For example, one might love beautiful music and through this love be inspired to create music. The three kinds of activities mentioned earlier, namely, gymnastics, money making, and philosophy, can also be loved and thus inspire creativity in these fields. Perhaps generativity occurs at its best when inspired by a relationship with a beloved person, but nothing in Plato's account precludes the "beloved" from being an abstraction. Plato would claim that one's love of the beauty of such objects carries within it a desire to realize one's own potential to create such lasting beauty. (Of course, one may choose not to do so or be incapable of doing so for a variety of reasons.)

As noted, in presenting the procreative model in the preceding passage, Plato asserted that "procreation must be in beauty," that is, the generative product germinates within the beautiful object. Even in the procreative realm, this model is limited; to the male, the child germinates in the beautiful object, but to the female, after the input of the beloved, the child germinates within the self. There are analogues to these processes in the mental realm; beautiful ideas may be placed within the mind of a beloved to germinate there either into later achievements by the beloved (as in teaching) or, more immediately, into stimulating conversation with the beloved that leads the lover to greater creative achievements. Creative projects can also come to fruition inside the lover rather than the beloved, as when one is inspired by the beloved to "give birth" to new ideas or virtuous actions.

"Birth in beauty" must be understood in the broad sense of "birth in the presence of—or inspired by—beauty." Thus interpreted, Plato's triadic scheme covers many varieties of generative relationships. The beloved may be a person or an abstraction and, if a person, may or may not be the vehicle for generating the product; the product can be a person, some other external object, a realization in oneself of virtuous traits, or a reputation that lives on after one. Whatever the variations, Plato's theory is distinctive for hypothesizing that generativity is closely linked to love in a tripartite relationship of individual, love object perceived as beautiful, and generative product.

The Love of Children and the Analogy to Animals

Plato buttressed his argument that erotic love is ultimately aimed at immortality by constructing an analogy between human and animal passions and their generative products:

> What is the cause, Socrates, of love and the attendant desire? See you not how all animals, birds as well as beasts, in their desire of procreation are in agony when they take the infection of love, which begins with the desire of union; whereto is added the care of the offspring, on whose behalf the weakest are ready to battle against the strongest even to the uttermost, and to die for them, and will let themselves be tormented with hunger or suffer anything in order to maintain their young. Man may be supposed to act thus from reason; but why should animals have these passionate feelings? . . . The mortal nature is seeking as far as possible to be everlasting and immortal; and this is only to be attained by generation because generation always leaves behind

a new existence in the place of the old. . . . Marvel not then at the love which men have of their offspring; for that universal love and interest is for the sake of immortality. (pp. 48, 49)

Why do people want to have children? Clearly, as Plato was well aware, there are instinctual processes underlying such desires; the animal analogy argues compellingly for this much. However, human beings often desire to have children, and that desire must result from a rational judgment that it is overall better to have children for one's happiness ("Man may be supposed to act thus from reason"); human beings routinely override instinctual urges that are not in their overall interest. One reason children conduce to happiness, Plato claimed, is that a degree of immortality comes with giving rise to offspring, both because one's name and virtues are remembered by one's descendants and because one's biological or psychological nature partly lives on in children one has sired or raised.

Plato convincingly argued that animal "love" and its attendant desires cannot be aimed at immediate satisfaction because animals will suffer and even die in the attempt to achieve sexual union and care for their young. Clearly, these strivings have some further function. Plato was laboring here under the burden of not having the theory of evolution to guide him in understanding animal behavior, but his conclusion is still recognizably evolutionary; animals are acting out of a principle that causes them to seek to generate young so that they (or, as we would say today, their genes) will live on after them. Plato took this generative goal to be a basic principle of all life, and he saw human desire for children as an expression of this principle.

One might point out that the animal analogy undermines Plato's case because it suggests that Erikson was right in saying that nurturance is an instinct; people want to have children simply because they instinctually enjoy nurturing them. In a manner analogous to the earlier "amputation" argument, Plato would no doubt reply that the pleasure of nurturing is not decisive in human decision making. Nurturant motives are easily overridden by judgments about whether the nurturance leads to a good result. Most people would not wish to nurture evil children or children who would not remember them or care about them. Although people do nurture other people's children (as in adoption) or even animals, the great majority of people would prefer to nurture their own biological children. This preference cannot be adequately explained as a general instinct to nurture. The best explanation, Plato held, is that people desire to perpetuate themselves and to achieve immortality, and that nurturance of children is a means to this end.

Why Generativity Confers Immortality: The Replacement Theory

Plato concluded the previously quoted passage with the observation that generation is the only way for a mortal creature to be immortal. He explained that "the mortal nature is seeking as far as possible to be ever-lasting and immortal; and this is only to be attained by generation" because "generation always leaves behind a new existence in the place of the old." This might be called the *replacement theory* of immortality. One's desire for immortality is to some degree satisfied or ameliorated, according to Plato's account, by generating something and leaving that thing in place of oneself—that is, by replacing oneself with that thing—when one dies.

However, why should replacement of oneself by something that lives on after one dies do anything at all to satisfy one's desire for immortality, when one is still going to die? This question goes largely unaddressed in contemporary theories of generativity, which tend to take symbolic immortality as a basic human desire. For example, the notion of symbolic immortality is at the heart of Kotre's (1984) account of generativity as the desire to "outlive the self." Kotre (pp. 10–11) noted that literal immortality—the satisfaction of the wish to live forever—is quite different from the symbolic immortality conferred by generativity, yet he offers no explanation of why people who want to live forever should be satisfied by mere symbolic immortality or generativity.

To his credit, Plato explicitly recognized this problem and offered an ingenious explanation for the link between generativity and immortality, in terms of the theory of personal identity:

> Nay, even in the life of the same individual there is succession and not absolute unity: a man is called the same, and yet in the short interval which elapses between youth and age, and in which every animal is said to have life and identity, he is undergoing a perpetual process of loss and reparation—hair, flesh, bones, blood, and the whole body are always changing. Which is true not only of the body but of the soul, whose habits, tempers, opinions, desires, pleasures, pains, fears never remain the same in anyone of us, but are always coming and going; and equally true of knowledge. And what is still more surprising to us mortals, not only do the sciences in general spring up and decay, so that in respect of them we are never the same; but each of them individually experiences a like change. For what is implied in the word 'recollection' but the departure of knowledge which is ever being forgotten and is renewed and preserved by recollection, and appears to be the same although in reality new, according to that law of succession by which all mortal things are preserved, not absolutely the same, but by substitution, the old, worn-out mortality leaving another new and similar existence behind—unlike the divine, which is always the same and not another? And in this way, Socrates, the mortal body, or mortal anything, partakes of immortality; but the immortal in another way. (p. 49)

Plato pointed out that human beings, unlike gods, stay alive over time by replacement of their parts. Thus, the perpetuation of oneself over time even during life consists of a sequence of related states that follow and replace each other, like the physical changes in one's body that occur from youth to old age or the changes in the beliefs that are in one's mind. Mortal beings have no real existence as constant, unchanging entities over time (that sort of unchanging nature is reserved for the gods, Plato contended); the continued existence of mortal beings is a construct from a sequence of things that substitute one for the other over time. Replacement is the only form of existence over time that mortals possess, and this form of existence, Plato argued, can be had to some degree after death.

Replacement after one is dead appears to confer an attenuated form of immortality. When living, one is replaced by new cells generated in one's body; after death, one is replaced by, for example, one's child's body, which is also initially generated in oneself, or the ideas one had while alive are replaced by similar ideas in the minds of others who know one's writings. In principle, the same sort of process is operating after death that conferred personal identity over the life span. The sense of immortality conferred by generativity is enhanced by the fact that replacement is a matter of degree; the limits of replacement during life are vague and form a "fuzzy set," allowing for peripheral cases in which replacement is less complete but still seems to preserve one's identity to some extent. Thus, through replacement, human beings possess an extension of the self into the future, and the mortal body or mind "partakes of immortality" in the sense appropriate to human beings. In effect, Plato here offered a psychological theory of the appeal of what others have called "symbolic immortality" (e.g., Kotre, 1984; McAdams & de St. Aubin, 1992).

Plato took a modern view in his account of memory in this passage. He maintained that to remember bits of knowledge is not to have one state continuously existing in the mind over time but for the bit of knowledge to be reconstructed by or reappear to the individual. Each time one remembers, one has a new experience that resembles in certain respects earlier experiences, but the experience is in fact a fresh construction that replaces what has come before.

It is not incidental that Plato spent so much of the passage considering the perpetuation of knowledge through memory and arguing memory is ever changing in new instances of recall. Although Plato was clearly right in saying that the body ages and changes over time, a critic might argue that one's mind remains constant and gives one a sense of personal identity over time and that this mental constancy ends abruptly at death. Plato systematically attacked this notion in his analysis of memory, thus attempting to make it possible for the replacement theory to be comprehensively applied to personal identity.

Mental replacement is critical to the overall theory of generativity. The two main ways to achieve immortality, according to Plato, are through human progeny, who physically replace one, and through the communication of various kinds of ideas (scientific, artistic, philosophical, or social) that live on as knowledge in others' minds after one dies. In the preceding passage, Plato subtly made his case that knowledge is no different in this essential respect from children. People express their physical nature in children, to whom they give a part of their physical being that lives on after them in the child's body. Analogously, they express their mental nature in teachings by which they give children, lovers, students, and others a part of their mental nature that lives on after them in the minds of these others.

Ironically, Plato had to emphasize the changing nature of knowledge to explain why teaching immortalizes the teacher's mental nature. Just as a child is not identical to the parent, so an idea passed on from its intellectual parent will evolve over time; however, this does not diminish the role that the parent played in the original genesis of the valuable product. Plato emphasized that discontinuity is the rule both within one mind and across minds; the fact that one's own memories are fresh constructions makes them all the more similar to the fresh constructions that occur in other people's minds. One's ideas live on after one is dead in other people's minds in more or less the same, ever-changing sense that they lived on in one's own mind while one was alive.

In addition to the many generative products, from laws and institutions to scientific knowledge and philosophical wisdom, that are perpetuated through knowledge, there is a second reason that Plato's account of memory plays a special role in his overall argument. Plato emphasized that people seek immortality by attempting to ensure that they possess a good reputation after they are gone. Indeed, he considered all generative products to be partly attempts to achieve an enduring reputation. Even children are valued not just because they physically replace one but even more because they keep one's memory alive. One's reputation is just a set of beliefs in the minds of other people. Thus, the replacement or replenishment of knowledge that constitutes others' memories of a person is the single most important element in achieving generativity.

Reputation is surely central to many forms of generativity; for example, the common practice of naming buildings, institutions, or other entities after those who gave money or otherwise made possible the creation of the entity seems to reveal a clear link between lasting reputation and generativity, as Plato suggested. To the modern ear, however, it may seem that Plato's emphasis on reputation is misguided and shallow. In modern culture, in which people are largely anonymous to one another and fame often results from exposure in the mass media, fame may or may not have a relationship to the degree of goodness or everlastingness of an individual's achievements. However, in the smaller communities of Plato's day, reputation may have been based on more direct knowledge of the person and his or her achievements. In any event, Plato assumed that reality and reputation are congruent, so that reputation, in the sense he intended, is *deserved* reputation. Under such circumstances, reputation need not have the questionable connotation that it does today.

Evidence That Other Forms of Generativity Are Aimed at Immortality

After arguing in the preceding passages that the desire for children is really a desire for immortality, Plato then defended the applicability of his analysis to other human pursuits. To support his claim that people who pursue a variety of activities seek immortality, he presented a quasi-empirical argument: Simply observe what they do, he said, and you will see that the devotion they show to their activities cannot be explained without recourse to a desire for immortality:

> Think only of the ambition of men, and you will wonder at the sense-lessness of their ways, unless you consider how they are stirred by the love of an immortality of fame. They are ready to run all risks greater far than they would have run for their children, and to spend money and undergo any sort of toil, and even to die, for the sake of leaving behind them a name which shall be eternal. Do you imagine that Alcestis would have died to save Admetus, or Achilles to avenge Patroclus . . . if they had not imagined that the memory of their virtues, which still survives among us, would be immortal? Nay, I am persuaded that all men do all things, and the better they are the more they do them, in hope of the glorious fame of immortal virtue; for they desire the immortal. (pp. 49–50)

Plato observed here that people are sometimes quite similar to animals in the seeming irrationality of their generative behavior. They are willing to sacrifice immediate pleasure and even health for great achievements, such as those attainable in the earlier mentioned pursuits of money making, gymnastics, and philosophy. Moreover, they are willing (like Alcestis) to sacrifice their lives for others. Within Plato's egoistic approach to human psychology, such self-sacrifice demands an explanation that eschews altruism as a motive. Plato's answer was that people sacrifice to ensure that others will lastingly think well of them. In claiming that people pursuing nonprocreative forms of generativity "are ready to run all risks greater far than they would have run for their children," Plato prepared the way for a radical claim he made later, that the eternal fame associated with other forms of generativity is often more desirable to people than procreation.

The last sentence of the preceding passage is particularly striking in attributing the immortality motive to all human actions. The sentence may be confusing; how can it be the case both that everyone does everything for immortality and that better people do more of what they do for immortality? Plato's point seems to be that everyone is to some degree concerned about immortality in every action they take (e.g., in considering how the action will affect their reputation) but that the better (i.e., the wiser and more virtuous) a person is, the more weight the person gives to such considerations over more immediate needs. From Plato's point of view, enhancing a reputation that can last thousands of years is always more desirable than obtaining immediate pleasure. No doubt Plato had in mind here Socrates's single-minded devotion to philosophy, but there are contemporary examples, as well; for instance, the mathematician Paul Erdos gave up all worldly ties to wander the world in pursuit of mathematical truth, and his devotion earned him such reknown that his recent death was reported on the front page of *The New York Times*.

A Typology of Generative Products

As I have noted, Erikson (1963) suggested that generativity encompasses three main kinds of activities: procreation, productivity, and creativity. He also mentioned that social concerns and even development of the self may express generative impulses. Kotre (1984) elaborated on Erikson's typology with his own division of generative products into four categories: biological (the bearing and nursing of the infant), parental (the nurturing and socializing of the child), technical (the teaching of skills), and cultural (the creating and passing on of the culture's symbols). There is a remarkable congruence between these typologies and the typology of generative products implicitly offered by Plato in passages such as the following:

> Those who are pregnant in the body only betake themselves to women and beget children—this is the character of their love; their offspring, as they hope, will preserve their memory and give them the blessedness and immortality which they desire in the future. But souls which are pregnant—for there certainly are men who are more creative in their souls than in their bodies—conceive that which is proper for the soul to conceive or contain. And what are these conceptions?—wisdom and virtue in general. And such creators are poets and all artists who are deserving of the name inventor. But the greatest and fairest sort of wisdom by far is that which is concerned with the ordering of states and families, and which is called temperance and justice. And he who in youth has the seed of these implanted in him and is himself inspired, when he comes to maturity, desires to beget and generate. He wanders about seeking beauty that he may beget offspring. (p. 50)

Plato maintained that, given the right conditions, at a certain age individuals desire to generate. He suggested that the particular form of generativity pursued by individuals depends both on the experiences and education of the individual (individuals have to have the right seeds "implanted" in them in youth) and on their innate nature and talent (individuals must be "inspired" and must be pregnant in the right way, soul or body). In seeming contradiction to his earlier, more optimistic statement that all people are potentially pregnant both in body and soul, Plato asserted here that some individuals are pregnant "in the body only," whereas others are more pregnant in the soul.

The same types of generative activities and their corresponding products mentioned by Erikson and Kotre can be found in Plato's discussion. First, there is "pregnancy of the body," or procreativity, with children as the products. Kotre (1984), like Plato, considered this to be one form of generativity. Although Erikson (1963) listed procreation as one form of generativity, he emphasized that sheer procreation is not sufficient; procreative generativity for Erikson requires not just producing children but also caring about and nurturing them so that their developmental needs can be satisfied and they can become capable of generativity. Erikson's concerns are reflected in Kotre's distinction between biological and parental generativity. The fuller, nurturant relationship to the child that Erikson required for procreational generativity is a second form of generativity in Kotre's typology. However, both agree that nurturance advances the generative content of parenting.

Despite the egoistic nature of Plato's view, he, too, implied that caring and not sheer procreativity is an element in generativity (not a necessary one, as Erikson claimed, but an additional one that advances generative aims, as Kotre specified) when he noted that the generative person "tends that which he brings forth." However, there is a difference between Plato's and Erikson's views of the motivation for providing care. Whereas Erikson saw this caring as instinctive, Plato saw it as an instrumental action aimed at ensuring that one's generative products are as good, long lasting, and reflective of the self as possible. Therefore, Plato's account of child rearing as egoistically motivated by personal longings for immortality seems to have what amounts to "altruistic" implications. The parent must take great pains to nurture and educate the child, develop the child's character and psychological capacities, and prepare the child to be a productive and generative citizen because to do less would not ensure that the child will preserve the parent's reputation into the far future and will reflect as favorably as possible on the parent. To some extent, Plato's claim that in seeking symbolic immortality one seeks to make one's generative product as "good" as possible (see the following) allows his theory to transcend the boundaries between the usual categories of agentic (narcissistic) and communal (altruistic) generative motives (Kotre, 1984; also see chapter 1, this volume).

In addition to procreativity, Plato postulated "pregnancy of the soul," which he said can lead to three kinds of mental generativity. First, the pregnant soul gives rise to the creative artists, such as poets or sculptors, who generate enduring objects that express or describe virtue and beauty.

This encompasses part of Erikson's "creativity" category and Kotre's "cultural symbols" category.

Second, the pregnant soul gives rise to artisans (i.e., craftspeople) and inventors, such as doctors and blacksmiths, who create useful skills or objects on the basis of their practical wisdom of specific disciplines and who pass on their technical skills. This category encompasses Erikson's category of productivity, at least when work is either productive of enduring artifacts or creative in a way deserving of lasting fame, as well as Kotre's category of technical generativity. However, Plato's account seems to exclude from the category of generativity routine productivity that contributes to the current maintenance of society but does not aspire to lasting contributions. To this extent, Plato rejected the notion advanced by Erikson, that sheer "maintenance of the world" is generative. On the other hand, Plato included a wide range of activities within the category of generative striving, including money making and sports, if those activities are motivated by a desire to become famous for one's admirable achievements, like today's financial gurus and sports heroes.

The third form of soul generativity, according to Plato, occurs when the individual comes to understand that families, social institutions, and laws order society and shape the young of future generations. The lover of wisdom and virtue wants to impart these qualities to others and thus plays an active role in the ordering of society's institutions and laws consistent with the ideal of justice, thus encouraging virtue in the citizenry. Such laws and institutions are the structures that nurture all of the procreation, productivity, creativity, and other virtues in a culture; therefore, social reform is a high form of generativity. From Solon to Lincoln, social reformers have earned their exceptionally long lasting and glorious reputations.

The theme of self-development is expressed in Plato's emphasis on realization of virtue as a route to generativity. Virtue is valued both for itself and for the immortality of reputation that it brings. Plato's focus on the development of virtue addresses a problem with Erikson's account. Erikson included self-development as a generative act, but he also argued that one indicator of failure of generativity is self-absorption. He never provided a criterion for distinguishing between these two types of involvement with the self. Plato suggested that only the development of virtue that can serve as a model for others through a good reputation can be classified as generative and not self-absorbed.

In a later passage, Plato placed science and philosophy above social reform as generative products:

> After laws and institutions he will go on to the sciences, that he may
> see their beauty, being not like a servant in love with the beauty of
> one youth or man or institution, himself a slave mean and narrow-
> minded, but drawing toward and contemplating the vast sea of beauty,

he will create many fair and noble thoughts and notions in boundless love of wisdom. (p. 51)

The "slave" metaphor reflects Plato's belief that a product becomes more generatively successful the more universal and therefore more potentially lasting it is. To produce something that is tied to one culture is to make one's generative fulfillment a slave to that culture's future, whereas to produce something of univeral human value, such as scientific or philosophical insight, is to achieve generative fulfillment that can transcend cultural boundaries and is therefore more lasting.

This passage also indicates what is clear throughout Plato's presentation, that generativity and wisdom are supposed to grow together. The basic idea appears to be that wisdom is the ability to choose long-term over short-term gratifications and that generativity is the ultimate in choosing for the longer term (i.e., longer than one's life span). In contrast, Erikson considered wisdom to be concerned mainly with accepting death rather than with guiding life. Generally, whereas Erikson conceptualized development in stages, Plato hypothesizes the integral, parallel development of love, wisdom, and generativity. Indeed, at a deep level, all three of these qualities come to mean much the same thing in Plato's theory. (The connections between these traits are related to Plato's broader doctrine of the "unity of the virtues," Vlastos, 1981b, aspects of which I consider elsewhere; see Wakefield, 1987, 1991.)

Theory of Generative Satisfaction and Evaluation of Generative Products

What makes a generative product more or less satisfying? Erikson has no real theory of generative satisfaction because he stops with the assertion that generative satisfaction is instinctual. He also does not attempt to provide an evaluative account of generative products. He does suggest that creativity and productivity are sublimations of procreative or erotic desires, but it is not clear whether this is supposed to imply that one kind of product is more satisfying or better than others. Other thinkers appear to have nascent accounts of generative satisfaction, but these accounts are not clearly worked out.

Plato implicitly offered an elegant theory both of the evaluation of generative products and of generative satisfaction; these are treated as the same thing because for Plato the evaluation of a generative product determines the degree of satisfaction conferred by the product. Plato needed such a criterion for his argument that some products are intrinsically more satisfying of generative strivings than others and thus represent a higher level of development of generative motivation.

One might think of Plato's account of the desirability of generative products as derived directly from his theory that the generative motive is to "possess the good forever." This formula suggests three criteria: (a) degree of possession (which might include such subcriteria as degree of connectedness to the self, uniqueness of connectedness to the self, and degree to which the connection is to essential rather than to superficial properties of the self), (b) degree of goodness, and (c) degree of immortality (i.e., how long lasting it is). These criteria make possible a rough ordering of kinds of generative products in terms of their generative value and satisfaction. Plato deployed these criteria in the following passage, in which he considered those who join together to beget mental "children":

> They are married by a far nearer tie and have a far closer friendship than those who beget mortal children, for the children who are their offspring are fairer and more immortal. Who, when he thinks of Homer and Hesiod and other great poets, would not rather have their children than ordinary human ones? Who would not emulate them in the creation of children as theirs, which have preserved their memory and given them everlasting glory? . . . There is Solon, too, who is the revered father of Athenian law; and many others there are . . . who have given to the world many noble works and have been the parents of virtue of every kind; and many temples have been raised in their honor for the sake of children such as theirs, which were never raised in honor of anyone for the sake of his mortal children. (pp. 50–51)

According to this passage, creative works are often more generatively satisfying than human children because such works have the potential to be both more beautiful in expressing or producing virtue (they are "fairer" then human children) and longer lasting (they are "more immortal") and thus more productive of eternal fame. Plato offered a striking challenge to conventional thought (as well as a risky empirical prediction) when he asked, "Who, when he thinks of Homer and Hesiod and other great poets, would not rather have their children than ordinary human ones?" Plato assumed here the "substitutability hypothesis": that one can choose between various generative products as if they satisfy the same urge and thus are interchangeable (Erikson also seems to come close to this position). Plato's theory suggests a variety of comparative questions that might be asked about the factors that affect the intensity of motivation for having children or doing creative work (e.g., If you knew that your child would not have any children, would that affect your motivation to have a child [degree of immortality]? If you knew that your child would turn out to be evil, would that influence your motivation [degree of goodness]? If you knew that your child would, after a certain age, not remember or know you, would that influence your motivation [degree of possession]?).

This completes my reconstruction of Plato's theory of generativity. I hope that the preceding exposition and interpretation have convinced the reader of what I believe: that Plato's theory rivals Erikson's in its elegance, insight, fruitfulness in raising questions, and even potential testability.

GENERATIVITY AND SYMBOLIC IMMORTALITY

There are many provocative claims in Plato's theory of generativity, such as that beauty brings out what is good within us and inspires creativity, that erotic love contains within it a desire for procreation, that erotic love is simply a particularly intense form of a more general desire to possess beauty, that different generative products are substitutable for one another, that most people would prefer to create great theory or great art than to procreate, and that generativity is essential to human happiness. Each of these claims, as well as others put forward by Plato or implied by his theory, requires careful examination to discover whatever measure of truth it may contain.

The central Platonic thesis is that generativity is motivated by a desire for a symbolic form of personal immortality. I noted earlier that both Kotre's (1984) and McAdams's (McAdams & de St. Aubin, 1992) theories of generativity postulate a longing for symbolic immortality as a motivation for generativity. However, no other theoretician has attributed generativity *entirely* to such motives, and without question Plato is the theoretician who most sytematically developed this thesis as the central element in a theory of generativity. In this section, I examine one aspect of this thesis in some depth.

The Puzzling Link Between Generativity and Immortality

Although it is taken as axiomatic by current "symbolic immortality" theories of generativity, Plato's claim that people desire to create and to procreate to achieve immortality is actually deeply puzzling. As I noted, this claim invites the question, why should the creation of generative objects satisfy one's desire for immortality, when in fact one dies and is not literally made immortal through one's generative works? The puzzle is expressed in Woody Allen's well-known remark: "I don't want to achieve immortality through my works; I want to achieve immortality by not dying." Put more starkly, the point is that no matter how much one generates, after a few years one will be dead anyway, and a dead individual is not literally immortal at all, to any degree, despite what he or she has left behind. Therefore, why should the desire for immortality be satisfied to any degree by leaving something behind? The very fact that one is dead implies that one's desire for immortality has gone unfulfilled.

This problem—namely, why symbolic immortality satisfies the desire for immortality—is not seriously addressed by any extant theory of generativity. Clearly, there are many possible psychological explanations for the satisfaction achieved from symbolic immortality and for people's *feeling* as though in some sense they are living on through their children and works. However, Plato's theory, because of its rationalistic structure, requires a logical link between the desire for immortality and the desire for generativity and thus forces one to ask whether or why such feelings are rationally warranted. I address the question here within this Platonic framework.

Note that this puzzle is related to a broader set of questions that face any theory of human nature: Why do people (especially within an egoist approach to psychology, which Plato accepts) care at all about what happens after they are dead? Why do people desire to have memories of themselves and of their works live on after their death? In particular, why do people care so much that they are remembered well or, in the case of public figures, that they are judged positively by history? The common explanation is that people crave immortality. However, it is apparent on reflection that before this explanation can be accepted, a more basic explanation is needed as to why events after one is dead would rationally satisfy to any degree the desire for immortality.

Plato's "replacement theory" and the "symbolic immortality" approach in general might be considered a "next best thing" answer to this puzzle: People really want immortality of the literal kind, but that is reserved for the gods; unable to obtain what they want, they instead pursue the next best thing, symbolic immortality, trying to ensure that, even if they cannot survive, some creation of theirs will "replace" them and live on after them. However, despite Plato's statement that through generativity people can partake of immortality, Plato's own text acknowledges the disparity between the literal immortality people want and the symbolic immortality they pursue. Plato asserted that "the mortal nature is seeking *as far as possible* [italics added] to be everlasting and immortal" and that "to the mortal creature generation is *a sort of* [italics added] eternity and immortality" (p. 48). He seemed to be implying that such an approximation is a good enough, second-best solution to the desire for immortality.

However, this "solution" just poses the puzzle over again in new terms. Symbolic immortality is not literal immortality. If one desires literal immortality, then symbolic immortality should not at all satisfy one's desire, any more than staring at a picture of an apple ("symbolic food") should satisfy one's hunger. The desire for immortality seems to be a situation in which the next best thing is just not good enough. Indeed, Plato's qualifying phrases are revealing: To be "as far as possible" immortal or "sort of" immortal is not to be immortal at all because immortality (in the literal sense of continuing to exist) is not a matter of degree. Thus, the link between generativity and satisfaction of the desire for immortality poses a fundamental puzzle for Plato's view.

There is a commonsense explanation of why we want, for example, a good reputation after we are dead, and this explanation entirely avoids Plato's problems. The explanation is that it makes people happy to know that they will be admired after they are gone for the same reason that it makes them happy to know that they are admired while they are alive by people they have never met; in fact, people just like to be admired, irrespective of where, when, or by whom. Thus, the knowledge that we have ensured that our good reputation will continue after we are dead brings us happiness. Even to Plato it would have been obvious that the desire for a good reputation need not be tied to the longing for generativity; the Greek gods are immortal, yet they want to be admired by humankind. The desire to ensure a good reputation after one is dead could simply be part of a general desire for a good reputation and have nothing to do with immortality.

However, this commonsense account is not sufficient because it does not explain the central psychological presupposition of Plato's argument, namely, that the prospect of posthumous fame to some degree or in some way reduces one's feelings of distress about the fact that one is going to die. Of course, most people do not want to die, irrespective of their generative accomplishments. However, Plato was pointing to a real phenomenon, I think, in claiming that there is some kind of connection between generative achievement and one's feelings about death and in observing that one's awareness of mortality is somehow involved in triggering generative motivation. (Erikson agreed with Plato that generativity is likely to lead to reduced fear of death, but for quite different reasons.) It is this relationship between generativity and feelings about death—specifically, that generativity can at least transiently take some of the pain out of the prospect of death—that needs explaining. The fact that everyone wants to be admired does not explain this special relationship between death and generativity.

Two facts remain: First, generativity assuages to some degree the longing for immortality and the fear of death. Second, generativity does not to any degree change the fact that one is going to die. A proper explanation of the relationship between generativity and immortality must explain how both facts can be comfortably true together.

Erikson on Generativity and the Sting of Death

Erikson postulated that the desire to nurture and create is an instinctual drive in its own right that requires no further explanation and cannot be reduced to any other motive, such as the desire for immortality. If Erikson was right, there is no direct connection between generativity and immortality and thus no puzzle. The answer to Plato's puzzle would be, "It is just intrinsically satisfying to leave something behind or to nurture future generations."

However, Erikson did postulate a relation between generativity and the fear of death in his account of the last developmental stage, integrity, which involves an acceptance of death. If one supposes that fear of death is correlated with desire for lasting life, then Erikson implicitly expressed a position about the relationship between generativity and the desire for immortality when he characterized the nature of integrity and its sources in earlier generative activity:

> Only in him who in some way has taken care of things and people and has adapted himself to the triumphs and disappointments adherent to being the originator of others or the generator of products and ideas—only in him may gradually ripen the fruit of these seven stages. I know no better word for it than ego integrity. . . . It is the ego's accrued assurance of its proclivity for order and meaning. It is a post-narcissistic love of the human ego—not of the self—as an experience which conveys some world order and spiritual sense, no matter how dearly paid for. It is the acceptance of one's one and only life cycle as something that had to be and that, by necessity, permitted of no substitutions. . . . Although aware of the relativity of all the various life styles which have given meaning to human striving, the possessor of integrity is ready to defend the dignity of his own life style against all physical and economic threats. For he knows that an individual life is the accidental coincidence of but one life cycle with but one segment of history; and that for him all human integrity stands or falls with the one style of integrity of which he partakes. The style of integrity developed by his culture or civilization thus becomes the "patrimony of his soul," the seal of his moral paternity of himself. . . . In such final consolidation, death loses its sting. . . . The lack or loss of this accrued ego integration is signified by fear of death: the one and only life cycle is not accepted as the ultimate of life. Despair expresses the feeling that the time is now short, too short for the attempt to start another life and to try out alternate roads to integrity. (Erikson, 1963, pp. 268–269)

Erikson's analysis here is quite contrary to Plato's. Erikson suggested that generativity reduces the fear of death (and thus the desire for immortality) by leading the individual to identify with the broader culture to which he or she has generatively contributed and to accept that this one culture, and this one life cycle within this culture, is all that is possible and thus all that can be desired. Plato implied, to the contrary, that it is precisely the desire to live on and to transcend one's life cycle and even one's culture that motivates the highest forms of generativity.

Erikson's account allows for several different routes to reduction of what he calls the "sting" of death. All these routes are at odds with Plato's account. First, Erikson suggested that fear of death subsides with the acceptance of the inevitability of one's unique life cycle and its accomplishments. Plato saw generativity rather as an expression of the desire to transcend one's life cycle. Second, Erikson saw solace in the identification with one's culture and its meaning system, within which one's generative contributions are defined; the very contingency of cultural meanings is claimed to trigger an acceptance of the limitations imposed by death. Plato held that one aspires to produce the most univeral, non–culturally contingent generative product one can, so one can live on independently of the fate of one's culture and thus transcend contingency to the degree possible. For Erikson, there is solace in a general postnarcissistic, nonegoistic, caring attitude involving loss of the boundaries of the self that develops at this stage and that makes personal survival less urgent. Plato emphasized that egoistic aspirations for personal immortality and happiness and the self's struggle to survive as a distinct entity are critical to generativity. Finally, for Erikson the relationship between generativity and immortality takes place after the generative stage is over, as a sheer matter of solace in assessing one's life after the fact. For Plato, issues concerning death and immortality are central to the motivation that fuels generativity itself.

As in Erikson's account of the developmental relationship between love and generativity (see the preceding discussion), it does not appear that Erikson considered generativity to be directly or logically linked to the fear of death or the desire for immortality. The relationship is indirect; generativity helps to promote a group of psychological traits, including acceptance of one's finiteness and one's unique life cycle, identification with one's culture, softening of the boundaries of the self, and acceptance of inevitability and contingency, that Erikson claimed reduce the sting of death. The postulated links between generativity and these traits and between these traits and reduction in the sting of death remain somewhat obscure. When Erikson claimed that "only in him who in some way has taken care of things and people and has adapted himself to . . . being the originator of others or the generator of products and ideas" will integrity be achieved and fear of death averted or controlled, the connection is a speculative psychological one, not the direct logical one that Plato postulated. Erikson's account therefore offers no clear solution to the puzzle of the rational connection that seems to exist between generativity and feelings about immortality.

Why Generativity Reduces the Sting of Death

There is, I think, a solution to this conundrum regarding the relationship between death and generativity, but it will take a bit more ground clearing to get to it. Recall that when Plato argued that people desire immortality, rather than asserting this fact as obvious he established it as a conclusion derived from the premise that people desire to possess the good forever. The logical structure of this argument reveals something important about the relationship between the desire for good things and the desire for immortality. As Plato would be the first to affirm, people do not value everlasting life itself as their penultimate good (the ultimate good being happiness); they value a good life, that is, a life filled with the possession of good things. People willingly end their lives (for example, those assisted in suicide by Dr. Kevorkian) when they see that there are insufficient good things in their lives anymore. Thus, Plato would claim, there is no desire for life as such; there is only a desire for a good life. (Plato referred to considered rational judgments; there may be a gut-level impulse to live no matter what, but people rationally override that impulse when a minimally good life is no longer achievable.) A good life does presuppose life, so the desire for a good life forever does presuppose a desire for life forever. However, Plato's apparent detachment of the desire for immortality from the desire for the possession of the good forever is misleading; the desire for a good life forever does not imply a desire for immortality as such but only for immortality in the context of a good life.

The critical point here is that life is a means, not an end in itself. Specifically, life is a means to a good life (i.e., a life that has at least a minimum of good things in it or perhaps a minimal balance of good over evil things in it), and if that goal cannot be achieved, then life is not of interest. This feature of the desire for immortality is obscured in Plato's presentation but implicit in the structure of his argument.

Life is desired as an instrumental means to possessing good things, therefore, such as a good reputation for one's achievements. Moreover, as in the argument about taking medicine and going to sea, instrumental means are valued only to the degree that they are needed to get to the desired end; one cares less about instrumental means if one can attain the end in some other way. Thus, if one is generative during life and one knows, for example, that one's good reputation will live on after one's death and that one's children will lead happy, generative lives after one's death, then one knows that one has already achieved some of the goals at which the continuation of life is aimed and that one would have pursued had one been alive. One thus manages to possess some of the goals of continued life without possessing continued life. *Although generativity does not allow one to partake of immortality, it does allow one to partake of the fruits of immortality.*

The means–end relationship between life and possession of good things provides an explanation of the effect of generativity on the sting of death. There are many important goods that cannot be possessed after death (e.g., health, awareness, pleasure, knowledge, friendship, and wealth), so no amount of generativity is likely to relieve substantially the horror of one's mortality. However, it does not seem quite as horrible to lose the means—namely, life—if one is assured of possessing at least some of the ends—for example, a good reputation and happy children in the future— for which the means are desired. Consequently, to the generative person death seems somewhat less disastrous than it otherwise would. By achieving some of the most important goals of the continuation of one's life, one feels somewhat less despair that one will not be alive to pursue those goals. Plato thus appears to be correct in claiming, contra Erikson, but in agreement with common intuition, that there is a direct logical relationship between generativity and reduction in the sting of death, despite the fact that generativity in no way confers immortality.

Plato's "immortality" argument is best construed as a nonliteral manner of speaking that emphasizes that one desires the possession of good things to last beyond one's death. The "replacement theory" is best taken as an account of why it is that certain kinds of things, such as reputation, children, and ideas, are perceived as connected to or "possessed by" oneself even after one dies. Generativity is the creation of such "immortal" possessions.

EXTERNALIZING THE SELF

In this section, I offer some critical comments on Plato's and Erikson's theories of generativity as well as some tentative suggestions concerning the directions that an integration of the two theories might take and how such an integration might avoid some of the problems I identify.

Generativity as Externalization of the Self

The theory of generativity starts with a compelling question: How does society perpetuate itself? Stated from a psychological perspective, the question becomes, how do people, each following his or her own motivational inclinations, manage to create and properly mold all the people, things, and ideas that are necessary to perpetuate society?

Erikson's answer, shaped by the psychoanalytic tradition of which he was a part, was that there is a specific instinctual drive to perform generative actions, in which the things needed for the perpetuation of society are themselves the "libidinal objects" of the drive. Plato's answer, shaped by rationalistic Socratic psychology, was that people generate what is necessary for the perpetuation of society as a rational strategy in attaining immortality and happiness.

Plato no doubt overemphasized the rational, instrumental component of generativity. He did not adequately develop an account of the instinctual urges that form the foundation of generative desires. Any theory of generativity must identify both the ultimate instinctual source of generative desires (if any) and the ways in which these urges emerge in action after interaction with the rest of the belief–desire "intentional" system (Wakefield, 1989). However, there are plentiful hints within Plato's work of the direction that an account of the instinctual sources of generativity might take. Plato's use of the analogy with animals suggests that the desire to give rise to replacements has an instinctual component. Plato spoke of people naturally being pregnant and wanting to give birth in soul and body "at a certain age," and this process appears to be an instinctual developmental occurrence. Plato also described the heat and passion of generative strivings, ranging from procreation and intense ambition to the sacrifice of one's life for an enduringly virtuous reputation, and he emphasized that one's insides "teem" with what needs to be born when in the presence of beauty. All this suggests instinctual sources of generativity.

What seems most basic and closest to an instinctual pleasure here, and also forms the heart of Plato's vision, is the urge to give birth to what is inside one. Plato referred here as much to the intense need to get onto paper the idea in one's head as he did to the need of the pregnant woman to bring forth what is in her womb. I use the term *externalization* to refer to the general process that Plato metaphorically called "birth," namely, the process of taking structures that have formed within and, in one way or another, placing them into the world or influencing the world to resemble them. Externalization is thus a broad concept, the results of which range from statues that resemble the self to ideas that come from the self and from teaching a child to live up to one's values to building an empire that is ruled by one's values.

In contrast to Erikson's claim that generativity is propelled by an instinctual satisfaction in nurturing, externalization theory suggests that generativity is propelled by an instinctual satisfaction in externalizing aspects of the self. From this perspective, nurturing would be, as Plato suggested, one means to the end of externalization. However, in contrast to Plato's single-minded emphasis on the rational pursuit of happiness as the source of generativity, externalization theory postulates the operation of a powerful instinctual level of motivation, as well. Of course, random externalization is neither sought nor satisfying. Earlier, I extracted a theory from Plato's text that possession, goodness, and long-lastingness are criteria by which externalizations are evaluated and by which they yield their satisfaction.

The Intentionalist Fallacy of Erikson and Plato

In postulating a specific generative instinct, Erikson was vulnerable to a common error. Even if there is a psychological mechanism with the function of producing generative outcomes, it need not consist of a motivational mechanism that gives rise to motives to produce generative outcomes. In coming close to postulating such a motivational system, Erikson may be accused of committing the "intentionalist fallacy" (Wakefield, 1989) of confusing the *natural function* of a motivational system—that is, the outcome the system is designed by natural selection to produce—with the *intentional content* of the resulting motives themselves. From the fact that the perpetuation of society is obviously a necessary outcome of human nature, Erikson appeared to infer that there must be an instinctual motivational mechanism that is designed to give people the motive to perpetuate society, and this inference is faulty. The fact that some task needs to be accomplished and is accomplished suggests only that it is a natural function of some mechanisms to bring about the accomplishment of the task; it does not necessarily mean that people are designed to have specific motives to accomplish the task. For example, we are not designed to have a specific motive to eat high-calorie foods; instead, we have a set of mechanisms that make foods like sweets and fats taste good and thus motivate us to eat sweets and fats; because these kinds of foods are high in calories, the function of getting us to eat high-calorie foods is accomplished. Motivational content and natural function need not coincide.

Plato's "immortality" account is subject to a similar fallacy. Lacking the theory of evolution, Plato seemed to confuse facts about biological functions, such as erotic love having the *function* of leading to procreation, with facts about the contents of motivational aims or desires, such as erotic love being itself a *desire* to procreate. Clearly, evolution often accounts for the accomplishment of a function with mechanisms that motivationally aim not directly at the function but rather at other goals that are correlated with the function. The relationship between erotic love and procreation is a prototypical example: Having sex is correlated with procreation; therefore, evolution builds in a sex drive, not a procreation drive. Generativity, too, could be a function of some motive, such as externalization, but not itself a specific motive.

Generativity: One Motive or Many?

Both Erikson and Plato saw generativity essentially in terms of one motive. Erikson was not precise about the intentional structure of this motive—whether it is a desire to nurture, to care for others, to perpetuate society, to assuage the sting of death, or something else—but it is clear that he considered all generativity to derive from this one motivational source through displacement and sublimation:

> There is, of course, always an alternative to pathogenic suppression, namely, *sublimation*; that is, the use of libidinal forces in psychosocial contexts. Consider only the increased capacity of some contemporary adults to "care" for some children not "biologically" their own. . . . And *generativity* always invites the possibility of an energetic shift to *productivity* and *creativity* in the service of the generations. (1985, p. 53)

Plato also saw all generativity as a manifestation of one basic desire, namely, the desire to achieve immortality. Both of these one-motive theories give rise to the substitutability thesis, that different kinds of generative products (e.g., children and theories) are motivationally equivalent and interchangeable. The implausibility of the substitutability thesis—people do not generally see creative work and having children as entirely substitutable for each other—is one objection to both approaches.

The idea that complex areas of human functioning are dominated by one motive is appealing to theorists but is implausible in the light of evolutionary considerations. The existence of a variety of motivational mechanisms with generative outcomes—for example, multiple submechanisms designed to maintain each area of procreative and creative endeavor—seems to be more likely.

However, this conclusion is in tension with another strong intuition, that all generative acts give one a distinctive kind of satisfaction. There is something similar about the satisfaction of nurturing one's child and the satisfaction of nurturing one's creative product beyond the metaphoric level. The commonality is not merely the fact that they are both acts of nurturing; there are many acts of nurturing that would not trigger the same kind of satisfaction. Rather, it appears to be the fact that, in shaping and bringing to fruition both one's child's development and one's creative work, aspects of the self are externalized. There is some degree of substitutability among such activities and products, although as noted, it is limited. The degree of substitutability seems to be due to the fact that both kinds of acts yield the same generative satisfaction, in addition to whatever more specific pleasures they yield. If a distinctive generative satisfaction exists, this suggests that some common motivational mechanism is being satisfied. Plato and Erikson may be understood as attempting to elucidate the nature of the motivational mechanism behind generative satisfaction.

There is a tension between two views. On the one hand, it seems implausible that a one-motive theory can explain the domain of generativity. The intuition here is that generativity as a unitary motive does not exist and that generativity is a basket of motives (e.g., procreativity and creativity) that have no inherent relationship except in how we categorize their outcomes. On the other hand, the phenomenology of generative satisfaction suggests the existence of one desire operating in all generative acts and domains. In the quest for an elegant theory of generative motivation, both Plato and Erikson emphasized the second intuition and played down the first. Indeed, because everyone knows about procreation, creativity, productivity, and so on, it is the very postulation of a relatively unified underlying motivational system that constitutes the construct of generativity. If no common motive exists, then it becomes questionable whether generativity as a theoretical entity (vs. an outcome) exists. However, this presupposition appears to be in tension with the manifest fact that generative activities are based on the operation of many disparate motivational mechanisms.

Externalization as a Metastage of Development

I believe that there is an appealing way to resolve the tension between one-motive and many-motive approaches to generativity. First, it is clearly true that there are many different motives with generative implications. Desires to nurture the young, to be remembered, to be productive, to compose a symphony, to discover scientific truths, to develop oneself to serve as a model of virtue and wisdom, to sacrifice oneself for one's society, and to achieve just laws and institutions are not derived from the same motivational mechanisms. Generativity is to this extent a bundle of mechanisms with varying specific functions.

However, there is also a truth to the one-motive theory. Motives that have generative implications, in addition to any idiosyncratic satisfactions they give, also yield a common generative satisfaction based on a higher order motivational mechanism. The substitutability of generative products exists to the extent and only to the extent that this generative satisfaction is common to all of them; substitutability is limited by the different satisfactions peculiar to each of the lower level mechanisms.

Why should such a common satisfaction be built into the functioning of a wide range of mechanisms? One may think of generative satisfaction as one half of an overarching developmental dichotomy. Roughly, it might be said that the early part of human life is absorbed primarily with what may be nature called "internalization"; the infant or child, through a variety of psychological processes, takes in information and structures from the social and physical environment that enable the child to gain competence, and he or she proceeds to master and integrate such internalizations. (Of course, such processes continue throughout life, but the dominant developmental challenge changes with age.) These internalizations range from memory for physical locales, perceptual development, and motor coordination to language learning, socialization, role acquisition, identity formation, and skill development. This "metastage" of internal structuralization relies on many different psychological mechanisms and processes that are each selected to solve a specific adaptive problem. These processes have in common only that the child "takes in" from the outside world and achieves the learning, inner structures, and skills that prepare him or her for adult roles and ultimately for generativity.

Despite the many different mechanisms involved in the internalization metastage, there seems to be a kind of generic motivation and consequent satisfaction involved in the learning, integration, and mastery process. It encompasses much of what has been referred to as the pleasure of effectance, or competence, and perhaps what Aristotle described as the pleasure of exercising one's faculties. When a child learns to sit up, to speak, to read, to play in organized sports, to learn adult ways, to become occupationally competent, and to do a myriad of other things that depend on learning and the skilled use of specific mechanisms, the child clearly feels a generic satisfaction in the mastery that the learning and internal structuralization have provided.

However, there comes a time when there arises a desire to produce something and no longer be a passive recipient and masterer of information and skills. This is the beginning of what might be considered the metastage of "externalization." Broadly speaking, when the adolescent finishes the tasks dominated by internalization, perhaps with occupational training and formation of an integrated identity within society's role structure as the last step, the rest of life is dominated by tasks that externalize what the individual's internalizations, transformed in accordance with the individual's unique internal nature, are capable of producing on behalf of society. The common generative motivation behind such actions can be obscured by the fact that, as noted, there are also more specific motives being satisfied. The desires to have children, to produce a good product, and to prove mathematical theorems are neither varieties of the same instinctual motive nor instrumentally chosen means to the same end, and the distinctive pleasures involved in these disparate activities provide one reason that people do not in fact see these activities as fully interchangeable alternatives. The motive to experience the pleasure of externalization has the function of producing generativity and perpetuating society, but it accomplishes these functions as a side effect. Creative writing is substitutable for having children, for example, only with respect to this one particular pleasure.

The externalization motive prompts one to place out into the world the results of the interaction of one's internalizations with one's unique nature. For this reason, people want not just to possess their individual ideas and values but to express them and see the world conform to them. They do not want only themselves to be immortal and thus want what lives after them to resemble them; more immediately, they want the intrinsic instinctual pleasure of externalizing what has formed within them and constitutes their unique nature and talent.

Therefore, the resolution of the tension between one-motive and many-motive approaches is that the one motive for externalization of the self—which is not specifically a motive to be generative but has the function of producing generativity—operates at a higher level than the many motives. The correlation between externalizing and generativity ensures society's perpetuation.

The externalization account can encompass Erikson's emphasis on nurturance, which is one of the best ways to project one's traits onto people who may live after one. Externalization theory also distinguishes generativity from altruistic urges, a challenge that Erikson's "nurturance" approach, as well as some more recent approaches, fails to address fully. Generative nurturance is in the service of externalizing the self (e.g., through procreation, teaching, or being a role model) or at least involves altruism toward future generations that thus expresses one's values after one is gone. Helping people in need out of altruistic regard for their suffering is of course admirable, but it is not generativity; a "birth" must be involved. (However, one may attempt to provide a model of generosity for others to follow or one may create altruistic institutions with the hope of enduringly influencing society's response to need; these are attempts to externalize one's altruism and are generative.)

Most of all, the externalization account expresses Plato's notion of generativity as "birth." Plato was correct in claiming that the generative moment comes when the individual wants to externalize his or her creations; simply having ideas, for example, is not enough. The urge is not just to live on through replacement but to do so specifically through the birthing of aspects of one's inner self. It is not implausible and deserves empirical testing that, as Plato suggested, externalized products are more satisfying if they are better, longer lasting, and connected to one's self. Concerning Plato's thesis that the birth is best inspired by beauty, it remains to be explored whether perception of beauty, in the broad sense that Plato intended, is indeed a potent trigger of the urge to externalize across a wide range of generative endeavors or whether Plato was here misled by the erotic–procreative model.

My hope, expressed at the beginning of this chapter, is that the field of generativity studies may be beneficially nurtured by the birth of some new theoretical ideas. Perhaps this may be so even if the new ideas are inspired by the beauty of Plato's theory and to this extent are very old indeed.

REFERENCES

Browning, D. (1975). *Generative man: Psychoanalytic perspectives*. New York: Dell.

De St. Aubin, E., & McAdams, D. P. (1995). The relations of generative concern and generative action to personality traits, satisfaction/happiness with life, and ego development. *Journal of Adult Development, 2*, 99–112.

Erikson, E. H. (1963). *Childhood and society* (2nd ed.). New York: Norton.

Erikson, E. H. (1964). *Insight and responsibility*. New York: Norton.

Erikson, E. H. (1985). *The life cycle completed: A review*. New York: Norton.

Erikson, E. H., Erikson, J. M., & Kivnick, H. Q. (1986). *Vital involvement in old age*. New York: Norton.

Freud, S. (1955). Group psychology and the analysis of the ego. In J. Strachey

(Ed. and Trans.), *The standard edition of the complete psychological works of Sigmund Freud* (Vol. 18, pp. 67–144). London: Hogarth Press. (Original work published 1921)

Jowett, B. (Trans.). (1956). *Plato's Symposium.* Indianapolis, IN: Bobbs-Merrill.

Kotre, J. (1984). *Outliving the self: Generativity and the interpretation of lives.* Baltimore: The Johns Hopkins University Press.

MacDermid, S. M., & Gillespie, L. (1992). *Generativity in multiple roles.* Paper presented at the Midwestern Psychological Association Convention, Chicago.

Mansfield, E. D., & McAdams, D. P. (1996). Generativity and themes of agency and communion in adult autobiography. *Personality and Social Psychology Bulletin, 22,* 721–731.

McAdams, D. P. (1985). *Power, intimacy, and the life story: Personological inquiries into identity.* New York: Guilford Press.

McAdams, D. P., & de St. Aubin, E. (1992). A theory of generativity and its assessment through self-report, behavioral acts, and narrative themes in autobiography. *Journal of Personality and Social Psychology, 62,* 1003–1015.

McAdams, D. P., de St. Aubin, E., & Logan, R. L. (1993). Generativity among young, midlife, and older adults. *Psychology and Aging, 8,* 221–230.

Peterson, B. E., & Stewart, A. J. (1993). Generativity and social motives in young adults. *Journal of Personality and Social Psychology, 65,* 186–198.

Santas, G. (1988). *Plato and Freud: Two theories of love.* Oxford, England: Basil Blackwell.

Snarey, J. (1993). *How fathers care for the next generation: A four-decade study.* Cambridge, MA: Harvard University Press.

Stewart, A. J., Franz, E., & Layton, L. (1988). The changing self: Using personal documents to study lives. *Journal of Personality, 56,* 41–74.

Vaillant, G. E. (1977). *Adaptation to life.* Boston: Little, Brown.

Vlastos, G. (1981a). The individual as an object of love in Plato. In *Platonic studies* (2nd ed., pp. 3–34). Princeton, NJ: Princeton University Press.

Vlastos, G. (1981b). The unity of virtues in the *Protagoras.* In *Platonic studies* (2nd ed., pp. 221–265). Princeton, NJ: Princeton University Press.

Wakefield, J. C. (1987). Why justice and holiness are similar: *Protagoras* 360–363. *Phronesis, A Journal for Ancient Philosophy, 32,* 267–276.

Wakefield, J. C. (1989). Levels of explanation in personality theory. In D. Buss & N. Cantor (Eds.), *Personality psychology: Recent trends and emerging directions* (pp. 333–346). New York: Springer-Verlag.

Wakefield, J. C. (1991). Vlastos on the unity of virtue: Why Pauline predication won't save the biconditionality thesis. *Ancient Philosophy, 11,* 47–65.

Wakefield, J. C. (1993). Is altruism part of human nature? Toward a theoretical foundation for the helping professions. *Social Service Review, 67,* 406–458.

II

GENERATIVITY IN SOCIETY, CULTURE, AND HISTORY

INTRODUCTION

The five chapters in Part 2 address the embeddedness of generativity in sociohistorical contexts. The first two of these chapters discuss the various social roles (parent, worker, community member) through which generativity is manifested and the social factors (gender, education, age) that shape generative expressions. The last three chapters each focus on a particular context (the gay community, Puritanism in the United States in the 1630s and the impact of the American Revolution after the 1770s, and Jewish Americans who survived the Holocaust) to explore unique forms of generativity.

Part 2 opens with *Generativity: At the Crossroads of Social Roles and Personality* (chapter 6) by Shelley M. MacDermid, Carol E. Franz, and Lee Ann De Reus. In this chapter, the authors examine the significance of social roles in terms of both social expectations and the behaviors of individuals in specific positions (or status groups in society) as conduits for the expression of generativity. These scholars implore generativity researchers to apply recent contributions to the social role literature to investigations of generativity. MacDermid, Franz, and De Reus provide a guide for future research in this area by outlining a set of propositions addressing the manner in which role *structures* and role *process* as well as role *opportunities* and *constraints* affect individual generativity. However, the authors offer more than these much needed conceptual linkages and advice by presenting the results of research that has begun to examine the theoretical propositions discussed. On the basis of three samples of women ($N = 181$), they demonstrate that experiences in multiple roles are interdependent but that generative expressions do indeed vary across social roles and that this variation has meaningful consequences for one's well-being. The chapter does much to alert scholars to the significance of social roles in conceptualizations of generativity and in attempts to relate generativity to outcome variables such as well-being.

It is this relation between generativity and well-being that is the crux of *Generativity in Adult Lives: Social Structural Contours and Quality of Life Consequences* (chapter 7) by Corey Lee M. Keyes and Carol D. Ryff. Employing a sample of over 3,000 adults (MacArthur Successful Midlife Development Project), these authors show that the study of generativity provides a crucial "sociopersonal" junction in the understanding of how society structures contemporary adults' health and well-being. Keyes and Ryff find that different aspects of generativity, as outcome variables, are shaped by the social factors of education (which motivates "generativity by instilling social concern and engendering the desire for reciprocity"), age, and gender. In addition to this look at how *society contours generativity*, the authors examine the process by which *generativity contours quality of life*. Separate measures of different components of generativity predict, in this sample, both psychological and social well-being. Finally, Keyes and Ryff explore the dynamics by which *generativity explains socioeconomic disparities in well-being*, noting that their data suggest that these dynamics shift considerably when age is taken into consideration. The authors display an impressive blend of research and theory in their use of a national probability sample (the first in generativity scholarship) to advance much needed theory addressing the social embeddedness of generativity.

The influence of the social context on individual manifestations of generativity is articulated through theory-building case study analyses in *Generativity, Social Context, and Lived Experience: Narratives of Gay Men in Middle Adulthood* (chapter 8) by Bertram J. Cohler, Andrew J. Hostetler, and Andrew Boxer. These authors begin the chapter with the presentation of a model by which scholars may study lives in context. This concise presentation of the *life course* approach to studying human development is perhaps the best we have seen. The authors next provide a discussion of generativity scholarship as perceived through this life course lens. Noting that "the narratives of gay men at midlife . . . provide fertile ground for exploration of the dialogic process between person and social order with respect to issues of generativity," these authors turn their attention to the structure and timing of the gay life course and embark on an in-depth exploration of generativity in the life stories of three gay men. The reader learns much about these three men and their generative commitments but also about the developmental barriers confronting gay men and lesbians who face social stigmatization, who face more personally than many others the plague of our time (HIV and AIDS), and whose lives are often off-time or entirely off-course. One also reads of the remedies for midlife adjustment that are part of the gay community context. Ultimately, one learns from this focused examination of three gay men how life course analyses shed light on the nature of generativity as expressed in different sociohistorical contexts.

The historical context of generativity is the focal point of Gerald F. Moran's *"Cares for the Rising Generation": Generativity in American History, 1607–1900* (chapter 9). Moran provides a history of generativity in the United States through historical case studies of two critical movements in U.S. history. He discusses the *Puritanism* that spread from England to the United States in the 1630s and the impact of the American Revolution on life and culture after the 1770s. Moran shows how the *regional* generative culture created by Puritans led to, in many ways, the *national* generative culture spurred by the revolution. However, the forms of generativity engendered by each historical force are quite distinct. Puritan generativity emphasized *parental generativity* because the family was the central conduit for religious socialization and the transmission of the covenant. Revolutionary generativity was built on secular values and English Libertarian thought and therefore stressed *public generativity* through public schooling and citizenship. The author profiles the differences between these separate forms of generativity and discusses the impact that each had on the people in the United States during these historical epochs.

Avi Kay also examines a unique form of generativity within a particular sociohistorical context in *Generativity in the Shadow of Genocide: The Holocaust Experience and Generativity* (chapter 10). Kay questions the relation between *genocide* and *generativity* through an examination of 20 Jewish Americans who were each living in Europe prior to the Holocaust. Ten of these adults are survivors of concentration camps. The other 10 form a contrast group in that each of these individuals relocated to either China or the former Soviet Union prior to the Holocaust and thus waited out this horror in relative isolation and safety until moving to the United States. Kay collected rich interview data from the participants and asked each to complete quantitative measures of generativity. What is it like, Kay asks, to try to care for the younger generation (generativity) when one has lived through a Holocaust that attempts to prevent the next generation from ever being born (genocide)? Kay offers insight as to why the generativity of the group of survivors is quite different from that of the refugees. For instance, the author explains why the survivors' generativity emphasizes the *creation* of a next generation, the *provision of material goods* to offspring, and the *lack of emotional connection* between survivors and their children. Furthermore, Kay describes how the *guilt* of the refugees in the contrast group stifles generative efforts.

6

GENERATIVITY: AT THE CROSSROADS OF SOCIAL ROLES AND PERSONALITY

SHELLEY M. MacDERMID, CAROL E. FRANZ, AND LEE ANN DE REUS

Generativity is vitally important to society. This is a strong statement on behalf of a theoretical construct given only passing attention by some scholars. Its sentiment is provoked by the tension between competing trends in popular culture. On the one hand, recent books (e.g., Edelman, 1992) exhort parents and youth to live lives of deeper moral commitment. Public service announcements on television cajole viewers to assist the less fortunate by mentoring children in the community or donating 5 hours per week to volunteer work. At the same time, however, welfare reform initiatives trumpet the importance of "personal responsibility," repeatedly reducing the tangible support for poor parents and promoting attitudes that disproportionately blame "welfare mothers" for national budgetary problems. Edelman argued that the "greatest threat to our ... future comes

This research was supported by a grant to Shelley MacDermid and Carol Franz from the Character and Competence Research Program, a grant to Shelley MacDermid from the Midlife Research Program of the Henry A. Murray Research Center, and a grant to Shelley MacDermid from the Purdue Research Foundation. The preparation of this chapter would not have been possible without the labor of Adena Altschul, a participant in the Purdue University MARC-AIM program, and Stephen Smith. We are grateful to Barbara Burek of the Institute for Human Development at the University of California at Berkeley and to Gabriela Heilbrun and Laura Gillespie de Haan for their contributions to the research presented here.

181

from no external enemy but from the enemy within" (p. 19). We believe that the "enemy within" is a lack of generativity and that a thorough understanding of generativity and its expression is essential to a well-functioning society.

"Generativity vs. stagnation" is the seventh the eight stages of psychosocial development proposed by Erikson (1968). Occupying the period of life between early adulthood and old age, the generativity versus stagnation stage is theorized to confront adults for about half their lives, longer than any other stage. In its essence, generativity involves a shift in individual interests from the focus on "I" and "me" during adolescence and young adulthood to a focus on the larger world—to "we" (Kroger, 1989). According to Eriksonian theory, generativity is expressed both inside and outside one's family in efforts to guide and care for subsequent generations and to "maintain the world" (Erikson, Erikson, & Kivnick, 1986, p. 73).

Although many scholars have provided important insights, one area of the landscape that is still poorly mapped is the consideration of generativity in the context of social roles, particularly in quantitative research. Our thesis in this chapter is that more differentiated and systematic approaches to social roles will yield important new insights about generativity. Specifically, we argue that generative expressions vary across social roles; that such variation is theoretically important and empirically related to important outcomes; and that this variation is the result, in part, of individuals actively selecting, managing, and manipulating opportunities for generative expression across their role systems. We believe that more differentiated and systematic approaches will help to untangle confusing patterns of change, stability, consistency, and variability in generativity observed by researchers so far (Bengtson, Reedy, & Gordon, 1985).

We begin our discussion by assessing the treatment of social roles in Eriksonian theory and research about generativity and by identifying trends in the adult development literature that have previously directed attention away from social roles. Next, we turn to the large body of theory and research about social roles to enhance our understanding of generativity. We consider both role structures and role processes, drawing on our discussion to develop a series of propositions to guide researchers in the study of social roles. Some of these propositions have been tested in our program of research, and we summarize the relevant results. Finally, we present the results of new analyses to stimulate future theory building and research about generativity in the context of social roles.

For the purposes of this chapter, we use an inclusive definition of *role*. We see roles as composed of both the cultural expectations for a position or status in society and the behavior of persons occupying such positions or statuses (Nye & Gecas, 1976). We focus primarily on a wide range of relatively public or formal roles shaped by shared expectations, as opposed to informal private roles (Stryker & Statham, 1985). Although Thoits

(1987) argued that roles are social by definition, we use the explicit phrase "social role" to emphasize our focus on generative expressions directed toward others.

SOCIAL ROLES IN THEORY AND RESEARCH CONCERNING GENERATIVITY

Social Roles in Theory

It is difficult to argue that involvement in various roles is *not* implicated in development given the amount of time adults spend as parents, partners, workers, friends, worshippers, and citizens. Indeed, the ability to select and maintain role commitments may be both a marker of a healthy identity and a mechanism for promoting further development (Franz & White, 1985; Grotevant, 1987; Helson, Elliott, & Leigh, 1990; Hornstein, 1986; Josselson, 1987; Kroger, 1989; Stewart & Gold-Steinberg, 1990; Waterman, 1982, 1988, 1992).

Role involvements figure prominently in the developmental perspectives on adulthood of Erikson and others (e.g., Bourne, 1978; Brooks-Gunn & Kirsh, 1984; Kotre, 1984; Levinson, 1980; see also Muuss, 1988). Hornstein (1986, p. 552), for example, called for a "dynamic model of identity that incorporates this notion of multiple role commitments." Juhasz (1989) proposed a triple-helix model of development embedded in the roles of family, work, and self. Levinson defined the entire "life structure" in terms of roles at work, in the family, and with other social groups and institutions (Levinson, 1980, cited in Wrightsman, 1994; Levinson, 1996).

Erikson also acknowledged the importance of participation in social roles. In his formulation, generativity is concerned primarily with "establishing and guiding the next generation" (Erikson, 1950/1963, p. 267). Generative expressions toward succeeding generations are not limited to the obvious parental role of bearing and rearing children: "The concept of generativity is meant to include such more popular synonyms as productivity and creativity, which, however, cannot replace it" (Erikson, 1950/1963, p. 267). Rather, healthy generative concerns extend beyond the family to the larger society:

> Matured adulthood, then, means a set of vital involvements in life's generative activities. . . . Some such combination [of generative ways] must assure the vitality of an order of care to those *wide* [italics added] areas of adult involvements which, according to a Hindu expression, guarantee the "maintenance of the world." All this, in short, leads to participation in areas of involvement in which one can learn to take care of what one truly cares for. (Erikson et al., 1986, p. 50)

Erikson's use of the word *wide* to describe desirable areas of involvement suggests that he considered participation in a diverse array of social roles important for optimal adult functioning. The necessity of participation in social roles for generative expression is especially clear when one observes the isolation inherent in self-absorption—the antithesis of generativity—defined by Erikson as "a lack of enriching interpersonal relations, and indulgence in oneself as one's own beloved only child" (1950; paraphrased by Bradley, 1988, p. 5).

Although social roles are assigned an important function in a number of developmental perspectives, this emphasis is not evident in most quantitative measures of generativity. In the following section, we illustrate this point by examining a number of existing measures.

Social Roles in Existing Measures of Generativity

Early quantitative measures of generativity were borrowed from inventories of personality traits. For example, Ryff and Migdal (1984) selected subscales of the Jackson Personality Inventory (JPI) to measure innovation and dominance as indicators of generativity. Because the JPI is intended for the "prediction of behavior in a wide variety of settings" (Jackson, 1976, p. 5), the items avoid systematic attention to any social role (e.g., "I am always seeking new ways to look at things"; Ryff & Migdal, 1984, p. 475).

A number of instruments have been developed specifically to measure generativity. Although most of these measures include items about particular social roles, they were not developed with the goal of systematic and balanced coverage. For example, the generativity items in Darling-Fisher and Leidy's (1987, 1988) Modified Erikson Psychosocial Stage Inventory (MEPSI) focus on "characteristic" patterns transcending particular roles or situations. The only item that specifically mentions social roles combines two of them: "I feel that I have left my mark on the world through my children/work" (Darling-Fisher & Leidy, 1987, p. 5). Similarly, Oschse and Plug (1986) explicitly mentioned only one role, devoting 4 of their 10 items to parenting.

Two measures include a broader range of social roles. Ryff and Heincke's (1983) generativity scale includes 3 items about work, 1 item about parenthood, 1 item about community organizations, and 5 items about younger people. The Loyola Generativity Scale (McAdams & de St. Aubin, 1992; McAdams, de St. Aubin, & Logan, 1993) consists of 20 items that do perhaps the best job in tapping the breadth of generative expressions, with at least one question about guiding younger people (including but not limited to one's own children), volunteer work, teaching, creative endeavors, productive efforts, and community work.

As we have shown, balanced and systematic attention to social roles is not pervasive in the measurement of generativity. Because this is so, it is reasonable to consider what advantages such attention offers. First, measures of generativity cannot be construct valid unless they fully represent the range of generative expressions acknowledged by Erikson. These include productive and creative activities, caring for younger or less experienced others (not necessarily parenting one's own children), maintaining societal institutions, and exhibiting care toward others (Erikson, 1950/1963; Erikson et al., 1986; Hulsizer et al., 1981).

A second advantage of balanced and systematic attention to social roles is the opportunity to replace unintentional assumptions made in the past with new empirical questions. For example, the traditional practices of asking global questions or aggregating generative expressions across social roles to create an overall total assumes that generative action in one social role is interchangeable with action in another. In addition, high generativity scores may be assigned more often to individuals who express generativity in many roles than to individuals who express generativity intensely in a smaller number of roles. Aggregation also prevents examination of the degree to which expressions of generativity are consistent across social roles and the implications of this consistency (or lack of it). Each of these issues should be resolved by analysis rather than assumption.

It also is important to consider *why* social roles have been sparsely studied by generativity researchers. Inattentiveness could be the result of careful deliberations determining that social roles are neither theoretically nor empirically significant, in which case our current interest would be considered unjustified. If inattentiveness to social roles were the result of biases or untested assumptions, however, scrutiny now might be especially important.

WHY HAVE SOCIAL ROLES RECEIVED LITTLE ATTENTION IN THE STUDY OF GENERATIVITY?

Lack of Comprehensive Attention to Psychological and Behavioral Expressions of Generativity

Erikson and others present Erikson's theory as a theory of personality development (e.g., Erikson, 1968; Wrightsman, 1988), and much of the research on generativity has been conducted by personality psychologists. There has been considerable debate, however, about how *personality* should be defined. When personality is considered purely a psychological phenomenon, behavior in social roles is less relevant. To the extent that researchers focus exclusively on behavior, the links between psychological expressions of generativity (and behavior in social roles) and the processes that produce generative behavior are irrelevant.

The study of generativity mirrors the conceptual literature in terms of varying emphases on its psychological and behavioral dimensions. The psychological emphasis is evident in the work of Carol Ryff, one of a few scholars who recently have conducted quantitative research on generativity, specifically on psychological perceptions of stability and change over time. Ryff and Migdal (1984) asked young adult and middle-aged women to characterize themselves at present, as they recalled themselves in the past, or how they anticipated themselves in the future. Generativity was measured using subscales of the JPI. A sample item of this personality inventory is the item "I feel confident when directing the activities of others." Because generativity was treated as a purely psychological aspect of personality, it was irrelevant to ask whether individuals scoring high on psychological generativity also expressed generativity behaviorally in their social roles.

Other researchers have adopted a more behavioral emphasis. Vaillant and Milofsky (1980), for example, classified members of their male sample as generative if they demonstrated responsibility for guiding the next generation by occupying roles such as "consultant, guide, mentor, or coach" (p. 1350). Although generative behavior was central to the measurement strategy, processes leading to it were excluded from consideration, as they were in Ryff and Migdal's (1984) study.

Although models incorporating both psychological and behavioral expressions of generativity are rare, an exception is that of McAdams and de St. Aubin (1992), who proposed that generative action is an outcome of the joint effects of motivation, thoughts, and plans. A number of McAdams's studies have demonstrated significant connections between psychological and behavioral manifestations of generativity (i.e., correlations were reported of .59, .32, and .20, respectively, by McAdams & de St. Aubin, 1992; McAdams et al., 1993; and Van de Water & McAdams, 1989). McAdams and de St. Aubin's framework is an important contribution to the literature on generativity because it begins to build a vision of the *processes* through which generative expressions are developed, selected, and implemented. The psychological elements of the model are more fully developed than the behavioral ones, however, and social roles are not given explicit attention. The observed empirical links between generative thoughts and generative actions vary in strength and are weak in some samples, leaving unresolved questions about how particular generative actions come to be expressed.

Another exception is Bradley's (in press; Bradley & Marcia, in press) recently developed Generativity Status Measure, which assigns individuals to one of five generativity styles or statuses on the basis of the degree to which their thoughts and actions are inclusive (i.e., defined in relation to the scope of caregiving activity) and involved (i.e., "the degree of active concern for the growth of oneself and others, a sense of responsibility for sharing skills and knowledge, and the ability to follow through with commitments"; Bradley, in press, p. 24). Again, although the inclusion of both psychological and behavioral expressions of generativity is commendable, Bradley's model excludes consideration of the relationship between the expressions and the processes that produce them.

Therefore, lack of attention to social roles in the study of generativity is at least in part due to the way that personality and generativity have been defined by researchers. Psychological emphases lead interest away from behavior in social roles, and emphases on behavior exclude links between psychological expressions of generativity and behavior in social roles that may be key to the processes that produce generative behavior. If the expression and production of generativity are to be thoroughly understood, not only its psychological and behavioral expressions but also the relationships between them deserve study.

Overemphasis in Personality Research on Stability (Over Time) and Consistency (Across Situations)

A second reason that social roles have been given little attention in quantitative generativity research is that the stability and consistency of personality have been emphasized over its variability in recent years (Emmons, 1995). From some perspectives, the term *personality development* almost seems an oxymoron when applied to adults—certainly according to McCrae and Costa (1990, p. 152), who have asserted that "personality does not change much after age 30." Overemphasis on personality traits (Helson & Stewart, 1994) and overgeneralization of consistency as a feature of personality traits (Zuroff, 1986) have sometimes resulted in change being defined more often as a failure to find stability than as a worthy phenomenon in its own right (Becker, 1968; Helson, 1993; Helson & Stewart, 1994; see also Mischel, 1990). Views of adult personality as stable over time and consistent across situations provoke little interest in generativity and how it may vary over time or across social roles. Because, theoretically, generativity develops during adulthood, the debate among personality psychologists concerning whether personality is stable or consistent over time also affects how generativity is studied.

It is difficult to assess the stability and consistency of generativity. Because the midlife period is several decades long and varies both historically and culturally, there are relatively few data sets that permit true longitudinal examination (i.e., without relying on retrospective judgments). Furthermore, the study of consistency has focused so far solely on variation in psychological expressions of generativity along multiple themes observed in written or verbal material. Behavioral consistency across social roles has not yet been studied. Nonetheless, like personality in general (e.g., domain-specific attitudes about the self, affective variables, intrapsychic processes, intellectual and ethical reasoning; Franz, 1994; Gilligan, Murphy, & Tappan, 1990; Haan, 1981; Haan & Day, 1974; Helson, 1993; Lachman, 1989; Neugarten, 1973), evidence is mounting that generativity changes over time and varies across situations or roles.

One innovative program of research that explores both the stability and the consistency of generative expressions has focused on the written works of Vera Brittain, a British writer and activist (Franz, 1988; Peterson & Stewart, 1990; Stewart, Franz, & Layton, 1988). Generative themes identified in Eriksonian theory (e.g., caring, productivity, and the need to be needed) were coded in Brittain's fiction and diaries. Over several decades, the generative themes ebbed and flowed in prominence (Peterson & Stewart, 1990). The patterns of change differed for each theme, rising and falling in concert with changes Brittain was confronting in her social roles of mother, wife, and writer. For example, the caring theme surged to very high levels during a wartime separation of Brittain from her children. Although intriguing, these patterns of change over time and variation across situations apply to only one person, and their generalizability is uncertain.

Opportunities to study the stability and consistency of generativity longitudinally in a large sample of men and women from various socioeconomic backgrounds have been provided by the data archive of the Institute for Human Development at the University of California at Berkeley. In a recent investigation, MacDermid, Franz, and De Reus (in press) examined data gathered on three occasions during a 20-year period in the lives of participants from two studies—the Oakland Growth Study and the Berkeley Guidance Study—who were from different birth cohorts. The dependent variables were Q-sort-based Generative Realization scores constructed using procedures developed by Peterson (Peterson & Kloehnen, 1995; Peterson & Stewart, 1993).

In group-level analyses, total generativity appeared quite stable over time. For example, participants in the Oakland Growth Study showed no change, on average, in generative realization during their 40s or 50s. The apparent stability at the group level was, however, the result of offsetting patterns of *instability* at the individual level. Among the Oakland birth cohort, equal numbers of participants increased or decreased at least one half of a standard deviation or displayed no change. Examination of individual trajectories of change revealed great diversity, including ascending and descending linear patterns and positive and negative quadratic patterns across the three data points.

Descriptive comparisons of men and women who increased or decreased in generativity during their fifth decade of life suggested that patterns of participation in social roles were related to trajectories of change in generativity. For men, conformity to traditional social expectations (e.g., getting married, having multiple children, and serving as the main breadwinner) appeared to accompany rising generativity. For women, however, increases in generativity were not consistently associated with conformity. Rather, increases were more likely for women who conformed to expectations for homemaking and motherhood or who *violated* expectations of marrying only once or having an employed spouse (MacDermid, Franz, & De Reus, in press).

These studies and others provide reliable evidence of change over time and variation across situations in both psychological and behavioral expressions of generativity. We also have tantalizing clues that social roles may be implicated in shifts in generative expressions. Lack of attention to social roles in the study of generativity, therefore, seems to have been the result of disproportionate emphasis on stability rather than careful theoretical decision making. Because our current interest appears to be justified, in the following section we examine the larger literature on social roles for propositions we might usefully extrapolate to the study of generativity.

ROLE THEORIES AND GENERATIVITY

Roles are among the most often-studied concepts in all of sociology and are a central feature of symbolic interactionism, a perspective developed to understand "how humans, in concert with one another, create symbolic worlds and how these worlds, in turn, shape human behavior" (LaRossa & Reitzes, 1993, p. 136). Formal roles are both positions and functions that individuals may serve in society (Nye & Gecas, 1976). As positions, roles are categories or statuses that have a recognized place in the social structure; "police officer" and "schoolteacher" are examples. Within positions, however, there are often multiple functions that individuals may choose or be expected to take on: "mentor" and "disciplinarian," for example.

Whatever their form, roles are shaped by expectations for particular behaviors, feelings, and emotions to be displayed by their occupants (LaRossa & Reitzes, 1993, p. 147). Expectations may be formal or informal (LaRossa & Reitzes) and may provide rewards and sanctions on the basis of the degree to which they are met. Individuals experience role expectations from outside themselves and from within, self-imposed consciously or unconsciously by internalized expectations learned through observation and socialization (Stryker & Statham, 1985).

Both role structures and role processes have been of interest to researchers (Nye & Gecas, 1976). Aspects of role *structure* include characteristics not only of individual roles but also of systems of multiple roles that are interdependent (Stryker & Statham, 1985). Especially relevant to generativity, and considered here, are the merits of role-specific (vs. global or aggregated) approaches; research on the degree to which commitments across the role system are balanced; the breadth, diversity, and quality of experiences in the role system; and characteristics of individual roles.

Role *processes* focus on the manner in which roles are socially constructed by interactions between individuals and situations and on the initiative of individuals in selecting, managing, and manipulating their role involvements (Burr, Leigh, Day, & Constantine, 1979; Stryker & Statham, 1985). Attention to the emergent property of roles is fundamental because "the meanings people assign to things ultimately organize their behavior" (Stryker & Statham, 1985, p. 320). Although there are many aspects of role processes, our major focus will be on the role of individuals in shaping their generative expressions.

Generativity and Aspects of Role Structure

Role-Specific Versus Global or Aggregated Approaches

Whereas experiences in particular roles have been linked to well-being, the study of generativity rarely has adopted a systematic approach to social roles in which multiple roles are given specific individual attention (for partial exceptions, see McAdams & de St. Aubin, 1992; Peterson & Stewart, 1992; Vaillant & Milsofsky, 1980). The literature on adolescent development, however, has much to offer the study of generativity in this area.

In the most influential expansion of Erikson's theory concerning the stage of "identity vs. role confusion," Marcia (1980) classified adolescents' levels of ego identity development according to the degree to which the adolescents had explored and made commitments to particular social roles. Dissatisfaction has arisen with "identity statuses," however, because they fail to take into account that individuals develop at different rates across role domains (Archer, 1992; Bandura, 1990; Cote & Levine, 1988; Kroger, 1989; Waterman, 1985).

In research that examined domains individually, Kroger and Haslett (1991) found significant variability among the domains of vocation, religion, politics, and relationships in adults' recollections from adolescence to adulthood. Waterman (1982) offered evidence of differential stability across domains and different patterns of participation in social roles as a function of identity status. As a result, there is now a well-established body of work on adolescence that adopts a domain- or role-specific approach in which identity development is measured separately in each of several roles. This strategy has allowed researchers to observe, for example, different decision-making processes across domains among adolescents selecting role commitments (Archer, 1992).

Although domain- or role-specific approaches are not well developed in the study of adulthood, the existing evidence is encouraging. For example, Lachman (1986) showed that domain-specific measures of control are more sensitive to changes related to aging and its correlates. Specifically regarding generativity, Peterson and Stewart (1993) found in a sample of young adults that various psychological motives were differentially linked to three types of generative action: parenting involvement, personal productivity, and societal concern. Although the measures of generative action were not sophisticated, intriguing differences were observed across domains. For example, generative action that conformed to traditional gender roles was related to motivations for power, whereas cross-gender generative activity was related to motivations for achievement. The researchers speculated that individuals motivated by power are seeking recognition and impact, which may be more forthcoming in response to conforming behavior, whereas individuals motivated by achievement may be seeking a sense of personal accomplishment yielded by nonconforming behavior. The fine-grained analysis and rich theoretical implications of this study would not have been possible without systematic and differentiated attention to multiple domains of both psychological and behavioral functioning.

Role-specific approaches offer opportunities to ask many new questions about generativity. For example, variability in generative expressions across roles can be explicitly examined, as can the implications of such variability. Because role-specific approaches have the potential to be more precise and fine-grained than global or aggregated approaches, they also are likely to be more effective in explaining variability in outcome variables. Our own research has examined this possibility; we describe our results in a later section.

Proposition 1: Domain- or role-specific approaches to generativity in social roles explain greater variability in psychological and behavioral outcomes than do global or aggregated approaches.

Degree to Which Role Commitments Are Balanced

Much of the research on multiple roles has been stimulated by William Goode's (1960) proposition that strain inevitably results from competing demands among individuals' various roles. Goode's view has been labeled the "role scarcity" hypothesis because it assumes finite energy: If one role receives attention, another necessarily must be denied. A competing view, the "role enhancement" hypothesis, was proposed by Marks (1977), who argued that roles may generate energy for one another. Empirical evidence suggests that both scarcity and enhancement may operate, but on different occasions across individuals, times, and situations (Baruch & Barnett, 1986; Tiedje et al., 1990; see also Moen, Dempster-McClain, & Williams's "role-context" approach, 1989, 1992).

A pervasive but untested assumption in the study of role scarcity and enhancement has been that role identities are organized hierarchically and that the salience of any one identity moderates its link to well-being (Nutt-brock & Freudiger, 1991; Thoits, 1992). It is not clear, however, that a hierarchy exists. For example, in an ambitious study of 17 different roles (Thoits), role salience was unrelated to psychological symptoms, either directly or in interaction with stress. Hierarchies that have been observed may have been methodological artifacts of the request that respondents rank order their roles.

Recently, Marks and MacDermid (1996) criticized the assumption that role systems are organized hierarchically, arguing that the holistic pattern of organization of the role *system* may be as important as or more important than the salience of any one role. Marks and MacDermid proposed "role balance" as a construct characterizing the degree to which one becomes "fully engaged in the performance of every role in one's total role system" (p. 418). From this perspective, role strain results from unbalanced patterns of over- and undercommitment to multiple roles. Using both single- and multiple-item measures of role balance, Marks and MacDermid found that respondents in two different samples (65 employed mothers and 303 male and female college students) who reported greater role balance also reported greater role ease, less role overload, higher self-esteem, and less depression. Individuals reporting higher role balance were not, however, any less busy than individuals reporting less balanced roles (i.e., employed mothers did not work fewer hours; college students were not taking fewer credit hours, working fewer hours, or seeing fewer friends).

Although the relationship between generativity and role balance has not yet been studied, balanced role systems may offer greater opportunities for generative expression and greater likelihood that such expressions will occur as a result. Because role balance is negatively related to role strain, individuals with more balanced commitments may feel more able to express generativity because they are under less strain.

Proposition 2: *Expressions of generativity are positively related to the degree to which patterns of commitment across the role system are balanced.*

Breadth and Diversity

Another aspect of role structure that is particularly interesting to developmentalists is the breadth and diversity of individuals' role systems: the number of roles in which individuals participate and the range of experience offered by those roles. Although early researchers worried that involvement in increased numbers of roles would have detrimental consequences for well-being, virtually all empirical evidence suggests that the breadth of the role system either enhances or is unrelated to well-being (Bronfenbrenner, 1979; Bronfenbrenner & Crouter, 1983; Moen et al., 1989; Nuttbrock & Freudiger, 1991). Hornstein (1986) and Fiske (1980), for example, observed both role additions (increasing the breadth of their role systems) and role substitutions (which would not increase breadth but could increase diversity) among well-functioning adults. Fiske (1980) observed well-functioning individuals in her sample who were involved in relatively few commitments throughout their lives.

Regarding generativity, Eriksonian theory suggests that breadth and diversity of role systems should be positively related to expressions of generativity. The emphasis on isolation in the antithesis of generativity underscores the importance of social involvement for healthy adult development. Larger and more diverse role systems provide more opportunities for generative expression, which in turn should result in greater likelihood of expression.

Proposition 3: Individuals whose role systems are larger, more diverse, or both are more likely to express generativity.

Quality of Experience

Studies have routinely found that the quality of experience in particular roles is as important as or more important than the number of roles occupied for psychological well-being (Barnett & Baruch, 1987; Baruch & Barnett, 1986; Heidrich & Ryff, 1993; Helson et al., 1990), physical health (Helson et al., 1990; Moen et al., 1992; Verbrugge, 1987), and longevity (Moen et al., 1989).

Research on multiple roles and the role enhancement perspective (Marks, 1977) suggest that the same role arrangements may be invigorating for some and stressful for others (Stryker & Statham, 1985). The time and energy available for individuals to devote to their role involvements vary widely and appear to be a function of their subjective experience more than of objective role demands or finite capacities (Marks). For example, individuals' feelings of control over the demands they face in their work and family roles are more important for their psychological and physical well-being than their family structure, number of overtime work hours, or income (Thomas & Ganster, 1995). Extrapolating this finding to the area of generativity, one might expect generative expressions to be less likely to occur when individuals feel strained or negatively evaluate their experience in a given role, regardless of its objective characteristics.

Proposition 4: Individuals are more likely to express generativity in roles in which they evaluate their experiences positively.

Variations in the Relative Importance of Roles

Researchers also have been interested in the *relative* importance of particular roles for well-being. For example, Moen et al., (1989, 1992) found that involvement in a particular role—membership in voluntary organizations—was notable in its reliable links to both health and longevity in a large longitudinal sample. Provocative suggestions have emerged from the study of adolescence that some parents may be "propelled" to confront the developmental tasks of midlife, such as generativity, by their children's adolescence (Colarusso & Nemiroff, 1982; Farrell & Rosenberg, 1981; Silverberg, 1989; Silverberg & Steinberg, 1987). At a time when midlife adults are confronting a generative need to guide the younger generation, younger individuals are striving for greater individuation and autonomy. Midlife adults may need to renegotiate their relationships simultaneously with their parents and their children (Erikson et al., 1986; Rodeheaver & Datan, 1981). For example, as midlife parents face declining sexual attractiveness and finite career prospects, they may be confronted with adolescents reaching their peak of physical development with entire careers before them. Each generation has its own "stake" in developmental issues (Colarusso & Nemiroff, 1982; Erikson, 1950/1963; Hulsizer et al., 1981; Lerner, 1986), and these stakes at times may compete (Kidwell, Fischer, Dunham, & Baranowski, 1983; McArthur, 1962). Supporting empirical evidence comes from Silverberg (1989), who found in a longitudinal study of 157 families that parents' reports of midlife concerns increased as a function of their same-sex child's emotional autonomy (although the relationship for mothers was bidirectional). Thus, some roles may be especially important during particular developmental periods.

Another contribution in this area has been the questioning of expectations that men and women each have "core" roles that are uniquely central to their well-being (Archer, 1992; Hornstein, 1986; Stewart & Gold-Steinberg, 1990). Specifically with regard to generativity, "it has been generally assumed that women's major generative role is motherhood" (Stewart & Gold-Steinberg, p. 544; see also Gergen, 1990; Neugarten, 1968). Such stereotypes have not been limited to women: "The core assumption has been that work is [men's] chief activity, their 'master role,' the very essence of what makes them men" (Cohen, 1987, p. 57).

A number of studies have shown, however, that both men's and women's well-being is linked to multiple roles that do not necessarily conform to gender-based stereotypes (e.g., Barnett, Marshall, & Pleck, 1992; Barnett, Marshall, Raudenbush, & Brennan, 1993; Coleman, Antonucci, & Adelmann, 1987). For example, Barnett, Marshall, and Pleck found that the quality of men's experiences in their work and family roles contributed equally to their psychological well-being. Thoits (1992) failed to find differences between men and women in the priority accorded 17 role identities, even after controlling for age, cohort, and life-cycle stage.

Current research and theory suggest that for both men and women, healthy generativity is characterized by a balance of instrumental (also called *agency, power, productivity, self-expansion,* and *self-centered life interests*) and expressive (also labeled *communion, intimacy, caring, self-sacrifice,* or *other-centered life interests*) concerns. Although these themes correspond to early conceptions of sex-linked roles in society (Parsons, 1955), recent findings emphasize balance over the specialization once thought optimal (Mansfield & McAdams, 1996). Thus, having a variety of roles is likely important for both men and women.

This possibility is foreshadowed in a recent study by Mansfield and McAdams (1996), in which 70 adults from various socioeconomic levels were classified as more or less generative on the basis of their involvement in teaching or unpaid volunteer work with young people and scores on measures of generative concern and generative behavior. The high- and low-generativity individuals were contrasted in terms of agency and communion themes and the integration of agency and communion evident in life-story interviews. The groups differed significantly in communion and in agency–communion integration. None of the findings appeared to be related to the gender of the respondents. Perhaps the integration of agency and communion was instead related to individuals' involvement in social or affiliative generative activities (e.g., volunteer work or teaching) as opposed to more solitary ones (e.g., creative or artistic work). Continued efforts to devote comprehensive and systematic attention to role behavior for both men and women, as manifested in this study, will yield important insights about the expression of generativity.

Proposition 5: Generative expressions in particular roles vary in their importance for developmental outcomes and individual well-being.

Interrelationships Among Roles

Other research has focused on the interrelationships among roles. For example, Baruch and Barnett (1986) found that the strength of links to well-being for women varied across parental, spousal, and work roles. Positive perceptions of experiences in one role also were found to compensate for negative experiences in another, except for the marital role: Nothing could compensate for negative experiences as a spouse. Barnett, Marshall, and Pleck (1992) found that positive experiences as husbands and fathers buffered men from negative mental health consequences of negative experiences on the job. Other research has identified interrelationships among specific elements of role experiences: Among 228 mothers who were practical nurses or social workers, a sense of challenge in the work role was associated with less disaffection in the parental role (Barnett, Marshall, & Sayer, 1992).

Because role-specific approaches have not been used previously in the study of generativity, there are no data that address the degree to which expressions of generativity across roles are interdependent. It seems important to know, however, whether difficulty with generative expressions in one role can be ameliorated by fulfillment in another. Prior research on multiple roles has suggested that this may be the case.

Proposition 6: Positive generative experiences in one role may compensate for negative experiences in another.

Developmental Sequences of Roles

Another aspect of social roles relevant to the study of generativity is change in their patterns over time. As the life course perspective emphasizes, widely held social expectations shape individuals' participation during their lives in an age-graded series of social roles (Bengtson & Allen, 1993; Caspi, 1987). This role participation occurs within multiple temporal (e.g., individual time and generational time) and social (e.g., family context and cultural context; Bengtson & Allen) layers.

Developmental progressions through social roles are evident in the work of Levinson (1980), Kotre (1984), and Snarey (1993). Kotre, for example, proposed four types of generativity based on particular activities: bearing children (biological), rearing and socializing children (parental), teaching skills to successors (technical), and passing the "culture" on to successors (cultural). These four types of generativity are thought to have a loose developmental order, in which biological generativity typically is exhibited before the other types and has a relatively short duration, whereas cultural generativity begins later in life and may occur over a longer period of time. Although biological and parental generativity occur within the parental role, technical and cultural generativity may occur in a wide variety of roles. Kotre wondered whether negative consequences may result from off-time or poorly coordinated expressions of different types of generativity, such as when teenagers bear children before they are prepared to rear and socialize them.

Snarey (1993) built on Kotre's work by examining progressions in biological, parental, and societal generativity across interviews conducted with 240 men when they were 25, 31, and 47 years old. Men who became fathers (either with no problem, after treatment for infertility, or by adoption) all scored significantly higher in societal generativity at midlife than did men who remained childless. Thus, parental generativity may indeed provide a foundation for societal generativity.

Proposition 7: There may be a developmental progression to generative expressions in particular roles, with generativity in more proximal roles (e.g., family) serving as a precursor to generativity in more distal roles (e.g., society).

Opportunities for, and Constraints on, Generative Expression

Another structural aspect of social roles is provided by the opportunities and constraints the roles pose for behavior (Cantor & Zirkel,

1990). According to Stryker and Statham (1985), individuals manage competing interests of imposition and improvisation. Impositions, or constraints, emerge from long-standing routines of interaction with others or cues based on prior experience (Caspi & Elder, 1992, call these "situational imperatives"). Improvisation is thought to be provoked by role structures that involve greater diversity (Stryker & Statham). In addition, role expectations are seldom completely clear, rigid, and invariant, leaving opportunities to improvise, negotiate, and compromise (Thoits, 1987). Improvisation may be suppressed, however, if role demands are overly challenging, that is, too ambiguous, excessive, conflicting, or overly complex (Peterson, 1987). Constraints also may be posed by aspects of the cultural context. For example, the standards for appropriate behavior and the range of opportunities available to individuals vary according to categories indexed by social class, gender, and marital status (Pearlin, 1980; Thoits, 1987). The study of such constraints must be undertaken carefully so that privileged social classes will not be favored (e.g., Neugarten, 1968). After all, Erikson (Hall, 1987, p. 134) admonished that the "generative contributions of a good plumber" should not be underestimated.

In the literature on social roles, Kohn's (1977) classic research on occupational self-direction is an excellent example of constraints and opportunities posed by a role setting. Kohn demonstrated that parents with few opportunities to exercise independent judgment at work experienced reductions in intellectual flexibility themselves and placed greater value on conformity in their children. As in occupational self-direction, it is likely that individuals are not free to express generativity in any role they choose; aspects of the role setting influence, although probably do not fully determine, generative expressions.

Proposition 8: Role settings both constrain and provide opportunities for expressions of generativity.

Conclusion

Our examination of the theory and research on multiple roles has led to a number of recommendations for studying generativity in the context of social roles and the structure of role systems. In the next section we consider role processes, specifically the role of individuals in shaping their generative expressions.

The Role of Individuals in Shaping Expressions of Generativity

Although the maturational nature of Erikson's theory suggests to some scholars that individuals are not influential (e.g., Lerner, 1986), Erikson emphasized both the enormous flexibility of developmental outcomes (Stevens-Long, 1990) and individuals' power to influence their own development. The active role of individuals in managing their own development is evident in the following excerpt by Erikson et al. (1986):

> In old age's final reworking of issues of lifelong nurturance and concern, older people must come to terms with the earlier-life choices they made about how to express generativity and how, for whatever reasons, not to express it. . . . Some . . . are taking advantage of the free time and diminished responsibilities of old age to develop creative and productive interests that have been dormant, often since late adolescence. Others, however, find themselves unable to take advantage of these later-life opportunities, and they experience some sense of stagnation. (p. 84)

The coding system developed by Bradley for the Generativity Status Measure (Bradley, 1988, in press; Bradley & Marcia, in press) also portrays an active individual. On the basis of a careful review of Eriksonian theory and detailed interviews, Bradley (in press) defined the generative style or status (the most developmentally optimal of the five categories) as follows:

> The Generative individual is conscious of being a guide to others, and feels the need to impart accumulated knowledge and experience, while remaining tolerant of other ways of being and other traditions. S/he is aware of her/his local community and larger issues, and feels a responsibility to contribute to the community, through involvement in professional associations and possibly volunteer work. The Generative individual displays consistency between stated beliefs and goals, and action towards those beliefs and goals. (p. 27)

Both of the preceding excerpts suggest that many individuals are aware, planful, and discerning in their efforts to express generativity. Thus, even within an Eriksonian model of epigenesis, adult development may be less deterministic and more probabilistic: "Developmental changes are determined by a multiplicative interaction of two sources of development, nature and nurture" (Lerner, 1986, p. 62). According to McAdams (1992), generativity is inherently transactional, existing between the person and the environment, rather than purely within or outside the individual. He likens generativity to constructs like attachment (McAdams & de St. Aubin, 1992), which are "relational and multiply contextualized" (p. 1004). "Adults may translate their conscious concern into generative commitment, taking responsibility for the next generation by making decisions and establishing goals for generative behavior" (McAdams & de St. Aubin, pp. 1005–1006).

Selecting and Managing Expressions of Generativity

The major psychological organizing structure that processes information and forms plans and goals for action has been called the *self* (Erikson,

1968; Markus, 1990), character (Baumrind, 1993; Stryker & Statham, 1985), identity (Erikson, 1968; Josselson, 1987; Markus & Nurius, 1986; Waterman, 1985), personal meaning (Reker & Wong, 1988), and a self-constructed theory of the self (Berzonsky, 1992). Common to all these formulations is a view of the self as interested in managing one's degree of personal consistency, one's purpose, and one's place vis-à-vis the larger culture (Josselson, 1987). Most conceptualizations ascribe three components to the self: one that is cognitive, one that is evaluative or affective, and one that is behavioral or conative.

Selecting Roles

The third component of the self constructs and manages plans for action to achieve desired goals (Bengtson et al., 1985; Cantor, 1990; Reker & Wong, 1988; Stryker & Statham, 1985). It is this behavioral or conative element that is thought to select roles or settings in which to participate and then to monitor and adjust performances in those roles or settings (Cantor, 1990; Nuttbrock & Freudiger, 1991; Waterman, 1992). Everyone probably has heard about individuals seeking new or different involvements in community activities so that they can "give something back"; such behavior may be a good example of individuals selecting roles to fulfill developmental needs.

Little (1983, 1993) applied the term *personal projects* to the sequences of activity individuals design and carry out to reach desired goals. These projects may be normative or individualistic, domain-specific or quite global. (Little also suggested useful strategies with which to assess personal projects.) A similar construct specific to midlife is the *generativity script*, a term coined by McAdams (1988, p. 65) to describe individuals' specific plans for generative action: "a vision of exactly what one hopes to put into life and what one hopes to get out of life before one is too old to be generative."

Of course, individuals are not completely free to participate in any role they wish. Age-graded societal expectations and other factors make some roles less discretionary than others. For example, most adults are expected to participate in the roles of worker, spouse, and parent. Unexpected or nonnormative life events such as unplanned pregnancies, widowhood, grandparenthood, or divorce may thrust individuals into roles against their wishes. Nonetheless, individuals still display considerable diversity in role involvements (Fiske, 1980; Hornstein, 1986), making decisions about which roles to participate in and to what degree (Bem, 1988; Caspi, 1987; Stryker & Statham, 1985). Although individuals tend, on average, to choose to participate in roles that are consistent with their self-perceptions (Caspi & Bem, 1990; Whitbourne, 1989), there also is evidence of individuals choosing role involvements that challenge them (Fiske, 1980), particularly when the new roles provide opportunities for successful functioning (Cantor, 1990).

Proposition 9: Persons select roles in which to participate on the basis of societal and individual preferences and constraints.

Monitoring and Adjusting Generative Expressions Within Roles

Once a particular role or setting has been selected for participation, individuals must monitor their performance in the role and make adjustments according to feedback they receive. Often, individuals encounter tension between their actual behavior and the behavior others expect of them or they expect of themselves (Rodeheaver & Datan, 1981; Stryker & Statham, 1985). A decision then must be made whether to improve the fit between actual and desired behavior and, if that is desired, how to proceed (Rodeheaver & Datan, 1981; Stryker & Statham, 1985). For example, individuals may choose to express generativity in socially conforming or nonconforming ways (Stryker & Statham, 1985).

Although it may seem that some roles allow individuals few opportunities to express generativity, the limited knowledge of the processes leading to generative expressions should make one hesitant to discount individual ingenuity. For example, the role of prison inmate does not seem on its face to offer individuals many opportunities to express generativity or to exercise initiative in doing so. Both are evident, however, in the following excerpt from an interview with "Lena," a 52-year-old woman serving her 5th of 20 years in prison for drug-related offenses (Pickens, 1994). Lena has five grown children and a 12-year-old son:

> I have a lot of inspiration from my minister who comes out and sees me once a week and always encourages me. He said, "You know what? You're goin' to be a shining light here in this prison." And I said to myself, "No, I can't. He doesn't know these women in here." I was thinkin' about the younger women, not the older women. This prison is full of young girls comin' in here. And I thought, "No, I couldn't. They're goin' to think, 'That's what she gets. She's a older lady and she should have known better and she can't tell me anything.'" And I was placed in this dorm and a young girl come to me and said, "Miss Lena, do you mind if I call you Mama?" And I thought, "Well, he's tellin' the truth. This is my chance." So every chance I got, I tried to encourage her too. You know, you're in prison, but you can also make a life for yourself and set your goals and keep them. . . . When I was in Miss G.'s class, people would talk about their gift, what they had. Some people can sing, and some people can sew. Some people can write poems. I said, "But I don't have a gift." She said, "Yes, you do." So now I see my gift. It's caring. It's mothering. I care for these young girls in the prison and it really makes me feel good when they come back and say, "Miss Lena. You know what you suggested. I tried it and it worked out." (pp. 79–80)

Proposition 10: Individuals actively manage their generative expressions. Within the constraints posed by the environment, individuals choose their generative expressions.

Working Toward Goals over Time

The choices individuals make form patterns over time. Although desires for self-consistency and self-esteem (George, 1990) may motivate individuals to choose familiar options, social transitions, new cognitive skills, and desires for self-enhancement and self-actualization may promote increasingly diverse choices (Helson & Stewart, 1994; Markus & Wurf, 1987). Future longitudinal research on the evolution of generative expressions could focus on individuals' patterns of choices over time, assessments of costs and benefits associated with various alternatives over time, and responses to emerging constraints and opportunities (Cantor, 1990).

Planful expressions of generativity over time have been observed in at least two studies. In his detailed qualitative study of eight individuals, Kotre (1984) observed that people's choices of generative expressions were sometimes motivated by their past experiences. For example, some individuals chose generative expressions that would correct damage caused by previous bad treatment from their parents and prevent future damage to their children. Kotre (p. 263) called this phenomenon the "transformation of defect."

Using an innovative conceptualization, Snarey (1993) observed that the choices men made in response to infertility (a threat to their biological generativity) were strong predictors of later generative expressions. Men who responded to infertility in self-centered ways displayed less societal generativity later in life than men who engaged in parentlike activities. Kotre's (1984) and Snarey's results suggest that McAdams's conception of generativity scripts may need to be amended to include not only visions and hopes but also strategies for achieving generative goals.

Proposition 11: Generative expressions form patterns over time that are partial functions of past experiences. These patterns may be the result of goal-directed generative activity.

Moving From Theory to Data

We now have presented our argument that the expression of generativity in social roles merits research interest, and we have suggested propositions to guide researchers in increasing systematic attention to social roles. A research program led by one of the authors (S. M.) has explored several of these propositions, and in the next section we summarize the relevant results of these explorations. We then present the results of some new analyses that suggest exciting possibilities for future propositions about generativity and social roles.

OUR APPROACH TO THE QUANTITATIVE
STUDY OF GENERATIVITY

A program of research led by the first author has focused on implementing a role-specific approach to the quantitative study of generativity (MacDermid, de Haan, & Heilbrun, 1996; MacDermid, Heilbrun, & de Haan, 1997; see also de Haan & MacDermid, 1995). To date, this approach has had several features. First, generativity is measured in two ways: (a) a role-specific method in which generativity is assessed separately in each of up to five roles and (b) the more traditional global, or aggregated, method. Second, respondents are asked to describe their perspectives about each role without being forced to create hierarchies by assigning priorities or rank ordering. Third, measures of generativity in each role include items acknowledging five generative themes reliably identified in Eriksonian theory: productivity; procreativity and the guiding of the next generation; creativity; care, or nurturance; and mastery, or achievement (Erikson, 1950/1963; Erikson et al., 1986; Hulsizer et al., 1981).

So far, we have focused on only five roles. Three of these might be considered "core" roles because they are the ones most consistent with traditional societal expectations: spouse, parent, and worker. The other two roles are more discretionary: worshipper and citizen (i.e., civic involvement). This array of roles is by no means comprehensive. For example, we especially regret the exclusion of the role of "friend," which was clearly important to many of our respondents. Our selection of roles for inclusion in our preliminary studies was intended to let us compare role-specific and global methods of assessing generativity as well as expand our examinations beyond the three core roles to which many earlier investigations were confined.

As mentioned previously, the generativity items for each role tapped multiple themes that are consistent with Eriksonian theory: procreativity, productivity, creativity, care, and mastery. *Procreativity* is central to Erikson's definition of generativity as a concern for "establishing and guiding the next generation" (Erikson, 1950/1963, p. 267). *Productivity* and *creativity* are explicitly mentioned as alternative expressions of procreativity (though not replacements) for procreativity (Erikson, 1963). Productivity may occur not only in "business" (Hulsizer et al., 1981, p. 255) but also in other settings; the "product" could conceivably be a good marriage. *Care* is mentioned explicitly as a strength or virtue associated with generativity (Erikson et al., 1986); we see care as nurturance directed toward others but without the expectation of guiding subsequent generations that procreativity requires (see also Bradley's, in press, notion of "inclusivity"). Finally, *mastery* is implicated in the work of generative individuals "to develop and maintain those societal institutions and natural resources without which successive generations will not be able to survive" (Erikson

TABLE 1
Role-Specific Generativity Items

Role	Rewards	Concerns
Worker Role	Helping others develop	Job doesn't fit my skills or interests
	Opportunity for advancement	Job conflicts with other responsibilities
	Helping others or being needed	Feeling that I'm not helping anyone
	Sense of accomplishment or competence	Not getting advancements I want or deserve
	Challenging, stimulating work	Job's dullness, monotony
Spouse or Partner Role	Spouse being a good parent	Conflicts about children
	Good communication	Poor communication
	Taking care of my spouse	Feeling that my affection is rejected
	Feeling competent	Not getting enough appreciation
	Doing creative things around the house	Boredom and monotony
Parent Role	Helping them develop	Worry about the teenage years
	Feeling proud of how they are turning out	Disappointment in what they are like
	Being the best caretaker for them	Too many arguments with them
	Taking pride in being a good parent	Not sure if I'm doing the right thing
	Being a creative parent	Feeling trapped/bored
Worshipper Role	Being able to teach my faith to younger people	Feeling that young people aren't interested in religious faith
	Feeling that my faith is getting stronger all the time	Feeling that my faith is getting weaker all the time
	Feeling that my faith enables me to help others	Feeling that my faith doesn't really help others
	Feeling that my faith enables me to handle difficult situations	Feeling that my faith isn't helping me to deal with difficult situations
	Developing new ways to make my faith meaningful	Feeling "dry" or that my spiritual life is in a rut
Citizen Role	Being able to be a role model for younger people	Feeling that younger people aren't interested in civic involvement
	Feeling that I am able to have a positive impact in my community	Feeling that I'm not making a difference in my community
	Feeling that my service to the community really helps others	Feeling that my service to the community doesn't help others
	Feeling that I am becoming more effective in the organizations I am involved in	Feeling that I'm not effective in the organizations I am involved in
	Developing new ways to make my community better	Feeling "burnt out," unable to generate new ideas

Note. Items are listed by theme in the following order: procreativity, productivity, care, mastery, and creativity.

et al., 1986, pp. 73–74.). Mastery, distinct from productivity, concerns one's own position as a "norm-bearer and decision-maker" (Neugarten, 1968, p. 93) and a sense of personal competence, as opposed to the production of a particular product.

Most of our studies so far have focused on women. In part, this is the undesirable result of sampling strategies that found many more women than men. It is also the case, however, that women's development during middle age has been sparsely studied (Gergen, 1990). Emphases on biological determinism and chronological age, which ignore much of the variability in women's lives, have slowed progress toward understanding women's adult development (Archer, 1992; Barnett & Baruch, 1978). Gergen (1990, p. 475) observed, that "to judge from the major studies on lifespan development at midlife, one would think only men survived the third decade of life." In addition, we have limited our consideration in most of our studies to women who were workers, wives, and mothers (i.e., who occupied all three core roles). This strategy allowed us to hone our focus on variations in generativity while controlling for role occupancy. Although we do not see these practices as necessary in the long term, they have been helpful in our initial explorations.

Three of the five role-specific measures of generativity used in this research program were constructed by borrowing items developed by Baruch, Barnett, and Rivers (1983) to describe the rewards and concerns experienced by respondents in the roles of wife, mother, and worker; new items were developed for the roles of citizen and worshipper (the items are shown in Table 1). We chose the initial items for several reasons. First, many of the rewards and concerns tapped by these items seemed directly related to generativity. In addition, because our measurement strategy was new, we wanted to use items with known properties and the measures of generativity that existed at the outset of our research program did not offer acceptable candidates. Finally, we planned to use Baruch, Barnett, and Rivers's original data set as a replication sample for our work and thus wanted to match the measures included there. Although our decision carries with it many of the difficulties common to secondary analysis, the results of our rating procedure and statistical replication across samples (described later) provided adequate evidence for construct validity. Future researchers should feel free to be guided more by the structure and focus of our method than by the exact content of the items.

Method

Constructing Our Role-Specific Measures of Generativity

A panel of judges assisted in the selection of the borrowed items most relevant to generativity (the selection process is described more fully by

MacDermid, de Haan, & Heilbrun, 1996). In each role, one reward and one concern item were identified for each of the five generative themes. For example, "feeling proud of how they are turning out" and "disappointment in what they are like" were the consensus choices for items related to the productivity theme. Rigorous confirmatory factor analyses using LISREL VII demonstrated statistical measurement equivalence using data from three diverse samples of women: 49 women employed at a bank; 87 women working at a large Midwestern university; and 45 women of diverse occupations from a study by Baruch et al. (1983) called Women of the Middle Years (MacDermid, de Haan, & Heilbrun, 1996; MacDermid et al., 1997).

Samples and Data Collection Procedures

Respondents in the sample of bank workers were employed at a medium-sized bank in a Midwestern community of 50,000, in a wide range of jobs. All employees ($N = 367$) were invited to participate in a study of families and jobs at work during work time. Screening questionnaires completed by the 257 (70%) employees who volunteered identified 68 women who had worked at the bank at least 6 months, who lived with a spouse or partner, and who had children no younger than 6 years; 90% of these women completed longer questionnaires. The final sample included the 49 mothers age 35 years or older.

To locate members of the university sample, researchers sent forms to uncover interest and eligibility to 1,000 employees in diverse units (e.g., education, administration, and health sciences) and occupational levels. Of the 536 employees who returned screening forms, the 298 who reported having youngest children at least 6 years old and who indicated willingness to participate were sent a questionnaire. Fifty-four percent ($n = 161$) of the eligible respondents returned completed questionnaires; of these, 87 were married mothers.

Baruch et al. (1983) gathered their data in a city near Boston whose inhabitants worked in a wide variety of jobs. Community voting lists were used to identify women age 35 to 55; the 6,000 women identified were contacted in random order to determine whether they met the criteria for the study (e.g., to qualify as employed, women had to have worked for pay at least 17.5 hours per week for the 12 weeks prior to data collection). Oversampling was used to ensure representativeness. Over 76% ($n = 238$) of the qualified women completed structured face-to-face interviews. Our research focuses on the 45 women from this group who were mothers, workers, and wives.

Although the questions asked of respondents varied somewhat from sample to sample, common to all measures were items concerning generativity, personal well-being, and demographic characteristics. To varying degrees, each study also asked questions about involvement in particular roles, such as time spent and perceived competence and satisfaction.

Results

Do Generative Expressions Vary From Role to Role?

Our earliest analyses (reported by MacDermid, de Haan, & Heilbrun, 1996; MacDermid et al., 1997) asked whether significant variation in generative expressions across social roles could be observed; such variation would be a criterion for the usefulness of a role-specific approach. In each of two studies, we ran a repeated measures analysis of variance on individuals' generativity scores across the three core roles: spouse, parent, and worker. "Role" was treated as a repeated measure. All analyses revealed significant though small differences, $F(2, 254) = 3.03$, $p < .05$ (MacDermid, de Haan, & Heilbrun, 1996); $F(2, 178) = 8.5$, $p < .001$ (MacDermid et al., 1997). Consistently, average levels of generativity in the parental role were significantly greater than in the spousal role. Generativity in the parental role also was consistently higher than generativity in the work role, although this difference was significant in only one study, the results of which are shown in Figure 1 (MacDermid, de Haan, & Heilbrun, 1996).

To verify these results, we conducted analyses to see whether women scoring above the median for generativity in one role were significantly more likely than other women to score above the median for other roles

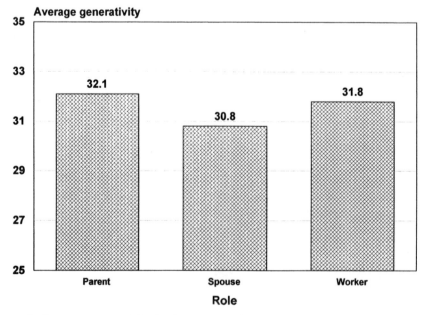

Figure 1. Average generativity in three core roles.

206   MACDERMID, FRANZ, AND DE REUS

(MacDermid et al., in press). Each woman in the bank worker and Boston samples was assigned to a "high" or "low" generativity group in each role using median splits. Using chi-square analyses, we found that women scoring above the median for generativity in one role were no more likely than other women to score above the median in the other core roles. On the basis of these findings, we concluded that there was significant variability in generative expressions across social roles, and we proceeded with further explorations.

Do Role-Specific Measures of Generativity Offer More Explanatory Power Than Global Measures?

Next, we tested the first proposition posed earlier: that role-specific measures account for greater variability in outcomes of interest, in this case psychological well-being, than global measures. (These analyses are described fully by MacDermid, de Haan, & Heilbrun, 1996, and MacDermid et al., 1997.) We compared our role-specific measures of generativity in each of the three core roles to two global measures: (a) 9 of the 10 items from the generativity subscale of the MEPSI (Darling-Fisher & Leidy, 1988; one item was omitted because it distorted the factor structure) and (b) the 16-item generativity scale developed by Ryff and Heincke (1983) to measure the degree to which an individual "expresses concern in establishing and guiding the next generation; possesses awareness of responsibilities to children or those younger in age; views self as a norm-bearer and decision-maker; shows awareness of leadership role and has a sense of maximal influence capacity" (Ryff & Heincke, 1983, p. 809).

We regressed multiple indicators of psychological well-being (four and three indicators in the bank and university samples, respectively) on each generativity measure in turn and compared the R-squared values obtained for the role-specific measures to those obtained using global measures. The results are shown in Figure 2. In our sample of bank workers, the role-specific measures of generativity accounted for significantly more variability in locus of control, depression, and life satisfaction than either of the global measures (MacDermid, de Haan, & Heilbrun, 1996). Role-specific generativity accounted for significantly more variability in self-esteem than did Ryff and Heincke's (1983) global measure. In our sample of university workers, role-specific measures accounted for significantly more variability than the MEPSI measure in one of three indicators of well-being (the Ryff and Heincke measure was not administered to this sample; MacDermid, de Haan, & Heilbrun, 1996). In the Baruch et al. (1983) sample, role-specific and average generativity accounted for equal variability in a Well-Being factor that represented locus of control, self-esteem, depression, and life satisfaction (MacDermid et al., 1997). Thus, the role-specific measure of generativity accounted for significantly more variability in psychological

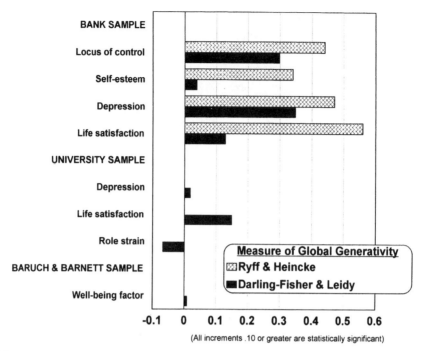

Figure 2. Increment to R-squared of role-specific over global measures of generativity.

well-being than did global measures in 7 of 12 comparisons. All but one of the significant results were observed in one of the three samples tested, however. Because we have been unable to identify any unusual features of this sample that might produce distorted results, we cautiously conclude that our first proposition received modest support.

Are Expressions of Generativity Related to the Breadth of the Role System?

We conducted some new analyses to assess support for Proposition 3, that individuals whose role systems are larger, more diverse, or both are more likely to express generativity. We collapsed the original samples from our bank and university studies, which included a total of 148 women who were employed, married, and had at least one child under 18 years living at home. Of these women, 117 also provided information about the roles of worshipper and citizen. Using t-tests, we compared the women who described five roles with the 31 women who provided information about the three core roles only. The two groups of women did not differ in terms of generativity averaged across all roles, global generativity, well-being, or satisfaction. These results are not consistent with Proposition 3 (although they are consistent with research described earlier that found no relationship between breadth of the role system and well-being). Before we amend or discard the proposition, more rigorous tests should be conducted using data that, unlike ours, permit comparison of a full range of role combinations varying in both breadth and diversity.

Is Generativity More Likely to Be Expressed When the Quality of Experience in a Role Is Positive?

Our fourth proposition predicts a positive relationship between generativity and individuals' subjective evaluations of their experience in a given role. In our earlier study of the bank worker and Baruch et al. (1983) samples (MacDermid et al., 1997), we conducted path analyses in which generativity in the three core roles was regressed on women's perceptions of competence and satisfaction in each role. Generative expressions in each core role were significantly and positively related to satisfaction (respectively for the parental, worker, and spousal roles, the standardized regression coefficients were .45, $p < .001$; .29, $p < .01$; and .49, $p < .001$). Generativity in the spousal role also was positively associated with satisfaction in the parental role. There were no significant links, however, between generativity and perceived competence.

Proposition 4 is supported by these findings. Generative expressions were consistently and positively related to subjective evaluations of satisfaction in each role. We note with interest the lack of significant relationships between generativity and perceived competence. *Feeling* good about one's involvement in a given role appears to be more important than *being* good at it for the expression of generativity. For example, one might choose to invest time and energy in socializing a less experienced colleague regardless of how competent one feels in one's own position. In the future, it will be useful for researchers to determine which indicators of role quality are and are not related to generativity.

Is Generativity More Important in Some Roles Than Others for Well-Being?

Proposition 5, introduced earlier, asserts that links between well-being and generative expressions vary across roles. The analyses we described earlier that compared role-specific and global measures of generativity also tested this proposition (MacDermid, de Haan, & Heilbrun, 1996). Generativity in the worker, spousal, and parental roles was regressed on multiple indicators of well-being in our samples of bank and university workers. Results showed clear variation across roles, consistent with the proposition. Perceptions of generativity in the spousal role were significantly and positively related to all but one indicator of psychological well-being in each sample. Generativity in the role of worker was significantly related to two indicators of well-being in each sample, although not as strongly as in the spousal role. Generativity in the parental role was not significantly related to psychological well-being; this was an unexpected result.

The results of these analyses support our proposition, demonstrating that links between generativity and well-being do appear to vary across roles. The analyses do not reveal, however, the implications of such variation. In a later section suggesting promising directions for future research, we report some new analyses examining the implications of the consistency of generative expressions across roles.

Are Expressions of Generativity in One Role Related to Those in Another?

Finally, we have been interested in the cross-role contingencies that were suggested by Proposition 6, wondering whether positive experiences in one domain might compensate for negative ones in another. In a 1995 study (MacDermid & Crouter), we tested the hypothesis that parents' emotional and temporal involvement in work might moderate relationships between children's transitions to adolescence and a measure of parents' midlife concerns (a precursor to our generativity measures). Data were gathered separately from fathers, mothers, and children age 10 to 13 in 135 families. Although the three indicators of midlife concerns (midlife crisis, centrality of parenting concerns, and resolution) did not directly tap generativity, they each tapped concerns related to turning points during midlife. Fathers' involvement in work appeared to serve a protective function for parents by moderating the intensity of midlife concerns, but only for families of boys. That is, parents of boys reported less severe midlife concerns when fathers spent more time or were more emotionally involved at work. In contrast, means for the families of girls were more consistent with an "exacerbation" model, whereby parents reported more severe midlife concerns when fathers were more emotionally involved in work.

Although these analyses do not examine generativity directly, they show that mothers' and fathers' experiences in the parental and work roles are related to each other and to midlife concerns. They also show that the interdependencies among roles can be quite complex, as evidenced by the interaction between fathers' work involvement and children's gender. We look forward to future research examining expressions of generativity in the context of influences from other roles.

Summing Up

In our research program, we have so far conducted preliminary explorations of five of the propositions advanced in this chapter. Our results are consistent with all but one, supporting the usefulness of role-specific approaches and demonstrating that expressions of generativity (a) appear to be more likely in roles in which individuals evaluate their experiences positively, (b) vary across roles in their importance for well-being, and (c) are interdependent across roles. The third proposition was not supported: Expressions of generativity did not appear to be related to the breadth and diversity of the role system. Of course, additional research is necessary to replicate our findings in other samples and to explore the propositions we have not yet tested.

The 11 propositions suggested here lay the groundwork for more systematic and differentiated attention to social roles in the study of generativity. Beyond them lie many intriguing directions for future research. In the next section, we present new analyses that are intended to stimulate interest in two such directions.

New Analyses Suggesting Future Research Directions

Generativity in the Marital Role

Greater attention to social roles as contexts for generativity will lead researchers to study quite specific aspects of particular roles. Although the marital relationship has received little attention from generativity researchers so far, considerable evidence highlights its potential importance for generative expression. Snarey (1993), for example, found that fathers' commitments to their marriages were strong predictors of their later expressions of parental generativity, particularly toward their daughters. The relationship between parenting satisfaction and midlife concerns observed by Koski and Steinberg (1990) was moderated by marital satisfaction. MacDermid and Crouter (1995) found that spouses' social support for each other ameliorated to some degree the implications for parents of their children's adolescence, highlighting the importance of the marital relationship when considering individual development in the context of family life.

We decided to pay more attention to marriage as a site for the expression of generativity using data gathered from about 70 couples in the well-known Oakland Growth and Berkeley Guidance studies (sample sizes varied slightly across analyses because of missing data in a handful of cases). The people who make up these two samples have been studied all their lives, since the early and late 1920s, respectively, for members of the Oakland and Berkeley cohorts. Our analyses used structured interview data gathered in the early 1970s and early 1980s, a data collection interval roughly bracketing the age decade of the 50s for Oakland participants and the 40s for Berkeley participants.

Q-sort ratings of data gathered in 1969 and 1970 were used to construct scores for generativity according to procedures developed by Peterson (Peterson & Kloehnen, 1995; Peterson & Stewart, 1992). Scores for Peterson's Generative Realization Index (Peterson & Kloehnen, 1995; Peterson & Stewart, 1992) were based on 13 items from the California Adult Q Sort, which was used by multiple observers to code data for each Oakland and Berkeley respondent. Three subscales emerged from principal-components analyses conducted during the validation study: *communal* generativity, represented by five items oriented toward nurturing other people; *agentic* generativity, represented by an orientation to be effective and productive (five items); and an *insight* component including three items focusing on social perceptiveness (Peterson & Kloehnen, 1995). These components correspond well to the blend of caring, productivity, and self-awareness in Erikson's notion of generativity. The validation study also found evidence of convergent and divergent validity in two groups of mid-life women (Peterson & Kloehnen, 1995).

From the 1982 interview, we selected two items that we thought reflected a logical outcome of generative expressions in marriage: "My spouse brings out the best in me" and "I cannot completely be myself" (reversed). For each item, individuals strongly agreeing or agreeing were assigned to an "agree" group, and individuals strongly disagreeing or disagreeing were assigned to a "disagree" group. The agree and disagree groups then were contrasted to see if individuals rated as generative in the context of marriage also had been rated as generative by clinical observers a decade earlier.

We conducted multivariate analyses of variance with two grouping variables, birth cohort (Oakland, Berkeley) and marriage rating (agree, disagree). The three generativity subscales served as dependent variables. We also conducted a univariate analysis of variance with total generative realization as the dependent variable. Separate analyses were conducted of each marriage rating for husbands and wives.

The univariate analyses of total generative realization revealed no significant differences between the agree and disagree groups of husbands or wives, regardless of which marital item was used to create the groups. The multivariate analyses revealed no differences in any of the generativity component scores indexed by husbands' ratings of their wives. In contrast, husbands who were characterized by their wives as "bringing out the best in me" had been rated significantly higher in communal generativity more than a decade earlier, $F(1, 69) = 5.84$, $p = .02$. Husbands whose wives felt that they "could be myself" scored significantly higher in both the communal, $F(1, 74) = 4.94$, $p = .03$, and insight, $F(1, 74) = 6.64$, $p = .01$, components of generativity. The mean scores for the agree and disagree groups, which differed significantly, are shown in Figure 3.

Wives' development (i.e., the degree to which they had been able to become the people they wished to be) appeared to depend in part on the generativity exhibited by their husbands in the context of marriage. It is not surprising that women's well-being and life experience may depend heavily on characteristics of their husbands. Because women occupy, on average, lower status positions both at home and at work, the ability of wives to negotiate successfully for conditions that favor them depends heavily on the attitudes and behavior of their husbands (Barnett, 1991;

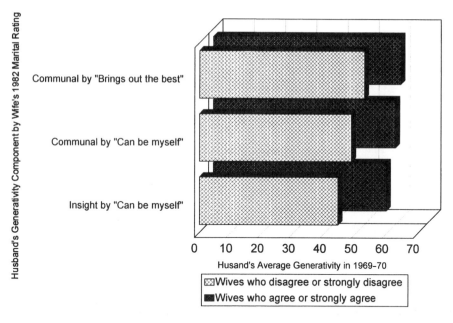

Figure 3. Average generativity scores in 1969–1970 by 1982 marital ratings.

Barnett & Baruch, 1978, 1987; McHale & Crouter, 1992). Support for this view comes from Barnett and Baruch's (1987) finding that negative experiences in the marital role could not be compensated for by positive experiences in other roles.

Because spouses typically spend more time with each other than with any other person, it is reasonable to assume that they are powerful influences on each other. Spouses shape one another's behavior as parents and perhaps also as developing adults. Marriage thus may be a major role setting for the expression of the care inherent in generativity. We look forward to future research assessing the developmental interdependencies operating within marital dyads to influence the generative expressions of both members.

Profiles of Generativity

A key premise in the argument in favor of more systematic attention to social roles is that generativity may not be expressed consistently across roles. A corollary is that the degree to which consistency is or is not present is meaningful. The existing literature does not take a clear stance (Becker, 1968), containing presumptions of both positive and negative consequences of inconsistency. For example, inconsistency could signal flexibility and differentiation (Bourne, 1978; Fiske, 1980) or lack of a coherent identity (Reker & Wong, 1988).

We decided to explore this issue by examining generativity "profiles" created by plotting individuals' levels of generativity in each of the five roles: parent, worker, spouse, citizen, and worshipper. We combined our bank and university samples ($n = 117$) of women, all of whom were employed, had at least one child under 18 living at home, and were married. We used cluster analysis (Ward's method) to identify groups of individuals with similar generativity profiles. Twelve observations were trimmed as part of the normal analytic procedure, resulting in a final sample size of 105. On the basis of various statistical indicators (e.g., scree plot, clustering criterion), we settled on three clusters that accounted for 46% of the variance. The average profile for each cluster is shown in Figure 4.

We tested for consistency of generative expressions across roles by conducting a repeated measures analysis of variance separately for each cluster. Results were significant in each of the three analyses, $F(4, 54) = 57.3$, $p < .001$; $F(4, 27) = 71.01$, $p < .001$; $F(4, 12) = 51.0$, $p < .001$, respectively, for the clusters shown from left to right in Figure 4), indicating that there was significant variability across roles for each cluster.

Follow-up t tests (with Bonferroni adjustments) comparing means within each cluster revealed that, on average, members of the first cluster (shown at the left in Figure 4) reported lower generativity in the role of "citizen" than in any other role. Average generativity scores for the role of spouse were significantly higher than for any other role; parental, worker, and worshipper generativity scores did not differ significantly from one another and were closer to spousal than to citizen scores. We conceptualize this cluster as favoring proximal or personal settings for the expression of generativity, as opposed to more distal societal settings, and labeled it "distributed personal." Cluster 2, the "concentrated parent" cluster, reported higher scores in the parental role than in the other four roles and partic-

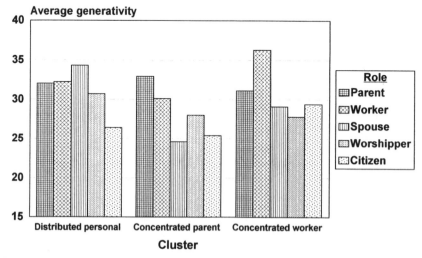

Figure 4. Average scores by cluster for generativity in each of five roles.

ularly low scores for generativity in the spousal role. We labeled the third cluster "concentrated work" because members of this cluster reported the highest scores, on average, for generativity in the work role, compared both to other clusters and to other roles within this cluster. With the exception of the roles of parent and worshipper, generativity scores for the other four roles did not significantly differ from one another.

We next used one-way analyses of variance to compare the clusters in terms of generativity scores in each role, global and average generativity, and personal well-being (i.e., satisfaction in core roles and with life, role strain, and depression). In terms of role-specific generativity, the clusters differed on three of the five roles included in the profile: worker, spouse, and citizen. The distributed personal cluster reported higher scores in the role of spouse than the other clusters and had intermediate scores in all other roles. The concentrated parent cluster reported significantly lower generativity scores in the roles of worker and spouse than either of the other clusters and lower scores than the concentrated work cluster in the role of citizen. The concentrated work cluster reported higher generativity in the worker and citizen roles than any other cluster.

In terms of well-being and average and global generativity, one-way analyses of variance revealed that individuals in the concentrated parent group were the least satisfied with their marriages and lives and were the most depressed. They reported the lowest overall average generativity (i.e., averaged across all five roles) and the lowest scores on the Darling-Fisher and Leidy (1988) measure of global generativity. The concentrated work and distributed personal clusters did not differ in terms of well-being or global, or average generativity.

Finally, we used one-way analyses of variance to verify that demographic differences among the clusters (e.g., respondents' ages, number of children, income, job prestige, and work hours) were not responsible for the differences we observed. No systematic differences were found.

These analyses revealed that differences among the women in our samples did not seem to be a function of consistency across the five roles studied. Of the two clusters with the highest well-being and global and average generativity, one showed a concentrated pattern of generativity centered on the work role, whereas the other displayed a more distributed pattern with similar levels of generativity across four of the five roles. Even though these two clusters displayed different levels of consistency, their members reported similar levels of well-being and global and average generativity. Individuals who were at least moderately generative on average, regardless of the level of consistency across roles, reported similar levels of well-being and global generativity. The concentrated parent cluster, however, displayed a pattern that was neither consistent nor at a moderate level; members of this cluster were the least satisfied and least generative. In our data, therefore, it appeared not to matter whether generative expressions were distributed evenly across roles if there was adequate generativity expressed in total.

The analyses presented in the last two sections are intended to stimulate the development of additional research questions and theory about generativity in the context of social roles. We look forward to future considerations of demands in specific roles, marriage among them. We also hope future researchers will undertake analysis of generativity profiles, including assessment of their diversity and the levels of generativity necessary for optimal well-being as well as further analyses of the implications of consistency or its lack.

CONCLUSION

Our thesis in this chapter has been that more differentiated and systematic approaches to social roles will yield important new insights about generativity. We have suggested that future generativity researchers make clear distinctions between the level of the role system and the level of individual roles because each level of analysis offers useful, but different, information. For example, role systems can be studied in terms of their breadth, the degree to which they are balanced, and the diversity and quality of experience they offer. The study of role systems offers opportunities to understand how individuals satisfy generative needs in the context of demands from multiple roles as they wend their way through each day. Examining the breadth, diversity, balance, and quality of generative experience across the role system also might improve the ability to predict reliably problematic versus optimal adult development.

Studying individual roles can inform professionals of the opportunities and constraints individuals confront in those roles. Understanding those opportunities and constraints might help in the understanding of the genesis of generative expressions. Comprehensive attention to individual roles also will improve the precision of explanations of well-being and developmental outcomes.

Greater attention to role processes is needed, particularly to the process of individuals actively selecting, managing, and manipulating opportunities for generative expression across their role systems. Questions remaining to be answered include the following: By what means does generativity come to be expressed? Under what circumstances are opportunities for generative expression likely to be realized? What characterizes individuals who seem to go out of their way to find (versus avoid) opportunities to express generativity? What generative expressions occur in unlikely places, and why or how? What characterizes the role settings within which frequent generative expressions occur? What (if any) are the minimum levels of generative expression required for optimal development?

We presented results from our research program that support several of our propositions and suggest new ones. In our data, for example, generative expressions vary across social roles, and that variation is empirically related to important outcomes such as psychological well-being. Expressions of generativity do not appear to be related to the breadth of the role system, but they do appear more frequently in roles in which participants evaluate their experiences positively. Experiences in multiple roles are interdependent: The quality of experience in one role depends in part on the quality of experience in another. We explored the marital role as a site for generative expression, suggesting that future research should attend to the likely developmental interdependencies among marital partners. Finally, we examined generative profiles, showing that the degree to which generativity is expressed consistently across the role system seems to matter only when the overall levels are low.

Our work is limited in a number of ways. Because we have conducted only preliminary explorations of only some of our propositions, we are able to offer only modest empirical evidence to support our case. We believe, that our argument has merit on theoretical grounds alone, however; our empirical investigations have served only to strengthen our commitment to it.

A more serious limitation of our perspective is that we have firmly grounded it in Western psychology. Although we suggest that generativity should be studied with greater attention to context, we do so presuming an individualistic cultural setting. In a more collectivist culture, our arguments regarding individual agency and the negotiability of role demands likely would stand on shaky conceptual and empirical ground.

We hope that the imaginations of other scholars are stimulated by our journey through the terrain of generativity and social roles. Attention to social roles will become more, not less, important in the future as the diversity of individual role patterns increases (Juhasz, 1989; MacDermid et al., 1997). For example, workers are now much less likely than they once were to spend their entire occupational careers with a single employer. Women are now much less likely to remain out of the paid labor force throughout their lives. Many workers now are expected to undergo periodic retraining, which may require temporary departures from paid work. Longevity has risen and fertility has fallen, increasing the likelihood of simultaneously providing care for dependent children and elders. Role demands and the complexity of role systems are rising now and will continue to do so, increasing the complexity of interdependencies among roles and the value of approaches that pay systematic and balanced attention to them.

The study of generativity can be highly abstract. It is not always clear from reading the research literature what the practical payoffs might be of greater attention to social roles in the study of generativity. If one accepts the premise, that generativity is necessary for societies to be maintained and to function well, however, the practical benefit of understanding how generativity comes to be expressed is immediately clear. Attending to social roles in the study of generativity could demonstrate how to remove constraints and create opportunities in role settings that would facilitate and nurture generative expressions. Professionals could learn to identify potential problems in fulfilling the developmental tasks of adulthood early enough to avoid them. We could learn how to teach others to be generative. Understanding motives, goals, and perceptions is well and good, but in the end we are interested in and depend on generative acts in everyday roles that truly do sustain the world.

REFERENCES

Archer, S. L. (1992). A feminist's approach to identity research. In G. R. Adams, T. P. Gullotta, & R. Montemayor (Eds.), *Adolescent identity formation* (pp. 25–49). Newbury Park, CA: Sage.

Bandura, A. (1990). Reflections on nonability determinants of competence. In R. J. Sternberg & J. Kolligan, Jr. (Eds.), *Competence considered* (pp. 315–362). New Haven, CT: Yale University Press.

Barnett, R. C. (1991). *Multiple roles, gender, and psychological distress* (Wellesley College Working Paper No. 233). Wellesley, MA: Wellesley College Center for Research on Women.

Barnett, R. C., & Baruch, G. K. (1978). Women in the middle years: A critique of research and theory. *Psychology of Women Quarterly, 3,* 187–197.

Barnett, R. C., & Baruch, G. K. (1987). Social roles, gender, and psychological distress. In R. C. Barnett, L. Biener, & G. K. Baruch (Eds.), *Gender and stress* (pp. 122–143). New York: Free Press.

Barnett, R. C., Marshall, N. L., & Pleck, J. H. (1992). Men's multiple roles and their relationship to men's psychological distress. *Journal of Marriage and the Family, 54,* 358–367.

Barnett, R. C., Marshall, N. L., Raudenbush, S. W., & Brennan, R. T. (1993). Gender and the relationship between job experiences and psychological distress: A study of dual-earner couples. *Journal of Personality and Social Psychology, 64,* 794–806.

Barnett, R. C., Marshall, N. L., & Sayer, A. (1992). Positive spillover effects from job to home: A closer look. *Women and Health, 19,* 13–41.

Baruch, G. K., & Barnett, R. C. (1986). Role quality, multiple role involvement, and psychological well-being in midlife women. *Journal of Personality and Social Psychology, 51,* 578–585.

Baruch, G. K., Barnett, R. C., & Rivers, C. (1983). *Lifeprints.* New York: Plume Books.

Baumrind, D. (1993, November). *Reflections on character and competence.* Address at the first meeting of the Character and Competence Research Program, Henry A. Murray Center, Cambridge, MA.

Becker, H. S. (1968). Personal change in adult life. In B. L. Neugarten (Ed.), *Middle age and aging* (pp. 148–160). Chicago: University of Chicago Press.

Bem, D. J. (1988). Putting persons back into the context. In N. Bolger, A. Caspi, G. Downey, & M. Moorehouse (Eds.), *Persons in context: Developmental processes* (pp. 203–216). Cambridge, England: Cambridge University Press.

Bengtson, V. L., & Allen, K. R. (1993). The life course perspective applied to families over time. In P. G. Boss, W. J. Doherty, R. LaRossa, W. R. Schumm, & S. K. Steinmetz (Eds.), *Sourcebook of family theories and methods: A contextual approach* (pp. 469–498). New York: Plenum Press.

Bengtson, V. L., Reedy, M. N., & Gordon, C. (1985). Aging and self-conceptions: Personality processes and social contexts. In J. E. Birren & K. W. Schaie (Eds.), *Handbook of the psychology of aging* (pp. 544–593). New York: Van Nostrand Reinhold.

Berzonsky, M. D. (1992). A process perspective on identity and stress management. In G. R. Adams, T. P. Gullotta, & R. Montemayor (Eds.), *Adolescent identity formation* (pp. 193–215). Newbury Park, CA: Sage.

Bourne, E. (1978). The state of research on ego identity: A review and appraisal, Part 1. *Journal of Youth and Adolescence, 7,* 223–251.

Bradley, C. L. (1988). *Generativity Interview and scoring manual.* Unpublished draft manual.

Bradley, C. L. (in press). Generativity-stagnation: Development of a status model. *Developmental Review.*

Bradley, C. L., & Marcia, J. E. (in press). Generativity-stagnation: A five category model. *Journal of Personality.*

Bronfenbrenner, U. (1979). *The ecology of human development.* Cambridge, MA: Harvard University Press.

Bronfenbrenner, U., & Crouter, A. C. (1983). The evolution of environmental models in developmental research. In P. Mussen (Ed.), *Handbook of child psychology* (pp. 357–414). New York: Wiley.

Brooks-Gunn, J., & Kirsh, B. (1984). Life events and the boundaries of midlife women. In G. Baruch & J. Brooks-Gunn (Eds.), *Women in midlife* (pp. 11–30). New York: Plenum Press.

Burr, W. R., Leigh, G. K., Day, R. D., & Constantine, J. (1979). Symbolic interaction and the family. In W. R. Burr, R. Hill, R. I. Nye, & I. L. Reiss (Eds.), *Contemporary theories about the family,* (Vol. 1, pp. 42–111). New York: Free Press.

Cantor, N. (1990). From thought to behavior: "Having" and "doing" in the study of personality and cognition. *American Psychologist, 45,* 735–750.

Cantor, N., & Zirkel, S. (1990). Personality, cognition, and purposive behavior. In L. A. Pervin (Ed.), *Handbook of Personality: Theory and Research* (pp. 135–164). New York: Guilford Press.

Caspi, A. (1987). Personality in the life course. *Journal of Personality and Social Psychology, 53,* 1203–1213.

Caspi, A., & Bem, D. J. (1990). Personality continuity and change across the life course. In L. A. Pervin (Ed.), *Handbook of personality: Theory and research* (pp. 549–575). New York: Guilford Press.

Caspi, A., & Elder, G. H. (1992). Studying lives in a changing society: Sociological and personological explorations. In R. A. Zucker, A. I. Rabin, J. Aronoff, & S. Frank (Eds.), *Personality structure in the life course* (pp. 276–322). New York: Springer.

Cohen, T. F. (1987). Remaking men: Men's experiences becoming and being husbands and fathers and their implications for reconceptualizing men's lives. *Journal of Family Issues, 8,* 57–77.

Colarusso, C. A., & Nemiroff, R. A. (1982). The father in midlife: Crisis and the growth of paternal identity. In S. H. Cath & A. R. Gurwitt (Eds.), *Father and child: Developmental and clinical perspectives* (pp. 315–327). Boston: Little, Brown.

Coleman, L. M., Antonucci, T. C., & Adelmann, P. K. (1987). Role involvement, gender, and well-being. In F. J. Crosby (Ed.), *Spouse, parent, worker: On gender and multiple roles* (pp. 138–153). New Haven, CT: Yale University Press.

Cote, J. E., & Levine, C. (1988). A critical examination of the ego identity status paradigm. *Developmental Review, 8,* 147–184.

Darling-Fisher, C. S., & Leidy, N. K. (1987). *The modified Erikson psychosocial stage inventory.* Unpublished instrument manual.

Darling-Fisher, C. S., & Leidy, N. K. (1988). Measuring Eriksonian development in the adult: The modified Erikson psychosocial stage inventory. *Psychological Reports, 62,* 747–754.

de Haan, L. G., & MacDermid, S. M. (1995). Is women's identity achievement associated with the expression of generativity? Examining identity and generativity in multiple roles. *Journal of Adult Development, 1,* 235–247.

Edelman, M. W. (1992). *The measure of our success: A letter to my children and yours.* Boston: Beacon Press.

Emmons, R. A. (1995). Levels and domains in personality: An introduction. *Journal of Personality, 63,* 341–364.

Erikson, E. H. (1963). *Childhood and society.* New York: Norton. (Original work published 1950)

Erikson, E. H. (1968). *Identity: Youth and crisis.* New York: Norton.

Erikson, E. H., Erikson, J. M., & Kivnick, H. Q. (1986). *Vital involvement in old age.* New York: Norton.

Farrell, M. P., & Rosenberg, S. D. (1981). *Men at midlife.* Dover, MA: Auburn House.

Fiske, M. (1980). Changing hierarchies of commitment in adulthood. In N. J. Smelser & E. H. Erikson (Eds.), *Themes of work and love in adulthood* (pp. 238–264). Cambridge, MA: Harvard University Press.

Franz, C. E. (1988). *A case study of adult psychosocial development: Identity, intimacy, and generativity in personal documents.* Unpublished doctoral dissertation, Boston University.

Franz, C. E. (1994). Does thought content change as individuals age? A longitudinal study of midlife adults. In T. F. Heatherton & J. L. Weinberger (Eds.), *Can personality change?* (pp. 227–250). Washington, DC: American Psychological Association.

Franz, C. E., & White, K. M. (1985). Individuation and attachment in personality development: Extending Erikson's theory. *Journal of Personality, 53,* 224–255.

George, L. K. (1990). Social structure, social processes, and social-psychological states. In V. W. Marshall, G. C. Myers, & J. H. Schulz (Eds.), *Handbook of aging and the social sciences,* (3rd ed., pp. 186–204). San Diego, CA: Academic Press.

Gergen, M. M. (1990). Finished at 40: Women's development within the patriarchy. *Psychology of Women Quarterly, 14,* 471–493.

Gilligan, C., Murphy, J. M., & Tappan, M. B. (1990). Moral development beyond adolescence. In C. N. Alexander & E. J. Langer (Eds.), *Higher stages of human development: Perspectives on adult growth* (pp. 208–228). New York: Oxford University Press.

Goode, W. J. (1960). A theory of role strain. *American Sociological Review, 25,* 483–496.

Grotevant, H. D. (1987). Toward a process model of identity formation. *Journal of Adolescent Research, 2,* 203–222.

Haan, N. (1981). Common dimensions of personality development: Early adolescence to middle life. In D. Eichorn, J. Clausen, N. Haan, M. Honzik, & P. Mussen (Eds.), *Present and past in middle life* (pp. 117–151). New York: Academic Press.

Haan, N., & Day, D. (1974). A longitudinal study of change and sameness in personality development: Adolescence to later adulthood. *International Journal of Aging and Human Development, 5,* 11–39.

Hall, E. (1987). *Growing and changing: What the experts say.* New York: Random House.

Heidrich, S. M., & Ryff, C. D. (1993). Physical and mental health in later life: The self-system as mediator. *Psychology and Aging, 8,* 327–338.

Helson, R. (1993). Comparing longitudinal studies of adult development: Toward a paradigm of tension between stability and change. In D. C. Funder, R. D. Parke, C. Tomlinson-Keasey, & K. Widaman (Eds.), *Studying lives through time: Personality and development* (pp. 93–120). Washington, DC: American Psychological Association.

Helson, R., Elliott, T., & Leigh, J. (1990). Number and quality of roles: A longitudinal personality view. *Psychology of Women Quarterly, 14,* 83–101.

Helson, R., & Stewart, A. (1994). Personality change in adulthood. In T. F. Heatherton & J. L. Weinberger (Eds.), *Can personality change?* (pp. 201–226). Washington, DC: American Psychological Association.

Hornstein, G. A. (1986). The structuring of identity among midlife women as a function of their degree of involvement in employment. *Journal of Personality, 54,* 551–575.

Hulsizer, D., Murphy, M., Noam, G., Taylor, C., Erikson, E., & Erikson, J. (1981). On generativity and identity: From a conversation with Erik and Joan Erikson. *Harvard Educational Review, 51,* 249–269.

Jackson, D. N. (1976). *Jackson Personality Inventory Manual.* New York: Research Psychologists Press.

Josselson, R. (1987). *Finding herself: Pathways to identity development in women.* San Francisco: Jossey-Bass.

Juhasz, A. M. (1989). A role-based approach to adult development: The triple-helix model. *International Journal of Aging and Human Development, 29,* 301–315.

Kidwell, J., Fischer, J. L., Dunham, R. M., & Baranowski, M. (1983). Parents and adolescents: Push and pull of change. In H. I. McCubbin & C. R. Figley (Eds.), *Stress and the family: Vol. 1. Coping with normative transitions* (pp. 74–89). New York: Brunner/Mazel.

Kohn, M. L. (1977). *Class and conformity: A study of values* (2nd ed.). Chicago: University of Chicago Press.

Koski, K. J., & Steinberg, L. (1990). Parenting satisfaction of midlife mothers. *Journal of Youth and Adolescence, 19,* 465–474.

Kotre, J. (1984). *Outliving the self: Generativity and the interpretation of lives.* Baltimore: The Johns Hopkins University Press.

Kroger, J. (1989). *Identity in adolescence: The balance between self and other.* London: Routledge.

Kroger J., & Haslett, S. J. (1991). A comparison of ego identity status transition pathways and change rates across five identity domains. *International Journal of Aging and Human Development, 32,* 303–330.

Lachman, M. E. (1986). Locus of control in aging research: A case for multidimensional and domain-specific assessment. *Journal of Psychology and Aging, 1,* 34–40.

Lachman, M. E. (1989). Personality and aging at the crossroads: Beyond stability versus change. In K. W. Schaie & C. Schooler (Eds.), *Social structure and aging: Psychological processes* (pp. 167–190). Hillsdale, NJ: Erlbaum.

LaRossa, R., & Reitzes, D. C. (1993). Symbolic interactionism and family studies. In P. G. Boss, W. J. Doherty, R. LaRossa, W. R. Schumm, & S. K. Steinmetz (Eds.), *Sourcebook of family theories and methods: A contextual approach* (pp. 135–163). New York: Plenum Press.

Lerner, R. M. (1986). *Concepts and theories of human development.* New York: Random House.

Levinson, D. J. (1980). Toward a conception of the adult life course. In N. J. Smelser & E. H. Erikson (Eds.), *Themes of work and love in adulthood* (pp. 265–290). Cambridge, MA: Harvard University Press.

Levinson, D. J. (1996). *The seasons of a woman's life.* New York: Knopf.

Little, B. R. (1983). Personal projects: A rationale and method for investigation. *Environment and Behavior, 15,* 273–309.

Little, B. R. (1993). Personal projects and the distributed self: Aspects of a conative psychology. In J. Suls (Ed.), *Psychological perspectives on the self: Vol. 4. The self in social perspective* (pp. 157–185). Hillsdale, NJ: Erlbaum.

MacDermid, S. M., & Crouter, A. C. (1995). Midlife, adolescence, and parental employment in family systems. *Journal of Youth and Adolescence, 24,* 29–54.

MacDermid, S. M., de Haan, L. G., & Heilbrun, G. (1996). Generativity in multiple roles. *Journal of Adult Development, 3,* 145–158.

MacDermid, S. M., Franz, Carol E., & de Reus, L. A. (in press). *Adult character: Agency, communion, insight, and the expression of generativity in midlife adults.* Chapter under consideration for inclusion in J. B. James (Ed.) volume from the Character and Competence Research Program of the Henry A. Murray Center.

MacDermid, S. M., Heilbrun, G., & de Haan, L. G. (1997). The generativity of employed mothers in multiple roles: 1979 and 1991. In M. E. Lachman & J. B. James (Eds.), *Multiple paths of midlife development* (pp. 207–240). Chicago: University of Chicago Press.

Mansfield, E. D., & McAdams, D. P. (1996). Generativity and themes of agency and communion in adult autobiography. *Personality and Social Psychology Bulletin, 22,* 721–731.

Marcia, J. E. (1980). Identity in adolescence. In J. Adelson (Ed.), *Handbook of adolescent psychology* (pp. 159–187). New York: Wiley.

Marks, S. R. (1977). Multiple roles and role strain: Some notes on human energy, time and commitment. *American Sociological Review, 42,* 921–936.

Marks, S. R., & MacDermid, S. M. (1996). Multiple roles and the self: A theory of role balance. *Journal of Marriage and the Family, 58,* 417–432.

Markus, H. (1990). On splitting the universe. *Psychological Science, 1,* 181–185.

Markus, H., & Nurius, P. (1986). Possible selves. *American Psychologist, 41,* 954–969.

Markus, H., & Wurf, E. (1987). The dynamic self-concept: A social-psychological perspective. *Annual Review of Psychology, 38,* 299–337.

McAdams, D. P. (1988). *Power, intimacy, and the life story: Personological inquiries into identity.* New York: Guilford Press.

McAdams, D. P. (1992). The five-factor model in personality: A critical appraisal. *Journal of Personality, 60,* 329–361.

McAdams, D. P., & de St. Aubin, E. (1992). A theory of generativity and its assessment through self-report, behavioral acts, and narrative themes in autobiography. *Journal of Personality and Social Psychology, 62,* 1003–1013.

McAdams, D. P., de St. Aubin, E., & Logan, R. (1993). Generativity among young, midlife, and older adults. *Pyschology and Aging, 8,* 221–230.

McArthur, A. (1962). Developmental tasks and parent-adolescent conflict. *Marriage and Family Living, 24,* 189–191.

McCrae, R. R., & Costa, P. T. (1990). *Personality in adulthood* (2nd ed.). New York: Guilford Press.

McHale, S. M., & Crouter, A. C. (1992). You can't always get what you want: Incongruence between sex-role attitudes and family work roles and its implications for marriage. *Journal of Marriage and the Family, 54,* 537–547.

Mischel, W. (1990). Personality dispositions revisited and revised: A view after three decades. In L. A. Pervin (Ed.), *Handbook of personality: Theory and research* (pp. 111–134). New York: Guilford Press.

Moen, P., Dempster-McClain, D., & Williams, R. M. (1989). Social integration and longevity: An event history analysis of women's roles and resilience. *American Sociological Review, 54,* 635–647.

Moen, P., Dempster-McClain, D., & Williams, R. M. (1992). Successful aging: A life-course perspective on women's multiple roles and health. *American Journal of Sociology, 97,* 1612–1638.

Muuss, R. E. (1988). Field theory and adolescence. In R. E. Muuss (Ed.), *Theories of adolescence* (5th ed., pp. 160–174). New York: Random House.

Neugarten, B. L. (1968). The awareness of middle age. In B. L. Neugarten (Ed.), *Middle age and aging* (pp. 93–98). Chicago: University of Chicago Press.

Neugarten, B. L. (1973). Personality change in late life: A developmental perspective. In E. C. Eisdorfer & M. Lawton (Eds.), *The psychology of adult development and aging* (pp. 311–335). Washington, DC: American Psychological Association.

Nuttbrock, L., & Freudiger, P. (1991). Identity salience and motherhood: A test of Stryker's theory. *Social Psychology Quarterly, 54,* 146–157.

Nye, F. I., & Gecas, V. (1976). The role concept: Review and delineation. In I. Nye & H. Bahr (Eds.), *Role structure and analysis of the family* (pp. 3–14). Beverly Hills, CA: Sage.

Ochse, R., & Plug, C. (1986). Cross-cultural investigation of the validity of Erikson's theory of personality development. *Journal of Personality and Social Psychology, 50,* 1240–1252.

Parsons, T. (1955). The organization of personality as a system of action. In T. Parsons & R. F. Bales (Eds.), *Family, socialization and interaction process* (pp. 133–186). New York: Free Press.

Pearlin, L. I. (1980). Life strains and psychological distress among adults. In N. J. Smelser & E. H. Erikson (Eds.), *Themes of work and love in adulthood* (pp. 174–192). Cambridge, MA: Harvard University Press.

Pervin, L. A. (1980). *Personality: Theory, assessment and research.* New York: Wiley.

Peterson, G. W. (1987). Role transitions and role identities during adolescence: A symbolic interactionist view. *Journal of Adolescent Research, 2,* 237–254.

Peterson, B. E., & Kloehnen, E. (1995). Realization of generativity in two samples of women at midlife. *Psychology and Aging, 10,* 20–29.

Peterson, B. E., & Stewart, A. J. (1990). Using personal and fictional documents to assess psychosocial development: A case study of Vera Brittain's generativity. *Psychology and Aging, 5,* 400–411.

Peterson, B. E., & Stewart, A. J. (1992, May). The assessment of generativity using the California Q sort. In E. de St. Aubin (Chair), *Emerging perspectives in adult personality development: Research concerning generativity*. Symposium conducted at the annual meeting of the Midwestern Psychological Association, Chicago.

Peterson, B. E., & Stewart, A. J. (1993). Generativity and social motives in young adults. *Journal of Personality and Social Psychology, 65*, 186–198.

Pickens, D. S. (1994). *Midlife women: Confronting the developmental challenge of formulating a generative identity*. Unpublished doctoral dissertation, Purdue University, West Lafayette, IN.

Reker, G. T., & Wong, P. T. P. (1988). Aging as an individual process: Toward a theory of personal meaning. In J. E. Birren & K. W. Schaie (Eds.), *Emergent theories of aging* (pp. 214–246). New York: Springer.

Rodeheaver, D., & Datan, N. (1981). Making it: The dialectics of middle age. In R. M. Lerner & N. A. Busch-Rossnagel (Eds.), *Individuals as producers of their development: A life-span perspective* (pp. 183–196). New York: Academic Press.

Ryff, C. D., & Heincke, S. G. (1983). Subjective organization of personality in adulthood and aging. *Journal of Personality and Social Psychology, 44*, 807–816.

Ryff, C. D., & Migdal, S. (1984). Intimacy and generativity: Self-perceived transitions. *Signs: Journal of Women in Culture and Society, 9*, 470–481.

Silverberg, S. B. (1989). *A longitudinal look at parent-adolescent relations and parents' evaluations of life and self*. Paper presented at the 10th biennial meeting of the International Society for the Study of Behavioral Development, Jyvaskyla, Finland.

Silverberg, S. B., & Steinberg, L. (1987). Adolescent autonomy, parent-adolescent conflict, and parental well-being. *Journal of Youth and Adolescence, 16*, 293–312.

Snarey, J. (1993). *How fathers care for the next generation*. Cambridge, MA: Harvard University Press.

Stevens-Long, J. (1990). Adult development: Theories past and future. In R. A. Nemiroff & C. A. Colarusso (Eds.), *New dimensions in adult development* (pp. 125–164). New York: Basic Books.

Stewart, A. J., Franz, C. E., & Layton, L. (1988). The changing self: Using personal documents to study lives. *Journal of Personality, 56*, 41–74.

Stewart, A. J., & Gold-Steinberg, S. (1990). Midlife women's political consciousness: Case studies of psychosocial development and political commitment. *Psychology of Women Quarterly, 14*, 543–566.

Stryker, S., & Statham, A. (1985). Symbolic interaction and role theory. In G. Lindzey & E. Aronson (Eds.), *Handbook of social psychology: Vol. 1. Theory and method* (3rd ed., pp. 311–378). New York: Random House.

Thoits, P. A. (1987). Negotiating roles. In F. J. Crosby (Ed.), *Spouse, parent, worker: On gender and multiple roles* (pp. 11–22). New Haven, CT: Yale University Press.

Thoits, P. A. (1992). Identity structures and psychological well-being: Gender and marital status comparisons. *Social Psychology Quarterly, 55,* 236–256.

Thomas, L. T., & Ganster, D. C. (1995). Impact of family-supportive work variables on work-family conflict and strain: A control perspective. *Journal of Applied Psychology, 80,* 6–15.

Tiedje, L. B., Wortman, C. B., Downey, G., Emmons, C., Biernat, M., & Lang, E. (1990). Women with multiple roles: Role-compatibility perceptions, satisfaction and mental health. *Journal of Marriage and the Family, 52,* 63–72.

Vaillant, G. E., & Milofsky, E. (1980). Natural history of male psychological health: IX. Empirical evidence for Erikson's model of the life cycle. *American Journal of Psychiatry, 137,* 1348–1359.

Van de Water, D. A., & McAdams, D. P. (1989). Generativity and Erikson's "belief in the species." *Journal of Research in Personality, 23,* 435–449.

Verbrugge, L. M. (1987). Role responsibilities, role burdens, and physical health. In F. J. Crosby (Ed.), *Spouse, parent, worker: On gender and multiple roles* (pp. 154–166). New Haven, CT: Yale University Press.

Waterman, A. S. (1982). Identity development from adolescence to adulthood: An extension of theory and a review of research. *Developmental Psychology, 18,* 341–358.

Waterman, A. S. (1985). Identity in the context of adolescent psychology. In A. S. Waterman (Ed.), *Identity in adolescence: Processes and contents* (pp. 5–24). New Directions for Child Development No. 30. San Francisco: Jossey-Bass.

Waterman, A. S. (1988). Identity status theory and Erikson's theory: Communalities and differences. *Developmental Review, 8,* 185–208.

Waterman, A. S. (1992). Identity as an aspect of optimal psychological functioning. In G. R. Adams, T. P. Gullotta, & R. Montemayor (Eds.), *Adolescent identity formation* (pp. 50–72). Newbury Park, CA: Sage.

Whitbourne, S. K. (1989). Comments on Lachman's "Personality and aging at the crossroads." In K. W. Schaie & C. Schooler (Eds.), *Social structure and aging: Psychological processes* (pp. 191–198). Hillsdale, NJ: Erlbaum.

Wrightsman, L. S. (1988). *Personality development in adulthood.* Newbury Park, CA: Sage.

Wrightsman, L. S. (1994). *Adult personality development: Theories and concepts.* Thousand Oaks, CA: Sage.

Zuroff, D. C. (1986). Was Gordon Allport a trait theorist? *Journal of Personality and Social Psychology, 51,* 993–1000.

7

GENERATIVITY IN ADULT LIVES: SOCIAL STRUCTURAL CONTOURS AND QUALITY OF LIFE CONSEQUENCES

COREY LEE M. KEYES AND CAROL D. RYFF

What are the contours and the consequences of generativity in adults' lives in the United States? Our inquiry originates with the larger question of how society structures adults' health and well-being. Framed by the social structure and personality perspective (House, 1981; Ryff, 1987), our study investigates the effects of age and educational stratification on generativity to understand how this aspect of adult life is shaped and

Support for writing this chapter and data for this study are from a multidisciplinary study of midlife development by the John D. and Catherine T. MacArthur Foundation Research Network on Successful Midlife Development, directed by Dr. Orville Gilbert Brim. We appreciate the support and stimulation of our MacArthur (Midlife) Network colleagues, especially our fellow members of the Social Class and Health Subgroup and the Social Responsibility Subgroup. We are grateful to Ronald C. Kessler for his assistance with matters related to the sample description. Alice S. Rossi, who guided many of the measures of social responsibility and generativity into the MacArthur Midlife Study, reviewed the chapter and constructively illuminated several important issues. We also gratefully acknowledge the helpful reviewer comments from Dan McAdams, Ed de St. Aubin, and the outside reviewer, Dan Mroczek.

touched by society. We hypothesize that generativity is shaped by social stratification processes embodied in educational attainment and aging. We also propose that having and acting on generative feelings influences the quality with which adults are able to lead their lives. Conceived of as a sociopersonal resource, generative feelings and behavior partly explain how social stratification affects adults' well-being as they age.

THE FACES OF SOCIETY AND SELF

Education and Age: Coordinates of Social Structure

According to Erikson (1950), generativity preoccupies midlife adults' hearts and minds. As the interest in guiding and molding the younger generation of individuals to become custodians of society (Kotre, 1984; McAdams & de St. Aubin, 1992), generativity is partly an ontological imperative. The reply to the generative invitation in middle adulthood depends on whether adults have established their identity and secured intimacy as young adults. Social structure, like age-graded processes,[1] shapes life by its constraints and opportunities. For example, as an accomplishment of late adolescence and young adulthood for many people, educational attainment is a launching pad for adult life (Karabel & Halsey, 1977). Education directly determines occupations and incomes (Sewell & Hauser, 1975, 1980) and indirectly affects numerous monetary sequelae (e.g., residence). Together, education and age are coordinates of social structure that, in concert, affect the quality of adults' lives, including their health and well-being.

How age and education intersect to influence quality of life has been examined from different theoretical perspectives, most of which have targeted physical health outcomes. The *divergence hypothesis* contends that social structural disparities in physical health increase as adults age. For example, Ross and Wu (1996) observed cross-sectionally and longitudinally that disparities in physical health and physical functioning between adults with different educational backgrounds diverge—and the divergence accelerates—with age. Divergence thus portrays social inequalities as worsening throughout life. The disadvantages of certain status characteristics and the advantages accrued from early opportunity and accomplishment are compounded with age. Similarly, the thesis of cumulative advantage (cf. Allison, Long, & Krauze, 1982) asserts that the fruits of education accumulate gradually with each added year of life. Social structural disparities in physical health represent an accelerating improvement for

---

[1]Development as purely ontogeny has been appended by life-span theorists (see Baltes, 1987; Dannefer, 1984, 1987; Featherman & Lerner, 1985), who cite the multiple determination of life through historical, social, as well as ontological, forces.

adults with more education as they age, whereas the health of older adults with less education gradually diminishes as they age. The theme of cumulative adversity is also evident in the double jeopardy thesis (Dowd & Bengtson, 1978) and in related studies of minority aging (Ferraro, 1987; Ferraro & Farmer, 1996), which examined the compounding of race and age-related discrimination as minorities become older adults.[2]

In contrast with the divergence hypothesis, the *convergence hypothesis* suggests that social structural differences in physical health and wellness diminish with age. The hypothesized convergence of educational disparities in physical wellness after middle adulthood could originate from structural lag (Riley, Kahn, & Foner, 1994) and the challenges of older adulthood (Dowd & Bengtson, 1978). The increase in the healthy life span of adults has not been accompanied, according to Riley and colleagues, by changes in social institutions that use the energy and talents of older adults. Without the opportunities to maintain and cultivate valued outlets, older adults are unable to engage in activities that are socially and personally rewarding.[3] Older adulthood might also consist of events and challenges that neutralize prior socioeconomic advantages. Aging creates, in effect, a level playing field. Even adults with cumulative advantages probably experience personal and physical losses that chip away at their physical health. Even if prior disadvantages are not neutralized with age, research now suggests that many adults successfully manage and adapt to life's vicissitudes. Theories posit and mounting evidence suggests that adults successfully age by amplifying assets and compensating for losses (Baltes & Baltes, 1990), as well as by choosing to spend time with people on the basis of the emotional closeness of the relationship (Carstensen, 1992). In short, a host of forces—institutional, biological, and psychological—could operate in concert to minimize the differences in physical health among older adults from various socioeconomic backgrounds.[4]

Studies show that convergence occurs during older adulthood (i.e., roughly after the ages of 60 to 65). Before converging in older adulthood, however, educational disparities in physical health actually diverge throughout younger and middle adulthood (House et al., 1990; House et al., 1994; cf. Maddox & Clark, 1992; cf. Taubman & Rosen, 1982). Social inequalities in health appear to mushroom during young and middle adulthood, becoming stagnant if not neutralized during older adulthood. The reduction of physical health inequalities is probably the result of processes

---

[2] See Smith and Waitzman (1994), who investigate the triple jeopardy of marital status, poverty status, and gender on the risk of mortality.
[3] For additional explanations (e.g., social policies) see Ferraro and Farmer (1996) and Ross and Wu (1995).
[4] It is plausible that structural lag is a jeopardizing condition that might promote educational disparities in health during older adulthood because it adds to and compounds pre-existing adversities.

leading up to (i.e., mortality), as well as defining (e.g., structural lag), older adulthood. The most impoverished and unhealthy adults are less likely to remain part of the population of older adults because they tend to die sooner than adults with better socioeconomic profiles (see e.g., Smith & Waitzman, 1994). Mortality starkly illustrates the gravity of social inequalities throughout the adult life span.

Generally missing from these prior literatures is discussion of the intervening processes that link age and education with health and well-being. That is, what are the mechanisms through which the social structural coordinates of age and education influence quality of life? As an aspect of the aging self, we see generativity as a possible route through which structural factors beget well-being. Toward illuminating the role of generativity in adults' lives, we investigate whether age and education shape generativity and whether, in turn, generative acts and feelings contribute to a sense of well-being. Elaborated next is our formulation of how generativity fits into and bridges the gap between social stratification and the quality of adult life.

Generativity as Nexus: Linking Society and Self

The question of the consequences of generativity (i.e., how it affects mental health and well-being) looms large, though it has been largely overlooked (cf. de St. Aubin & McAdams, 1995; MacDermid, De Haan, & Heilbrun, 1996). Reflecting its developmental profile (Erikson, 1950), research has focused on either the structure and meaning (Kotre, 1984; McAdams & de St. Aubin, 1992) or age trajectories of generativity (Ryff & Heincke, 1983; Ryff & Migdal, 1984; Peterson & Klohnen, 1995; Peterson & Stewart, 1993). This work suggests that generativity is a multifaceted construct that may be manifest in distinct ways. The issue of the personal use of generativity, however, receives little attention. Do generative adults benefit from feeling and acting generatively? We believe so because generativity exhibits individuals' longing to feel socially instrumental—needed by others and capable of creating positive results for others (see, e.g., Adler, 1979; Bakan, 1966; McAdams, 1996; Stewart, Franz, & Layton, 1988). By conception, generativity is the desire for and act of benefiting others. The personal ramifications of generativity are therefore often overlooked, remaining embryonic parts of theoretic developmental stages. Successful resolution of the generativity imperative paves the way for resolving the integrity task of older adulthood. Thus, seen as vital both socially (i.e., intergenerationally) and personally (i.e., developmentally), generativity should, we assert, explain variation in adults' health and well-being.

Invoking a social structural perspective, we propose that the question of generativity's consequences must be accompanied by consideration of the forces that contour the expression and experience of generativity. As agents of generativity, adults and their behavior are shaped by context. Societal opportunities and constraints are structural factors that motivate or deter generative beliefs and action (McAdams & de St. Aubin, 1992). Reflecting accomplishment and expanding opportunity, educational attainment in particular might motivate generativity by instilling social concern and engendering the desire for reciprocity. Alternatively, lack of education and its associated privations and inequalities might create various forms of alienation and diminish personal agency (Mirowsky & Ross, 1989). Education can therefore shape generative feelings and behavior by contouring social interest and feelings of agency about generative action. Education-linked occupational and earnings disparities (Sewell & Hauser, 1975, 1980) also affect the distribution of personal resources (e.g., skills) that can be instrumental for guiding and assisting the next generation. Taking these observations together, we hypothesize that the amount of generativity—behaviors, commitments, and self-conceptions—will be greater among adults who have more, compared with fewer, years of education.

Turning to consequences, we further propose that generativity illuminates social structural disparities in adults' well-being. For us, generativity is a theoretical hybrid between the interpretive lens through which the self is viewed and the awareness of one's personal resources. With regard to the former, social–psychological theory delineates numerous avenues through which the self is conceived (e.g., social comparison and reflected appraisal; see House, 1981; Rosenberg, 1979). The ways of construing oneself explicate how forces of social stratification and inequality can undermine self-conception (see, e.g., Gecas & Schwalbe, 1983; Gecas & Seff, 1990; Rosenberg & Pearlin, 1978), thereby frustrating the allegedly universal motive to protect and maintain favorable self-imagery. Following these formulations, we see generativity as a lens of self-evaluation, drawing potentially on social comparisons ("What am I able to do for my children or community compared to others?") and reflected appraisals ("Am I seen by others as a person to whom others would come for advice?").

Awareness of personal resources is another route by which social structure factors, through generativity, influence life quality. Although everyone at some time experiences serious stressors and life events, the resources with which to deal with the vagaries of life are not distributed randomly. Higher socioeconomic status means that individuals have better personal (e.g., health care) and social (e.g., social support networks) resources to offset stress and life events (see House, Landis, & Umberson, 1988; Kessler, House, Anspach, & Williams, 1995; Ross & Wu, 1995, 1996; Williams, 1990). Our claim is that the self-perception that one has such resources is part of both the experience of generativity (e.g., "I am able to do for others") and the mechanism through which it enhances, or its absence undermines, well-being. Unlike traditional resources, generativity is a personal resource given to society and the next generation, not necessarily used to extinguish the fires of one's own stress and life events (cf. Midlarsky, 1991). As a resource for others and as a way of viewing oneself favorably, generativity may explain some of the educational disparity in quality of life.

PSYCHOLOGICAL AND SOCIAL WELL-BEING: BAROMETERS OF SELF AND SOCIETY

Well-being is an under-used class of outcomes for monitoring the quality of adults' lives. Most studies of social stratification employ physical functioning, physical health, or risk of mortality as dependent measures, ignoring more positive features of physical and mental health (cf. Marmot, Ryff, Bumpass, Shipley, & Marks, 1997). In the subjective well-being literature, numerous studies document educational and age differences in well-being (Diener, 1984; Herzog, Rodgers, & Woodworth, 1982). Few studies, however, explore the theoretical intersection of education and age. Theoretical conceptions of well-being as anything more than life satisfaction or personal happiness are also scarce. Research even shows that almost everyone feels relatively happy (Diener & Diener, 1996), suggesting that many extant measures of well-being do not adequately capture or reach into the deeply divisive and powerful social conditions in society. However, considerable theory, organized along disciplinary lines, provides blueprints regarding the criteria of life and its qualities.

Sociological theory, for example, is replete with examples of the uncertain and laborious fit of individuals and society. The quality of our ties to one another and society affects us personally and likewise affects the machinations of society. Social wellness originates in the classic themes of anomie (Durkheim, 1951; Mirowsky & Ross, 1989; Seeman, 1959, 1983) and alienation (Israel, 1971; McLellan, 1977). The issue of solidarity is carried forward from classic sociology to queries about the unity and sympathies of individuals with society. Drawing on these theoretical roots, we explored multiple operational dimensions of social well-being (see Keyes, 1995, 1996a for more detail).

Each dimension of social wellness represents challenges that people face as social beings. People must try to cultivate a genuine sense of belonging in a world where they do not live their entire lives basking in the unconditional love of family or friends (social integration). Adults struggle to feel like and be valuable contributors to a world that does not value them equally or value them merely for being human (social contribution). People also work toward making sense of what is a complex world (social coherence). Another challenge is to see some growth and evolution in a world that does not automatically change or improve (social actualization). Lastly, adults grapple with accepting other people, most of whom are strangers (social acceptance). Favorable resolution of these social challenges represents positive social functioning.

Psychological theory is also saturated with criteria of individual health and wellness. The continuity of themes in psychological well-being center around recognizing and striving to realize talents and potential (Waterman, 1993). The eudamonic quest is personified by self actualization (Maslow, 1968), full functioning (Rogers, 1961), individuation (Jung, 1933; Von Franz, 1964), and maturity (Allport, 1961), as well as stages of adult development (Erikson, 1959) and fulfillment of developmental tasks (see Ryff, 1982, 1984 for detailed reviews).

Each dimension of psychological well-being (see Ryff, 1989a, 1989b; Ryff & Keyes, 1995) indicates the challenges individuals encounter as they strive to function fully and realize their unique talents. Adults must strive to feel good about themselves, while facing complex and sometimes unpleasant personal aspects (self-acceptance). They attempt to develop and maintain warm and trusting interpersonal relationships in contexts that do not always engender warmth or trust (positive relations with others). People also seek some degree of self-determination and personal authority, in a society that sometimes surreptitiously desires submission and blind obedience (autonomy). Another challenge includes striving to shape the immediate environment into what one needs and desires, despite a world that often resists shaping (environmental mastery). Adults also endeavor for a direction in life when the world offers none or provides unsavory alternatives (purpose in life). Lastly, people encounter the challenge of growing personally and realizing their potential because it is often easier but much less rewarding to remain the same but unhappy person (personal growth). Rising to life's psychological challenges elevates positive psychological functioning.

In summary, our research investigated whether and how generativity matters in adults' lives. As a sociopersonal resource, generativity is the capacity to give to others with the goal of maintaining society through the next generation. Society through social stratification structures adults' feelings of personal and social worth and capabilities to assist others. Generativity also matters because it affects self-evaluation and how adults feel about their lives. As generative adults, people realize their potential as a valuable resource that, when imparted to others, maintains and improves the quality of society. Feelings and expressions of generativity therefore address the psychological challenge toward self-realization and the social challenge of solidarity. Psychological and social wellness should therefore be higher among individuals who report higher levels of each component of generativity. Lastly, generativity is a potential explanation of how education affects well-being. People with more education report higher levels of social and psychological well-being because they possess more social interest and view themselves as generative resources capable of helping others and the next generation. In short, social stratification helps to determine whether people perpetuate the quality of their lives and the quality of society through generative feelings and behavior.

The following sections of this chapter provide a description of the national probability sample with which we investigated the questions outlined above and provide a summary of our operational measures of key constructs. We then present the research findings on the social structural contours of generativity and its consequences for life quality.

RESEARCH SAMPLE

Underscoring our emphasis on how societal forces shape generativity, we conducted this research with a national probability sample showing wide diversity on key variables and constructs of interest (age, education, generativity, social, and psychological well-being). The sample, drawn with random-digit dialing procedures, consisted of noninstitutionalized, English-speaking adults, age 25 to 74, who resided in the 48 contiguous states, and whose household included a least one telephone. The first stage of the multistage sampling design selected households with equal probability through telephone numbers. Disproportionate stratified sampling was used at the second stage to select respondents. The sample was stratified by age and sex, with oversampling of men between the ages of 65 and 74. Working but nonhousehold numbers (e.g., business) were eliminated by definition. Working numbers that were unsuccessfully contacted 10 times (i.e., no answer by human or answering machine) were also eliminated as elements of the population. Field procedures were initiated in January 1995 and lasted approximately 13 months. With a response rate of 70% for the telephone phase and a response rate of 87% for the self-administered questionnaire phase, the sample consisted of 3,032 adults.

Adults who agreed to participate in the complete study were administered a computer-assisted telephone interview lasting 30 minutes on average. Adults were then mailed two questionnaire booklets requiring about 1.5 hours on average to complete. All respondents were offered $20, a commemorative pen, periodic reports of study findings, and a copy of a final study monograph as incentives for participation in all phases of the study.

Table 1 reports the demographic characteristics of the sample

TABLE 1
Sample Characteristics (N = 3,032): MacArthur Foundation's
Successful Midlife National Study

Demographic Variable	Breakdown	Unweighted %	Weighted %
Age*			
	Young Adults, 25–39	33.2	40.5
	Midlife Adults, 40–59	46.0	40.3
	Older Adults, 60–74	20.8	19.2
Gender			
	Males	48.5	43.5
	Females	51.5	56.5
Education			
	12 Years or Less	39.2	51.5
	13 Years or More	60.8	48.5
Marital Status			
	Married	64.1	68.1
	All Others	35.9	31.9
Race			
	Caucasian	87.8	83.8
	African American	6.8	11.4
	All Other Races	4.4	5.7

Note. Sample weight consists of a poststratification component to match the sociodemographic distribution of the United States on the basis of the October 1995 Current Population Survey.
*Average age of the unweighted sample is M = 47.0 (SD = 13.1) and, when the sample is weighted, M = 45.3 (SD = 13.5).

when unweighted and when weighted. The sample weight adjusts for unequal probabilities of household selection and unequal probabilities of respondent selection within households. Moreover, the sample weight poststratifies the sample to match the October 1995 Current Population Survey proportions of adults on the basis of gender, age, race, education, and marital status, as well as the proportions of adults residing in metropolitan (nonmetro) areas and regions (Northeast, Midwest, South, and West) of the United States. On the one hand, the unweighted sample misrepresents the U.S. population in terms of most demographic characteristics. On the other hand, all components of the weighting variable are functions of independent variables, and multivariate estimates that were based on the unweighted sample should therefore be unbiased and efficient (Winship & Radbill, 1994) provided the model is correctly specified. Because conclusions of multivariate analyses (ANOVA and regression) are unchanged by weighting, we reported analyses of the unweighted sample.[5]

---

[5]One of a possible 21 two-way interactions of mean-level generativity by age, education, and gender varied with sample weighting. The interaction went from statistically significant (p < .05, weighted sample) to marginally statistically significant (p = .10, unweighted sample). We do not discuss the weight-contingent interaction because no other estimate was affected by sample weighting.

OPERATIONAL DEFINITIONS

Generativity

We measured behavioral, normative, and self-construed generativity (McAdams & de St. Aubin, 1992). The *behavioral measures* attempt to represent Erikson's (1950) notion of the expansion of care beyond oneself toward others. Respondents indicated whether they give emotional support (defined for respondents as comforting, listening to problems, or giving advice) in an average month to any of three generative targets. Subsequently, respondents indicated whether they provide, in an average month, unpaid assistance (defined for respondents as help around the house, transportation, or childcare) to any of three generative targets. The targets of emotional support and unpaid assistance are (a) children or grandchildren; (b) other family members or close friends; and (c) anyone else, such as neighbors or people at church. Each behavioral measure of generativity therefore ranges from 0 to 4, where 0 means a respondent does not give, for example, emotional support, and 4 means a respondent does give emotional support to all generative targets. As such, our behavioral measures of generativity reflected the extensiveness of individuals' expressions of generativity through emotional support and unpaid assistance.

We operationalize *generative commitment* through felt normative obligations to the primary domain and the civic domain of society. Our conception is more sociological, compared with McAdams' psychological conception (see McAdams, Hart, & Maruna, chapter 1, this volume) of generative commitment as personal investment in goals to act generatively. In our study, respondents were given a list of hypothetical situations and asked to rate how much obligation they would feel if the situation happened to them, on a scale from 0 (no obligation at all) to 10 (a very great obligation). The primary domain measured individuals' commitments to assist and care for other people in need. Three examples of the eight items measuring primary obligation are: (a) to raise the child of a close friend if the friend died, (b) to take your divorced or unemployed adult child back into your home, and (c) to drop your plans when your children seem very troubled. On the same scale from 0 to 10, respondents then indicated how much obligation they felt toward civic expressions of their commitments. Three examples of the six items comprising the scale of civic obligation are: (a) to serve on a jury if called, (b) to keep fully informed about national news and public issues, and (c) to work hard even if you don't like or respect your employer or supervisor. Higher scores on each scale indicate more obligation.

Lastly, generativity consists of *self-construal*, of which we measured three facets. First, our measure of *generative concern* consisted of three items that tap expectations for, control over, and thought and effort into one's contributions to others. Looking 10 years into the future, respondents evaluated the quality of their contribution to the welfare and well-being of other people on a scale from 0 (worst) to 10 (best). Moreover, respondents judged the amount of control, on a 0 (no control at all) to 10 (very much control) scale, they think they have over their contributions to the welfare and well-being of other people. Lastly, each respondent indicated how much thought and effort, on a scale from 0 (no thought and effort) to 10 (very much thought and effort), they put into their contributions to the welfare and well-being of others these days. Higher scores indicate more concern for generativity toward others.

In turn, we used a reduced and slightly modified version of the Loyola Generativity Scale (R-LGS; original scale is LGS; McAdams & de St. Aubin, 1992) to measure what we call *generative qualities*. Respondents indicated whether six descriptive statements described them, on a scale from 1 (a lot) to 4 (not at all). Respondents evaluate whether others would say (a) that you have made unique contributions to society, (b) that you have important skills you can pass along to others, (c) that many people come to you for advice, (d) that you feel that other people need you, (e) that you have had a good influence on the lives of many people, and (f) that you like to teach things to people. Higher scores indicate that respondents view themselves as having more generative qualities. Keep in mind that McAdams and de St. Aubin (1992) conceived of the LGS as a measure of generative concern. We believe that the LGS in general and our R-LGS in particular measures self-conception ("Am I generative?") and that our measure of generative concern comes closer to operationalizing concern about one's generativity (i.e., "Do I think about whether, when, and how much I am generative?").

Last, we measured a constellation of personal characteristics that represents a putative facilitator of generativity. Respondents indicated how much, on a scale from 0 (not at all) to 10 (very much), they are (a) caring, (b) wise, and (c) knowledgeable. We believe that care, wisdom, and knowledge are a constellation of traits that define the essence of a generative personality and self-definition. Higher scores indicate the subjective assessment of the possession of more characteristics that delineate generative self-conception and probably encourage generative behavior.

Table 2 presents the descriptive statistics of the generative variables and scales. The scales possess adequate internal (α) reliabilities, ranging from .73 to .84. All scales and variables indicating components of generativity correlate positively, suggesting that individuals who express generativity to more people also feel more primary and civic obligations and also view themselves as more generative individuals with generative concerns, capabilities, and qualities. The correlations also suggest that our parsing of the generativity domain was reasonable and replicated McAdams and de St. Aubin's (1992) conceptual model. That is, the two behavioral

TABLE 2
Correlations and Descriptive Statistics of Generativity

Generativity	1	2	3	4	5	6	7
1. Emotional Support	—	.46	.18	.14	.18	.22	.09
2. Unpaid Assistance		—	.15	.12	.15	.20	.08
3. Primary Obligation			—	.44	.30	.22	.27
4. Civic Obligation				—	.29	.27	.31
5. Generative Concern					—	.42	.31
6. Generative Qualities (R-LGS)						—	.34
7. Generative Traits							—
M	2.0	1.2	59.9	47.0	20.7	17.0	23.9
SD	1.0	1.0	13.5	10.1	6.0	3.8	3.8
Range	0–4	0–4	0–80	0–60	0–30	0–24	0–30
Alpha Reliability	—	—	.83	.80	.78	.84	.73

All correlations are statistically significant at $p < .01$ (two−tailed).
Note. All variables and scales scored in positive direction; — means indicators do not form a scale measuring a latent construct.

components correlate more highly than with the normative and self-construal components, the two normative obligation scales correlate more highly than with the behavioral and self-construal components, and the scales of self-construed generativity intercorrelate more highly than with most other components.

Well-Being

Psychological well-being is measured with Ryff's (1989b) six dimensions of positive psychological functioning (see Exhibit 1 for scale definitions and items). In a prior national probability sample (Ryff & Keyes, 1995), the same 3-item scales used in this study replicated the proposed theoretical structure and age and gender profiles as obtained with the original 20-item scales. Social well-being is measured with Keyes' (1995) five dimensions of positive social functioning (see Table 3 for scale definitions and items). The 3-item scales used in this sample replicated the theoretical structure of social wellness using more extensive measures in a local probability sample (Keyes, 1996a). Moreover, the larger scales and the current 3-item scales exhibit construct validity (Keyes, 1996a). All social well-being scales correlate modestly with dysphoria and global well-being (happiness and satisfaction) and correlate minimally with physical health and perceived optimism. The scales of social wellness correlate strongly with measures of social health and functioning like anomie, perceived external control, perceived neighborhood quality, as well as with a measure whether individuals engage in prosocial community activities.

For present purposes, we investigated the consequences of generativity by using a composite index of psychological well-being (i.e., sum of 6 psychological well-being scales) and social well-being (i.e., sum of 5 social well-being scales).[6] Higher scores indicate more positive levels of well-being. The internal (α) reliability of the overall psychological wellness scale is .80, and the overall social wellness scale is .81. The correlation of social and psychological well-being is $r = .52$. ($p < .001$). The objectives of this study and the lack of theoretical specificity at this time argue against hypotheses of relationships of social structure and generativity with specific dimensions of psychological or social well-being. For practical reasons as well, we chose to elaborate the nuances of social structure and the multiple components of generativity, while working with two broad constructs of well-being as outcomes. Maintaining multidimensionality and complexity

---

[6]Respondents with missing data on only 1 of the 3 items on a scale were imputed the mean of the 2 items with data present. Respondents with missing data on 2 of the 3 items were imputed the value of the 1 item with data present. Respondents with missing data on all 3 items for a scale were omitted from the study. Only 35 (1.1%) respondents were omitted from the overall psychological well-being scale, and 52 (1.7%) were omitted from the overall social well-being scale.

EXHIBIT 1

Operational Definitions (High Scorers) and Indicators of Theory-Guided Well-Being Dimensions

Psychological	Social
Self-Acceptance: possess positive attitude toward the self; acknowledge and accept multiple aspects of self; feel positive about past life.	*Social Acceptance*: have positive attitudes toward people; acknowledge others and generally accept people, despite others' sometimes complex and perplexing behavior.
1. I like most parts of my personality (+).	1. People who do a favor expect nothing in return (+).
2. When I look at the story of my life, I am pleased with how things have turned out so far (+).	2. People do not care about other peoples' problems (−).
3. In many ways I feel disappointed about my achievements in life (−).	3. I believe that people are kind (+).
Personal Growth: have feeling of continued development and potential and are open to new experience; feel increasingly self-knowledgeable and effective.	*Social Actualization*: care about and believe society is evolving positively; think society has potential to grow positively; think society is realizing potential.
1. For me, life has been a continuous process of learning, changing, and growth (+).	1. The world is becoming a better place for everyone (+).
2. I think it is important to have new experiences that challenge how I think about myself and the world (+).	2. Society has stopped making progress (−).
3. I gave up trying to make big improvements in my life a long time ago (−).	3. Society isn't improving for people like me (−).
Purpose in Life: have goals and a sense of direction in life; present and past life are meaningful; hold beliefs that give purpose to life.	*Social Contribution*: feel they have something valuable to give to society; think their daily activities are valued by their community.
1. Some people wander aimlessly through life, I am not one of them (+).	1. I have something valuable to give to the world (+).
2. I live one day at a time and don't really think about the future (−).	2. My daily activities do not produce anything worthwhile for my community (−).
3. I sometimes feel as if I've done all there is to do in life (−).	3. I have nothing important to contribute to society (−).

Environmental Mastery: feel competent and able to manage a complex environment; choose or create personally suitable contexts.

1. The demands of life often get me down (−).
2. In general, I feel I am in charge of the situation in which I live (+).
3. I am good at managing the responsibilities of daily life (+).

Autonomy: are self-determining, independent, and regulate behavior internally; resist social pressures to think and act in certain ways; evaluate self by personal standards.

1. I tend to be influenced by people with strong opinions (−).
2. I have confidence in my own opinions, even if they are different from the way most other people think (+).
3. I judge myself by what I think is important, not by the values of what others think is important (+).

Positive Relations With Others: have warm, satisfying, trusting relationships; are concerned about others' welfare; capable of strong empathy, affection, and intimacy; understand give-and-take of human relationships.

1. Maintaining close relationships has been difficult and frustrating for me (−).
2. People would describe me as a giving person, willing to share my time with others (+).
3. I have not experienced many warm and trusting relationships with others (−).

Social Coherence: see a social world that is intelligible, logical, and predictable; care about and are interested in society and community.

1. The world is too complex for me (−).
2. I cannot make sense of what's going on in the world (−).
3. I find it easy to predict what will happen next in society (+).

Social Integration: feel part of community; think they belong, feel supported, and share commonalities with community.

1. I don't feel I belong to anything I'd call a community (−).
2. I feel close to other people in my community (+).
3. My community is a source of comfort (+).

Note. A negative sign indicates an item that is reverse-coded. The response option is *agree* or *disagree* (*slightly, moderately,* or *strongly*) that the item is self-descriptive.

simultaneously across all facets of generativity and all components of psychological and social well-being produces an unwieldy analytic and interpretive challenge.

Social Structure

Age and education were the two primary social structural coordinates in our analysis. Age was coded into young adulthood (ages 25 to 39), midlife (ages 40 to 59), and older adulthood (ages 60 to 74) to represent periods of adult life (e.g., see Levinson, 1978). Education was measured as the highest grade of school or year of college completed. We coded education into a dichotomy, coded 0 for respondents with 12 or fewer years of education and coded 1 for respondents with 13 or more years of education. Dichotomizing education slightly reduces the correlation between education and well-being but better represents what we feel is one of the deeper divisions to originate from education (e.g., occupational stratification into blue and white collar).

Our regression models also included several social structural control variables that might affect both educational attainment and wellness and could affect both generativity and wellness. We adjusted our regressions for gender, marital status (married or cohabiting = 1; else = 0), parental status (have biological or adopted children = 1; none = 0), employment status (working or self-employed = 1; other = 0), racial status (Whites = reference category; all others dummy coded separately—Black; Native American or Aleutian Islander/Eskimo; Asian or Pacific Islander; Multiracial; and Other Race). Last, we controlled for self-perceived physical health 10 years ago and current physical health, measured on scales from 0 (worst) to 10 (best).

RESEARCH FINDINGS

Our presentation of research findings begins with investigation of the social structural shape of generativity. Of interest is whether our age and educational groups showed differences on the various measures of generativity. To answer these questions, we conducted multiple, followed by univariate, ANOVAs, which test mean-level differences of each component of generativity by education and age, adjusting for any gender differences. We then investigate the consequences of generativity with regression procedures, attempting to illustrate the purported positive association of generativity with well-being and the extent to which generativity explains educational differences in well-being.

The interactive effects of education and age on well-being are also examined to investigate the divergence and the convergence hypotheses of social structure. Cross-sectionally, the convergence and divergence hypotheses predict a positive main effect coefficient of the regression of well-being on education. However, the convergence hypothesis predicts a negative, whereas the divergence hypothesis predicts a positive, coefficient reflecting the interaction of education with age. The negative interaction coefficient signifies how much the beneficial effect of more, compared with less, education diminishes with age; a positive interaction reflects how much more beneficial educational attainment is for adults as they age.

The Social Structural Contours of Generativity

We provide graphic summaries of how various aspects of generativity are shaped by age and education (see Table A, Appendix, for descriptive statistics of each dimension by education, gender, and age). The figures are organized according to the statistical findings; that is, we graph age and education differences, or their interaction, only if they emerge as statistically significant effects in the multivariate and subsequent univariate analyses. Moreover, though not part of the theoretical focus of this chapter, gender played a prominent role in the expression of generativity, and its effects on well-being are, therefore, presented (the gender effects are substantively interpreted in the discussion). Multivariate (ANOVA) tests revealed statistically significant mean-level differences in aspects of generativity by education, Wilks $F(7, 2877) = 12.9$, $p < .001$; by age, Wilks $F(14, 5756) = 23.1$, $p < .001$; and by gender, Wilks $F(7, 2877) = 25.6$, $p < .001$. Subsequent univariate tests showed that age shapes all aspects of generativity. Education, too, structures most dimensions of generativity. In some instances, the impact of education and age on generativity depends on gender.

Figure 1.a plots the social contouring of the *extensiveness of emotional support to others*. Women, compared with men, extend their emotional support to more people; for gender main effect, $F(1, 2952) = 69.2$, $p < .001$. Gender differences in the extensiveness of emotional support parallels research showing that mothers, compared with fathers, provide more types of help to their children (Rossi & Rossi, 1990; see chapter 9). In general, emotional support is more extensive among midlife and older adults—for age main effect, $F(2, 2952) = 16.7$, $p < .001$, and among more educated adults—for education main effect, $F(1, 2952) = 21.9$, $p < .001$. The effects of education and age on emotional support are interactive; for age by education, $F(2, 2952) = 13.2$, $p < .001$. As Figure 1.a reveals, the interaction shows that education does not structure emotional support for younger adults. Perhaps young adults invest their energy and attention in their careers and their families, suggesting that the demands of young adulthood could level the educational differences in the behavioral expression of generativity.

Figure 1.b illustrates a different, and more simplistic, pattern of find-

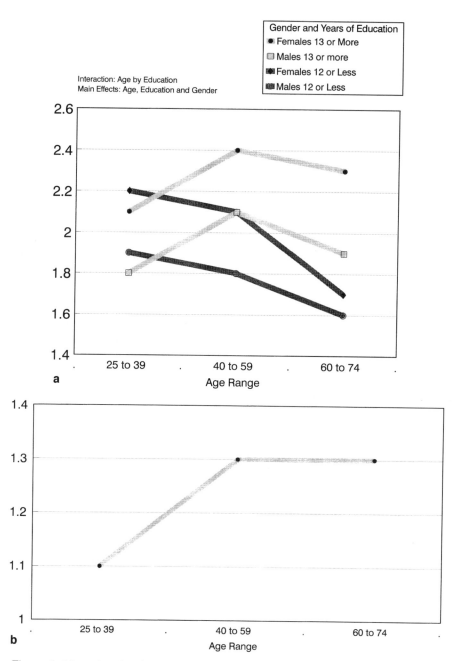

Figure 1. Mean levels of generative behavior. a, mean extensiveness of emotional support; b, mean extensiveness of unpaid assistance.

ings for the second behavioral indicator of generativity: *extensiveness of unpaid assistance to others*. Here, there is only a main effect of age, $F(2, 2952) = 13.8$, $p < .001$, with the figure showing that younger adults provide unpaid assistance to fewer people. We note, however, that all adults are generative for at least one other person—all age groups report providing support or assistance to at least one person on average. Among midlife and older adults, more than one other person is the recipient of generative emotional support and assistance, a trajectory perhaps reflective of weaker or more specific commitments and obligations during young adulthood.

Analysis of the normative components of generativity suggests, however, that generative norms and social commitments are not uniformly lower among young adults. For example, as illustrated in Figure 2.a, younger adults feel more *primary obligation* than midlife and older adults; for age main effect, $F(2, 2952) = 11.8$, $p < .001$. Our findings therefore suggest that younger adults appear to be more invested in the specific familial domain. Younger adults, in other words, feel a greater obligation to help other people and children. Women also feel more obligation than men to assist other people; for gender main effect, $F(1, 2952) = 89.1$, $p < .001$. Primary obligations are felt equally, however, by adults of each educational background. Regardless of educational attainment, commitment to the intimate circle of people and children appear palpable and salient.

Alternatively, Figure 2.b shows that younger adults feel less *civic obligation* than midlife and older adults; for age main effect, $F(2, 2952) = 61.6$, $p < .001$. Education also contours civic obligations, with those of higher educational levels feeling more obligated to assist society and its institutions; for education main effect, $F(1, 2952) = 23.8$, $p < .001$. Perhaps because of the inequalities experienced and social value imputed to individuals of different educational backgrounds, adults with more education feel more obligation and commitment to society (see also Mirowsky & Ross, 1989). Finally, gender contours civic obligations, with women reporting higher levels than men; for gender main effect, $F(1, 2952) = 6.0$, $p < .001$. Women therefore feel more obligated than men to assist social institutions as well as people.

Analyses of the first component of self-construed generativity, *generative concern*, revealed significant differences by age, $F(2, 2886) = 8.8$, $p < .001$; education, $F(1, 2886) = 18.0$, $p < .001$; and gender, $F(1, 2886) = 48.9$, $p < .001$; as well as revealed an interaction of the effect of age by gender, $F(2, 2886) = 6.4$, $p < .01$, on generative concern. As shown in Figure 3.a, adults with 13 years or more of education feel more concern for others' welfare and well-being than adults with 12 or fewer years of education. Moreover, younger and midlife adults report more concern than older adults. Although women generally report more generative concern than men, older men and older women report about the same level of concern. Thus, although they do not extend their generativity to as many

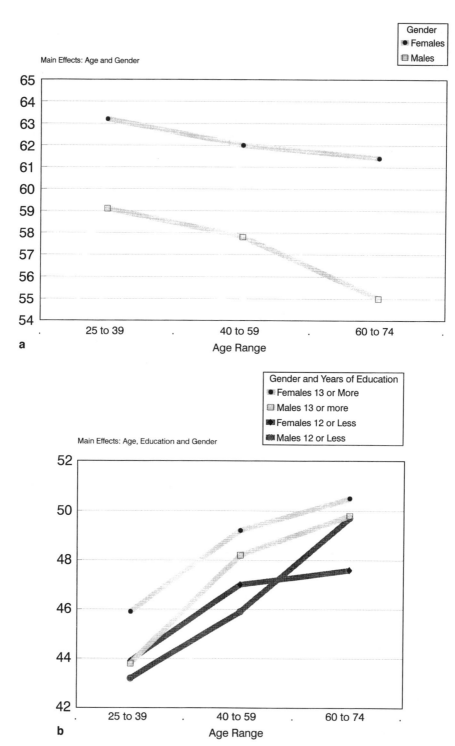

Figure 2. Mean levels of generative commitment. a, primary; b, civic obligations.

people or feel as much obligation to society as midlife adults, young adults think about, try, and expect to contribute to others' welfare and well-being as much as midlife adults. Education also appears to structure concern, perhaps by instilling self-reflection or the feeling that one's educational advantage should be reciprocated socially.

Analysis of self-construed *generative qualities* (i.e., R-LGS) also revealed main effects of age, $F(2, 2886) = 8.6$, $p < .001$; education, $F(1, 2886) = 63.0$, $p < .001$; and gender, $F(1, 2886) = 11.1$, $p < .001$; along with an interaction of the effect of education by gender, $F(1, 2886) = 8.7$, $p < .01$. Figure 3.b shows that midlife adults perceive themselves as greater resources for teaching, guiding, and assisting others than younger and older adults. Moreover, the educational disparity in the perception of oneself as a generative resource is greatest for women. More education appears to promote everyone's generative self-conceptions, but education seems a particular enhancement to women's self-images as people who can guide and teach others and to whom others come for advice.

Last, analysis of trait-like characteristics that *facilitate generativity* showed main effects of age, $F(2, 2886) = 6.8$, $p < .001$; and gender, $F(1, 2886) = 17.1$, $p < .001$; as well as an interaction of education by gender, $F(1, 2886) = 3.9$, $p < .05$. Figure 3.c illustrates that, with age, adults view themselves as increasingly caring, wise, and knowledgeable. Moreover, women with more education define themselves as a more characteristically generative than women with 12 or fewer years of education. However, higher educational attainment does not coincide with increased generative qualities for men. In fact, men with more education tend to feel less personally generative than men with 12 or fewer years of education.

The Life Quality Consequences of Generativity

What are the personal benefits and possible costs of generativity? Does generativity explain the relationship of education, as well as age, with overall wellness? We performed hierarchical regression of psychological and social well-being onto the indicators of social structure and each set of measures reflecting the components of generativity. Step 1 regresses each composite of well-being (psychological or social) onto the control variables and education, age, and the interaction term (computed by multiplying education by the age dummy variables). If the interaction of education and age was not statistically significant at any step, we reestimated the final set of equations omitting the interaction term. We note that our order of the entry of each generativity components—behavioral aspects are entered before normative and self-construal aspects—is not an implicit causal argument. Although our cross-sectional design does not permit testing of causal

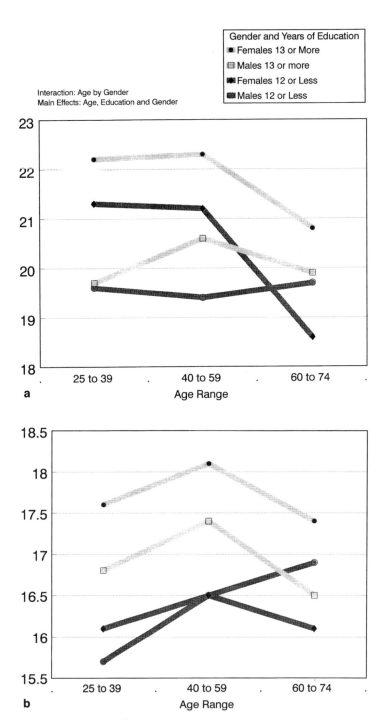

Figure 3. Mean levels of generative self-conception. a, generative concern; b, generative qualities (R-LGS); and c, civic obligation.

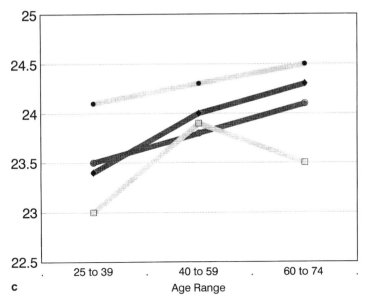

c

Figure 3 Continued.

directionality, we see the various components of generativity working reciprocally and interactively through time.

The top of Table 3 presents the hierarchical regression of psychological well-being onto the independent variables. The disparities of psychological well-being by education neither diverge nor converge with age. The interaction of education and age was therefore dropped from the final models. However, adults with 13 or more, compared with 12 or fewer, years of education feel psychologically healthier. Older adults at each educational level, with all other variables held constant, report higher levels of overall psychological well-being than do younger adults; midlife and younger adults report similar overall psychological well-being profiles. Moving to step 4, the final model shows that nearly all measures of generativity predict psychological well-being. Supporting more people emotionally, feeling more obligated to civic society, having more generative concern for others' welfare and well-being, seeing oneself as more of a generative resource, and possessing more generative personal qualities correspond with higher levels of psychological well-being. Thus, generative behavior, generative social obligations, and generative self-definitions are key ingredients in the recipe for psychological wellness.

Generativity also explains social structural differences in psychological wellness. The difference in psychological well-being between older and younger adults is not explained by behavioral generativity at step 2. Rather, the age difference disappears when psychological well-being is

TABLE 4
Hierarchical (Ordinary Least Squares) Regression of Well-Being

Regressors	Step 1 b	Step 1 β	Step 2 b	Step 2 β	Step 3 b	Step 3 β	Step 4 b	Step 4 β
Psychological Well-Being (N = 2,888)								
12 Yrs or Less Education	—	—	—	—	—	—	—	—
13 Yrs or More Education	4.2**	.14	3.9**	.13	3.5**	.12	3.0**	.10
Young Adults	—	—	—	—	—	—	—	—
Midlife Adults	.40	.01	.35	.01	-.17	-.01	-.73	-.03
Older Adults	2.0**	.05	2.2**	.06	1.4	.04	1.2	.03
Extensiveness Emotional Support			1.6**	.11	1.2**	.08	.61*	.04
Extensiveness Unpaid Assistance			.61**	.04	.40	.03	.04	.01
Primary Obligation					.09**	.08	.02	.02
Civic Obligation					.22**	.16	.09**	.06
Generative Concern							.15**	.06
Generative Qualities (R-LGS)							.74**	.20
Generative Traits							.82***	.22
intercept	70.9		68.7		57.1		39.9	
R^2	.16		.17		.21		.32	

Social Well-Being (N = 2,891)

	Model 1		Model 2		Model 3		Model 4	
Education by Midlife Adults	1.0	.03	.75	.03	.58	.02	.75	.03
Education by Older Adults	3.6**	.08	3.1*	.07	2.9*	.07	3.7**	.08
12 Yrs or Less Education	—	—	—	—	—	—	—	—
13 Yrs or More Education	4.4**	.16	4.2**	.16	3.8**	.14	2.8**	.11
Young Adults	—	—	—	—	—	—	—	—
Midlife Adults	1.8*	.07	1.8*	.07	.70	.03	.27	.01
Older Adults	1.0	.03	1.5	.05	-.37	-.01	-.59	-.02
Extensiveness Emotional Support			1.6**	.11	1.2**	.09	.61*	.04
Extensiveness Unpaid Assistance			1.1**	.08	.86**	.07	.43	.03
Primary Obligation					-.01	-.01	-.06**	-.06
Civic Obligation					.34**	.26	.24**	.18
Generative Concern							.29**	.13
Generative Qualities (R-LGS)							.74**	.21
Generative Traits							.23**	.07
intercept	44.9		42.3		30.7		20.4	
R^2	.11		.14		.20		.28	

Note. All models adjust for marital, parental, employment, and racial status, as well as gender, current health, and health 10 years ago. Results are based on unweighted data.

*p < .05; **p < .01 (two-tailed).

regressed onto generative obligations at step 3. Although mean-level analyses reveal that older adults engage in more extensive generative behavior, the heart of the difference in overall psychological well-being between younger and older adults is that older adults feel less obligated to care for other people but feel more obligated to care for society and its institutions. Step 2 through step 4 also show that the generativity components explain about one-third of the relationship between education and psychological well-being. Behavioral generativity at step 2 reduces the education coefficient by only 7%. Generative norms, at all levels of generative behavior, reduce the educational coefficient another 10% at step 3. Net of generative behavior and norms, the self-construal measures of generativity reduce the educational coefficient by another 17% at step 4.

In contrast to psychological well-being, disparities in overall social wellness by education diverge with age. The step 1 regression equation reveals a positive interaction coefficient of education by age. Adults with more education feel socially healthier than adults with 12 or fewer years of education. However, the educational disparity in social well-being increases dramatically among older adults. The final model at step 4 reveals that all generativity components predict social well-being. Providing emotional support to more people and having more civic obligation, more generative concern, more generative resources, and more generative qualities coincide with better overall social well-being. Every element of generativity that predicts better psychological well-being also predicts better social wellness. The one glaring difference is that feeling more primary obligation, all other things being equal, corresponds with lower social well-being. Some commitments may exact personal costs, perhaps because feeling obligated to care for others prevents individuals from rising to the challenges of social well-ness.

Generativity explains social structural differences in social well-being. As with psychological wellness, the age difference in social well-being (between midlife and younger adults) is not explained by behavioral generativity at step 2. Instead, the age difference reduces to zero, when social well-being is regressed onto generative obligations at step 3.

Midlife adults are socially healthier than younger adults, apparently because midlife adults are relieved of primary obligations and free to be obligated to civic society—and that is regardless of the extensiveness of their emotional support and unpaid assistance to others. Moreover, step 2 through step 4 show that the generativity components explain upwards of 40% of the relationship between education and social well-being. At step 2, behavioral generativity reduces the main effect of education by only 5%, while generative norms reduce the main effect of education by another 10% at step 3. Self-construals of generativity reduce the main effect of education by as much as 26% at step 4. On the other hand, the educational disparity among older adults (i.e., the interaction) is reduced 14% by behavioral generativity at step 2 and only 6% by generative norms at step 3. Generative self-conception does not explain the divergence in older adulthood. Insofar as divergence reflects the cumulative advantage of valuable resources, the educational gap in social health for older adults is best explained by the transmission of one's own resources (e.g., emotional support) to more people, rather than flattering self-conceptions as generative.

DISCUSSION AND FUTURE DIRECTIONS

Individuals are embedded and stratified in society. The objective of our research is to move toward understanding how social stratification affects adults' health and well-being. Because social stratification connotes personal worth and shapes personal experiences and access to resources, one's position in society can be a blessing or a curse. Social placement affects whether and how much adults perceive that they have valuable skills and knowledge that they can impart to others. In other words, all forms of generativity (i.e., self-conception, norms, and behavior) are central to understanding how social stratification affects health and well-being. Generativity is therefore noteworthy from the angles of social science as well as the helping professions and politics for at least three reasons.

First, society contours generativity. Midlife and often older adults, adults with more education, and women tend to exhibit greater levels of diverse aspects of generativity than young adults, adults with fewer years of education, and men. In two instances, young adults show more generativity through generative concern for others' welfare and well-being and much more obligation to primary ties than midlife and older adults. Consistent with Erikson's (1950) argument that younger adulthood demands identity and intimacy, we believe that younger adults' lower levels on most other aspects of generativity reflects pressures from career and family. Perhaps relieved of primary obligations, midlife and older adults give emotional support and unpaid assistance to more people and feel less primary but more civic obligations.

Such a simple summary belies the complexity of social structural effects on self-conceived generativity. Perhaps representing another potent social force (i.e., position), gender also was found to contour all levels of generativity, and some of the effects of age and education on self-conception depend on gender. Prior theory (e.g., Gilligan, 1982) and literatures (see, e.g., Helson, 1997) have argued for and have tended to show the importance of social relationships and caring for women. Consistent with the posited priority of caring and of relationships for women, our data and findings show that women report higher levels than men on nearly all aspects of generativity (the exception is the extensiveness of unpaid assistance). Beyond providing more emotional support and feeling more obligated for primary relationships, the women in the MacArthur Midlife study also report feeling more obligated than men for the maintenance of civic society. Thus, women also extend their care beyond immediate familial relationships to the larger sphere of society, perhaps reflecting the changing patterns of women's dual roles as parent and employee. Moreover, our findings show that women also define and perceive themselves more generatively than men. Women appear to think more about (i.e., concern for) their generative acts, they see themselves as greater generative resources and they define themselves with more generative traits than men.

But, gender also intermingles interactively with age and education. Prior to older adulthood, women exhibit more generative concern than men. Older men and women show the same amount of generative concerns, perhaps because they now have common experiences (e.g., structural lag) that affect their self-images. Education, too, generally promotes more positive generative self-conceptions. Compared with men, women with more education see themselves as greater generative resources and as more caring, knowledgeable, and wiser than women with less education. Women apparently receive a self-concept boost from education, which drives a deeper socioeconomic wedge among women than among men. The greater educational disparity among women possibly creates inequalities in the distribution of generative resources. Insofar as women remain the primary caretakers that directly guide and mold their children (see, e.g., Rossi & Rossi, 1990), the relatively deeper socioeconomic disparity in generativity among women implies a downward spiral. That is, results suggest that children born into lower socioeconomic conditions should be unlikely to receive the kind of guidance that increases their odds of becoming adults who, in turn, will generatively act to perpetuate their own health and a healthy society.

Second, generativity contours quality of life. Generative behavior, generative norms, and generative self-conception predict and possibly promote psychological and social well-being. The strong relationship of generativity and well-being reflects, we believe, the fact that generativity is fundamental to individuals feeling good about themselves and for judging their lives as worthwhile and meaningful. The embodiment of generativity is feeling that one has something valuable to give to society and is able to do for others. Guiding and assisting others, in turn, probably both reflects and promotes one's own feelings of social integration. Through generativity, adults act as custodians of society and probably gain the feeling that they are integral to perpetuating their communities. Perhaps for such reasons and more, we find in our study that all aspects of generativity predict well-being. Having extensive generative emotional support and generative obligations to society, focusing more concern on being generative, and possessing more generative personal qualities predict better overall psychological and better overall social well-being. In only one instance did an aspect of generativity prove to be costly. Feeling more obligated to primary ties seemed to suppress adults' overall social well-being. In general, though, all components of generativity appear to be effective responses to the psychological challenges (e.g., self-acceptance) and the social challenges (e.g., social contribution) of life.

Third, generativity explains socioeconomic disparities in well-being. The presence or absence of generative feelings and behavior explain in part how social inequalities possibly promote or hinder adults' health and well-being. As an explanatory mechanism, generativity is a theoretical hybrid that combines nuances of self-perceived personal worth and resources. Education purportedly affects adults' agency and self worth, which translates into less extensive generative behavior, normative (e.g., civic) obligation, and less flattering images of oneself as generative. With more education, adults feel that they have valuable skills and experience. With education, adults feel more committed and obligated to society—in essence, they feel more vital to making society work. With education, adults assist and encourage more people and children—in essence, they become a vital part of society. The impact of social stratification is therefore profound and far-reaching. That is, stratification affects the quality of adults' lives by affecting whether they are likely to behave in ways (e.g., generative assistance to others) that undoubtedly affect the health of the social system.

Generativity does not, however, appear to have the same amount of explanatory power throughout adulthood.[7] That is, generativity explained anywhere from about 33% to 40% of the variance between education and well-being for younger and midlife adults. On the other hand, generativity explained only about 25% of the variance between education and well-being of older adults. The differential explanatory power of generativity by age contradicts mean-level results because younger adults report lower levels on most aspects of generativity than midlife and older adults. Two important implications stem from the explanatory role of generativity. First, as a source for social renewal—a concern shared by sociologists (Durkheim, 1897/1947)—generativity has the capacity to reduce socially stratified dis-

---

[7]The analysis separately regressed the composite scale of well-being onto education and age, as well as the control variables, for each age group of adults. Subsequently, the composite scales of well-being were regressed onto education and age, the controls, and all (i.e., all 7 components) indicators of generativity for each age group of adults. Our intent was to observe whether and what aspects of generativity explained educational disparities in well-being for each age group of adults. Results are available on request.

parities in well-being. Because generativity is shaped by as fundamental a process as education, the implication is that the perpetuation of a healthy society depends, as always, on assurance of educational opportunity and healthy schools. The role of generativity suggests a new story line in these frequently heard messages. Greater educational opportunity and attainment can surely create healthier wage earners and tax payers. If political trends away from national toward more local governance and involvement continue, the relationship of education and generativity becomes increasingly salient because education affects the predilection for ordinary individuals guiding and assisting the next generation.

The second implication is theoretical. The differential explanatory power of generativity by age suggests that educational disparities in quality of life are less amenable to explanation and reduction with age. This does not appear to reflect mean-level differences of generativity by age. Though it is possible that we could find a different set of explanatory variables that work well for all age groups, the point is that age-graded tasks and activities are implicated in how social structural processes affect lives throughout adulthood. Life-span issues, as well as cohort experiences, can dictate the types of processes that explain social structural differences in health and well-being. Moreover, there is an inverse and complex relationship between the process and products of education and aging. With age, educational attainment becomes increasingly distal. The effects of education, as adults age, become increasingly proximal. Thus, the apparent resistance of education to being explained in older adulthood could reflect our efforts to explain educational attainment rather than the effects of education in older adulthood. Put differently, as we age, education has more effects. Researchers, however, attempt to explain the same structural designation (i.e., years of education) for all adults. What this argues for is more process models like the social structure and personality framework that use developmentally sensitive explanatory variables such as generativity. In short, future research on adult development and successful aging should focus attention on the impact of social structure. At the same time, we would argue for a life-span perspective to the study of social stratification. Does social stratification affect adults' lives in the same ways throughout adulthood? Illustrating the relevance of classic theory, Erikson's conceptions of developmental tasks point to possible age-graded explanatory constructs.

Extant theories of the intersection of education and age focus on the mutual effects of education and age on health and wellness rather than focus on the explanation of educational differences with age. Double jeopardy and cumulative advantage theories argue that the educational disparities in health and wellness diverge with age, whereas structural lag, age as a levelling status, and processes of successful aging argue that educational disparities converge with age. Our study supports the divergence hypothesis. However, we observe that differences in social, but not psychological, well-being between adults with different educations diverges in older adulthood. What this suggests is that the ability of adults of different educational backgrounds to handle the psychological challenge of self-realization is constant at all ages. Whatever psychological challenges are possibly added with age are apparently managed successfully by most adults. However, aging may introduce social challenges that older adults simply cannot or do not care to manage.

This study is one of the first attempts to investigate generativity in a large probability sample of adults. Future research would nonetheless benefit from longitudinal assessments to permit disentangling the relationships of generativity and well-being. Moreover, researchers should measure the purported explanatory aspects of generativity—the interpretative and resource aspects that help to explain the relationship of social structure and well-being. For example, the interpretive side of generativity could be ascertained through social comparisons of generative resources, reflected appraisals of generative traits, and self-perceptions that are based on generative behavior. We also know relatively little about the unique class of resource mechanisms in which people give valued resources to others rather than use the resources themselves (e.g., social networks and supports) to stave off stress (see Keyes, 1995, 1996b). Understanding how guiding and helping others directly affects adults' health and well-being would fill a void in the conception and understanding of how giving and getting resources touches the lives of adults (see also Marks, 1990; Midlarsky, 1991). Research on all fronts will help to explicate the role of generativity in adult lives—its social structural contours and quality of life consequences.

APPENDIX

TABLE A
Mean Generativity Dimensions by Education, Gender, and Age

Generativity	12 Years or Less						13 or More Years					
	Males			Females			Males			Females		
	25–39	40–59	60–74	25–39	40–59	60–74	25–39	40–59	60–74	25–39	40–59	60–74
Emotional Support	1.9	1.8	1.6	2.2	2.1	1.7	1.8	2.1	1.9	2.1	2.4	2.3
	(1.0)	(1.1)	(1.2)	(0.9)	(1.0)	(1.2)	(1.0)	(0.9)	(1.0)	(0.9)	(0.8)	(0.9)
Unpaid Assistance	1.1	1.2	1.2	1.1	1.3	1.1	1.1	1.2	1.4	1.1	1.4	1.4
	(1.0)	(1.1)	(1.1)	(1.0)	(1.1)	(1.2)	(0.9)	(1.0)	(1.1)	(0.9)	(1.1)	(1.1)
Primary Norms	58.9	57.2	54.6	64.4	62.9	60.8	59.4	57.6	55.1	62.7	61.1	61.5
	(12.7)	(14.4)	(18.6)	(12.4)	(12.9)	(15.8)	(12.4)	(13.0)	(13.2)	(11.8)	(12.8)	(12.4)
Civic Norms	43.2	45.9	49.7	43.9	47.0	47.6	43.8	48.2	49.8	45.9	49.2	50.5
	(10.3)	(10.6)	(10.7)	(10.6)	(11.2)	(11.2)	(10.1)	(8.7)	(9.9)	(9.0)	(8.6)	(9.1)
Concern	19.6	19.4	19.7	21.3	21.2	18.6	19.7	20.6	19.9	22.2	22.3	20.8
	(6.0)	(6.8)	(7.0)	(5.9)	(5.8)	(7.9)	(5.6)	(5.5)	(5.6)	(4.8)	(5.2)	(7.1)
Qualities	15.7	16.5	16.9	16.1	16.5	16.1	16.8	17.4	16.5	17.6	18.1	17.4
	(3.7)	(3.7)	(4.2)	(3.7)	(3.8)	(4.0)	(3.6)	(3.8)	(3.6)	(3.4)	(3.7)	(3.8)
Traits	23.5	23.8	24.1	23.4	24.0	24.3	23.0	23.9	23.5	24.1	24.3	24.5
	(4.0)	(3.9)	(3.9)	(4.6)	(4.0)	(4.6)	(3.7)	(3.5)	(3.9)	(3.3)	(3.5)	(3.5)
Unweighted N	156	239	129	184	277	174	329	435	157	323	413	154

Note. Standard deviation in parenthesis. Unweighted Ns are averaged over the Generativity dimensions.

REFERENCES

Adler, A. (1979). *Superiority and social interest.* New York: Norton.

Allison, P. D., Long, J. S., & Krauze, T. K. (1982). Cumulative advantage and inequality in science. *American Sociological Review, 47,* 615–625.

Allport, G. W. (1961). *Pattern and growth on personality.* New York: Holt, Rinehart & Winston.

Bakan, D. (1966). *The duality of human existence: Isolation and communion in Western man.* Boston: Beacon Press.

Baltes, P. B. (1987). Theoretical propositions of life-span developmental psychology: On the dynamics between growth and decline. *Developmental Psychology, 23*(5), 611–626.

Baltes, P. B., & Baltes, M. M. (1990). *Successful aging: Perspectives from the behavioral sciences.* New York: Cambridge University Press.

Carstensen, L. L. (1992). Social and emotional patterns in adulthood: Support for socioemotional selectivity theory. *Psychology and Aging, 7,* 331–338.

Dannefer, D. (1984). Adult development and social theory: A paradigmatic reappraisal. *American Sociological Review, 49,* 100–116.

Dannefer, D. (1987). Aging as intracohort differentiation: Accentuation, the Matthew Effect, and the life course. *Sociological Forum, 2*(2), 211–237.

Diener, E. (1984). Subjective well-being. *Psychological Bulletin, 95,* 542–575.

Diener, E., & Diener, C. (1996). Most people are happy. *Psychological Science, 7*(3), 181–185.

Dowd, J. J., & Bengtson, V. L. (1978). Aging in minority populations: An examination of the double jeopardy hypothesis. *Journal of Gerontology, 33*(3), 427–436.

Durkheim, E. (1947). *The elementary forms of the religious life.* New York: Free Press. (Original work published in 1911)

Durkheim, E. (1951). *Suicide.* New York: Free Press. (Original work published 1897)

Erikson, E. H. (1950). *Childhood and society.* New York: Norton.

Featherman, D. L., & Lerner, R. M. (1985). Ontogenesis and sociogenesis: Problematics for theory and research about development and socialization across the life-span. *American Sociological Review, 50,* 659–676.

Ferraro, K. F. (1987). Double jeopardy to health for black older adults? *Journal of Gerontology, 42*(5), 528–533.

Ferraro, K. F., & Farmer, M. M. (1996). Double jeopardy to health hypothesis for African Americans: Analysis and critique. *Journal of Health and Social Behavior, 37,* 27–43.

Gecas, V., & Schwalbe, M. L. (1983). Beyond the looking-glass: Social structure and efficacy-based self-esteem. *Social Psychology Quarterly, 46,* 77–88.

Gecas, V., & Seff, M. A. (1990). Social class and self-esteem: Psychological centrality, compensation, and the relative effects of work and home. *Social Psychology Quarterly, 53*(2), 165–173.

Gilligan, C. (1982). *In a different voice: Psychological theory and women's development.* Cambridge, MA: Harvard University Press.

Helson, R. (1997). The self in middle age. In M. E. Lachman & J. B. James (Eds.), *Multiple paths of midlife development* (pp. 21–43). Chicago: The University of Chicago Press.

Herzog, A. R., Rodgers, W. L., & Woodworth, J. (1982). *Subjective well-being among different age groups.* Ann Arbor: University of Michigan, Institute for Social Research, Survey Research Center.

House, J. S. (1981). Social structure and personality. In M. Rosenberg & R. H. Turner (Eds.), *Social psychology: Sociological perspectives* (pp. 525–561). New York: Basic Books.

House, J. S, Landis, K. R., & Umberson, D. (1988). Social relationships and health. *Science, 241,* 540–545.

House, J. S., Kessler, R. C., Herzog, A. R., Mero, R. P., Kinney, A. M., & Breslow, M. J. (1990). Age, socioeconomic status, and health. *The Milbank Quarterly, 68*(3), 383–411.

House, J. S., Lepkowski, J. M., Kinney, A. M., Mero, R. P., Kessler, R. C., & Herzog, A. R. (1994). The social stratification of aging and health. *Journal of Health and Social Behavior, 35,* 213–234.

Israel, J. (1971). *Alienation: From Marx to Modern Sociology.* Boston: Allyn.

Jung, C. G. (1933). *Modern man in search of a soul* (W. S. Dell & C. F. Baynes, Trans.). New York: Harcourt, Brace & World.

Karabel, J., & Halsey, A. H. (1977). *Power and ideology in education.* New York: Oxford University Press.

Kessler, R. C., House, J. S., Anspach, R. R., & Williams, D. R. (1995). Social psychology and health. In K. S. Cook, G. A. Fine, & J. S. House (Eds.), *Sociological perspectives on social psychology* (pp. 548–570). Boston: Allyn and Bacon.

Keyes, C. L. M. (1995). *Social functioning and social well-being: Studies of the social nature of personal wellness.* Unpublished doctoral dissertation, Department of Sociology, University of Wisconsin, Madison.

Keyes, C. L. M. (1996a). *Social well-being.* Manuscript submitted for publication.

Keyes, C. L. M. (1996b, April). *A contributive model of well-being: The relationship of prosocial community involvement with psychological and social well-being.* Paper presented at the meeting of the Midwest Sociological Association, Chicago.

Kotre, J. (1984). *Outliving the self: Generativity and the interpretation of lives.* Baltimore: The Johns Hopkins University Press.

Levinson, D. J. (1978). *The seasons of a man's life.* New York: Knopf.

MacDermid, S. M., De Haan, L. G., & Heilbrun, G. (1996). Generativity in multiple roles. *Journal of Adult Development, 3*(3), 145–158.

Maddox, G. L., & Clark, D. O. (1992). Trajectories of functional impairment in later life. *Journal of Health and Social Behavior, 33,* 114–125.

Marks, N. F. (1990). *Giving and getting in adulthood: Social role-related differences in psychological well-being.* Unpublished doctoral dissertation, Department of Sociology, University of Wisconsin, Madison.

Marmot, M., Ryff, C. D., Bumpass, L. L., Shipley, M., & Marks, N. F. (1997). Social inequalities in health: Converging evidence and next questions. *Social Science and Medicine, 44,* 901–910.

Maslow, A. H. (1968). *Toward a psychology of being* (2nd ed.). New York: Van Nostrand.

McAdams, D. P. (1996). Explorations in generativity in later years. In L. Sperry & H. Prosen (Eds.), *Aging in the twenty-first century: A developmental perspective* (pp. 33–58). New York: Garland Publishing.

McAdams, D. P., & de St. Aubin, E. (1992). A theory of generativity and its assessment through self-report, behavioral acts, and narrative themes in autobiography. *Journal of Personality and Social Psychology, 62,* 1003–1015.

McLellan, D. (1977). *Karl Marx: Selected writings.* Oxford, England: Oxford University Press.

Midlarsky, E. (1991). Helping as coping. In M. S. Clark (Ed.), *Prosocial behavior* (pp. 238–264). Thousand Oaks, CA: Sage.

Mirowsky, J., & Ross, C. E. (1989). *Social causes of psychological distress.* New York: Aldine de Gruyter.

Neugarten, B. L. (1968). The awareness of middle age. In B. L. Neugarten (Ed.), *Middle age and aging* (pp. 93–98). Chicago: University of Chicago Press.

Neugarten, B. L. (1973). Personality change in late life: A developmental perspective. In C. Eisdorfer & M. P. Lawton (Eds.), *The psychology of adult development and aging* (pp. 311–335). Washington, DC: American Psychological Association.

Peterson, B. E., & Stewart, A. J. (1993). Generativity and social motives in young adults. *Journal of Personality and Social Psychology, 65*(1), 186–198.

Peterson, B. E., & Klohnen, E. C. (1995). Realization of generativity in two samples of women at midlife. *Psychology and Aging, 10*(1), 20–29.

Riley, M. W., Kahn, R. L., & Foner, A. (1994). *Age and structural lag: Society's failure to provide meaningful opportunities in work, family, and leisure.* New York: Wiley.

Rogers. C. R. (1961). *On becoming a person.* Boston: Houghton Mifflin.

Rosenberg. M. (1979). *Conceiving the self.* New York: Basic Books.

Rosenberg, M., & Pearlin, L. I. (1978). Social class and self-esteem among children and adolescents. *American Journal of Sociology, 84,* 53–77.

Ross, C. E., & Wu, C-l. (1995). The links between education and health. *American Sociological Review, 60,* 719–745.

Ross, C. E., & Wu, C-l. (1996). Education, age, and the cumulative advantage in health. *Journal of Health and Social Behavior, 37,* 104–120.

Rossi, A. S., & Rossi, P. H. (1990). *Of human bonding: Parent-child relations across the life course.* New York: Aldine de Gruyter.

Ryff, C. D. (1982). Successful aging: A developmental approach. *Gerontologist, 22,* 209–214.

Ryff, C. D. (1984). Personality development from the inside: The subjective experience of change in adulthood and aging. In P. B. Baltes & O. G. Brim (Eds.), *Life-span development and behavior* (Vol. 6, pp. 244–281). New York: Academic Press.

Ryff, C. D. (1987). The place of personality and social structure research in social psychology. *Journal of Personality and Social Psychology, 53,* 1192–1202.

Ryff, C. D. (1989a). Beyond Ponce de Leon and life satisfaction: New directions in quest of successful aging. *International Journal of Behavioral Development, 12,* 35–55.

Ryff, C. D. (1989b). Happiness is everything, or is it? Explorations on the meaning of psychological well-being. *Journal of Personality and Social Psychology, 57,* 1069–1081.

Ryff, C. D., & Heincke, S. G. (1983). Subjective organization of personality in adulthood and aging. *Journal of Personality and Social Psychology, 44,* 807–816.

Ryff, C. D., & Migdal, S. (1984). Intimacy and generativity: Self-perceived transitions. *Signs, 9,* 470–481.

Ryff, C. D., & Keyes, C. L. M. (1995). The structure of psychological well-being revisited. *Journal of Personality and Social Psychology, 69*(4), 719–727.

Seeman, M. (1959). On the meaning of alienation. *American Sociological Review, 24,* 783–791.

Seeman, M. (1983). Alienation motifs in contemporary theorizing: The hidden continuity of the classic themes. *Social Psychology Quarterly, 46*(3), 171–184.

Sewell, W. H., & Hauser, R. M. (1975). *Education, occupation, and earnings: Achievement in the early career.* New York: Academic Press.

Sewell, W. H., & Hauser, R. M. (1980). The Wisconsin Longitudinal Study of social and psychological factors in aspirations and achievements. In A. C. Kerckhoff (Ed.), *Research in sociology and education* (pp. 59–99). Greenwich, CT: JAI.

Smith, K. R., & Waitzman, N. J. (1994). Double jeopardy: Interaction effects of marital and poverty status on the risks of mortality. *Demography, 31*(3), 487–507.

de St. Aubin, E., & McAdams, D. P. (1995). The relations of generative concern and generative action to personality traits, satisfaction/happiness with life, and ego development. *Journal of Adult Development, 2*(2), 99–112.

Stewart, A. J., Franz, E., & Layton, L. (1988). The changing self: Using personal documents to study lives. *Journal of Personality, 56,* 41–74.

Taubman, P., & Rosen, S. (1982). Healthiness, education, and marital status. In V. R. Fuchs (Ed.), *Economic aspects of health* (pp. 121–140). Chicago: University of Chicago Press.

Von Franz, M. L. (1964). The process of individuation. In C. G. Jung (Ed.), *Man and his symbols* (pp. 158–229). New York: Doubleday.

Waterman, A. S. (1993). Two conceptions of happiness: Contrasts of personal expressiveness (eudaimonia) and hedonic enjoyment. *Journal of Personality on Social Psychology, 64*, 677–691.

Williams, D. R. (1990). Socioeconomic differentials in health: A review and redirection. *Social Psychology Quarterly, 53*(2), 81–99.

Winship, C., & Radbil, L. (1994). Sampling weights and regression analysis. *Sociological Methods and Research, 23*(2), 230–257.

8

GENERATIVITY, SOCIAL CONTEXT, AND LIVED EXPERIENCE: NARRATIVES OF GAY MEN IN MIDDLE ADULTHOOD

BERTRAM J. COHLER, ANDREW J. HOSTETLER,
AND ANDREW M. BOXER

Widely noted demographic changes in the industrialized West, including the general aging of the population, have been accompanied by increasing academic and popular interest in the ways in which individuals experience patterns of change and continuity in their lives, from young adulthood to oldest age. This search for the meaning of personal and shared experience must be understood against a backdrop of shared cultural expectations regarding the appropriate timing and outcome of life transitions that are presumed to be integrated into a unitary and coherent experience of the self. Like stories, lives are assumed to have a beginning, a middle, and an end, with increasing complexity and a predictable, ordered plot. The experience of continuity over time, so essential for positive adjustment

From the Committee on Human Development, the Department of Psychiatry, and the Evelyn Hooker Center for Gay and Lesbian Mental Health. We thank our colleagues Gil Herdt and Rick Shweder and the student participants in the workshop on culture and mental health for their incisive comments regarding both the framework for studying lives and the particular issues posed by the study of the life course of gay and bisexual men and women.

and the maintenance of morale, reflects a narrative action founded in the search for the meaning of lived experience (Cohler & Cole, 1996, McAdams, 1985, 1993, 1996; see also chapter 1, this volume).

Efforts to portray the course of lives in terms of predefined, sequential, and age-ordered stages, phases, or tasks have provided little lasting understanding of the manner in which people maintain the experience of personal integrity or continuity over time. The course of development is much less clearly ordered than such stage theories would predict and cannot be understood apart from either larger social and historical trends or unique events within particular lives. Certain sequentially negotiated tasks across the adult life course, related to work, intimate partnership, providing for the next generation, and dealing with the finitude of life, appear to be ubiquitous within contemporary society, yet no simple checklist can capture the full range of variation in developmental pathways or the ways in which certain tasks and prescribed social roles are experienced.

In contrast to intrinsic stage models of development, the life course perspective in the social sciences provides a nuanced and situated approach to individual development. Integral to the life course perspective, the concept of cohort suggests that people who experience similar social and historical circumstances represent a convoy of consociates (Kahn & Antonucci, 1981; Plath, 1980) who interpret expectable role transitions in similar, predictable ways. From leaving school to the advent of parenthood, retirement, or widowhood, responses to life transitions are intelligible only within the larger context of historical events taking place over time. The related concepts of social time and age norms (Durkheim, 1912/1995; Hagestad & Neugarten, 1985; Neugarten, 1979; Neugarten & Hagestad, 1976; Neugarten, Moore, & Lowe, 1965/1996; Sorokin & Merton, 1937) point to the historically specific social imperatives of the institutionalized life course, as well as the subjective experience of being developmentally "on-time" or "off-time" regarding expected life transitions (Festinger, 1954; Hagestad & Neugarten, 1985; Roth, 1963). Cross-cultural accounts have also contributed to an understanding of the course of development as located within a particular social and historical context, highlighting shared cultural meanings related to person, the passage of time, and the expectable course of life, as well as the patterns of human relationships that these generate (Geertz, 1973a, 1973b). Finally, the narrative perspective has illuminated the ways in which people selectively interpret and appropriate shared discourses and in so doing construct a unique and continuously renegotiated sense of self (Gergen, 1994; Gergen & Gergen, 1983; Hermans & Kempen, 1993; McAdams, 1989, 1991, 1993; Sarbin, 1986).

Positing a view of adult development as taking place among particular, unique persons confronting socially constructed tasks or challenges within contemporary bourgeois culture, this chapter focuses on the lives of urban gay men in the midst of the transition to midlife (Cohler & Lieberman, 1979; Lieberman & Falk, 1971; Neugarten, 1973, 1979). The present discussion focuses on the life stories of three gay men at midlife, selected from a group of more than 35 interviews with gay men and women that focused on the management of personal integrity and identity, as well as the changing experience of self and others, across the years of middle adulthood. The three men are from disparate social backgrounds and are somewhat unusual in that at the time of the interview not one of them is involved in a long-term partnership and each is explicitly and self-consciously concerned with issues relevant to the transition to midlife, including generativity. These life histories highlight the shared challenges the men have faced as well as the distinctive manner in which each has chosen to confront these challenges.

STUDYING LIVES IN CONTEXT: COHORT, SOCIAL TIME, AND PERSONAL NARRATIVE

The modern era has been defined by unprecedented social change, the proliferation of technologies, and cataclysmic world-historical events that have worked together to transform the life course of the individual. There is perhaps no better example of this than the change that has taken place in concepts of gender identity and in relations between men and women, which are understood in markedly different ways than they were even three decades ago. More generally, the period between 1965 and 1975 represented a "watershed" in social life in the United States; values, behaviors, and attitudes all showed dramatic change over this 10-year period (Duberman, 1993; Echols, 1989; Gitlin, 1987; Tipton, 1982). It is important to recognize both the dramatic nature of this change and, more generally, the role of linked concepts of cohort and generation in explaining such social change. This time of rapid social change has also been reflected in a significant change of focus in the study of lives from a life-span or life-cycle to a life course perspective, a transition characterized by decreasing attention to intrinsic developmental stages and increasing attention to social context, individual narrative, and lived experience.

Life Course and Personal Narrative

Whereas the life-cycle approach to developmental study focuses largely on presumed intrinsic, age-ordered and stage-ordered processes, the life course perspective assumes an open system shaped by social and historical process as well as by expectable and eruptive life changes within individual lives (Elder, 1992, in press-a, in press-b; Elder & Caspi, 1988; Hagestad & Neugarten, 1985; Neugarten, 1979; Neugarten & Hagestad, 1976; Pearlin & Lieberman, 1979). The life course perspective makes few assumptions regarding necessary tasks or issues to be resolved or negotiated over time. According to this more recent perspective, individual developmental challenges or concerns are inevitably shaped by the present social order (Dannefer, 1984).

On a related note, the life course perspective provides a unique opportunity for the study of the manner in which shared cultural meanings become the foundation for the construction of particular lives (Plummer, 1995; Riessman, 1993). These shared meanings are appropriated by individuals and portrayed in a story, or narrative, that also integrates particular life circumstances, such as encounters with unexpected adversity. Encounters with adversity initiate a renewed search for meaning, leading to continued renarration of the life story according to a "followable" account of lived experience (Gubrium, Holstein, & Buckholdt, 1994; Ricoeur, 1977; Schafer, 1980, 1981). The life-story, or narrative, approach to the study of lives is rooted in both the contributions of the Chicago School of Sociology, particularly Thomas and Znaniecki's (1974) masterful study of the impact of migration on the lives of Polish peasants moving to the New World, and a long tradition of ethnographic inquiry, summarized in reviews by Langness and Frank (1981) and Watson and Watson-Frankie (1985). In general, the narrative approach to the study of lives reveals the discursive boundaries of the interplay of person and social order. Over time, social and historical change may lead to quite different renderings of the life story, both within individual lives and across generations, with the life stories of earlier generations influencing those of later generations. This is dramatically illustrated in the collections of gay men's narratives, which span several generations, compiled by the Hall Carpenter Archives (1989) and by Porter and Weeks (1991). Among the specific tools the life course perspective provides for understanding lives in the context of these social and historical processes are the concepts of generation, cohort, and social timing.

Generation, Cohort, and Life Course

The concept of generation is central to the life course perspective (Cain, 1964; Ryder, 1965). Following the work of Mannheim (1928), life course researchers (e.g., Bengtson, Furlong, & Laufer, 1974; Laufer & Bengtson, 1974; Troll, 1970) have typically defined generation with reference to three age-linked characteristics: position within a cluster of four or five groups alive contemporaneously; period or point in the course of life, such as youth or middle age; and cohort, or group of persons of a given birth year who have experienced similar social and historical events. The age distribution in a given society at any one time creates groups of individuals with particular understandings of self and others, determined in part by shared interpretations of historical events. These collective interpretations, in conjunction with expectable and eruptive life changes, largely shape the course of individual development over time (Cohler & Boxer, 1984; Pearlin, 1980; Pearlin, Menaghan, Lieberman, & Mullan, 1981).

It is particularly important in the study of lives to focus on the distinction between period and cohort in life course study and to recognize the significance of social and historical change in governing the sequence of transitions into and out of major social roles across the course of adult life (Dannefer, 1984; George, 1993, 1996; Hogan, 1981; Hogan & Astone, 1986; Marini, 1984). Generation understood as cohort refers to a unit of developmental analysis founded on birth year or years (Elder, 1974, 1992, in press-b; Elder and Caspi, 1990; Schaie, 1984; Tuttle, 1993). For example, Easterlin (1987) showed that people growing up within particularly large birth cohorts face enhanced competition all their lives for resources ranging from places in preschool programs to adequate medical and social services in later life. Easterlin noted that one of the consequences of membership in the large "baby boom" cohort has been enhanced because of lifelong competition for resources and rewards. From college application to finding a job and marital partner (Guttentag & Secord, 1983) to anticipated problems providing health care and social services for an emerging, unusually large cohort of elders in the middle of the 21st century, the misfortune of having been a part of a large birth cohort, constantly competing for a place, has taken its toll on morale.

The capacity to understand the impact of social change within particular lives may be tied to recognition of cohort as a critical variable affecting the manner in which people understand self and social order. Schaie's (1984) summary of his work on the Seattle Longitudinal Study highlighted cohort differences in psychometric test performance. It was the pioneering work of Glen Elder and his colleagues (Elder, 1974, 1992, in press-a, in press-b; Elder & Caspi, 1988, 1990), however, that firmly established the significance of cohort-related factors for individual development. Reanalyzing archival data from the longitudinal studies at Berkeley's Institute of Human Development, Elder (1974) was able to show the differential impact of the Great Depression on the adjustment of groups of preschool and adolescent boys and girls. As Elder and Caspi (1990) observed, age understood as an index of birth year serves to locate people in history and provides an index of the range of events likely to have an impact on particular lives.

Elder and Caspi (1990) further suggested that the "pileup" of such events in a particular sequence may also have a specific impact. A prime example of the effects of such a pileup is provided by individuals born after World War II, who arrived at mid-adolescence during the turbulent years of the 1960s and whose subsequent adult lives were shaped by the totality of this tumultuous era. The adolescent experiences of this "60s generation" were vastly different from those of adults who were adolescents both 10 years earlier, during the prosperous and peaceful Eisenhower years, and 10 years later, during the era of conservative backlash and ultraindividualism. Furthermore, Tuttle (1993) showed that preschool children respond quite differently to such catastrophes as war or natural disaster than teenagers or middle-aged adults, leading to some common experiences in the subsequent course of life. Reports by Livson and Peskin (1980), Schuman and Scott (1989), and Clausen (1993) suggest that both particular life circumstances and sociohistorical events taking place during adolescence influence lived experience across the second half of life.

In summary, there may be little value in portraying modal personality patterns or developmental tasks for any given age or point in the life course except in terms of cohort-specific sociohistorical changes and events. However, it is also important to acknowledge Rosow's (1978) caution regarding the difficulty of determining the boundaries, or the number of years, that separate one cohort from another. In a similar vein, as Elder (in press-b) emphasized, there are significant intracohort effects that must also be considered. Life circumstances affect members of a particular birth cohort in different ways. For example, conscription for military service has a differential impact on individuals depending on socioeconomic and marital–parental status (Elder, 1986, 1987; Elder & Hareven, 1993; Elder, Shanahan, & Clipp, 1994; Sampson & Laub, 1996). The life-history, or narrative, method provides a means for disentangling the impact of various demographic variables on individual development, as well as a more reliable method for sorting individuals into cohorts.

Social Time, Expectable Transitions, and the Organization of Personal Experience

Whereas the concept of cohort organizes people into relatively distinct groups of consociates, social time organizes individual lives into patterns of sequential role positions. In conjunction with cohort-specific effects, the subjective experience of social time helps to determine the manner in which individuals understand the sequence and timing of both expectable and eruptive events across the course of life. Informed by Durkheim's (1912/1995) discussion of time and the ritual life of the community, research on the ways in which people understand the course of life suggests that they maintain an internal timetable regarding expectable role transitions and associated life changes (Hagestad & Neugarten, 1985; Hazan, 1980; Neugarten & Hagestad, 1976; Neugarten et al., 1965/1996; Roth, 1963; Sorokin & Merton, 1937). Neugarten and her colleagues (Neugarten et al., 1965/1996) demonstrated agreement regarding the definition of age categories among concurrently living generations. Although older adults are somewhat more tolerant than younger adults of variation in the timing of certain role transitions, there is broad agreement on what constitutes childhood, adolescence, adulthood, and later life.

Across the course of life, people continually compare their own development, including realization of particular, expected social roles, to a socially shared timetable of expectable events. From these comparisons they determine whether they are on-time or either "early" or "late" off-time. Even very young children are familiar with the sequence of expectable life transitions, from first entrance into school through graduation, first job, advent of parenthood, retirement, widowhood, and death (Farnham-Diggory, 1966). This expectable sequence of life changes provides the context for understanding personal experience. Even unpredictable life circumstances—both adverse and positive—occur in the context of these expectable life changes. More eruptive life events, such as widowhood in the fourth versus the eighth decade of a woman's life, pose particular problems both because there are fewer consociates to provide support and assistance (Kahn & Antonucci, 1981; Plath, 1980) and because there has been little time to rehearse this life change through observation of others in a similar position (Neugarten, 1979).

Seltzer (1976) and Cohler and Boxer (1984) have suggested that the experience of positive morale, or life satisfaction, is largely determined by the sense of being on-time for expectable role transitions or life changes. The sense that life changes occur expectedly and on-time—or consistent with the timing for other members of a cohort or generation—contributes to an enhanced sense of personal congruence and well-being. Being early off-time poses specific problems related to the lack of both preparation for change and consociates to provide support. Although, as Furstenberg, Brooks-Gunn, and Morgan (1987) suggested, individuals may in later life overcome difficulties associated with early off-time transitions, the initial adjustment may be extremely challenging. On the other hand, being late off-time apparently has certain advantages. As Nydegger (1980, 1981) and Daniels and Weingarten (1982) have observed, men who make a late off-time transition to parenthood are more settled in their careers and more comfortable with themselves than men who make this transition on-time.

Hagestad (1994) discussed a fourth possibility, that of being "outside" or "out" of time, a not uncommon experience among those whose life trajectory is markedly outside the norm or those who are terminally ill or expecting death imminently. On the basis of her own experience of prolonged illness and her sense of being excluded from professional and social events, Hagestad described the feeling of living outside the continuity of time. Whereas her friends and colleagues may have been acting out of consideration for her welfare, not wishing to burden her during her illness, the result was a strange sense of depersonalization. However, there is another aspect to Hagestad's portrayal, in which individuals may be "out" of time in both senses of the phrase. This is the experience of many of those with a terminal illness of uncertain duration, who live out of time in the sense that it is difficult to plan for a future with an unknown terminus. Not only are these people off-time in the sense of confronting their own mortality and the very finitude of life earlier in life than has been characteristic of recent cohorts of men and women, but they are also out of time in the sense that it is difficult to reckon time when its future duration is unclear and unpredictable. In other words, they are outside of time as reckoned, and, more literally, they are running out of time. This is clearly the situation at the present time among men and women who are HIV-positive or have AIDS.

It is also important to recognize that there may be differences in definition and timing of role transitions, both *within* cohorts—according to race, class, education, and a variety of other demographic characteristics—and *across* cohorts. Within the generation of young adults who were born in the late 1960s and early 1970s—the so-called Generation Xers—the underemployment characteristic of the current economy seems to be shifting the onset of careers to the late 20s, leading to further postponement of such expectable role transitions as marriage and parenthood (George, 1993, 1996; Hogan, 1981; Hogan & Astone, 1986; Marini, 1984). Comparing their own attainments to those of preceding generations, these young adults experience lowered morale and express frustration at being late off-time for this particular role transition. However, when comparing themselves to other members of their generation, things appear much less bleak, leading to improvements in morale. When one recognizes the impact of both cohort and social timing, it becomes clear that lives cannot be studied apart from their historical context. It is also apparent that the impact of cohort or generation and of social timing may be best understood through the study of the ways in which these building blocks of lived experience are reflected in the individual life story, which itself inevitably changes across the course of life.

GENERATIVITY, LIVED EXPERIENCE, AND MIDDLE ADULTHOOD

Across the adult years, physical maturation—so crucial in shaping preadult experience—is largely superseded in importance by cultural and social determinants of development. The adoption of a characteristic adult role portfolio, focused on work, realization of intimate partnership, and provision for the next generation, assumes particular significance in the maintenance of a sense of coherence and well-being over time. Men and women at midlife are thought to be primarily concerned with fostering the well-being of the next generation within the worlds of family and work (Levinson, 1978, 1996). This concern, initially identified by Erikson (1958,

1950/1963) as "generativity," has become the subject of ongoing interest in the study of adult lives (McAdams, 1985, 1993, 1996; McAdams & de St. Aubin, 1992; McAdams, de St. Aubin, & Logan 1993; McAdams, Ruetzel, & Foley, 1986; Peterson & Klohnen, 1995; Peterson & Stewart, 1996; Snarey, 1993; also see chapters 1 and 3, this volume).

Much of this research has assumed expectable transitions across adult life, including entrance into work or career, marriage and parenthood (Hogan, 1981; Hogan & Astone, 1986; Marini, 1984), and retirement. The present study concerns the place of generativity within the lives of gay men and lesbians, whose adult life course may be other than what is normatively expected. Although many gay and lesbian couples have children or are foster parents, others have elected partnership but not parenthood or have not been able to realize enduring intimate ties. The study of nonnormative life course trajectories raises important questions regarding both the significance of generativity across the adult years and the variation in the expression of generativity. It is also important to consider the ways in which the study of adult lives of gay men and women might inform the broader study of adult lives within contemporary bourgeois society.

The Systematic Study of Generativity: Construct, Timing, and Social Change

To date, the study of generativity has been largely concerned with resolving the following four conceptual and methodological issues: First, it has been difficult to arrive at a common understanding of generativity. Second, it remains unclear whether generativity is a developmental issue relevant to a particular point in the life course or an individual attribute varying in salience among adults. Related to both of these issues is the status of parenthood as a defining characteristic of generativity. Third, it has not been clear whether generativity, as portrayed in the research literature, is a function of a particular cohort of successful middle-aged and middle-class adults or is characteristic more generally of lives across cohorts. Finally, on a related note, there is the question of whether concern with productivity and social commitment merely reflects conformity to middle-class norms or whether it reflects spontaneous achievement motivation.

First, uncertainty regarding what constitutes generativity can be traced back to Erikson's reluctance to provide a precise definition. Concern for the next generation and personal accomplishment have been highlighted as particularly significant elements of the definition. The most thorough explorations of Erikson's (1958, 1950/1963, 1982) concept have been provided by Kotre (1984), McAdams and his colleagues (McAdams, 1985; McAdams & de St. Aubin, 1992; McAdams et al., 1993; McAdams et al., 1986; Van de Water & McAdams, 1989), and Stewart and Peterson and their colleagues (Peterson & Klohnen, 1995; Peterson & Stewart, 1990, 1993, 1996; also see chapter 3, this volume).

Employing the life stories of eight men and women, Kotre (1984) attempted to construct a coherent account of generativity, extending Erikson's initial focus on the specifically midlife task of resolving the conflict of "generativity vs. self-absorption." Although caring for the next generation is central to Kotre's (1984) discussion of generativity, Kotre challenged Erikson's rather deterministic reliance on sexual reproduction and parenthood as the inspiration for generative concern. In addition to the biological and parental components of generativity, Kotre added two more, related, forms of generativity to his typology: technical (teaching skills and larger cultural traditions) and cultural (tending, modifying, and conserving culture). Kotre's (1984) inclusion of cross-generational transmission of specific skills as an intrinsic element of generativity is echoed by Peterson and Stewart (1990). In contrast, Vaillant (1993) and Vaillant and Milofsky (1980) distinguished between concern for the next generation, concern with personal accomplishment—which is inherently more egocentric— and concern with preservation of culture. They argued that the latter concern is more directly associated with the subsequent developmental task of keeping the meaning versus rigidity.

Extending Kotre's (1984) observations and revisiting Erikson's initial formulation of the epigenetic perspective, McAdams and his colleagues tried over the course of more than a decade to clarify, revise, and rework the concept of generativity. In one study (1986, p. 806), for example, they included the wish to feel close to and supportive of others as an important component of generativity and midlife development. More recently, McAdams (1996) highlighted teaching, mentoring, and creating products that benefit the next generation and foster the well-being of others (apparently resolving what was a contradiction to Vaillant, 1993, who saw the creation of products as potentially egocentric). Nevertheless, for McAdams and his colleagues, parenthood continues to be a defining characteristic of generativity, at least for women. According to chapter 1, this volume, as well as articles by Peterson and Stewart (1993, 1996) and Peterson and Klohnen (1995), parenthood appears to be a prerequisite for inclusion among groups of highly generative women (nearly three quarters of a group of women studied had at least one child).

The second problem posed by the systematic study of generativity concerns whether this developmental issue is primarily relevant to particular points in the life course or is a more enduring attribute of individual lives. Vaillant (1993) viewed generativity as closely associated with the attainment of midlife and argued that generative concern is evoked by both the crisis of finitude and the "shock" of having adolescent children. As a consequence of these changes, midlife adults are likely to express increased concern for sharing their accomplishments with the next generation. Neugarten and Datan (1974), Ryff and her colleagues (Ryff & Heincke, 1983; Ryff & Migdal, 1984), and to some extent Peterson and Stewart (1993, 1996) also found an association between the attainment of midlife and enhanced generative concern. Whereas some accounts treat generativity as a personal disposition arising in response to increased realization of mortality at midlife (Jaques, 1965, 1980; Marshall, 1975, 1986; Münnichs, 1966; Neugarten & Datan, 1996), other accounts suggest that it is the nature of the midlife role portfolio, particularly care for the next generation of children and grandchildren and mentorship at work (Levinson, 1978, 1996), that primarily determines the increased preoccupation with generative commitments across the second half of life.

McAdams and his colleagues, while remaining somewhat committed to the idea of midlife salience of generativity, have recently recognized the difficulty of differentiating between generativity as a personal attribute, which may become particularly salient in middle adulthood as a consequence of social timing, and generativity as a relatively distinct developmental stage (McAdams 1996, p. 144). To this end, they have begun more intensive study of adults characterized as generative, irrespective of age, in an effort to understand better those attributes associated with generativity (Mansfield & McAdams, 1996; McAdams, 1996; McAdams & de St. Aubin, 1992; McAdams, Hoffman, Mansfield, & Day, 1996). In their model of generativity, McAdams and de St. Aubin (1992) have suggested that generative actions result from the interplay of personal attributes related to generativity and socially constructed expectations and that they are incorporated into the individual's narrative, or life story, where they influence subsequent generative actions. It is significant that McAdams and de St. Aubin (1992, p. 1004) rejected the view of generativity as necessarily linked to midlife except as a reflection of contemporary societal expectations concerning responsibility for the next generation. Most recently, McAdams (1996) focused on generativity as a "quality of living that can be manifest at virtually any point in adulthood" (p. 145).

In an attempt to reconcile recent investigations with previous research on generativity, Stewart and Vandewater (chapter 3, this volume) suggested that the primary developmental focus of midlife should be the realization and satisfaction of generative strivings; the need for generativity, however, should have appeared earlier in the adult life course, presumably along with motivation for parenthood. Whereas early adulthood—a time for family formation—should reflect the desire for generativity, midlife marks the ascendance of generativity, which is expressed through a broadening of concern from parenthood to the larger community and is accompanied by an enhanced sense of personal effectance.

With regard to the third conceptual issue, it is quite probable that research on the role and salience of generativity within adult lives has been bounded by sociohistorical circumstance. In his biographical illustrations of individual generative commitments, Kotre (1984) acknowledged that processes of social and historical change across generations have led him to qualify his account. Kotre also recognized the considerable variation in the life stories of his informants, who ranged from a Black teacher and civil rights worker to a Lebanese immigrant, a former alcoholic, and a proselytizer for twelve-step programs, thus highlighting the peril of theoretical generalization.

The epigenetic, or spiral, conception of lives by Erikson and his colleagues (Erikson, 1982; Erikson, Erikson, & Kivnick, 1986), Vaillant and his colleagues (Vaillant, 1977, 1993; Vaillant & Koury, 1993; Vaillant & Milofsky, 1980; Snarey, 1993), and Levinson (1978, 1996) has been grounded in the study of people who arrived at middle adulthood in the period following World War II. Furthermore, most research on generativity has been based on groups of successful men and women and graduates of elite liberal arts colleges. Racially and economically inclusive studies of more recent cohorts of men and women might further clarify the relationships among age, cohort, and generativity. As already indicated, there is reason to believe that the sequencing of adult careers (George, 1993, 1996; Hogan, 1981, Marini, 1984) may have been more predictable for this cohort than for present cohorts. Also contributing to a different experience of midlife are higher divorce rates, later first marriages with delayed advent of parenthood (Daniels & Weingarten, 1982; Nydegger, 1981), and increasing acceptance of both voluntary childlessness and nontraditional sexualities (Cornett & Hudson, 1987; Houseknecht, 1979; Jacobson & Heaton, 1991; Veevers, 1979).

On the other hand, a comparative study of elite college graduates and working-class counterparts has suggested similar concern with generativity at midlife (Snarey, 1993; Vaillant, 1993, Vaillant & Milofsky, 1980). It should be noted, however, that this study employed a narrower definition of generativity, focusing exclusively on care and concern for the next generation, than that adopted by both McAdams and his colleagues and Peterson and Stewart and their colleagues. Taken together, research on the sociohistorical contexts of midlife development raises questions regarding the definition, salience, and timing of generative concern, at least as traditionally understood (see chapter 3, this volume).

Finally, as Marcia, Kowacz, and Bradley (1990) cautioned, echoing Vaillant (1977, 1993), emphasizing cultural reproduction as a defining element of generativity may reflect simple social conformity, or what Winnicott (1960) portrayed as a "false self." This false self, which is expressed in excessive concern with social conformity and the opinion of others, may reflect avoidance of painful issues concerning the search for personal coherence or integrity when confronted by, among other things, increased personalization of death and enhanced realization of the finitude of life

(Jaques, 1965, 1980; Kotre, 1984; Marshall, 1975, 1986; Neugarten & Datan, 1996).

This discussion suggests that the concept of generativity, like many of the creative ideas of Erikson, has been elusive. Attempts to define generativity and to place it within a sequence of life course tasks have had mixed results. As portrayed in Peterson and Stewart's (1993, 1996) study of women both in young adulthood and at midlife, parenthood appears to be central to the definition of generativity. However, at a time when many men and women elect not to have children, the relationship between generativity and realization of the parental role must be reconsidered. Rather than focusing on generativity as a task that is primarily salient at a specific point in the course of life, it might be more instructive to place a discussion of generative concern within the broader context of the socially structured adult life course and situated within specific, unique lives, as emphasized in the present chapter. Among other things, such an approach would require recognition of the ways in which opportunities to provide and care for future generations are socially structured and regulated. Not only are creative products judged worthy or unworthy on the basis of certain cultural standards, but access to future generations is often restricted.

Generativity, Middle Adulthood, and the Gay Man

The narratives of gay men, whose experience is outside the norms on which so much of life course theory has been grounded, provide a fertile ground for exploration of the dialogic process between person and social order with respect to issues of generativity at midlife. The study of people who have adopted a nontraditional erotic identity—primarily those who identify themselves according to the contemporary categories of lesbian, gay, or bisexual—raises important questions regarding the meanings of generativity and its place within adult development. Foremost among these questions are those concerning the structure and timing of the gay life course. The study of generativity among gays and lesbians necessitates consideration of the effects of societal stigma and discrimination, as well as the historical and social movements and events particular to the gay community. More specifically, the study of lesbian and gay midlife development must address the experience of being outside normative social time without benefit of a gay-specific social timetable, as well as the enormous cohort differences in lived experience that have resulted from dramatic social change and the emergence of AIDS.

The study of gay development across the course of life must begin, of course, with recognition of the importance of historical events and cohort effects. The organization of same-sex desire around a homosexual and, later, a lesbian or gay identity became possible only during the course of the present century (Foucault, 1990; Weeks, 1985). The cohort currently in middle adulthood came of age during an era in which there were no visible gay role models or other cultural resources to support early development. Many of these men and women did not resolve issues of identity and sexuality until well into their 20s or even 30s, placing them well off-time with respect to their heterosexual counterparts. Nontraditional sexual orientation has also presented career challenges for many lesbians and gay men, who have been faced with a choice between deceit and discrimination. These problems have often been further complicated by issues related to race, gender, and class. Unfortunately, the present chapter is able to address only the concerns of middle-class gay men at midlife.

Lesbian- and gay-identified persons not only are likely to be off-time with respect to certain normative life events and developmental tasks but also have constructed different developmental norms. The lack of institutional support for and modeling (Antonucci, 1990; Kahn & Antonucci, 1981; Plath, 1980) of same-sex relationships and the emergence of alternative subcultural expressions of intimacy have also contributed to a somewhat unique gay experience of young adulthood.

As they enter middle adulthood, the cohort of gay men with whom the present study is concerned are facing new obstacles, but they are also making new contributions (Isay, 1996). The challenge of being off-time or out of time with respect to normative developmental schedules has been intensified by the AIDS pandemic, which has hit this cohort of men the hardest. AIDS has shortened the expectable life course for many men, leading to telescoping of developmental concerns, including the loss of loved ones and the realization of the finitude of life (Bennett & Thompson, 1991; Borden, 1989, 1992; Kelly, 1980). Emphasis within the gay community on youth, although perhaps overstated, also has not made the midlife transition any easier. In addition, opportunities to be generative are further limited by the heavy cultural (and academic) emphasis on parenthood, which is out of reach for many gay men and simply not chosen by others, and by the hysteria of those who would prohibit any contact between adult gay men and younger generations. Nevertheless, many gay men reach out to future generations through teaching, social work, activism, and other forms of mentoring (Isay, 1996).

The relationship between sexual orientation and generativity is further complicated by the widely acknowledged fluidity of erotic identity. Many men and women at some point in their lives adopt a heterosexual identity and set of social roles, marrying and having children, and at another time adopt a same-gender erotic identity. Parenthood is common among gay and lesbian couples, with many gay and lesbian couples serving as foster or adoptive parents or providing care for children from a previous marriage of one or both partners. Increasingly, women within lesbian relationships elect to become pregnant. Kertzner and Sved (1996) suggested that gay men and women are actively involved in generative activities. Indeed, the relationship between parenthood and generativity among young and middle-aged couples is as complex within the lives of gay men and women as among straight counterparts (Blumenstein & Schwartz, 1983).

Cornett and Hudson (1987) discussed generativity within the lives of gay men and women at midlife who elected to remain childless. They observed that gay men and women seek equivalent expressions of parental care. However, at least one problem posed by this effort to identify equivalent contributions, as well as by similar efforts to fit gay and lesbian lives within the generativity paradigm, is that the authors effectively equated generativity with parenthood; although many gay men and women are also parents, efforts to find parallel generative experiences for gays and straights ignore the complex nature of generativity as an expression of broader concern for succeeding generations. Much of this critique is addressed in the present volume. However, it must also be acknowledged that, given the popular cultural ideal that equates full adulthood with parenthood, not all generative acts are considered to be equal. Lesbians and gay men who are unable or choose not to become parents, like childless heterosexuals, must contend with this cultural ideal, one way or another, in the construction of their adult lives. Although some researchers take the view that all generative efforts apart from parenting are simply redirections of a blocked need, we prefer to adopt a different, broader perspective.

The present study, based on the work of McAdams (1985, 1993, 1996), adopts a working definition of generativity that emphasizes belief and action reflecting commitment to the well-being of the next generation. This commitment is demonstrated through efforts to make life better for the next generation; it may include political and social activism, teaching, mentoring, work in public health, support for environmentalism and conservation, and volunteering and leadership in social organizations providing assistance to others. Although there may be specific products associated with generativity, this perspective emphasizes the enhancement of opportunity for the next generation and the transmission of important institutions and ways of life. Although parenthood may be an important avenue for the realization of generativity, it is neither necessary nor always sufficient.

McAdams (1996) also suggested that highly generative persons enact a *commitment script*, which often depicts victory over earlier adversity. In response to prior challenges, some individuals become increasingly concerned with the welfare of others. Cohler and Schiff (1997) found such concern to be particularly marked among individuals who survived Shoah. A similar outcome may be found among the cohort of gay men and lesbians now in midlife who have struggled to overcome the adversity of stigma and discrimination. One important outlet for this generative concern has been social activism. In contrast to the cohort of older gay men and lesbians, who had sought to avoid notice, the present generation of middle-aged gay men and women have rallied around the cause of gay liberation. Determined that future generations avoid suffering such stigma, many gay activists have focused on changing mores and laws to facilitate equality of participation. Other activists work directly with youth, focusing their efforts on creating and maintaining "safe spaces" for gay teenagers to explore their feelings and receive support from others. Organizations that cater to lesbian and gay youth are staffed by both young and middle-aged persons concerned with the welfare of the next generation.

The AIDS epidemic has both provided new opportunities for generative expression and highlighted the socially structured nature of generativity. For those who care for present generations of gay men living with and dying from AIDS, providing for the needs of future generations may seem like a luxury. At least among the current cohort of middle-aged gay men, AIDS has led to a foreshortened sense of time (Borden, 1989, 1992). Gay men now arriving at midlife have already confronted concerns related to "outliving the self" (Kotre, 1984) that are more commonly characteristic of adults who are well into middle adulthood; however, such concerns appear inseparable from the welfare of the next generation. A major concern of AIDS activists has been to curtail the epidemic so that the next generation does not become infected. Among gay women, breast cancer prevention groups have adopted a similar mission of concern for the health of the next generation.

Finally, to the extent that people have achieved some degree of seniority in their work by midlife and, through lived experience, have attained a larger perspective, we believe this point in the course of life may be more salient than earlier periods for the expression of generative concern. However, it is possible for some young adults to be particularly concerned with and committed to the welfare of the next generation.

GENERATIVITY IN THE LIFE STORIES OF THREE GAY MEN

Inspired by both an interest in the sociohistorical context of lives and a commitment to the narrative perspective, a group of investigators at the University of Chicago has been engaged for the past 4 years in a study of lesbians and gay men at midlife and beyond. Although much is known about the "coming out" experiences of lesbian and gay youth (see, for example, Herdt, 1989; Herdt & Boxer, 1993; Savin-Williams, 1990), there has been less study of the course of adult lives among middle-aged and older gay men and lesbians (Berger, 1996; Cruikshank, 1990; Friend, 1991; Kehoe, 1989; Kimmel, 1993; Kimmel & Sang, 1995; Reid, 1995; Sang, 1993; Vaccha, 1985). There have been several notable accounts of gay men's life stories (Hall Carpenter Archives, 1989; Kantrowitz, 1996; Nardi, Sanders, & Marmor, 1994; Porter & Weeks, 1991; Vaccha, 1985), but these collections provide little theoretical reflection and fail to address the larger social and historical context of the life stories.

Participants in our study were recruited through advertisements in a local gay newspaper, through a professional organization for older gay men, and through snowballing effects. Interviews were based on an open-ended protocol, beginning with a brief life history and including questions on a wide range of topics. Interviews took place primarily in the homes of the participants, were audiotaped and later transcribed, and were up to 4 hours in length. The three life histories reviewed here were selected to represent the diversity of perspectives and life experiences both within the larger sample and within the gay community in general. These men are typical, but not necessarily statistically representative, of middle-aged gay men who are not presently in partnered relationships (in a recent survey of 160 Chicago-area gay men and women over the age of 45, 46% of the gay men reported currently being in a same-sex partnered relationship, with an average duration of 10.2 years; Herdt, Rawls & Beeler, 1997).

These three life stories focus on the identification of generative themes as well as the contextualization of generative efforts within the broader midlife concerns and experiences of the three gay men. We do not employ a quantitative coding scheme, but rather highlight the three men's efforts to endow their midlife experience with meaning. Each of the three men reports struggling with issues related to care and concern for the next generation and personal mortality. One of these men is HIV-positive and has experienced a series of tragic losses, whereas the other two have been less personally affected by the AIDS epidemic.

Mark: A Life Deferred

A Brief Life History

Mark is a 45-year-old African American adoptive father of two adolescent boys, the biological children of a cousin. He works as an administrator at an urban vocational college. The oldest of two sons born to middle-class parents, he moved with his family from the city to the suburbs when he was in grade school. He described himself as somewhat of an "oddity" during his school years because he was advanced in his studies and a straight "A" student. He found himself the frequent object of teasing, apparently unrelated to gender and sexual issues. He characterized his early family life as stable and supportive. He recalled being only vaguely aware of attraction to other men until the age of 13, at which time he had his first sexual experience with a 14-year-old boy. Mark observed that he did not "put it all together" until he was 18 or 19 and in college, when he found himself uninterested in initiating a sexual relationship with the girl to whom he had become engaged. He broke off the engagement and, for the first time, began to see himself as gay. This entailed the difficult realization that, among other things, he would not be "continuing the family line."

He remained mostly "closeted" and removed from gay life until he became involved with a profeminist men's group early in the 1970s that included several other gay men. He formed close friendships with some of these men, which facilitated his "coming out" process. In graduate school, he met a heterosexual man with whom he fell deeply in love, an unrequited relationship that motivated him to seek counseling. His therapist advised him to disclose his feelings to his friend, which he did. Although the friend reacted relatively well, he was unable to return Mark's feelings in kind. Eventually the friendship fizzled, and it took Mark a long time to get over this romantic rejection.

One of the few Black graduate students at his university, Mark felt generally unsupported, and he left without his degree to take care of his mother when she was diagnosed with cancer in the early 1980s. A few years after his mother's cancer diagnosis, his father also became ill, debilitated by severe diabetes. At about the same time, his cousin abandoned her two small boys, ages 2 and 3 at the time, and he was able to adopt them. For over a decade now, Mark has been caring for both of his aging, infirm parents and his adoptive sons, in addition to balancing career demands. About 2 years ago, he decided it was time to rearrange his priorities before his whole life passed him by. In the past year, he has more actively sought out sexual partners, with the goal of achieving greater intimacy in his life, and is becoming more involved with the lesbian and gay community. He also recently changed jobs so that he could work in the city.

Mark's sons are still his primary concern, and he continues to care for his parents, but he also makes time to pursue his own interests. His sons are aware of his sexual orientation and are basically very accepting, although the issue is not discussed outside the family setting. He worries that, given the pressures of being adolescent and male, they might experience some difficulty in their peer group; however, the boys seem to have a healthy attitude about the situation. Students at a Christian academy, they come home on occasion to report what they were "taught" about homosexuality at school; fortunately, Mark is able to provide his sons with the other side of the story. He said that ensuring that his sons receive a good education is "tantamount to [their] survival" and that his own life will become his top priority only when they are in college.

Analysis of Narrative Themes

Mark's developmental trajectory, which is at once similar to and different from the pathways followed by other middle-aged gay men, sharply illustrates the complex intertwining of group characteristics and unique events in the construction of a life. To begin with, Mark's development—like that of all other members of late-modern, bourgeois culture—unfolded against a shared backdrop of expectations about the normative course of life. Like most gay men of his cohort, who were denied adequate structural and symbolic resources to support their development, Mark was clearly a late bloomer—or off-time—with respect to the resolution of sexual and identity concerns. However, unlike many of his White peers, his coming out was further complicated by his subcultural and religious background. Even more important is the fact that Mark's adult life took an unexpected direction as a result of unpredictable life course events.

Mark's early development was not entirely dissimilar from that of other (mostly White) gay men of his generation. Like many of these men, he reported a difficult and trying set of childhood experiences, although he did not connect these experiences to an emerging sense of erotic identity. Instead, Mark related his early experience of difference, of standing out in a crowd, to his academic prowess, something that was not necessarily expected, by either White or Black peers, from a young male African American. If it was difficult for a young White man with same-sex desires to arrive at a positive gay identity, it was perhaps that much more of an accomplishment for a young Black man, who was also forced to contend with the powerful influence of a church not accepting of his sexual preference, as well as with the more general perception that being gay is a "White thing." In addition, he was much influenced, as we have already mentioned, by strong cultural and familial expectations regarding the continuation of the family name. Mark himself explicitly acknowledged, that this particular life course expectation—and the fear that he would have to forsake it—was a major obstacle to the development of a gay identity: "Part of the thing I found sad was when I realized that I was gay, I thought that I would have to give that part of my life [desire to be a father] up." For this and other reasons, Mark was unable to understand or acknowledge his same-sex feelings until he entered college, and even then the process of coming to terms with these feelings was gradual.

Like many other gay men who experience being different or who pursue an adult trajectory that is off-time or even out of expectable time, Mark struggled to understand his own development. He questioned academic and folk theories concerning the "cause" of homosexuality and, like other gay men and women, created his own developmental theories. Lacking a developmental timetable of expectable transitions and attempting to make his life story coherent, Mark has been actively involved in creating his life-world. To this end, he has been involved with encounter groups and, during graduate school, psychotherapy with the explicit purpose of addressing concerns related to intimacy and sexuality. This self-examination was interrupted by his parents' unexpected illnesses and the arrival of his adopted sons. These unanticipated life events contributed to an off-time developmental pattern with respect to his peers; he did not return to typical developmental concerns for many years.

Although these events were clearly unpredictable, it is not merely coincidental that the responsibility for caring for members of these two generations fell on the shoulders of a single, unattached, and professionally successful family member—not an uncommon constellation of traits for a gay man or woman. It is most remarkable that, the "chance" events that led to the adoption represented the fulfillment of the fondest desire of his life:

> The most tremendous impact of having my children, they fulfilled what had been a lifelong dream. I wanted to be somebody's father. I had a father and a grandfather, and all of those examples were part of my life, and I wanted to do that. So that was very important to me.

Mark also displayed an unusual level of self-consciousness when talking about the ways in which fatherhood contributed to his own development:

> When I got them [his adopted sons], I felt anchored in time and space, and there was a real serenity connected with that. And that's because my generativity needs have been met. And gay men have that . . . you know, that's a big issue, and there isn't much modeling of that at all.

As a result of agreeing to care for his adopted sons, therefore, Mark adopted a conventional pattern of generativity, complemented by teaching, mentoring, and activism. In addition to being a committed father, he considers himself a social activist—a family tradition—and is also dedicated to his job, which, among other tasks, involves counseling students. He says he is particularly dedicated to his lesbian and gay students, who are often in desperate need of mentoring:

> In dealing with my students and counseling my students, young gay men and lesbians and bisexual students, they just amaze me. They fascinate me, because their experience is different from my experience. And I try to be aware of those differences, and let that reflect the guidance and counseling that I'm called upon to give them, whenever that's necessary.

Apparently, the lack of visible role models for lesbian and gay youth has produced a new set of opportunities for gay adults to be generative, although the age-structured nature of gay life sometimes leads to missed opportunities. At the same time, as Mark indicated, cohort differences forced him to work that much harder to understand the developmental needs of his students.

His "generativity needs hav[ing] been met," Mark, now 45, is finally making time for himself and for concerns that he has not addressed until the present time:

> And this last year, I said, I'm not getting any younger, it's time to get on with life, and I decided to make some changes . . . I decided to . . . start focusing more on my own personal life. . . . it's been a really cataclysmic time, because I had to come out and do something or else I was just going to . . . spend the next how many years I had, just going along, and it would just be over . . . I've really been supporting everybody and that's been really difficult . . . [I've been] overwhelmed by my responsibilities, and I have anger connected with that, and I have a real . . . and I had no idea that it would take this long. And of course, even the children, who were very much wanted. I always wanted to be a father, but the children were unexpected, and so I never got a chance to prepare for leading, you know, my life, where I was the main focus, and taking on all of these other responsibilities, so I have a lot of deferred stuff.

With respect to his continuing difficulties in establishing an intimate relationship, Mark seemed cautiously optimistic about the future. Whether or not he meets "Mr. Right," Mark has worked a lifetime to build close relationships, and like many gay men, his friendship network will remain important to him regardless of his relational status. For instance, he described a group of former co-workers in the following way: "I have a group of former assistants, when I worked in housing at the university . . . we were literally like a big family. And that relationship has continued. And many of them I can turn to at the same time." About his gay friends in general, Mark said the following: "There's a certain intimacy that's manifested in humor, amongst close friends [in the gay community], that I enjoy." He also has a close gay male friend whom he speaks to almost every day, as well as close relationships with the members of his somewhat nontraditional family.

Mark has positive feelings about the future and has no regrets about having elected to care for his adopted sons rather than focus on his own development as a gay man. He is HIV-negative and intends to remain so; however, he has lost several friends to AIDS and has long been around illness and death. These experiences have contributed to his reflective and philosophical outlook, which is consistent with expectable midlife concerns with generativity:

> [When my sons go to college] I will be 50 years old, so it will look a lot different than when I was 33 years old and my family responsibilities started. I'm looking forward to seeing where I come from . . . I was really quite excited on my last birthday of turning 45 . . . I was reminded in the midst of illness and death that there is a lot of living left to be done. No I'm not a young man anymore, but I'm not necessarily ready to check out either. There's wonderful potential over the

next 20 years ... I played the hand I was dealt and I did OK. I still got plenty of time.

Tim: A Second Life at Mid-Life

A Brief Life History

Tim is a 49-year-old White, former Catholic brother (nonordained) who has been teaching at the same urban Catholic school for the past 25 years. The second oldest of six in a traditional Irish Catholic family, Tim dated his first awareness of being different to grade school, but it took him 30 more years to identify the precise nature of his difference. He had a "sense" that he was a sissy as a child, and he was singled out for ridicule by his peers. In the eighth grade, he narrowly escaped being elected the junior high equivalent of prom queen, but he was still forced to stand before his entire class as the runner-up, an experience he found humiliating. Adding to this early trauma was his mother's death from brain cancer when he was only 12 years old. The illness was brief, and his father managed to conceal it from the family. As a consequence, Tim was not able to prepare for and grieve this early loss. It was only many years later, as a result of psychotherapy, that Tim was finally able to come to terms with his mother's death.

In the years following the loss of his mother, Tim became the model son. He recalled being driven by the desire not to be a burden on his father, who had already suffered so much. He attended an all-boys Catholic high school, where he found his niche relatively quickly, getting involved in drama, the glee club, and the school newspaper. He recently discovered that several of his friends from high school are also gay; but he had had no idea of their sexual preference during high school. After his freshman year in high school, Tim made the decision to join the Catholic brothers. He continued to attend the same school, but he lived away from home. He was inspired to join the order responsible for instruction in his high school, whose members he described as wonderful role models. In retrospect, he also acknowledged that the idea of being in an all-male environment had been strangely appealing.

He remained with the brothers throughout his college years and graduate school, and eventually he began teaching himself religion and philosophy, which he has always enjoyed immensely. He claimed that during his years with the brothers he was almost completely unaware of his sexual feelings. He interpreted his strong attachments to certain brothers in terms of friendship, community, and spirituality. It was only in his mid-30s that he began to interpret his feelings for other men in a sexual way, and the need to explore this side of his life eventually led him to leave the order at the age of 38, still a virgin.

His initial encounters with gay life were a little disappointing, discouraging, and even frightening. He moved into a largely gay neighborhood, living alone for the first time in his life, and was almost immediately mugged and physically assaulted in a gay-related attack. It is not surprising that he began to question whether he had made the right decision. His first experiences in the gay social and sexual scene were also somewhat negative. He misinterpreted his first one-night stand as the start of a love relationship, and he experienced additional frustration and rejection in the bar scene, all of which led to a rude awakening. He later learned that he was going to the "wrong" bars (i.e., bars primarily for younger men) and made the appropriate adjustment. More important, he discovered a gay Catholic organization, where he met many of the close friends who now make up his support network.

Presently unpartnered, Tim is still teaching high school, and he recently bought a condominium in the city's predominantly gay neighborhood. He remains close to the siblings nearest in age to him and enjoys the role of uncle. He has become more politically involved, but he has not yet disclosed his sexual orientation at the Catholic school in which he teaches. About half of his gay friends are in long-term relationships, but he says he remains ambivalent about partnering. He seems to enjoy his relatively new-found independence. However, he and several of his single gay friends who are in his age group have discussed the possibility of a group living arrangement for the future. He has no regrets about his late start in gay life, and he values all the years he had with the brothers. At the same time, he is equally glad he made the change.

Analysis of Narrative Themes

Tim's story provides another compelling argument for understanding lives in terms of culturally and historically endowed meanings, an approach that also contends with variation and individual contributions to the art of living. For gay men of Mark and Tim's generation, the adoption of an adult homosexual lifestyle had begun to be a viable (if stigmatized) option only while they were growing up, and the homosexual world was far removed from and largely invisible to the childhood and adolescent worlds in which they were raised. Clearly stigma has produced a general delay in the sexual development of more than one generation of individuals with same-sex desires.

Simply to say that Tim was off-time with respect to his adolescent and early-adult development, although this is undeniably true in part, is to miss what is unique about his life. In an important way, Tim has lived two lives, and he would not trade in either of them. Like Mark, Tim struggled self-consciously during his early-adult years to decide how he might best serve his community. At midlife Tim was ready to embark on a different kind of journey, one of personal, sexual, and relational exploration. His story also highlights some uniquely gay variations on life course development.

Although Tim was very much aware of being different and of feeling marginalized as a child, he never connected this difference to sexual matters. It is nevertheless somewhat telling that his primary role models were members of an all-male religious order; as we already stated, he retrospectively acknowledged the implicit sexual appeal of this environment and lifestyle. Still, he claimed little awareness of sexual desire during most of his years with the brothers:

> I wasn't even thinking about straight sex. That whole part of me was so low developed at least on the conscious level. I think things were happening—I look back and say, well, this, this, and this. I know there were certain brothers I liked being around and I enjoyed when they paid attention, but then I just said they were nice people. I don't think I blocked it out—there wasn't anything to block, or at least consciously. I figured my sexual issues were solved when I went through religious life.

Despite his assertions to the contrary, one cannot help but wonder the extent to which Tim's lack of sexual awareness was related to his not wanting to rock the boat in the wake of his mother's death. Regardless of the reasons that brought him to the order, Tim found life with the brothers rewarding, both personally and spiritually; as he approached midlife, however, he began to feel as though something were missing. He entered therapy and began to address not only his growing sexual and affectional stirrings but also the loss of his mother, for whom he had never fully mourned. He eventually decided to make some changes in his life. He described his state of mind before and during the transition in this was:

> I just felt fulfilled. I love what I'm doing, I love teaching. I'm a good teacher and I enjoy being with the kids and this group of brothers. It was a happy time. I made the right decision for my life. Late into the 70s I began to get a little bit—saying there's some part that's not happening. But I said, oh well, that's just typical. . . . There's some part of me that's not being realized and not happening. I needed just something to do where I'd have some time to think and to step and explore, 'cause I had never [even] written a check, plus my sexual identity was really coming to the forefront much more than it had ever before.

Although the events immediately following his departure from the brotherhood were somewhat traumatic—particularly the gay-bashing incident—his transition was facilitated by a network of supportive and understanding friends, both new and old. The initial difficulty of this transition to an openly gay life was clearly exacerbated by the lack of role models and other important kinds of formal support for someone coming out at midlife. Among the many things he had to learn on his own was not to "read a wedding ring and a picket fence" from a one-night stand.

Through his teaching and spiritual counseling, Tim dedicated much of his early adulthood to "caring for the next generation." Moreover, despite the relatively recent changes in his life, he maintained his commitment to caring for others and improving the world around him. He continues to enjoy teaching, and he is aware that he is a role model, if a quiet one, to his young gay students. He says he has no desire to have children of his own, but his involvement in the gay community has provided other opportunities to be generative: He volunteers with political and AIDS organizations.

In fact, the AIDS crisis—and the lesbian and gay community's necessary response to it—provides perhaps the most poignant example of the culturally structured nature of generativity. Like other gay men within his cohort, Tim manages to balance caring for men of his own cohort—both dying and living with AIDS—and nurturing the growth of his gay and straight students. These expressions of generativity have been at some personal cost; overwhelmed by the magnitude of the epidemic, he is currently taking a respite from his volunteer work with AIDS patients.

Tim also reflected on the telescoping effect the AIDS crisis has had on gay life course development and the way it heightens and adds a sense of urgency to gay men's search for meaning:

> I think you have more appreciation for the time you are together. Appreciation for each other. Among the people I hang around with, "live for today" is not "and forget tomorrow." I think, no, not at all. The group tends to have more of a spirituality. They look at life as a spectrum. It's important to enjoy the moment but not to say the hell with what else is gonna happen . . . I feel I'm making a contribution, so I don't feel I'm waiting around.

Tim's experience of intimacy has also been somewhat unique. For more than 20 years he enjoyed the companionship of the brothers and being part of a spiritual community. After living in this community for so long, he was more than ready to experience independence. For this reason, he says he is somewhat ambivalent about finding a long-term romantic relationship:

> I really go back and forth on that. For all those years I didn't—sometimes I really value that. Some of my friends are in relationships. I just don't know where I stand. On the one hand, I'll say yes I want one, on the other I'll say I like my independence.

At the same time, Tim acknowledged failure in achieving the romantic intimacy he desires. He claimed that his late start in gay life left him "playing catch-up" and that he still has much to learn about relationships: "The whole relationship part is still not—you know, I still do irresponsible things [sexually] because I still haven't dealt with all that piece of my life yet in terms of the whole sexuality." Tim also admitted that he is fearful about the possibility of living alone and becoming incapacitated. Like Mark and many other mature gay men, however, Tim has a strong and extensive support network, and he and a group of his closest friends are considering entering into a group living arrangement at some point in the future. He jokingly claimed to have the "busiest calendar in the Midwest." Tim even suggested that the intimacy gay men experience with their friends, both male and female, may give them an advantage over their heterosexual counterparts in confronting life crises: "[For gay men] there might be more of a support system. For a straight man if you are in crisis a lot can't go to their friends and say, I'm experiencing a crisis . . . It's just not culturally set up that way for straight men." On the other hand, he is also very much aware that ageism in the gay community can make growing "gay and gray" difficult at times, not to mention the ways in which it hinders intergenerational contact and exchange:

> Older people sometimes seem to be left out of the picture. It's hard for those . . . in younger years who really struggled for things and some people are reaping the benefits of that. In a bar, lack of acknowledgment, the sense of an older person's talking to me, he wants to get into my pants.

Generally, Tim is satisfied with his life, his many friends and his professional and political commitments. He has no regrets about his late coming out, but he also seems more than happy with his decision to change his life. He summed up his coming out experience, which also served as his "midlife crisis," in the following way:

> I think it was a freeing up . . . I learned a lot about life beforehand and about dealing with people and I brought that with me. I certainly loosed a lot of things in myself . . . I just felt more complete. I was concerned about the issues gays and lesbians were facing and I wanted to speak about it and I wanted to speak about it as someone who could admit he was.

Edward: Finding Peace, Staying Sober, and Living with HIV

A Brief Life History

Edward is 43, White, and HIV-positive. Like Tim, Edward is from a large Irish Catholic family native to a large Midwestern city. His parents raised 11 children, 10 biological and 1 adoptive. Edward's father died of lingering cancer while Edward was in high school; his mother is still alive but afflicted with Alzheimer's disease. One of Edward's brothers is also gay, but despite their similar sexual orientation, they are not close. Edward recently retired because he felt job-related stress was causing his health to deteriorate. He never had a career, per se, but instead held several jobs related to food and beverage management over the course of his professional life. At different times he has been a bartender, a manager in a food-store chain, and the owner of his own catering business.

Edward's childhood was particularly adverse. He was still very young when his mother gave birth to triplets, who received the lion's share of the family's attention. He claimed this was the beginning of his "abandonment issues." When he was 13, a game of strip poker with several neighborhood boys turned violent, and Edward became the target of a gang rape. He was driven into a state of isolation for an extended period of time, and he never again spoke to the perpetrators, some of whom had been trusted friends. Although he had always been somewhat of a "sissy," a perception exacerbated by his lifelong weight problem, it was only in the wake of the sexual assault that he began to think of himself as sexually different from other boys. He was confused for a long time about whether he was raped because he was gay or whether the rape "caused" him to be gay, and thus he alternated between self-blame and hatred for his attackers. He also started drinking after the incident. On top of all this, his alcoholic father was physically abusive, although he learned from his older brothers' mistakes and was often able to avoid his father's wrath.

Despite having to repeat his freshman year—another aftershock of the rape—Edward managed to enjoy himself during high school. He made several friends, became involved with theater, and began to experiment sexually with other boys. Throughout his high school years he worked in grocery stores, and he continued to do so after graduation while also attending college part-time. Apparently unmotivated to finish his degree and eager to be out from under his parents' control, he got a new job and moved to a different part of town. At the same time that he began to explore gay life, he was also seriously involved with a couple of women, to one of whom he became engaged. His closest male friend at the time, with whom he was sexually involved, also got engaged. When Edward realized that he could not serve as the friend's best man because he was in love with him and not with his own fiancée, he broke off his engagement. Shortly thereafter, he became a regular on the gay bar scene, eventually taking work as a bartender.

Although working and constantly socializing in bars contributed to what had become a chronic problem with alcohol, Edward was able to make a lot of new friends, and for the first time, he became politically involved through a group of local bartenders. However, a vacation in Florida and his first "taste of the high life" contributed to the start of a cocaine addiction, which eventually led to several financial crises. Drinking, drugging, and severe problems with his back—necessitating several surgeries—served to disrupt and destabilize his work life. He was in and out of therapy, but it did not seem to be helping. Edward's father came to his financial rescue on at least one occasion, but new tensions entered their relationship when Edward came out to him. Despite their troubles, he and his father were able to come to some sort of mutual understanding with the assistance of the family priest before his father's death.

After his father died, Edward's life continued its downward trend. He went on cocaine binges; went through several destructive, short-term relationships with men; and spent almost all his time in bars. It was at this time that his friends began to die of the then unknown disease that, along with his alcoholism, would soon become the central focus of his life. He abruptly failed to make a go of a painting business he started because he was drunk or high most of the time. Finally, nearly suicidal, he "bottomed out" one day when he realized that he had no idea how or where he had spent the last several days. He found his way to Alcoholics Anonymous (AA) and eventually Narcotics Anonymous (which he has since left), and through much hard work and with the support of a new network of friends, he has remained sober since.

Part pop-psychologist, part philosopher, Edward finally seems to have achieved a degree of peace, despite or perhaps as a result of becoming HIV-positive in 1989. He has lost countless friends over the years, nursing some of them through the terminal stages of their illnesses. He deals with his grief through therapy, through AA and other support groups, and with the help of his many remaining friends. He started what became a successful catering business in the early 1990s, but he was happy with his decision early in 1995 to retire. He is currently living with a man with whom he was romantically involved for many years but who now is more of a friend and a companion. He keeps busy with his volunteer work, his responsibilities as an AA sponsor, and his many social engagements. At one time pessimistic and defeated, Edward currently is positive and hopeful about the future.

Analysis of Narrative Themes

Edward's developmental trajectory clearly overlaps a great deal with those of Mark and Tim. Coming to terms with his sexuality, which has preoccupied him throughout his adolescent and adult life, was complicated by a series of uncontrollable and often traumatic life events. Although alcoholism and childhood abuse are closely associated in his mind with his experience of being gay, the relationship among these issues is far from apparent. Whereas being a "sissy" clearly made him a potential target for the kind of physical and sexual abuse he suffered and gay bar culture undoubtedly contributed to his alcoholism, other factors are certainly implicated, including familial and perhaps hereditary factors in the latter case and the pure randomness of life events in the former. These difficult developmental issues, in conjunction with his HIV diagnosis, have produced a midlife experience for which normative theories of adult development simply cannot account. The heightened sense of developmental self-consciousness of certain gay men, to which we have already alluded, is particularly evident in Edward's reflection on his life and was certainly amplified through his years of therapy and involvement with AA. According to Edward's own elaborate narrative, his troubles began with the birth of the triplets, and his developmental fate was seemingly sealed by the rape, about which he was silent until he entered therapy 20 years later. He traced all his problems to these two events and to his childhood experience in general, from his fear of abandonment and consequent "fear of commitment" to his internalized homophobia and his problems with drugs and alcohol. His adult life would become one big attempt to overcome his childhood and his own self-hatred. In his words,

> a lot of the reasons that I drank and drugged was to stuff a lot of those feelings I had from being a kid, from the stuff that happened or didn't happen. But the most important thing that I learned at that point was that I had to take care of me, and that I had to be me, and that I had to live and function as a gay man, which is what I am. I had to stop this homophobic behavior, and, although I had always thought that I was pretty much out there, the reality of my own homophobia really came out after I got sober.

Although Edward was aware of his same-sex desires and was sexually active with men throughout high school, the influence of shared community expectations delayed his identification as a gay man. He dated women out of "fear of realizing what I was all about," and he fully expected to be "the father of a big family and . . . happily married." Despite the emergence of a highly visible lesbian and gay subculture, there has been little study of gay and lesbian lives over time; consequently, there is little agreement regarding an expectable gay life course, a state of affairs evidenced by Edward's uncertainty about the future course of his life. Even after coming out, he was guided by what he now sees as naive life expectations, expectations that are now making his midlife adjustment more difficult:

> Life was going to be very different. What I wanted to be, and what I really thought it was going to turn out to be, were two very different things, are completely different than what it is today. I always anticipated that I was going to meet some man and fall in love and we were going to be together forever . . . everyone that I ever dated was going to be Mr. Right and we were going to be together forever.

Edward also feels that his career expectations were influenced by his sexual orientation. He said his professional choices were dictated by the desire not to be "inhibited by [his] sexuality," and he sometimes wonders about other career paths he might have taken.

Despite realizing a degree of self-acceptance after coming out in his early 20s Edward's young adulthood was consumed by drugs, alcohol, and sex without intimacy. Edward's work as a bartender, and the fact that he was a habitué of gay club culture, facilitated his substance abuse, even lending it an air, at least at first, of social legitimacy. It would take more than 10 years, a handful of severe financial crises, and several failed relationships before he hit "rock bottom." The turning point he narrated is not unlike those of others who eventually find their way to AA:

> I was to the point of suicidal behavior. And I woke up one day and realized I had been on this binge and I had no idea where I'd been for the last week, what I had done, where all my money went, whether I'd been robbed. My rent was late, my gas was shut off in my apartment, it was November. It was cold. My phone didn't work. They would be shutting my electricity off at any moment, and I woke up thinking, why am I doing this?

In the early days of his recovery, he went to AA five to seven times a week and saw his therapist once a week. Since the age of 33, AA and other twelve-step groups have been the primary source of new friends and a constant source of support.

Complicated by the many developmental difficulties he faced, Edward's experience of intimacy and communion has been somewhat similar to the experiences of Mark and Tim, although there are important differences. Although all three men reported that approximately half of their gay friends were currently partnered, each is presently single, and Edward seems the most dissatisfied of the three with his relational status. Before his 5-year relationship with Tony, currently his roommate, Edward was involved in many short-term relationships, some of which, in retrospect, he still cannot understand:

> There was another relationship in there that . . . once it was over, I thought to myself, how did I ever get involved with this person? What was the reason, where did it come from, where did he come from? I realized I had no idea why I was putting up with him, or anything that he was about. He was so totally different than myself. But I needed him, I needed someone, anyone at that time. And it was awful.

However, Edward now views another past relationship as the love of his life, and he often regrets not telling this man how he really felt until it was too late.

At the same time, AIDS and other things have changed the way he thinks about and approaches relationships. Here he tells the story of how he met Tony:

> It was during that year that my friend Gail passed away, my friends Bill and Kevin passed away. Two of my other very good friends got

sick. I didn't have time for a boyfriend. I didn't want one, and Tony pursued it much harder than I did.

With respect to his current attitude about relationships, Edward observed the following:

> I don't know that I would get into a relationship at this point in my life, although I miss having that person next to me in bed. I miss having that intimate relationship with someone. But I keep a lot of people in my life, and so a lot of those needs get met.

Despite his unfavorable, if somewhat ambivalent, evaluation of his relational history and future prospects, Edward feels surrounded by people who care about him. In addition to his ex-partner, Tony, he knows he can rely on his many friends from AA and his HIV support groups, who are at least "as important . . . [to each other as] our real blood families." Comparing gay men with straight men, Edward says, "I think gay men have a much different network, whether they have partners or not. They don't have that fear so much of being alone, as a [specifically] gay stipulation."

Of course, having so many friends with AIDS has necessitated his rebuilding his friendships on more than one occasion, but he knows that doing so is absolutely essential to his continued survival and well-being: "After this series of losses happened, I went through a period of depression, and one day I woke up and realized that my phone doesn't ring anymore. And what am I going to do about this?" Edward responded by calling a friend who was in the same boat and who became his "partner" in "reaching out to new people."

We hoped this vignette would demonstrate that Edward has also managed to be a generative person. Even during his days as a bartender, he was concerned with making the gay community more responsive to the needs of its members and thus a better place for all generations:

> The biggest thing we did was really make people aware. We formed an organization . . . it was a gay bartenders' association. And what we did was got bartenders from gay bars and other gay people who worked in the restaurant and bar industry together to do things to make it more of a responsible situation. We gave classes on how to be a responsible bartender to your customer, how to be responsible to the community, how to be responsible to yourself.

Edward currently volunteers with AIDS and lesbian and gay rights organizations, and he is a committed uncle to his many nieces and nephews. He believes that being single enables him to relate to his nieces and nephews in a way that their married relatives cannot; they treat him as a confidant and not as an out-of-reach authority figure.

The most significant aspect of Edward's midlife development is his HIV status. The developmental telescoping common to individuals living with AIDS is striking within Edward's recounting of his life story. We have already indicated that Edward recently retired. Although he seems to be adjusting relatively well and he is able to fill his days with a variety of activities, the initial transition was a little difficult: "I really struggled with my time and my structure and my fears of what's going to happen if I don't have enough money to live on, and what's going to happen, you know."

AIDS has, of course, also made Edward aware, on a daily basis, of the finitude of life. The ravaging nature and often rapid deterioration associated with AIDS leads many gay men both to question the meaning of life and the justice of the world and to invest every day with new value. However, on some days, Edward is overwhelmed by emptiness or fear:

> I thought I was dealing with it. I thought I was dealing with it so well. And then one day, about 1993, I woke up and I just couldn't get out of bed. . . . The really fearful part of that was that most of those people that were my friends that got sick, got sick today and died tomorrow. It was a month, a year, some of them—one of them was 4 days. He went into the hospital on Friday and on Monday he was dead.

Like Tim, Edward has spent a great deal of time caring for the dying, including a pair of lovers who were ill at the same time, for whom he prepared free gourmet meals so they would not have to eat hospital food. Unfortunately, normative theories of generativity and midlife development typically do not allow room for this kind of necessary care and attention to the present generation, an attention that precludes an exclusive focus on the succeeding generation.

Despite the devastation of his generation and his own HIV diagnosis, Edward's morale is generally high, and his health, at present, is relatively good, something that he attributes to "not bombarding [himself] with all these [AIDS-related] drugs." He explained how his doctor recently helped him out of a funk and how this changed his attitude about the future:

> I think the reality of me and my life slapped me in the face last year, when the doctor said, "This is it, you have a choice here. You can either participate or not." When he told me that he thought that up to that point I wasn't participating, and that the only way it was going to be different is if I made it different, then I realized I didn't want to die, and it wasn't over, and it didn't have to end like this. And that was when I really started thinking. . . . What I'm recently seeing in my life, in 10 years? I see myself actively working, participating . . . I've changed my whole thinking process. . . . Two years ago, there was no future. Today, big time!

Although such an approach to his illness might be termed denial, it seems likely, given recent improvements in his health and his state of mind, that it is the right approach. Edward summed up his thoughts about midlife, his own and others, in the following way:

> I think that the fact that when you get to be middle-aged, let's say that's 40, if you acknowledge your life and the parts of your life, good, bad or indifferent, being able to be comfortable with who and what you are at that point, is real important.

Perspectives on Generativity Among Gay Men at Midlife

The perspective adopted in the present chapter, founded on the study of lives across time and generations (Boxer & Cohler, 1989; Cohler & Boxer, 1984; Dannefer, 1984; Elder, 1992, in press-b; George, 1996; Hagestad & Neugarten, 1985; Hogan, 1981; Hogan & Astone, 1986; Neugarten, 1979; Neugarten & Hagestad, 1976; Pearlin, 1980; Sorokin & Merton, 1937), maintains that the course of adult lives is largely determined by socially shared expectations regarding the timing and sequence of role transitions. In taking seriously the dialectic process between the individual and his or her life-world, this perspective also acknowledges that the whole of lived experience is far more than the sum of its socially structured parts and that persons are capable of changing the social order even as they live within it. The three life stories reviewed in this chapter are served well by this approach to the study of lives.

Expression of Generativity Themes Among the Three Men

The life course of many gay men and lesbians is outside of time as appropriate timing is traditionally defined by bourgeois society and cultural standards. A combination of cultural factors, including the strange and inexplicable hatred often inspired by intimacy between persons of the same gender (Meyer, 1996; Phillps, 1996; Young-Bruehl, 1996), has created a set of developmental barriers that have made the lesbian and gay experience less than positive and always distinctive. Often arriving at midlife at least off-time—if not entirely off-course—for expectable life events and role transitions, many lesbians and gay men face serious challenges to their continued growth and development. At the same time, the gay community has developed some of its own solutions and alternatives both to common concerns and to those distinctive to gay men and women facing midlife at the present time. On the basis of McAdams's (1996) work, we have posed a view of generativity emphasizing care and concern for the well-being of the next generation.

Among these three men, Edward has perhaps experienced the greatest adversity, and of the three men, his midlife experience most closely resembles McAdams's (1996) "commitment script." At a time when Mark and Tim were preoccupied with school, Edward was in the vanguard of the first openly gay generation, and he participated actively in this emerging public culture. He combined this involvement with continuing dedication to the welfare of the next generation, as reflected in his activism, his leadership in AA, and his volunteer work with organizations promoting "safer sex."

In a much less dramatic way, but nevertheless outside the normative social timetable, the two other men have also demonstrated a variety of commitments, generative and otherwise. Mark and Tim have expressed their generative concerns directly, through their work with the next generation: Mark as the primary caregiver for his two young children, and Tim through his enduring commitment to education of inner-city youth. In addition to being a doting father, Mark is dedicated to the young students he counsels, particularly gay and lesbian students seeking an idealized role model. The need among lesbian and gay youth for such adult role models cannot be overstated, and this relatively new gay adult role provides an opportunity for the expression of generativity in a manner similar to that found in Levinson's (1978, 1996) portrayal of the mentoring of younger employees by older employees. At the same time, Mark's generative commitments have come at the cost of certain of his own unmet needs. Like many middle-aged heterosexual women, Mark is finally making some time for his own interests and concerns, while at the same time expressing great satisfaction with the joy his family and friends bring to him.

Tim's commitment to the care of the next generation also began somewhat off-time for his cohort, as part of his long teaching career. Like Mark, Tim also hopes to serve as a role model for gay and lesbian students. Clearly, teaching is an important part of Tim's commitment script (McAdams, 1996; Tomkins, 1987). However, attainment of this generative goal has been made more complex as a result of the real prospect of discrimination; Catholic schools are not generally known for their tolerance or acceptance of openly gay teachers. Having been a member of a celibate Catholic order for much of his adult life, Tim is also off-time with respect to sexual and intimacy concerns. On the other hand, he relishes his newfound independence and enjoys his relationships with his colleagues, his family, and his particularly tight-knit group of friends, who have even discussed the possibility of a group living arrangement, an option increasingly considered by middle-aged and older gay men and women. Nevertheless, it must be acknowledged that Tim's search for intimacy, like that of Edward and Mark, drains time and energy that might otherwise be directed toward generative commitments. That is the unfortunate price of being off-time.

These three life stories highlight some of the many ways in which gay men confront the challenges of middle adulthood while at the same time contributing to the world around them and maintaining a sense of integrity. The view of generativity provided in the present chapter appears sufficiently inclusive to accommodate not only individuals who are off-time or off-course with respect to normative development but also men and women who lead more traditional lives. Clearly, there are many more stories to be told. If little is known about the lived experience of gay men, less is known about lesbians, not to mention gays and lesbians of different races and social classes. Whereas individuals who have related their life stories to us thus far have been primarily White, middle-class men and women, the larger study from which these reports were drawn seeks a demographically diverse sample of lesbians and gay men. We hope others will join in the narrative study of aging and sexual orientation, a research endeavor that will contribute to a broader understanding of lives.

NEXT STEPS IN THE STUDY OF GENERATIVITY

Reviewing the lives of a cohort of Harvard men who entered college in the late 1930s, Vaillant (1977) mused on the life of an intermittently alcoholic gay man, a poet living on a houseboat on the San Franscisco Bay. Although Poe was clearly unlike his more explicitly achieving counterparts, Vaillant was troubled by an apparently successful midlife man who had suffered so much and yet seemed so much more reflective about his lived experience than his former classmates. Ultimately, Vaillant was unable to make sense of Poe's life.

Poe immediately acknowledged his homosexuality to Vaillant. Noting that he had read all of the papers thus far generated by the study he was a part of, Poe pointed out that Vaillant and his colleagues had classified homosexuality as a mental illness, alongside alcoholism and psychosis (Vaillant, 1977, p. 352). Indeed, Poe himself had succumbed for some time to alcoholism and had seen the "bottom" of life in ways uncharacteristic of his classmates. At the same time, he had been originally employed as a high school English teacher, had attained modest success as a poet, and dedicated part of each day to writing. Following several decades of personal struggle, Poe had achieved a sense of integrity that contrasted markedly with the experience of many of his contemporaries. After reviewing their conversation, Vaillant conceded that what mattered most was that Poe "was happy and that he cared" (Vaillant, 1977, p. 366).

Perhaps the most important question in the study of generativity and sexual orientation concerns the impact of a nontraditional, or nonnormative, life trajectory (Hogan & Astone, 1986). Closely related to this question is the effect on lived experience of stigma (Kantrowitz, 1996; Meyer, 1996; Young-Bruehl, 1996), which may produce a marked sense of being different and lead to different expressions of generativity. Vaillant recognized that difference in life experience alone may have fostered Poe's profound introspection, which exceeded that of his former classmates. Despite the personal turmoil in his life, Poe, unlike many of the other men in the study, had achieved a remarkable sense of peace with himself. This observation suggests that the intertwined issues of morale and generativity are also central to the life course study of individuals whose erotic identity departs from heterosexist expectations (Chodorow, 1992; Young-Bruehl, 1996). In addition, the future study of generativity and erotic identity should highlight more general issues, including both the definition of generativity and its salience across the course of life, the impact of aging and cohort effects on the expression of generativity within lives over time, and the differentiation of generativity from social conformity, or the "false self." The lives reviewed in this chapter have raised these questions in detail.

A final point about cohort effects should be noted: As this chapter is being written, there is much encouragement from initial clinical reports of a combination of medications designed to reduce viral load and support the immune system, results that may transform AIDS from a death sentence into a chronic illness. Should this initial effort prove successful, there will be a lengthening of the expected life course of many gay men, thereby altering, once again, the midlife experiences of gay men.

CONCLUSION

A revolution in the study of lives has occurred over the past two decades, leading to a more nuanced understanding of the dynamics of the life course. Rather than a fixed series of stages or tasks, the course of life is best understood as a story that is retold over time as a consequence of particular life experiences taking place at a particular time within a particular social context and told to particular others. Providing the building blocks for this story, the socially structured course of development consists of an implicit (and sometimes explicit) timetable learned in earliest childhood and maintained across time as a means of social comparison. With attainment of adulthood, this timetable takes the form of a series of expectable adult roles assumed and later surrendered or even taken away, as in the situation of forced retirement or widowhood. Development is characterized less by a set of sequential, purely psychological tasks than by a series of transitions into and out of expectable roles at expectable times. Along these lines, generativity is less of a psychological issue than a characteristic role that is significant across the course of adult life. Because opportunities for generative behavior are socially regulated, and to the extent that certain individuals live off-time with respect to expectable adult role transition, generativity may be experienced in distinctive ways and at different points of the adult life course.

The complexity of any given period in the life course cannot be captured by a single developmental concern. All persons confront a variety of challenges throughout life, made more or less difficult by the resources at their disposal. At least within late-modern society, therefore, development may be best understood metaphorically as water running downhill to join a stream (Waddington, 1956). Along the way it encounters obstacles that threaten its integrity and coherence, such as the loss of a parent through death or divorce, social unrest and conflict, or the experience of stigmatization. However, it is precisely the meanings that are made of such adversities that give the course of development and the life story its distinctive form.

REFERENCES

Antonucci, T. (1990). Social supports and social relationships. In R. Binstock & L. K. George (Eds.), *Handbook of aging and the social sciences.* (pp. 205–227). San Diego, CA: Academic Press.

Bengtson, V., Furlong, M., & Laufer, R. (1974). Time, aging, and the continuity of social structure: Themes and issues in generational analysis. *Journal of Social Issues, 30,* 1–30.

Bennett, K., & Thompson, N. (1991). Accelerated aging and male homosexuality: Australian evidence in a continuing debate. In J. A. Lee (Ed.), *Gay midlife and maturity* (pp. 65–75). New York: Haworth Press.

Berger, R. (1996). *Gay and gray: The older homosexual man* (2nd ed.). New York: Haworth Press.

Blumenstein, P., & Schwartz, P. (1983). *American couples: Money, work, sex.* New York: Morrow.

Borden, W. (1989). Life review as a therapeutic frame in the treatment of young adults with AIDS. *Health and Social Work, 14,* 253–259.

Borden, W. (1992). Narrative perspectives in psychosocial intervention following adverse life events. *Social Work, 37,* 135–141.

Boxer, A., & Cohler, B. (1989). The life-course of gay and lesbian youth: An immodest proposal for the study of lives. *Journal of Homosexuality, 17,* 315–355.

Butler, R. (1963). The life-review: An interpretation of reminiscence in the aged. *Psychiatry, 26,* 65–76.

Cain, L. (1964). Life-course and social structure. In R. Faris (Ed.), *Handbook of modern sociology* (pp. 272–309). Chicago: Rand McNally.

Chodorow, N. (1992). Heterosexuality as a compromise formation: Reflections on the psychoanalytic theory of sexual development. *Psychoanalysis and Contemporary Thought, 15,* 267–304.

Clausen, J. (1993). *American lives: Looking back at the children of the Great Depression.* New York: Free Press.

Cohler, B., & Boxer, A. (1984). Middle adulthood: Settling into the world—

person, time, and context. In D. Offer & M. Sabshin (Eds.), *Normality and the life-cycle* (pp. 145–204). New York: Basic Books.

Cohler, B., & Cole, T. (1996). Studying older lives: Reciprocal acts of telling and listening. In J. Birren, G. Kenyon, J-E Ruth, J. J. F. Schroots, & T. Svensson (Eds.), *Aging and biography: Explorations in adult development* (pp. 61–77). New York: Springer.

Cohler, B., & Lieberman, M. (1979). Personality change across the second half of life: Findings from a study of Irish, Italian and Polish-American men and women. In D. Gelfand & A. Kutznik (Eds.), *Ethnicity and aging* (pp. 227–245). New York: Springer.

Cohler, B., & Schiff, B. (1997). *Shoah, life-stories, and later life response to adversity.* Chicago: Committee on Human Development, University of Chicago.

Coleman, P. (1986). *Ageing and reminiscence: Social and clinical implications.* New York: Wiley.

Cornett, C., & Hudson, R. (1987). Middle adulthood and the theories of Erikson, Gould, and Vaillant: Where does the gay man fit? *Journal of Gerontological Social Work, 10,* 61–73.

Cruikshank, M. (1990). Lavender and grey: A brief survey of lesbian and gay aging studies. In J. A. Lee (Ed.), *Gay midlife and maturity* (pp. 77–87). New York: Haworth Press.

Daniels, P., & Weingarten, K. (1982). *Sooner or later: The timing of parenthood in adult lives.* New York: Norton.

Dannefer, D. (1984). Adult development and social theory: A paradigmatic re-appraisal. *American Sociological Review, 49,* 100–116.

Duberman, M. (1993). *Stonewall.* New York: St. Martin's Press.

Durkheim, E. (1995). *The elementary forms of the religious life* (K. Fields, Trans.). New York: Basic Books. (Original work published 1912)

Easterlin, R. (1987). *Birth and fortune: The impact of numbers on personal welfare* (2nd ed.). Chicago: University of Chicago Press.

Echols, A. (1989). *Daring to be bad: Radical feminism in America, 1967–1975.* Minneapolis: University of Minnesota Press.

Elder, G. H., Jr. (1974). *Children of the Great Depression.* Chicago: University of Chicago Press.

Elder, G. H., Jr. (1986). Military times and turning points in mens' lives. *Developmental Psychology, 22,* 233–245.

Elder, G. H., Jr. (1987). War mobilization and the life course: A cohort of World War II veterans. *Sociological Focus, 2,* 449–472.

Elder, G. H., Jr. (1992). Life course. In E. Borgatta & M. Borgatta (Eds.), *Encyclopedia of sociology* (Vol. 3, pp. 1120–1130). New York: Macmillan.

Elder, G. H., Jr. (in press-a). Human lives in changing societies: Life course and developmental insights. In R. Cairns, G. H. Elder, Jr., & E. Costello (Eds.), *Developmental science: multiple perspectives.* New York: Cambridge University Press.

Elder, G. H., Jr. (in press-b). The life-course and human development. In R. M. Lerner (Ed.), *Handbook of child psychology: Volume I: Theory.*

Elder, G. H., Jr., & Caspi, A. (1988). Human development and social change: An emerging perspective on the life course. In N. Bolger, A. Caspi, G. Downey, & M. Moorehouse (Eds.), *Persons in context: developmental processes* (pp. 77–113). New York: Cambridge University Press.

Elder, G. H., Jr., & Caspi, A. (1990). Studying lives in a changing society: Sociological and personological explorations. In A. I. Rabin, R. A. Zucker, R. A. Emmons, & S. Frank (Eds.), *Studying persons and lives* (pp. 201–247). New York: Springer.

Elder, G. H., Jr., & Hareven, T. (1993). Rising above life's disadvantage: From the Great Depression to war. In G. H. Elder, Jr., J. Modell, & R. Parke (Eds.), *Children in time and place: Developmental and historical insights* (pp. 47–72). New York: Cambridge University Press.

Elder, G. H., Shanahan, M., & Clipp, E. (1994). When war comes to men's lives: Life course patterns in family, work, and health. *Psychology and Aging, 9,* 5–16.

Erikson, E. H. (1958). *Young man Luther: A study in psychoanalysis and history.* New York: Norton.

Erikson, E. H. (1963). *Childhood and society.* New York: Norton. (Original work published 1950)

Erikson, E. H. (1982). *The life-cycle completed.* New York: Norton.

Erikson, E. H., Erikson, E., & Kivnick, H. (1986). *Vital involvement in old age: The experience of old age in our time.* New York: Norton.

Farnham-Diggory, S. (1966). Self, future, and time: A developmental study of the concepts of psychotic, brain injured and normal children. *Monographs of the Society for Research in Child Development, 33* (Whole no. 103).

Festinger, L. (1954). A theory of social comparison processes. *Human Relations, 7,* 117–140.

Foucault, M. (1990). *The history of sexuality: An introduction* (Vol. 1). New York: Vintage Books/Random House.

Friend, R. (1991). Older lesbian and gay people: A theory of successful aging. In J. A. Lee (Ed.), *Gay midlife and maturity* (pp. 99–118). New York: Haworth Press.

Furstenberg, F., Brooks-Gunn, J., & Morgan, S. (1987). *Adolescent mothers in later life.* New York: Cambridge University Press.

Geertz, C. (1973a). The impact of the concept of culture on the concept of man. In *The interpretation of cultures* (pp. 33–54). New York: Basic Books.

Geertz, C. (1973b). Person, time and conduct in Bali. In *The interpretation of cultures* (pp. 360–411). New York: Basic Books.

George, L. (1993). Sociological perspectives on life transitions. *Annual Review of Sociology, 19,* 353–373.

George, L. (1996). Missing links: The case for a social psychology of the life-course. *The Gerontologist, 36,* 248–255.

Gergen, K. (1994). *Realities and relationships: Soundings in social construction.* Cambridge, MA: Harvard University Press.

Gergen, K., & Gergen, M. (1983). Narratives of the self. In T. Sarbin & K. E. Scheibe (Eds.), *Studies in social identity* (pp. 245–273). New York: Praeger.

Gitlin, T. (1987). *The Sixties: Years of hope, days of rage.* New York: Bantam Books.

Gubrium, J., Holstein, J., & Buckholdt, D. (1994). *Constructing the life-course.* Dix Hills, NY: General Hall.

Guttentag, M., & Secord, P. (1983). *Too many women: The sex ratio question.* Beverly Hills, CA: Sage.

Hagestad, G. (1994). *On-time, off-time and out of time.* Paper presented at the annual meetings of the Gerontological Society of America, Atlanta, GA.

Hagestad, G., & Neugarten, B. (1985). Age and the life course. In R. Binstock & E. Shanas (Eds.), *Handbook of society and aging* (2nd ed., pp. 35–61). New York: Van Nostrand Reinhold.

Hall Carpenter Archives. (1989). *Walking after midnight: Gay men's life stories.* New York: Routledge.

Hazan, H. (1980). *The limbo people: A study of the constitution of the time universe among the aged.* London: Routledge & Kegan Paul.

Herdt, G. (Ed.). (1989). *Gay and lesbian youth.* New York: Haworth Press.

Herdt, G., & Boxer, A. (1993). *Children of horizons.* Boston: Beacon Books.

Herdt, G., Rawls, T., & Beeler, J. (1995). *The Horizons Mid-Life Study: Report from the survey.* The Committee on Human Development and the Evelyn Hooker Center for Gay and Lesbian Mental Health. Manuscript in preparation.

Hermans, H., & Kempen, H. (1993). *The dialogical self: Meaning as movement.* New York: Guilford.

Hogan, D. (1981). *Transitions and social change: The early lives of American men.* New York: Academic Press.

Hogan, D., & Astone, N. (1986). The transition to adulthood. *Annual Review of Sociology, 12,* 101–130.

Hostetler, A. (1996). *Beyond identity in lesbian and gay developmental theory: Cohort, cultural meaning and the context of life-course development.* Unpublished manuscript, Committee on Human Development, University of Chicago.

Houseknecht, S. (1979). Timing of the decision to remain voluntarily childless: Evidence for continuous socialization. *Psychology of Women Quarterly, 4,* 81–96.

Isay, R. (1996). *Becoming gay: The journey to self-acceptance.* New York: Pantheon Books.

Jacobson, C., & Heaton, T. B. (1991). Voluntary childlessness among American men and women in the late 1980s, *Social Biology, 138,* 79–93.

Jaques, E. (1965). Death and the mid-life crisis. *International Journal of Psychoanalysis, 46,* 502–514.

Jaques, E. (1993). The midlife crisis. In G. Pollock & S. Greenspan (Eds.), *The course of life: Vol. V. Early adulthood* (pp. 201–231). Madison, CT: International Universities Press.

Kahn, R., & Antonucci, T. (1981). Convoys of social support: A life-course approach. In S. Kiesler, J. Morgan, & V. Oppenheimer (Eds.), *Aging: social change* (pp. 383–405). New York: Academic Press.

Kalish, R. (Ed.). (1989). *Midlife loss: Coping strategies*. Newbury Park, CA: Sage.

Kantrowitz, A. (1996). *Under the rainbow*. New York: St. Martin's Press.

Kehoe, M. (1989). *Lesbians over 60 speak for themselves*. New York: Haworth Press.

Kelly, J. (1980). Homosexuality and aging. In J. Marmor (Ed.), *Homosexual behavior: A modern reappraisal* (pp. 176–193). New York: Basic Books.

Kertzer, R., & Sved, M. (1996). Midlife gay men and lesbians: Adult development and mental health. In R. Cabaj & T. Stein (Eds.), *Textbook of homosexuality and mental health* (pp. 284–304). Washington, DC: American Psychiatric Press.

Kimmel, D. (1993). Adult development and aging: A gay perspective. In L. D. Garnets & D. C. Kimmel (Eds.), *Psychological perspectives on lesbian and gay male experiences* (pp. 517–534). New York: Columbia University Press.

Kimmel, D., & Sang, B. (1995). Lesbians and gay men in midlife. In A. D'Augelli & C. Patterson (Eds.), *Lesbian, gay, and bisexual identities over the lifespan: Psychological perspectives* (pp. 190–241). New York: Oxford University Press.

Kotre, J. (1984). *Outliving the self: Generativity and the interpretation of lives*. Baltimore: The Johns Hopkins University Press.

Langness, L., & Frank, G. (1981). *Lives: An anthropological approach to biography*. Novato, CA: Chandler & Sharp.

Laufer, R., & Bengtson, V. (1974). Generation, aging and social stratification: On the development of generational units. *Journal of Social Issues, 30*, 181–206.

Levinson, D. (1978). *The seasons of a man's life*. New York: Knopf.

Levinson, D. (1996). *The seasons of a woman's life*. New York: Knopf.

Lieberman, M., & Falk, J. (1971). The remembered past as a source of data for research on the life cycle. *Human Development, 14*, 132–141.

Livson, N., & Peskin, H. (1980). Perspectives on adolescence from longitudinal research. In J. Adelson (Ed.), *Handbook of adolescent psychology* (pp. 47–96). New York: Wiley.

Mannheim, K. (1928). The problem of generations. In K. Mannheim (Ed.), *Essays on the sociology of knowledge* (pp. 276–322). London: Routledge and Kegan Paul.

Mansfield, E., & McAdams, D. (1996). Generativity and themes of agency and communion in adult autobiography. *Personality and Social Psychology Bulletin, 22*, 721–731.

Marcia, J., Kowaz, A., & Bradley, C. (1990). Industry and generativity: New directions for present and future research on psychosocial development. In C. Vanderplas-Holper & B. Campos (Eds.), *Interpersonal and identity development: New Directions* (pp. 113–117). Porto, France: ICPHD and Louvain-La Neuve: Academia.

Marini, M. (1984). Age and sequencing norms in the transition to adulthood. *Social Forces, 63,* 229–244.

Marshall, V. (1975). Age and awareness of finitude in developmental gerontology. *Omega, 6,* 113–129.

Marshall, V. (1986). A sociological perspective on death and dying. In V. Marshall (Ed.), *Later life: The social psychology of aging* (pp. 125–146). Newbury Park, CA: Sage.

McAdams, D. (1985). *Power, intimacy, and the life-story.* Homewood, IL: Dorsey Press.

McAdams, D. (1989). The development of a narrative identity. In D. Buss & N. Cantor (Eds.), *Personality psychology: Recent trends and emerging directions* (pp. 160–174). New York: Springer-Verlag.

McAdams, D. (1991). Self and story. In A. Stewart, J. Healy, Jr., & D. Ozer (Eds.), *Perspectives in personality: A research annual* (Vol. 3, Part B, pp. 133–160). London: Jessica Kingsley.

McAdams, D. (1993). *Stories we live by: Personal myths and the making of the self.* New York: Morrow.

McAdams, D. (1996). Narrating the self in adulthood. In J. Birren, G. Kenyon, J-E Ruth, J. J. F. Schroots, & T. Svensson (Eds.), *Aging and biography: Explorations in adult development* (pp. 131–148). New York: Springer.

McAdams, D., & de St. Aubin, E. (1992). A theory of generativity and its assessment through self-report, behavioral acts and narrative themes in autobiography. *Journal of Personality and Social Psychology, 62,* 1003–1015.

McAdams, D., de St. Aubin, E., & Logan, R. (1993). Generativity among young, midlife and older adults. *Psychology and Aging, 8,* 221–230.

McAdams, D., Hoffman, B., Mansfield, E., & Day, R. (1996). Themes of agency and communion in significant autobiographical scenes. *Journal of Personality, 64,* 339–377.

McAdams, D., Ruetzel, K., & Foley, J. (1986). Complexity and generativity at mid-life: Relation among social motives, ego development, and adults' plans for the future. *Journal of Personality and Social Psychology, 50,* 800–807.

Meyer, I. (1996). Minority stress and mental health in gay men. *Journal of Health and Social Behavior, 36,* 38–56.

Münnichs, J. (1966). *Old age and finitude: A contribution to psychogerontology.* New York: Karger.

Nardi, P., Sanders, D., & Marmor, J. (1994). *Growing up before Stonewall: Life stories of some gay men.* New York: Routledge.

Neugarten, B. (1973). Personality change in late life: A developmental perspective. In C. Eisdorfer & M. Lawton (Eds.), *The psychology of adult development* (pp. 311–338). Washington, DC: American Psychological Association.

Neugarten, B. (1979). Time, age, and the life-cycle. *American Journal of Psychiatry, 136*, 887–894.

Neugarten, B., & Datan, N. (1996). The middle years. In D. Neugarten (Ed.), *The meanings of age: Selected papers of Bernice Neugarten* (pp. 135–159). Chicago: University of Chicago Press.

Neugarten, B., & Hagestad, G. (1976). Age and the life course. In R. Binstock & E. Shanas (Eds.), *Handbook of aging and the social sciences* (pp. 35–55). New York: Van Nostrand Reinhold.

Neugarten, B., Moore, J., & Lowe, J. (1996). Age norms, age constraints, and adult socialization. In D. Neugarten (Ed.), *The meanings of age: Selected papers of Bernice Neugarten* (pp. 24–33). Chicago: University of Chicago Press. (Original work published 1965)

Nydegger, C. (1980). Role and age transitions: A potpourri of issues. In C. Fry & J. Keith (Eds.), *New methods of old age research: Anthropological alternatives* (pp. 127–145). Loyola University of Chicago: Center for Urban Studies.

Nydegger, C. (1981). On being caught up in time. *Human Development, 24*, 1–12.

Pearlin, L. (1980). Life strains and psychological distress among adults. In E. Erikson & N. Smelser (Eds.), *Themes of work and love in adulthood* (pp. 174–192). Cambridge, MA: Harvard University Press.

Pearlin, L., & Lieberman, M. (1979). Social sources of emotional distress. In R. Simmons (Ed.), *Research in community and mental health* (Vol. 1, pp. 217–248). Greenwich, CT: JAI Press.

Peterson, B., & Klohnen, E. (1995). Realization of generativity in two samples of women at midlife. *Psychology and Aging, 10*, 20–29.

Peterson, B., & Stewart, A. (1990). Using personal and fictional documents to assess psychosocial development: A case study of Vera Brittain's generativity. *Psychology and Aging, 5*, 400–411.

Peterson, B., & Stewart, A. (1993). Generativity and social motives in young adults. *Journal of Personality and Social Psychology, 65*, 186–198.

Peterson, B., & Stewart, A. (1996). Antecedents and contexts of generativity motivation at midlife. *Psychology and Aging, 11*, 21–33.

Phillps, A. (1996). *Terrors and experts*. Cambridge, MA: Harvard University Press.

Plath, D. (1980). Contours of consociation: Lessons from a Japanese narrative. In P. B. Baltes & O. G. Brim, Jr. (Eds.), *Life-span development and behavior* (Vol. 3, pp. 287–305). San Diego, CA: Academic Press.

Plummer, K. (1995). *Telling sexual stories: Power, change, and social worlds*. New York: Routledge.

Porter, K., & Weeks, J. (1991). *Between the acts: Lives of homosexual men, 1885–1967*. New York: Routledge.

Reid, J. (1995). Development in later life: Older lesbian and gay lives. In A. D'Augelli & C. Patterson (Eds.), *Lesbian, gay, and bisexual identities over the lifespan: Psychological perspectives* (pp. 215–240). New York: Oxford University Press.

Ricoeur, P. (1977). The question of proof in Freud's psychoanalytic writings. *Journal of the American Psychoanalytic Association, 25,* 835–872.

Riessman, C. K. (1993). *Narrative analysis.* Newbury Park: CA: Sage.

Rosenwald, G. (1993). Conclusion: Reflections on narrative self-understanding. In G. Rosenwald & R. Ochberg (Eds.), *Storied lives: The cultural politics of self-understanding* (pp. 265–290). New Haven, CT: Yale University Press.

Rosow, I. (1978). What is a cohort and why? *Human Development, 21,* 65–75.

Roth, J. (1963). *Timetables: Structuring the passage of time in hospital treatment and other careers.* Indianapolis, IN: Bobbs-Merrill.

Ryder, N. (1965). The cohort as a concept in the study of social change. *American Sociological Review, 30,* 843–861.

Ryff, C., & Heincke, S. (1983). Subjective organization of personality in adulthood and aging. *Journal of Personality and Social Psychology, 44,* 807–816.

Ryff, C., & Migdal, S. (1984). Intimacy and generativity: Self-perceived transitions. *Signs: Journal of Women in Culture and Society, 9,* 470–481.

Sampson, R., & Laub, J. (1996). The military as a turning point in the lives of disadvantaged men. *American Sociological Review, 61,* 347–367.

Sang, B. (1993). Existential issues of midlife lesbians. In L. D. Garnets & D. C. Kimmel (Eds.), *Psychological perspectives on lesbian and gay male experiences* (pp. 500–516). New York: Columbia University Press.

Sarbin, T. (1986). The narrative as a root metaphor for psychology. In T. Sarbin (Ed.), *Narrative Psychology* (pp. 3–21). New York: Praeger.

Savin-Williams. R. (1990). *Gay and lesbian youth: Expressions of identity.* Washington, DC: Hemisphere Publishing.

Schafer, R. (1980). Narration in the psychoanalytic dialogue. *Critical Inquiry, 7,* 29–53.

Schafer, R. (1981). *Narrative actions in psychoanalysis* (Vol. 14, Heinz Werner Lecture Series). Worcester, MA: Clark University Press.

Schaie, K. W. (1984). The Seattle longitudinal study: A 2-year exploration of the psychometric intelligence of adulthood. In K. W. Schaie (Ed.), *Longitudinal studies of personality* (pp. 64–135). New York: Guilford Press.

Schuman, H., & Scott, J. (1989). Generations and collective memories. *American Sociological Review, 54,* 359–381.

Seltzer, M. (1976). Suggestions for examination of time-disordered relationships. In J. Gubrium (Ed.), *Time, roles and self in old age* (pp. 111–125). New York: Human Sciences Press.

Shlaes, J. (1995). *Generativity and object relations,* Unpublished doctoral dissertation, Department of Counseling Psychology, Northwestern University.

Snarey, J. (1993). *How fathers care for the next generation: A four-decade study.* Cambridge, MA: Harvard University Press.

Sorokin, P., & Merton, R. (1937). Social time: A methodological and functional analysis. *American Journal of Sociology, 42,* 615–629.

Thomas, W. I., & Znanecki, F. (1974). *The Polish peasant in Europe and America*. New York: Octagon Books/Farrar, Straus & Giroux. (Original work published 1918)

Thompson, P. (1988). *The voice of the past*. (2nd ed.). New York: Oxford University Press.

Tipton, S. (1982). *Getting saved from the sixties: Moral meaning in conversion and social change*. Berkeley: University of California Press.

Tomkins, S. (1987). Script theory. In J. Aronoff, A. I. Rabin, & R.A. Zucker (Eds.), *The emergence of personality* (pp. 147–216). New York: Springer.

Troll, L. (1970). Issues in the study of generations. *International Journal of Aging and Human Development*, 9, 199–218.

Tuttle, W., Jr. (1993). America's home front children in World War II. In G. Elder, J. Modell, & R. D. Parke (Eds.), *Children in time and place: Developmental and historical insights* (pp. 27–46). New York: Cambridge University Press.

Vacha, K. (1985). *Quiet fire: Memoirs of older gay men*. Trumansburg, NY: Crossing Press.

Vaillant, G. (1977). *Adaptation to life*. Boston: Little, Brown.

Vaillant, G. (1993). *The wisdom of the ego*. Cambridge, MA: Harvard University Press.

Vaillant, G., & Koury, S. (1993). Late midlife development. In G. Pollock & S. Greenspan (Eds.), *The course of life. Vol. 6: Late adulthood* (pp. 1–22). Madison, CT: International Universities Press.

Vaillant, G., & Milofsky, E. (1980). Natural history of the male psychological life-cycle: IX. Empirical evidence for Erikson's model of the life cycle. *American Journal of Psychiatry*, 137, 1348–1358.

Van de Water, D., & McAdams, D. (1989). Generativity and Erikson's "belief in the species." *Journal of Research in Personality*, 23, 435–449.

Veevers, J. (1979). Voluntary childlessness: A review of issues and evidence. *Marriage and Family Review*, 2, 1–26.

Waddington, C. (1956). *Principles of embryology*. London: Allen & Unwin.

Watson, L., & Watson-Frankie, M. B. (1985). *Interpreting life-histories: An anthropological inquiry*. New Brunswick, NJ: Rutgers University Press.

Weeks, J. (1985). *Sexuality and its discontents: Meanings, myths, and modern sexualities*. Boston: Routledge & Kegan Paul.

Winnicott, D. W. (1960). Ego distortion in terms of the true and false self. In *The maturational processes and the facilitating environment* (pp. 140–152). New York: International Universities Press.

Young-Bruehl, E. (1996). *The anatomy of prejudices*. Cambridge, MA: Harvard University Press.

9

CARES FOR THE RISING GENERATION: GENERATIVITY IN AMERICAN HISTORY, 1607–1900

GERALD F. MORAN

The history of generativity has yet to be written. Although historians were introduced to Erik Erikson's theories on the subject well over two decades ago, surprisingly few have explored the history of generativity in any systematic way (Hoffer, 1983). Even family and life-span historians have failed to exploit the concept. However, materials for the historical study of generativity abound. Since the 1960s, historians, influenced by new social–scientific methods, have been amassing evidence concerning the history of family, parenthood, and childhood, expanding opportunities for the study of generativity in past time. This is particularly the case for the history of the United States, an area in which social history has acquired striking sophistication.

I propose in this essay to sketch the history of generativity in the United States from 1607 to the late 19th century. I organize the study around what I have identified as two highly creative, generative time periods in U.S. history: the era of Puritanism, a movement that began in England but was transmitted to the United States in the 1630s; and the period of the American Revolution, which was initially directed against the English but went on to transform U.S. life and culture after the 1770s. Each movement provided distinctive definitions of generativity; promoted "concern in establishing and guiding the next generation" (Erikson, 1963, p. 267); and nourished compatible generative institutions, social structures, and practices. Each movement also gave rise to a generative culture, in which social demands, individual concerns, and adult commitments and actions were focused on providing for the next generation (see chapter 1, this volume). Although both movements produced mixed results, they nevertheless left generative legacies that survived well beyond the lifetimes of their founders.

Puritans and revolutionaries did not use the term *generativity*, but they were not strangers to ideals and concerns that social scientists today identify as "generative." Indeed, as this chapter argues, the Puritans were a generative people who managed, amid the disruptions of transmigration and resettlement, to provide as much for the next generation as background and circumstances allowed. The revolutionaries were also a generative people and were able to nurture on a national level as strong and viable a generative culture as the Puritans had created on a regional level.

There are good reasons for arguing these points. With respect to the Puritans, they were the first biblical people to migrate to British America; after organizing their movement around the ideal of the covenant, they created in New England forms of life (some old, some new) that they hoped would nourish piety and pass on the divine blessing to future generations. That the family was considered the carrier of the covenant meant that it was the focal point of Puritan generative ideals and acts. However, the ideal of the covenant so pervaded the society and its system of symbols that few facets of social life lacked generative meaning. Although I primarily focus on Puritan generative ideals and behavior found within the family, I note that Puritan generativity surely contained other aspects of the "anatomy of generativity" described in this volume, including desires, beliefs, and particularly narrative constructions, which inform many of the diaries, autobiographies, and narratives of conversion of the settlers (see chapter 1, this volume). In contrast to other, contemporary colonial settings, such as the Caribbean, where high mortality rates rendered generational development impossible and turned the region into "the white man's grave—and the black man's, too" (Dunn, 1972, p. 302), New England produced a highly generative culture.

The revolutionaries were as generative as their Puritan forebears, albeit for different reasons. Although revolutionary generativity had roots in Puritanism, it drew especially on secular, political values that had their gestation in 17th-century England and were transmitted to the colonies, through the writings of John Locke and other English libertarians, during the mid-18th century. As Table 1 indicates, the character of revolutionary generativity was also different, focused, as it was, not on the region, the

TABLE 1
Revolutionary Versus Puritan Generativity

Aspect	Revolutionary	Puritan
Type	Technical	Parental
Source	Political ideology	Religious ideology
Scope	National	Regional
Goal	Citizenship	Sainthood
Vehicle	School	Family
Target	Students	Children
Parent	Mother	Father

family, children, and covenantal relationships, but on the nation, public schooling, students, and republican citizenship.

Puritanism and the revolution together gave the United States a dual generative legacy, one centered on parenthood, the other on public education. Despite their differences, both the revolution and Puritanism mobilized individuals and communities around similar generative concerns and commitments that gave birth to new patterns of life and behavior invested in providing for future generations.

COLONIAL VIRGINIA AND THE CRISIS OF GENERATIVITY

Developmental time and generativity are nourished and sustained by stable family and generational relationships; social forces affecting family life may disrupt and even dissolve developmental timetables and the generative goals of individuals or a society. Erikson observed the following regarding the developmental disruptions accompanying one social force—transmigration:

> The danger of any period of large-scale uprooting and transmigration is that exterior crises will, in too many individuals and generations, upset the hierarchy of developmental crisis and their built-in correctives; and that man will lose those roots that must be planted firmly in meaningful life cycles. For man's true roots are nourished in the sequence of generations and he loses his taproots in disrupted developmental time, not in abandoned localities. (1964, p. 96)

For many of the 100,000 people who migrated from England to North America in the 17th century, the process of resettlement as well as of transmigration disrupted family formation, generational development, and developmental schedules. Historian Bernard Bailyn observed the following concerning the impact of "alien soil" on Old World family forms and culture:

> European culture endured a severe shock upon its first contacts with the American environment and in subsequent adjustment to it. The

institutional structure of society which had supported culture in Europe and effected its transfer from generation to generation was severely damaged in the course of transplantation. . . . The critical point was the process of transfer, the transmission of the culture to the young. (1960, p. 73)

Because the New World also attracted "the wrong kind of people"— adventurers, traders, freelancers (mercenary soldiers), and planters who were interested less in the transfer of family to the New World than in the transfer of wealth to the Old—they often failed to provide the setting for the kind of "heroic effort" required of settlers for the successful transmission of culture to the young.

Consider, for example, the case of Colonial Virginia, where ideals, environment, and practice all militated against family formation, generational development, and provisions for the well-being of the young. Established in 1607 as England's first and ultimately largest overseas colony, Viginia was primarily, if not entirely, designed to produce a profit for investors. When, during a period of trial and error, it was discovered that money could be made from the cultivation and sale of tobacco, the colony devoted itself almost exclusively to producing and exporting the staple crop.

Caught up in the scramble for the land and labor necessary to produce tobacco, Virginians often gave little thought to young people beyond rational calculation of their economic worth. The demand for labor to work the plantations was insatiable, and because English youth were in good supply, Virginians continued to import and exploit them throughout the 17th century, taking them on as indentured servants under contract to labor for them for 7 years. If the young people had remained in England, they would have been protected by English labor laws governing the treatment of "life-cycle servants" (Galenson, 1981). By going to the colonies, they put themselves at the mercy of masters who were unrestrained by social legislation and were likely to abuse them.

This practice, combined with an unhealthy environment, resulted in a society in which mortality rates among youth were extremely high and the opportunities for marrying and establishing stable generational relations were quite low. Well over 50% of the youth died before they completed their term of servitude. Those who survived servitude and were free to marry either died before having the chance to marry or had difficulty finding spouses, given the heavy importation of male youth, which caused an imbalanced sex ratio. If few people lived long enough or had the opportunity to marry, even fewer survived to become parents; those who were fortunate enough to have children rarely lived beyond the birth of one or two. Parents who survived the death of a spouse usually remarried, forming, if they lived long enough, complex families (reminiscent of today's), composed of stepparents, stepchildren, and stepbrothers and stepsisters. Often both parents died young, a circumstance that steadily added to the number of orphans in the society. In Middlesex County, for which data recently have been compiled, 20% of the children born between 1650 and 1689 were orphaned before their 13th birthday, and 37% before their 18th (Rutman & Rutman, 1984, p. 114). Given the rarity of stable family life and generational relationships, anyone with family connections automatically had a leg up over kinless competitors in the race for social standing and status. So thoroughly did discontinuities mark the colony's development that "each generation of Virginians seems to have started anew, paying little attention to what had preceded it" (Breen, 1980, p. 165). Virginia's settlers "focused their attentions on what they called the colony's 'present state,' a dynamic present flowing continuously into a future that bore no resemblance to the past" (Breen, 1980, p. 169).

Originating as the very antithesis of a generative culture, Virginia society had by the mid-18th century become settled enough to maintain a steady sequence of generations and to raise prospects of generativity. However, planters' norms and values continued to work against the well-being of the young. Although it had become easier to plan and provide for education, parents still placed little value on learning. In fact, some planters educated sons less as a reflection of their interest in education than as a sign of family status and achievement. Instead of trying to institute schools, most planters hired tutors to teach their sons at home. Because Virginians failed to establish a broad system of schools, most children received little education, and many did not even acquire literacy (Vinovskis, 1995, p. 9).

Planters' labor practices also continued to work against the well-being of the young. Although Virginians by this time had scrapped the system of indentured servitude, they replaced it with an even more exploitive and heinous form of youthful labor: African slavery. That by the 1770s over 40% of Virginia's population was enslaved boded ill for the future of generativity in that society or, for that matter, in the other regions of the Colonial South, where slavery had become an integral part of everyday life (Morgan, 1980).

PURITAN GENERATIVITY: THE 17TH CENTURY

If Anglo-America could thus prove harmful (even lethal) to the young, it could also offer people opportunities for recreating and even improving on Old World family forms and generational relations. The history of Colonial New England demonstrates that the disruptions of transmigration and transplantation could be overcome and that a generative culture could be instituted in the New World.

What made New England different from the other regions of Anglo-America was the presence of Puritanism. Started in the mid-16th century in England, Puritanism was a religious reform movement that was aimed at purifying the English church and society. As reformers, Puritans operated outside the formal structures of the society and relied almost exclusively on the family to organize relationships and propagate values and faith. As a biblical people, the Puritans subscribed to the ideal of the covenant and viewed the family as God's vehicle for perpetuating faith and religious obligations. They developed a new conception of the family, one that enhanced the importance of paternal power and parenthood. Viewing the family as "a little monarchy," they gave fathers the ultimate authority in all matters related to the household, acknowledging them as the absolute, uncontrollable authority over children (Norton, 1996, p. 98). In addition to heading and running the household, fathers were expected to elicit unquestioning obedience from the young. In this way, children would instinctively defer to their superiors in church and society (Norton, 1996, p. 42).

At the same time, the Puritans placed severe generative demands on fathers. They were expected to care for their children and to provide for their future well-being. They were supposed to "preserve, feed, and clothe" them, and to educate them. This included teaching them how to read and write, at least to the extent of their own literacy (Demos, 1986, p. 44). Fathers were also supposed to provide for their children's moral and religious education, and in the absence of the minister, lead them in prayer and exhort them to piety. In raising children in the faith, fathers had many other responsibilities, including setting the right example; as one minister put it, "many a chosen vessel, that when he hath beheld his Fathers love to Christ, and faithfulness to the interest of God, Zeal, Patience, Holiness, that hath been a special means of Conviction and Conversion" (Mather, 1679, p. 24).

Puritans assigned the mother a complementary but lesser role. She was expected to submit to her husband and serve as his domestic "helpmeet . . . keeping at home, educating . . . her children, keeping and improving what is got by the industry of the man." In one respect, however, she was nearly his equal, and this was in respect to children and servants:

> If God in his Providence hath bestowed on them Children or Servants, they have each of them a share in the government of them; tho' there is an inequality in the degree of this Authority, and the Husband is to be acknowledged to hold a Superiority, which the Wife is practically to allow; yet in respect of all other in the Oeconomical Society, she is invested with an Authority over them by God; and her Husband is to allow it to her, and the others are to carry it to her as such. (Quoted in Morgan, 1966, p. 45)

However, historian N. Ray Hiner (1973) appropriately pointed out that "hardly any attention was devoted to mothers in 17th-century recitations of parental duties." Indeed, "if the Puritan father had a relatively equal teaching partner, it was not the wife but the minister" (Hiner, 1973, p. 12). When it came to establishing and guiding the next generation, the responsibility rested squarely on the shoulders of the father.

Because efforts to reform England failed, the Puritans decided that their children would be better off in Colonial America. Among their motives for migrating to New England was the interest in ensuring the future well-being of posterity. As William Bradford, a founder of Plymouth Plantation, explained it, a primary reason for the removal of the pilgrims to Colonial America was that "children . . . were drawn away by evil examples into extravagant and dangerous courses" and that parents "saw their posterity would be in danger to degenerate and be corrupted" (Bradford, 1952, p. 25). John Winthrop, first governor of Massachusetts Bay, offered similar sentiments: "The Fountaines of Learning and Religion [in England] are so corrupted," he said, that "most children . . . are perverted, corrupted, and utterlie overthrown by the multitude of evil examples" (quoted in Axtell, 1974, p. 203). A half century later, Increase Mather echoed Bradford's and Winthrop's observations, noting that "our Fathers came hither" for "their Off-Spring," and did so "that they might leave their Children under the special blessing of God in Jesus Christ" (Mather, 1679, p. 22).

The Puritans acted to ensure that the migration would proceed in as orderly a fashion as possible. Although the "exodus" to New England was "the largest folk migration in the history of New World settlement" (Stout, 1990, p. 966; involving the transmigration of over 20,000 people in just a single decade, the 1630s), it was also the best organized. Desiring to avoid the instability plaguing Virginia at the time, the organizers of the venture only reluctantly imported youth and instead systematically recruited heads of households and other adults for the voyage (most migrants were age 20–39). Their efforts paid off. Most migrants left England, crossed the Atlantic, and resettled in New England in family groups, maintaining a pattern known as "chain migration."

After surviving the trials of the Atlantic crossing and the tribulations of resettlement, the migrants preferred to live out the rest of their lives within the comparatively stable and peaceful confines of their new communities. In the process, they developed an environment that fostered and nourished family life and generational relations. Although immigration remained low after the Great Migration, population increased rapidly in response to highly favorable conditions of life. Because of the abundance of land, a relatively equal sex ratio, a low rate of epidemic diseases, and a low population density, New Englanders enjoyed a high ratio of married to unmarried women, comparatively low ages at marriage (women averaging 20 years of age at marriage, men 27 years of age), low mortality, rising longevity, and an unusually high rate of fertility. For the remainder of the 17th century, New England women gave birth to an average of 10 children,

7 of whom lived to adulthood. That New Englanders produced completed families averaging in excess of 7 children made their region a unique demographic environment; nowhere else in England, Europe, or in the West for that matter did completed families approach the size of those in Puritan America. As a result, New England's population soared, rising from just over 30,000 in 1660 to over 90,000 by 1700 (Greene, 1988).

As New England aged and the population grew, opportunities for inter- and cross-generational contacts in households and communities multiplied. Because New England women bore children through their early 40s (the age of onset for menopause), they and their husbands lived with members of the next generation until their late 60s and early 70s, when it was time to prepare for death. Most households had some children under age 18, and most husbands and wives spent little time without children in the home. There were few child-free years in New England and even fewer "empty nests." There were numerous opportunities for the practice of parental generativity, certainly more numerous than in any other society in Anglo-America.

Communities as well as households contained unusually high concentrations of young people. A rare Colonial census reveals the youthfulness of New England towns. In some communities, the population under age 10 was as high as 35% of the total, and the population under age twenty was as high as 60% of the total (Trumbull, 1850–1890, pp. 485–491). New England was also a society in which cross-generational as well as intergenerational contacts were common. Computing the numbers of people in the over 60 cohort allows one to gauge the chances for cross-generational contact between grandparents and children. Because the percentage of the population in the over 60 cohort ranged between 4% and 7% from one community to the next, and because the average New England town contained 500 inhabitants, the number of elderly in such places must have ranged between a low of 20% and a high of 35% (Demos, 1986, p. 151). However, these figures underestimate the numerous opportunities available for grandchildren–grandparent interaction and for the exercise of grandparental generativity. In one New England community, over 80% of children and youth under the age of 19 had at least two living grandparents (Demos, 1986, p. 154). New England proved conducive to the development of intimate grandparent–grandchildren relationships. "Grandfathers are more affectionate towards their children's children than to their immediates," wrote Reverend John Robinson, "as seeing themselves further propagated in them" (quoted in Demos, 1986, p. 153). Historian John Demos (1986) argued that "there was much interest and affection" in the grandparent–grandchild relationship, "at least on the side of the grandparents; occasionally, there was co-residence and mutual dependence" (p. 154). So different was New England in this regard that it "might have been responsible," according to one historian, "for a simple but tremendously important invention, at least in terms of scale—grand-parents" (Murrin, 1972, p. 238).

Puritan concerns for and commitments to the young were thus planted in a child-rich soil. The result was the germination of Puritan generative activity that gave life to familial, educational, religious, and economic institutions for the young. From the start of settlement, Colonial authorities stressed the importance of educating children at home and closely supervised heads of households in this regard (Norton, 1996, p. 55). Legislation was also adopted protecting children from parental neglect and abuse. The Massachusetts Body of Liberties of 1641 contained a section, "Liberties of Children," that was the first of its kind enacted in the Western world. One provision prohibited parents from exercising "any unnatural severitie" toward children. If unnatural severity took place, children were accorded "free libertie to complaine to Authorities for redresse" (Pleck, 1987, p. 22). When one considers that the 17th century was an age when parenthood was disparaged and children battered, one can appreciate the Puritans' achievement in the area of child protection.

In addition, public schooling was established to provide a supplement and corrective to household education. At first New England towns took the initiative in establishing local schools for children, but beginning in 1647 the colonies themselves accomplished the task. In that year Massachusetts passed its famous "Old Deluder Satan" law, requiring every town of 50 "families or householders" to "appoint one within their own town to teach all such children as shall resort to him to write and read" and every town of 100 families to "set up a grammar school, the master thereof being able to instruct youth, so far as they may be fitted, for the University." In 1650 and 1658 the colonies of Connecticut and Plymouth respectively followed suit. At the same time, in 1636, Harvard College was founded, for the purpose of teaching New England youth the Gospel and how to preach it. As one historian aptly wrote about this development, "there had been no comparable achievement in the history of modern colonization" (quoted in Cremin, 1970, p. 210).

New Englanders provided for the religious well-being of their children by including them fully in the new religious system; whereas other Protestant reformers did away with infant baptism, New Englanders not only kept it but also elevated it to a status commensurate with the only other sacrament of the church, the Lord's Supper. In addition to granting children high sacramental status, New England churches provided for their religious growth and development. A number of local churches set up catechetical schools or classes for teaching religion to youth and children who were as young as 7 years or encouraged ministers to visit families to teach children congregational doctrine at home (Stout, 1986).

New Englanders also instituted new inheritance structures that reveal their commitment to securing the economic as well as the religious future of their children. Rejecting English inheritance laws and practices that confined bequests of land to the eldest son (known as primogeniture), the colonies adopted laws that in intestate cases dictated that the widow receive a third of the property and all surviving children, both male and female, the other two thirds. In this system of partible inheritance, which represented a radical departure from English and European practice, a double portion went to the eldest son and single portions to his sisters and younger brothers (Karlsen, 1987, p. 82).

Although New Englanders made distinctions among stages of life, there was no idea of specific, age-appropriate behavior. Stages of life were marked, not by the arrival of a particular age, but by the movement of individuals into a specific status, denoted by the absence or exercise of powers appropriate to that status. Middle age was considered a protracted period of life (from about age 30 to about age 60), the time for the exercise of "generative power," particularly over grown children who still occupied a dependency status. For the purpose of this chapter, it is important to inquire into how this power was used with respect to children; the answer should shed light on the issue of New Englanders' personal generative goals and intentions (Demos, 1986, p. 124).

Psychologist John Kotre (1984) demonstrated the importance of distinguishing between two modes of generativity: *agentic* generativity, in which the focus is the generative subject, and *communal* generativity, in which the focus is the generative object. In early New England the two forms coexisted, often in tension, and even for the same individuals. There is considerable evidence in family documents for parental solicitude for and love of children as children. Samuel Willard, a New England minister, expressed the characteristically Puritan concern for children in this way:

> The Love of Parents of their Children is such as admits not of suitable words to express it, it being so intense and influential, so that God himself is pleased to resemble His Love to His Children by this, there being no Comparison that better resembleth it." (1726, p. 601)

There is also much evidence of self-interest in the father's personal handling and treatment of children, however, and of resultant tension and conflict between the generations (Greven, 1970), which shows up especially in the testamentary behavior of New England fathers. As social historians discovered while searching New England probate court and land records, landowning fathers, although abandoning primogeniture and entail for partible inheritance practices, nevertheless retained title to and full ownership of property even after their sons had become adults and had married. Although they were willing to loan their sons land when the sons needed it, they resolutely refused until death to grant them ownership, at which point the land was turned over to sons by probated will (Greven, 1970).

320   GERALD F. MORAN

What motivated fathers to follow this practice? According to Thomas Hooker, founder of Connecticut, fathers kept land from sons to ensure their submission:

> Thus the Lord deales with us as a wise father doth with his child, he seeth if he had his portion in his hands he would be riotous and car-lesse, and therefore it is wisdome not to trust him with his estate, but to keep him low, and to keep him upon dependance, that he may have better subjection from his hands." (1637, p. 133)

John Locke, the son of Puritans, echoed Hooker:

> There is another *Power* ordinarily *in the Father*, whereby he has a tie on the Obedience of his Children. . . . And this is the Power Men generally have to *bestow their Estates* on those, who please them best. . . . It is commonly in the Father's Power to bestow it with a more sparing or liberal hand, according as the Behavior of this or that Child hath comported with his Will and Humour. (1965, p. 357)

That New England fathers were not at all reluctant to disinherit or reward children who had angered or pleased them suggests their support for the Lockean notion that inheritance was "no small Tye on the Obedience of Children" (Locke, 1698/1965, p. 358).

Fathers also used land and personal property to control family for-mation. Historian Lawrence Stone wrote of one Michael Wentworth, who in 1558 mandated in his will that if any of his daughters did not accept the spousal choice of the executors "but of their own fantastical brain bestow themselves upon a light person" their inheritance would be lowered from 100 to 66 pounds (in Degler, 1980, p. 10). This "powerful posthumous economic blackmail" was behavior New England fathers did not hesitate to stoop to follow. In one New England community, for example, fathers who owned land used it to influence, if not to shape, their sons' decisions about marriage. By withholding title to the land, fathers could determine when and perhaps whom their sons would marry (Greven, 1970).

PURITAN GENERATIVITY: THE 18TH CENTURY

The pattern of paternal self-interest (and possibly accompanying gen-erational tension) may explain why New England institutions that were intended to propagate generational values produced, over the long run, mixed results. Harvard declined both qualitatively and quantitatively as the century progressed; by the 1670s the school was enrolling perhaps no more than 20 students altogether (Silverman, 1985, p. 17). The early school laws for which New England became famous were often ignored; by the 1660s, only one third of the 50-family towns had complied with the petty-school requirements; thereafter, as new towns reached the mandated sizes, they tended to disregard the requirement (Cremin, 1970, p. 182), forcing parents to continue to rely on the resources of the family to educate children. With respect to piety, religious conversion and church membership failed to keep pace with population growth and the maturation of the second generation, a development for which one historian holds the founding fathers of New England responsible: "Only unusual Puritans seem to have been capable of raising children who knew how to love their fathers. In the absence of this love, full conversion became difficult for most and impossible for many" (Murrin, 1972, p. 239).

However, the positive response of New England fathers to a succession of generational crises may provide the last word on paternal intentions regarding children and on the direction of generative change. One such crisis involved the generational transmission of piety. When New England's leaders realized that children were going unbaptized because their parents (the second generation) were failing to join the church, they decided to adjust the religious system to fit the needs of the children. The result was the ingenious device known as the halfway covenant, which allowed the children of church members to obtain baptism for their children by acquiring knowledge of doctrine and joining the church as a halfway member. Although the measure took time to take hold in individual churches, its use was widespread by the early 18th century. When it became apparent that the halfway covenant, which was supposed to serve as a stepping-stone to full communion, was not working the way it was intended to work, New Englanders adjusted the system again, developing a new religious persuasion that rejected the idea of conversion as an adult experience of life and emphasized instead the religious capacities of youth. The result was the Great Awakening of the 1740s, which was the first religious revival in Colonial American history and was marked by a rash of youthful religious conversions and church admissions. Henceforth, religious revivalism was a primary vehicle for the intergenerational transmission of piety and church membership.

Fathers' responses to generational crises involving the transmission of land also shed light on the question of generative intentions and results. In this case the problem was the rising pressure of population on shrinking land resources. By the time of the maturation of the fourth generation, families had begun to run out of the land resources necessary to sustain previous, partible inheritance practices. Their response was not to alter the treatment of children but to change the inheritance system itself, bringing it into line with the changed needs of the new, less fortunate generation. Fathers either apprenticed sons, at family expense, to relatives or craftsmen; prepared them for nonfarm work through formal education; or gave them a gift of money or a deed to land in a newly developed settlement. One historian has gone so far as to argue that such paternal adaptations to the land crisis marked the emergence of new, more equitable generational relations:

> Underlying all of these expedients was a new conception of parental duty and authority. Fathers had begun to consider their role not as that of patriarchs grandly presiding over an ancestral estate and minutely controlling the lives of their sons and heirs, but rather as that of benefactors responsible for the future well being and prosperity of their offspring. The delicate balance between the two traditional concerns of agrarian families—preservation of their holding and provision for their children—had been tipped decisively in favor of the latter. Once, the farm had been an end in itself; now it was the means to another and a more important end. This tendency for parents to find the fulfillment and justification of their own lives in the success of their children marked the appearance of a new and different type of family life, one characterized by solicitude and sentimentality toward children and by more intimate, personal, and equal relationships. (Henretta, 1973, p. 30)

THE AMERICAN REVOLUTION: THE CIVIC IMPULSE

The American Revolution placed generativity at the center of the life of the new nation and redefined and secularized it. Like the founders of New England, the leaders of the new nation never tired of discussing the importance of what they were doing to the well-being of posterity. At the moment of independence, Thomas Paine argued in *Common Sense* that

> as parents, we can have no joy, knowing that [the English] government is not sufficiently lasting to ensure any thing which we may bequeath to posterity: And by a plain method of argument, as we are running the next generation into debt [by submitting to English taxes], we ought to do the work of it [the revolution], otherwise we use [posterity] meanly and pitifully. (1776/1982, p. 87)

When it looked as if the revolution was entering a critical phase, George Washington observed that the future behavior of the American states would decide "whether the Revolution must ultimately be considered a blessing or a curse, not to the present age alone, for with our fate will the destiny of unborn Millions be involved" (Morgan, 1980, p. 68). In the Constitution of the United States appears the ultimate, public affirmation of revolutionary generativity: "We the People of the United States, in Order to form a more perfect Union, . . . and secure the Blessing of Liberty to ourselves and our Posterity, do ordain and establish this Constitution for the United States of America."

Although they were as committed to posterity as their Puritan forebears, the new nation's leaders had generative values, ideas, and goals that differed from theirs. Whereas New England Puritans hoped to raise pious and faithful sons, American revolutionaries wished to rear loyal and virtuous citizens.

As I demonstrate, the revolution gave rise to a national debate over the future of the country, one that centered on education and the issue of how to transmit the nonmonarchical, democratic values to new generations. Although public schooling was emphasized over parental education and the revolution even stimulated antipatriarchal rhetoric, the family remained important as a generative site despite simultaneously experiencing changes that altered the traditional generative roles of the parents.

The central element of revolutionary generativity was education. Noah Webster quoted the French philosopher Montesquieu to explain the importance of education in the new republic:

> It is observed by the great Montesquieu that "the laws of education ought to be relative to the principles of government." In despotic governments the people should have little or no education, except what tends to inspire them with a servile fear. Information is fatal to despotism. In monarchies education should be partial and adapted to the rank of each class of citizens. But "in a republican government," says the same writer, "the whole power of education is required." Here every class of citizen should *know* and *love* the laws ... and an attachment to the laws may be formed by early impressions upon the mind." (Rudolph, 1965, p. 65)

The Revolution had turned the subject of education into "an object of vast magnitude" (Rudolph, 1965, p. 45).

According to Peter Hoffer (1983), there was a developmental aspect to revolutionaries' rising commitment to education. Because many of them were becoming parents when the reform era in education was inaugurated, they were likely to construe education as a "generative challenge":

> During the 1770s and early 1780s education was not as high upon their list of priorities; later in their lives, it assumed far greater importance. An answer is obvious: they became much more concerned with education when they themselves became parents, particularly when their children were old enough to read. With children whose education they directed and could take pride in surrounding them, they began to examine more generational educational questions. (Hoffer, 1983, p. 71)

Hoffer continued with the following observation:

> The late 1780s and early 1790s found the generation of 1776 acutely sensitive to the challenge of transmitting their values to others. Their own parents were dead or retired, making the once-young men of 1776 into the heads of families and leaders of the nation. (pp. 71–72)

In this regard, it is possible to point to Benjamin Rush as typical of the educational leaders of his generation. Born in 1745 and a graduate of the College of New Jersey (Princeton) in 1760, he was a Philadelphia physician and a father of three young children when he initiated public discussion of education in the United States with the publication of a pamphlet in 1786 on the need for educational reform. Arguing that it was necessary "to convert men into republican machines" so that they could "perform their parts properly in the great machine of the government of the state," Rush called for an extensive, even comprehensive system of public schools, one that would touch all people and embrace all levels of schooling. Addressing specifically the citizens of his home state of Pennsylvania, he proposed that a pyramidal, four-stage system of education be developed. The base would consist of "free schools" in every township, and the middle would involve an academy in each county "for the purpose of instructing youth in the learned languages and thereby preparing them to enter college." Topping it off would be four colleges and one university. Thusly, he reasoned, "the whole state will be tied together by one system of education" (Rudolph, 1965, p. 5).

During the next 15 years, other educators joined Rush in what became this country's first national dialogue on education. Although there was some disagreement over whether the nation or the states should control the process of education, all agreed with Rush that the revolution had made public schooling a civic necessity. There was also general agreement on the great benefits to be gained from such a system of public education. Samuel Harrison Smith, a 1787 graduate of the University of Pennsylvania (at age 15) and editor of *The National Intelligencer*, a Jeffersonian newspaper, was among the first writers to make the connection between public education and the survival of the principles inscribed in the Declaration of Independence: "The effects of such a system on the United States . . . would be giving perpetuity to those political principles so closely connected with our present happiness" (Rudolph, 1965, p. 221).

Educational reformers felt, however, that before a "new model" system of education could be built, the old school order had to be dismantled or at least refitted to the new political reality. Republican pedagogues such as Rush and Smith pushed the benefits of public education, but they also presented a critique of the prevailing, Colonial forms of education and schooling.

Among the institutions marked for criticism was the private school. "Should education be public or private?" Smith asked in *Remarks on Education*, published in 1798 (Rudolph, 1965, p. 205). John Locke had lavished praise on private instruction, and Southern planters had grown fond of having their children educated at home. Still, Smith's own answer to the question was a resounding no to private education. Smith reasoned that the revolution had made education essential to the survival of freedom, equality, and the people's happiness and that education could not be left to personal whim and private resources. Robert Coram, librarian of the Library Company of Wilmington, Delaware, agreed, observing that "by turning private schools into public ones, every citizen has an equal opportunity of acquiring knowledge," and that "the burden" of public schooling is "easiest maintained" as it "falls upon all the citizens" (Rudolph, 1965, p. 138).

Educators also singled out the system of "country schools" (as opposed to "seaport" schools) for criticism. Coram leveled the most serious charges against this form of schooling. He complained that

> the country schools through most of the United States, whether we consider the buildings, the teachers, or the regulations, are in every respect contemptible. The buildings are in general sorry hovels.... The teachers are generally foreigners, shamefully deficient in every qualification necessary to convey instruction to youth and not seldom addicted to gross vices.... A blind adherence to British policy seems to have pervaded [the system]. (Rudolph, 1965, pp. 136–138)

Most important, the call for public schools accompanied a general critique of parenthood (the locus of Puritan generativity), one that focused on the weaknesses of family government and on parental negligence regarding childhood education. These concerns were expressed from the start of the educational reform movement. After recommending that "the authority" of schoolmasters be made "as *absolute* as possible," Rush made the following observation:

> I am satisfied that the most useful citizens have been formed from those youth who have never known or felt their own wills till they were one and twenty years of age, and I have often thought that society owes a great deal of its order and happiness to the deficiencies of parental government being supplied by those habits of obedience and subordination which are contracted at schools. (Rudolph, 1965, p. 16)

Coram considered the defects in family government to be a compelling reason for replacing it with public schools, arguing that "education should not be left to the caprice or negligence of parents" (Rudolph, 1965, p. 113). Amanble de Lafitte du Courteil, a French emigré who arrived in the United States in 1796, echoed Coram, observing that in the United States there was "a kind of negligence of children ... whether because parents are occupied with their affairs or through apathy or a mistaken tenderness, all the youth of both sexes is absolutely neglected" (Rudolph, 1965, p. 239). Samuel Knox, an Irish emigré who entered the United States in 1795, agreed:

> In many parts of this country, owing either to a want of proper seminaries of instruction, to the mistaken fond indulgence of parents, or both, youth have the greatest part of their education to acquire when it ought to be nearly completed. Under such circumstances little solid

improvement of any kind can be gained. .... Indeed, nothing can be more hostile in any country to the interests of the education of youth than the pampered treatment and imprudent fondness of luxurious and indulgent parents. (Rudolph, 1965, p. 303)

As Smith said, "it is the duty of a nation to superintend and even to coerce the education of children." He also noted that "high considerations of expediency not only justify but dictate the establishment of a system which shall place under a control, independent of and superior to parental authority, the education of children" (Rudolph, 1965, p. 210).

On the other hand, Smith saw public education as the vehicle both for freeing children from parental dependence and for strengthening the family through the enhancement of children's "mental powers." He argued that state schools would "withdraw the mind of the child from an entire dependence on its parents" and would "place it in situations demanding the exercise of its faculties." This would "strengthen, instead of weakening, its attachment to domestic scenes." If ever there was a time for public education, he concluded, this was it: "The indulgence of parental tenderness should now be exchanged for the patient and unobstructed exercise of the mental powers" (Rudolph, 1965, pp. 206–207).

During the 19th century, the state's role in education was expanded, schools multiplied in number and scope, and mass public elementary and common schools were developed (Vinovskis, 1995, p. 74). At the same time, as patriotic fervor waned and national unity gave way to bitter party disputes, the purity of government was called into question, and its capacity to exercise impartiality in educational matters was thrown into doubt. Despite questions about parental government, educators realized that for public education to succeed, the support of families had to be cultivated and nourished. The advantages of public schools would "be lost to the community" without support from "the wise and well-directed authority of parents and guardians" (Rudolph, 1965, p. 303). Thus, in the midst of the campaign against patriarchy and the debate over parenthood in the United States, many leaders looked to the family to help the new nation realize republican values and principles. In addition, the family itself was changing; a rapidly shifting social reality was reshaping generational relations, family formation, child rearing, and the respective roles of parents. These changes were part of the social process that has come to be known as "the rise of the modern American family" (Degler, 1980). It had its gestation in the Northeast among middle-class families, and it affected the character and outcomes of revolutionary generativity.

As I have shown, generational relations began to change during the mid-18th century, when New England fathers, faced with shrinking land resources, decided to exercise paternal power less to control than to provide for needy sons and their families. However, what began as a matter of individual choice and personal preference became, in the postrevolutionary period, a paradigm for generational relations. The advice John Locke offered fathers to loosen the leash on sons as they came of age and reason made sense to those who had freed themselves from a tyrannical king who had tried to keep them under his thumb despite their maturity as colonists. This reworking of generational relations contributed, in the postrevolutionary period, to the decline of parental control over grown children and to the corresponding improvement in the children's freedom of choice in marriage. Increasingly, self-determination by the partners became the basis of family formation (Degler, 1980, p. 10).

At the same time, child rearing became the primary focus of the family, even "its reason for being, its justification as it were" (Degler, 1980, p. 66). For the first time, children began to be seen as special, particularly with respect to their capacity to be shaped into good citizens. They were viewed as developing individuals, whose education must be appropriately attuned to their stages of development (Vinovskis, 1995, p. 19). Hence, they were increasingly seen as worthy and deserving of special treatment. Children were expected to have a right to develop reason and conscience and to have the capacity to become independent and free on reaching adulthood. Accordingly, attitudes toward the physical treatment of children as recorded in child-rearing literature changed, shifting from general to limited support for corporal punishment (and psychological methods of discipline were condoned and even encouraged). In 1862 the first child-rearing book was published that condemned the physical punishment of children under all circumstances (Pleck, 1987, pp. 34, 39). Children were also punished less severely; according to a statistical study of personal reminiscences of childhood, spanking replaced whipping as the corporal punishment of parental choice during the first half of the 19th century.

The idea that children needed special and loving care reflected and in turn reinforced another aspect of the U.S. family at that time: the fall in White women's fertility. The "decline in fertility" in the 19th-century United States, historian Degler has argued, "is certainly the single most important fact about women and the family in American history" (Degler, 1980, p. 181). The total fertility rate (the average number of children a woman bears before the age of menopause) declined 50% between 1800 and 1900. More specifically, the fertility rate fell from 7.04 children in 1800 to 3.56 in 1900. Although the decline during a later period (1900–1936) was steeper—a fall of 41% in just 36 years—at no time in U.S. history has the decline been as steep as in the 19th century (Degler, 1980, p. 181).

The steepness and steadiness of the decline in fertility have prompted historians to search for explanations. Most recently, the search has led to the realm of values, specifically to the question, "What new motives or purposes might have arisen at the end of the 18th century?" (Degler, 1980, p. 187). To answer this question, historians have examined the effects of two changes on the lives of U.S. women. On the one hand, women, having digested the revolutionary ideology of self-determination, became increasingly conscious of themselves as individuals (Kerber, 1980; Norton, 1980). As they awakened more to self, they sought to control the aspects of life, including fertility and family size, that they could control. On the other hand, as children were increasingly seen as innocent and precious, women were identified by themselves and by men as the primary parent for bringing up children to reflect this novel and special view. Whereas in the Colonial period fathers had been depicted as the primary rearers of children, by the late 18th and the 19th centuries the mother was being identified as the crucial figure in children's development.

The rise of women's domestic role—the process known as the separation of the spheres (Cott, 1977; Kerber, 1980; Norton, 1980)—was reinforced by economic changes such as commercialization and industrialization that pulled fathers from homes and into the marketplace and workplace, leaving the women behind to tend to the *domus*. As early as the 1780s, educators realized that parental roles were separating along lines of gender and that education would have to be adjusted to accommodate that fact. Benjamin Rush observed the following in one of this country's first treatises on female education, published in 1787:

> From the numerous avocations to which a professional life exposes gentlemen in America from their families, a principal share of the instruction of children naturally devolves upon the women. It becomes us therefore to prepare them, by a suitable education, for the discharge of this most important duty of mothers (Rudolph, 1965, p. 22)

In the period from 1840 to 1870, numerous manuals were published for mothers who were devoting more time to the raising of fewer children. Catherine Beecher's *A Treatise on Domestic Economy* was the first to present the full view of motherhood that we associate with the Victorian era and with "the feminine mystique" of the 1950s. Beecher devoted whole chapters to a broad range of "domestic" topics, including health, clothing, cleanliness, early rising, domestic exercise, the care of infants, the management of children, and social duties. She said the following in defense of the idea of "domestic economy":

> The success of democratic institutions, as is conceded by all, depends upon the intellectual and moral character of the mass of the people. If they are intelligent and virtuous, democracy is a blessing; but if they are ignorant and wicked, it is only a curse, and so much more dreadful than any other form of civil government, as a thousand tyrants are more to be dreaded than one. It is equally conceded, that the formation of the moral and intellectual character of the young is committed mainly to the female hand. The mother writes the character of the future man; the sister bends the fibres that hereafter are the forest tree;

the wife sways the heart, whose energies may turn for good or for evil the destinies of a nation. (Beecher, 1841/1977, p. 13)

What of the fathers? Was there anything left for them to do in the 19th century? The separation of spheres, while engendering parental labor and fostering its division and specialization, did not lessen the importance of the role fathers played in families. Fathers remained at the head of the family, which meant that they still made the key decisions regarding running the household. Moreover, they were the breadwinners, and it was their work that supported the household economy. Indeed, beginning in the early 19th century in middle-class families, "fatherhood, breadwinning, and manhood were inextricably linked in American culture: men organized their lives and their identity around fatherly breadwinning" (Griswold, 1993, p. 222). Fathers also served in capacities that put them more directly in touch with their children, especially their sons. One of these was the role of primary disciplinarian. Another was that of preparing sons in a practical sense for entry into the world. They were expected, for example, to assume responsibility for their sons' education and to assist them on their choice of a calling. Finally, they were supposed to support their wives in teaching children virtue (Griswold, 1993; Rotundo, 1993).

To be sure, fathers were increasingly willing to defer to their wives and their local schools in the rearing and educating of their children, but these processes were counterbalanced by the expectations that fathers would assume new roles in complementary areas of family life. However, parental roles were further segmenting along lines of gender: Mothers and fathers were expected to enter children's lives at different, age-appropriate stages of their development. Changes in the respective roles of fathers and mothers during the 19th century left enduring legacies of various engendered and age-appropriate generativities.

Since the 19th century, social, economic, cultural, and demographic changes have brought about profound alterations in generativity in the United States. Both the entry of women into the workforce and the rise of political feminism have at once expanded parental generative options for individual men (those, that is, who express an interest in becoming more involved in their children's lives) and broadened cultural and technical generative opportunities for individual women. At the same time, the contraceptive revolution, combined with demographic changes such as later marriages, greater longevity, and higher divorce rates, has greatly reduced the amount of time some people, especially men, spend in environments where children and youth are present (Griswold, 1993, p. 229). Even as some men invest more, and others less, in parenting, an increasing number of fathers are fleeing family and paternity; this "flight from the family" (Griswold, 1993, p. 228) is contributing to a crisis of paternal generativity among certain segments of the population. Concomitantly, as more and more women enter the workforce, female contributions to technical and cultural generativity grow and widen, adding further to the diversity of contemporary generativity in the United States. Even as men and women exchange domestic and economic roles that were prescribed by the Victorian family, tensions between the family and public education—the dual legacy of Puritanism and the revolution—persist, forming, in fact, a central theme in the history of generativity in the United States.

REFERENCES

Axtell, J. (1974). *The school upon a hill: Education and society in Colonial New England.* New York: Norton.

Bailyn, B. (1960). *Education in the forming of American society: Needs and Opportunities.* Chapel Hill: University of North Carolina Press.

Beecher, C. (1977). *A treatise on domestic economy* (K. K. Sklar, Ed.). New York: Shocken Books. (Original work published 1841)

Bledstein, B. J. (1976). *The culture of professionalism: The middle class and the development of higher education in America.* New York: Norton.

Bradford, W. (1956). *Of Plymouth Plantation.* New York: Modern Library.

Breen, T. H. (1980). *Puritans and adventurers: Change and persistence in early America.* New York: Oxford University Press.

Cott, N. F. (1977). *The bonds of womanhood: "Women's sphere" in New England, 1780–1835.* New Haven, CT: Yale University Press.

Cremin, L. (1970). *American education: The Colonial experience, 1607–1783.* New York: Harper & Row.

Degler, C. (1980). *At odds: Women and the family in America from the revolution to the present.* New York: Oxford University Press.

Demos, J. (1986). *Past, present, and personal: The family and the life course in American history.* New York: Oxford University Press.

Dunn, R. S. (1972). *Sugar and slaves: The rise of the planter class in the English West Indies, 1624–1730.* New York: Norton.

Erikson, E. (1963). *Childhood and society.* (Rev. ed.). New York: Norton.

Erikson, E. (1964). *Insight and responsibility: Lectures on the ethical implications of psychoanalytic insight.* New York: Norton.

Fliegelman, J. (1982). *Prodigals and pilgrims: The American revolution against patriarchal authority, 1750–1800.* Cambridge, England: Cambridge University Press.

Galenson, D. (1981). *White servitude in Colonial America: An economic analysis.* Cambridge, England: Cambridge University Press.

Greene, J. P. (Ed.). (1975). *Settlements to society, 1607–1763: A documentary history of Colonial America.* New York: Norton.

Greene, J. P. (1988). *Pursuits of happiness: The social development of early modern*

British colonies and the formation of American culture. Chapel Hill: University of North Carolina Press.

Greven, P. J., Jr. (1970). *Four generations: Population, land, and family in Colonial Andover, Massachusetts.* Ithaca, NY: Cornell University Press.

Griswold, R. L. (1993.) *Fatherhood in America: A History.* New York: Basic Books.

Henretta, J. (1973). *The evolution of American society, 1700–1815: An interdisciplinary analysis.* Lexington, MA: Heath.

Hiner, N. R. (1973). The cry of Sodom enquired into: Educational analysis in seventeenth-century New England. *History of Education Quarterly, 13,* 3–22.

Hoffer, P. C. (1983). *Revolution and generation: Life cycle and the historical vision of the generation of 1776.* Athens: University of Georgia Press.

Hooker, T. (1637). *The soules implantation.* London: Young.

Karlsen, C. F. (1987). *The devil in the shape of a woman: Witchcraft in Colonial New England.* New York: Norton.

Kerber, L. K. (1980). *Women of the republic: Intellect and ideology in revolutionary America.* Chapel Hill: University of North Carolina Press.

Kotre, J. (1984). *Outliving the self: Generativity and the interpretation of lives.* Baltimore: The Johns Hopkins University Press.

Locke, J. (1965). *Two treatises of government* (P. Laslett, Ed.). New York: New American Library. (Original work published 1698)

Lockridge, K. A. (1974). *Literacy in Colonial New England: An inquiry into the social context of literacy in the early modern West.* New York: Norton.

Mather, I. (1679). *Pray for the rising generation.* Boston: John Foster.

Moran, G. F., & Vinovskis, M. A. (1992). *Religion, family, and the life course: Explorations in the social history of early America.* Ann Arbor: University of Michigan Press.

Morgan, E. S. (1966). *The Puritan family: Religion and domestic relations in seventeenth-century New England* (Rev. Ed.). New York: Harper & Row.

Morgan, E. S. (1975). *American slavery, American freedom.* New York: Norton.

Morgan, E. S. (1980). *The genius of George Washington.* New York: Norton.

Murrin, J. M. (1972). Review essay. *History and Theory, 21,* 226–272.

Norton, M. B. (1980). *Liberty's daughters: The revolutionary experience of American women, 1750–1800.* Boston: Little, Brown.

Norton, M. B. (1996). *Founding mothers and fathers: Gendered power and the forming of American society.* New York: Knopf.

Paine, T. (1982). *Common Sense* (I. Kramnick, Ed.). New York: Penguin Books. (Original work published 1776)

Pangle, L. S., & Pangle, T. C. (1993). *The learning of liberty: The educational ideas of the American founders.* Lawrence: University of Kansas Press.

Pleck, E. (1987). *Domestic tyranny: The making of American social policy against family violence from Colonial times to the present.* New York: Oxford University Press.

Rotundo, E. A. (1993). *American manhood: Transformations in masculinity from the revolution to the modern era.* New York: Basic Books.

Rudolph, F. (Ed.). (1965). *Essays on education in the republic.* Cambridge, MA: Belknap Press.

Rutman, D. B., & Rutman, A. H. (1984). *A place in time: Middlesex County, Virginia, 1650–1750.* New York: Norton.

Shammas, C., Salmojn, M., & Dahlin, M. (1987). *Inheritance in America: From Colonial times to the present.* New Brunswick, NJ: Rutgers University Press.

Silverman, K. (1985). *The life and times of Cotton Mather.* New York: Columbia University Press.

Stone, L. (1977). *The family, sex, and marriage, 1500–1800.* New York: Harper & Row.

Stout, H. S. (1986). *The New England soul: Preaching and religious culture in Colonial New England.* New York: Oxford University Press.

Stout, H. S. (1990). Puritanism. In D. G. Reid (Ed.), *Dictionary of Christianity in America.* Downers Grove, IL: Interuniversity Press.

Trumbull, J. H. (1850–1890). *The public records of the colony of Connecticutt.* Hartford, Case, Lockwood, and Brainard.

Vinovskis, M. A. (1995). *Education, society, and economic opportunity: A historical perspective on persistent issues.* New Haven, CT: Yale University Press.

Willard, S. (1726). *A complete body of divinity.* Boston: Green and Kneeland.

10

GENERATIVITY IN THE SHADOW OF GENOCIDE: THE HOLOCAUST EXPERIENCE AND GENERATIVITY

AVI KAY

And Noah and his sons left the Ark, Noah's wife and his sons' wives (separately). Even though God had decreed that they might now procreate; Noah did not act on this privilege. For he said: but what will happen if Mankind continues to sin and the flood waters come once again and destroy all existence? (Noah asked) why should one have children and fear they will be destroyed—until God swore not to ever bring the flood waters again. *Taken from the biblical commentary of the "Klee Yakar" on Genesis.*

Generativity is a term proposed by Erikson (1963) to describe a concern with "establishing and guiding the next generation" (p. 267). *Genocide* is an attempt to exterminate an ethnic or racial group to ensure that there will be no "next generation" of the targeted group. This chapter considers the impact of what may be the most infamous case of attempted genocide—the Holocaust—on the generative behavior of survivors of the German concentration camps. If under normal circumstances individuals are driven to ensure the future of their progeny and culture—and through them their own immortality—what might be the consequences of attempted genocide on survivors' concern for personal, familial, and cultural continuity?

This inquiry can be placed within the expansive literature on the psychological ramifications of the Holocaust experience (see Kay, 1995, for a review of that literature). It has as its aim the description of the nature and role of generativity in the Holocaust survivor population. The thoughts and conclusions presented are based on research undertaken with 20 European-born Jews currently residing in the United States: 10 concentra-

335

TABLE 1
A Demographic Description of the Sample Population

Item	Holocaust survivors	Refugees
Age		
Range of group members	63–73	63–75
Group average	69.5	68.5
Marital Status		
Married	10	9
Widowed	0	1
Number of children		
1	0	3
2	3	3
3	5	4
4	2	0
Average	2.9	2.1
Education		
High school or less	9	9
College	1	1
Employment experience		
Were or are self-employed	9	8
Current employment status		
Employed full-time	2	2
Employed part-time	2	3
Retired	6	5

tion camp survivors and 10 individuals who, having fled Europe immediately prior to World War II, spent the war years either in the interior areas of the former Soviet Union or in China. The latter group, who resembled the survivors except with regard to their Holocaust period experiences, served as a contrast group in the explication of the impact of that experience on generativity among Holocaust survivors (see Table 1 for a description of the demographics of the two groups).

The data were culled from both qualitative and quantitative measures. The qualitative data were generated by responses to a series of images from the Thematic Apperception Test (TAT) and an in-depth interview that focused on issues related to generativity. The quantitative data were generated by two measures: the Loyola Generativity Scale (LGS) and the Generative Behavior Checklist (GBC), which provide self-reports concerning the presence of, respectively, generative concerns and generative behaviors (see McAdams & de St. Aubin, 1992, for a description of these measures).

HISTORICAL BACKGROUND CONCERNING
THE HOLOCAUST EXPERIENCE

There has been a Jewish presence in Europe since the time of the Roman Empire. As Western culture expanded into the hinterlands of Central and Eastern Europe, so did the Jewish population. By the eve of World War II, in 1939, there were no less than 8 million Jews in Europe (including the Soviet Union), with most residing in Eastern Europe. They had a ubiquitous presence in European capitals such as Berlin, Budapest, Paris, Vienna, and Warsaw. Moreover, the German, Hungarian, Polish, Rumanian, and Russian countryside was dotted with towns and villages where Jews constituted a large percentage of the population. By 1945 6 million of these people would be dead.

Of the millions who passed through the German camp system, it is estimated that only about 75,000 survived the extensive system of forced-labor, concentration, and death camps in which most of European Jewry found their doom (Porter, 1980). This population of survivors served as the focus of this study.

PSYCHOLOGICAL CONSEQUENCES OF THE HOLOCAUST EXPERIENCE

Overview

The literature dealing with the psychological ramifications of the Holocaust experience can be roughly divided into three "subliteratures," which are briefly presented in order of their chronological emergence (see Bergmann & Jacovy, 1982; Kay, 1995; Krystal, 1968, for a more expansive review of this literature).

The Traditional Approach

The early work concerning the psychological impact of the Holocaust experience was clinical in nature and based on the experiences of psychiatrists employed by the West German government in the early 1960s as part of the process by which Holocaust survivors were to be considered deserving of reparations from the German government (Chodoff, 1984; Krystal, 1968; Niederland, 1961).

The approach taken by these mental health professionals can be termed a "deficit" approach to Holocaust survivors; it has as its aim the identification and examination of what were seen as psychopathological, maladaptive consequences of the Holocaust. This stream of literature is associated with the "survivor syndrome" (Niederland, 1961), and the proponents of this approach typically believed that the psychological damage associated with incarceration in the German concentration camps was chronic, very often severe, and nearly irreversible. It was believed to be virtually an inevitable outcome of the concentration camp experience.

The survivor syndrome was seen as a multifaceted entity spanning numerous categories of the *Diagnostic and Statistical Manual of Mental Disorders* (American Psychiatric Association, 1994). The literature on the survivor syndrome speaks of the following outcomes: anxiety, disturbances of cognition and memory, chronic depressive reactions, survivor guilt, alterations of personal identity, psychophysiological symptoms (such as gastrointestinal conditions, peptic ulcers, and headaches), a lifelong sense of heightened vulnerability and increased awareness of dangerous situations, and permanent psychotic changes in personality.

Two elements of the traditional approach are particularly germane to generativity. First, survivors were expected to suffer from psychological and experiential dislocation resulting from the severed ties that characterize their lives (Hoppe, 1984). This characteristic was seen as leading to a natural psychological wound that would appear due to "the break in the sense of connection men have long felt with vital and nourishing symbols of their cultural traditions; symbols revolving around family, idea systems, religions, and life cycles in general" (Lifton, 1969, p. 43).

Extensive work was also done regarding the impact of the Holocaust experience on family relations in general and parental behaviors in particular. What were seen as "hasty marriages," undertaken in the shadow of the Holocaust experience to create a sense of belonging and love, led to a supposed tension between the "fear of bringing another generation into being" and the "need . . . to undo the destruction magically by creating a family as soon as possible" (Krystal, 1968, p. 192).

Survivor parents were seen by many as lacking, at least partially, in the ego functions necessary for child rearing. Others (Aleksandrowicz, 1973; Klein, 1973) noted affective "flatness," self-involvement, and ineffective parenting in survivors, who failed to establish basic trust in the world for their children or to prepare their children for healthy separation.

Alongside the reported inability of survivor parents truly to engage their children, the former were seen as viewing their offspring as "overvalued representation(s) of all the relatives lost in the holocaust of European Jewry" (Sigal & Rakoff, 1971, p. 393).

Although there has been criticism of the traditional approach on both methodological (e.g., Harel, 1983; Solkoff, 1981) and conceptual (e.g., Terry, 1980) grounds, it nevertheless remains the basis for the view of Holocaust survivors held by both many mental health professionals and the public at large.

The Empirical Approach

The preceding description reflects what has been considered "common knowledge" concerning the psychological reality of the Holocaust survivor for many years. Because of the "popularity" (for the lack of a better word) of the survivor syndrome, by the 1970s, a clear picture of what a

Holocaust survivor was "supposed to be like" developed. In fact, following extensive interviews with Holocaust survivors, Rabinowitz (1976) noted that one of the most surprising discoveries arising from her work with survivors was the variability that she found in survivors and in their coping mechanisms.

The traditional, clinical-based approach to the psychological study of Holocaust survivors gradually gave way to work that, although also anchored in the "deficit" approach, sought to examine the maladaptive traits of Holocaust survivors from an empirical perspective (e.g., Eaton, Sigal, & Weinfeld, 1982; Leon, Butcher, Kleinman, Goldberg, & Almagor, 1981). The findings of this line of research have been much more equivocal in nature with regard to the post-Holocaust psychological adjustment of survivors.

Although some empirical studies confirmed earlier conclusions concerning anxiety and cognitive constriction among survivors (Eaton et al., 1982; Kohn Dor-Shav, 1978; Shanan & Shachar, 1985), other "accepted" characteristics of the survivor syndrome appeared more tenuous (Leon et al., 1981; Zlotogorski; 1983).

Recent Developments

Over the past decade a new approach has emerged with regard to the study of the effects of the Holocaust experience on survivors. A prominent figure in this approach has been Robert Lifton, a psychiatrist who has done much work on survivorship. Lifton sought to change the focus from the impact of the trauma suffered to an understanding of how the survivor coped with that trauma.

In some of his recent work, Lifton (1988) considered generativity to be the pivot on which much of the posttraumatic existence of survivors rests. Without citing or referencing even one work on generativity, Lifton provided a view of the role and predicament of the survivor that is clearly influenced, at the very least, by the works of Erikson (1963) and Kotre (1984):

> If we review some of our experiences with Vietnam War veterans and other groups who have undergone severe trauma, we find in each case a struggle to reinstate a larger human connectedness or a sense of being "on the great chain of being." This is one of the most poignant and difficult struggles that accompanies the recovery process. We symbolize immortality—our historical and biological connectedness to those who have gone before, those who we assume will follow. We do this through our limited life span, whether through children, our works, our influences, or through nature, or whether some spiritual principle, or even through experiences of transcendence. (pp. 8–9)

This approach has taken center stage with the surge in both written memoirs and oral histories on the part of Holocaust survivors (Langer, 1990). As noted, this approach is perhaps best viewed as shifting the focus from the consequences of suffering to the consequences of surviving. One consequence of survival was the need of survivors to find meaning and purpose in survival. Whereas "meaning" may be seen as denoting a philosophical wresting with one's existence, "purpose" seems to be more action- and future-oriented. One purpose may be investment in children, work, and other activities that an individual can bring into the world, as well as the knowledge and wisdom that they can bequeath others. In other words, the individual desires to leave a legacy and undertake actions that can be summed up in one word: *generativity*.

GENERATIVITY AND THE GENERATIVE WORLD OF THE HOLOCAUST SURVIVOR

Although the term *generativity* was initially used by Erikson some 40 years ago, it has been only in recent years that attempts have been made to explicate this construct. The research presented here was informed by the work of Kotre (1984), regarding the various avenues generativity may take, and of McAdams and de St. Aubin (1992), regarding the ways in which generativity may unfold and take form in one's life.

More specifically, the generative lives of the Holocaust survivors and the refugee contrast group mentioned earlier were examined along the lines of Kotre's (1984) typology, which suggested that generativity could be expressed through four avenues of generative behaviors: (a) *biological*, the biological parenting of a child; (b) *parental*, the social parenting of a child; (c) *technical*, the transmission of skills and symbols of a society; and (d) *cultural*, the creating of new or transmission of existing elements of a culture (see Kotre, 1984, for a discussion of the specific components). In addition, it was proposed that the Holocaust survivor population may express yet another, unique form of generativity: (e) *universal*, the creation and transmission of a unique message arising from the Holocaust experience to humanity as a whole.

As in Kotre's work (1984), an effort was made to understand more fully the role of generativity in the lives of the individuals studied by means of an explication of the relative importance of *communion* and *agency* needs (Bakan, 1966) in their generative behavior. In terms of generativity, the need of communion can be seen in an individual's desire to participate in interpersonal relationships and become part of a larger social reality in which generative objects are created and allowed to evolve and grow as independent entities. Agency, for its part, represents the self-expansion of the individual by means of generative behavior in which the generative object (e.g., a child, a cultural innovation) becomes a monument to itself.

It can be expected that in most generative actions both communion and agency needs come into play.

In addition, the generative lives of the Holocaust survivors and the refugee group were examined along the lines of the work of McAdams and de St. Aubin (1992), which focused on the timing, possible purpose, and differing expressions of generativity. This work offers a model of generativity that focuses on understanding the sources of generativity and traces the evolution of generativity in the individual from the first apprehension of the possibility of generative activity, to the way in which generativity may be acted on, through how the individual's personal "generative story" may be constructed. In the next section I delineate the impact of this model, and of Kotre's (1984) typology of generativity, on the generative world of Holocaust survivors.

The Generative World of the Holocaust Survivor

Perhaps the most striking finding of this research was the vigor with which generativity was present in the lives of the Holocaust survivors examined. Indeed, it is virtually impossible to address the self-concept of the Holocaust survivors who participated in this study separately from their generative world. The robustness of the generativity expressed by the Holocaust survivors was particularly conspicuous when compared with the information offered by the refugee contrast group. This difference is present in both the interview protocols and the results of the LGS (see Kay, 1995). Although the two groups studied here are admittedly small, it is nevertheless worthwhile to note that the survivor group far outscored both the refugee sample and a similar aged group studied by McAdams et al. (1993).

As suggested by McAdams (1985), the psychosocial development of the individual need not follow a strict Eriksonian path in which the stage of "generativity vs. stagnation" appears only when issues of identity are settled. Rather, it was suggested that for some, generativity may be a vehicle around which identity is formed. Such seems to be the case for the Holocaust survivors studied here, who exhibited a great deal of generativity in three of the four categories suggested by Kotre (1984): biological, parental, and cultural generativity.

It is worthwhile to note that in the protocols of the generativity interview a clear difference emerges between the survivor group and the refugee group with regard to not only the number of *generativity-related* elements expressed but also the *general attitude* of the two groups toward their personal history. Refugees did not seem to view their personal history as containing elements that were particularly profound. They typically "delegitimized" their own stories of travail and upheaval, commenting that "compared to others" (whom they referred to as "the survivors") they had it easy. This self-perceived lack of "legitimacy" concerning their own loss and a possible sense of guilt seemed to diminish the importance of their life experiences in their eyes and to suppress their desire to transmit their own personal stories.

Early Sources of Generativity

The relative psychological disengagement of the refugees from their past can be witnessed early on in their generative development. It is only in the material presented by the survivors that one can identify references that tie early socialization (the "social demand" for generativity described in the model of McAdams and de St. Aubin) to later generativity. Although refugees made some mention of the pre-Holocaust years, those references were oblique and in no way related to generative beliefs or actions.

For the survivor group, the pre-Holocaust world served as a palpable backdrop to the lives they lived and the goals and dreams that drove their generative actions. The distinctive focus of the survivors on their early development is not surprising. Krystal (1968) noted the tendency of survivors to idealize their childhood is an attempt to reconnect to the people, places, and patterns they were torn away from and forever deprived of. Particularly central to these memories were references to the importance of family ties, a focus that can be seen as reinforcing one of the basic norms of pre-Holocaust culture of the Eastern European Jewish community described in Zborowski's (1965) seminal work on that milieu. The authors noted that a widely accepted truth of that society was that "it is the business of every person to become a parent; and it is the business of every parent to make people out of their children" (p. 335). This drive toward family became a central element of the generative world of the Holocaust survivor.

Generativity During the Holocaust Period

Additional differences in the evolution of the generative world of the two groups can be seen in their comments concerning the Holocaust years. For the refugee group, the Holocaust period was one of "watchful waiting." Like the general population of Jewish refugees who fled Europe prior to the Holocaust, the refugees spent the war years with their families distant from the Nazi war machine. Following are the words of three individuals from the refugee group who offered typical comments concerning their experiences during the war years. Carl, a store owner who sat out the war with his family in a small town in the north of China, made these comments:

> Again, life for me in China was just a 9-year waiting period. Nothing creative or anything like that happened. We just sat out the war—

that's what we did. That's all. That's all I can say. There's no Holly-
wood movie script here. People say, "Oh, he must be able to write a
book." But it was a boring life. There was no radio. There was a Japanese supervised newspaper, in English, but that had the Japanese party
line.

A similar tone is present in the words of Marvin, another individual
from the refugee group, who spent the war years in the Yakutsk region of
the former Soviet Union, "1000 miles east of Moscow":

We were all together, my family. My father and mother worked in
munitions. We did not have books too much, but we learned a little
to write in Russian, we learned a little math. And the Jews learned a
little Torah, a little religion. We were cut off, we did not know what
was happening in the war, we heard rumors of the camps but did not
really know anything, we were so far away.

Finally, Hal remembered the war years he spent in China as "a great
piece of luck, if a waste. We lived off charity. We were, of course, the lucky
ones. But I cannot help but to regret the waste of 5 years."

In contrast to these accounts, the Holocaust years for the survivor
group were, of course, a period of almost unimaginable deprivations and
trauma. The reality they faced seems to have pushed issues of generativity
to the forefront. From the interview data it is clear that it was during the
Holocaust that the survivors, most of whom were adolescents at the time,
had their first generative thoughts.

Jacob, the elder statesman of the survivor group, was all of 20 years
old at the beginning of World War II in 1939; he remembered his thoughts
in the moments before he fell asleep at night in the concentration camp.
Jacob's comment contains the kernels of both biological and cultural generativity:

In *lagger* [the Yiddish term for "concentration camp"] I would go to
sleep at night think[ing] how weird it would be not to wake up. But
in the morning I'd open my eyes and say: "Hah, they're not going to
destroy the whole Jewish people. Some of us will survive. Maybe I will
be the lucky one. By me we [the Jewish people] will survive." It made
for a future to look for.

The seeds of cultural generativity and, perhaps, universal generativity
can be seen in the words of the following two survivors, Max and Norman.
Max recalled a conversation he had with his father as the latter made his
way toward his certain death:

My father, when he went to the gas chambers. He said, "Don't forget,
what happened to us, what is happened to you. Don't forget, if you
live, tell, tell the story." [Pauses, with tears in his eyes] Then, I knew
I would live.

Norman, a rather thoughtful and loquacious individual, almost bristled at my attempt to thank him for his time:

> A.K.: I would like to thank you for finding the time to speak with me.
> Norman: [Interrupting] No, no . . . I do not participate to do a favor.
> I do not do it for me. I do it for them.
> A.K.: For who?
> Norman: For my friends. . . . We were three and we always said that if any of us [were to] live, then we will talk . . . we will tell what happened. I didn't think I would live. But it is me . . . it is me who now tells the story.

The emergence of generative thoughts among the survivors during the Holocaust may simply be a natural outcome of an unnatural situation in which the young survivors were forced to take responsibility for issues of personal and community survival. Many spoke of a vow to "bear witness" if they were to survive. However, the emergence of generativity in the lives of the Holocaust survivors may have had an additional and critical psychological role in the lives of these individuals both during and after the Holocaust.

The generative thoughts presented here can perhaps be seen as a means somehow to escape the despair of the survivors' Holocaust reality. The overwhelmingly adverse reality that threatened to overcome the survivors' capacity to function encouraged an "escape" to some future time when current travails would no longer exist. This phenomenon repeated itself at different points in the survivors' lives. Indeed, this finding is in line with those of Dasberg (1987), who noted that the survivors with whom he spoke coped with adverse conditions at various points in their lives by disengaging from their present situation and projecting themselves into a more benevolent future.

It seems clear that, for survivors, another way of projecting themselves into a happier future was to contemplate the possibility of having children, who in turn would beget other children. Thus, during the seemingly endless nightmare of their Holocaust existence, when their immediate existence may have seemed uncertain, many survivors interviewed thought of some distant place and time in which they would once again be surrounded by family. Indeed, the belief that they might not only survive the concentration camp but also achieve immortality through the children has been deemed to be one of the principal coping mechanisms used by survivors (Dimsdale, 1980).

The refugees may be considered to have been in a state of "suspended animation" during the Holocaust period. Generativity-related elements were completely absent from their recollections of the period. Also absent were recollections of feelings of concern or upheaval, which may have been expected to emerge in the wake of the major changes that occurred in their young lives during that period. This lack may be related to the previously mentioned tendency of the refugee group to "discount" the importance of their own personal experiences owing to guilt about what happened to those who were left behind. For, as Hal noted, "we were, of course, the lucky ones."

In contrast, for the survivors the Holocaust was the period that defined and shaped their subsequent existence. They clung to what the psychological literature refers to as "generative thoughts" to escape an oppressive present. As I will show, the generativity that emerged in the darkness of the Holocaust continued to be the light that shone on the paths the survivors subsequently took in life.

Generativity in the Post-Holocaust Period

Although the generative world of the refugees remained rather static during the post-Holocaust period, the survivors passed through a number of different stages with regard to their generative selves. In this section I address both the evolution and the nature of the generative world of these individuals.

Biological Generativity

In Erikson's (1950) first approximation of generativity, much emphasis was put on the psychobiological drive to procreate and, thus, to ensure the physical survival of the species. The Holocaust survivors interviewed here can be seen as initially being driven by a strong impulse to conceive children. Indeed, biological generativity is the most significant theme of the survivors' early post-Holocaust generative development. As opposed to the refugee group, most of the survivors emerged from the Holocaust period as either sole survivors or one of a very few in their extended family who remained alive. As such, it is not surprising that the survivors seemed to view themselves as an "endangered species."

Support for the preceding proposition can be found in Helmreich's (1992) work on the post-Holocaust development of survivors. He noted that the survivors with whom he spoke commented that after the Holocaust they were alarmed about the future of the Jewish people because "there were no Jewish children." This may help explain why, at first, it seemed enough for the survivors that there be a generation to carry on after them. Witness the words of Jacob:

> Why did I want to have children? Because I thought God save[d] me. I don't know why. The whole family perished. So, I thought if I'm alive, so maybe God wants me to be a saving place out. So I thought, you're alive then you must leave a *dor* ["generation" in Hebrew] after you.

In fact, remnants of this theme can also be found in the responses of the survivors to an item in the LGS concerning adoption. Survivors seemed rather equivocal with regard to the proposition of adopting children if they were unable to have children of their own. They seemed to value the continuation of their family (what sociobiologists refer to as their "gene pool") through the creation of another generation physically—not only emotionally, socially, or culturally—linked to the historical familial chain from which they emerged. To put it bluntly, survivors were less interested in raising "Jewish children" than in having individuals with "genuine" Jewish genes repopulating the world.

Members of the refugee group seemed far less ardent concerning the biological aspect of generativity. In addition, as I show in the next section, there also existed significant and telling differences in the characteristics of parental generativity between the survivor group and the refugee group. The differences in the role and nature of family relations between the two groups were evident in the interview, the TAT responses, and the LGS results.

Parental Generativity

The creation of the family unit—the conceiving of children and concern for their subsequent well-being—is clearly the most central element of the post-Holocaust generative world of both the refugee group and the survivor group interviewed here. The most prevalent behaviors for both groups on the GBC related to the strengthening of family relations. However, as I previously noted, there was a significant distinction between the groups concerning how parental generativity was conceived and practiced.

The motivation of the refugee group toward parental generativity was rather normative. Carl, who was quoted concerning the years he spent in northern China, commented that he wanted children because "it gets kind of lonesome without kids around. When you have kids you feel strong, you have a family like everyone else."

Marvin, who spent the war years in the interior of Russia, said that having children was "to have a continuation of family. A natural phenomenon of preservation." Murray, another former refugee who was in China, remarked that the reason to have children is "to perpetuate yourself. Carry on from generation to generation . . . to have someone to talk to." All these comments, reflective of the overall approach of the refugees, can be clearly categorized as communal in nature, with an emphasis on establishing relationship.

The preceding comments contrast sharply with those of the survivors. Far from being "deeply ambivalent" about raising children and reentering a family framework (Krystal, 1968), the survivors saw that outcome as a central goal of their lives. In fact, the survivors expressed a type of generative desire that simply has not been recorded elsewhere in the generative literature. Survivors expressed a type of generative desire that, in reality, is unachievable: a desire to change the past. Initially, all of the survivors viewed parental generativity as a contribution to their past as much as a contribution to their future.

In this context, it is important to recall how survivors explained their desire to have children during this period. Following are a few comments regarding this matter that are typical of the group. First, consider the words of Henry, who survived Mauthausan:

> You form another family . . . I lost all my family. Now I have a family back. A man looks for safety, with family you are not alone. I wanted a family back—it is the only thing that you can hold.

Daniel, the most Americanized of the survivors, spoke of his motivation for children as follows:

> By having kids part of our family is still here. You know . . . [the] cycle of life. Not only life affirming, but you reclaim your past by giving them the names [of deceased relatives].

Max, who previously recalled his last meeting with his father, recalled the years after the Holocaust and noted the following:

> The main important thing was to raise a family again. When you go out from the camps and nobody was there to say anything, nobody was there, eh, to comfort you or do anything for you. So you naturally want to build a family. Want to build back what it was before. You don't *want* [a family] . . . you *need* [a family].

The preceding comments are in line with a tendency of survivors to view the family in an almost mythical fashion (e.g., Krystal, 1968); for these survivors, the ability to create a post-Holocaust family somehow undid some of the events of the Holocaust period. Other writers noted the inevitable disappointment felt by survivors they treated when they realized that having children was not a cure-all for their inner pain.

Another aspect of parental generativity worth noting is related to the nature of the relationship between the generative agents (the participants in this study) and the generative objects (their children). One of the main components of parenting is "nurturing," a basic ingredient of *maintaining* a generative creation. Members of the refugee group spoke of two major elements of "good parenting": an interpersonal and a material aspect. In the former, the parent was to serve as a guide for the child. The role of guide entailed speaking with the child, advising the child, and preparing the child for the challenges to be faced as an adult in the world. In addition, the parent needed to provide material things for the child (including a good education) that would help sustain the child. The statements of the refugee group concerning this matter contain themes of both communion with the children and agency in their drive to be the "good provider."

Accordingly, the comments offered by members of the refugee group in response to an inquiry concerning what it means to be a good parent reflect those two parameters. Witness the following statements:

Carl: A good parent raises his children to be a good, honest person. He helps them into this world and prepares them for all the good and bad that might come his way.

Murray: A good parent is close to the child. He talks to him, helps him learn things.

Leo: Kids don't come into this world by themselves, you're responsible for them, put them on their feet. Show them the way.

Percy: A good parent tells the kid what's right, what's wrong.

Ralph: A good parent . . . I tried to give my daughter a good beginning.

Zev: That's constantly watching over them, advising them, helping them grow up.

The preceding statements contrast greatly with the manner in which survivors characterized a good parent. Following are some of these responses:

Joseph: The important thing is to love your children, you teach them. You make sure that they have all what they need.

Henry: You bring children into this world and you have to be able to make a living, and try to give them as best you can give it to them, with work, with clothes, you try to give them an education of their own.

Daniel: A good parent puts food on the table, a roof over the head, gives them an education . . . take care of their needs.

Irwin: You have to help your children, get them up. Give them . . . buy what they need for the house, for school.

Norman: It's [being a parent] more the obligations than love . . . Well, a good parent, you talk to your children, have a dialogue. You give them an education—that they can't take away.

Ted: It's your obligation to put your kid on his feet. That's your obligation.

Mel: You have to take care of your kids. That they should have what to eat, that they should have an education. We [survivors] worked hard so that our kids will have it good here [in the United States].

These statements point to the fact that, for the survivors, good parenting was a much more narrow and concrete matter than for the refugees. The responses of the survivors concerning what constitutes a good parent were focused on the provision of the material needs of the children. A good parent put food on the table, provided a roof for the family, and gave the children what they needed. This finding is in accordance with the conclusions of a variety of investigators (e.g., Rakoff, Sigal, & Epstein, 1966; Rosenberger, 1973) who examined the relationship between survivors and their children. Indeed, Helmreich (1992) commented that there was an overwhelming tendency among survivors with whom he spoke to emphasize material possessions as tangible expressions of love. The drive toward material well-being probably is related to the extreme material deprivation of the Holocaust period.

In addition, the role of "provider" may have taken on even more importance (and on an unconscious level, attraction) for the survivor. It may have allowed the survivor to explain his zealousness to work in terms of the material necessities of the future he was working toward rather than of the past from which he was trying to escape.

Further support for the proposition that the survivors were particularly driven to "be needed" can be found in responses to the LGS. The items on that scale for which the survivors received the highest scores had to do with being a productive member of society, such as doing volunteer work, helping others, and making commitments to others.

In fact, perhaps the major element of the interpersonal relationships of the survivors had nothing to do with their partner in the relationship but rather with the role they themselves played in the relationship. It was important for the survivor to be a provider, to be needed by others. Indeed, such an interpretation might help explain the responses of the survivors to the query, "Do others need you?" That question served as a point of unexpected tension in the interview process, eliciting responses of "I hope so" and, most often, a nervous laugh.

This observation may offer an insight into the previously mentioned results of the LGS. The need to prove one's worth can be seen to be a product of the Holocaust experience, in which survivors were virtually bereft of any control over their situation. It is important to remember that in the Holocaust world Jews remained alive as long as their existence was seen as productive and useful to the German Third Reich. To be unproductive, therefore, may be tantamount to being expendable and replaceable.

It is interesting to note that the focus on material needs and the ensuing striving to satisfy those needs may have been most adaptive for the survivors in the period after the Holocaust. It has been suggested (Krystal, 1968) that one means by which survivors avoided directly confronting unhealed scars of their memory was through immersion in the travails and challenges of work and economic advancement. Krystal also suggested that, as the challenges of the working world fade, the survivors are forced to reconfront unresolved thoughts and feelings, resulting in a period of unquiet senescence.

Another element of the parent–child relationship worth noting concerns the nature of communication between parent and child. As noted, the refugee group seemed to engage their children on an emotional, inter-personal level more than did the survivor group. However, neither group, on the whole, spoke freely about their personal life experiences. The refugees seemed to refrain from speaking about their past owing to a tendency to devalue the legitimacy and importance of their experiences. This held true whether the audience was their own children or others.

Regarding the tendency of the survivors to find it difficult to engage their children on an emotional level, the responses of the survivors to the TAT images are informative. First, survivors tended to offer responses that were much more past-oriented and negative (in terms of affect) than those of the refugee group. Also, survivors typically offered responses that were standard, and even blase, on the surface, followed by content that was emotionally laden and "disturbing" in nature. This "dual tier" response is reminiscent of the words of a survivor interviewed for the Yale University Holocaust Archives (Langer, 1990): "We had to educate our children and we had to guide our children and be nice people and make parties and everything. But all that was make believe" (p. 141).

It is worthwhile to reflect on the preceding comment for a moment. It can be stated that the survivors did battle with the demands of the present while held captive by the injuries of the past. To some degree, the survivors seemed to perform their parental duties in a fashion similar to that of worshippers who, familiar with liturgy and custom, no longer have faith in the efficacy of their words and actions.

Another element of the TAT responses worth noting is related to the sense of "miscommunication" between people of different generations (who were present in a number of the TAT images presented). Survivors' TAT responses told of the difficulty the parents and children in the images experienced in understanding one another. Similarly, communication with children, in general, and concerning the Holocaust experience, in particular, was difficult for the survivors. With regard to the Holocaust experience, three different types of communication patterns emerged. Although survivors representing all three types felt that they *should* transmit their story, they differed in how they dealt with that obligation. First, there were those who chose not to speak to their children owing to the emotional strain resulting from such an action, such as Henry:

> I didn't tell them [his children] anything. I mean they knew I was in the camps, and they knew they didn't have a grandpa or grandma, but no details. I couldn't do it—I didn't want to relive it. When they came to me and said, "Dad, please we need to know," I started to tell. I don't know, maybe I was selfish. I don't know.

Other survivors noted that they chose to refrain from telling their stories to their children because of the way that it might affect the children.

Irving, who claimed during the interview that survivors knew that they must survive to tell their stories, noted the following:

> Until recently, my kids did not know anything. When they were small I did not want to tell them. How could they understand? It would only make them sad, they couldn't really understand. I didn't want to be emotional in front of the kids. Maybe they will feel sorry for me, be sad. But now, they are adults, I have told them about the camps, I see that they need to know. I won't be around forever.

Similarly, Daniel, the only college-educated survivor offered this recollection:

> No, I didn't really tell them everything. They knew a little about my home, a little about where I was in the war and how I got here [the United States]. But a lot I did not pass on. I didn't want them to hate. They could not really understand what happened, they . . . it would be too much for them.

Finally, there were others who told their children about their experiences in an open fashion. However, it was clear that these individuals were uncertain that the information was understood. Norman, who is the most active in institutionalized Holocaust remembrance projects, commented as follows:

> The kids can't understand. Sometimes it is so difficult, unbelievable. How can they believe it? It's impossible to believe it. I can't understand what happened. I tell them, but can they understand? That is what I am afraid of.

The uncertainty of the interviewees concerning the ability to share their life experiences with their children was also present in other parts of the interview protocols. When the interviewees were queried concerning what message, if any, from their life they wished to relate to their children, typical answers included the advice to "be honest," "work hard," and "respect others." None of the refugees spoke of any message related to the refugee experience, and only one survivor suggested that he sought to communicate to his children a message that was Holocaust-related.

On the face of it, refugees and survivors seemed to be "in the same boat." Neither group sought to transmit to their children messages or "lessons from life" from what can reasonably be seen to be a central element in the parents' development. However, the explanation for this situation is different for refugees than for survivors.

The refugees were seen to discount the magnitude of their experiences. The years of "delegitimatizing" a need they have had to share with others their pain may have been the cause of what seemed to be a lack of affect and connection to their own personal history. The refugees interviewed seemed to believe that they did not have a right to "hurt" in light of the much greater loss sustained by those who stayed behind during the Holocaust period. This hesitation to gain ownership of their pain led them to decide not to share their past with their children because they perceived that others would also view that story as insignificant.

The last thing that the survivors can be accused of is viewing their story as lacking importance to others. Similarly, far from disconnecting from their past they seemed, for better or worse, tremendously linked to their past. However, like the survivors interviewed by Helmreich (1992), the interviewees hesitated to try to express to their children the total nature of their personal Holocaust experience. This can be deemed to be a result of a paradoxical situation in which the survivors feared that the children could not absorb the full intensity of the experience or, conversely, might absorb it too well. The consequence of this was that although survivors wanted their children "to remember," they found it hard to relay to the children a coherent message about the Holocaust that could serve as a remembrance.

Technical Generativity

One aspect of generativity that is almost completely absent from the lives of the individuals interviewed in this study is that of technical generativity. This lack may be related to the fact that only a handful of the interviewees could be said to have a profession. Even fewer had received a high school education, not to speak of postsecondary studies. It is not surprising, therefore, that the overwhelming majority of the participants worked in fields that did not demand any training. Responses on the LGS and the interview protocols indicate that they did not feel that they had any special skills to transmit to others. On the whole, work for this population had little to do with skills or occupational pride. The survivors worked to provide for family. As such, the only motivation to teach another a skill was to make the business more efficient and allow the individual to take even better material care of the family.

Numerous authors (e.g., Helmreich, 1992; Rabinowitz, 1976) have noted the relative financial security achieved by Holocaust survivors. A possible explanation for that is a drive for success and activity that overcompensated for the impotence and helplessness experienced in the Holocaust (Charney, 1992). The drive toward mastery is an example of an agentic drive, in which the skills developed or transmitted serve to strengthen the generative agent's sense of self-efficacy. As previously noted, this drive toward material well-being and accomplishment was adaptive for the survivors in that it provided them escape from memories and a means to engage their children on a plane more accessible than that of emotional interaction. Following are some typical comments concerning different aspects of technical generativity:

> Arthur: Yes, I like teaching others—the more the workers know, the more I can stay away.
> Henry: What was a good job? If you could make it [financially], it was a good job.
> Irving: The best part of work? I worked and I was happy to give my children what they need. A roof over their head, clothes to wear, food to eat. I was happy to give my children an education.

All the interviewees placed great emphasis on higher education. Education can be seen as a proxy for technical generativity for the interviewees, in the absence of possession of technical skills of their own to pass on to their children. This attitude may also have had the effect of giving increased value and legitimacy to the striving for material success in the eyes of the survivors. Perhaps in reference to the vicissitudes of their own lives, the provision of an education for the children was an example of agentic strivings of the survivors to "empower" their offspring; many of the Holocaust survivors noted that others "could not take an education away from you."

It is interesting that the fathers were equipping the generative object with tools for survival without addressing the underlying motivations for doing so. As such, it is perhaps not surprising that an examination of the interview protocols indicates that this message was not verbalized to their children. This unspoken message is yet another example of the nature of the communication between father and son.

Cultural Generativity

After emerging initially in the Holocaust period among the survivors, cultural generativity played a secondary role in the lives of the interviewees. The main and overriding generative commitment to provide material support for children overshadowed issues of cultural continuity. Given their religious background and later Holocaust experience, survivors may be likened to a ship afloat without a home port. The cultural world from which they emerged was destroyed. Although they were no longer, by any means, religious, less traditional, "American brands" of Judaism (e.g., Conservative and Reform) were foreign to them. In addition, it has been claimed that survivors felt estranged from the larger Jewish community in the United States and its institutions (Rabinowitz, 1976).

However, with time, the survivors—as opposed to the refugees—came to place increased emphasis on providing their children with at least a rudimentary religious background. Whereas all the survivors noted that it was important to them that their children receive a religious education, the refugees were divided on the matter. Typically, this desire was not due to feelings of faith among the survivors; it was more past-oriented and fueled by a drive to create a continuity by linking their offspring to the world and family from which they had emerged. Max, who was previously quoted concerning his last conversation with his father in a concentration camp, was typical:

> We suffered because we were Jews. My family died because they were Jews. I wanted my kids to know about what was, Jewish history, about the holidays. I grew up that way and that's what I pass along. It makes for continuation.

The one clear "Jewish belief" that was exhibited by both refugees and (particularly) survivors was Zionism. Indeed, if religion did not serve as a personally significant credo for refugees and survivors, Zionism did. Members of both groups took great pleasure in their activities related to Zionism and spoke of the visits that they and their children had made to Israel. It was clear that the survivors took some solace from the belief that the suffering of the Holocaust provided the groundwork for the subsequent creation of a Jewish state. For all of the interviewees, the price of Israel's creation was the Holocaust, and its *raison d'être* was to prevent another Holocaust. As such, Zionism motivated tremendous emotional and financial investment on their part.

These findings are in line with the findings of others, such as Brenner (1980), who discovered that events in Israel had a particularly potent impact on the Holocaust survivors with whom he spoke. As the survivor group became increasingly established and financially secure, survivors could be found at the forefront of Israel-related political and economic activities. This progression from Zionist beliefs to action should be viewed as an important process in the post-Holocaust development of the survivors. These activities provided meaning to suffering and salvaged "heroism," à la Becker (1973), from degradation and shame.

Another venue through which survivors have contributed to the cultural milieu of the communities in which they live relates to Holocaust remembrance. For nearly 30 years after the Holocaust, survivors seemed to be in a "latency period" and did not, by and large, attempt to interest others in Holocaust remembrance. In addition, during this period, the general Jewish community and others did not exhibit tremendous interest in their stories. However, over the past two decades, survivors have become pivotal in transforming their personal experiences into a central focus of (primarily Jewish) education and consciousness. The Holocaust has evolved into a new Exodus; a story to be told from generation to generation.

Universal Generativity

Earlier, I suggested that the survivors exhibited a unique form of generativity, termed *universal generativity*, composed of the creation and transmission of a unique message to all of humanity, arising from the Holocaust experience. I noted further that a deep and resolute determination to "bear witness" emerged among the survivors during the Holocaust period. However, despite the widespread institutionalization of Holocaust remembrance, the message arising from the Holocaust experience cannot be considered to be universal in nature. Rather, the message "Never Again," which became a slogan of the Holocaust, was aimed at Jews and had as much to do with the past as with any possible future.

Quite understandably, the survivors interviewed did not want others to forget their suffering and the suffering of those who perished during the Holocaust. The lesson of this suffering will, like most lessons, be interpreted and reinterpreted by others in a myriad of different ways. It is already clear that others, both from within the Jewish community and from without, see the Holocaust as a historical episode that must be taught and researched to prevent other, similar tragedies from occurring elsewhere, against other innocents. However, on the basis of the data from this study, survivors may be too close to this experience truly to disengage and view it in a more universal nature.

CONCLUSION

The generative lives of the individuals studied were indelibly marked by the Holocaust. For the refugee group, the Holocaust period was recalled, to some degree, as a vacuum in which little of significance occurred. Their lives were interrupted, and any significant education or training ended. In addition, although they all emerged with their families intact, the community and society from which they emerged were no longer in existence. However, it has been suggested that despite these circumstances, the relative ease with which these individuals survived the period may have led to the creation of their own type of "survivor guilt."

This sense of guilt seems to have hampered the development of these individuals as generative beings. Overall, they expressed less generativity than both the survivor group of the present study and a group of similar ages presented by McAdams et al. (1993). Although the refugees greatly valued the creation of families and invested their principal efforts in the advancement of the family unit and offspring, they seemed to feel that they had neither important messages nor significant life experiences to convey to their children. There was something barren in the affective lives of these individuals, yielding some constriction in their ability truly to engage those around them. Although these individuals did not, by any measure, seem haunted by their past, the shadows of this past seemed clearly visible on the lives they have led.

The survivors, on the other hand, emerged from the data culled here as extremely generative beings. The hold the past had on their lives, in general, and on their generative lives, in particular, was unmistakable. The generative energy that was so potent in these individuals emerged from the deep wells of their Holocaust experience. This energy drove the survivors to seek to create a new reality in which to live their lives after having lost the family, community, and culture from whence they had emerged. Through this new reality, with its foundation of the creation or recreation of the family framework, the survivors sought somehow to undo the past and regain what had been lost.

Despite their strong desire to immerse themselves in the family framework, the survivors interviewed seemed unable to engage their children fully. They seemed uncertain whether, how, and when to share with their children memories of the most potent experience in their life, their Holocaust experience. The difficulty that the survivors had in engaging their children on the emotional plane can be seen as both a cause and a result of their emphasis on providing the children with material goods. Ultimately, the survivors' main expression of generativity was the biological creation of a new generation of Jews and their subsequent sustenance.

The survivors seemed concerned about whether and how their children would understand their stories and what they would think of them and the world in which they lived. Some survivors may have felt that by shielding their children from the true story of their life they saved their children from having to confront the evils and fears from which they, themselves, were not saved. This temptation to censor exceedingly traumatic life experiences in an effort to protect the generative object may be expected to be present in the lives of other generative agents who have experienced extreme experiences. Although such a decision may be driven by a purely generative concern, it can be expected to result in a chasm in the interaction of parent and child.

When the survivors finally felt ready to tell their story, it was most often in the context of institutionalized memorializing of the Holocaust. In this context it seems worth noting that a number of the children of the survivors interviewed approached me with a request for a copy of the interview so they could learn about their fathers' Holocaust experience.

As in all work based on the recollection of the life lived, it is worthwhile to pause to consider the importance to the storyteller of the nature of the story told. Kotre (1995) noted that, in old age, an increasing element of "myth" may enter the individual's recollections. As an individual is distanced from the actual events and people who made up one's early life, these figures and actions gain historic and heroic proportions. However, for victims of extreme trauma, what is sometimes termed the *narrative myth* is not necessarily the product of a life review. Rather, the "myth" may be an extension of an earlier existing "heroic self" that Becker (1973) suggested individuals seek to deny their ultimate, inevitable demise.

For those incarcerated in concentration camps during the Holocaust, death was not a philosophical problem to confront as one engaged in life, but a likely outcome of their immediate circumstances. As noted earlier, it has been suggested (Dasberg, 1987; Dimsdale, 1980) that survivors coped with this overwhelming and immediate prospect by "projecting" themselves into another, more favorable future. The generative self presented by the survivors interviewed for the present study was the product of this search and the vehicle to a future that had within it the seeds of eternity. The hopes, acts, and memories of generativity seemed to provide the survivors a reason to live both during and after the Holocaust.

Ironically, the very characteristics of the Holocaust experience responsible for the robust generativity of the survivors were associated with a congenital defect that limited the full expression and enjoyment of that generativity. The focus on generativity as a means to undo part of their personal history may be responsible for the sense that the survivors interviewed here, like those interviewed by Gill (1988), seemed to suffer more than they showed. Although they exhibited remarkable resilience to the attack on their body and spirit and often achieved significant personal and material success, the survivors were unable to alter the one most menacing peril to their happiness and well-being: their past.

REFERENCES

Aleksandrowicz, D. (1973). Children of concentration camp survivors. In E. Anthony & C. Koupernik (Eds.), *The child and his family* (pp. 385–392). New York: Wiley.

American Psychiatric Association. (1994). *Diagnostic and statistical manual of mental disorders* (4th ed.). Washington, DC: Author.

Bakan, D. (1966). *The duality of human existence: Isolation and communion in Western man.* Boston: Beacon Press.

Becker, E. (1973). *The denial of death.* New York: Free Press.

Bergmann, M., & Jucovy, M. (Eds.). (1982). *Generations of the Holocaust* (pp. 287–310). New York: Basic Books.

Brenner, R. (1980). *The faith and doubt of Holocaust survivors.* New York: Free Press.

Charney, I. (Ed.). (1992). *Holding on to humanity—the message of the Holocaust survivors: The Shamai Davidson Papers.* New York: New York University Press.

Chodoff, P. (1986). Survivors of the Nazi Holocaust. In R. Moos (Ed.), *Coping with life crisis: An integrated approach* (pp. 407–414). New York: Plenum Press.

Dasberg, H. (1987). Psychological distress of Holocaust survivors and offspring in Israel, forty years later: A review. *Israel Journal of Psychiatry and Related Sciences, 24,* 243–256.

Eaton, W., Sigal, J., & Weinfeld, M. (1982). Impairment in Holocaust survivors after 33 years: Data from an unbiased community sample. *American Journal of Psychiatry, 139,* 773–781.

Erikson, E. (1963). *Childhood and society.* New York: Norton.

Gill, A. (1988). *The journey back from hell: Conversations with concentration camp survivors. An oral history.* New York: Avon Books.

Harel, Z. (1983). Coping with stress and adaptation: The impact of the Holocaust on survivors. *Social Welfare, 5,* 221–230.

Helmreich, W. (1992). *Against all odds: Holocaust survivors and the successful lives they made in America.* New York: Simon & Schuster.

Hoppe, K. (1984). Severed ties. In S. Luel & P. Marans (Eds.), *Psychoanalytic reflections on the Holocaust: Selected essays* (pp. 95–112). New York: KTAV.

Kay, A. (1995). *Genocide and generativity: The effects of the Holocaust experience on generativity.* Unpublished doctoral dissertation, Northwestern University, Evanston, IL.

Klein, H. (1973). Children of the Holocaust: Mourning and bereavement. *Yearbook of the International Association for Child Psychiatry and Allied Professions, 2,* 393–410.

Kohn Dor-shav, N. (1978). On the long-range effects of concentration camp internment on Nazi victims. *Journal of Consulting and Clinical Psychology, 46,* 1–11.

Kotre, J. (1984). *Outliving the self: Generativity and the interpretation of lives.* Baltimore: The Johns Hopkins University Press.

Kotre, J. (1995). *White gloves: How we create ourselves through memory.* New York: Free Press.

Krystal, H. (Ed.). (1968). *Massive psychic trauma.* New York: International Universities Press.

Langer, L. (1990). *Holocaust testimonies.* New Haven, CT: Yale University Press.

Leon, G., Butcher, J., Kleinman, M., Goldberg, A., & Almagor, M. (1981). Survivors of the Holocaust and their children: Current status and adjustment. *Journal of Personality and Social Psychology, 41,* 503–516.

Lifton, R. (1969). *Boundaries: Psychological man in revolution.* New York: Vintage Press.

Lifton, R. (1988). Understanding the traumatized self: Imagery, symbolization, and transformation. In J. Wilson, Z. Harel, & B. Kahana (Eds.), *Human adaptation to extreme stress: From the Holocaust to Vietnam* (pp. 7–34). New York: Plenum Press.

McAdams, D. (1985). *Power, intimacy and the life story: Personological inquiries into identity.* New York: Guilford Press.

McAdams, D., & de St. Aubin, E. (1992). A theory of generativity and its assessment through self-report, behavioral acts, and narrative themes in autobiography. *Journal of Personality and Social Psychology, 62,* 1003–1015.

McAdams, D., de St. Aubin, E., & Logan, G. (1993). Generativity among young, midlife, and older adults. *Psychology and Aging, 8,* 221–230.

Niederland, W. (1961). The problem of the survivor: The psychiatric evaluation of emotional disorders in survivors of Nazi persecution. *Journal of Hillside Hospital, 10*, 233–247.

Porter, J. (1980). Social-psychological aspects of the Holocaust. In B. Sherwin & S. Ament (Eds.), *Encountering the Holocaust: An interdisciplinary survey* (pp. 189–222). Chicago: Impact Press.

Rabinowitz, D. (1976). *New lives: Survivors of the Holocaust in America.* New York: Knopf.

Rosenberger, L. (1973). Children of survivors. *Yearbook of the International Association for Child Psychiatry and Allied Professions, 2*, 375–378.

Shanan, J., & Shachar, O. (1985). Cognitive and personality functioning of Jewish Holocaust survivors during the midlife transition (46–65) in Israel. *Archives of Psychology, 135*, 275–294.

Sigal, J., & Rakoff, V. (1971). Concentration camp survival: A pilot study and effects on the second generation. *Canadian Psychiatric Association Journal, 16*, 393–397.

Solkoff, N. (1981). Children of survivors of the Nazi Holocaust: A critical review of the literature. *American Journal of Orthopsychiatry, 51*, 29–42.

Terry, J. (1980). The damaging effects of the survivor syndrome. In S. Luel & P. Marans (Eds.), *Psychoanalytic reflections on the Holocaust: Selected essays* (pp. 134–164). New York: KTAV.

Zlotogorski, Z. (1983). Offspring of concentration camp survivors: The relationship of perceptions of family cohesion and adaptability to levels of ego functioning. *Comprehensive Psychiatry, 24*, 345–354.

III

APPLICATIONS: GENERATIVITY IN BIOGRAPHY AND CLINICAL WORK

INTRODUCTION

The four chapters in the final part of this book explore the applications of generativity to understanding individual lives and to intervention strategies that seek to improve human lives. These chapters speak to the uses of generativity within the therapeutic context of healing and in single-case psychobiographies. This part addresses the manifestations, transformations, and rehabilitations of generativity in particular lives experienced within specific contexts.

John Kotre and Kathy B. Kotre consider the possible applications stemming from an understanding of the dynamics surrounding generative *buffers* in "Intergenerational Buffers: 'The Damage Stops Here'" (chapter 11). An intergenerational buffer is an individual who achieves generativity by choosing *not to pass on* a toxic legacy. It is an adult who has suffered from intergenerational damage but decided that "it stops here; it ends with me." The introduction of this new concept to the generativity literature is couched with John Kotre's larger theoretical contributions in two important ways. First, the chapter employs J. Kotre's taxonomy of generativity domains and discusses the existence of buffers in each of the four areas: *biological, parental, technical,* and *cultural.* The chapter authors provide insight for each of these domains concerning the personal resources that allow one to buffer and the very real costs of living the buffer role. Second, the portraits of buffers highlight the *dark side* of generativity, a notion missing in Erikson's writing on the subject but given extensive analysis in J. Kotre's past scholarship. The authors view generativity as an impulse that may be channeled into vice as well as virtue. Buffers have suffered from other persons' generative vices but have themselves achieved generative virtue by terminating the negative legacy passed on to them.

Ed de St. Aubin finds plenty of evidence of both generative virtue and generative vice in "Truth Against the World: A Psychobiographical

Exploration of Generativity In the Life of Frank Lloyd Wright" (chapter 12). This chapter continues the rich tradition of employing psychobiography to articulate, explore, and construct generativity theory. The life of the architect Frank Lloyd Wright (1867–1959) is ideal for a psychobiographic exploration into generativity because it both illuminates existing theory and leads to further theory development. De St. Aubin offers analyses of the three life domains in which Wright was afforded the opportunity to influence, care for, and contribute to younger generations: *architecture*, *fatherhood*, and the *fellowship* he established to pass on his ideas and techniques to younger apprentices. In examining the architecture domain, de St. Aubin contends that the evolution of Wright's design patterns speaks to the development of generative content during adulthood. The actual forms and patterns of his architecture capture the maturation of his generative concerns. De St. Aubin discusses the dynamics involved in the maturation of generativity as evidenced in the evolution of Wright's architecture.

A second psychobiographic assessment of generativity is furnished by Susan A. Lee in "Generativity and the Life Course of Martha Graham" (chapter 13). The life of Martha Graham (1894–1991), the great modern dancer, is replete with examples of the contextualized nature of generativity and the generative tensions that are inherent in the life of a creator. The dominant context of Graham's generativity was the *world of dance*, where the generative products one creates for others to enjoy are ephemeral performances that by their very nature do not exist beyond the immediate time frame. Lee explains Graham's initial reluctance to allow her dance to be filmed—film is the one medium through which current generations benefit directly from Graham's legacy. The dance world is unique in other ways as well (e.g., its emphasis on youth and physical prowess), and Lee details the form of generativity that Graham exhibited in this context. The author captures the complex generative tensions within Graham's *mentoring efforts*. Hundreds of dancers who studied under Graham evolved into world-class performers and choreographers, yet Graham was far from a purely altruistic mentor. She could not "let go" of her favorite dance roles and refused to let others perform these. Lee pulls from the writing of other generativity scholars to demonstrate that the *dark side* of Graham's generativity resulted from the tensions between her *communal* efforts to pass on a form of movement and her *agentic* strivings, which led to an egotistical control and hoarding of her generative products.

The final chapter of the book, called "Family Generativity and Generative Counseling: Helping Families Keep Faith With the Next Generation" (chapter 14), is by David C. Dollahite, Brent D. Slife, and Alan J. Hawkins. These authors both extend generativity theory and apply generativity scholarship to the therapeutic context with the introduction of two concepts: *family generativity* and *generative counseling*. The authors are careful to provide a solid philosophical foundation for the practical techniques they hope counselors will begin to employ in working to improve the generative lives of adult clients. The six core concepts that undergird family generativity and generative counseling are *holism* (sustaining generative connections), *morality* (keeping generative commitments), *capability* (developing generative capabilities), *temporality* (initiating generative changes), *agency* (making generative choices), and *spirituality* (maintaining generative convictions). Dollahite, Slife, and Hawkins supply specific counseling applications for each of these concepts and argue convincingly that the gestalt that emerges, generative counseling, is superior to the medical model that informs so much of current psychotherapy.

11

INTERGENERATIONAL BUFFERS: "THE DAMAGE STOPS HERE"

JOHN KOTRE AND KATHY B. KOTRE

There is a paradoxical aspect to generativity that was once articulated powerfully for a television audience by a woman near death from AIDS. She had already lost her husband to the disease, and she had little time left. However, she drew a great deal of strength from knowing that when she died, the HIV virus would die with her. There would be a little less of it in the world. The damage, and the sequence of injustice that brought it to her, would not be passed on.

Many people—probably more than one imagines—receive a crippling or even life-threatening legacy from the past, absorb it, and try to live so that none of it infects others. Some parents who suffered terrible forms of abuse as children, for example, insist that what happened to them will never happen to their offspring. These people, like the woman dying from AIDS, strike us as possessing many of the seven features of generativity described by McAdams and de St. Aubin (1992). At the very least they show generative concern, commitment, and action. Paradoxically, they express a good deal of their generativity by *not* passing something on to others. Although they themselves may bear scars, they say of a sequence of intergenerational damage, "It stops here. It ends with me." These individuals, serve as what we have termed *intergenerational buffers*.

In this chapter we introduce a new concept, that of buffering, to the growing discourse on generativity. Our hope is that the concept will be researched in academic settings and applied, when appropriate, in clinical ones. The possibility of application is particularly intriguing. In the literature so far, a few researchers have identified a generative dimension in midlife transitions: Levinson (1978) spoke of "creating a legacy"; Kotre (1984, 1996) and Snarey (1993) told of "reworking a heritage"; and McAdams (1985) wrote of "rewriting a generativity script." A few articles recently have appeared that include considerations of generativity in descriptions of therapeutic intervention (e.g., Kleinberg, 1995; Shane & Shane, 1995). As issues of generativity receive greater attention in therapy, the concept of buffering may prove to be quite beneficial. It may also prove helpful outside the clinic, assisting in the understanding of cultural and historical change.

Our approach is built around the four types (or domains) of generativity outlined by Kotre (1984, 1996) in *Outliving the Self*: biological, parental, technical, and cultural. This typology has been employed with one adaptation—the collapsing of technical and cultural generativity into a single category—by Snarey (1993) in his intergenerational study of fathering. With a different adaptation—the positing of a fifth category of universal generativity—it is used by Kay in his study of Holocaust survivors (chapter 10, this volume). Parts of the typology have also been used to interpret significant, self-defining moments in the lives of teachers (Weber, 1990) and to discuss the quest for "personal redemption" in later life (Manheimer, 1995).

Biological generativity refers to the begetting, bearing, and nursing of children—the passing on of living substance (genes, blood, milk) from one generation to the next. *Parental* generativity involves the rearing of children and their initiation into a family's traditions. It is distinct from biological generativity because people sometimes raise children who are not their genetic offspring. *Technical* generativity is expressed in the teaching of skills and techniques: how to read, how to repair a car, how to perform a healing ritual, how to write a legal brief, and so on. *Cultural* generativity, the fourth type, refers to the conservation, renovation, or creation of collective meaning systems, be those systems religious, artistic, ideological, scientific, or commonsensical (Geertz, 1973). A meaning system may be thought of as the "mind" of a culture, just as related skills, techniques, and rituals may be considered its "body." Although they are conceptually distinct, "mind and body" are nearly always passed on in tandem. In telling someone "how to do it" (technical generativity), one also teaches her or him "what it means" (cultural generativity).

What follows are the stories of individuals who have buffered in each of the four domains of generativity. In these accounts we focus on processes of discovery, definition, and intervention; we comment on resources that helped the person to be a buffer; and we explore the cost of living that role. Following the presentation of the stories, we discuss the practical side of interpreting an experience as buffering. At what point in therapy is such an interpretation best introduced? Are there times when a person's experience cannot bear such an interpretation? How do people deal with the recognition, on the one hand, that they have failed to buffer and, on the other, that the time has come to cease buffering? The "dark side" of generational continuity has often been neglected in research, although history bears ample witness to its power (Kotre, 1995). Our objective throughout this chapter is to demonstrate that one expresses generativity when stopping the propagation of this dark side.

BIOLOGICAL GENERATIVITY

Biological generativity refers to the passing on of living substance from one generation to the next; its target of concern is not only what is conceived—the growing fetus, the newborn—but also one's genetic line. The example involving AIDS at the outset of this chapter brings out, for one person, the meaning of arresting the spread of biologically infectious material. The story we present here is analogous, although the material involved is not a virus but defective genes. The people involved were brought to our attention by a genetics counselor and interviewed by one of the authors (J. Kotre).

A young couple, whom we will call Karen and Don, wanted to start a family but were troubled by a puzzling coincidence. A few years before, Don's sister had given birth to a daughter with abnormalities that matched a pattern in Don's younger brother: a heart defect, a double thumb, a club foot, and severe mental retardation. One child like this in the family could be attributed to "accident" or "fate," thought the couple, but two could not. Karen and Don went to a human genetics clinic and began a process of *discovery*. With the help of a counselor, they constructed a family tree (called a *pedigree*), identified potential carriers of the disorder in Don's family, and persuaded these family members to get a blood test. Don's test confirmed the young couple's worst fear: He was a carrier of the disorder, and potential children were at risk.

The disorder in question was a chromosomal translocation. At some point in Don's genetic past, a piece of one chromosome had broken off and become attached to another chromosome. Copies of the misplaced material had been passed on for generations in his family, manifesting themselves from time to time in abnormalities like those suffered by his younger brother and niece.

The impact of these discoveries on Don's family was profound. When blood testing revealed that his mother was not a carrier, she was relieved of a burden of guilt she had secretly carried for years. She had always thought that she was the cause of her son's and her granddaughter's abnormalities. The same information implicated Don's father; his reaction to the news can be gauged by his refusal to have a blood test. Don's sister, who had just given birth to a normal child, had a tubal ligation. Don himself fell into a guilty silence. Not only was he the carrier of a genetic defect, but he was also disappointing his wife, who desperately wanted to have a baby. He thought of artificial insemination, rejected the idea, and came close to abandoning altogether the idea of having children. Then, suddenly and surprisingly, after the couple began to look into adoption, Karen discovered she was pregnant. (The two had also been having problems with infertility.) When she came to this part of her story, Karen's words were ominous: "You just never think it's going to happen to you."

Now the process of discovery was extended one generation down, as Karen underwent amniocentesis to determine the status of her unborn fetus. Along with discovery there occurred a process of *definition*: In this case "damage" would be considered to exist if her child had the same pattern of problems that existed in the afflicted members of Don's family. Definition is important because in matters of buffering people often make different and even conflicting judgments. Karen's mother provides an example. She would not tolerate an abortion. According to Karen, "She kept saying, 'There is no way that you will terminate your pregnancy if you get bad news. There is just no way.' She didn't tell anyone I was pregnant." To an opponent of abortion, "damage" is not a child with an abnormality but the ending of fetal life. One who buffers damage in one domain and from one point of view, therefore, may inflict it in and from another.

A process of *intervention* began for Karen and Don when amniocentesis revealed that theirs was to be a child with severe abnormalities. "Maybe I should go ahead and have the child," Karen remembered thinking, "because it could be the only one I'll ever have." However, the couple had already decided under what conditions they would terminate the pregnancy: "If the fetus had been a carrier, then we were going to go ahead and go full term and have the child. But we did not want to have a child that we knew would have physical deformities and be mentally retarded." They had to inform their families of their intentions, including Karen's mother. "When we called and said, 'It's bad news, and I'm terminating the pregnancy,' she just couldn't believe it."

Karen's abortion was no easy matter for her. "It's not like I just lost the baby; I had a miscarriage. I willfully went in and terminated a pregnancy, and it was hard for people to deal with it. Some people think it was the kind of thing . . . you go in and you're knocked out and you wake up and you're not pregnant anymore. And that's not the way it was at all.

They induced labor, and I was in labor for 10 hours and I delivered a child. I was awake. My mother called to find out how I was doing afterwards but then dropped the subject. When I went back to work, everyone acted like things should be normal, like nothing had ever happened, and I was definitely mourning."

The experience left Karen more determined than ever to have a baby. She and Don talked again of artificial insemination, but Don knew he could not accept a child that his wife had conceived through that process. Karen had corrective surgery to help her become pregnant and began taking fertility drugs. Three months later, she conceived once again. "Although the odds were that it wouldn't happen again, we were very, very reserved," she said. "I never thought past the amniocentesis. It was: I'm not going to buy any baby clothes. I'm not going to get a crib. I'm not going to do anything until I know everything is okay." They got the results from amniocentesis on a memorable Friday morning. "The phone rang," said Karen, "and when I talked to the nurse, I tried to read into her voice whether it was good or bad. And she said, 'I've got good news. Everything is fine.' The baby was not even a carrier. And then I asked the sex. I thought if any human being knows, then I'm going to know. So we found out it was a boy. We started planning and we started coming up with names. When he was born, they took a blood sample and double-checked. He was perfectly normal."

Karen later gave birth to another child, a girl whom they knew would be a carrier of the family's genetic defect, although she herself would not be affected. One of their reasons for going through with the pregnancy was a belief that advances in genetic medicine would give their daughter far more reproductive options, when she became an adult. They were surely correct in this assumption; the technique of amniocentesis has already been augmented by that of chorionic villus sampling, which can provide genetic information about a fetus in the first trimester of pregnancy rather than the second. Still in the experimental stage is preimplantation diagnosis (Emery & Mueller, 1992; Handyside, Lesko, Tarin, Winston, & Hughes, 1992), which is done just a few days after insemination. A mature egg is fertilized with sperm in vitro and allowed to develop to the four- to eight-cell stage. One or two cells are then removed and examined (the loss of the cells apparently has no effect on later development). If no defects are found, the embryo is subsequently implanted in the mother's uterus. No abortion is required if problems are discovered during examination of the cells.

Early in the 21st century, according to Pergament (1990), the human genome will have been completely mapped. Sometime later, devices will be created to scan an individual's entire genetic code to see if there are any mutations that will lead to serious health problems. Gene therapy will be performed on embryos. Throughout the next century, the questions that faced Karen and Don as a couple will face all humans. How much do we want to *discover* about our genetic makeup? What will we *define* as damaging within it? And how far will we wish to go when we *intervene* in its workings? It may be well to remember in this larger context what Karen and Don's genetics counselor has learned from dealing with individual clients: "No one really knows how they're going to act on information until they're in the situation where they have to act on it."

In this story, the damage in question was biological and hidden. In the next—an example from the domain of parental generativity—the damage was a family tradition plain for all to see. That made matters of discovery and definition quite different.

PARENTAL GENERATIVITY

"Growing up in my family was pretty scary," said a middle-aged woman who was a client of one of the authors of this chapter (K. Kotre). We identify her as Sandra. Her story illustrates buffering in *parental* generativity: stopping a tradition of damage in the raising of children. It also illustrates what makes "buffering" different from "reworking" (Kotre, 1984, 1996; Snarey, 1993). The term *reworking* is best applied to legacies that are a combination of good and bad, whereas *buffering* is best reserved for those that are purely malignant, here, two abusive parents rather than one.

Sandra's father was a violent man. As a child she would wait each evening to see when he would come home and in what state, attentive to the "messages"—how he pulled into the driveway, how he approached the door—that revealed how drunk he was. "It was my responsibility to read those messages and get everybody out of danger," she recalled. That responsibility was not occasional but a way of life. Sandra remembered the night her father broke an iron skillet with a swing meant for her mother. She recalled the many times she and her younger sisters thought they were going to die—and the one time her father actually said they would: "He was screaming, 'I'm going to kill you all,' and he broke a lamp and cut himself, and he seemed to get real fascinated with his own blood, and he was flipping his arms around, and the blood was splattering all over the walls and all over us." On another occasion, Sandra thought he had killed her mother. During the fight, Sandra had been cowering behind a chair in the corner of the room, her little sister behind her, terrified at the grotesque shadows created by a fallen lamp. Her mother was trying to phone for help, but her father ripped the phone off the wall—it was a heavy, old-fashioned phone—and beat her unconscious. Eventually, an ambulance came and took her mother away. She was pregnant at the time, and Sandra did not know if she was dead or alive.

Horrendous as this legacy was, what Sandra received from her mother may have been more insidious, because it was so deeply internalized. Her mother constantly disparaged Sandra. She was too short, too dark, too coarse, too stupid, too "plain." Sandra remembered being 6 years old and shining her shoes with a sponge applicator. When she got the black polish all over herself, her mother became furious and used a stiff brush to scrub her face with bleach and bathroom cleanser. Once adolescence came along, Sandra's mother repeatedly told her that no boy would ever want her. Her younger sister was attractive; the boys were "hot" for her but not for Sandra. "Maybe there's something wrong with you," her mother would say. Even when her first boyfriend date-raped her, Sandra's mother said she was a fool to "let him get away" because he was from a family who had some status in the community.

Sandra's mother convinced her that she was inadequate, but Sandra, the oldest of four, was in fact the family's "little adult." A memory from the age of 5 has her sitting on the couch with her mother, listening to a tearful litany of complaints, patting her mother on the back and assuring her that everything would be all right. "I was my mother's mentor," she said, looking back from the perspective of middle age. By the age of 12, Sandra was earning money doing laundry, ironing, and housecleaning for neighbors. Often it was she who put food on the table, not either of her parents. If her father became angry, it was Sandra's fault; she, the oldest, had forgotten to put something away or to keep her younger siblings quiet.

Sandra found occasional refuge from all this in a church. When she was in kindergarten, she started going to a Pentecostal gathering with a girl who lived near her grandmother's house. Sandra was white; her friend and the other church members were black. Sandra spoke of the "wild, uninhibited love" in that church, a contrast with the wild, uninhibited violence at home. A gospel passage struck her: "I've prepared for you a room." She thought, "I have a place," a safe place. In the third grade she was baptized at that church. "I ran home the next day after spending the night at my friend's house, and when I went in the door and said, 'Mom, I'm going to get to go to heaven,' she just flipped out. 'How dare you go to that holy roller nigger church and get baptized? How dare you embarrass us like that?' She beat me with a shoe. It was a long time before I went to church with joy again."

When Sandra reached adulthood, there was no need to *discover* a legacy of damage or to *define* it as such. It was evident for anyone to see and judge. That was part of the humiliation: The whole neighborhood had witnessed scenes of vulgarity and violence. *Intervention* began as soon as Sandra had children. She had gotten pregnant right after high school, married the baby's father, and given birth to a little girl. Four years later, she had a second child, a boy. With blind persistence, Sandra worked at being the opposite of her mother, trying to be perfect to keep danger at bay, trying to instill the sense of safety and well-being that she had missed.

"We were always together. I would do special things for them. When I'd make pudding, I'd put it in little cups with little wrappers on top so you peeled off the top. Just motherly things. And learning things—take them to the zoo, take them to museums. I might have overdone it."

As Sandra's two children were growing up, both she and her husband worked hard and spent carefully. They bought a house and took good care of it. Her husband was unaware of what lay in her background; he simply saw her as an intense woman who kept a perfect house. However, as Sandra was approaching 40, he left her for another woman. Many months later, with a divorce imminent, he decided to return. Sandra tried to forgive him, tried not to "fall apart," but the wound was deep. She began to have a variety of physical complaints: stomach pains, severe headaches, sleep-lessness, and fits of uncontrolled crying. When she was promoted at work and given extensive new responsibilities, she began to have panic attacks in which she would "check out" or "float away," dissociating the way she had as a child. At this point she sought counseling. "I figured I was going to die if I didn't get help." Her diagnosis was complex, including posttrau-matic stress syndrome and depression. After a few weeks of treatment, the depression began to lift and her anxiety became manageable. However, she remembered little of her childhood, certainly none of the events recounted here. She generalized and made sweeping evaluative statements, but she did not recall specific episodes of abuse.

Now Sandra began a different kind of *discovery*, in the form of recov-ering memories and trying to authenticate them. With her husband at her side, she revisited the apartment of her childhood. As memories came to the surface, she made connections. She always had to sleep curled up and facing a wall, with a pillow at her back. Now she knew why: It was a position to protect against a nighttime beating. She connected the feeling of dissociation at work with the feeling in her memory, and she understood why the feeling came back. She questioned her mother, divorced now from her father, and learned that the history of abuse in her family went back at least one more generation. Her mother was not only a victimizer; she herself had been a victim.

As this intergenerational perspective was developing, Sandra's ther-apist helped her to see that while she carried the scars of abuse, and prob-ably would for life, she had not passed them on to her children. She had not done what her mother had. This was a cognitive reframing, a redefin-ition of her place in life that had positive effects on Sandra's self-image. It is also the moment that gave birth to the concept of *buffer*.

At first Sandra resisted seeing herself in the suggested role. She thought of all the occasions on which she had not been the "perfect" mother. Over time, however, she began to comprehend what she had ac-complished, what strength of character it took to absorb such badness and give such goodness. She had lived with a sense of dread for her children's future, fearing her mother's prediction: "Some day, you'll get yours. You'll understand what I'm going through." When her children were born, she could not bear to take a first look at them, so sure was she of finding them deformed. Now they were grown, and they had turned out well. How, then, could she be the stupid, inadequate person her mother always said she was?

The realization that she was an intergenerational buffer allowed Sandra to make peace with herself. Her therapy progressed rapidly after that. The religious dimension of her problem was addressed, as was her relationship with her husband. He had seen so much improvement in her that he was willing to participate in the counseling. Sandra was able to make peace with him, and a short time later her therapy came to an end.

Two questions can be asked of Sandra's story and indeed of any story that involves buffering. The first is, what *resources* enabled her to buffer? The second is, what was the *cost* of the buffering? In the case of Karen and Don, the most important resource was their unyielding desire to have a normal baby. The cost was estrangement from Karen's mother and the emotional pain of an abortion. Sandra's first resource was religious faith or, as she said, "Jesus. Finding Jesus very early in my life," referring to her childhood experiences in the Pentecostal church. Other ingredients were a persistent temperament and a keen intelligence, although she never knew she had the latter. Her relationship with her husband, strong enough to survive a serious break, was also a factor; it gave her strength and her children a second parent. From a developmental perspective, however, Sandra's most significant resource may have been that she had been a buffer all her life. "I was the one responsible for getting the children out of danger." Her mother had cast her in that role, but so had her younger siblings: "On scary nights when we weren't sure what was happening, my sister would come in the top bunk and sleep behind me. Because I would be in front of her, she wouldn't have to worry." When Sandra became a parent, her buffering took on an intergenerational character. Now it was her children, not her brothers and sisters, whom she was called on to protect.

The cost of being a buffer all her life was great. Not only did she carry in her person the results of the original damage, but she suffered a developmental loss. "I never really felt like a child. I do not know how to relax and play. I spent all of my 20s and half of my 30s not enjoying life like I should have. I was robbed, really robbed. I can make it up, but I was robbed."

TECHNICAL GENERATIVITY

It happens that in our third and fourth stories, the protagonists do not themselves bear the scars of the original intergenerational damage, as

Sandra did. They witness it in others. The damage is not passed on within families, either biologically or parentally, but in the wider sphere outside the family.

The third story centers on *technical* generativity; it involves skills and techniques—here, medical procedures—that one learns from the previous generation and teaches to the next. The procedures in question are two whose use on women have been significantly curtailed: dilatation and curettage (D&C) and hysterectomy (Keyser, 1988; Mushinski, 1996). These procedures are related: A D&C removes the lining of the uterus, and a hysterectomy removes the uterus itself. For a number of years, the routine treatment for abnormal vaginal bleeding was a D&C. If several D&Cs did not solve the problem, the uterus (and often the ovaries as well) was removed. Thaddeus Zwirkoski was a physician who saw unnecessary risk in these procedures, defined them as damaging when others did not, and found an alternate way to treat his patients. Born of Polish immigrants in Winnipeg, Manitoba, Canada, Zwirkoski was educated at Ottawa Medical School and completed his residency in Detroit. Now 70, he has practiced in the Detroit area all his life. He was interviewed by both of this chapter's authors.

The roots of this story go back to Dr. Zwirkoski's reasons for becoming a gynecologist in the first place. He had what he called a "close heart" to women. "My mother was sick since I was 3 or 4 years old. My sister suffered from a lot of menstrual cramps. I was a few years younger than she was, and I didn't understand why she was having troubles." Because he did not understand such things, he talked to women about them, a theme that runs through his entire narration. One of the many part-time jobs he took to help pay his school expenses was singing at parties. When there was a break, "instead of talking with the men, I sat and talked with the women. I wanted to know how married people react, why women were complaining. Is it fact? Is it fiction? Are they making it up?" He had "platonic relationships" with his girlfriends, having vowed not to marry until he became a specialist; he talked with them about their experience of being female. From early on, he educated himself by communicating with his future patient population, and he believed what they told him. In particular, he believed what they told him about their monthly cycles.

This self-education may be seen as part of a process of *discovery*. It continued in medical school. Because the European professors there were strict and uncommunicative, Zwirkoski became the "question box," asking what other students were reluctant to bring up. When he wanted to learn more about endocrinology, he took extra courses, connecting what he was learning there with what he was learning from conversations with women. Even before his clinical years, he was making trips to the operating room to observe technique.

Early in his clinical training, Zwirkoski began to question some standard practices, in particular the automatic use of the D&C. In a D&C, the lining of the uterus is scraped off—this is the "curettage"—and examined for signs of polyps, fibroids, and other abnormalities. Although its purpose is diagnostic, in the 1950s it was also being used as a form of treatment, to stop excessive bleeding. The procedure was expedient and financially rewarding. In Dr. Zwirkoski's emerging view, however, it did not address the root cause of most abnormal bleeding, which was hormone imbalance. No one, he recalled, was trying to regulate the endocrine system. No one was taking the time to talk to patients. After 3 to 6 months, many of the women who had had D&Cs were again bleeding excessively.

As a resident, Zwirkoski came to *define* what he was being taught as poor technique. Few agreed with him. "I used to argue with doctors. I couldn't figure out why nothing else was done for the woman." The technique was more than poor; it had the potential for damage. There was the risk of a perforated uterus, as well as the risk associated with any procedure that required anesthesia. In Zwirkoski's view, a D&C was "totally unnecessary because the problem could have been corrected by communication with the patient and by medication."

At the time Zwirkoski was turning 30 and he was developing an alternative approach: using natural hormones to correct imbalances. He had found several local doctors who took that approach and he learned from them. What they were doing proved to be compatible with his own study of endocrinology and with the knowledge he had gathered from talking to women. However, as a resident, his ability to *intervene* was limited. He was not the final authority in matters of patient care, and the hospital's pharmacy did not carry the medications he would require. "When I got into private practice, I did it my way." He began his own practice in 1958, when he was 32 years old. What enabled him to buffer from the very beginning—what was a primary *resource*—was the alternate approach (and hence the identity) that he had already established. At the age of 32 there was no doubt in his mind. He knew himself to be a doctor who listened closely to his female patients, gave them knowledge about their bodies, and used hormone replacement as a first line of treatment. He was "Doctor Z."

D&Cs were in their heyday when he began to practice. "I would do 1 a week, and the other guy would do 10, 15, 20." Zwirkoski's D&Cs were limited to cases in which there were other than hormonal causes. When he was in a position to supervise residents, he preached the benefits of hormone replacement therapy and, more important, of communication. "I don't think there's 1 or 2% of doctors who believe their primary function is to give their patients knowledge and remove fear." When there was no choice but to do a hysterectomy, he would remove the uterus but not the ovaries. "I had a lot of problems with residents and even surgeons who did not respect tissue. The residents would start putting their clamps on and grabbing stuff, and I'd say, 'Who told you we were taking out the ovaries?'" The answer was always that the patient might get ovarian cancer when she was older. "So I said, 'Fine, if you think that way, why don't you get your testicles removed because you might get cancer of the testes? It may not be as common, but you're still at risk.'"

Zwirkoski wanted to keep the ovaries intact because of their role in the endocrine system. He received confirmation of his approach when his patients told him it worked and when he was often called on to treat the casualties of other approaches, "castrated" women, he called some of them. Added confidence in his definition of damage and his ability to repair it strengthened his buffering and kept him on an independent course. When birth control pills came out in the 1960s, he would not prescribe them until the size of the doses came down. Even then he would not use them for hormonal regulation. Although the pill form made them convenient for that purpose (natural hormones required injections), he was cautious about using synthetic hormones. Later, when fetal monitoring became routinely available, he objected to the "skyrocketing" rates of caesarean sections to which it led. He objected all along to dismissing postpartum depression and what is now known as premenstral syndrome (PMS) as problems that were merely "in the head." He treated postmenopausal women long before the replacement of estrogen for such women was considered routine.

Zwirkoski's buffering entered the realm of generativity when he became a teacher of residents. However, he was not out to change medical practice on a wider basis: "I figured I was doing better for my patients than other people would, but I couldn't change society." Talking about hormone replacement at conferences was like "talking to air." To have the credibility he needed, he said, he would have had to teach and conduct research at a medical school. "But I have to be with people. People to me are better than any book. And I read many books every day through people." Besides, he was suspicious of academicians who did not have personal knowledge of how hormones affect both mind and body. "You think the guy that's got all the degrees knows everything. He knows baloney because he doesn't know how to talk to a woman."

At 70, Dr. Zwirkoski has had the satisfaction of seeing academic research support a number of the stands he had taken earlier in his career. He has seen a decline in the use of the techniques he once warned against: Both D&C and hysterectomy now require extensive, documented justification. He has not, however, seen a corresponding rise in the number of physicians practicing hormonal regulation. Medical students are not being taught enough endocrinology, he said. Besides, his approach takes time: time, in some cases, to learn what is happening to a woman almost every day and then to explain it to her. This is one reason his approach is not more widespread. "Ninety percent of the time, it's too much work." The time-consuming nature of his approach is one of the *costs* Dr. Zwirkoski has borne, although cost was rarely mentioned in his narrative. When pressed, he spoke of patients he had lost because he would not do "convenience" hysterectomies and of "hassles" with his peers, but that was all. Had he lost income by doing far fewer surgeries than others? "I didn't go into medicine for money."

It is clear from this story that one does not buffer in the realm of technical generativity without getting into the realm of cultural generativity—into issues of meaning, value, and (in this case) scientific theory. As Dr. Zwirkoski tried to teach his residents, "there's more to medicine than just surgery or lab tests." Convictions about the place of women, the place of patients, and the place of income provided a background for his generativity, offering what McAdams (1985) has called an ideological setting. Another part of the background was provided by hypotheses about the functioning of the human body. In the next case, culture comes out of the background and into the fore, where it becomes the direct target of buffering. The buffering did not extend throughout a career, as it did in the case of Dr. Zwirkoski; it occurred, rather, at a particular historical moment.

CULTURAL GENERATIVITY

The fourth type of generativity, *cultural*, refers to the conserving, renovating, or creating of a meaning system: the "mind" of a culture as opposed to its "body." In practice, mind and body are virtually inseparable, as we noted in the case of Dr. Zwirkoski and as our final story illustrates. In the 1960s the Catholic church reconsidered its stance on birth control, primarily with regard to the newly developed pill but also with reference to any "artificial" technique. The concrete "how to's" of contraception were inextricably tied to abstract conceptions of religion, law, ethics, history, and institutional self-definition. Technique was tied to a collective "mind" that had perdured for centuries.

A participant in the process of reconsideration, one of the few women involved, was Patty Crowley. The subject of a biography by John Kotre (1979; see also McClory, 1995), she was reinterviewed by him for the present chapter. Although she would not have phrased it as such, she served in the role of intergenerational buffer. Patty and her husband Pat, now deceased, were asked to serve on the Special Study Group on Population and Birth Control convened by Pope Paul VI in 1964. Popularly known as the birth control commission, the group was assigned the task of looking into the matter of contraception, so that the pope, "supported by the light of human science," might decide on its morality. The church was already on record as being opposed to contraception; in the view of

Catholic conservatives, it had spoken infallibly and its stand could not be reversed. However, the opening of the Second Vatican Council in 1963 had led many Catholics to wonder whether this "infallible" teaching could be—indeed, would be—changed.

The Crowleys were in their early 50s when they were asked to serve on the birth control commission. They never knew why they had been selected, although the most likely reason was their leadership of the Christian Family Movement (CFM), an international organization of Catholic laypersons that they had founded almost two decades before. All the other members of the commission were experts of one kind or another: demographers, economists, sociologists, psychiatrists, gynecologists, philosophers, and theologians. The Crowleys were one of three married couples present; Patty was one of five women (out of a total of 57 delegates). Although no one realized it at the time, all three of the married women were incapable of bearing children. When they received the invitation to sit on the commission, the Crowleys were unquestioning believers in the church's traditional teaching. They had never practiced birth control in their marriage and had had no need to: After the birth of their fourth child, Patty had been left sterile by a near-fatal episode of hemorrhaging. Unlike other intergenerational buffers, she herself had borne few, if any, of the effects of the legacy in question.

Because they were the only nonexperts on the commission, the Crowleys decided that their role was to speak for "plain married couples." They began the process of *discovery* by undertaking, with the help of a sociologist, several surveys of CFM membership and by placing a request in the Catholic press for readers to mail in their comments about the church-approved rhythm method. What the Crowleys discovered about cultural damage overwhelmed them. The general attitude of some 3,000 responding couples from 18 countries was one of controlled frustration. What truly moved Patty, and changed her *definition* of damage, were the "awful stories" that came in the mail, such as the following:

> The maintenance of temperature charts is much too awkward in the social environment of the average Indian home. Where a number of people live and sleep together in one room, a couple have often to choose a late hour at night or a very early hour at morning—say 1 or 2 a.m.—for the conjugal relationship, at a time when everyone else is fast asleep. (Kotre, 1979, p. 95)
>
> I am on the verge of a nervous breakdown with worry, and my doctor also tells me that it would be unwise to have more children. My husband suffers from colitis, which is a nervous disorder aggravated by continual worry of this immense problem. Total abstinence, is this our only answer? Does the Church approve of this state? If so, we will accept its ruling. (Kotre, 1979, p. 94)
>
> My husband has a terrible weakness when it comes to self-control

in sex and unless his demands are met in every way when he feels this way, he is a very dangerous man to me and my daughters. Apart from these times he is completely normal and tries in every way he knows, such as morning Mass, sacraments, prayers, etc., to accumulate grace. (McClory, 1995, p. 91)

Following my 3rd pregnancy in 2 years I almost smothered the baby with a pillow because I couldn't stand its crying. Now in a few years we will have to abstain entirely, perhaps for years, when I become more irregular due to menopause. I am very depressed and becoming more so. What will another baby do to me at this age? (Kotre, 1979, p. 97)

It was patent that the writers of these "awful stories" were not ordinary Catholics but among the most devout. Like 78% of those in the surveys at large, they believed that the church should change its position. It was also clear that most of the story writers were women. How could the Crowleys bring their voice—the voice of sexual females—into the celibate male bastion of Rome?

The Crowleys sent copies of the letters they had received to other commission delegates in the United States and Canada and to the commission secretary in Rome in the hope that they would eventually reach the pope. At a meeting of the commission in April of 1966, the second meeting they had attended, Patty realized that the time for her *intervention* had come. However, she was still in awe of her surroundings. "Here were all these learned men from all over the world," she remembered. "My inclination would have been to say little and sit down. But I had come a long way at that point" (McClory, 1995, p. 102). When the women present were asked to address the assembly, Patty presented "A Woman's Viewpoint." "Is rhythm unnatural?" she asked. "Yes," she answered. She read excerpts from the letters she and Pat had received. "No amount of theory by men will convince women that this way of making and expressing love is natural," she said in conclusion. "We think it is time for a change" (Kotre, 1979, p. 99).

The work of the panel concluded in early June of 1966 with a report calling for change. It was endorsed, according to some sources, by a vote of 52 to 4. The Crowleys left Rome with a peaceful feeling that an immense amount of work had borne fruit, indeed that they had helped to make history. All that remained was an official proclamation from the pope.

What the Crowleys did not know, however, was that conservative forces connected with the commission were working behind the scenes to undo its work. These members had already written a minority report to stand against the majority report. For several years Paul VI agonized over a decision. Then, on July 29, 1968, he announced his conclusion in the encyclical *Humanae Vitae*: The church would not change its position. The Crowleys did not learn of the pope's declaration until a reporter called them at 4 o'clock in the morning to ask for their comments. They were stunned, incredulous. Within a few weeks they had joined 200 Catholic scholars in signing a statement that took exception to the encyclical and encouraged Catholics to decide for themselves.

Now the Crowleys began to bear the *cost* of being buffers. Even before the release of the encyclical, they had tried to share their enthusiasm about the commission's conclusions with a priest who had been their longtime mentor; he reprimanded them and said only, "We'll wait and see what the pope says." After their public stand in opposition to the encyclical, they were cut off from him and from many in the church hierarchy who had been friends, supporters, and guides of the CFM. That movement, their "baby," began to lose momentum as married couples became disillusioned with the Catholic church in general. Today CFM is a fraction of its original size and in the hands of leaders who blame the Crowleys' refusal to accept *Humanae Vitae* for its decline. "I get frustrated when I see what's happened to CFM," said Patty, 25 years later, adding, "I guess I'm a little bitter. No priest ever talked to me about *Humanae Vitae*. No one ever discussed what we had done or why it turned out the way it did. No one asked how we felt. We never even got a letter of thanks from the Vatican" (McClory, 1995, p. 164). The stony silence in the wake of the encyclical extended even to their fellow commissioners, with whom the Crowleys lost contact. Three years after the appearance of the encyclical, Pat was diagnosed with cancer; he died in 1974. Said Patty in retrospect, "If Pat and I hadn't had each other, we could never have made it through this period" (McClory, 1995, p. 165). Her relationship with her husband was one of her primary *resources*. In 1995 Patty Crowley was still a loyal Catholic and active in her parish. "No one is going to kick me out," she said, although the emotional scars of the commission's aftermath were still with her.

The major source of conflict throughout the Crowleys' experience on the birth control commission was over the definition of damage: Church conservatives did not see it the way the Crowleys and the other members of the commission did. The former were concerned about damage to a tradition of papal infallibility, the other about damage to married couples. The commission was effective, however, in stopping the damage it saw. It effected change not in the official culture of Catholicism but in its unofficial, popular culture. The fact that a commission was created in the first place had set U.S. Catholics of a particular generation thinking: why would the pope convene such a group if the rule was not revocable? The fact that the commission subsequently recommended a change furthered their thinking. By the time Pius VI made his official proclamation in 1968, it was too late. The majority of Catholics in the United States had made up their mind, not only to practice unapproved forms of contraception but also to reconsider their view of the pope, their definition of the church, and in some cases, their affiliation with it. It was a profound cultural shift.

When one serves as a buffer in the transmission of cultural elements, one rarely acts in isolation, simply because the extent of a culture is so vast and its adherents so many. Rarely does cultural change center in one person, as it did in the cases of the famous persons—Martin Luther and Mahatma Gandhi—who were the subjects of Erikson's biographies (Erikson, 1958, 1969). The Crowleys were not the figureheads that Luther and Gandhi were; they were not even principal players on the commission. Perhaps more than any other commission member, however, they were deeply in touch with the suffering caused by the church's rule on contraception. They played a role in stopping the suffering, although not in the way they had planned.

DISCUSSION

It should be clear from this chapter that we see the removal of a particular moral prohibition from intergenerational transmission in the same light as the removal of a piece of genetic material. There are differences, of course. In one case, one is dealing with an abstract element of culture, and in the other, one is dealing with a concrete element of biology; one case involves the human spirit, and the other, human tissue. However, in both instances a buffer says, "The damage stops here." In both, other people contest the buffer's definition of damage, so moral conflict ensues.

In our presentation of these cases we have attempted to highlight processes of discovery, definition, and intervention. We have also touched on the costs to buffers and the resources that helped them to bear those costs. We have suggested that there are benefits to seeing buffering as a generative act. We should remember, however, that none of the people whose stories we have told used the concept spontaneously in their personal narration. It was only in retrospect that any of them saw their role as buffers, and in only one case, that of Sandra, did the terminology truly make a difference.

Sandra's internalization of the concept is instructive. It occurred within the framework of an existing therapeutic process in which a strong alliance had been formed with a counselor. We believe these conditions are essential to such internalization. Unless a foundation of safety and trust has been established, it is unlikely that a client will reveal the true depth of damage, or the dark side, of his or her experience. It is equally unlikely that the client will integrate into autobiographical memory a generative interpretation of that experience.

Even when a strong therapeutic alliance is present, the concept of buffering cannot simply be "dropped into" a client's life story. Such a profound shift in meaning can take place only when the client is processing memories in some depth—the kind of depth that is measured, for example, by the Experiencing Scale (Klein, Mathieu-Coughlan, & Kiesler, 1986). Without deep processing, change may occur in generic memories—scripts, schemas, memory clusters (Barsalou, 1988)—but not in the "self-defining" memories that deal with specific episodes (Singer & Salovey, 1993). Change in the latter is essential. Many people who have suffered damaging early-life experiences have a general awareness of these experiences but no specific recollections of them. Sandra was typical in this regard. During the early stages of her therapy, she could relate generic memories and the meanings she attached to them, but she had little access to the concrete events from which she derived those meanings. It was only later in therapy that she was able to get in touch with specific incidents and discuss them in relation to their meanings. It is at this point, when specific episodes are being processed at a deep level, that a therapist can best offer an alternate interpretation.

Still, all a therapist can do is offer. Even when conditions lend themselves to introduction of the concept of buffering, it is ultimately the client who determines what meanings his or her narrative will contain. Lehman, Ellard, and Wortman (1986) reported that survivors who found meaning in sudden and irrevocable loss fared better than those who did not. However, that meaning ("It was God's will," for example) could not be imposed from the outside. It was helpful only when the bereaved persons found or created it for themselves. Similarly, a therapist can offer a generative interpretation of damaging life experiences, but that is as far as she or he can go. The rest is up to the client.

Clients respond in different ways to the idea of buffering, and so do people outside of therapy. When the concept was explained to one middle-aged woman, it prompted the realization that she had *failed to buffer*. Sexually abused by her father, she was unable to prevent him from inflicting the same damage on the generation that came after her. What he had done to her she thought of as an "accident," an exception to his true character; she was able to end the abuse gradually, but she never told anyone about it. "I did not face reality in time to prevent abuse to my daughters." It had never occurred to her that they would be at risk.

When one of this woman's daughters was 11, she told her mother that her grandfather had been acting strangely. Another daughter left a paper titled "Grandpa" on the kitchen table.

> The woman said the following: I read, in effect, 'I trusted you and you hurt me.' I knew I had let my daughters down, should have known better, protected them better, asked questions and informed their father of what I knew. I told my daughter I had read her paper, asked her to forgive me for not protecting her, told her I had had enough experience with my father to serve as a warning. And I admitted that I had never told her father, so he had been deprived of the opportunity of protecting her.

For this woman, the impact of her failure to buffer was worse than the damage that she herself had suffered. However, the pattern of abuse in her immediate family stopped, largely because an 11-year-old did what she herself was unable to do. "She did not deny what happened," the woman said. "She did not make excuses, and she did not choose silence." When she became an adult, this same child convinced her mother to tell her husband what had taken place within his family. (The secret had been kept from him.) Although this child let her mother know that the abuse was more severe than she had indicated initially, she has done much to assuage her mother's guilt. "She assured me that I did serve to some degree as a buffer because she knew I would listen and understand," the mother said. "And she pointed out that the power of a grandfather isn't quite as strong and ever present as that of a father." This woman sees her daughter as "the intergenerational buffer I failed to be."

In this case a sequence of intergenerational damage was stopped because the knowledge of it was passed on. Is this a universal feature of buffering: Stop the damage by transmitting the knowledge? Or are there times when the damage is so extreme that even the knowledge of it is crippling? One victim of the Nazi Holocaust began telling her son of her death camp experiences when he was 4. By the time he was a teenager, he was seeing a psychiatrist because of recurring nightmares that were directly related to the stories he had heard. His mother's transmission of knowledge was clearly premature. Sandra waited until her children were in their 20s before beginning to talk about her past. "They can't back up and absorb it now," she said. "They're in the safety zone." This is close to what Sidney Bolkosky, an oral historian of the Holocaust, has stated: The late teens are early enough for the children or grandchildren of surviving victims to hear of their forebears' experience (Bolkosky, personal communication, 1996). At that point it is safe to cease buffering with regard to the knowledge of damage.

Bolkosky (1987) has been recording the stories of Holocaust survivors since 1981. Before that time, hardly any survivors spoke of their experiences, except to each other. There were a number of reasons for their silence. As immigrants to the United States, many were told to forget about the past and start afresh. One of them recalled going on a trip to see his cousin in California. He had just gotten off the plane when his cousin said, "I don't want to hear about it. I don't want to know what happened. I've seen the newsreels." Language was another problem, not because of the difficulty of translating into English, but because common, easily translatable words (e.g., bunk, cold) had such different reference points in and outside a concentration camp (Langer, 1991). In addition, there was the pain and the abject humiliation to which survivors had been subjected and the awful choices some were forced to make. There was the desire to protect their children and, later, the fear that their children, like everyone else, would not understand.

In about 1980, the silence began to break. A popular television series on the Holocaust that was aired in 1978 and a massive gathering of surviving victims in Jerusalem in 1981 provided a cultural impetus. Survivors themselves were also getting ready to talk. They were aging; it was now or never. Their children, now adults, were old enough to hear; the buffering could cease. Many survivors made audio or video recordings in which they told of their experiences, and they continue to do so. "So it will never happen again," they say, or "to defeat the Holocaust deniers"; in other words, so the damage will stop. However, Bolkosky believes that "never again" is not the real reason survivors speak: It is because the events themselves were so compelling, because the Holocaust was the most significant thing that happened to them, because their history was a part of the world's history. As they neared the end of their life, they could not *not* speak, and they found various ways of speaking. One woman made an audiotape of her experiences and went for a walk while her children listened to it. They were stunned. They had not even known that she was a victim (personal communication, 1996).

Each new case makes one sensitive not only to differences of kind in buffering but also to differences of degree. Some individuals have suffered more than others at the hands of previous generations; some have blocked the transmission of damage more completely; some have paid a higher price to do so. Some have had experiences that were so humiliating and so devastating that they cannot, from the inside, sustain a definition of buffering.

Although he did not employ the concept of buffering in his study of Holocaust testimonies, Langer (1991) brought out the difference between inside and outside perspectives on trauma. From the inside, he noted, in the depths of "unheroic" memory, the victim often feels the concentration camp experience is unredeemable, devoid of meaning, and impossible to restore to generational continuity. Much as an outsider, or even a loved one, might wish it otherwise, no generativity is possible. (Impossible also, we might add, is the consolation of seeing oneself as a buffer.) However, interviewers—outsiders—often try to redeem the experience, give it meaning, and restore it to the flow of generations.

Langer (1991) provided many illustrations of the contrast between internal and external points of view. In one taped segment he observed two interviewers attempting to make a heroine of a former victim, telling her that she had survived through pluck and guts. She said no, it was through luck and sheer stupidity. The interviewers could not comprehend and could not reconcile their perspective with hers, and the interview seemed to end, said Langer, "with the defeat of the witness, or at least of her language" (p. 63). Another interviewer told a survivor, "You are one of the greatest optimists I've ever met" (p. 59)—just after the victim spoke of the harsh truths she knows in her deepest being, of her complete lack of faith in humans, of her extreme pessimism. This interview ended, too, with unreconciled perspectives. Even children who grew up in the homes of surviving victims find it difficult to bridge the gap. The adult daughter of one couple said that her parents' ordeal has left her with strength and a sense of connection with a rich Jewish heritage. Her parents, however, who from her perspective are the very channels of strength and connection, have no sense of being so. What have they been left with? "Loneliness," said the mother. "As long as we live, we are lonely." Said the father: "Nothing to say. Sad" (p. ix).

An awareness of differences in perspective should accompany any attempt to interpret another's experience as buffering. The risk in employing the concept is that a person's experience may not be able to bear it, that he or she will not be understood. Its use may reflect the inability of outsiders to hear what lies beyond normal human boundaries. Some of life's happenings are so abject that the insider believes he or she can never recross the boundary and reenter the flow of generational continuity, not even under the rubric of buffering.

Will a given individual benefit from seeing a damaging life experience as buffering? It is a matter of case-by-case judgment. The work of Kay (chapter 10, this volume) offers a different picture of concentration camp survivors than does Langer; his participants might well profit from such an interpretation, whereas Langer's might not. However, something more general can be said: If generativity is to emanate from individuals who have had damaging experiences, something akin to buffering must work its way into their conceptual framework. McAdams, Hart, and Maruna (chapter 1, this volume) found that "redemption sequences" characterize the life stories of highly generative adults. To consider oneself a buffer is to locate oneself in the middle of such a sequence, albeit one that extends beyond any individual life. It is an interpretation that appears to fit the narrative inclinations of those striving to be generative.

Although we have leaned in our discussion toward practical applications of the notion of buffering, we do not wish to overlook its theoretical potential. The concept can be used in the analysis of historical change, as in the case of Patty Crowley, and it may prove fruitful in the study of biography and autobiography. Kenyon (personal communication, 1996), for example, suggested an investigation of "biographical buffering"—cases in which people deny access to material about their life, such as by burning personal documents. The principal value of the concept, however, whether on a practical or theoretical level, is that it keeps one alert to generativity's dark side. Buffering deserves a place in our vocabulary if only to honor the price people pay, often silently and sometimes without consolation, to protect future generations.

REFERENCES

Barsalou, S. W. (1988). The content and organization of autobiographical memories. In U. Neisser & E. Winograd (Eds.), *Remembering reconsidered: Ecological and traditional approaches to the study of memory* (pp. 193–243). New York: Cambridge University Press.

Bolkosky, S. (1987). Interviewing victims who survived: Listening for the silences that strike. *Annals of Scholarship, 4,* 33–51.

Emery, A. E., & Mueller, R. F. (1992). *Elements of medical genetics* (8th ed.). Edinburgh, Scotland: Churchill Livingstone.

Erikson, E. (1958). *Young man Luther: A study in psychoanalysis and history.* New York: Norton.

Erikson, E. (1969). *Gandhi's truth: On the origins of militant nonviolence.* New York: Norton.

Geertz, C. (1973). *The interpretation of cultures.* New York: Basic Books.

Handyside, A. H., Lesko, J. G., Tarin, J. J., Winston, R. M., & Hughes, M. R. (1992). Birth of a normal girl after in vitro fertilization and preimplantation diagnostic testing for cystic fibrosis. *New England Journal of Medicine, 327,* 905–909.

Keyser, H. (1988, May). All about D&Cs. *Prevention, 40,* 71–73.

Klein, M. H., Mathieu-Coughlan, P., & Kiesler, D. J. (1986). The experiencing scales. In L. S. Greenberg & W. M. Pinsof (Eds.), *The psychotherapeutic process: A research handbook* (pp. 21–71). New York: Guilford Press.

Kleinberg, J. L. (1995). Group treatment of adults in midlife. *International Journal of Group Psychotherapy, 45,* 207–222.

Kotre, J. (1979). *Simple gifts: The lives of Pat and Patty Crowley.* Kansas City, MO: Andrews & McMeel.

Kotre, J. (1995). Generative outcome. *Journal of Aging Studies, 9,* 33–41.

Kotre, J. (1996). *Outliving the self: Generativity and the interpretation of lives.* New York: Norton. (Originally published in 1984)

Langer, L. (1991). *Holocaust testimonies: The ruins of memory.* New Haven, CT: Yale University Press.

Lehman, D. R., Ellard, J. H., & Wortman, C. B. (1986). Social support for the bereaved: Recipients' and providers' perspectives on what is helpful. *Journal of Consulting and Clinical Psychology, 54,* 438–446.

Levinson, D. (1978). *The seasons of a man's life.* New York: Knopf.

Manheimer, R. J. (1995). Redeeming the aging self: John Kotre, George Drury, and cultural generativity. *Journal of Aging Studies, 9,* 13–20.

McAdams, D. P. (1985). *Power, intimacy, and the life story: Personological inquiries into identity.* New York: Guilford Press.

McAdams, D. P., & de St. Aubin, E. (1992). A theory of generativity and its assessment through self-report, behavioral acts, and narrative themes in autobiography. *Journal of Personality and Social Psychology, 62,* 1003–1015.

McClory, R. (1995). *Turning point: The inside story of the papal birth control commission, and how Humanae Vitae changed the life of Patty Crowley and the future of the church*. New York: Crossroad.

Mushinski, M. (1996, January–March). Hysterectomy charges: Geographic variations, United States, 1994. *Statistical Bulletin*, pp. 2–12.

Pergament, E. (1990). Reproductive genetics in the 21st century: Fact and fantasy. In B. A. Fine, E. Gettig, K. Greendale, B. Leopold, & N. W. Paul (Eds.), *Strategies in genetic counseling: Reproductive genetics and new technologies* (pp. 24–30). New York: March of Dimes Birth Defects Foundation.

Shane, E., & Shane, M. (1995). Generativity versus personal ambition: The feminine dilemma seen in the light of new motivational systems. *Psychoanalytic Inquiry, 15*, 514–528.

Singer, J. A., & Salovey, P. (1993). *The remembered self: Emotion and memory in personality*. New York: Free Press.

Snarey, J. (1993). *How fathers care for the next generation: A four-decade study*. Cambridge, MA: Harvard University Press.

Weber, S. (1990). The teacher educator's experience: Cultural generativity and duality of commitment. *Curriculum Inquiry, 20*, 141–159.

Photograph courtesy of the Library of Congress,
Prints and Photographs Division, LC-710034-262-
36384.

12

TRUTH AGAINST THE WORLD: A PSYCHOBIOGRAPHICAL EXPLORATION OF GENERATIVITY IN THE LIFE OF FRANK LLOYD WRIGHT

ED DE ST. AUBIN

The legacy that Frank Lloyd Wright (FLW)[1] created in his seven decades as an active architect stands as a powerful testament to the creative potential of the individual. The genius manifested in his more than 430 completed architectural projects marks him, more than 35 years after his death, as possibly the most influential U.S. architect ever. Through an integration of originality and productivity, FLW made a lasting contribution to future generations. He was, to use a term introduced by the psychologist Erik Erikson (1963), an exceptionally *generative* man. Yet many of his core attributes and behaviors were decidedly nongenerative, even antigenerative. FLW was verbally abusive toward his children at times and appeared unable to care for them as a generative father would. Although he attracted hundreds of apprentice–disciples to his fellowship at Taliesin,

---

[1] I follow Gill's (1987) lead here in referring to Frank Lloyd Wright as FLW throughout this chapter. It is less cumbersome for the reader and requires less space without conveying any less information.

FLW was a poor teacher who mentored but a handful of students who went on to achieve independent and significant careers as working architects. Furthermore, FLW was a philanderer and self-serving prevaricator whose narcissistic tendencies stifled his generative potential.

It was these extremes in generativity that first attracted me to FLW as a candidate for a psychobiographic exploration. The guiding questions of this investigation concern the manifestation of generativity within the life of FLW as well as the development of his generativity over time. I provide analyses of the generativity dynamics inherent in three pertinent life domains (fatherhood, mentorship, and architecture) and explicate the evolution of generativity within the architecture (physical and theoretical) of FLW.

GENERATIVITY THEORY AND PSYCHOBIOGRAPHIC METHODS

Psychobiography and related methods have been integral to the study of generativity. Indeed, the very emergence of generativity as a concept is wedded to psychobiography. Erikson was one of the most prominent psychobiographers to have practiced the craft (Runyan, 1982), and he was the originator of generativity theory. He applied his theoretical conceptualizations concerning generativity and his larger psychosocial theory of human development to book-length psychobiographies of Martin Luther (Erikson, 1958) and Mahatma Gandhi (1969).

Erikson (1950/1963) conceived of generativity as a midlife psychosocial phase wherein an individual's desire to create and care for the younger generation is matched by cultural expectations that one begin to do just that. Although generativity emerges from the full expression of mature intimacy in the production and raising of children, Erikson included creativity and productivity in his definition and emphasized the plasticity and potential scope of this mode, "which may genuinely include works, plans, and ideas generated either in direct connection with the task of securing the life of the next generation or in wider anticipation of generations yet to come" (1954/1987, p. 274). Furthermore, he felt compelled to stress the cultural (see also Browning, 1975, and Bellah, Madsen, Sullivan, Swindler, & Tipton, 1991) and individual benefits of generativity. Whereas traditional models of socialization are unidirectional in that the older generation is viewed as influencing the younger, Erikson wrote of generativity as fulfilling the adult's need to be needed, and he said it was "as indispensable for the renewal of the adult generation's own life as it is for that of the next generation" (1988, p. 251). Through psychobiography, Erikson (1958, 1969) made clear that the generative adult is one who creates legacies of self that benefit future generations while at the same time providing meaning and purpose to one's adult life.

The advancement of generativity theory and the deciphering of individual lives were next paired in John Kotre's (1984) *Outliving the Self: Generativity and the Interpretation of Lives*. The life-story approach Kotre applied in this study is psychobiographic in that it uses psychological methods and insight in "collecting, analyzing, and discerning stories about persons' lives" (McAdams, 1988, p. 1; see also Runyan, 1988). In a "thick analysis" of generativity using eight rich life stories, Kotre (1984) addressed what he believed to be the two major shortcomings of Erikson's writings concerning generativity: (a) that Erikson did not sort out the different types of generativity and (b) that he failed to see the potential dark side of generativity. In addressing the first weakness in generativity theory, Kotre divided the concept into an eight-celled classification system with two possible modes of generative expression (agency and communion), both of which exist at one of four levels (biological, parental, technical, and cultural). In contrast to the optimistic tone inherent in Erikson's discussions of generativity, Kotre believed that generativity often points to the multifaceted capacity for the perversity of human nature. The legacy that one creates may well be toxic. It is best, argued Kotre, to view generativity as a "desire to invest one's substance in forms of life and work that will outlive the self" (p. 10), an impulse that may be channeled into vice as well as virtue.

Generativity theory experienced a growth spurt in 1993, when three separate books containing pivotal scholarship in this area were published: (a) John Snarey's *How Fathers Care for the Next Generation: A Four-Decade Study*, (b) George E. Vaillant's *The Wisdom of the Ego*, and (c) Dan P. McAdams's *The Stories We Live by: Personal Myth and the Making of the Self*. Each author combines idiographic analysis with nomothetic data to advance or explicate generativity theory, although Snarey's book is the only one dedicated entirely to the notion of generativity. Drawing from longitudinal and intergenerational data, Snarey demonstrated empirical evidence for the predictors (boyhood precursors and concurrent variables) and results (midlife consequences and outcomes measured in one's child) of different types of adult male generativity. The quantitative studies presented in the book are combined with qualitative portraits revealed in life-narrative interviews with fathers and their children. Again, life-story and psychobiographic methods are merged with the construction of generativity theory.

Vaillant's contributions to generativity scholarship are offered within his larger research concerning adult ego development and the maturation of the ego defense mechanisms (1977, 1993; Vaillant & Milofsky, 1980). His use of psychobiography in adult development research is perhaps the most poetic to date, displaying clinically insightful appraisals of well-known individuals (Leo Tolstoy, Eugene O'Neill), characters from literature (Goethe's Faust, Arthur Miller's Willy Loman), and research participants. All provide fertile material for Vaillant, who integrated his psychobiographic work with analyses of longitudinal data to explore generativity theory. One of Vaillant's significant contributions to the understanding of generativity is his contention that it is best understood as two separate steps. Generativity begins with caring for one or a few specific younger persons in a direct manner such as in a mentorship role but then, in a second generative phase, becoming a "keeper of the meaning" who guides entire collections of persons and unknown others in the preservation of cultural values and past traditions. For Vaillant, it is the scope of generativity that increases as one matures through adulthood.

Like Vaillant's (1993) contribution, McAdams' (1993) scholarship in generativity is embedded within a larger theory construction effort, though McAdams has focused exclusively on generativity in many of his empirical investigations. Moving away from the Eriksonian insistence on the sequentiality of discrete developmental stages in adulthood, McAdams' "Life Story" model incorporates generativity issues under the rubric of identity concerns. For McAdams, the psychosocial construction of self (identity) is the fundamental and enduring mode of adult personality development and the "generative script" (one element of identity) is the self defining story one narrates regarding his or her efforts to create lasting contributions (1985, 1993). McAdams' research is psychobiographic in that his investigations nearly always begin with the intense analysis of individual life-story interview data.

A final integration of generativity theory and psychobiography (see also Susan Lee's chapter in this volume) is represented in the work that Abigail Stewart, Bill Peterson, and their colleagues (Peterson & Stewart, 1990; Stewart, Franz, & Layton, 1988) have completed regarding the generativity of Vera Brittain, a British feminist and pacifist writer born in 1893. These scholars content analyzed the personal documents and published writings Brittain produced at different periods of her life for themes of generativity (as well as other adult personality modes) to track Brittain's psychosocial preoccupations over time. This research is psychobiographic in that it applies existing psychological theory (in this case Erikson's psychosocial theory as it relates to adult development) to the investigation of a single life. It is quite different from most psychobiography in that the investigators conduct statistical analyses based on the systematic quantification of themes such as generativity found within the products (in this case writings) of one individual.

It is evident from this brief outline of relevant research that generativity scholarship and psychobiographic methods have been closely linked in the past. The advancement of generativity theory requires scholarship that engages in the intense study of individual lives as well as that involving large-scale longitudinal and intergenerational research. Although psychobiography is a useful research methodology, even its most ardent enthusiasts highlight its potential pitfalls (Elms, 1994; Runyan 1982, 1984, 1988). Two of the possible shortcomings that Elms (1988, 1994) discusses (both outlined and both committed in Freud's 1910 psychobiography of Leonardo da Vinci) are particularly relevant to this psychobiography of generativity within the life of FLW: (a) Avoid pathologizing the psychobiographic subject, and, (b) avoid idealizing the psychobiographic subject.

The vast majority of writings on the life and architecture of FLW fall squarely within this second category. Often written by former apprentices, this work reads more as fawning adulation than objective analysis, usually glossing over or entirely omitting those component's of FLW's life that demonstrate any of his negative qualities as a human or as an architect. It is just these attributes that make it difficult, particularly for a psychologist, not to pathologize FLW. He was a brilliant architect, yet he was also prone toward narcissism, callousness, obtuseness, elitism, and dishonesty. In my study of his life and work, I vacillated between vilifying and deifying FLW, though I hope to avoid such extremes in my final analysis.

This leads to a third difficulty inherent in the psychobiographic process: Not to invest too much of one's own personal "issues" in the interpretation of another's life. Irving Alexander, who has discussed problems of reliability in psychobiographic interpretation (1988, 1990), has demonstrated the manner in which Erikson's psychobiographical work reveals dynamics of his own personality (1996). Furthermore, Elms (1988) believes that Freud's errors in his *Leonardo* are all traceable to "idiosyncratic sources bound up in Freud's personal conflicts." Psychobiographers must recognize this reality and try to remove as much partiality as possible, even as one acknowledges that the inherently intense one-interpreter-to-one-life processes of psychobiography are likely to lead to biasing dynamics such as projection.

A fourth obstacle I faced in this study concerns what Anderson (1988) referred to as examining subjects from a distance. I am unable to interview FLW, and I must rely to a great extent on the biographical scholarship of others, which I have already noted is typically less than objective. Carlson (1988) suggested that psychologists engage in an "invisible collaboration" with biographers by using a specific biography as the central piece of data. This is feasible only to the extent that the biography is objective, comprehensive, and insightful. Of the dozens of commentaries on FLW, none meets all of these criteria.

Other standard sources of information for psychobiography include personal documents such as correspondence and diaries (Allport, 1942; Wrightsman, 1981), and these have been used extensively in FLW scholarship (Gill, 1987; Secrest, 1992). Creative artists produce objects, and these objects may be assessed in psychobiography. FLW designed well over 600 building projects (not all of them built) in his 91 years of life. Thus, much of his generative energy resulted in design schemes or constructed buildings. Some have argued that there is a definite pattern to the temporal transformations in his physical architecture (Hoppen, 1993). Although this observation is not accepted by all FLW scholars, most agree that there were specified shifts in his architectural theory over time. The evolution of FLW's design patterns and his ideas regarding architecture speak to the development of generative content during adulthood. The actual forms and ideas inherent in his architecture capture the patterned maturation of his generative concerns. I discuss the dynamics involved in the maturation of generativity as evidenced in the evolution of the architecture of FLW.

A final procedural note concerns the scope of this project. I follow Alexander's (1988) advice in narrowing the focus of my psychobiography by seeking in the available data the answer to a specific question. Rather than attempt to account for all aspects of an entire life, I concentrate my exploration, as Anderson (1981) did in his analysis of William James's period of depression. Begin with a manageable question, suggested Alexander (1988), for the search will surely expand with time. My question concerns the manifestation and development of generativity within the life and work of FLW.

GENERATIVITY AND THE LIFE OF FRANK LLOYD WRIGHT

The three domains in which FLW's generativity may be examined are architecture, fatherhood, and the fellowship he established to pass on his ideas and techniques to younger apprentices. These are the areas in which FLW was afforded the opportunity to influence, care for, and contribute to younger generations. A selective chronology of the significant events in FLW's life is provided in the appendix as an overview because the objectives and allotted space of this chapter precluded coverage of all significant life events. This chronology serves as a backdrop to the discussion supplied in the text.

Fatherhood

Parenting is perhaps the most common manifestation of generativity. It is a core aspect of Erikson's writings and has been examined in several research studies (most comprehensively by Snarey, 1993). Some have suggested that fatherhood is less directly attached to generativity than motherhood because men have less of an immediate, or biological, connection to their children (Hawkins, Christiansen, Sargent, & Hill, 1995). Others have reported evidence that men who are fathers are more preoccupied with generative concerns than are men without children (McAdams & de St. Aubin, 1992).

As in his architecture, FLW was prolific in fatherhood: He produced seven children and adopted one. His first marriage (to Catherine Tobin) resulted in six offspring: Lloyd, John, Catherine, Frances, David, and Robert Llewelyn. He sired one daughter (Iovanna) with his third wife (Olgivanna Milanov Hinzenberg) and adopted the child (Svetlanta) she had borne in her previous marriage. Despite his large brood, FLW expressed confusion about the very concept of fatherhood. In his 1932 autobiography, FLW wrote the following:

> Is it a quality? Fatherhood? If so, I seemed born without it. And yet a building was a child. I have had the father-feeling, I am sure, when coming back after a long time to one of my buildings. That must be the true feeling of fatherhood. But I never had it for my children. I had affection for them. I regarded them as with me and play-fellows, comrades. (Quoted in Gill, 1987, p. 105).

This professed confusion regarding fatherhood may be interpreted as self-protective annulment, a coping strategy that FLW was to employ often in his life. He could not be held accountable for something that he did not understand or that he apparently was "born without." FLW was a negligent father, and his behaviors caused much pain for his children, although he rarely acknowledged this.

During the two decades framing the turn of the century, FLW and his young family lived in Oak Park, an extremely conservative Chicago suburb. The inhabitants of this town conformed closely to social conventions. However, FLW embraced his emerging role as the iconoclast, living a flamboyant lifestyle that included relatively open sexual affairs with other women. As if this were not humiliating enough for the children (see John Lloyd Wright, 1992), the tabloids of the time carried amplified reports of FLW's behaviors. It was his affair with Mamah Cheney that ended his first marriage. As his father had when FLW was 16, FLW left his children and wife to pursue other commitments and pleasures.

The separation clearly affected each child differently. Gill (1987) suggested that David and his sister Catherine were most severely damaged by the separation, never forgiving FLW for his cruelty toward their mother. When Catherine (the mother) died just a few weeks before FLW died in 1959, son David intentionally waited a full day before telling FLW the news. When FLW asked David why he didn't tell him as soon as he knew, David replied, "Why should I have bothered, you never gave a god-damn for her when she was alive" (quoted in Gill, 1987, pp. 498–499).

It would be inaccurate to consider FLW an abusive father. If anything, he was an indulgent parent who genuinely enjoyed "playing" with his children. His return visits to the Oak Park home after the marital separation were motivated by a desire to be with his children. However, these were short and infrequent visits. FLW did not place a high priority on his obligations to his children. Intimate love and architecture came first.

Both Lloyd and John, the two eldest, maintained close contact and partial loyalty to FLW throughout their lives, and each worked in various capacities as an architect with FLW when they were adults. John was instrumental in the Midway Gardens project (1913) and was head assistant to FLW during the construction of the Imperial Hotel in Japan (1915), until FLW fired him. Lloyd, who was trained as a landscape architect, was instrumental in helping FLW devise the "textile" block system of reinforced patterned concrete blocks. Lloyd also served as supervisor (a "go-between," or mediator, between FLW and his clients) in many of the later California projects, particularly in Los Angeles.

Although he often took the bully mode with clients and apprentices, FLW felt especially entitled to belittle his sons in their professional roles, using fatherhood as manipulative leverage. When John protested that FLW had failed to pay him his promised salary for work, FLW submitted to John a bill with a complete accounting of how much John had cost FLW over his entire lifetime, including childhood expenses and obstetric costs. A few years later, John was faced with a similar situation when working on the Imperial Hotel. When John decided to take part of his pay out of a check that a client had given to John to pass along, FLW shot back a telegram that began, "You're fired! Take the next ship home" (John Lloyd Wright, 1992, p. 99) and sent his ex-wife, Catherine, a letter accusing her of raising a thief.

In a letter to son Lloyd, who was growing uneasy in his position between unhappy clients in Los Angeles and the expensive but inaccessible architect they had hired (FLW was at Taliesin in Wisconsin much of this time), FLW wrote the following:

> You are "spongy" and you don't know just why. But I will tell you why. It is because you are not really reliable. You will say a thing is so when you only think it is so. You will promise and not keep it. You will buy when you can't pay. You will attempt anything and blame failure on others. . . . You are sentimental but not kind. . . . I think you would carelessly do wrong to anyone when you ought to be more careful. You are quick to impute to others the quality that is rankling in your own soul . . . You are absolutely the worst mannered young man I know. I enjoy being with you for a while, but soon I find myself vulgarized somehow by the lack of consideration or whatever it is that emanates from you. . . . The value of a dollar is blank to your mind. Your sense of time is loose. Your step is loose. Your grasp of your work is loose. Your sense of justice is loose . . . I have been your "excuse" for too long, my son! Too long! (Quoted in Gill, 1987, p. 275).

Such onslaughts of insults did not sway Lloyd from the earnest and enduring loyalty he displayed toward FLW. John's view of his father, however, is best understood as profoundly ambivalent. At the age of 54, John wrote a biography of his 78-year-old father titled *My Father Who Is on*

Earth. It is a quirky book written from several perspectives (John as a four-year-old, FLW speaking to St. Peter at the Pearly Gates, FLW speaking to John from the dead). It leaps from justifying FLW's lifestyle, to anger at FLW's callousness toward his children, to worship of FLW's godlike qualities. The ambivalence is most evident in John's writings about FLW's fathering generativity, although he does not couch his feelings in these terms. He wonders out loud to his audience why FLW claimed never to have wanted to be a father yet produced seven children. He wonders why FLW left Catherine and the children, why he did not say good-bye, and why he did not leave sooner. Although John's pain is implicit in the words he chose, he more explicitly rationalized and sanitized FLW's lifestyle, casting FLW as the misunderstood romantic whose passions run counter to an overly moralistic and confining culture. (It is an image that FLW slowly came to embrace as well.) In a bizarre twist of logic, John portrayed Catherine as the antagonist in the Oak Park story: a stifling force trying unsuccessfully to domesticate the beautiful and wild FLW.

Although he admitted that his father was a poor teacher of architecture, John suggested he had "inherited" FLW's talent. Regarding his first house and FLW's influence, John wrote that: "the strength of his genius so charged the environment that I had been subjected to all my life that, before I had had an architectural training, I had unconsciously been impregnated with ideas that enabled me to bring a reflection of one of his buildings into being" (John Lloyd Wright, 1992, p. 66). Unable to form his own sense of genuine architecture, John had created a structure with all of the classic trimmings of a Prairie style home yet with none of the warmth or singularity that characterized FLW's structures: It was a poor imitation. Although neither John nor Lloyd achieved a reputation as a significant architect that was independent of his father's, both contributed significantly to certain aspects of FLW's architectural efforts, which represents a blending of career and paternal generativity that appears to have been rare in the great creators of modern time.

In 1925, at the age of 58, FLW began a second phase of fathering with the birth of Iovanna, who was born to him and Olgivanna, then 27 years of age. FLW married Olgivanna 3 years later, and he adopted her daughter, Svetlanta, at that time. The four family members lived with FLW's mother, Anna, and a few dozen apprentices, artists, and workers at Taliesin in Spring Green, Wisconsin, a home and work studio that FLW had originally created for his mistress, Mamah Cheney, in 1911 (it subsequently burnt to the ground in 1914 and then was rebuilt, only to be damaged by fire again later).

The similarities between the two phases of fathering are that FLW maintained a feverish work pace that left little time or energy for parenting and that his iconoclastic public image greatly affected his children's development. The difference, of course, was that Olgivanna and her two daughters had no expectations of normality. FLW was by then a powerful worldwide force in architecture with renowned buildings in Japan and a well-received book of his ideas and work in Germany, to say nothing of his growing popularity in the states. Olgivanna was an exceptionally well-read international traveler with decidedly unconventional beliefs about family life and the proper role of a father. FLW's public image worked to foster the home environment Olgivanna was attempting to create.

Catherine Tobin, conversely, was a young and impressionable woman from a well-connected but conventional family who had married a charismatic boy from Wisconsin with some talent and ambition in architecture. All that he became worked against her image of domestic life. Furthermore, the social milieu of Oak Park in the 1890s was as different from that of Taliesin in 1925 as Catherine was from Olgivanna. The same behaviors that ostracized FLW in Oak Park were embraced and reinforced at Taliesin.

The relation between fatherhood and architecture in the life of FLW is captured in Gardner's (1993) "Faustian bargain" metaphor. In the analysis of seven modern creators (Freud, Einstein, Martha Graham, Picasso, Stravinsky, T. S. Eliot, Gandhi), Gardner argued that each struck a conscious deal whereby their responsibilities and care in their personal relationships were to be sacrificed for the greater good of their work. All were great enough creators to shift the entire paradigm of their respective disciplines, yet in doing so all wreaked havoc in the lives of those closest to them.[2] As a modern creator, FLW also caused pain to many in his life. In the name of architecture, he neglected his fatherly duties, which are fundamental to generativity.

Fellowship

One way that many women and men express generativity is through the role of mentor (Kleiber & Ray, 1993; Vaillant, 1993), whereby one passes along one's skills to younger members of a profession, craft, or trade. FLW mentored hundreds of individuals through the fellowship that he began in 1932 at Taliesin in Spring Green, Wisconsin. Five years later this group began to split the year, traveling back and forth between Wisconsin (summers) and FLW's Taliesin West (winters) for which construction began in the Arizona desert in 1937. Over 200 former FLW apprentices returned to Taliesin West in 1987 to celebrate the 50th anniversary of its birth (Hoppen, 1993). There are 70 active members of the Taliesin Fellowship today.

---

[2] I highly recommend this book. The themes in FLW's life parallel many of the themes Gardner found in the lives of his seven modern creators. In fact, I believe that FLW's life fits the portrait of the prototypical modern creator (an amalgamation of the life patterns of the seven creators investigated) that Gardner presents toward the end of the book as closely as any of the seven individuals discussed in that book.

In this section, I discuss FLW's motivation (generative and otherwise) behind beginning the fellowship, the structure and climate of the fellowship, and the core generativity inhibitor involved in this inherently generative life domain.

Motivation

FLW and Olgivanna began thinking seriously about beginning an architectural school in the late 1920s. Organizational plans were drafted and attempts were made to raise start-up funds. Plans were almost completed through a partnership with the University of Wisconsin, but they fell through when FLW refused to agree to the terms offered (Johnson, 1990), which he felt failed to grant him sufficient autonomy and income. The initial conceptualization for such a school was an idealistic blend of FLW's generative desire to pass on his architectural vision and Olgivanna's attempt to spread the teachings of Georgi Ivanovich Gurdjieff, a charismatic Greek-Armenian religious leader she had studied under in France (whose greatest proselytizer was the Russian mathematician P. D. Ouspensky, especially regarding the book *In Search of the Miraculous*). Gurdjieff had begun the Institute for the Harmonious Development of Man, and Olgivanna hoped to incorporate many of its teachings into the fellowship. She saw parallels between Gurdjieff's "holistic" ideas of living and the "organic" architectural vision of FLW.

At 64 years of age when the fellowship officially began, FLW had definite beliefs as to what constituted good architecture, and he was beginning to form his ideas regarding the role of architecture in society. At this time he was starting to speak and later to write about his vision of utopia, which was a type of architecturally dominated democracy promoting fierce individualism. The fellowship was an avenue by which FLW could drive his ideas into younger minds, thus increasing his current popularity and guaranteeing that these notions would survive after his death.

FLW served as apprentice to Louis Sullivan for nearly 7 years as a young man, and he repeatedly acknowledged the positive influence that Sullivan had on his life and architecture. Referring to his relationship with his mentor, FLW described his position in the architectural firm of Adler and Sullivan as "the pencil" in the hands of the *Lieber Meister*. Now was his chance to help spark and nurture young architectural minds and to continue these intergenerational threads of generativity he had experienced.

The generative impetus behind the fellowship was lofty indeed, and genuinely so, but there were also more pragmatic reasons for luring dozens of young men and women to the Wisconsin countryside. One reason was that these people were willing to pay FLW money to work for him at a time when FLW was bringing in few commissions. According to Hoppen (1993), there had been only three projects in the past 7 years, and FLW had begun to sell off his treasured Japanese prints. FLW was unable to afford or find motivated workers to help with the continual additions and restructuring he planned for his Taliesin buildings. Using fellowship members was better than employing cheap labor. He had a labor source that signed personal checks over to the Master.

FLW had formed an atelier of talented artists and apprentices in the style of the European Renaissance masters when he first opened his own office at the age of 26. He was able to surround himself with gifted sculptors and craftspeople while in Oak Park and Chicago from 1893 to 1911. However, the isolation he chose by creating Taliesin and the serious economic consequences of the stock market crash in late 1929 left him without the elements that had become essential to his life: architectural commissions and skillful workers to help him complete his building designs. Unlike poets or other creative artists, architects are unable to perform their craft without patronage and the expensive resources of material and labor. The fellowship was to provide all three.

The creation of a fellowship also figured prominently in Olgivanna's self-appointed position as public relations agent for FLW. She began an ambitious project in about 1930 to rejuvenate FLW's career and to publicize his life and his philosophy of architecture. It was she who convinced FLW to write his autobiography, which was published in 1932. This book brought FLW's work and ideas to the attention of a wide audience and stimulated several of its readers to sign up as Taliesin fellows. Perhaps more important, it resulted in contracts for architectural projects. For example, Edgar Kaufmann, Sr., who was to become one of FLW's leading patrons (he commissioned the Broadacre model and, later, Fallingwater), first heard of FLW through his son Edgar Kaufmann, Jr., who became an apprentice after reading the autobiography. Furthermore, Olgivanna believed that surrounding FLW with young and fertile minds would invigorate his career by channeling his energy.

The fellowship helped FLW and Olgivanna to legitimize their lifestyle at Taliesin to themselves and others. Hertz (1995) contended that FLW,

> essentially a moralist at heart, was never happy in the role of pariah cast upon him by the media in the 1920s. Now he had access to the minds of young architects who chose to work under his direction in a stable environment, in the context of a harmonious home life. (p. 96).

In the same way that he built Taliesin and openly moved in with his mistress, Mamah Cheney, in 1911, FLW wrote a letter "to the countryside" (Gill, 1987), informing his neighbors of his honest relationship with Olgivanna. A second letter advertised the opening of the Taliesin Fellowship. The several motivational forces that led to the opening of the fellowship in 1932 included generative aspirations, pragmatic concerns, attempts at rejuvenation, and needs for legitimacy.

Structure and Climate

Hertz (1995) described fellowship life as an immersion experience. Apprentices were to take part in all components of work and life at Taliesin: digging ditches, washing dishes, cleaning barn stalls, lugging building materials, producing plays, hosting parties, entertaining clients, occasionally drafting designs of the Master (FLW), packing and caravanning across the country twice a year, and always helping to reconstruct the various Taliesin (and Taliesin West) buildings. Curtis Besinger (1995), who was an apprentice from 1939 until 1955,[3] attested to the fact that most apprenticeship activities were not directly related to architecture. It was typical that an apprentice spend the first 6 months completing "grunt" work before being allowed into the drafting room.

Influenced by the romantic notions surrounding self-sufficiency and holistic living, FLW was not interested solely in teaching his apprentices the particular skills needed to perform architecture; he hoped also to instill in his apprentices a love of architecture as a way of life. His philosophy of organicism applied to life modes as well as design schemes. Apprentices were to incorporate the various areas of life into one organic whole and to learn architecture by living architecture. However, not all inhabitants of Taliesin were architectural apprentices. There were, coming and going at different periods, poets, artists, musicians, and actors to add to the lively atmosphere.

A revealing quotation relayed by Gill (1987) captures the atmosphere of the fellowship well. FLW said to his old friend Carleton Smith, who was visiting Taliesin, "You know Carleton, a perfect democracy flourishes here at the Fellowship. When I get hungry, we all eat" (p. 170). Meant for its comic effect, the quip hints at the tension between FLW's desire to maintain an egalitarian mode within the fellowship and his self-serving tendencies.

From the early 1930s until his death in 1959, FLW developed and refined his concept of Broadacre: a utopian community of planned living that embodied what he felt were the most noble ideals held in the United States—individual freedom grounded in a strong work ethic and the love of beauty in nature and the arts. The fellowship served as a laboratory experiment for his theories. Although architecture was seen as the supreme integration of all things great, appreciation for music and art were as central to life at Taliesin as caring for crops and livestock. No man or woman at the fellowship was above physical labor, and all were encouraged to participate in the more cultured activities such as choir and theater.

Despite what was purported to be an egalitarian collective, a hierarchy

---

[3]Besinger took a short hiatus from the fellowship between 1943 and 1946 when he was forced to enter into the U.S. "Work of National Importance" program as a conscientious objector to World War II.

existed, and several forces divided the fellowship members into definite cliques. In general, the longer an apprentice "stayed on," the higher up the hierarchy he or she moved. If one stayed long enough (estimated at between 4 and 7 years), he became a "senior" and, instead of paying tuition, received a small stipend (Besinger recalls his being $30 a month). This practice of seniority did not appear to affect the social milieu of the fellowship negatively (Besinger, 1995).

It was the forceful spreading of Gurdjieff's philosophy by Olgivanna and especially by the Wrights' daughter Iovanna that Besinger noted to be the most damaging and divisive influence. Besinger (1995) openly expressed his discontent regarding this issue and portrayed both Olgivanna and Iovanna quite negatively. He believed that the Gurdjieff component of the fellowship headed by these two women worked against the efforts of FLW to pass on his architectural wisdom. Besinger related a conversation he had with Olgivanna in which she suggested that the fellowship would improve after the death of FLW because it would then be able to focus more heavily on the philosophy of Gurdjieff! Within the fellowship, there were those who followed the Gurdjieff track through soul searching "movements" (a form of collective musical yoga and meditation) and discussions of his teachings. Although all activities were supposedly voluntary, those who chose not to attend were ostracized. The fractioning intensified in 1949 when Gurdjieff died and Iovanna returned from her studies with him in Paris to Taliesin. For Besinger, this was the beginning of the end of any hope that the fellowship might serve its primary function of architectural training.

It is interesting that Besinger viewed Svetlanta, Iovanna's half sister, as the social glue at Taliesin; she gracefully built bridges between the different groups that were forming. Her death in 1947 in a strange single-car accident that also took the life of her son Daniel was devastating to the collective Taliesin spirit. The palpable doom created by her death led to an exodus of apprentices from the fellowship.

Forced into a Spartan existence, many apprentices felt exploited by FLW, who maintained his lavish lifestyle. Several senior apprentices left in 1941 because they disagreed with FLW's decision to stop allowing individual apprentices to accept architectural commissions through the fellowship. It had long been agreed that funds secured through these commissions would be divided: one third to FLW, one third to the fellowship, and one third to the architect. A client commented to FLW that he would rather hire an apprentice than FLW because the apprentice was just as talented and more conscientious with schedules and budgets. FLW burst into the drafting room at Taliesin that afternoon and announced that all documents created there were to bear his name as head architect and that any work not approved by him personally would be considered a forgery and subject to legal action (Gill, 1987).

This episode is but one of many that characterize FLW's undesirable combination of hot temper and arrogance. Those who read the fellowship literature and came to Taliesin in hopes of finding a holistic way of life through organic architecture were often surprised to find a tyrant barking out orders. Although his wish was to foster the individual creativity of his apprentices, FLW's authoritarian style coerced many into blind conformity.

Generativity Inhibitor

In John Lloyd Wright's biography of FLW, St. Peter at the Pearly Gates expresses approval of FLW's architecture but chastises him for his failure to pass on his talents:

> You do a good job building your buildings in keeping with your ideal. But you have been weak in your support of others in their desire for this same attainment. Although there is nothing to show that you ever depressed or quenched any rising genius, neither can there be shown that you ever stood behind one and helped him up. (1992, p. 172)

It is amazing, Gill (1987) noted, that few of the hundreds of FLW apprentices went on to achieve significant, independent careers as practicing architects. I believe that FLW's generative potential could have been more fully realized in this area had it not been for his poor pedagogy. FLW's instructional techniques were misguided, and his implicit theories regarding the learning process and the development of talent were erroneous. His son John simply referred to FLW as a "bad teacher" (1992, p. 131). FLW's desires in this area were generative in that he wished to mentor young architects, but he was ultimately ineffective as a teacher or guide to younger apprentices.

FLW was critical of the university system. He felt that its mass production method of stamping formulas into the minds of pupils stifled the natural proclivities and desires a student might have concerning architecture. He believed, instead, that one must learn by doing and by harvesting one's intrinsic love of beauty in form and material. He refused to refer to himself as a teacher, to Taliesin as a school, or to his apprentices as students. Although many might agree with these sentiments and characterizations of traditional passive models of instruction, FLW's alternative proved to be no better.

Gill (1987) referred to FLW's system as the "watch the genius" method. Rather than supply lessons to his apprentices regarding techniques and theories in architecture, he "performed" greatness in this area and expected somehow to imbue those around him with his genius. His architectural precocity precluded his ability to empathize with his struggling students. FLW did not have the perspective necessary to understand his students' inability to grasp a concept. Employing what might be considered the "Nike form of pedagogy," he simply commanded them to "just do it."

Furthermore, he lacked the necessary patience and care of a good teacher. It was quicker to be critical than constructive in evaluating an apprentice's work. Void of what Baltes, Staudinger, Maercker, and Smith (1995) referred to as the "strategic knowledge" of a wise adult, FLW would sooner belittle than encourage the efforts of his apprentices. In discussing FLW's teaching, John Lloyd Wright recalled that "he taught me not to say "old antique" by laughing at me when I said it" (1992, p. 131). Apprentices sometimes spent months fashioning small models and drawings for a highly anticipated Christmas morning ritual. The Master would walk through and survey the presents inside each "box" the students had designed and con-structed, often with no commentary or with a cryptic comment such as "it looks upside down" (Hoppen, 1993).

FLW's failures as a teacher stemmed in part from his belief that ar-chitectural talent was an innate gift: "You can't get into the riches and depths of human expression unless you're born with something that is rich enough and strong enough to get there" (in John Lloyd Wright, 1992, p. 158). FLW was to express this belief often: One was either born an archi-tect or was not. In his more elitist moments, he would add that few are endowed with such a gift. Training was for nothing other than to encourage a God-given talent of the chosen ones. What percentage of the apprentices did he feel were born architects? For what purpose were the others at Taliesin?

To be fair to FLW, his aspirations in this area were quite high. Rather than simply teach his apprentices how architecture had been done in the past, he professed a desire to give them a much more encompassing gen-erative gift: a way of life. Architecture was a mode of living, not simply a way of building. He hoped that his notion of organicism would foster each apprentices' unique sense of beauty in life and work. FLW wrote the fol-lowing in a 1950 issue of the *Architectural Forum*:

> I still hope to see these basic principles more comprehended. No man's work need resemble mine. If he understands the workings of the prin-ciples behind the effects he sees here, with similar integrity he will have his own way of building. . . . Personally, I believe architects are born. And I don't think they are made. . . . This is good soil in which it can sprout. Instead of imitating effects, search for the principle that made them original and own your own efforts. (Hoppen, 1993, p. 165)

FLW's teaching style contradicted the spirit of these words. Only the most resilient student was able to weather FLW's callousness as a mentor. He was an authoritarian teacher who stifled the creative attempts of his apprentices and unknowingly created a conformist mode whereby students strove for his approval by replicating or closely approximating his work. The large gap between FLW and his students in talent, lifestyle, and fame rendered genuine identification, an integral part of a mentoring relationship, nearly impossible. That FLW was such a poor teacher is especially ironic given that many of his ancestors were celebrated educators.

To say that FLW was inadequate as a teacher is not to denounce the Taliesin Fellowship as a failure. Most former apprentices cherish their Taliesin years. Furthermore, it was a productive force in the world of architecture, allowing FLW to maintain his increasingly prolific mode in that area. FLW simply was not effective in his generative attempts to pass on his architectural vision to younger generations.

Architecture

FLW was effective, however, in producing great buildings. Because it was within the realm of architecture that FLW was most profoundly generative, I leave this analysis for last and treat it in the most detail. I begin with a brief discussion of the vicissitudes inherent in FLW's architecture: the contexts and dynamics that promoted change in his architectural thought and production. In the remaining five segments of this section, I present a developmental scheme that captures the generative movement of his architecture over the 70-year period that he spent practicing that craft.

My exploration of the work of FLW revealed that his architectural mission began as a (a) *search for truth* in which he attempted to synthesize his experiences, proclivities, and design influences into a unified idea of "good architecture"—architecture that had integrity. This (b) *truth* that he began to refer to as "organic architecture" led to a larger, (c) *grand vision* of architecture's role in promoting a democratic society and individual freedom. Although inherently theoretical, this (d) *partially realized* utopia was expressed in several of his models and buildings and in one large university campus project. In the final (e) *playful retrospectives* phase, FLW returned to his beginnings as his creativity drew on the original sources of his architectural inspiration.

The Vicissitudes of Generativity

At the age of 47 FLW experienced what Snarey (1993; also see chapter 2, this volume) referred to as "generativity chill." This occurs when a generativity-threatening experience, such as a child's death or near-death, startles one into facing the reality (and fear) of death. It may have the effect of activating or reenergizing one's generativity as one attempts to reduce the death anxiety by creating a legacy.

FLW built his most personal structure to date when he created Taliesin in Spring Green, Wisconsin. Removed from the intrusive press and from a chaotic Chicago, this was to be his getaway, where he could spend time with his new-found love, Mamah Cheney. In 1914, 3 years after FLW built Taliesin, tragedy struck. Julian Carleton, a fundamentalist from Barbados who was employed as the cook at Taliesin, boarded up all the windows and doors but one and then set the structure afire. As his victims emerged through the door to escape the fire, he slaughtered them with an ax. In all, Carleton killed Cheney, her two daughters who were visiting, four of Wright's employees, and himself.

FLW was, by all accounts, completely devastated by the event. His son John, who rode with FLW and Mamah's husband (all in the same train compartment) from Chicago to Spring Green, remarked that he had never seen his father so lifeless as during this incident. It was the first nadir point in an enduring pattern of personal and architectural death and rebirth cycles in FLW's career. Disaster was to strike often, but it always led to rejuvenated creativity. Taliesin was to incur damage by fire again in 1925 and then again in 1952. Each time, designs were drawn and reconstruction begun the next day. Some (Hoppen, 1993) have argued that the great fire of 1871 that destroyed so much of Oak Park was instrumental in gaining Wright important residential commissions early in his career.

Fire was not the only force of destruction. Miriam Noel blistered FLW's career as well. Officially his second wife, Noel met FLW soon after the death of Cheney (Noel wrote a kind of seduction note to FLW expressing her sympathies). The most turbulent of FLW's four significant relationships, this one was a lethal mix of clashing personalities and bizarre events that included FLW's starting rumors that Noel was a heroin addict, FLW's indictment for unlawfully transporting women (Noel) across state lines (Clarence Darrow got the case dismissed), Noel's sadistic and violent nature, FLW's insecurities turned to hatred, and physical violence between the two (Gill, 1987). FLW barely survived the relationship, but in the depths of its horror he created the Imperial Hotel in Tokyo, a magnificent structure.

Perhaps the lowest FLW ever sank architecturally occurred in the years between 1924 and 1933 when he completed only two projects. His awakening began in the late 1920s with the help of Olgivanna (his third and final wife), the beginnings of the Ocotillo camp in Arizona for his workers, the publication of his autobiography in 1932, and the changing tide of public opinion, best represented in the positive profile of FLW in a 1930 *New Yorker* article (Hertz, 1995).

FLW was back. He was revitalized and now had the benefit of young minds and bodies to work with (the Taliesin Fellowship opened in 1932), but the country was in the midst of the Great Depression. As a result, he lost some important commissions, and much of his energy was channeled into designs, models, and writings. Those who did have money for a building by FLW at this point were rewarded immeasurably. The Edgar Kaufmann, Sr., home (Fallingwater, in Pennsylvania), completed in 1935, is considered "the best-known private home for someone not of royal blood in the history of the world" (Storrer, 1992, p. 230). Quite different in design but equally representative of this rebirth are the Hanna residence (Honeycomb House, in Stanford, California) and the Johnson Administration Building (Racine, Wisconsin), both completed in 1936.

Aware of the dramatic pattern of destruction leading to rejuvenation in his architecture, FLW likened himself to the phoenix, the mythical bird that consumes itself and then rises in youthful freshness out of its own ashes (John Lloyd Wright, 1992). These outbursts of creativity occurred in much shorter time frames as well. Several apprentices have related stories of different incidents that have the same basic plot: Pressure builds when FLW fails again to meet a deadline on promised designs for a client; the client threatens to back out of the project; and then—BAM!—FLW churns out many weeks' worth of design schemes in an hour or two. Working at a feverish pace the apprentices do all they can to keep him supplied with enough sharp pencils, and the client is won over by the greatness of the plan. The most often retold episode is of FLW drawing the complete set of plans for Fallingwater in less than 2 hours.

From mental germination to creative outburst, FLW played with the possibilities of form, material, and location until that "thrilling moment in any architect's experience. He is about to see the countenance of something he is invoking with intense concentration. Out of this inner sense of order and love of the beauty of life something is to be born" (FLW, quoted in Hoppen, 1993, p. 150).

This metaphor of giving birth through his architectural efforts demonstrates well the tension several theorists have noted between agentic and communal modes within generativity (Kotre, 1984; Mansfield & McAdams, 1996; McAdams, 1985; Peterson, 1993). The full expression of generativity requires both an extension of self (agency) and a blending with and through others (communion). The generative adult takes pride in fashioning a unique gift or creating products in one's own image, a form of healthy self-adulation. He or she must also "let go" and offer these products up to the larger community. FLW was consistently agentic in his architecture but rarely communal.

FLW's buildings were designed as manifestations of his greatness. As a young man he said,

> Not only do I intend to be the greatest architect who has yet lived, but the greatest who will ever live. Yes, I intend to be the greatest architect of all time, and I do hereunto affix "the red square" and sign my name to this warning. (Quoted in John Lloyd Wright, 1992, p. 33)

The healthy self-adulation of the generative adult often slipped into arrogance for FLW. It wasn't simply the brash pride of an ambitious young man. A vision of his arrogance is captured in the videos of the famous "column test," which occurred when FLW was 70 years of age. The Wisconsin state building code would not allow for the construction of the Johnson Wax building as designed unless FLW could prove that his unorthodox "dendriform" columns could support 12 tons of weight each. The columns were but 6 inches in diameter at the base, and few believed that his reinforced concrete would withstand the test. They were to be disappointed. Once the 12 tons had been placed on the large disk on top of the column, FLW motioned with his cane for more sandbags and pig iron to be loaded. As members of the press (called out by FLW; he was beginning to use the press for his profit) and the code inspectors looked on from a safe distance, FLW occasionally strolled up to the bottom of the column and gave it an exaggerated kick. The column collapsed only after 60 tons had been piled onto it.

Further evidence of his conceit in architecture is abundant. Insecure with his height of 5' 5" (Hertz, 1995), FLW designed many of his buildings (Fallingwater and the school at Taliesin are two prime examples) such that anyone over 6' would have to stoop to get through some of the passageways. He said that tall people, like weeds, were a waste of material. There is no doubt that his buildings were extensions, in his mind, of his greatness. But what of the communal aspect of generativity?

FLW found it difficult to offer his products to a wider audience, including the clients who paid for them. Regardless of legal ownership, he considered any building designed by him as belonging to him. Hoppen (1993) related an incident in which FLW took a group on a tour of a home he had designed many years earlier. He walked through the front door unannounced and proceeded through each room, including the dining room where the residents were having their dinner, without pause, all the time pointing out details of his work and discussing how he would change things now. Never acknowledging the family at the dinner table, he and his group strolled out the door without bothering to close it. Similarly, he retained ownership of gifts he had given to friends or family. His initial generosity might be followed up by a return visit years later when he would reclaim the gift, suggesting that he had a better spot for it at his home.

The communal aspect of generativity did not come naturally to FLW. He found it difficult to let go of his products in a genuine way. It was not difficult, however, for him to improve on the gifts others created, including his attempts to "improve" valuable Japanese prints with colored pencils and crayons.

Like the great modern creators studied by Gardner (1993), FLW resisted stagnation, the other side of Erikson's generativity dialectic. Had he continued throughout his life to make variations of the Prairie style home he had perfected in the first two decades of the century, FLW would have achieved both wealth and fame. The same could be said regarding Picasso's blue period. Great creators are not satisfied with redundancy, however, and they must move on. When asked which of his buildings was his favorite, FLW typically responded, "The next one."

The Search for Truth

As a young architect, FLW's primary quest was to discover a genuine combination of form and function. Although his mentor, Louis Sullivan, held that "form follows function" in good architecture, FLW contended that the two are the same. FLW's mode here is captured well in his mother's family (the Lloyd Jones) motto, which he heard often in his childhood: "truth against the world." His search for truth in architecture, like this maxim, assumed an antagonistic stance against the world. Although he had not yet settled on his own unique version of the truth in architecture, he knew that it was not to be found in the design and building conventions of the time. For example, he refused a generous grant to study at the prestigious Beaux Arts Paris because of its emphasis on classicism.

These larger architectural standards and norms represented the "world" that he railed against. He despised traditional styles such as Queen Anne and disliked anything derivative. This is not to say that he did not experiment with these forms himself or that he invented his ideas regarding true architecture from scratch. Instead, his sense of truth came from the many styles that he experimented with during this early period of his career.

Although FLW was positively influenced by many architects and architectural traditions, he gave credit only to Sullivan, whom FLW worked for from the time he was 20 until he was 26. In a fortunate intersecting of the historical and the personal in time and place, FLW applied for a position with the firm Adler and Sullivan at a time when the firm was not seeking to employ more draftspersons but when Sullivan was hoping to find a sketch artist who could do justice to his intricate designs. FLW was hired to work closely with Sullivan, and 2 years later the firm began planning for its part in the 1893 Chicago World's Columbian Exposition, which was to display architecture from around the world.

The fair was held at the midway of the University of Chicago, which was also founded that year, on the south side of Chicago. Many of the core components of FLW's eventual formula for true architecture were present at this fair: indigenous Native American and Central American architecture, the urban planning of Daniel Burnham and John Wellborn Root, the use of emerging technologies in building, the landscape architecture of Frederick Law Olmsted, the Turkish pavilion, and, of course, the Japanese tradition. Equally as important, many of his "enemies" were represented as well. Partly defining himself through repudiation, FLW was exposed to productions of academic neoclassicism (dominated by Easterners) and of Beaux Arts Paris. FLW viewed these derivative designs as unoriginal and thus false.

Sullivan's contribution to the exposition, the transportation building that FLW worked so closely on, was certainly not derivative. The intricate ornamentation in the shrinking arches of the "golden doorway" was not well received at the time, but later it was recognized for its significance in the historical progression of architecture. This would serve as a good model for belated or intrinsic rewards to those like FLW who adhered to "truth against the world."

The several buildings that FLW designed while working with Sullivan, both the official projects that he headed for the firm and the several "bootlegged" designs he completed, are best described as eclectic. He drew liberally from the different architectural influences to which he had been exposed. He toyed with different styles even after he was fired from Adler and Sullivan for moonlighting in 1893. Houses designed within the same time period are often completely different from one another, and sometimes completely different styles exist side by side in the same house. The Moore house of 1895, for instance, combines a Tudor roof line with both detailed Gothic and clean-lined Japanese-style windows (portions were later redesigned and built after a 1922 fire). FLW was extremely prolific during these years, completing over 50 projects within the first decade after leaving Sullivan's mentorship.

FLW received the attention of a wide audience when he appeared in the *Architectural Record* in 1905. He received international attention when his work and ideas were published in a Wasmuth edition in Germany 5 years later. FLW's search for truth was beginning to culminate in the mature Prairie style homes and the significant nonresidential commissions of the Larkin Company Administration Building (1903, Buffalo, New York) and Unity Church (1904, Oak Park, Illinois). The Willits house (1901, Highland Park, Illinois) is considered the first true Prairie home, and the Robie House (1906, Chicago) is considered the prime example of this style. Describing the Willits house and the Prairie style in general, Gill (1987) writes the following:

> Despite the rather too obvious efficiency of its plan, the Willits house has the warmth and charm that Wright was able to introduce into all his best houses by dint of their detailing—the bejeweled art-glass windows, the peek-a-boo wood screens that lure one from room to room, the broad brick hearths that promise the primordial consolations of firelight and tribal gatherings. It was not the actual prairie that these houses summoned up, but the expression of some essential goodness in family life that could be imagined as existing (or having once existed) on the American prairie. (p. 136)

The Prairie style FLW championed at this time was not the truth he had been seeking but a manifestation of it. His explorations during these years did not lead to a type of home, Prairie or any other, but culminated in his beliefs regarding the underlying principles and ideals on which all true architecture could be built. The Prairie style was an important aspect of FLW's creative development because it was the first to adhere to his tenets of architectural truth, but he went on to discover other styles that also followed the philosophy he constructed.

Truth

FLW's philosophy was best captured in his concept of "organic architecture," which is expressed in its nascent stage in the introduction he wrote for the 1910 German Wasmuth edition. FLW developed this philosophy over the years. In its mature form, the tenets of FLW's doctrine of architectural truth include the following:

1. *An organic relationship is to exist between an architectural structure and the surrounding land it inhabits.* A building should not conquer nature but embrace it symbiotically. This is captured in FLW's remark that a house should be "of" a hill and not "on" a hill. This concept also is reflected in FLW's insistence on using construction materials that are indigenous to the area of the building. He used local lava in his Japanese projects, for example, and sand-based concrete in Taliesin West in the Arizona desert. Hertz (1995) commented that FLW's "Emersonian organicism made him a twentieth century environmentalist, an anachronism in terms of Modernist ideology, but a prophet in relation to architectural concerns of the late twentieth century" (p. 1).

2. *An architect is to be inspired not from past architecture which is (derivative) but from forms in nature.* FLW implemented the abstractions of organic structures such as trees or cacti and natural formations such as mountain ranges into his building designs.

3. *Organic architecture is elemental and nonpretentious.* It is elemental in that it addresses the fundamental aspects of structure such as the destruction of the box as the pivotal form, the reinvention of the column, and the removal of the superfluous to intensify the essential. FLW said "five lines where three is enough is stupidity" (quoted in John Lloyd Wright, 1992, p. 68). It is nonpretentious in that it does not lie. A material is used to represent itself and nothing else.

4. *The meaning and integrity of a structure derives from its geometric essence.* All buildings should have a unifying geometry, and this geometry should be expressed organically in that the whole relates to the parts and the parts to the whole, as in the geometric consistency of a Japanese print. Furthermore, specific geometric forms are representative of human modes

and sentiments. The horizontal line is the line of domesticity. The square (FLW's self-assigned symbol) represents integrity. A circle denotes infinity. The triangle stands for unity. A spire is aspiration. At 90, FLW could still imagine the feel of the Froebelian geometry blocks he played with as a child. All form was, in essence, geometric.

5. *Technology must be used for aesthetic purposes.* Amazed at the failure of his fellow artisans to see the potential uses of modern tools and machinery in their craft, FLW embraced technology. He referred to steel as a "miracle of strength for its weight and cost." Reinforced concrete was to appear in several different guises in his architecture: as textile blocks, as his beloved cantilevers, and as strong but narrow "dendriform" columns.

Positing these five tenets is reductionistic to be sure, but they capture the central aspects of FLW's elusive writings concerning architectural truth. His plan to overthrow the architectural establishment was founded on these convictions. The forces within architecture working against this plan were classicism, commercialism, and academism (Hertz, 1995). Although he had the talent to back up his battle call of "truth against the world" within the realm of architecture, these tenets of truth were noticeably missing in his personal life. Here one finds little evidence of the organic modes he spoke of, such as integrity and nonpretension.

There was no truth in his image of himself. His 1932 autobiography reads like the rantings of an egomaniacal liar. There was no truth in his desire to meet the stated requests of his clients. He advised his son John to give the client what you deem they need, not what they say they want (John Lloyd Wright, 1992). There was no truth in his marriage vows. There was no truth in his false erudition. His writings are filled with misguided interpretations, confusion of thought, and fabrications. There was no truth in his imagined persecution. The press did pester him, but not to the extent he professed. Make-believe heroes need make-believe villains.

He had, however, found truth in architecture. There was no falseness in the beauty of his buildings. FLW seemed aware of this contradiction at some level. Speaking of his philandering ways, he told Hoppen (1993) that "God might have been testing my character, but he knew that in architecture I always gave my best" (p. 54). If he was to be judged, he told journalists, let it be by his architecture. There were no lies there.

A Grand Vision

Having firmly established his vision of architectural truth as it applied to the individual building, FLW's generativity in this domain broadened in scope as he began to redirect his architectural efforts to the larger concerns of society. He was beginning to discuss his vision of utopia. He wrote 4 books and 14 articles between his 61st and 65th years—in all, he published over 20 books—most of which address his utopian vision in one way or another. His public addresses were important avenues for his proselytizing as well. Like his minister father, who was a gifted orator, FLW was capable of charming the most unsympathetic audience member. His utopian views are the dominant theme of the six lectures he delivered at Princeton in 1930 (which were recycled in addresses given at the Chicago Art Institute and other places) and an important component of his London lectures in 1939.

Although FLW's idea of utopia is discussed in most of his publications, the books that are primarily about his vision of the good society include *The Disappearing City* (1932) and its expanded revision, *When Democracy Builds* (1945), as well as *The Living City* (1958) and *Architecture and Modern Life* (1937), which FLW co-authored with Baker Brownell, a professor of sociology. Although the vision shifted somewhat in the nearly 30 years between the Princeton lectures and the publication of *The Living City*, the global portrait that FLW painted of the desired community was generally consistent.

"Usonia" was the name he chose for his utopia and it had Broadacre City as its capital. One dominant theme in this vision was the oppressiveness of the city. City dwellers are forced to live in artificial verticals. FLW felt that there was an innate human need to live in open horizontals; he referred to the horizontal as the line of domesticity. The city lacks soul and it removes humans from nature, which is a primary source of inspiration and beauty. The population must be decentralized, spread across the vast expanse of land. Every Usonian citizen was to be granted one "broad acre." This decentralization, made possible through technological advances such as telephones and automobiles, would help diffuse the central authority of the government and encourage individualism and self-sufficiency through contact with and ownership of the land.

Fierce individualism promoted through holistic living with the land was a major aspect of FLW's utopia. Unlike many socialist or religion-based utopias, which emphasize the surrender of individual uniqueness to the group or to a greater power, Usonia was designed such that individual talents and ambitions could be fully realized. One step toward this goal was to raze completely the existing system of education. FLW often said that if he were rich he would buy all the universities and burn them to the ground. There were no professors in Usonia because professors transform students whose wonder seeks originality into dullard clones. Instead, there are "father confessors" who relate their views without stifling students' unique innovative tendencies. In this way those who have talent may rise. Not surprisingly, it was the gifted and wise architect who had a central role in Usonian society, which created an odd mixture of a benevolent totalitarian architect leader of an otherwise egalitarian democracy. As in the Taliesin Fellowship, there was a tension between FLW's desire for equality between all and his inflated perspective of himself and architecture.

FLW was genuine in his hopes to achieve democracy through his architecture. He railed against the divisive class structure he saw in European hegemony and against the traditional prejudices that thwarted the freedom of the individual (Johnson, 1990). In Usonia, all citizens are seen as worthy of benefiting from great architecture. Consonant with the emphasis on the "common man" in the United States beginning in the 1930s, FLW declared that all persons, from every rank and background, should live and work in beautiful buildings. Aware of the financial constraints caused by the Great Depression that began in late 1929, FLW sought ways to use technology and inexpensive building materials to construct affordable housing.

As in FLW's version of "the truth" in architecture, his grand vision is defined through the forces it opposes (modern city, class structure, big government) as much as through what it embraces (open horizontals, fierce individualism, egalitarianism, affordable housing, machine as liberator). Hertz (1995), who has written of FLW's Usonia extensively, found great wisdom in this utopian vision. He lamented the fact that FLW's utopian writings have not drawn more interest, even from FLW scholars. Le Corbusier, the French architect and contemporary of FLW, had utopian views that have been thoroughly studied, yet Usonia remains relatively unexamined. Gill (1987), offering a different view, equated FLW's utopia with a monstrously enlarged Oak Park—"a single immaculate and homogeneous non-city" (p. 338)—void of the charm offered by neighborhoods and of the energy that emanates from the dense population of a city.

Partial Realizations

FLW's grand vision of utopia was an idealistic end state to which he could direct his generative energy in architecture. It was the type of society FLW wanted to create and leave to younger generations. It was a blueprint of how to set up society such that all members could live fulfilling lives. However, it was unattainable in its complete form. Usonia was not to be achieved but approximated. Mature generativity requires one to work with what is at hand to approximate the completion of larger dreams. As the popular slogan has it, one must "think globally and act locally." Theories of how the world should be left to younger generations are wonderful but "doing" generativity requires both flexibility and pragmatism. FLW's utopia is partially realized in several different projects.

One physical manifestation of FLW's utopian writings was the 12-square-foot model of Broadacre City that he and his apprentices constructed during the early 1930s. Eager to play with a tangible representation of his utopian vision, FLW lured two patrons into funding his efforts in the midst of the Depression, when commissions were rare. The model is a detailed depiction of four square miles of Broadacre. Once completed, it traveled the world on exhibition. It is currently on display at Taliesin in Spring Green, Wisconsin.

A second, and more pragmatic, realization of FLW's utopian vision consists of what were known as Usonian homes. The first Usonian home was built for Herb Jacobs in 1936; its defining characteristic was its inexpensiveness. It was Wright's response to the affordable housing obstacle in his utopia. Later, during the 1950s, the Usonian "automatic house" was developed. It was a prefabricated home made of inexpensive materials and affordable to nearly every person in the United States. Hundreds of them were bought and constructed. Usonian homes contain only the essentials. There are no light fixtures, basements, or gutters, for example. Furthermore, a Usonian home was nearly always constructed of horizontal wood slats and built facing away from the street with doors opening up to large gardens. This was consonant with FLW's views on horizontality, individuality, and attunement to nature. Usonian homes did not pretend to be anything other than what they were: simple yet beautiful homes affordable to middle-class people. Wright compared Usonian homes to a country girl who is content to wear clothes that fit her status and her labor.

Wright also implemented other inexpensive building techniques made possible by technology, such as his beloved concrete textile block. This method was used extensively in the Florida Southern University (FSU) design, which was the closest FLW came to fulfilling his utopian vision in one project. FSU contains the largest collection of FLW buildings on one site. The 1938 design included 18 buildings, although only 10 were constructed (between 1938 and 1959). Ludd Myrl Spivey, the president of FSU, was like FLW in many respects: he was a slender bundle of energy willing to connive and able to charm to achieve his lofty dream—to turn an unknown regional Methodist seminary into a prestigious "great education temple" (Gill, 1987, p. 397). The project afforded FLW the opportunity to build a Usonian community. Adhering to the notion of decentralization, the buildings are spread out over the entire 87-acre campus. Horizontality is achieved in that the buildings hug the ground and are connected by a series of covered esplanades that replicate the horizontal linearity of the surrounding orange groves. The Florida sunlight dances with the blocked glass that is woven into the concrete textile blocks. An integration of the use of inexpensive building materials and holistic living principles was expressed in a peculiar way when FLW had the student-builders donate their urine to a mix used in oxidizing the copper detailing on the buildings.

FLW's grand utopian vision was partially realized in the Broadacre model, the Usonian homes, the use of inexpensive building materials and techniques, and the campus of FSU. It was through the "doing" aspect of generativity that these completed projects represent FLW's approximation of his larger, idealistic generativity plan.

Playful Retrospectives

Hertz (1995) viewed the FSU project as transitional:

A stable rectangle, rotated, becomes a hexagon. Rotated still faster and further, it finally becomes a circle. Thus the vibrant interpenetration of diverse forms—superimposed combinations of hexagons, rectangles and circles—in Wright's work at Florida Southern can be viewed as a transitional achievement leading to the circles, arches and ovals of his last years. (p. 111)

In the final phase of his architectural generativity, FLW returned to his beginnings as his creativity drew on the original sources of his architectural inspiration. His last visions were captured in architectural drawings, the medium in which he began and the very talent that landed him his job with mentor Louis Sullivan.

FLW began to play with geometry, as he first did with his Froebel blocks as a child, in a whimsical manner. His use of crystallized rotation —twisted repetitions of a unified geometry—throughout his designs is one manifestation of this phase. These buildings, most of which were constructed during the 1950s, pull one in and through the structure. One is drawn into the multiple perspectives offered by the rotational pattern. At 81 years of age, FLW designed 3 one-room cottages for his sister, Marginel Wright Barney. Again playing with shapes, each building is based on a different geometry. At 85, FLW designed three lines of furniture, one circular, one rectangular, and one triangular-hexagonal (Besinger, 1995).

FLW's manipulation of geometry led to his late-life fascination with the curvilinearity of arches and spirals that Sullivan so cherished. In *Genius and Mobocracy*, published when FLW was 82, he discussed the significant influence that Sullivan had on him and placed himself within the generational lineage of Sullivan and Sullivan's major influence, Henry Richardson. FLW was returning to the teachers of his past. This is most clearly manifested in the several curvilinear designs of this period: the David Wright residence of 1950, the Greek Orthodox church of 1956, the Marin County civic center of 1957, and the Gammage Memorial Auditorium of 1959. All these designs are curvilinear.

Perhaps the best example of this phase in FLW's career is the Guggenheim Museum of Art in New York City. The story of the Guggenheim project, which was initiated in 1943, is complex and lengthy. It begins with the assumption of the curator, Hilla Rebay (Baroness Hildegard Rebay von Ehrenwiesen), that FLW was dead, and the assumption of FLW, once he was hired, that Rebay was a man—he invited Rebay and her wife to Taliesin! Examples of other complications include the death of Solomon R. Guggenheim in 1949, which all but ended the project; picketing of the construction site by groups of artists in protest of FLW's design; and the halting of construction by city inspectors for failure to meet building codes. However, the Guggenheim was eventually completed, officially opening 6 months after FLW's death in 1959.

The museum was to house abstract "nonobjective" art. The one unified downward sloping ramp that forms the spiraling interior of the building was meant to capture the unfolding of an artist's chronology of creativity. The spiral widens as it rises toward the sky. FLW referred to it as an "an optimistic ziggurat." The Guggenheim is the best physical representation of Erikson's theory of psychosocial development that I can imagine, each separate ring symbolizing a phase of life. Looking downward from the interior top, one looks back over the entire life as lived. From this vantage point, I imagine FLW surveying his past, including the unfolding of his generativity from quest to truth, from vision to fulfillment.

CONCLUSION

The evolution of FLW's generativity within the realm of architecture was surely not as orderly as the outline presented indicates. The five identified phases in the growth of FLW's architectural projects and ideas are best understood as parts of a general pattern of development. These capture the most salient aspects of FLW's architecture at different points in his life. The reality of human development is too messy to suggest that any one issue or mode completely dominates any specified period within a life. Erikson knew this well. His notion of epigenetic development (Erikson, 1950/1963) maintains that all developmental issues are present at all times but that modes such as identity formation or generativity emerge as psychosocially most salient during specified phases of development. This is not to suggest that, for example, the generative adult whom Erikson situates within the seventh psychosocial stage at midlife is not at some level working on identity issues that dominate young adulthood. Identity, like all psychosocial issues, is never "achieved" completely.

One finds nascent generativity in the child just as one observes elders who struggle to some extent with childhood issues such as a sense of competence (Erikson's fourth stage, which occurs during late childhood, "industry vs. inferiority"). Likewise, there is ample evidence of the existence of modes in FLW's architecture that do not fit neatly into the five-phase scheme. For instance, his concerns regarding affordable housing were most prominent during late midlife when he worked on the Usonian home (partial realizations of a grand vision), although Gill (1987) noted that FLW was already "determined to provide the best possible housing for the largest possible number of people at the lowest cost" at the age of 34. Gill referred to a 1901 *Ladies Home Journal* article wherein FLW included a complete set of housing designs that could be sold for the low cost of $5. Furthermore, the spiral is most fully realized in FLW's last architectural phase, but FLW noted its meaning in *The Japanese Print: An Interpretation*, which he published at the age of 45. The point is that the concern for affordable housing may have been a consistent aspect of FLW's architectural generativity but was most salient during late midlife. He was clearly aware of curvilinearity his entire life, but it was not until he was an old man that he fully implemented spirals, arches, and circles into his architecture. Rather than view such examples as inconsistent with the general developmental pattern, these and other such instances represent epigenesis in the development of FLW's architectural generativity.

Few would wish to emulate all aspects of FLW's generativity. As noted, he was an apathetic father and a poor teacher. His life and work demonstrate the complexity of generativity. One may be generative in one life domain but not another. One may possess characteristics that act as inhibitors to one's generative desires. Within the domain of architecture, however, FLW was extremely generative.

In his design patterns, FLW took the detailed floral designs of Sullivan and abstracted them into geometric forms. For instance, he re-created trees in many of his window designs as clusters of rectangles. To abstract is to leave out the details. It is possible to do the same in discussing generativity theory with regard to the details of one life. Abstracting from the particulars of FLW's architecture, one discovers that his generativity in this area required focus on specified projects; an ideology regarding the ideal society; the use of state-of-the-art technology to create partial fulfillments of this ideology; and a perspective of how one's self fits into the larger social and historical context. These abstractions read as aphorisms for a generative life. The generative adult employs the materials at hand to achieve approximations of his or her view of how the world should be left to younger generations.

Asked by an apprentice if he was afraid of death, FLW replied, "Not at all. There is not much you can do about death. What is immortal will survive" (quoted in Hoppen, 1993, p. 160). Much has survived his physical existence. The "outcome" (Kotre, 1995) of his generativity includes both dark remnants such as the pain he caused his children and the remarkably positive legacy that is his architecture. The buildings FLW created represent his version of the truth, which he chose to leave to a world that he battled against his entire life.

APPENDIX

Selective Chronology of the Life of Frank Lloyd Wright

This Chronology is selective in that it lists only a small fraction of FLW's completed architectural projects (of which there are over 430), publications (there are approximately 20 books and many smaller publications such as magazine articles), public addresses (there were hundreds, if one includes those delivered to the fellowship at Taliesin), travels, personal life events, and awards received (there were dozens). Although I admit to a certain degree of arbitrariness in final decisions regarding the inclusion and exclusion of items in this chronology, each was based on the convergence of views from independent sources concerning which FLW products are most significant or representative.

Year	Age	
1867		Born June 8 in Richland Center, Wisconsin, to William Wright (minister born in 1825; first wife died in 1864) and Anna Lloyd Jones (daughter of idealistic Unitarian farmers; born in 1842). FLW, the first of three children, spent a large portion of the 1870s in New England, living the nomadic life imposed by father's occupation.
1885	18	Parents divorce. Father wins court settlement, and FLW has no further contact with his father. FLW lives with mother and her family in Spring Green, Wisconsin.
1887	20	*Hillside Home School*, a private school in Spring Green where his aunts Nell and Jane taught. FLW's first completed architectural project.
	20	FLW moves to Chicago after a brief stay at the University of Wisconsin, where he receives practical experience in building under the guidance of Allan D. Conover, a professor of engineering. In Chicago, he is employed first in the offices of J. L. Silsbee, the architect and friend of FLW's uncle, Jenkin Lloyd Jones, an established Chicago minister. Soon after, FLW is hired as a draftsman in the Adler and Sullivan architectural firm. Referring to his relationship with his mentor, Louis Sullivan, FLW described his position here as "the pencil" in the hands of the *Lieber Meister*.
1889	22	FLW marries Catherine Tobin (also 22 years of age). This marriage produced six children: Lloyd, John, Catherine, Frances, David, and Robert Llewelyn.
	22	*FLW residence*: Oak Park, Illinois. FLW continually redesigned and reconfigured this structure, with major changes being the playroom addition in 1893 and the studio in 1895.

Appendix continues

Year	Age	
1893	26	FLW fired from Adler and Sullivan for moonlighting (what he referred to as bootlegging): He designed as many as 10 houses between 1890 and 1893 on his own, typically not assigning his name to these projects as a protection from committing a breach of his employment contract.
	26	*Winslow residence and stables*: River Forest, Illinois. First independent commission after leaving Adler and Sullivan.
1896	29	*Romeo and Juliet Windmill*: Spring Green, Wisconsin.
1901	34	Delivers *The Art and Craft of the Machine* to the Chicago Arts and Craft Society at Jane Addams's Hull House. Although most members of the powerful arts and craft movement of this period viewed technology as a menacing force that stifles all that is beautiful and artistic in human endeavors, FLW embraced modern technological advances (captured in the "machine" metaphor) in this address as expanding human artistic potential. Not surprisingly, the speech was not well received.
	34	*Ward W. Willits residence*: Highland Park, Illinois. Considered the first true Prairie style house.
1903	36	*Larkin Company administration building*: Buffalo, New York.
1904	37	*Unity Church*: Oak Park, Illinois. Introduces the use of reinforced concrete construction in a large-scale building.
1905	38	Travels to Japan with wife and another couple for 3 months. FLW purchases several rare textiles and art objects. He becomes a major collector of Japanese prints, twice having them displayed in Chicago Art Institute exhibitions. Begins to receive national attention for his architectural designs, appearing in *Architectural Record* during this year.
1906	39	*Robie House*: Chicago, Illinois. An excellent example of the mature Prairie style that FLW had been creating.
1909	42	FLW generates public uproar by openly traveling to Europe with his mistress, Mamah Borthwick Cheney, who is the wife of one of his clients. This scandalous eschewing of the conventions costs him potential clients. He and Cheney work on *Ausgefuhrte Bauten und Entwurfe*, a book illustrating FLW's architecture published by Wasmuth in 1910. FLW writes preface to the introduction titled "Sovereignty of the Individual and the Causes of Architecture."

Year	Age	
1911	44	*Taliesin*: Spring Green, Wisconsin. FLW created this residence for himself, his lover Mamah Cheney, and his mother, on whose property it was constructed.
1912	45	Published *The Japanese Print: An Interpretation*.
1913	46	*Midway Gardens*: Chicago, Illinois. Encompassing an entire city block, this open space for entertainment and dining has been described as a mix of U.S. cafe, German beer garden, Japanese sculpture garden, and teahouse.
1914	47	Julian Carleton, a fundamentalist from Barbados who was employed as the cook at Taliesin, locked all but one door and then set fire to Taliesin. As his victims emerged through the door to escape the fire, he slaughtered them with an axe. In all, he killed Cheney; her two daughters, who were visiting; four of Wright's employees; and himself.
1915	48	FLW meets Miriam Noel soon after the tragedy of the fire. She moves to Taliesin. Noel is a rich (from divorce settlement) 43-year-old with three children.
	48	Taliesin is rebuilt; Noel leaves FLW (moves to Chicago) 9 months later.
	48	*Imperial Hotel*: Tokyo, Japan.
1917	50	*Arizona Biltmore Hotel and cottages*: Phoenix, Arizona.
1920	53	*Aline Barsdall Hollyhock house*: Los Angeles, California. Poured concrete structure suggestive of a Mayan temple.
1922	55	Catherine grants FLW the divorce he was seeking for 13 years.
1923	56	Mother (Anna Lloyd Wright) dies.
1924	57	FLW marries Miriam Noel.
	57	Louis Sullivan dies.
	57	FLW meets Olgivanna Milanov Hinzenberg, a 26-year-old mother of one, who is seeking a divorce from a Chicago architect.
1925	58	Olgivanna and FLW give birth to Iovanna.
	58	Another fire strikes at Taliesin.
1927	60	Noel grants FLW a divorce.
	60	FLW becomes incorporated to solve financial problems.
1928	61	FLW marries Olgivanna and adopts Svetlanta, Olgivanna's daughter from a previous marriage. FLW and Olgivanna remain married until his death in 1959.

Appendix continues

Year	Age	
	61	*Ocotillo Desert Camp*: Chandler, Arizona. A forerunner to the later Taliesin West, this camp was to house FLW and his crew while they worked on various projects for Dr. Alexander Chandler. The stock market crash of 1929 brought these commissions to a halt.
1930	63	Alfred Kahn lectures delivered at Princeton University, titled "Modern Architecture."
1932	65	Publishes *Autobiography*.
	65	Publishes *The Disappearing City*.
	65	Taliesin Fellowship opens.
	65	FLW and apprentices construct 12-square-foot model of *Broadacre City*.
1936	69	*Edgar J. Kaufmann, Sr., residence (Fallingwater)*: Ohiopyle, Pennsylvania.
	69	*Paul Hanna house (Honeycomb house)*: Palo Alto, California.
	69	*Johnson Wax administration building*: Racine, Wisconsin.
1937	70	Publishes *Architecture and Modern Life*, with Baker Brownell.
	70	*Taliesin West*: Scottsdale, Arizona.
	70	*Herbert Johnson residence (Wingspread)*: Wind Point, Wisconsin.
1938	71	Begins *Florida Southern University* project. FSU contains the largest collection of FLW buildings on one site. The 1938 design included 18 buildings of which only 10 were constructed (between 1938 and 1959).
1939	72	Publishes *An Organic Architecture: The Architecture of Democracy*.
	72	Delivers "Four Evenings on an Organic Architecture, the Architecture of Democracy," through the Sir George Watson Lectures before the Royal Institute of British Architects.
1941	74	King George VI awards FLW His Majesty's Gold Medal of the Royal Institute of British Architects.
1943	76	Expanded edition of *Autobiography* appears in print.
	76	Beginning of *Guggenheim Museum of Art* project—completed in 1959.
1945	78	Publishes *When Democracy Builds*.
1947	80	*Unitarian Church*: Shorewood Hills, Wisconsin.
1948	81	*Morris Gift Shop*: San Francisco, California.
1949	82	FLW receives American Institute of Architects Gold Medal.
	82	Publishes *Genius and Mobocracy*.
1950	*83*	*David Wright residence*: Phoenix, Arizona.

APPENDIX   (*Continued*)

Year	Age	
1952	85	*Price Company Tower.* Bartlesville, Oklahoma. A 19-story office building constructed of reinforced concrete and cantilevered floors with gold-tinted glass exterior.
1953	86	Publishes *The Future of Architecture.*
1954	87	Publishes *The Natural House.*
	87	*Beth Sholom Synagogue:* Elkins Park, Pennsylvania.
1956	89	*Annunciation Greek Orthodox Church:* Wauwatosa, Wisconsin.
1957	90	Publishes *A Testament.*
	90	*Marin County Civic Center.* San Raphael, California.
1959	91	FLW dies on April 9. Tombstone that he designed reads, "Love of an idea is the love of God."
1959		Guggenheim Museum opens 6 months after FLW's death.

REFERENCES

Alexander, I. E. (1988). Personality, psychological assessment, and psychobiography. In D. P. McAdams & R. L. Ochberg (Eds.), *Psychobiography and life narratives* (pp. 265–294). Durham, NC: Duke University Press.

Alexander, I. E. (1990). *Personology: Method and content in personality assessment and psychobiography.* Durham, NC: Duke University Press.

Alexander, I. E. (1996). On the origins of militant nonviolence [Review of Erik Erikson's Gandhi's truth]. *Contemporary Psychology, 41(4),* 311–315.

Allport, G. W. (1942). *The use of personal documents in psychological science.* New York: Social Science Research Council.

Anderson, J. W. (1981). Psychobiographical methodology: The case of William James. In L. Wheeler (Ed.), *Review of personality and social psychology* (Vol. 2, pp. 245–272). Beverly Hills, CA: Sage.

Anderson, J. W. (1988). Henry A. Murray's early career: A psychobiographic exploration. In D. P. McAdams & R. L. Ochberg (Eds.), *Psychobiography and life narratives* (pp. 139–172). Durham, NC: Duke University Press.

Baltes, P. B., Staudinger, U. M., Maercker, A., & Smith, J. (1995). People nominated as wise: A comparative study of wisdom-related knowledge. *Psychology and Aging, 10,* 155–166.

Bellah, R. N., Madsen, R., Sullivan, W. M., Swindler, A., & Tipton, S. M. (1991). *The good society.* New York: Knopf.

Besinger, C. (1995). *Working with Mr. Wright: What it was like.* Cambridge, MA: MIT Press.

Browning, D.S. (1975). *Generative man: Psychoanalytic perspectives*. New York: Dell.

Carlson, R. (1988). Exemplary lives: The use of psychobiography for theory development. In D. P. McAdams & R. L. Ochberg (Eds.), *Psychobiography and life narratives* (pp. 105–138). Durham, NC: Duke University Press.

Elms, A. C. (1988). Freud as Leonardo: Why the first psychobiography went wrong. In D. P. McAdams & R. L. Ochberg (Eds.), *Psychobiography and life narratives* (pp. 19–40). Durham, NC: Duke University Press.

Elms, A. C. (1994). *Uncovering lives: The uneasy alliance of biography and psychology*. New York: Oxford University Press.

Erikson, E. H. (1958). *Young man Luther: A study in psychoanalysis and history*. New York: Norton.

Erikson, E. H. (1963). *Childhood and society*. New York: Norton. (Original work published 1950)

Erikson, E. H. (1969). *Gandhi's truth: On the origins of militant nonviolence*. New York: Norton.

Erikson, E. H. (1987). The dream specimen of psychoanalysis. In S. Schlein (Ed.), *A way of looking at things: Selected papers from 1930 to 1980 Erik H. Erikson*. New York: Norton. (Original work published 1954)

Erikson. E. H. (1988). On the generational cycle: An address. In G. H. Pollock & J. M. Ross (Eds.), *The Oedipus papers: Classics in psychoanalysis* (pp. 241–259). Madison, CT: International Universities Press.

Gardner, H. (1993). *Creating minds: An anatomy of creativity seen through the lives of Freud, Einstein, Picasso, Stravinsky, Eliot, Graham, and Gandhi*. New York: Basic Books.

Gill, B. (1987). *Many masks: A life of Frank Lloyd Wright*. New York: Ballantine Books.

Hawkins, A. J., Christiansen, S. L., Sargent, K. P., & Hill, E. J. (1995). Rethinking fathers' involvement in child care: A developmental perspective. In W. Marsiglio (Ed.), *Fatherhood: Contemporary theory, research, and social policy* (pp. 41–56). London: Sage Publications.

Hertz, D. M. (1995). *Frank Lloyd Wright in word and form*. New York: Simon & Schuster.

Hoppen, D. W. (1993). *The seven ages of Frank Lloyd Wright*. Santa Barbara, CA: Capra Press.

Johnson, D. K. (1990). *Frank Lloyd Wright versus America: The 1930's*. Cambridge, MA: MIT Press.

Kleiber, D. A. & Ray, R. O. (1993). Leisure and generativity. In J. R. Kelly (Ed.), *Activity and aging* (pp. 106–117). London: Sage Publications.

Kotre, J. (1984). *Outliving the self: Generativity and the interpretation of lives*. Baltimore: The Johns Hopkins University Press.

Kotre, J. (1995). Generative outcome. *Journal of Aging Studies, 9*, 33–41.

Mansfield, E. D., & McAdams, D. P. (1996) Generativity and themes of agency and communion in adult autobiography. *Personality and Social Psychology Bulletin, 22,* 721–731.

McAdams, D. P. (1985). *Power, intimacy, and the life story: Personological inquiries into identity.* New York: Guilford Press.

McAdams, D. P. (1988). Biography, narrative, and lives: An Introduction. In D. P. McAdams & R. L. Ochberg (Eds.), *Psychobiography and life narratives* (pp. 1–18). Durham, NC: Duke University Press.

McAdams, D. P. (1993). *The stories we live by: Personal myths and the making of the self.* New York: Morrow.

McAdams, D. P., & de St. Aubin, E. (1992). A theory of generativity and its assessment through self-report, behavioral acts, and narrative themes in autobiography. *Journal of Personality and Social Psychology, 62,* 1003–1015.

Peterson, B. E. (1993). Generativity and social motives in young adults. *Journal of Personality and Social Psychology, 65,* 186–198.

Peterson, B. E., & Stewart, A. J. (1990). Using personal and fictional documents to assess psychosocial development: A case study of Vera Brittain's generativity. *Psychology and Aging, 5,* 400–411.

Runyan, W. M. (1982). *Life histories and psychobiography.* New York: Oxford University Press.

Runyan, W. M. (1984). Alternatives to psychoanalytic psychobiography. In W. M. Runyan (Ed.), *Psychology and historical interpretation* (pp. 219–246). New York: Oxford University Press.

Runyan, W. M. (1988). Progress in psychobiography. In D. P. McAdams & R. L. Ochberg (Eds.), *Psychobiography and life narratives* (pp. 295–326). Durham, NC: Duke University Press.

Secrest, M. (1992). *Frank Lloyd Wright.* New York: Knopf.

Snarey, J. (1993). *How fathers care for the next generation: A four-decade study.* Cambridge, MA: Harvard University Press.

Stewart, A. J., Franz, C., & Layton, L. (1988). The changing self: Using personal documents to study lives. *Journal of Personality, 56,* 41–47.

Storrer, W. A. (1992). *The architecture of Frank Lloyd Wright: A complete catalog* (2nd Ed.). Cambridge, MA: MIT Press.

Vaillant, G. E. (1977). *Adaptation to life.* Boston: Little, Brown.

Vaillant, G. E. (1993). *The wisdom of the ego.* Cambridge, MA: Harvard University Press.

Vaillant, G. E., & Milofsky, E. (1980). The natural history of male psychological health: IX. Empirical evidence for Erikson's model of the life cycle. *American Journal of Psychiatry, 137,* 1348–1359.

Wright, J. L. (1992). *My father, Frank Lloyd Wright.* New York: Dover. (Unabridged and revised republication of *My father who is on earth,* published in 1946 by Putnam, New York).

Wrightsman, L. S. (1981). Personal documents as data in conceptualizing adult personality development. *Personality and Social Psychology Bulletin, 7,* 367–385.

Photograph courtesy of the Library of Congress, New York
World-Telegram and Sun Collection, Prints and Photographs
Division; LC-USZ62-117523.

13

GENERATIVITY AND THE LIFE COURSE OF MARTHA GRAHAM

SUSAN A. LEE

In this chapter, I discuss Martha Graham's adaptive strategies and developmental challenges, her role as change agent in the dance world, her mentoring of several generations, and the magnitude of her legacy to society. This view of Martha Graham's life is presented against an analysis of the influential artistic milieu—the dance world as a social system. A developmental perspective frames this inquiry into Graham as a generative adult.

Graham began her journey of producing dances of substance at a time when most work in dance could be characterized as superficial, frivolous, or emotive. In the 1920s dance venues in the United States were limited to vaudeville, Broadway, and exhibitions of ballroom dance. Professional ballet was largely imported from Europe. This professional scene was also the arena for the new expressive Greek-inspired forms of Isadora Duncan and the Far Eastern motifs of Ruth St. Denis.

In her dance dramas, Graham continually reflected universal themes of the human condition as well as the forces in her life, including her personal frustrations in developing gratifying, long-term relationships. She brought a singular voice to the craft of choreography, transforming it into

429

a powerful vehicle for emotional content, theatrical device, and storytelling.

A comprehensive assessment of Graham's work reveals multifaceted achievements unrivaled by other dance artists. She was a truly commanding presence on stage. She pioneered a movement vocabulary grounded in essential technical training; she choreographed complex, personal work; and she changed the face of modern dance in the United States. Her dance works reveal her rich inner life. She externalized and gave form to the depths of her experience through choreography. Although she rejected the mantle of "feminism," Graham may be most remembered for her achievements in positioning women at the center of heroic sagas.

The examination of the life of Graham must be more than a simple chronicle of amazing performances and choreographic longevity. To the beneficiaries of her rich creative outpourings, the immense price exacted for her life course was not revealed. She made a tremendous impact as a generative adult in the scope of her artistic products, yet she seemed incapable of nurturing her own well-being in a sustained way. It is perhaps the tension between the artistic bounty and the poverty of personal accomplishment in so many areas of adult development that makes her story so compelling to those striving to understand the challenges to the human spirit presented by the seeking of generative fulfillment.

This interpretation of the life of Graham aims to illuminate a coherent story while avoiding eulogizing or pathologizing of the subject. The highly narrative dance theater created by Graham makes her a magnificent candidate for psychobiographic inquiry. Graham's choreographic works illustrate her ongoing dynamic processes psychologically and developmentally. Although these movement archives are a rich source of psychobiographic data, they must be understood as constructed revelations that demonstrate the rational manipulation and reworking of themes for the creative individual, not simply unfiltered outpourings of the unconscious (Rothenberg, 1990). It is beyond the scope of this chapter to interpret or analyze the depth and breadth of Graham's choreography. I will, however, chronicle the evolution of her choreography as it relates to her progress as a generative agent, following narrative and psychobiographic research traditions (McAdams & Ochberg, 1988; Wrightsman, 1988). Whereas many of her choreographic works have been analyzed, Graham's life remains to be examined and understood as a text.

The unfolding tale of an artist's life is mediated by the developmental tasks and phases, or stages. Who the artist is to become is also influenced by the social systems in which the personal developmental processes are embedded (Lee, 1989). The life of Graham must be set, therefore, against the relationships that populated it and the institutions that served as a context and must be framed against the historical and cultural moment in

430   SUSAN A. LEE

time. Influenced by but not limited to the work of both Erik Erikson (1963, 1969) and Daniel Levinson (1986, 1991, 1996), this research has been stimulated by the advancements in theorizing by the many contributors to this volume, especially McAdams and de St. Aubin (1992) and Kotre (1984).

This case study is drawn from a variety of sources of data including secondary biographical sources such as newspaper articles and other archival documents, Graham's (1991) autobiographical sketchings, Graham's choreography experienced in performance and reviewed on film and videotape, interviews with Graham Dance Company members representing several generations of dancers, participant observation at the Graham school, and hours of transcribed data following my personal interview with Graham during her 90th birthday celebration season.

Marker events for Graham from age 17 to 96 are presented in the life history time line in the appendix. Following establishment of a brief historical perspective on her career, this chapter focuses on the critical middle adulthood years and addresses Graham's life as a model of generativity that gives evidence of the potentially destructive power of an all-consuming drive to make art. This study also presents an example of the imperfection or perversion of generative yearnings as described by Kotre (1984). Gardner (1993) also identified a pattern in creative individuals of trading the personal longings for happiness for a lifetime of brilliance. He found that, in one way or another, the creative individuals he examined were embedded in some kind of bargain, deal, or Faustian arrangement as a means of ensuring the preservation of their unusual gifts. Gardner also accurately identified Graham as an artist who had contracted for greatness at considerable psychological and interpersonal cost.

A BRIEF HISTORY

Graham was born in Allegheny, Pennsylvania, on May 11, 1894, the oldest daughter of three girls in a Scotch-Irish family. Martha was described as a serious child with a clear sense of individuality (Stodelle, 1984). Her father, who specialized in the fledgling medical discipline of psychiatry, stimulated Martha's inquiring mind while simultaneously setting a tone of discipline in their Presbyterian home. The Puritan element in the household was further countered by the influence of the Graham family nanny, a young Irish woman only a few years older than Martha. Lizzie was responsible for introducing Martha to dramatic parlor games as well as to the ritual and spectacle of the Roman Catholic mass.

Martha's baby brother died from the measles before his second birthday, leaving her mother, Jennie, despondent. Her family moved to Santa Barbara in response to the health needs of her sister and now somewhat fragile mother. California provided an environment of striking contrasts to the East, an inviting sensuous and cultural landscape. The themes of constriction and regulation versus freedom and indulgence would be played out again and again both in Martha's life and in her work.

Captivated by a show poster of the great exotic dancer Ruth St. Denis, Graham implored her parents to let her see the performance. Although her family, like so many Victorians, disapproved of dancing, on a trip to Los Angeles with her father in 1911, Graham attended the concert. At age 17, it was the image of the divine Miss Ruth that first beckoned to Graham to construct a vision of herself as a dancer. Graham was considered plain by the standards of beauty of her time, and it may have been the transformative potential of the concert stage that sealed her fate (McDonagh, 1973). Despite protests from her father that she pursue a life of scholarship, Graham enrolled at the Cumnock School in Los Angeles to work in "creative expression." Following her father's death she enrolled at Denishawn, the school founded by Ruth St. Denis and her husband, Ted Shawn, in California.

Graham's short stature, lack of "elegance" in technique, and circumspect nature did not win her the attention of St. Denis. She was delegated instead to work most closely with St. Denis's young husband, Ted Shawn. Shawn was an ambitious young man who wrestled with his rivalry with his famous wife. He organized a New York City tour, and Graham was invited to join, performing the kinds of work associated with Denishawn. During the tour Graham became involved with Denishawn music director Louis Horst. Horst, 10 years Graham's senior, was married to another dancer. Graham and Horst never married each other, yet the turbulent, 20-year Graham–Horst collaboration changed the face of modern dance.

In 1923, following a brief interlude working with the Greenwich Follies, Graham was hired as co-director of the Eastman School of Dance and Dramatic Action in New York. She surrounded herself with students dedicated to her aesthetic, women able to match her drive and vision for contemporary dance. Graham's life demonstrates the difficulties and hardships associated with the early years in making modern dance.

In 1926 Graham and Horst gave their first independent concert. Modern dance in general and Graham's particular vision for this revolutionary form were not readily welcomed by the public. Her craft, vitality, and charisma kept a small faithful audience coming back, however, and made a convert of at least one significant critic of the time. Even in the early days of her work, seeds of the themes that would dominate her ballets could be seen: the distilled essence of an American spirit; myth and morality; men and women in relationship; journeys of the human spirit; and an endless parade of powerful female figures including the Brontë sisters, Emily Dickinson, Joan of Arc, Jocasta, and many others.

Graham made dances for the members of her company as well as her own solos. Whereas her early works were imitative of the Denishawn style, her continuing need to find her own unique voice as an artist drove her efforts. She succeeded in inventing a new dance language that would later be the Graham signature. This dance vocabulary was angular and dynamic, driven in part by the powerful use of torso in the signature contraction and dramatic falls. Unlike ballet, which is preoccupied with classical lines and an ornamental manipulation of the limbs, Graham's dancers moved with action initiated from the center of the body. The female form in her dance was not a fragile ethereal creature balancing on pointe, but was firmly grounded and connected, barefoot, to the floor.

In response to Louis Horst's influence, Graham was exposed to leading composers of the time. She worked primarily with new scores composed for her dances. She eliminated unnecessary or distracting ornamentation in stage settings and costumes. She designed and executed many of the dance garments that also became associated with her style. The integrity of image, sound, costume, and use of the body is magnificently represented in her dance *Lamentation* created in 1930, at age 36. McDonagh (1973) described the scene as follows:

> In "Lamentation" Graham sat on a low platform and stretched the material of her costume into long diagonal folds, first on one side and then on the other, while she assumed leaning positions that seemed to defy the stability of a seated figure. All that was visible of her body was her two bare feet, her hands and a narrow expanse of face, such as would be revealed by a traditional nun's habit . . . a dance of anguish, expressed through stress lines on the fabric, much as the passage of emotional waves leave their traces on the lines of the face. (p. 69)

Having accomplished what she could with an all-female ensemble, Graham struggled to expand the work. The women of her company begrudgingly allowed for the incorporation of male performers. Erick Hawkins, a new student at the school, got a good deal of attention. Graham's attraction to him was palpable (DeMille, 1991). Hawkins's ambition was especially irksome to many within the Graham organization, including Louis Horst. Owing to great conflict in their intimate relationship yet intense connection as partners in a single-minded obsession with the value and significance of Graham's work, the relationship between Graham and Horst had devolved to one of fondness from a distance.

At age 50, Graham developed one of her most well-known works, *Appalachian Spring*, as a gift to Hawkins. To a score by Aaron Copland, and set by Noguci, this dance drama depicts a Quaker couple on their wedding day. After years of secretly living with Hawkins, Graham married him in Santa Fe in 1949. Their marriage was short-lived, ending in separation in 1950.

As a mature dancer (56 years old), Graham continued to attempt some of her most demanding roles despite the urgings by Hawkins and others to reconsider. In what would become a crisis of substantial proportion, Graham was unable to perform in London because of a knee injury. Her physical pain, however, was far out-classed by her reaction to Hawkins's abandonment of the company. Her inner turmoil was expressed in her complete withdrawal and descent into depression. She did not dance for 2 years.

Many dancers are tempted to perform past their prime because of the powerful, seductive lure of the ecstatic transformation that can be achieved when the body feels like a sublime expressive instrument (Lee, 1995). In this regard, Graham was addicted to the experience. In commenting in 1984 on her view of contemporary choreography, Graham captured what had been a key issue in her personal drama, stating, "I miss the star very often . . . the star person, the person who knows too much and takes you by the throat and almost kills you if you don't accept their words."

The death of her career as a performer in the context of her ongoing struggle to come to grips with the failure of her relationship with Erick Hawkins taxed Graham's adaptive capacities to the breaking point. Although she emerged from that journey determined to continue on her chosen path, she was clearly scarred. Alcohol abuse became a dominant theme in her older adulthood. Just as she had not recognized the impending rupture of her relationship with Hawkins, she denied the extent of her drinking problem. Graham began a pattern of increased, self-imposed isolation.

It is unclear how much of her behavior in later life was directly attributable to alcoholism. It is amazing that in her 60s she continued to produce enduring works of art. At 64 she premiered her first evening-length dance drama, Clytemnestra. This work was recognized worldwide as one of the great choreographic contributions to modern theater. "Running through Graham's work, as through her life, was the theme of unruly passion versus the constraints of duty" (McDonagh, 1973, p. 251). She was not able to perform one or two works at each concert owing to the increasing pain of arthritis. With growing agitation in the dance world to persuade her to retire from the stage, Graham raged, but the rage was futile (Horosko, 1991). Her body was going, whether or not she would accept the fact. Her friend and confidant, Carroll Russell (personal communication, 1983), reported that "Mrs. Wickes [Graham's Jungian analyst] gently told her 'Martha, you are not a goddess, you are human. You are not immortal.' To which she responded, 'we'll see about that.'" Her final performance as a dancer was at age 74. The following year she hovered near death from alcohol-related liver damage (DeMille, 1991).

It was characteristic of a woman determined to script her fate that Graham recovered. Miraculously, at age 78 she resumed her place in the center of her dance world. She swooped like an avenging angel on anyone she perceived as attempting to thwart her control or influence on her empire. In what was a kind of reign of terror, she fired or dismissed even her most loyal disciples. Graham regained her choreographic voice, but much of her contact with the company and the outside world was managed by Ron Protas. A Graham soloist reported (1995) that "the Graham organization was re-invented guided behind the scenes by a young man of considerable ambition." Martha Graham died in April 1991, before the completion of *Maple Leaf Rag*. The company was caught by surprise by her passing because of their willing participation in the myth of her immortality.

GRAHAM AND GENERATIVITY

Developmental Conflicts

Generativity is but one aspect of human identity formation, but it is an area in which Graham demonstrated measurable achievement; she left an artistic legacy. In spite of forces that could inhibit generative potential, such as pervasive self-preoccupation or overwhelming losses and setbacks, Graham produced both art products of world-class stature and a cadre of artistic offspring who would carry her vision into the future. One measure of generativity involves assessing the ability to adapt to major developmental hurdles, which allows the individual to focus critical psychic energy on a generative task. An important challenge is to demonstrate a range of adaptive mechanisms that are appropriate to the changing needs of adulthood.

Some artists devoted to dance, often referred to as the "boys and girls of the company," find themselves trapped in a dependent position (Lee, in press). The dancer can be developmentally frozen in a permanent state of young adulthood, not expected to carry the burden of adult responsibilities, focusing instead on the physical demands of performing and touring. The lack of connection to mainstream life and the lack of skills for life beyond the studio serve the dance world well in maintaining the myth of endless adolescence. Graham was treated like an "acrobat of the gods," in that she was allowed to avoid aspects of day-to-day life. She did not drive, manage her financial affairs, maintain property, or concern herself with the operation of the school. She came to rely heavily on trusted "others" so that she could be free to create. The situation made her vulnerable to exploitation and manipulation as she aged.

Like many young adults, Graham was often locked in battle with her inner conflicts in forging her identity. Graham was not completely free of the internalized image of herself as a traditional woman of her era, an image that was pitted against her all-consuming passion to achieve greatness through her art. She was not able to find a life script or expansive enough identity to allow her to contain more then a unidimensional version of herself. Traditional domestic life and mature relationships eluded her. She lived instead with the constancy of creating dances within the narrow confines of her school, rehearsal studio, and nearby apartment. Some of the themes embodied in her dances portray her changing interior land-scape. Some of her heroines appear to be held captive, tragically, by self-limiting definitions. However, other works depict women of power and domination or present women poised and ready for the challenges of full adulthood, such as *Frontier* and *Appalachian Spring*.

Levinson (1996) has explained that for some people, early and middle adulthood is primarily a time of increasing vitality and fulfillment (although not without struggle and pain), whereas for others it is a time of increasing triviality, stagnation, and inner deadness. Sometimes propelled by the quest for meaning in life and by death awareness, middle adulthood plays a critical role as a passage that can be successfully navigated toward generativity. In middle adulthood there appears to be a developmental need to fill in the blanks of what was omitted in earlier passages. It can be an opportunity to empower underdeveloped aspects of the self and realize components of the dream that have not yet been realized (Lee, 1997). In the case of Graham, the missing piece was a relational partner who could make her feel fully connected, mirrored, and satisfied. Instead, her two important romantic relationships could be described as a clash of the titans. Louis Horst offered her unwavering dedication to the quality of her craft and insight into her work, but he kept himself unavailable for a permanent relationship. The two remained linked as though by destiny and main-tained a connection, however painful. Graham needed him artistically. Horst came the closest to serving as her mentor: shaping her work, toler-ating her rages, and encouraging her when she was in despair.

Her life with Hawkins could be seen as an example of the blurring of role-appropriate behavior between mentor and student. As often hap-pens in opposite-sex pairings, the intimacy, stimulation, and shared vision for making dances became hopelessly confused with a love relationship. Hawkins was masterful on the stage and aspired to be her equal artistically, but his work was hopelessly eclipsed by her talent. He brought discipline and energy to the management of the company and stability to the school that was desperately needed. He also brought youth, physical passion, and the promise of a commitment, aspects that had been missing with Horst. Graham encouraged Hawkins's artistic individuation from her, knowing at some level that the relationship could not survive without it. It would seem that when they each possessed the long desired, idealized other, the reality of married life was a role for which they were both woefully unpre-pared. Hawkins could not exist in her shadow as a choreographer.

Some of the early literature on life course development holds that all human beings strive for an ultimate realization of autonomy and self-actualization (Levinson, 1986). Contemporary views of female development encourage a redefining of agency. The goal is to achieve not a separate sense of self but a more complex sense of self grounded in interdependent relationships (Jordan, Kaplan, Miller, Stiver, & Surrey, 1991). Graham's life demonstrates how difficult it was for her to achieve such connection in personal relationships. However, her capacity as a mentor may have allowed her gratification through strong affiliation with her dancers.

Graham as Mentor

At the center of a synergistic web was Graham as the "sorceress," casting a spell on all who entered. She could model the "good mother," doing what she could to ensure the survival of the company. In this regard she came to rely heavily on the financial contributions of supporters (Bethsabée de Rothschild, Robin Howard, Lila Wallace, Halston, and others) who were captivated by her vision. She could also be the "bad mother," living in fear of the young female rivals and turning cruelly against those who wanted to separate completely from the company to pursue their own work (DeMille, 1991). She set standards for herself, however, that were demanding and brutal. For many mentor–novice relationships, the only possible resolution is a painful, disruptive split (Lee, 1996).

A kind of sisterhood held the women together in the early days. As with dance organizations then and now, the dancers survived on poverty wages, being paid only when the company had performances and living on unemployment through significant portions of each year. Although it was an honor to be chosen to work with Graham, the dancers increasingly wanted more in return. Graham was deeply offended by the trend of dancers expectations. She was demanding and cruel, insisting that her dancers sacrifice as she did to make dances happen.

Like most charismatic leaders, Graham had great influence; those who fell under that influence suffered, although they were usually glad to do it. Scores of individuals described themselves as having studied with or been influenced by Graham, although some were in her presence for no more than one class. She also developed a following among actors and actresses who recognized the power they could harness for their stage performance by studying with Graham. One of these was Bette Davis, whose words follow:

> I worshipped her. She was all tension-lighting. Her burning dedication gave her spare body the power of 10 men. She would, with a single thrust of her weight, convey anguish. Then, in an anchored lift that made her 10 feet tall, she became all joy. (Lee, 1984b, p. 5)

In observing the development of her role as mentor, as in other aspects of Graham's life, one notices shifts and tensions (Helpern, 1994). Over time she learned how to draw on the talents of her performers to compensate for her declining ability to create the movement herself. It is essential for master teachers in dance to pull great talent around themselves and produce the next generation of bodies—to prepare dancers to become the living instrument of a great choreographer. Graham perfected the process of allowing the dancers to produce some sections of the work; they always used her vocabulary and set the movement to Graham's wishes and specifications. In this capacity she developed her dancers and furthered her reach to the next generation.

Another achievement, born in part of necessity, was the model of a dance organization that evolved to support Graham's needs. This nexus of artistic interaction fused Graham with the school and the dance company. A master teacher attracts talent like a magnet, and the talent matures through the training provided by the school. Dance company performers can be selected from that talent pool. Company members can also go on to become teachers, completing the circle. Everyone is exposed to the choreographic vision of the charismatic leader. As a result, the environment is highly charged with a strong commitment to the work. This organizational structure remains as a model of synergistic potential.

One of Graham's gifts was to pass on the need to express oneself through movement, not simply as the instrument of another artist but in one's own voice. A list of those who studied with Graham and went on to have significant choreographic careers reads like the "who's who" of dance. Even in her later years, she had a profound impact on her dancers, which made it possible for them to accept her bargain. A Graham Dance Company member (personal communication, 1996) of many years enthusiastically recalled the experience of working with Graham:

> It was not just what she said, I was informed by a kind of body to body talking, the use of her eyes and body language. She invited me to investigate my potential as long as it was in her direction. She pulled things out of me along the way. Her ultimate legacy is that we became thinking dancers, to be ourselves, not puppets like Balanchine's dancers.

As an aging matriarch of a huge dynasty, Graham's hold on the young participants changed. Although loyalty was always demanded, "family members" were allowed to leave and have outside experiences in the dance world as long as they quietly returned home. The male members were in high demand for other work because of the virile, athletic style the technique produced. Graham was especially demanding of the dedication of the female members of her company.

Graham was fortunate that she remained within a world with predictable structures for producing her dances. She came to enjoy a kind of safety net of supporters who allowed her to go into the studio and create. Most artists find the lack of institutional support to be a primary impediment to their continued artistic productivity. Her choreographic works demonstrate an obsession with capturing female protagonists attempting to overcome fatalistic forces in the universe. Graham revisited her own life script for rich source material. When assessing Graham as a model of generativity, one may conclude that the most unconflicted realm of her contribution was her role as change agent, as the next section demonstrates.

Graham as Change Agent in Dance

The life history time line in the appendix to this chapter reflects the awe-inspiring drive that took Graham from the popularly acclaimed and uplifting works like *Frontier* (1935) to the darkly dramatic Greek cycle, including *Errand Into the Maze* (1947) during middle adulthood. The scope of Martha Graham's contribution to dance, however, extends well beyond the approximately 200 works she choreographed (Horosko, 1991). She made the transition relatively quickly from being a dancer engaged in the process of making her own compositions to becoming an innovator. Although she did not set out on a course to create a dance technique, that became a singular achievement (Helpern, 1994).

Graham composed a series of codified movements that yielded a systematic approach for making dances, analogous to the system of classical ballet. Dance technique has two purposes: preparing the body for the demands of professional dance and establishing a movement language for communication. Graham began to articulate her plan for the training of the body through the somewhat revolutionary approach of working on the floor to harness the forces of gravity in relation to the spine. She needed a movement language for her dance, a language produced by the limitations and strengths of her body. Her search for sources in gesture that could support the universal themes she tackled meant rejecting the dance fashion of the time of doing "steps."

Her dance dramas, sometimes described as angular, tense and explosive, evoked a new awareness of the pelvis as a point of initiation, the lower torso as a vital site of life and animation. The development of her technique can be traced, along with the evolution of her choreography. Graham was a woman of deep passion, and her sensuality revealed itself in her dances. Her dance vocabulary was often criticized as being too erotic.

Graham borrowed generously from her earlier works. There was a kind of linear connection. She would say what she had to say in a piece and leave it, moving on but employing similar devices to tackle the next preoccupation. The essence of her creativity was summarized by a Graham Company member (personal communication, 1996) as follows:

> She did not really take the work to a new level, but she would move forward. When a project was identified, there was no way of knowing where it would go. She would lock herself in the studio until it was done. Each birth had its unique features and, as she would tell her dancers, "You don't determine what the baby will look like."

Graham blazed new trails by creating a matriarchal social system that came to characterize much of modern dance, unlike that of ballet, which to this day remains mostly the choreographic property of men. Women, with some notable exceptions like Margot Fonteyn, have relatively short performing careers and disappear in relative obscurity. The modern dance world as shaped by Graham produced strong family connections to a choreographic approach and movement technique that could be used successfully to sustain the careers of men and women as artistic directors, teachers, and choreographers.

Graham and the Life Course

Although generativity is not viewed rigidly as a stage of life, a life course developmental perspective is an important lens for considering the impulses, processes, and products of the generative adult. Is the potential for successful generativity contingent on "successful" navigation of the life course? In striving for a generative dream, how many paths will be disrupted or derailed? Snarey (chapter 2, this volume) describes the impact of "generative chill" when it is necessary to rebuild one's legacy after failure. Who will falter in light of such impediments and who will triumph? Gutmann (1990) described an "active mastery style" as a developmental attribute that allows the individual to turn troubles into strengths. Other such challenges to adult adaptive capacities should be delineated, including the unique issues confronting the creative artist.

For so many people in the dance world, dancing is not a career but a core component of personal identity (Lee, 1989, 1995). This experience of the self as dancer is not shed when the body is no longer able to perform. Dancers face the polarity framed by Erikson of "generativity vs. stagnation" (1963). This developmental challenge was further explored by Levinson (1996), who recognized the difficulty of breaking out of a flawed life structure to allow for improving one's life and becoming "one's own woman" in the second half of life.

Middle adulthood affords an opportunity to reflect on one's life and make "midcourse corrections." It is not known whether Graham felt empowered or motivated to make major changes in how she worked and lived. Professionally, she received countless indications affirming her genius, supporting or encouraging the life choices she was making. Personally, the failure of her relationships with both Horst and Hawkins assaulted her self-esteem and confidence in her direction. The disparity between these two aspects of her experience must have loomed in Graham's self-assessment.

Each dancer must negotiate developmental hurdles with the goal of continued growth, integrating the new aspects of the self, in the context of mourning the loss of the ability to perform, a core part of identity. Graham did not set out to be known as a great choreographer; she wanted to dance. She scripted herself as destined to dance. In 1984 she stated once again the view she held of being chosen:

> You don't select it [to be an artist, a dancer] . . . it fastens itself to you. You become a channel and are used. It is a very terrible and deeply rewarding experience. The preparation of a dance is one of the agonies of life . . . but you have no say, it walks behind you, the ancestral footsteps prod you forward, upstairs, downstairs, anyplace, but you have to have that appetite for danger. I don't mean death danger, but the death of not being able to do the things you envision. And that of course is a great tragedy. (Lee, 1984a)

Graham dismissed any romantic notions of aging as a glorious time to turn one's attention toward some existential connection to society. The sheer number of works Graham choreographed may indicate her desire to achieve a form of immortality through an artistic legacy. She was determined to defy aging and perhaps counter her own death anxiety by persevering in a field dominated by youth and beauty:

> Despite similarities in meaning, however, generativity and immortality are not coterminous; and not all symbols of immortality entail creating something in one's own image. No one has captured the difference in meaning better than Woody Allen, who said on one occasion, "I don't want to achieve immortality through my works. I want to achieve immortality by not dying." (Kotre, 1984, p. 11)

Again and again Graham reminded the world that she could overcome the fate of most professional dance artists and continue to define herself as performer first, long after most dance careers would have evolved into teaching, administration, or choreography. She wrapped herself in the myth of immortality. She was not concerned with being remembered for the dances she made; she wanted the opportunity to perform another great role, yet one more time.

Throughout her life, she strove to be present in the here and now, stating, "I'm very bad about time. I don't think about the past time very much. I think about what I've got to do and what I want to do in the future" (Lee, 1984b). This feature of her personality contributed in part to the kind of psychological hardiness needed for generativity.

Over the course of her life, she single-mindedly established a stable life structure to achieve the dream for herself of being a major artist of contemporary dance. Her psychological self seemed immobilized by the unfulfilled dreams and losses. The study of adult development inevitably goes beyond the focus on the self and requires examining the life course and engagement of the self in the world:

> The life structure forms a boundary between self and the world and mediates the relationship between them. The life structure is the framework within which external aspects and internal aspects are interwoven. It is important to distinguish between the development of the life structure and the development of the self. (Levinson, 1996, p. 24)

Martha Graham provides a rich example of life structure appropriate for making great art yet unsuitable for fulfillment or growth of other aspects of the self. This particular nexus of self and life structure is a useful construct for examining other case examples to advance the understanding of creative individuals. According to Levinson (1996, p. 375), "a disproportionate number of women find that their work, even if to some extent rewarding, is demeaning, empty or damaging to the self. The dissatisfaction may be expressed in alcoholism, depression, early retirement, or the search for youthful excitement." Graham did not retire from the work that dominated her life, but she deadened herself to a fuller range of life experiences.

What modifications are needed in the artist's world to allow for a juncture of self and work that is not destructive? Especially for women, the balance and tension between competing roles of mother, partner, and artist must be assessed. Is generativity in art pitted against generativity as parent? Greenacre (1960) postulated that creativity is the correlate of childlessness. Gedo (1983) pointed out that the great majority of women geniuses have, indeed, been childless, although this fact may or may not be causally related to their accomplishments. Limited data exist concerning the interplay of the demands of childbearing and child rearing and "giftedness" in artistic spheres. Bepko and Krestan (1993, p. 25) stated that "for women 'Innovators,' having children is just another form of creative energy." However, these authors also stated that "the dichotomizing of the two aspects of female energy, caretaking versus generative action, has been the dominant impact of the cultural narrative about love" (p. 25). In a letter to her analyst in 1951, Graham wrote the following:

> I had always joked a little about my next incarnation and that I should be a dancer again . . . a ballet dancer and do Swan Lake. But I knew yesterday that was not it . . . that I would have children. I think I could never say that before. I never could release myself to become the most simple and elemental instrument of life. I had to be in control or govern even over nature. (Graham, 1991, p. 192)

It is impossible to speculate whether, if Graham had had a viable relationship, she would have considered procreation as well as creation. Graham was not alone in sensing the potential threat to her kind of generativity that childbearing might impose. The role shift could be dramatic, and Graham had already evidenced the ways in which she would choose life structures that "fit" with her view of herself as "dancer."

In her famous address to the National Endowment for the Arts in 1950, Graham poetically outlined the essence of such a definition of self:

> I am a dancer. I believe that we learn by practice. Whether it means to learn to dance by practicing dancing or to learn to live by practicing living, the principles are the same. In each it is the performance of dedicated precise set of acts, physical or intellectual, from which comes the shape of achievement, a sense of one's being, a satisfaction of spirit. One becomes in some area an athlete of God. Practice means to perform, over and over again in the face of all obstacles some act of vision, of faith of desire. Practice is a means of inviting the perfection desired. (Graham, 1991, p. 3)

Through the combination of a professional persona and living a solitary existence outside the walls of her school and studio, Graham kept much of herself hidden from the prying eyes of the world. Like a high priestess she remained at arm's length, worshipped or feared but not truly known. Added to the power of her reputation were her chiseled features and resonant voice, which gave her even greater authority. In many ways, her underlying grandiose self allowed her to persevere in spite of the obstacles of living in an art world. The devaluation, contempt, and financial threats to the very existence of her organization, which would have been the undoing of many talented artists, were overcome again and again.

Although Graham occasionally experienced self doubt in relation to her work, she would go back into the studio and create. Her grandiosity and determination shielded her so that she seemed untouched by the changing currents of audience approval. She had developed a way of dismissing negative responses, but evidence suggests that some messages penetrated to her core. In identifying her passion and determination, Carroll Russell (personal communication, 1983) reported that "Martha defiantly retorted to an audience during a tour of Italy, 'You can boo me, but you can't stop me.'"

She continued to believe in her chosen artistic path, but an underlying depression characterized a significant portion of her adult life, fueled in part by her unmet relational needs. When Graham approached opportunities to rework what had been learned at earlier developmental periods, she persisted instead in maintaining the script she had started. The theme of isolation that may accompany greatness, as well as mourning and loss, loom large in her life story.

CONCLUSION

The life course of Martha Graham represents a path of generational continuity, forged by one of the greatest modern dance artists of the 20th century. Although she was profoundly ambivalent about attempting to preserve a temporal art form, she was finally persuaded that her dances should live beyond her ability to perform them. In the beginning there were few films. Dances were passed on through a personal tradition, taught by the former occupants of the roles. Even with the advent of videotapes, Graham was preoccupied with making new works while she could. Most of the early work has been lost.

It is in the arena of passing on her dances that the destructive potential in Graham can be identified. She loved her dances, and she could not bring herself to "let go" of some of her most cherished roles so that they could be performed by others. As a mentor, she abandoned a whole generation of performers. She did not coach them or help them bring their unique talents to the roles. The historical implications are significant for the dance world because so much of dance is passed on in an oral tradition, from one artist to another.

This reluctance serves as one example of the conflict Graham experienced between the agentic and communal modes of generativity described by Kotre (1984):

> If the life of the progenitor assumes greater weight, if the creation is simply a clone or a monument to the self, we may speak of an agentic mode of generativity. On the other hand, if life-interest is transferred to the generative object with the result that its life becomes more important than the progenitor's, we may speak of a communal mode. (p. 16)

Graham emerged from this conflict, however, and began to choreograph new dances in the 1970s and 1980s that were a significant departure from the kinds of work Graham had choreographed for herself. Works such as *Acts of Light* reveal a new emphasis on technical virtuosity much more akin to ballet performance than to her modern dance. With Graham's role confined to choreographing, new company members came from a more eclectic preparation and training in dance. The shift toward having a company that did not have the benefit of the extensive teaching by Graham can be viewed as a natural, evolutionary process in a dance organization.

Kotre's (1984) challenge that one must not equate generativity with virtue serves as an effective frame for contextualizing Graham's gifts compared to those other generative agents:

> Whether fruit is nourishing or poisonous, it still issues from a mechanism of reproduction. Failing to classify monuments of destruction as the products of fertility closes our eyes to the full reach of this pervasive

human motive. Though doing so calls for changing a semantic habit, it would be better to view generativity as an impulse that can be channeled into vice as well as into virtue. (Kotre, 1984, p. 9)

By contemporary standards, within which women strive to achieve balance in career and relational components of adult life, Graham heartily failed. Her life is a chilling tale about a human spirit valiantly raging to preserve an artistic empire and vision in a field in which the work vanishes with the last gesture. Her story, with the descent to alcoholism and her cloistered existence, speaks to the concerns of what happens to a life when the desire for love, affiliation, and family is in mortal conflict with the demands of the profession.

Graham's life story supports the view presented by McAdams, Hart, and Maruna (chapter 1, this volume) that generativity is a multifaceted construct that must be examined in the context of the individual generative narration. Across the life course of Graham, there is evidence of ambivalence about the care and commitment of the next generation as well as fierce loyalty. She was experienced both as preoccupied with self and exploitive and as a master teacher who imparted great inspiration in her charges. Her life story for many in the field of dance, when offered up as a model for the next generation, still shines like a warning beacon about the destructive potential of the generative impulse. Nevertheless, Graham emerged later in life to achieve some measure of a "satisfying sense of ending" (McAdams, 1993, p. 203). However unpopular she may have been, Graham surrounded herself with individuals who ensured the survival of the Graham Company and maintained the integrity of the continued teaching of the dance technique. For society, Graham filled the role of contemporary storyteller, creating for herself the life script of new myth maker. She is a compelling example of the human ability to focus all capacities on a singular goal, overcoming societal norms and personal loss in the doing. This case study serves as a reminder of the continuing need to understand the nature of the task of producing art in the United States, to analyze the life course of artists, and to establish theory that can embrace the complexity of generativity as a construct for men and women.

APPENDIX

Graham Life History Time Line

Age	Marker Event
17	Sees St. Denis perform
20	Dr. Graham dies
22	Begins classes at Denishawn
27	Begins relationship with Louis Horst
30	Performs with Greenwich Village Follies
32	Gives first independent concert
36	*Lamentation*
37	*Primitive Mysteries*, with recognizable Graham style
41	*Frontier*, begins to work with collaborators and use scenic elements
44	*American Document*, casts Erick Hawkins
50	*Appalachian Spring*, a gift to Erick Hawkins
52	Greek cycle begins
53	*Errand Into the Maze*; some solos performed by company members
55	Marriage to Hawkins
56	Failed European tour owing to injuries; separation from Hawkins
58	Divorce
64	Mother dies; *Clytemnestra*, full evening-length work
65	*Episodes*, intended as a collaboration with Balanchine
68	Successful European tour
70	Louis Horst dies
73	Analyst (Mrs. Wickes) dies
74	Final dance performance
75	Hospitalized with cirrhosis
78	Rebuilds the Graham organization
79	Begins to choreograph again
81	Creates *Lucifer* to star Nureyev
87	*Acts of Light*, homage to the Graham technique
90	*The Rite of Spring*
96	*Maple Leaf Rag*

REFERENCES

Armitage, M. (1966). *Martha Graham*. New York: Dance Horizons.

Bepko, C., & Krestan, J. A. (1993). *Singing at the top of our lungs: Women, love, and creativity*. New York: HarperCollins.

DeMille, A. (1991). *Martha: The life and work of Martha Graham*. New York: Random House.

Erikson, E. H. (1963). *Childhood and society* (2nd ed.). New York: Norton.

Erikson, E. H. (1969). *Gandhi's truth: On the origins of militant nonviolence*. New York: Norton.

Gardner, H. (1993). *Creating minds*. New York: Basic Books.

Gedo, J. E. (1983). *Portraits of the artist*. New York: Guilford Press.

Graham, M. (1991). *Blood memory*. New York: Doubleday.

Greenacre, P. (1960). Woman as artist. In *Emotional Growth* (Vol. 2). New York: International Universities Press.

Gutmann, D. (1990). In J. Kotre (Ed.), *Seasons of life*. Ann Arbor, MI: WQED.

Helpern, A. (1994). *The technique of Martha Graham*. New York: Morgan & Morgan.

Horosko, M. (1991). *Martha Graham: The evolution of her dance theory and training, 1926–1991*. Chicago: A Cappella Books.

Jordan, J. V., Kaplan, A. G., Miller, J. B., Stiver, I. P., & Surrey, J. L. (1991). *Women's growth in connection: Writings from the Stone Center*. New York: Guilford Press.

Kotre, J. (1984). *Outliving the self: Generativity and the interpretation of lives*. Baltimore: Johns Hopkins University Press.

Kotre, J. (1990). *Seasons of life* [Video]. Ann Arbor, MI: WQED.

Lee, S. A. (1984a). *Interview with Martha Graham*. Unpublished manuscript, Chicago.

Lee, S. A. (1984b). Martha Graham: 90 years of genius. *Arts and Events, 3*(2), 4–6.

Lee, S. A. (1989). Adult development and female artists: Focus on the ballet world. *Medical Problems of Performing Artists, 4*(1), 32–37.

Lee, S. A. (1995). Women's lives in ballet: A psychological perspective. *Impulse, 3*, 229–237.

Lee, S. A. (1996). *Mentoring and women in authority*. Paper presented at the meeting of the Illinois Psychological Association, Chicago.

Lee, S. A. (in press). Women's lives in dance: A developmental perspective. In S. Friedler & S. Glazer (Eds.), *Dancing female: Lives and issues in contemporary dance*. The Netherlands: Harwood Academic Press.

Levinson, D. J. (1986). A conception of adult development. *American Psychologist, 41*, 3–14.

Levinson, D. J. (1991, October). *Middle adulthood: The least explored season of the life cycle*. Lecture presented at Northwestern University, Evanston, IL.

Levinson, D. J. (1996). *The seasons of a woman's life*. New York: Knopf.

McAdams, D. P. (1993). *Stories we live by: Personal myths and the making of the self*. New York: Morrow.

McAdams, D. P., & de St. Aubin, E. (1992). A theory of generativity and its assessment through self-report, behavioral acts, and narrative themes in autobiography. *Journal of Personality and Social Psychology, 62*, 1003–1015.

McAdams, D. P., & Ochberg, R. (Eds.). (1988). *Psychobiography and life narratives*. Durham, NC: Duke University Press.

McDonagh, D. (1973). *Martha Graham: A biography*. New York: Praeger.

Rothenberg, A. (1990). *Creativity and madness*. Baltimore: The Johns Hopkins University Press.

Stodelle, E. (1984). *Deep song: The dance story of Martha Graham*. New York: Schirmer Books.

Wrightsman, L. S. (1988). *Personality development in adulthood*. Newbury Park, CA: Sage.

14

FAMILY GENERATIVITY AND GENERATIVE COUNSELING: HELPING FAMILIES KEEP FAITH WITH THE NEXT GENERATION

DAVID C. DOLLAHITE, BRENT D. SLIFE, AND ALAN J. HAWKINS

Counselors who are concerned with strengthening and healing relationships between generations can draw on the concept of generativity to assist them. This chapter invites counselors to grant a more prominent place for generativity in clinical work with families by (a) presenting the concept of *family generativity* as a logical extension of the generativity concept and (b) presenting some initial ideas on a new approach to clinical work designed to help families develop and sustain family generativity, which we call *generative counseling*. Generative counseling is illustrated by use of a clinical example, which is introduced briefly in a subsequent section and then discussed in relation to the major ideas we present throughout the chapter. Although the ideas presented in this chapter have not yet been systematically tested for clinical effective-

We express our appreciation to Edward Kimball, Stephanie Morris, Wes Burr, Tom Draper, Dan McAdams, Ed de St. Aubin, and two anonymous reviewers for helpful comments and suggestions on a previous draft.

ness, we have found them helpful in our clinical and educational work.

There are many well-articulated approaches to clinical work with families (Gurman & Kniskern, 1991). However, it appears that in the current professional counseling context, conceptual and practical eclecticism reigns. Eclecticism allows clinical flexibility of strategy but can ignore serious incompatibilities in assumptions about human beings, families, and the change process. We believe there is a critical need for additional integrative conceptual frameworks of counseling that are constructed on firm philosophical ground with attendant clear and coherent assumptions and practices based on these core philosophical concepts. This approach facilitates ongoing theory development and application of the ideas to research and practice (Lavee & Dollahite, 1991; Slife & Williams, 1995). Therefore, we expend considerable effort outlining the core philosophical ideas on which we build our clinical conceptual framework and practical suggestions, and we compare them with other philosophies of science and intervention.

GENERATIVITY AND FAMILY GENERATIVITY

Generativity

We assume that most readers of this volume have at least some degree of familiarity with the concept of generativity, so we provide only a brief discussion of the basic concept here (see chapter 1, this volume, for an in-depth discussion). According to Erikson, generativity is the primary developmental task of adulthood. Establishing and learning to care for the next generation is central to mature and healthy adulthood. Although Erikson identified many avenues for achieving generativity, he said that "parenthood is, for most, the first, and for many, the prime generative encounter" (Erikson, 1950/1963, p. 130). Casting parenting in this way— as a developmental task that produces the virtue of caring—creates a useful tool for understanding men and women in families (Hawkins, Christiansen, Sargent, & Hill, 1995; Hawkins & Dollahite, 1997).

Seeing life, marriage, and parenting through the lens of generativity links child development and child well-being with adult development and adult well-being; active parental care of children that increases children's well-being simultaneously serves to increase the parents' growth and well-being (Snarey, 1993). For parents, an ethical commitment to care for their children and a relational bond to nurture their children's development become significant parts of the path to healthy adulthood. Parental failure to develop generativity can lead to both a pervading sense of stagnation and self-absorption for the parent and difficult developmental challenges for children (Erikson, 1982a, 1982b). This lack, in turn, can lead to issues counselors encounter frequently, including depression and low-self esteem as well as marital and intergenerational distance, conflict, and dissatisfaction. Therefore, an understanding of and attention to issues of generativity are relevant to many issues in the clinical context.

Although Erikson was an eminent theoretician and clinician, and his ideas on the importance of developing trust, identity, and intimacy have become part of the clinical rubric, his ideas on generativity have not been adopted by clinicians in general or, more surprisingly, among marriage and family therapists in particular.[1] Although family therapy theories have included intergenerational concepts (e.g., differentiation, triangulation, legacy, and invisible loyalties), the concept of generativity (Erikson, 1950/1963) and interventions to help adults develop it have been neglected in psychotherapy in general and in marriage and family therapy in particular. Indeed, the concept of generativity has been almost dormant in clinical family scholarship. One notable exception is the work of Boszormenyi-Nagy and his colleagues (Boszormenyi-Nagy, Grunebaum, & Ulrich, 1991; Boszormenyi-Nagy & Spark, 1984), which emphasizes the importance of intergenerational connections and obligations to family well-being in clinical work, including ethical obligations across generations; these authors cite Erikson's ideas on generativity. Generativity is perhaps considered by clinicians to be merely a developmental concept that is not particularly relevant to the types of dysfunction present in families that come for counseling. By not including generativity among important clinical ideas, however, clinicians working with individuals, couples, and families may be overlooking an important potential aid to understanding their clients' challenges, not to mention a valuable source of clients' motivation for constructing solutions that attend to the needs of the next generation while enhancing their own development.

The work of Snarey (1993), Hawkins and Dollahite (1997), and the authors in this volume suggests a timely awakening of interest in Erikson's concept of generativity as it pertains to helping individuals and families meet the needs of the next generation. Some recent theoretical work on generativity in fathers (Dollahite, Hawkins, & Brotherson, 1996, 1997; Hawkins & Dollahite, 1997; Snarey, 1993) emphasizes the ethical and relational dimensions implicit and explicit in Erikson's concept of generativity as opposed to the psychosocial needs that a generative drive serves. That is, rather than stress the more individualistic desire of "outliving the self" (Kotre, 1984) through one's biological or cultural progeny that generativity serves, these authors have highlighted the sense that generativity is achieved through "sociomoral commitments that are freely made, but

---

[1]For example, the term *generativity* does not appear in Gurman and Kniskern's (1991) two-volume *Handbook of Family Therapy*.

ethically binding" (Snarey, 1993, p. 27). Dollahite et al. (1997) developed a "conceptual ethic of fathering as generative work" that emphasizes the ethics of fathers' care for the next generation. Dienhart and Dollahite (1997) provided an application of generative theory to the understanding and strengthening of father–child relationships. In this chapter, we build on this work, introducing the concept of family generativity and the practice of generative counseling.

Family Generativity

Scholars usually frame generativity as an individual characteristic, desire, motivation, or drive. We wish to focus attention on the concept of generativity as something present (or not) in the family system as well. Thus, in this chapter we propose the concept of *family generativity*. We define family generativity as *the moral responsibility to connect with and care for the next generation that resides in the family and extended family systems and in adult family members*. Thus, family generativity includes the sense of obligation for the next generation that is experienced in various family relationships (marriage of parents, grandparents, adult siblings) and also encompasses the personal generative motivations that parents and other adult family members experience as individuals.

We propose that family generativity involves family systems (including extended family members and systems) and adult family members who are seeking to meet the needs of the next generation by working collectively and individually in *maintaining generative convictions, sustaining generative connections, keeping generative commitments, making generative choices, initiating generative changes,* and *developing generative capabilities.* We develop these and other ideas throughout the chapter.

GENERATIVE COUNSELING: BEYOND THE MEDICAL MODEL OF PSYCHOTHERAPY

Social science historians have generally acknowledged the dominating influence of medicine in current formulations of psychopathology and psychotherapy (Leahey, 1992; Viney, 1993, Yanchar & Slife, 1997). In much the same way that social scientists looked to the natural sciences as their model for scientific method, applied social scientists looked to the applied natural sciences, primarily medicine, as their model for psychopathology and psychotherapy. The medical model of psychotherapy has influenced generations of counselors in their conduct of all aspects of counseling. Even though many aspects of this model are rarely acknowledged in psychotherapy, this model's style of "patient" care and its general presumptions regarding "disease" or "illness" still pervade the "mental health" arena.

In recent years, many have questioned the appropriateness of this model for the social and behavioral sciences (Polkinghorne, 1983; Robinson, 1985; Sarbin, 1996; Slife & Williams, 1995, 1997). Indeed, the impetus for the family therapy movement was, in large measure, an explicit challenge to the medical model of psychotherapy (Becvar & Becvar, 1988; Hoffman, 1981). Family systems thinking and postmodern approaches have challenged various concepts of traditional psychotherapy to the extent that many counselors, for various reasons, have moved away from certain elements inherent in this model. However, we believe that many assumptions of the medical model remain influential as part of the philosophical and practical environment of the mental health system. At various places in this chapter, therefore, we compare the core philosophical concepts of generative counseling with the core philosophical assumptions of the medical model of psychotherapy.

Interventions derived from the medical model of psychotherapy have, of course, been successful in helping clients with various types of issues. However, we find the model less effective as a basis for helping counselors work with families to establish and sustain meaningful intergenerational relationships across the life course and for helping resolve the lingering intergenerational distance, grief, and longing often felt in families who seek counseling. The generative counseling approach we present is a way of conceiving of and conducting the clinical process such that emphasis is given to community and temporal context, choice and capability, and spiritual and moral dimensions in relation to sustaining and strengthening intergenerational relationships. Generative counseling explicitly and systematically seeks to transcend the medical model in these contexts.

A CLINICAL EXAMPLE

Here we provide a hypothetical clinical example to ground the philosophical discussions that follow. We regularly refer back to this case example to illustrate the clinical possibilities of generative counseling, thus *linking theory and story* (Dollahite et al., 1996) to present our ideas.

Art and Rebecca Jenson sought help from a counselor on behalf of their daughter, Leslie, 16. During the first few counseling sessions, Art, Rebecca, and Leslie presented the following account: Leslie had done well in elementary and junior high schools but had grown to despise high school because it was "irrelevant to real life," and now she wanted to drop out. Her sense of self-worth had dropped considerably, which was a surprise to her parents, and she was very moody.

She also was set on moving out of the house to get out from under parental control. Leslie had been a relatively obedient and helpful child but now chafed at any attempts of her parents to exercise authority over her. Over the past 2 years, Art and Rebecca had given Leslie more and more freedom. They recently dropped requirements that she be home for dinner and attend church services with the family. Art and Rebecca were frustrated and hurt by Leslie's apparent rejection; Rebecca believes her recent increased drinking is a result of that rejection. The Jensons saw Leslie making a foolish decision to drop out of school when she had so much going for her, and they suspected that she was drinking quite a bit now as a result of her association with a small group of older friends.

Art and Rebecca are highly educated professionals who value education deeply. Rebecca is a professor, and Art has his own organizational consulting business. Art says he is a workaholic and fears this has damaged his relationship with Leslie. He has on several occasions reduced his workload temporarily to accommodate a semester increase in Rebecca's teaching load or to spend a little more time with Leslie. Rebecca enjoys teaching and has excelled in that, although it has cost her in terms of reduced research productivity. The Jensons' marital relationship could be adequately described as cooperative although it lacks fun, warmth, and intimacy. Rebecca and Art would like their relationship to be more than it is, but they do not know how that could be achieved in the face of pressures from work and family.

The Jensons admit that their communication skills are lacking. Art is quiet and has a hard time discussing his feelings. Rebecca sometimes starts "packing her bags" mentally when Art directs criticism her way. There are also significant differences in their approaches to parenting. Art's approach to Leslie's problems has been to let her make her own choices if she will not listen to reason. Rebecca's approach is not as laissez-faire: "Leslie doesn't know how good she has it," Rebecca often says to Art, "and she needs to wake up and smell the coffee."

Rebecca's parents divorced when she was 9. Her father occasionally abused Rebecca, both emotionally and physically. After the divorce, her mother worked at two and sometimes three jobs at a time to provide for her daughters. Rebecca did not have much money or parental time growing up. Her mother passed away in her early 50s from some serious health problems, leaving Rebecca feeling empty and sad at her death. Rebecca voluntarily lost contact with her father. Art grew up in a strong, politically active family. His aging parents are still nearby, and Art cares for them dutifully, without much direct help from his siblings.

The Jensons attend church together as much as possible, but that is the extent of their shared activities now. Rebecca is a devout Baptist, and she feels deeply the religious duty to care for her family. Her own upbringing left her feeling like she did not know how to be a good mother. More than anything, Rebecca wants to provide her children with a better home life than she had. Art's spiritual feelings are more eclectic and less institutional. He values the moral education religion provides children, but he is more concerned with the need for people to act charitably rather than avoid a list of sins. The social aspect of church is what Leslie seems to value most.

CORE CONCEPTS OF FAMILY GENERATIVITY AND GENERATIVE COUNSELING

We propose six philosophical ideas that together form the core concepts of family generativity and generative counseling. These are *holism, temporality, agency, capability, spirituality,* and *morality.* Although these six core concepts are inextricably interwoven and form an integrated construct, we discuss each of them in turn and then briefly suggest how the ideas are integrated afterward. In each of the six sections we (a) develop

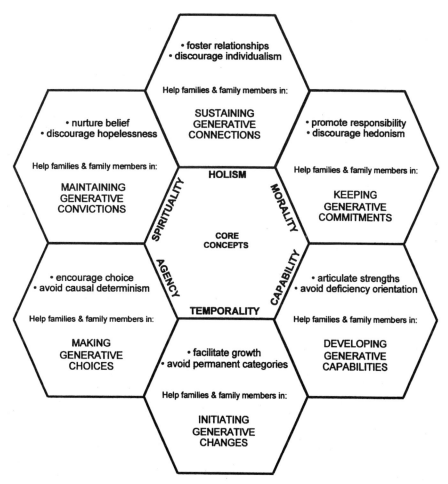

Figure 1. Core concepts and activities of family generativity and generative counseling.

the concept of family generativity, comparing it with other perspectives on generativity; (b) develop our ideas about counseling from a generative perspective, including a comparison of the ideas with the medical model of psychotherapy; and (c) suggest clinical practices that devolve from the core philosophical ideas, using the earlier clinical example to illustrate these ideas and a set of clinical questions that may be asked. Figure 1 depicts the core concepts of family generativity and generative counseling and the associated activities that we suggest emerge from them and are consistent with them.

Before describing those concepts and activities, however, we mention an important caveat: No systematic empirical or clinical research has been conducted to gauge the effectiveness of these activities in clinical settings. Because we are still developing these ideas and practices, we place them into the clinical literature tentatively and with caution. Our belief that these practices may be helpful flows from their logical relation to several sources that are associated with the therapeutic enterprise: (a) philosophical concepts that we believe are more consistent with the human intergenerational experience than is the medical model; (b) our awareness of the clinical value of certain practices that seem to be consistent with our ideas, such as narrative therapies and solution-focused therapies; (c) our own counseling and educational experiences; and (d) our own spiritual convictions, moral values, and ethical commitments.

HOLISM IN FAMILY GENERATIVITY AND GENERATIVE COUNSELING

Holism and Family Generativity

Family generativity is a holistic concept because it is inherently familial, intergenerational, relational, and communal. Family generativity involves the care of the rising generation by the generations ahead of it, including the parent generation (parents, aunts, uncles) and the grandparent generation (grandparents, great-aunts, and great-uncles), not simply as individuals but also as couples, sibling groups, and the extended family group that makes up the "older generation." Family generativity depends on and contributes to connections, care, and commitments among family members and between family adults and the broader community. Family generativity, of course, also includes the motives and actions of members in the family acting as individuals, but it emphasizes collective and coordinated action. However, because *family generativity*, by definition, resides in the relationships between generations, rather than only within individuals, it is conceptually distinct from most other conceptualizations of generativity, which focus on individual motivations deriving from an internal drive, need, or developmental imperative.

The activity of family generativity that is consistent with the core concept of holism is *sustaining generative connections*. Generative connections are relationships that families have with people and communities that contribute to the care and well-being of the next generation.

Holism and Generative Counseling

Finding the atoms of matter was the principal goal of the natural sciences for many years, whether the "atom" was the atom (or quark) of physics or the cell of biology. In medicine, the qualities of a human organism are thought to stem directly from the smaller organs, cells, and atoms that make up the organism. The "disease" model, for instance, postulates a number of smaller, atomistic entities, such as viruses and bacteria, that initiate the deleterious effects of the disease. The assumption is that once these atomistic entities are completely understood, the larger units of disease will also be understood.

In the behavioral sciences, the medical model has entailed a similar focus on the smaller entities of social systems. This focus was part of the original objection to the medical model by family therapists: The medical model attended primarily to the individuals of the family rather than to the family as a unit. The family was not ignored, but its qualities were viewed as stemming directly from the qualities of the individuals who make up the family. Moreover, individuals were considered to be self-contained entities, whether their qualities derived from nature, nurture, or some interaction of the two. This individualism has allowed such characteristics as personality traits to be viewed as relatively stable from context to context, because such individual qualities are thought to dominate.

Generative counseling, on the other hand, assumes a holistic theoretical stance. Rather than postulating that the whole is derived from more fundamental, atomic parts, the generative perspective asks one to consider that the parts themselves depend on the whole for their very existence. Generative counseling, relative to the medical model, is holistic because this relatedness of the parts includes time as well as space. That is, the understanding of any individual requires an understanding not only of the individual's present relationship with others across "space" (e.g., cohort, family) but also of the individual's relationship with others across generations, past, present, and future (Dollahite et al., 1997; Slife, 1993).

The medical model *does* permit a "relating" of the various individuals who make up a system. However, this relating assumes that individual qualities dominate and thus produce the system from their various combinations and interactions. A generative perspective, by contrast, assumes that the relational individual comes first, both developmentally and ontologically. That is, most of the qualities and characteristics of individuals stem not from what is inherent "in" individuals but from how they are related to other people "outside" themselves. In this sense, the whole, rather than the part, dominates, and the individual cannot be understood or treated without some understanding of the whole, both within the generation and across the generations.

Generative Interventions

Generative counselors *foster relationships, avoid individualism,* and *help families and family members in sustaining generative connections.* They look for generative relationships that already exist or that are created through generative change and help to nourish them. To promote family generativity, counselors can strengthen and help change relationships between adult extended family members so that generative care may flow more freely to resolve conflict or reduce distance between family members. Generative counseling also works to connect families and children with the communities of commitment and care that can surround them (Pipher, 1996). It helps clients create or restore connections with communities of faith, service, education, and so forth, so that they can both receive help from other generative people and act on their generative commitments for the well-being of the next generation. Because individuals themselves are dependent on relationships, according to this holistic perspective, an individual's own identity and self-image are strengthened through such commitments and such communities (Bellah, Madsen, Sullivan, Swindlen, & Tipton, 1985). We discuss generative communities in greater depth later. This contextual and holistic approach is consistent with systems therapies in general and with contextual therapy (Boszormenyi-Nagy et al., 1991) and integrative therapy (Duhl & Duhl, 1991) in particular.

Clinical example for holism. In the case example presented earlier, relational and intergenerational connections are central to the Jensons' challenges. Art and Rebecca feel that Leslie is severing her relationship with them. It is interesting that Rebecca severed connections with her own abusive father, and the lost connection with her deceased mother is a source of sadness. Although they are clearly committed to each other, Art and Rebecca need to attend to and work on the quality of their connection. Art remains actively involved with his aging parents, and the Jensons are connected to a religious community from which they draw strength. Perhaps Art and Rebecca could draw on Art's parents as a source of help for Leslie, as well as religious teachers and leaders whom Leslie respects. These resources might help Rebecca to allow the separation that Leslie seems to need in her relationship with her parents while feeling that her daughter is connected to generative communities and individuals who can guide her. It may help Rebecca to work on the sadness she feels at the loss of her mother and the distance she feels with her father to deal more effectively with the relational challenges she is facing with Leslie. Leslie might benefit indirectly if she sensed greater warmth and intimacy between her parents. Leslie also might benefit from Rebecca's generative "historical" work regarding her own parents because Rebecca would learn to see Leslie less as a "willful child," with personality characteristics she does not understand, and more as a person in a dynamic relationship with her. That is, Rebecca would begin to see how her own intergenerational issues affect how she sees and interacts with Leslie.

Clinical questions for holism. Clinical questions such as the following can help generative counselors foster healthy relationships and avoid individualism to sustain generative connections:

- Who do you consider to be part of your "family," broadly defined?
- What are your ideas of the ways "strong families" work together to care for the next generation?
- What kinds of things do you do to maintain a sense of intergenerational family togetherness?
- What do you value most about your children's connections with members of your extended family?
- How does your family interact with and depend on communities in which you participate?
- As parents, how can you draw on the strength of your extended family to help your children?
- Are there people in your community you can draw on to help you resolve this concern with your children?

TEMPORALITY IN FAMILY GENERATIVITY AND GENERATIVE COUNSELING

Temporality and Family Generativity

Temporality refers to time and context. Family generativity does not assume stable traits or characteristics of either individuals or family systems but emphasizes that lives and the stories people tell about them can and do change—gradually or dramatically (Mair, 1988; McAdams, 1985; Parry & Doan, 1994; White & Epston, 1990). Lives and relationships are full of time and context. Family generativity is contextual because it is focused on meeting the needs of those of the next generation, who live in a world that changes across contexts and time. Eriksonian theory suggests that individuals typically focus on generativity in adulthood, which makes the temporal nature of family generativity consistent with Erikson's ideas. However, we propose that family generativity, in addition to being a motivation or trait that is triggered and then remains relatively stable (but changes across time and context), is also a set of generative connections, convictions, commitments, choices, and capabilities that must be continually and contextually nurtured. This conceptualization of family generativity, therefore, shares significant similarities with the conceptualization presented by McAdams, Hart, and Maruna (see chapter 1, this volume), which emphasizes the temporal and contextual processes that operate within generative action.

The activity of family generativity that is consistent with the core concept of temporality is *initiating generative changes.* By generative changes, we mean changes in attitudes, desires, beliefs, concerns, commitments, actions, thoughts, habits, patterns, structures, and narratives in the members of the older generation, individually and collectively, in manifesting care for the younger generation to take into account their living in a changing world.

Temporality and Generative Counseling

The consideration of temporality as an issue of critical concern for generative counseling is inspired by philosophers such as Heidegger (1962), who have contended that "being" requires temporality and who specifically address models, such as the medical model, that have traditionally assumed the superiority of atemporal explanations. *Atemporal* explanations are explanations that are essentially "timeless," or unchanging and universal in their basic nature (Faulconer & Williams, 1985; Slife, 1996; Slife & Williams, 1995). Although our perceptions and the natural world exhibit changes, science has traditionally sought the unchanging laws that lie "behind" this natural world and govern these perceptions. For instance, gravity governs the behavior of falling bodies; this law is atemporal because it is unchanging across time and space.

The use of atemporal explanations came to psychotherapy through medicine (Yanchar & Slife, 1997). The medical profession has always endeavored to discover the atemporal biological principles that lie behind the symptoms of disease. Tubercle bacillus, for instance, is thought to affect the body and be cured in certain ways, regardless of the time or place in which it is contracted. The mental health field has essentially adopted this view; its diagnostic system is borrowed from medicine and clearly exhibits atemporality. Categories of the *Diagnostic and Statistical Manual* (DSM) used by most psychotherapists are usually viewed as stable sets of general classifications that do not vary across time or space. Although in recent versions of the DSM it has been acknowledged that definitions of mental disorder can change over time and differ across cultures, even these versions contain categories that are considered to cross contexts and thus are essentially atemporal. Schizophrenia, for example, is considered to be a category that crosses cultures and eras. If it were not so considered, there would be little point in searching for the biological causes of this disorder (e.g., Johnstone, 1996).

Of course, practitioners of generative counseling acknowledge that some conditions have biological origins and that many clinical problems seem stable across time and context. However, these counselors look for and emphasize temporal explanations and meanings that are *full* of time, rather than atemporal explanations and meanings that are time*less* (Faulconer & Williams, 1985; Slife, 1993; Slife, Hope, & Nebeker, 1997). Temporal explanations are full of the era and context of their construction and interpretation. Era, generation, culture, circumstance, situation, and relational context all matter, and clinicians must take these into account in any helping process. Each generation must be situated within its own era and culture to be truly understood and helped. In this sense, meanings of phenomena such as symptoms are inextricably tied to context and culture. These meanings have no special universal or atemporal status beyond their cultural and narrative embeddedness.

This embeddedness points to another aspect of temporality that is seen in generative explanations, a "temporary" quality. Because each generation should be understood in its own context, and because contexts constantly change and evolve, the explanations about people within a generational context cannot be permanent or universal. A temporal explanation is also a "humble" explanation. Much like atemporal explanations, temporal explanations simplify people's rich experience to reduced categories of explanations (e.g., the "moral" of the story). However, unlike atemporal explanations that presume objective contact with and representation of a permanent reality, temporal explanations contain within themselves the possibility of their own negation; implicit is the assumption that they are inherently context-bound and thus potentially inapplicable to another context. This explanatory humility allows an openness to change that is difficult to achieve in atemporal approaches (Yanchar & Slife, 1997). An atemporal approach prompts counselors to look for sameness and universality across contexts—to fit the unchanging categories of explanation—whereas a temporal approach prompts counselors to be open to change, because contexts and situations can gradually or suddenly be altered.

Generative Interventions

Generative counselors *facilitate growth, avoid permanent categories*, and *help families and family members in initiating generative changes*. They work to avoid placing their clients in atemporal (unchanging, pervasive) categories, even though the medical model of psychotherapy encourages diagnostic categorization. This approach is consistent with the narrative therapy tool of "externalizing," which locates problems outside of clients (White & Epston, 1990). Categorizing is probably one of the most difficult clinical tendencies to avoid, even for those who may be ideologically opposed to clinical classification on other grounds, because many professionals believe they must use diagnostic categories to help their clients (e.g., to obtain third-party reimbursement or to "give them a name for their problem"). Even when diagnostic categories are used for pragmatic purposes, a generative counselor avoids perceiving and relating with a family or individual as an occupier of a permanent category (e.g., stereotype) but conceives of people and families as in continual development and aids in that development by helping them initiate generative changes.

Clinical Example for Temporality

In the specific case study presented earlier, the Jensons are facing challenges that are "full" of time and context. Thus, a generative counselor must see the Jensons in their specific context and must be wary of relating the Jensons' issues too readily to those of other families she or he has counseled or to categories of families or individuals. The Jensons' problems and solutions are unique to their context, at least to some degree. The specific configuration of Rebecca's issues with her parents, in relation to Art's dutifulness with his parents, in relation to Leslie's issues with her parents, possesses many recognizable clinical themes; however, the "whole" of their relationships is also unique. By the same token, the Jensons' problems are not static. They are not, for instance, a "dysfunctional family" in the conventional categorical sense of this term. First, there are undoubtedly many aspects of their "functioning" that are not problematic that could be recognized and strengthened. Second, even the "dysfunctional" aspects of their family "system" are likely to change under different sets of circumstances. For example, Rebecca and Leslie tend to see their relationship in categorical, dysfunctional terms, yet the generative counselor can call attention to this "overgeneralizing" and "stereotyping" of their evaluation. The counselor can facilitate and point to the times—both in the session and outside—that Rebecca and Leslie have evidenced positive relations, including generative commitments to one another. Art, too, may be using acontextual categories that block meaningful change. For example, he describes himself as a workaholic and is worried that he has permanently damaged his relationship with Leslie. The generative counselor can note the evidence that he willingly moderates his activities for important family purposes. If it were needed to meet the current challenge, Art clearly has the capacity and willingness to devote more time to family. Similarly, Rebecca does not think she is a "good mother" because she grew up in a "dysfunctional family" with an "abusive father" and an "unavailable mother." Clearly, however, Leslie's early educational success and sense of self-worth reflect well on Rebecca's parenting, and her deep generative desires toward Leslie are a strong source of change.

Clinical Questions for Temporality

Clinical questions such as the following can help generative counselors facilitate growth and avoid atemporal categorizations to initiate generative changes:

- Has there been a time or instance when you feel you truly met the needs of the next generation?
- How has that changed over time?
- How have you made important changes in the past to improve caring for the next generation?
- Have there been labels applied to you or your children by yourself or by professionals that are inconsistent with your desires and efforts to care for the next generation?
- If so, how can you draw on your strengths to act in ways that belie those labels?
- If you were writing (or speaking) about the changes you've made toward family generativity 1 or 2 years from now, what do you hope you can write (or say)?

AGENCY IN FAMILY GENERATIVITY AND GENERATIVE COUNSELING

Agency and Family Generativity

The concept of family generativity emphasizes human agency over the functioning of internal drives and response to cultural pressures. Although there are certainly biogenetic, psychological, and sociocultural factors that encourage older family members to care for younger ones, we propose that caring for the next generation is ultimately a *choice* that family members make, separately and together. Family generativity is thus an agentic concept because family members are able to choose whether to be generative in their overall family life orientation as well as with respect to individual daily actions (see chapter 7, this volume).

The activity of family generativity that is consistent with the core concept of agency is *making generative choices*. By generative choices we mean both large and small choices that benefit children. These choices are often made in a nongenerative cultural context (Dienhart & Daly, 1997) that puts significant constraints on acting generatively (chapter 7, this volume) and in which seeking one's own pleasures, goals, and happiness is emphasized. These choices are usually not easy ones, and it is possible even for caring adults to allow children's significant and changing needs to receive less attention than they deserve and family members would like to provide.

Agency and Generative Counseling

The medical model establishes a firm deterministic foundation for its explanations and understandings of the world, whereas generative counseling has an agentic perspective (cf. Slife & Fisher, 1997). *Determinism* is the assumption that all events are caused and thus cannot have happened otherwise. *Agency* is the assumption that events *could* have occurred otherwise, all other factors but the exercise of will remaining the same. That is, agency is the assumption of a world of possibility, or "coulds," whereas determinism is the assumption of a world of necessity, or "musts."

The determinism of the medical model is inherent in its conceptions of disease, atemporality, and atoms. It assumes that these atoms operate according to unchangeable laws that determine all events and entities of the natural world. Medical practitioners are the first to admit that they do not know all the causal factors involved in health and pathology. Still, the assumption of the medical model is that such factors exist and that they operate in a deterministic manner. No one seriously posits, for example, that a disease entity has the ability to choose its own biological path. These entities are determined by a complexity of factors that may not be presently known but *are* determined.

The medical model has, at least traditionally, provided a similar deterministic foundation for the behavioral sciences. Although the causal events may differ from those studied by the natural sciences, many psychosocial and behavioral theories presume that antecedent events cause present social or psychological events (Hoffman, 1981; Slife, 1993). This presumption means that individual or familial behavior is determined by the past. Thus, many psychotherapies suggest that one begin counseling by taking a "history" of the client or the family, assessing what are often perceived as stable, deterministic traits of the individual or family. If the problem is caused by events in the client's past (e.g., family experiences, reinforcement history, childhood trauma, or cognitive programming), treatment would need to take into account these historical events.

Generative counseling, however, does not assume this form of determinism but assumes that human beings can choose, within some constraints, what they think, feel, do, and believe (Williams, 1992). Thus, rather than trying to find a way to "cure" people or families, this approach calls for generative choices to be made, individually and collectively. Family therapists have expressed their own difficulties with the concept of individualistic linear causality (Hoffman, 1981). They have viewed it as ultimately focusing attention on the individual, who supposedly possesses a unique causal and experiential history. However, there is also a kind of determinism in many family system conceptions (Slife, 1993); although these conceptions are often focused on the present, rather than the past, they also assume a world in which events necessarily (and deterministically) occur, in this case, as a result of properties of the system (boundaries, rules, feedback mechanisms, and so on). The holism of generative counseling is different because it presumes a whole of possibility (and temporality) rather than a system of necessity (Bohman, 1993; Heidegger, 1926/ 1962; Slife & Williams, 1995). In other words, generative counseling affirms the importance of the agent's context (or relationship with the whole) but does not assume that this context is a "force" against which the individual or family is relatively helpless.

Generative Interventions

Generative counselors *encourage choice, avoid causal determinism,* and *help families and family members in making generative choices.* Generative counselors see people as agents who, within constraints, make choices about how they think, feel, believe, and act, rather than as beings who are wholly or mostly determined by factors outside their control. Many times clients in psychotherapy see themselves as locked in, stuck, powerless, destined to fail, or hurt because of their past or current situation; their family upbringing;, their personality; or their current social, economic, or psychological condition. Counselors can encourage and assist families and individuals to make generative choices in spite of such challenges and constraints—to choose to "rework situations" (see chapter 2, this volume) and take action that flows from their desires and commitments to care for the next generation.

Clinical Example for Agency

Agency is crucial to the Jensons' challenges. Art suspects his over-commitment to work may be directly responsible for Leslie's desire to leave home. Rebecca believes that her family-of-origin experiences made her an unskilled mother. Perhaps they both worry that the current low level of intimacy in their marital relationship is shaping Leslie's diminished respect for and interest in her parents. As is common in counseling situations, the Jensons feel "trapped" by these circumstances, present and past. A generative counselor can work with the Jensons to avoid the perception that the past is determinative. Although the past must be taken into account in the present, it does not prohibit anyone from adopting different relational styles or holding people responsible for their behaviors. In this sense, Leslie, Art, and Rebecca are all capable of making choices to change the current situation, and each is also responsible, to some degree at least, for his or her own behavior. Leslie, particularly, can be held responsible for her poor decisions and her poor judgment. Past issues certainly may act as constraints on the ease with which choices are made, but these can be addressed in counseling to make generative choices more likely. In this way, a generative counselor can work with the Jensons to reinforce their abilities to choose to stay connected to Rebecca, both by establishing responsible boundaries and by nurturing her.

Clinical Questions for Agency

Clinical questions such as the following can help generative counselors encourage self-chosen action and avoid the pessimism of determinism to support individuals' and families' abilities to make generative choices:

- Do you believe that you and your children can change in ways that will help resolve these issues?
- What constraints make it difficult for you to choose ways to meet your children's needs?
- How have you made choices that resolve the tough dilemmas you face in deciding between meeting your needs and those of your children?
- If you were to take one action right now that would benefit your children, what would it be?

CAPABILITY IN FAMILY GENERATIVITY AND GENERATIVE COUNSELING

Capability and Family Generativity

We assume that most families are capable of being generative, that is, of meeting the needs of the next generation. Capabilities are usually present even when they are not realized. However, our emphasis on presumed capabilities does not ignore the fact that some people lack capabilities and that most people have weaknesses in caring for the next generation. We believe that, given awareness and effort, even weaknesses can be improved significantly. This assumption of capability is generally consistent with most other formulations of the generativity construct; usually there is the presumption that adults have the inherent ability or moral direction to care for the next generation in most circumstances (Dollahite et al., 1997; also see chapter 7, this volume), even in challenging circumstances (Brotherson & Dollahite, 1997; see chapter 11, this volume).

The activity of family generativity that is consistent with this core concept is *developing generative capabilities*. By generative capabilities we mean desires, concerns, beliefs, and actions that are concerned with the well-being of the next generation.

Capability and Generative Counseling

One of the more obvious contrasts between the medical model of psychotherapy and generative counseling concerns the issue of practitioner emphasis, or focus. The medical model leads mental health professionals to look for and treat deficiencies in functioning, making them "pathology sniffers," to use Yalom's (1985, p. 128) term, whereas generative counseling leads professionals to look for and develop the capabilities and strengths of their clients. The medical model is, of course, based on a "disease" conception of abnormality. That is, the medical model assumes that something is wrong "inside" the individual and that this wrongness leads the person to be "disordered" or "dysfunctional." Wrongness traditionally has been emphasized and conceptualized in a variety of ways in the behavioral sciences, ranging from intrapsychic conflicts to learning deficits to irrational cognitions to dysfunctional family structures.

Generative counseling, on the other hand, assumes that nearly all clients have generative capabilities and strengths and that personal and family generative strengths can be developed to enhance generative action, which is consistent with the skill training approach in family counseling (L'Abate, 1991). Although this approach does not deny the reality of deficiencies and weaknesses, it does not emphasize the correction of these deficits and weaknesses as the focus of counseling. Rather, it attempts to discover and develop the strengths clients and families bring to counseling. Doherty (1991) argued that clinicians are generally more helpful when they build from strengths rather than from deficiencies. When people and families come for counseling, they have likely forgotten some things they once knew or neglected to do some things they can do and have done before (Furman & Ahola, 1992). Generative counselors believe that people have the capacity to "generate" constructive relationships as well as to care about "generational" issues (Dienhart & Dollahite, 1997). Even when there is a "deficiency" in the generating and generational relating, the focus is on what is positively happening in these arenas and on how to develop those capabilities, instead of on what is not happening or how to eliminate deficiencies.

Generative Interventions

Generative counselors *articulate strengths, avoid a deficiency orientation, and help families and family members in developing generative capabilities.* Generative counselors avoid thinking, speaking, and feeling about their clients in ways that emphasize deficiency and dysfunction; rather, they work to facilitate the empowering articulation of clients' strengths by both the client and the counselor. They work to help the client develop generative capabilities, both manifest and hidden strengths they already possess and new strengths that may develop during the course of counseling.

Clinical Example for Capability

Art and Rebecca Jenson present many strengths that lend themselves to generative capabilities. Rebecca has a deep concern for her daughter and a desire to give her a better home life than she herself had. In other words, Rebecca has the desire to be what the clinical literature calls a "transitional character," also termed an "intergenerational buffer" (chapter 11, this volume). Her love of teaching and firm religious beliefs evidence strong generative capabilities. Although Art describes himself as a workaholic, he uses the flexibility in his employment situation to accommodate his wife and spend more time with his daughter, and he still finds the time to care for his aging parents (a kind of reverse generativity). In virtually all of their interactions and recent challenges with Leslie, they have adapted their parenting and have tried to maintain a positive relationship. These strengths are a solid foundation for continued efforts to deal with their current family challenges. A generative counselor would reflect, reinforce, and build on these strengths.

Clinical Questions for Capability

Clinical questions such as the following can help counselors articulate strengths and avoid focusing on deficiency to develop generative capabilities:

- What do you do well in your nuclear or extended family to care for the next generation?
- What are your greatest strengths in meeting your children's needs as a family?
- May I join you in a search for capabilities in your family that you can develop to contribute better to your children's development?
- If you could build on one of your strengths to benefit your children, what would it be?

SPIRITUALITY IN FAMILY GENERATIVITY AND GENERATIVE COUNSELING

Spirituality and Family Generativity

Spirituality involves a rising above or going beyond the ordinary limits of materiality and the tendencies of humanity, usually as a result of strongly held beliefs and convictions. It may describe rising above our natural world to relate with a divine being, going beyond our own physical state to affect some heightened awareness of ourselves, or connecting to others in ways that cannot be explained solely by material factors. Commonly, scholars and clinicians exploring this spirituality have described it as a type of *transcendence* (Anderson & Worthen, 1997; Bahr & Bahr, 1996; Hart, 1994; Slife, Nebeker, & Hope, 1996).

Anderson and Worthen (1997) have suggested that "every human relational event can be viewed as spiritual" (p. 5); we believe this is particularly true for intergenerational relationships. Hart (1994) asserted that whereas "it is true that for most people, spirituality is nurtured within the context of organized religion . . . we are spiritual whether or not we belong to a religious denomination" (p. 23). Spirituality permeates human lives and human relationships and is often, although not necessarily, associated with religious belief and practice.

Spirituality has been discussed or implied by a number of scholars recently in their formulations of generativity (Allen & Connor, 1997; Dollahite et al., 1997; Hawkins, Dollahite, & Rhoades, 1993; McAdams, Dimond, de St. Aubin, & Mansfield, 1997, Snarey, 1993; also see chapters 1 and 11, this volume). We define *generative spirituality* as a transcendent connection with the next generation that flows from and encourages convictions of abiding care for that generation. Although others may not view generative care in spiritual terms, we view *family generativity* as inherently spiritual because, in our definition, it involves transcending selfishness, the demands of the present, and the attractions and distractions of one's own generation. For many families and family members, religious belief encourages generative commitments and religious practice, and the religious community supports their generative actions. Of course, there are many families and individuals who are generative but do not define themselves as religious.

The activity of family generativity that is consistent with the core concept of spirituality is *maintaining generative convictions*. We believe that, in most cases, a spirituality of *everyday* life has great potential to deepen and enrich family generativity. This "prosaic" approach to generative spirituality suggests that small acts of care matter greatly (Morson, 1988), especially when they happen frequently and with transcendent meaning. Generative spirituality thus involves adult family members, in concert with others and individually, abiding by their deep convictions to maintain transcendent connections with the next generation. These connections, in turn, encourage adults to form or strengthen convictions to transcend the cultural power of expressive individualism that often leads them toward self-absorption and away from abiding commitments to care (Bellah et al., 1985).

Spirituality and Generative Counseling

The medical model, stemming as it does from the natural sciences, affirms the ideology of materialism. Diseases and the tissues they infect are understood to be material entities, and the primary means of treating such diseases are themselves material interventions (surgery, physical manipulations, medication). Materialism posits that reality consists only of the visible and tangible things of the world that exist independently of the observer (Slife et al., 1997); the validity of mental impressions that do not stem from material objects—and thus do not come through our senses— is, by definition, suspect. In counseling, then, nonmaterial events and entities, such as spiritual ones, cannot be given much credence or significance.

Some professionals have begun to question the exclusivity of material (medical) assumptions and the type of therapy they lead to. Recent scholarship has pointed to the importance and value of a spiritual dimension in counseling (Anderson & Worthen, 1997; Brothers, 1992; Gorsuch, 1988; Hart, 1994; Moore, 1994; Richards & Bergin, in press; Shafranske, 1996). Anderson and Worthen (1997) asserted that, although a transcendent spiritual dimension may not be *required* for effective counseling to occur, the presence of a spiritual dimension opens possibilities for understanding and transformation that may not exist without the spiritual dimension. According to Anderson and Worthen (1997), the absence of this dimension can lead a family therapist to treat marriages and families as "a mechanical or technological 'system' to be diagnosed as a mechanic diagnoses a car, devising structural interventions to repair its 'interpersonal mechanics'" (p. 6). Hart (1994), like Anderson and Worthen, has called for clinicians to view and relate with families and individuals in more spiritual and less mechanistic ways, with the expectation that new sources of hope, strength, and transformation will become available to counselors and clients.

Generative counseling emphasizes the transcendent spiritual dimension of human families, human relationships, and human beings. A spiritual dimension can encourage family members to create connections and convictions that can help them transcend intergenerational distance or conflict. This transcendence is not atemporal or contextless but connotes a type of intergenerational relationship that is deeply contextual. In this sense, the context of the relationship is not itself transcended; rather, people in relationship are helped to transcend the limits of individual weakness, selfishness, or anger (Dollahite et al., 1997; Slife, 1993).

A generative approach in no way denies the reality or importance of the material; however, unlike the medical model, it does not assume that the material realm contains all that can be considered real or important. Consideration of a spiritual dimension opens the door to a profound respect for what is outside, and harder to grasp than, the material, the ordinary, or the mundane. We suggest, therefore, that counselors view intergenerational relationships as *sacred* and *enduring*: sacred because they are singular, highly significant, and to some extent, capable of helping people transcend the mundane concerns of the self, and enduring because they have a boundless quality to them, in terms of both time and importance.

The generative counselor does not conceive of or conduct counseling simply as a bounded, rational, technical, and scientific enterprise. We believe that generative counselors best serve people and the intergenerational relationships they create when they approach them with a deep appreciation, even a reverence, for the sacred and enduring nature of those relationships. A spiritual approach invites counselors to "listen meditatively or contemplatively" to the concerns clients bring to counseling and respond with hope and compassion, believing that deep transformation can occur, often not merely as a result of one's own expertise and efforts but also through spiritual influences (Anderson & Worthen, 1997, p. 9). We do not believe that a counselor needs to be an outwardly "religious" or "spiritual" person to take a spiritual stance with clients concerning their intergenerational relationships; rather, the counselor simply needs to recognize and communicate to the clients that there are sources of insight and inspiration beyond the knowledge and skills of the counselor and clients that can be accessed in the counseling process.

Generative Interventions

Generative counselors *nurture belief, avoid hopelessness,* and *help families and family members in maintaining generative convictions.* Generative counselors recognize and value the transcendent spiritual aspirations and convictions of human beings and families and nurture that spirituality in its varied forms. They help clients maintain generative convictions by assisting them to identify, clarify, or challenge beliefs about themselves, their children, their lives, what is important, their potential as parents and grandparents, and the meaning and value of generative activity.

Clinical Example for Spirituality

Art and Rebecca Jenson demonstrate important spiritual resources. Art appreciates the moral education that flows from religious teachings and believes acts of charity are the essence of a spiritual life. Rebecca has deep religious convictions in a specific faith that believes in a God who is spiritually involved in the lives of His creations. Leslie enjoys being with other people in an organized religious setting. A generative counselor could draw on these spiritual resources to counteract the hopelessness that the Jensons seem to feel. The Jensons feel trapped, or stuck, and a counselor can help them believe that a commitment to spiritual sources and meanings "outside" themselves will enable them to move outside the trap they feel. The counselor may invite the Jensons to pray together, seek guidance from religious texts and religious advisors, and attend to spiritual impressions they may receive. The counselor would believe, and help the clients to believe, that significant change is possible, although the form of that change may be unexpected, because spiritual transformation usually is not neatly controlled or predicted.

Clinical Questions for Spirituality

Clinical questions such as the following can help generative counselors nurture belief and avoid hopelessness to maintain generative convictions:

- What are your deepest and strongest spiritual beliefs?
- In what ways do these beliefs influence your relations with the next generation?
- Are there spiritual resources that you can draw on in this situation to transcend the obstacles to caring well for the next generation?
- What is it about your spiritual convictions that motivates you to continue to try to resolve the challenges you face including those with your children or other members of the rising generation?
- In the past when doubt and fear have overtaken you, what spiritual beliefs and practices have helped you?
- What is your extended family's greatest spiritual strength and how can you draw on that now to benefit both your children and others in need of care?

MORALITY IN FAMILY GENERATIVITY AND GENERATIVE COUNSELING

Morality and Family Generativity

Family generativity has a moral dimension that flows from the assumption that older generations have ethical and moral obligations to younger generations. These obligations exist because parents bring children into being and the younger generation is dependent on adult family members for their care, love, acceptance, and mentoring. We assume that people have an inherent "moral sense" (Wilson, 1993) that encourages generativity, although this does not negate the possibility that parents and other family adults can choose to be oriented toward ideals other than the welfare of the rising generation; agency is necessary to morality (Slife & Williams, 1995). The moral dimension of family generativity suggests that, in spite of the transcendent connection most adults feel to the next generation, the degree of adult-oriented, hedonistic expressive individualism present in Western cultural norms and practices (Bellah et al., 1985; Slife, 1997) results in the need for reminders of adults' generative responsibility.

These reminders often, but not always, flow from authentic spiritual traditions or religious communities. Most spiritual traditions teach that placing the needs of others ahead of oneself is the essence of spirituality and morality; thus, spiritual connections and convictions often influence people to make and keep generative commitments. The Jewish ethical philosopher Immanuel Levinas (1985, 1987) placed the needs of "the other" as the prime ethical imperative. Christian thought suggests that "whoso would save his life must lose it" (Holy Bible, Mark 8:35), a concept consistent with family generativity but at odds with much contemporary self-oriented psychology. The work on generativity of Erikson (1950/1963, 1982b), Snarey (1993), Dollahite et al. (1997), and McAdams, Hart, and Maruna (chapter 1, this volume) certainly illuminates moral and ethical dimensions, and our concept of family generativity is consistent with these views.

The activity of family generativity consistent with the core concept of morality is *keeping generative commitments*. By generative commitments, we mean the bonds and connections that have been freely and continuously made and that focus on action to benefit the next generation.

Morality and Generative Counseling

The assumptions and treatments of the medical model are typically viewed as neither moral nor immoral because they are tied to naturalism. Naturalism assumes that the world is governed by natural laws and that these laws are indifferent to morality; they are neither good nor bad, they just are. The application of naturalism to psychotherapy historically has resulted in many benefits. "Demons" are no longer exorcized from people manifesting symptoms of schizophrenia, and "witches" are no longer burned at the stake. Mental disorder is viewed as part of the natural world and thus is not subject to moral or religious judgments. The naturalism of the medical model has led many traditional psychotherapists into believing they should not take an explicit moral stance relative to client choices and lifestyles except insofar as neglect or abuse of others is concerned. Effective treatment usually is thought to involve the reserving of moral judgment, particularly when it concerns judgments about how clients *ought* to live their lives. Of course, the medical model has, in a sense, adopted the moral obligation to help clients (or at least to do no harm), and there are numerous ethical obligations that apply to the counseling setting.

The generative counseling perspective, by contrast, possesses an explicitly moral dimension. Generative counseling assumes that therapists *cannot* and *should not* avoid making moral judgments and promoting moral responsibility (Doherty, 1995; Slife, 1997). Frequently, therapeutic conversations explore what one "ought" to do or what constitutes the "good life." Generative counseling also attempts to make implicit moral judgments explicit, so that they can be dealt with more openly and honestly.

Generative counseling is also straightforward in its promulgation of a particular morality; indeed, by its very definition, family generativity implies that people *ought* to care for subsequent generations (Dollahite et al., 1997). Parenting is the prototype of this care, of course, but this moral imperative is not exclusive to parents; it extends to grandparents, aunts, uncles, and other adult family members as well as members of the community. Generative counseling suggests that all people *should* be involved in aiding the next generation, whether through example, education, or mentoring. Moreover, family generativity implies that people *ought* to avoid self-absorption in doing this caring. That is, one does not care for the next generation because one is attempting to benefit oneself; one cares for another because one *ought* to care for another, even if that caring entails self-sacrifice or suffering. Counselors can therefore exert meaningful moral influence and skilled intervention to help families be generative in an often nongenerative culture (Dienhart & Daly, 1997; Dienhart & Dollahite, 1997).

Generative Interventions

Generative counselors *promote responsibility, discourage hedonism,* and *help families and family members in keeping generative commitments.* Generative counselors encourage clients to make responsible moral choices on behalf of the next generation that transcend personal comfort, convenience, or preference. They help clients keep generative commitments that they have already made or that they choose to make during the course of counseling. They encourage their clients to engage in moral reflection about the effect of their actions on the next generation and work to help clients make and keep commitments that place the needs of the next generation above personal needs and wants. In so doing, counselors assist those they work with to live in the world with integrity (Erikson's final developmental task). For example, counselors using this approach feel comfortable calling forth generative sacrifice; they know that people in crisis and afraid may act in ways that seem to preserve personal happiness at the expense of the best interests of the next generation.

Clinical Example for Morality

Art and Rebecca's sense of moral obligation to the next generation is strong and a rich resource to draw on in facilitating change. Spiritual convictions, values that highlight the importance of families, and desires to help others are all evident in the Jensons' lives. The problem the Jensons have brought to counseling is complex and difficult to resolve and will undoubtedly require some sacrifice on their part. In the face of this difficulty, there is a strong temptation to avoid responsibility. Art's resignation in letting Leslie learn from her own mistakes may be a sign of this avoidance. Rebecca's increased drinking also may partly be an effort to escape responsibility. A generative counselor would continually encourage the Jensons' efforts to avoid nonresponsible ways out and to focus on what is best for Leslie, even if that includes significant personal discomfort and sacrifice. Rebecca and Art should be asked to make these sacrifices because it is the best thing to do, not because they will receive any personal benefit from them (although the counselor knows that generative sacrifices usually result in an increased sense of integrity for those who make them).

Clinical Questions for Morality

Clinical questions such as the following may help generative counselors promote responsibility and discourage selfish desires to keep generative commitments:

- What values are most important for you to pass along to your children?
- In what ways have you sacrificed for your family?
- What sacrifices could you make now to give your children what they most need?
- What commitments on behalf of the next generation have you made in the past that are being challenged now?
- How can you draw on your communities to help maintain your generative commitments?
- What new commitments can you and your family make to benefit the next generation?

INTEGRATION OF FAMILY GENERATIVITY AND GENERATIVE COUNSELING

The main activities of generative counseling are intended to sustain and encourage family generativity. Generative counseling is holistically integrated, and the various parts are related to one another and to the central idea of family generativity. In the interests of space, we give only two examples of this integration. *Generative agency* is holistic (choice is embedded in a web of other choices, contexts, and constraints), temporal (choices and constraints change over time), spiritual (choice is enhanced and challenged by spiritual connections and convictions), capability-oriented (the exercise of choice brings greater capabilities), and moral (people are accountable for their choices). Therefore, generative counselors do not assume that people are wholly and always free to do whatever they please; rather, they work with clients as "contextual agents" (Dienhart & Dollahite, 1997; Dollahite et al., 1997) by exploring the ways in which clients' choices are constrained and influenced but open to the exercise of agency in meeting the needs of the next generation.

Similarly, *generative morality* is agentic (people choose their commitments), capability-oriented (people have the capacity to be moral), holistic (generative morality exists in a web of connections with other people, places, ideas, and cultures), temporal (morality is embedded in context and era), and spiritual (morality draws life from spiritual connections and convictions). Generative counselors encourage moral reflection and action within these contexts, with a clear emphasis on making moral choices to meet the needs of the next generation, but they also recognize that a sense of moral responsibility alone is insufficient to sustain generative action.

GENERATIVE COMMUNITIES AS RESOURCES IN GENERATIVE COUNSELING

One of the strengths of the medical model of psychotherapy is that it is clearly embedded in a broader system of support for patients and a community of colleagues for professionals. For generative counseling to progress, there needs to be support in the broader culture for the philosophy and practice of generative counseling. Generative communities and other resources[2] are crucial in assisting counselors who are endeavoring to maintain and strengthen generative action. We believe there are extant paradigms, institutions, and communities that are consistent with the six core concepts of family generativity and generative counseling. Generative counselors and their clients should be able to draw on these communities for support and encouragement.

On the basis of the six core concepts of family generativity and generative counseling, a generative community would need to acknowledge that (a) connection with a community of care helps the next generation (holism); (b) generative transformation is possible, and understanding is contextual (temporality); (c) human beings can choose to grow and change in generative ways (agency); (d) people and families can, with support, develop their inherent potential for care (capability); (e) spiritual reality exists and is relevant to caring for the next generation (spirituality); and (f) there are ethics and morals that can guide parents in caring for their children (morality).

---

[2]Counselors who seek assistance in working from a generative perspective with fathers can consult a web site called *FatherWork*, which can be accessed at http://fatherwork.byu.edu.

Generative communities can include schools, churches and syna-
gogues, fraternal and other benevolent orders, cultural and ethnic communities, and community organizations such as the YMCA and YWCA.
In our view, the most significant and widely available aids for parents and
other family adults in actualizing family generativity stem from religious
communities. Some recent literature has suggested that religious beliefs,
motivations, experiences, and communities serve both to encourage and to
support people in generative commitments and actions (Dollahite et al.,
1997; Pipher, 1996; Shafranske, 1996). Members of religious communities
typically consider themselves bound by a coherent and meaningful set of
beliefs, practices, and supportive connections to others that give purpose
and aid to a family's efforts to care for the next generation.

There are several reasons that religious communities are likely to offer
valuable support for generative counselors. First, religious beliefs can give
a sense of conviction in life that supports *generative faith*. Religious beliefs
frequently connote the possibility and desirability of transcendence and
transformation, both of which are integral to family generativity and generative counseling. Second, religious practices can give a sense of agency
that can encourage *generative hope*. Such practices include participation in
sacred rituals and the retelling of sacred stories, both important tools of
counselors in helping families believe that generative change can happen.
Third, religious communities can give a sense of transcendent connection
with others, regarding the past as well as the future, that motivates *generative care*. These communities often make covenants and sacrifices that
bind the members of the community to one another in generative commitments and convictions. It is interesting to note that Erikson (1982b)
himself saw a vital connection among his three major developmental
tasks—trust, fidelity, and care—and the Christian virtues of hope, faith,
and charity (Holy Bible, I Corinthians 13:13). Together, religious beliefs,
practices, and community can help families and individuals transcend antigenerative forces and choose to create and continually nurture the next
generation.

Generative counselors can encourage clients both to benefit from and
to contribute to these supportive communities by (a) helping clients to
make holistic generative *connections* through meaningful and joyful participation in a religious community, (b) helping clients to initiate generative
changes by drawing on religious beliefs and images that involve the possibility of transformation, (c) helping clients to maintain generative spiritual
convictions through reference to religious beliefs and stories that focus on
transcendent realities, (d) helping clients to develop generative *capabilities*
by drawing on religious stories that depict people in difficult circumstances
discovering strengths, (e) helping clients to keep generative *commitments*
by encouraging adherence to religious covenants that emphasize keeping
faith with God and with one's community through sacrifice and service,

and (f) helping clients to exercise their agency to make generative *choices* by referring to religious beliefs that emphasize choosing goodness in times of struggle and trial. We believe that generative counselors can and should draw on generative communities, particularly communities of faith, to assist the families they work with better meet the needs of the next generation.

CONCLUSION

Taken as a whole, the concepts and activities of family generativity and generative counseling create a paradigm of theory and approach to practice that we believe is significantly different from many forms of behavioral science and clinical intervention. In an increasingly postmodern counseling context, with family systems theory in particular becoming more accepted, many clinicians have already adopted a philosophy and set of practices that include aspects of the perspectives we have described. We hope that they and others will see the potential of family generativity and generative counseling to frame and inform the work they are doing with their clients so that the bonds between generations can be sustained and strengthened.

REFERENCES

Anderson, D. A., & Worthen, D. (1997). Exploring a fourth dimension: Spirituality as a resource for the couple therapist. *Journal of Marital and Family Therapy, 23,* 3–12.

Allen, W. D., & Connor, M. (1997). An African American perspective on generative fathering. In A. J. Hawkins & D. C. Dollahite (Eds.), *Generative fathering: Beyond deficit perspectives* (pp. 52–70). Thousand Oaks, CA: Sage.

Bahr, H. M., & Bahr, K. S. (1996). A paradigm of family transcendence. *Journal of Marriage and the Family, 58,* 541–555.

Becvar, D. S., & Becvar, R. J. (1988). *Family therapy: A systematic integration.* Boston: Allyn & Bacon.

Bellah, R. N., Madsen, R., Sullivan, W. M., Swindler, A., & Tipton, S. M. (1985). *Habits of the heart: Individualism and commitment in American life.* Berkeley: University of California Press.

Bohman, J. (1993). *New philosophy of social science.* Cambridge, MA: MIT Press.

Boszormenyi-Nagy, I., Grunebaum, J., & Ulrich, D. (1991). Contextual therapy. In A. S. Gurman & D. P. Kniskern (Eds.), *Handbook of family therapy* (Vol. 1, pp. 200–238). New York: Brunner/Mazel.

Boszormenyi-Nagy, I., & Spark, G. M. (1984). *Invisible loyalties: Reciprocity in intergenerational family therapy.* New York: Brunner/Mazel.

Brothers, B. J. (Ed.). (1992). *Spirituality and couples: Heart and soul in the therapy process*. New York: Haworth Press.

Brotherson, S. E., & Dollahite, D. C. (1997). Generative ingenuity in fatherwork with young children with special needs. In A. J. Hawkins & D. C. Dollahite (Eds.), *Generative fathering: Beyond deficit perspectives* (pp. 89–104). Thousand Oaks, CA: Sage.

Dienhart, A., & Daly, K. (1997). Men and women co-creating father involvement in a nongenerative culture. In A. J. Hawkins & D. C. Dollahite (Eds.), *Generative fathering: Beyond deficit perspectives* (pp. 147–164). Thousand Oaks, CA: Sage.

Dienhart, A., & Dollahite, D. C. (1997). A generative narrative approach to clinical work with fathers. In A. J. Hawkins & D. C. Dollahite (Eds.), *Generative fathering: Beyond deficit perspectives* (pp. 183–199). Thousand Oaks, CA: Sage.

Doherty, W. J. (1991). Beyond reactivity and the deficit model of manhood: A commentary on articles by Napier, Pittman, and Gottman. *Journal of Marital and Family Therapy, 17*, 29–32.

Doherty, W. J. (1995). *Soul searching: Why psychotherapy must promote moral responsibility*. New York: Basic Books.

Dollahite, D. C., Hawkins, A. J., & Brotherson, S. E. (1996). Narrative accounts, generative fathering, and family life education. *Marriage and Family Review, 24*, 349–368.

Dollahite, D. C., Hawkins, A. J., & Brotherson, S. E. (1997). Fatherwork: A conceptual ethic of fathering as generative work. In A. J. Hawkins & D. C. Dollahite (Eds.), *Generative fathering: Beyond deficit perspectives* (pp. 17–35). Thousand Oaks, CA: Sage.

Duhl, B. S., & Duhl, F. J. (1991). Integrative family therapy. In A. S. Gurman & D. P. Kniskern (Eds.), *Handbook of family therapy* (Vol. 1, pp. 483–513). New York: Brunner/Mazel.

Erikson, E. H. (1963). *Childhood and society*. New York: Norton. (Original work published 1950)

Erikson, E. H. (1982a). *Identity and the life cycle*. New York: Norton.

Erikson, E. H. (1982b). *The life cycle completed*. New York: Norton.

Faulconer, J., & Williams, R. (1985). Temporality in human action: An alternative to positivism and historicism. *American Psychologist, 40*, 1179–1188.

Furman, B., & Ahola, T. (1992). *Solution talk: Hosting therapeutic conversations*. New York: Norton.

Gorsuch, R. L. (1988). Psychology of religion. In M. R. Rosenzweig & L. W. Porter (Eds.), *Annual Review of Psychology* (pp. 201–221). Stanford, CA: Annual Reviews.

Gurman, A. S., & Kniskern, D. P. (Eds.). (1991). *Handbook of family therapy*. New York: Brunner/Mazel.

Hart, T. (1994). *Hidden spring: The spiritual dimension of therapy*. New York: Paulist.

Hart, H. M. (1997). *Generativity and social involvement among African-American and white adults*. Unpublished doctoral dissertation, Department of Human Development and Social Policy, Northwestern, Evanston, IL.

Hawkins, A. J., Christiansen, S. L., Sargent, K. P., & Hill, E. J. (1995). Rethinking fathers' involvement in child care: A developmental perspective. In W. Marsiglio (Ed.), *Fatherhood: Contemporary theory, research, and social policy* (pp. 41–56). Newbury Park, CA: Sage.

Hawkins, A. J., & Dollahite, D. C. (Eds.). (1997). *Generative fathering: Beyond deficit perspectives*. Thousand Oaks, CA: Sage.

Hawkins, A. J., Dollahite, D. C., & Rhoades, C. J. (1993). Turning the hearts of the fathers to the children: Nurturing the next generation. *BYU Studies, 33,* 273–291.

Heidegger, M. (1962). *Being and time* (J. Macquarrie & E. Robinson, Trans.). San Francisco: Harper & Row. (Original work published 1926)

Hoffman, L. (1981). *Foundations of family therapy: A conceptual framework for systems change*. New York: Basic Books.

Johnstone, E. C. (1996). A concept of schizophrenia. In B. D. Slife (Ed.), *Taking sides: Clashing views on controversial psychological issues* (pp. 222–230). Guilford, CT: Dushkin/Brown Benchmark.

Kotre, J. (1984). *Outliving the self: Generativity and the interpretation of lives*. Baltimore: The Johns Hopkins University Press.

L'Abate, L. (1991). Skill training programs for couples and families. In A. S. Gurman & D. P. Kniskern (Eds.), *Handbook of family therapy* (pp. 631–661). New York: Brunner/Mazel.

Lavee, Y., & Dollahite, D. C. (1991). The linkage between theory and research in family science. *Journal of Marriage and the Family, 53,* 361–374.

Leahey, T. H. (1992). *A history of psychology: Main currents in psychological thought* (3rd ed.). Englewood Cliffs, NJ: Prentice-Hall.

Levinas, E. (1985). *Ethics and infinity*. Pittsburgh, PA: Duquesne University Press.

Levinas, E. (1987). *Time and the other* (R. A. Cohen, Trans.). Pittsburgh, PA: Duquesne University Press.

Mair, M. (1988). Psychology as storytelling. *International Journal of Personal Construct Psychology, 1,* 125–137.

McAdams, D. P. (1985). *Power, intimacy, and the life story: Personological inquiries into identity*. New York: Guilford Press.

McAdams, D. P., Dimond, A., de St. Aubin, E., & Mansfield, E. D. (in press). Stories of commitment: The psychosocial construction of generative lives. *Journal of Personality and Social Psychology*.

Moore, T. (1994). *Soul mates: Honoring the mysteries of love and relationship*. New York: HarperCollins.

Morson, G. (1988, Autumn). Prosaics: An approach to the humanities. *American Scholar*, pp. 515–528.

Parry, A., & Doan, R. E. (1994). *Story re-visions: Narrative therapy in the postmodern world*. New York: Guilford Press.

Pipher, M. (1996). *The shelter of each other: Rebuilding our families*. New York: Putnam.

Polkinghorne, D. (1983). *Methodology for the human sciences*. Albany: State University of New York Press.

Richards, P. S., & Bergin, A. E. (in press). *A theistic/spiritual approach to counseling and psychotherapy*. Washington, DC: American Psychological Association.

Robinson, D. N. (1985). *Philosophy of psychology*. New York: Columbia University Press.

Sarbin, T. R. (1996). Toward the obsolescence of the schizophrenia hypothesis. In B. D. Slife (Ed.), *Taking sides: Clashing views on controversial psychological issues* (pp. 231–240). Guilford, CT: Dushkin/Brown Benchmark.

Shafranske, E. P. (1996). *Religion and the clinical practice of psychology*. Washington, DC: American Psychological Association.

Slife, B. D. (1993). *Time and psychological explanation*. Albany: State University of New York Press.

Slife, B. D. (1996, August). *Problems and perils of eclecticism in psychotherapy: A hermeneutic alternative*. Paper presented at the meeting of the American Psychological Association, Toronto, Ontario, Canada.

Slife, B. D. (1997). *Modern and postmodern value centers for the family*. Unpublished manuscript.

Slife, B. D., & Fisher, A. (1997). *Avoiding impalement on the horns of the free will/ determinism dilemma in psychotherapy*. Unpublished manuscript.

Slife, B. D., Hope, C., & Nebeker, S. (1997). *Examining the relationship between religious spirituality and psychological science*. Unpublished manuscript.

Slife, B. D., & Williams, R. N. (1995). *What's behind the research? Discovering hidden assumptions in the behavioral sciences*. Thousand Oaks, CA: Sage.

Slife, B. D., & Williams, R. N. (1997). Toward a theoretical psychology: Should a formal subdiscipline be recognized? *American Psychologist, 52*, 117–129.

Snarey, J. (1993). *How fathers care for the next generation: A four-decade study*. Cambridge, MA: Harvard University Press.

Viney, W. (1993). *A history of psychology: Ideas and context*. Boston: Allyn & Bacon.

White, M., & Epston, D. (1990). *Narrative means to therapeutic ends*. New York: Norton.

Williams, R. N. (1992). The human context of agency. *American Psychologist, 57*, 752–760.

Wilson, J. Q. (1993). *The moral sense*. New York: Free Press.

Yalom, I. D. (1985). *Inpatient group psychotherapy*. New York: Basic Books.

Yanchar, S., & Slife, B. (1997). *Categorizing people: Temporal and atemporal reductionism*. Unpublished manuscript.

EPILOGUE: EMERGING THEMES
AND FUTURE DIRECTIONS

Each of the chapters in this volume offers unique insights into the meaning and manifestations of generativity in adult lives. The authors have proposed new theoretical frameworks for understanding the different features of generativity; its developmental course; and its role in society, culture, and history. They have distinguished among different facets of generativity, such as generative concern and generative commitment; they have identified different motivations for generativity, such as the desire for symbolic immortality, the need to be needed, and the cultural demands of age-graded norms; they have distinguished among generative motivations, capacities, and accomplishments in considering the development of generativity over the life course; and they have proposed provocative new constructs such as generativity chill, intergenerational buffers, and universal generativity to capture the difficult challenges that generativity poses in modern lives. The authors have introduced innovative new ways to measure and evaluate generativity, and they have described new research findings linking generativity to mental health and well-being, patterns of parenting, friendships and social support, religious and political involvements, volunteer activities, and social roles. Casting an unusually wide and interdisciplinary net, the contributors to this volume have studied generativity in nationwide samples and individual lives, examining the manifestations of generativity among contemporary adults in the United States and the citizens of colonial New England; among gay middle-aged men and female graduates of a private college; in the father–son relationship and in the dynamics of extended families; and in the lives of Holocaust survivors, reformed criminals, and distinctively creative individuals such as the architect Frank Lloyd Wright and the dancer Martha Graham.

483

No capsule summary can capture the richness and depth of the psychological, sociological, historical, and biographical analysis offered by the contributors of this volume. Each chapter speaks eloquently for itself. In this epilogue, therefore, we do not aim to summarize what has come before. Instead, we seek, first, to identify a few common themes running through a number of the different offerings and converging on an emergent new understanding of generativity. We do this with an eye toward identifying advances in knowledge about generativity, spelling out what we believe we have learned about generativity through the investigations reported in this book. Second, we seek to articulate new questions raised by the authors— new challenges, puzzles, and conundrums—that may point to new directions for theory, research, and applications with respect to generativity and adult development.

In general terms, we have identified four main themes that characterize an emergent understanding of generativity coming out of this book.

1. *Generativity is a central psychosocial feature of adult lives and centrally implicated in psychological well-being, social adaptation, and mental health.* In chapter 1, McAdams, Hart, and Maruna review studies linking generative concern to high levels of life satisfaction, self-esteem, and a sense of coherence in life and to low levels of depression and anxiety. In chapter 3, Stewart and Vandewater show that generative accomplishment, as assessed in Q sorts, is positively associated with measures of psychological well-being. Keyes and Ryff (chapter 7) conceive of generativity as a "socio-personal resource" that links society and the self. They describe new data from a nationwide sample of adults showing that generative behavior, generative norms, and generative self-conceptions predict and possibly promote psychological and social well-being. The strong connection between generativity and well-being, they argue, reflects the fact that generativity is fundamental to feeling good about oneself in adulthood and for judging one's life as worthwhile and meaningful. Highly generative adults feel that they have something valuable to give to society and that they are able to do good things for other people. Because generativity is differentially expressed in different domains of an adult's life, domain-specific measures of generativity prove especially predictive of well-being, as MacDermid, Franz, and De Reus show in chapter 6. In addition, the confidence that generativity instills in one realm can spill over to promote success and well-being in other realms: Snarey and Clark (chapter 2) report that fathers who score high on parental generativity may also enjoy enhanced occupational mobility and greater marital satisfaction. It is indeed partly because generativity appears to be such a salient factor in psychological and social well-being that Dollahite, Slife, and Hawkins (chapter 4) place family generativity in the heart of their model for family counseling.

2. *Generativity follows a variegated developmental course.* Although Erikson was probably right to situate generativity roughly as an issue of "mid-

dle" adulthood, the conventional reading of his model to suggest that "generativity vs. stagnation" fits neatly into a midlife "stage" assumes more order and regularity than both common sense and the data suggest. Over 2,000 years ago, Plato anticipated the difficulty of neatly delineating stages of identity, intimacy, and generativity in the adult years when he conceived of generativity as inextricably tied to love (see chapter 5). In contemporary U.S. adults, act–frequency measures of generative actions have shown the predicted peak in midlife, relative to scores for younger and older adults; however, open-ended measures of generative commitments show low scores for young adults and relatively high scores for *both* midlife and older adults (see chapter 1).

Grand stage models for adult development are especially problematic in considering the lives of women and members of racial or ethnic minority groups. Examining data from two longitudinal studies of women, Stewart and Vandewater (chapter 3) and Peterson (chapter 4) make a strong case for a more complex developmental model regarding generativity. Generativity *motivation*, they argue, is high in young adulthood and may decrease somewhat later on; the *capacity* for generativity, by contrast, starts at a relatively low level but builds to a crescendo in the middle-adult years and decreases in older age; generative *accomplishment*, or *realization*, increases linearly from youth to old age. MacDermid, Franz, and De Reus (chapter 6) propose a developmental sequence whereby generativity within proximal (family) roles tends to precede generativity within more distal (societal) roles. Cohler, Hostetler, and Boxer (chapter 8) argue for a life course perspective that allows for on-time developmental tasks and off-time disruptions, irregularities, and enhancements that help to determine the unique trajectory of a human life. Adult lives are less orderly and predictable than stage models suggest, although adults typically seek to impose order on their lives by constructing life stories that integrate the reconstructed past, perceived present, and anticipated future. The psychosocial construction of generativity can follow an idiosyncratic course in any individual life, as de St. Aubin's (chapter 12) psychobiographic examination of the life of Frank Lloyd Wright makes abundantly clear.

3. *Generativity is many different things, expressed in many different domains, and motivated by many different sources.* Since publication of the writings of Kotre (1984), theorists of generativity have endeavored to articulate the construct further, dividing it into different components, features, facets, and processes. Not only does generativity fail to fit neatly into a single stage, therefore, but the concept of generativity itself also fails to fit neatly into a simple conceptual category. There appear to be many different ways to divide up the concept of generativity.

One common approach is to divide generativity into its familial and societal aspects, corresponding to what MacDermid, Franz, and De Reus (chapter 6) identify as proximal and distal roles, respectively. Snarey and

Clark (chapter 2); Moran (chapter 9); Kay (chapter 10); and Dollahite, Slife, and Hawkins (chapter 14) concern themselves mainly with generativity as expressed in family parental roles; in contrast, Peterson (chapter 4); Keyes and Ryff (chapter 7); Cohler, Hostetler, and Boxer (chapter 8); de St. Aubin (chapter 12); and Lee (chapter 13) focus as much on the more public expressions of generativity in work and art, in community involvements, and in political and religious activities. General measures of generativity often predict generative functioning in particular domains. For parenting, therefore, overall generative concern is positively associated with parental investment in education (see chapter 1) and with a parenting style that is both warm and authoritative (Peterson, Smirles, & Wentworth, 1997). Outside the family, various measures of generativity predict political and community involvements as well as an overall sense of social responsibility. In some cases, generativity in one domain may be associated with generativity in another, as Snarey and Clark (chapter 2) show when they report a positive correlation between ratings of parental and societal generativity in fathers. In other cases, one is struck by the unevenness in generativity across domains. Frank Lloyd Wright was, by all accounts, a terrible father, but he expressed generativity in powerful and beautiful ways through his architecture. Even within the role of master teacher, Wright presents a mixed story when it comes to generativity; his talented protégés learned a great deal from him, but they did not receive the kind of nurturance and freedom that might have enhanced their growth and talents further (chapter 12).

A second way to differentiate concepts in the sphere of generativity is to distinguish between agentic and communal forms (Bakan, 1966; Kotre, 1984; McAdams, 1985). McAdams, Hart, and Maruna (chapter 1) distinguish between agentic and communal sources of generativity motivation: Generativity may spring from desires for symbolic immortality (agentic) and from desires to nurture others in need (communal). Wakefield (chapter 5) juxtaposes the agentic and communal in suggesting that Plato viewed generativity in terms of a general human desire for immortality that is part and parcel of love. The prototypical expression of generativity, furthermore, appears to blend agency and communion, in that the individual seeks to generate some product or outcome that serves as an extension of the self (agency) and then seeks to nurture and care for that which has been generated, ultimately offering it up as a gift of the self (communion). Problems in generativity, furthermore, may result from an overemphasis on the agentic or the communal at the expense of the other. Lee (chapter 13) portrays Martha Graham's generativity in sharply agentic terms. Graham's self-promoting passion to generate new artistic forms exacerbated her tendency to exploit others, including her protégés, in the service of self.

Third, various authors of chapters in this volume seek to enrich the discourse on generativity by proposing conceptual distinctions within the process of generativity and offering new constructs that capture especially problematic aspects of generativity. McAdams, Hart, and Maruna (chapter 1) offer a seven-feature model that divides generativity into desire, demand, concern, belief, commitment, action, and narration. Furthermore, they suggest that generative acts can be roughly grouped into those in the service of creating, maintaining, and offering. Stewart and Vandewater (chapter 3) distinguish among generative motivation, capacity, and accomplishment (realization). Although they do not offer a new theoretical model of generativity, Keyes and Ryff (chapter 7) operationalize generativity through a number of different measures. Snarey and Clark (chapter 2) propose a new concept, *generativity chill*, and Kotre and Kotre (chapter 11) write provocatively of *intergenerative buffering* in generativity, whereby an individual seeks to stop the transmission of a negative legacy from one generation to the next.

4. *Although generativity may be a human universal, it is exquisitely contoured and contextualized by culture.* The commitment stores and reform tales identified by McAdams, Hart, and Maruna (chapter 1) are life-narrative forms constructed by highly generative adults living in a particular time and place. As such, these life narrations reflect cultural assumptions about how stories should be told about lives. Highly generative adults differ from their less generative counterparts with respect to the ways that they appropriate the literary forms that exist in their society for making sense of a human life in time. Cohler, Hostetler, and Boxer (chapter 8) provide moving accounts of how gay men make narrative sense of their own generative efforts in the United States in the late 20th century. Kay (chapter 10) describes how experiences from World War II shape the way Holocaust survivors make sense of their own efforts to pass on parts of themselves to the next generation. Lee (chapter 13) describes the subculture inhabited and produced by modern dancers and shows how Martha Graham shaped and was shaped by that fiercely competitive world.

In a more general vein, MacDermid, Franz, and De Reus (chapter 6) argue that generativity exists at the crossroads of personality and social roles: Individuals actively assume and negotiate role structures that offer varying opportunities for generative behavior. Analyzing nationwide survey data on behavior and well-being, Keyes and Ryff (chapter 7) conclude that the quality of adults' lives in the United States is shaped by the stratification processes embodied in education: More highly educated American adults enjoy higher levels of well-being partly because they are able to develop more meaningful and efficacious expressions of generativity. Age and gender contextualize the issue further. Midlife and older adults, adults with more education, and women tend to exhibit greater levels of diverse aspects of generativity compared to young adults, adults with fewer years of education, and men. In the words of Keyes and Ryff, whereas generativity contours the quality of life, society contours generativity. Pushing the cultural analysis a bit further, Moran (chapter 9) raises the possibility that some societies are more generative than others.

The chapters in this book show that a great deal is known about the meanings and manifestations of generativity. However, there is a great deal more to learn. There also appear to be a number of large holes in the study of generativity—potential areas of inquiry that have heretofore been left virtually untouched. Furthermore, many of the authors have raised new and unexpected questions and puzzles about generativity and adult development. We conclude our wrap-up by posing four questions that reflect interesting problem areas in the study of generativity. We invite the reader to generate more.

1. *What are the developmental antecedents of generativity?* With the exception of Snarey and Clark (chapter 2), the authors are virtually silent about the issue of how it is that some people become more generative than others. Data reported by Snarey (1993) suggest that fathers who become highly and positively involved with their children's social and emotional development during adolescence tend to be men whose own fathers were distant or nonnurturant but who showed a significant degree of occupational achievement enabling them to be good family providers. Snarey and Clark (chapter 2) speculate that childhood modeling and the reworking of early experience in adulthood are instrumental in the making of the generative father. Suggestive hints about early experience also come from narrative reconstructions of childhood obtained by McAdams, Hart, and Maruna (chapter 1), but such retrospective accounts are not reliable sources for what actually happened long ago; they serve instead as narrative windows into one's current self-conception. Long-term longitudinal studies are needed to tease out what early factors, if any, may predict generativity in the adult years. Possible explanations here appear to be almost limitless, ranging from those invoking temperament and infant attachment to those examining parenting styles, experiences in school, and other determinants involving families, neighborhoods, churches, and other institutions.

2. *What is the relation to creativity and leadership?* Erikson (1963) suggested that the concept of generativity shares space with the concepts of creativity and leadership, among others. Many expressions of generativity appear to involve some form of creativity, as in the pro*creation* of children and the making of products and outcomes designed to outlive the self. One might ask whether highly creative people are especially generative. In some ways they are, and in some ways they are not, as the case studies of Frank Lloyd Wright (chapter 12) and Martha Graham (chapter 13) show. Part of the indeterminacy here comes from the difficulty in defining *creativity*. Gardner (1993) suggested that creativity exists not so much within a single individual as in the nexus of the individual, the

domain, and the field. Creative individuals work within a particular domain of expression that exists as part of a rule-governed field. The field's rules are determined by various experts such as literary critics and book reviewers (for the field of literature) and granting agencies and peer review panels (for sciences). To a large extent, the experts decide who and what is creative in a given field. In a loose sense, the same might be said for generativity, although it is perhaps more difficult to determine who the experts are and how the rule-governed fields may operate for the different domains of generative expression. However, the parallels between generativity and creativity bring up the question of the precise relation between the two. Even less is known about the relation between leadership and generativity. It seems intuitively right that some kinds of highly effective leaders owe their success to their generative capacities and inclinations. Major failings in leadership may signal shortcomings in generativity, as well. To our knowledge, however, no research or theorizing has focused explicitly on the relation between generativity and leadership.

3. *What are the limits, costs, and excesses of generativity?* Kotre (1984) was the first to suggest that generativity may have a dark side. Because generativity involves the creation and the passing on of products and outcomes from one generation to the next, the extent to which a community views particular generative expressions as "good" depends on the shifting social constructions of the potential worth embodied in those products and outcomes. Madmen and tyrants may view their own efforts as especially generative, in that they aim to craft enduring legacies for what they may consider to be "the good." Even the best generative expressions can certainly go wrong, for one cannot control what one's product will lead to in the future, even if one cares for and nurtures those products in a wise and compassionate way. In chapter 11, Kotre and Kotre make another significant contribution to theorizing about generativity by identifying the phenomenon of intergenerational buffering, which is generativity in the service of *not* transmitting something from one generation to another. In their words, the buffer insists that "the damage stops here." On the other hand, damage is sometimes the main result of one's best generative efforts. Beyond the work of the Kotres, this troubling conundrum has not generally been addressed.

To date, investigators have not examined the problem of how to "let go" of one's generative products—how to grant one's children (literal and figurative) lives of their own. Many of the shortcomings in generativity exhibited by Frank Lloyd Wright and Martha Graham appear to stem from difficulties in letting go. Neither have investigators asked hard questions about the personal costs of generativity. The positive empirical association between measures of generativity and of well-being is not so strong as to rule out the possibility that excessive generativity sometimes comes at a price. Such a price has been identified by Gardner (1993) in the lives of creative geniuses. He argued that certain exceptionally creative individuals, such as Einstein and Picasso, have felt compelled to make Faustian bargains for the sake of their creative work. Intimate relationships, family fulfillments, and even overall happiness may be sacrificed to the gods of artistic or scientfic achievement. To what extent do the Einsteins and Picassos of generativity experience the same phenomenon? Hints that such a comparison may be especially apt come from Erikson's (1969) portrait of the ever-generative Gandhi.

4. *What is the role of suffering in generativity?* Snarey and Clark (chapter 2) define *generativity chill* as the anxiety experienced when one encounters the possibility of losing either the fruits of one's generative efforts or one's very powers to be generative. From the realm of parental generativity come such obvious examples as infertility and facing the possibility of losing one's child. Snarey and Clark found that the most generative fathers were those who had, at one time or another, encountered an episode of generativity chill. In a similar vein, Kay (chapter 10) intimates that the Holocaust experience seemed to intensify the generative strivings of survivors, who showed much stronger generative inclinations than a matched group of adults who were refugees (rather than concentration camp inmates) during World War II. Peterson (chapter 4) suggests that midlife women who showed high levels of both generativity motivation and generativity realization seemed to be compelled to continue their substantial efforts to achieve generative goals because of "tension or frustration" in an area of strong personal concern. McAdams, Hart, and Maruna (chapter 1) report that highly generative adults tend to construct life stories that emphasize early recollections of the suffering of others and numerous examples in their own lives in which suffering paved the way for growth, insight, and fulfillment.

Is it necessary to experience deep suffering to be especially generative? Is generativity enhanced or undermined by suffering? One can imagine examples of both: ways in which personal anxiety, frustration, or deprivation might help to make a person more generative or might contribute to stagnation, self-preoccupation, and despair. What is the relation between experiencing personal misery or witnessing the misery of others on the one hand and what Erikson identified as the "belief in the species" that sustains the necessary faith for generativity on the other?

As the contributors to this book make clear, when one thinks hard about generativity, one is challenged to ask some of the most important questions about the psychological, social, ethical, and existential meanings of one's own life and of life in general. We, the editors, hope that the ideas offered in this volume have generated questions like these for the reader.

REFERENCES

Bakan, D. (1966). *The duality of human existence: Isolation and communion in Western man*. Boston: Beacon Press.

Erikson, E. H. (1963). *Childhood and society* (2nd ed.). New York: Norton.

Erikson, E. H. (1969). *Gandhi's truth: On the origins of militant nonviolence*. New York: Norton.

Gardner, H. (1993). *Creating minds*. New York: Basic Books.

Kotre, J. (1984). *Outliving the self: Generativity and the interpretation of lives*. Baltimore: The Johns Hopkins University Press.

McAdams, D. P. (1985). *Power, intimacy, and the life story: Personological inquiries into identify*. New York: Guilford Press.

Peterson, B. E., Smirles, K. A., & Wentworth, P. A. (1997). Generativity and authoritarianism: Implications for personality, political involvement, and parenting. *Journal of Personality and Social Psychology, 72*, 1202–1216.

Snarey, J. (1993). *How fathers care for the next generation: A four-decade study*. Cambridge, MA: Harvard University Press.

AUTHOR INDEX

Adelmann, P. K., 194, *220*
Adler, A., 230, *259*
Ahola, T., 467, *479*
Aleksandrowicz, D., 338, *357*
Alexander, I. E., 395, 396, *425*
Allen, K. R., 196, *219*
Allen, W. D., 469, *478*
Allison, P. D., 228, *259*
Allport, G. W., 233, *259*, 395, *425*
Almagor, M., 339, *358*
American Psychiatric Association, 338, *357*
Anderson, D. A., 469–471, *478*
Anderson, J. W., 395, 396, *425*
Anspach, R. R., 231, *260*
Antonucci, T., 266, 271, 278, *301, 305*
Antonucci, T. C., 194, *220*
Archer, S. L., 190, 194, 204, *218*
Aristotle, 171
Armitage, M., *446*
Astone, N., 269, 272, 297, 299, *304*
Auge, S., 23, *39*
Axtell, J., 317, *331*
Azarow, J., 23, 27, 28, *41*, 90, *98*

Bahr, H. M., 469, *478*
Bahr, K. S., 469, *478*
Bailyn, B., 313, *331*
Bakan, D., 10, *39*, 230, *259*, 340, *357*, 486, *491*
Baltes, M. M., 229, *259*
Baltes, P. B., 228, 229, *259*, 406, *425*
Bandura, A., 190, *218*
Baranowski, M., 194, *222*
Barnett, R. C., 191, 193–195, 204, 213, *218*
Barsalou, S. W., 384, *388*
Baruch, G. K., 191, 193, 195, 204, 205, 207, 209, 213, *218*
Baumeister, R. F., 29, *39*
Baumrind, D., 199, *219*
Becker, E., 10, 25, 29, *39*, 354, 356, *357*
Becker, H. S., 187, 213, *219*

Becvar, D. S., 453, *478*
Becvar, R. J., 453, *478*
Beecher, C., 329–330, *331*
Beeler, J., 281, *304*
Bellah, R. N., 12, *39*, 46, *73*, 392, *425*, 458, 469, 473, *478*
Bem, D. J., 199, *219, 220*
Benedek, T., 71, *73*
Bengston, V., 268, *301, 305*
Bengtson, V. L., 182, 196, 199, *219*, 229, *259*
Bennett, K., 278, *301*
Bepko, C., 442, *446*
Beresford, B., *72*
Berger, R., 280, *301*
Bergin, A. E., 470, *481*
Bergmann, M., 337, *357*
Berzonsky, M. D., 199, *219*
Besinger, C., 403, 404, 418, *425*
Biernat, M., *226*
Bledstein, B. J., *331*
Block, J., 102, *128*
Blumenstein, P., 279, *301*
Bohman, J., 465, *478*
Bolkosky, S., 385, *388*
Borden, W., 278, 280, *301*
Boszormenyi-Nagy, I., 451, 458, *478*
Bourne, E., 183, 213, *219*
Bowlby, J., 13, *39*
Boxer, A., 269, 271, 280, 297, *301, 304*
Bradford, W., 317, *331*
Bradley, C., 276, *305*
Bradley, C. L., 184, 186, 187, 198, *219*
Bray, D., 84, *97*
Breen, T. H., 315, *331*
Brennan, R. T., 194, *218*
Brenner, R., 354, *357*
Breslow, M. J., 229, *260*
Bronfenbrenner, U., 192, *219*
Brooks-Gunn, J., 183, *219*, 271, *303*
Brothers, B. J., 470, *479*
Brotherson, S., 48, *73*
Brotherson, S. E., 451, 466, *479*

Duhl, F. J., 458, *479*
Dunham, R. M., 194, *222*
Dunn, R. S., 312, *331*
Durkheim, E., 232, 255, 259, 266, 270, *302*
Duvall, R., *72*

Easterlin, R., 269, *302*
Easterline, R., *302*
Eaton, W., 339, *357*
Echols, A., 267, *302*
Edelman, M. W., 181, *220*
Elder, G. H., 197, *220*
Elder, G. H., Jr., 269, 270, *302, 303*
Elder, G. J., Jr., 270, 297, *303*
Elder, G., Jr., 267, 269, 270, *302, 303*
Ellard, J. H., 384, *388*
Elliot, L. B., 84, *100, 183*
Elliott, T., *221*
Elms, A. C., 395, *426*
Emery, A. E., 371, *388*
Emmons, C., 187, *226*
Emmons, R. A., 11, 24, *40, 220*
Epston, D., 459, 462, *481*
Erdos, P., *156*
Erikson, E. H., 7, 9, 11, 12, 16, 17, 22, 26, 29, 31, 35, *40*, 46, 47, 62, 65, 69, 72, *73*, 75–85, 87, 94–96, *97*, 101, 102, 105, 106, 123, 126–128, *129*, 133–140, 144, 149, 151, 156–161, 163–165, 167–170, 172, 173, *173*, 182, 183, 185, 194, 198–199, 202, 204, *220, 222*, 228, 230, 233, 236, 253, 256, 259, 272–274, 276, *303*, 311–313, *331*, 335, 339, 345, *358*, 383, *388*, 391, 392, 395, 419, *426, 431*, 440, 446, 450, 451, 473, 477, *479*, 488, 490, *491*
Erikson, J., *222*
Erikson, J. M., 65, *73, 77, 97*, 137, *173*, 182, *220*
Espin, O., 83, *97*
Evans, R., 78, *97*

Falk, J., 267, *305*
Farmer, M. M., 229, *259*

Farnham-Diggory, S., 271, *303*
Farrell, M. P., 194, *220*
Faulconer, J., 460, 461, *479*
Featherman, D. L., 228, *259*
Feld, S. C., 88, *99*
Ferraro, K. F., 229, *259*
Festinger, L., 266, *303*
Fischer, J. L., 194, *222*
Fisher, A., 464, *481*
Fiske, M., 192, 193, 199, 213, *220*
Flavell, J. H., 17, *40*
Fliegelman, J., *331*
Foley, J., 273, *306*
Foley, J. M., 14, *41*, 79, *98*
Foner, A., 229, *261*
Foote, H., *72, 73*
Foucault, M., 278, *303*
Frank, G., 268, *305*
Franz, C., 394, *427*
Franz, C. E., 60, *73*, 78, 83, 85–88, 96, 97–99, 102, 107, *129, 131, 183*, 188, 189, *221, 223, 225*
Franz, E., 10, *42*, 134, *174*, 230, *262*
Freud, S., 77, 144, 145, *173*
Freudiger, P., 192, 199, *224*
Friend, R., 280, *303*
Furlong, M., 268, *301*
Furman, B., 467, *479*
Furstenberg, F., 271, *303*

Galenson, D., 314, *331*
Ganster, D. C., 193, *226*
Gardner, H., 400, 410, *426, 431*, 446, 488, 490, *491*
Gecas, V., 182, 189, *224*, 231, *259*
Gedo, J. E., 442, *446*
Geertz, C., 266, *303*, 368, *388*
George, L., 269, 272, 276, 297, *303, 304*
George, L. K., 201, *221*
Gergen, K., 266, *304*
Gergen, K. J., 16, *40*
Gergen, M., 266, *304*
Gergen, M. M., 194, 204, *221*
Giddens, A., 16, 26, 28, 29, *40*
Gill, A., 357, *358*
Gill, B., 391, 395, 397, 398, 402–405, 408, 412, 416, 417, 419, *426*
Gillespie, L., 134, *174*
Gilligan, C., 47, *73*, 188, *221*, 253, *260*

Gitlin, T., 267, *304*
Glueck, E., 47–49, 53, 72, *73*
Glueck, S., 47–49, 53, 72, *73*
Goffman, E., 64, *73*
Goldberg, A., 339, *358*
Gold-Steinberg, S., 127, *131*, 183, 194, *225*
Gomez, C. A., 83, *97*
Goode, W. J., 191, *221*
Gordon, C., 182, *219*
Gorsuch, R. L., 470, *479*
Gough, H. G., 91, *97*
Graham, M., 431, 442, 443, *447*
Greenacre, P., 442, *447*
Greene, J. P., 318, *331*
Greven, P. J., Jr., 320, 321, *332*
Griswold, R. L., 51, *73*, 330, *332*
Grotevant, H. D., 183, *221*
Gruen, W., 79, 80, 82, *97*
Grunebaum, J., 451, *478*
Gubrium, J., 268, *304*
Gurdjieff, G. I., *401*
Gurman, A. S., 450, 451, *479*
Gutmann, D., 120, *129*, 440, *447*
Guttentag, M., 269, *304*

Haan, N., 188, *221*
Habermas, J., 16, *40*
Hagestad, G., 266, 267, 270, 271, 297, *304*, *307*
Hagestad, G. O., 10, *42*
Hall, E., 128, *129*, 197, *221*
Hall Carpenter Archives, 268, 281, *304*
Halsey, A. H., 228, *260*
Hampes, W. P., 58, *74*
Handyside, A. H., 371, *388*
Harel, Z., 338, *358*
Hareven, T., 270, *303*
Harrison, B. M., 26, *42*
Hart, B., 107, *129*
Hart, H. M., 22, *40*, *480*
Hart, T., 469, 470, *479*
Haslett, S. J., 190, *222*
Hauser, R. M., 228, 231, *262*
Hauser, S., 79, *99*
Havighurst, R., 79
Hawkins, A. J., 47, 48, 62, 69, 71, *73*, *74*, 396, *426*, 450, 451, 469, *479*, *480*

Hazan, H., 270, *304*
Healy, J. M., Jr., 107, *129*
Heaton, T. B., 276, *304*
Heidegger, M., 460, 465, *480*
Heidrich, S. M., 193, *221*
Heilbrun, G., 109, *129*, 202, 205–207, 209, *223*, 230, *260*
Heincke, S., 275, *308*
Heincke, S. G., 17, *42*, 80, 99, 102, *130*, 184, 207, *225*, *262*
Helgeson, V. S., 10, *40*
Helmreich, W., 345, 349, 352, *358*
Helpern, A., 438, 439, *447*
Helson, R., 10, *40*, 85, 93, 94, 97-99, 107, 118–120, *129-131*, 183, 187, 188, 193, 201, *221*, 253, *260*
Henretta, J., 323, *332*
Herdt, G., 280, 281, *304*
Hermans, H., 266, *304*
Hermans, H. J. M., 28, *40*
Hertz, D. M., 402, 403, 408, 410, 413, 414, 416, 418, *426*
Herzog, A. R., 229, 232, *260*
Hill, E. J., 396, *426*, 450, *480*
Hiner, N. R., 316–317, *332*
Hoffer, P. C., 311, 324, *332*
Hoffman, B., 275, *306*
Hoffman, B. J., 30, *41*
Hoffman, L., 453, 464, *480*
Hogan, D., 269, 272, 273, 276, 297, 299, *304*
Hogan, R., 13, *40*
Holstein, J., 268, *304*
Hooker, T., 321, *332*
Hope, C., 461, 469, *481*
Hoppe, K., 338, *358*
Hoppen, D. W., 396, 400, 401, 406, 408–410, 414, 420, *426*
Hornstein, G. A., 183, 192, 194, 199, *222*
Horosko, M., 434, 439, *447*
Hostetler, A., *304*
House, J. S., 227, 229, 231, *260*
Houseknecht, S., 276, *304*
Howard, A., 84, *97*
Howard, G. S., 28, *40*
Hudson, R., 276, 279, *302*
Hughes, M. R., 371, *388*
Hulsizer, D., 185, 194, 202, *222*

Isay, R., 278, 304
Israel, J., 232, 260

Jackson, D. N., 184, *222*
Jacobson, C., 276, 304
James, W., 396
Jaques, E., 275, 277, *304, 305*
Jenkins, S., 86, 99
Jenkins, S. R., 86, 97, 98
Johnson, D. K., 401, 416, *426*
Johnstone, E. C., 461, *480*
Jones, C. J., 85, 98
Jordan, J. V., 437, *447*
Josselson, R., 183, 199, *222*
Jowett, B., 135, *174*
Jucovy, M., 337, 357
Juhasz, A. M., 217, *222*
Jung, C. G., 77, 233, 260

Kahn, R., 266, 271, 278, *305*
Kahn, R. L., 229, *261*
Kalish, R., *305*
Kantrowitz, A., 281, 299, *305*
Kaplan, A. G., 437, *447*
Karabel, J., 228, 260
Karlsen, C. F., 320, *332*
Kay, A., 335, 337, 341, *358*
Kehoe, M., 280, *305*
Kelly, J., 278, *305*
Kempen, H., 266, 304
Kempen, H. J. G., 28, *40*
Kenyon, G. M., 28, *40*
Kerber, L. K., 329, *332*
Kertzer, R., 278, *305*
Kessler, R. C., 229, 231, 260
Keyes, C. L. M., 232, 233, 239, 257, 260, 262
Keyser, H., 376, *388*
Kidwell, J., 194, *222*
Kierkegaard, S., 62, *74*
Kiesler, D. J., 384, *388*
Kimmel, D., 280, *305*
Kinney, A. M., 229, 260
Kirsh, B., 183, *219*
Kivnick, H., 276, 303
Kivnick, H. Q., 65, *73*, 77, 97, 137, *173*, 182, 220
Kleiber, D. A., 400, *426*

Klein, H., 338, 358
Klein, M. H., 384, *388*
Kleinberg, J. L., 368, *388*
Kleinman, M., 339, *358*
Kloehnen, E., 188, 211, 212, *224*
Klohnen, E., 273, 274, 307
Klohnen, E. C., 79, 84, 87, 90, 94, 98, 102–104, *130*, 230, *261*
Kniskern, D. P., 450, 451, *479*
Knox, S., 326
Koestner, R., 105, *130*
Kohn, M. L., 197, *222*
Kohn Dor-shav, N., 339, *358*
Koski, K. J., 211, *222*
Kotre, J., 9, 10, 12, 15, 35, 40, 47, 65, 74, 82, 98, 102, 117, 128, *129*, 134, 135, 152, 153, 156, 157, 161, *174*, 183, 196, 201, *222*, 228, 230, 260, 273, 274, 276, 277, 280, *305*, 320, 332, 339–341, 356, *358*, 368, 369, 372, 379–381, *388*, 393, 409, 420, *426*, 431, 441, 444, 445, *447*, 451, *480*, 485, 486, 489, *491*
Koury, S., 276, *309*
Kowaz, A., 276, *305*
Krauze, T. K., 228, *259*
Krestan, J. A., 442, *446*
Kroger, J., 182, 183, 190, *222*
Krystal, H., 337, 338, 342, 346, 347, 349, *358*
Kuehne, V. S., 79, 99

L'Abate, L., 467, *480*
Lachman, M. E., 188, 191, *222*
Landis, K. R., 231, 260
Lang, E., 226
Langbaum, R., 29, *40*
Langer, L., 340, 350, *358*, 385–387, *388*
Langland, L., 85, 99
Langness, L., 268, *305*
LaRossa, R., 189, *222*
Laub, J., 270, *308*
Laub, J. H., 48, *74*
Laufer, R., 268, 301, *305*
Lavee, Y., 450, *480*
Layton, L., 10, 42, 83, 86, 87, 99, 102, *131*, 134, *174*, 188, 225, 230, 262, 394, *427*

SUBJECT INDEX

CFM. *See* Christian Family Movement
Cheney, Mamah, 397, 399, 402, 407–408
Child rearing, 13, 137. *See also* Parenting–parental generativity
  active (case study), 52–57
  in early American history, 328–330
Children
  love of, in Plato's theory of generativity, 150–151
  rights of Puritan, 319
  singling out of, 31
China, 11
Christian Family Movement (CFM), 380, 382
Citizen role, 203
Civic obligation, 245, 252
Coding, generativity, 87–88
Cohorts, 266, 268–270
Colonial Virginia, 313–315
Columbian Exposition, 411
Commitment, generative, 8, 11, 24–26, 139, 236
  balancing of, 191–192
  scripts and stories, 33–35, 279
Communal generativity, 14–15, 212, 320, 486
Communion desires, 13–15, 340–341
Communities, generative, 476–478
Concern, generative, 8, 20–23, 236–237
Contamination sequences, 33
Convergence hypothesis, 229
Copland, Aaron, 433
Coram, Robert, 326
Counseling. *See* Generative counseling
Course of generativity, 75–96, 484–485. *See also* Life stories
  case studies, 82–84
  cross-sectional studies, 79–82
  and desires vs. accomplishments, 86–92
  and Erikson's theories, 75–79
  and felt capacity for generativity, 92–94
  longitudinal studies, 84–89
    coding, 87–88
    desires, over time, 88–89
    measurement, 86–87
Courteil, Amanble de Lafitte du, 326
Creation and creativity, 25, 202
  and leadership, 488–489
Criminal behavior, 35

Cross-sectional studies, of generativity in adulthood, 79–82
Cultural demand, 8, 9, 11, 15–19
Cultural generativity, 274, 368, 487
  among Holocaust survivors, 353–354
  and intergenerational buffering, 379–383

Davis, Bette, 437–438
Death, fear of, 163–167
Degler, Carl, 328
Demos, John, 318
Desires, generativity. *See also* Inner desire
  accomplishment vs., 89–94
  over time, 88–89
Development
  and social roles, 196
Development, and social roles, 183. *See also* Course of generativity; Life stories
Diagnostic and Statistical Manual, 460–461
Distortion of generativity, 65
Divergence hypothesis, 228–229
Division of labor, 139
Domestic economy, 329–330
Duncan, Isadora, 429

Early American history, generativity in, 311–331
  American Revolution, 323–326
  and child rearing, 328–330
  Colonial Virginia, 313–315
  and education policies, 324–327
  Puritans, 315–323
    in 17th century, 315–321
    in 18th century, 321–323
Education
  age, relationship to, 228–229, 242–243
  among Puritans, 319
  as coordinate of social structure, 228–230
  in early American history, 324–327
  mean generativity dimensions by, 258
  social structural contours of generativity, 242–256
  and technical generativity, 353
  Frank Lloyd Wright on, 405
Egoloss, 139

504   SUBJECT INDEX

Einstein, Albert, 400
Eliot, T. S., 400
Epigenesis, 76
Eriksonian theory of generativity, 7, 450–451
    belief in the species, 11, 26–27
    course of generativity, 75–79
    and fatherhood, 46–47
    fear of death in, 163–165
    intentionalist fallacy in, 168–169
    love in, 135–140
    and midlife, 16, 17
    motivation in, 169–170
    Plato's theory of generativity vs., 134–140, 163–165, 167–173
    and psychobiography, 392–393
    shortcomings of, 135–136
    social roles in, 183–184
Ethics, generative, 69–71
Evolution, 136
Experiencing Scale, 384
Externalization of self, 167–168, 171–173

False self, 276–277
Family generativity, 449, 452
    and agency, 463–464
    and capability, 466–467
    core concepts of, 455–456
    and generative counseling, 475–476
    and holism, 456–457
    and morality, 472–473
    and spirituality, 468–469
    and temporality, 459–460
Fathering and fatherhood, 21–22, 25–26
    among Puritans, 316–317, 322–323
    case study of, 45–73
        active child rearing, examples of, 2–57
        autonomy, development of, 58–59
        and Erikson's theories, 46–47
        ethics, generative, 69–71
        and generativity chill, 61–63
        humor, role of, 58
        and intergenerational conflict, 63–65
        and modeling–reworking, 65–69
        sociohistorical context, 49–52
        study sample, 47–49
        and upward mobility, 59–60
    in early American history, 330

in Eriksonian theory, 78
and technical generativity, 353
Frank Lloyd Wright and, 396–400
Faustian bargain, 400, 431
Felt capacity for generativity, 92–94
Fidelity, 139
Freud, Sigmund, 395, 400

Gandhi, Mahatma, 82–83, 383, 392, 400
Gardner, H., 431
Gay men, generativity in, 273, 277–301
    future research directions, 299–300
    life stories (case studies), 280–299
        Edward, 290–298
        Mark, 281–286, 297–298
        Tim, 286–290, 297–298
    methodology, 277–280
    and socially shared expectations, 297
GBC. See Generative Behavior Checklist
Gender. See also Men; Women
    and agentic–communal desires, 14–15
    in early American history, 328–331
    in Eriksonian theory, 78
    as social structural contour of generativity, 243–249, 253–254, 258
Generation, 268, 269
Generation Xers, 272
Generative agency. See Agency–agentic generativity
Generative Behavior Checklist (GBC), 25, 30, 336
Generative commitment. See Commitment, generative
Generative counseling, 449–450, 452–478
    and agency, 464–466
    and capability, 467–468
    clinical example, 453–455
    core concepts of, 455–456
    and family generativity, 475–476
    generative communities as resources in, 476–478
    and holism, 457–459
    and morality, 473–475
    and spirituality, 470–472
    and temporality, 460–463
Generative morality, 476
Generative narrations, 82
Generative Realization Index, 211
Generativity, 450–452
    behavioral expressions of, 186

Intentionalist fallacy, 168–169
Intergenerational buffers, 367–387
  among Holocaust survivors, 385–386
  and biological generativity, 369–372
  and cultural generativity, 379–383
  definition of, 367–368
  and internal–external points of view,
    386–387
  and memory processing, 383–384
  and parental generativity, 372–375
  and technical generativity, 375–379
Intergenerational conflict, 63–65
Intimate partnerships, 77

Jackson Personality Inventory (JPI), 184,
  186
James, William, 396
JPI. See Jackson Personality Inventory

Kaufmann, Edgar, Jr., 402
Know, Samuel, 326–327
Kotre, John, 393, 444–445

Leadership, and creativity, 488–489
LGS. See Loyola Generativity Scale
Life course perspective, 266–268, 440
Life stories, 9, 11–12, 28–36, 265–266.
    See also Course of generativity
  and buffering, 383–384
  highly generative adults, 30–35
  reform stories, 35–36
Lifton, Robert, 339
Locke, John, 312, 321, 325, 328
Loevinger, J., 22–23
Longitudinal studies, of generativity in
    adulthood, 84–89
  coding, 87–88
  and desires over time, 88–89
  measurement, 86–87
Love
  in Eriksonian theory, 135–140
  in Plato's theory of generativity, 140–
    147
    children, love of, 150–151
    and desire for happiness, 143–145
    and desire for immortality, 145–147
    and desire to possess the beautiful,
      141–143

Loyola Generativity Scale (LGS), 20–23,
  30, 87, 90, 92, 184, 237, 336,
  341, 346, 349, 352
Luther, Martin, 383, 392

Marriage, 212–213
Mastery, 202, 204
Mather, Increase, 317
McAdams, D. P., 394
McClelland, D. C., 106
Medical model of psychotherapy, 452–
  453
Men. See also Fathering/fatherhood; Gay
    men, generativity in
  longitudinal study of generativity in,
    84–85
  response of, to infertility, 201
Mentoring
  by Martha Graham, 437–439
  by Frank Lloyd Wright, 400
MEPSI. See Modified Erikson Psychoso-
    cial Stage Inventory
Middle time, of life cycle, 16–17
Midlife generativity, 16–19, 76, 101
  and adolescent children, 194, 274
  case studies, 82–83
  cross-sectional studies, 80–82
  longitudinal studies, 84–85, 90–94
  and social health, 252–253
Miller, Arthur, 393
Mills Longitudinal Study, 85
Modeling, 65–69
Modified Erikson Psychosocial Stage In-
    ventory (MEPSI), 184, 207
Montesquieu, 324
Morality
  and family generativity, 472–473
  generative, 476
  and generative counseling, 473–475
Mothering and motherhood
  among Puritans, 316–317
  in Eriksonian theory, 78
Motivation, 13–19
  and cultural demand, 15–19
  in Erikson's theory, 169–170
  generativity in women with high, 111–
    118
  generativity in women with low, 118–
    124
  and inner desire, 8, 9, 11, 13–15

Motivation (*continued*)
  in Plato's theory of generativity, 169–170
  TAT as measure of, 103, 105

Narration of generativity, 9, 11–12. *See also* Life stories
Narrative myth, 356
Next generation, concern for, 8, 20–23
Noel, Miriam, 408
Noguci, 433

Oakland Growth Study, 85, 188, 211–212
O'Neill, Eugene, 393
Ouspensky, P. D., 401

Paine, Thomas, 323
Parenting and parental generativity, 80, 274, 368, 450–451. *See also* Fathering
  among gay and lesbian couples, 278–279
  with Holocaust survivors, 346–352
  and intergenerational buffers, 372–375
  and Puritans, 316–317
  and role of parent, 203
Partner role, 203
Paul VI, Pope, 379, 381, 382
Performance sequences, 19–28
  and belief in the species, 26–27
  and commitment, 24–26
  and concern for next generation, 20–23
Personality, 185, 187–189
Personal narration, 268
Personal projects, 199
Personal strivings, 24–25
Physical health, inequalities in, 229–230
Picasso, Pablo, 400, 410
Platonic theory of generativity, 133–173
  desire for immortality in, 155–156
    love, role of, 145–147
    replacement theory, 151–155
    symbolic immortality, 161–167
  Eriksonian theory vs., 134–140, 163–165, 167–173
  and externalization of self, 167–168, 171–173

generative products, 156–161
  evaluation of, 159–161
  typology of, 156–159
intentionalist fallacy in, 169
love in, 140–147
  children, love of, 150–151
  and desire for happiness, 143–145
  and desire for immortality, 145–147
  and desire to possess the beautiful, 141–143
motivation in, 169–171
procreation in, 147–149
and replacement theory of immortality, 151–155
and triadic character of generativity, 149–150
as unrecognized theory, 133–134
value of, 134
Private roles, 182
Procreation and procreativity, 78–79, 137, 147–149, 157, 202
Productivity, 80, 202, 204
Protas, Ron, 435
Psychobiography, 392–396, 430–431
Psychotherapy, medical model of, 452–453
Puritans, 312, 315–323
  in 17th century, 315–321
  in 18th century, 321–323

Q sorts, 87, 90, 92, 94, 102–109, 111, 115, 117–119, 122, 126
Qualities, generative, 237
Quality of experience, and roles, 193

Radcliffe Longitudinal Study of the Class of 1964, 85–92, 107–108
Realization. *See also* Performance sequences
  generativity desire vs., 89–94
  generativity in women with high, 111–114, 118–122
  generativity in women with low, 114–118, 122–124
Rebay, Hilla, 418–419
Redemption sequences, 32, 33, 124
Reform stories, 35–36
Rejectivity, 47
Religion. *See also* Spirituality

of Puritans, 316, 322
and worshipper role, 203
Replacement theory of immortality, 151–155, 162
Reputation, 154
Reworking, 372
Ritual life, 270
Robinson, John, 318
Role balance, 192, 194–195
Role enhancement hypothesis, 191
Roles. *See* Social roles
Role scarcity hypothesis, 191
Root, John Wellborn, 411
Rush, Benjamin, 325, 329
Russell, Carroll, 434, 443

Seattle Longitudinal Study, 269
Self
externalization of, 167–168, 171–173
false, 276–277
selection–management of generativity expressions by, 198–199
Self-perception of generativity, 80–81
Sexual abuse, 384–385
Sexual orientation, 277–279
Shawn, Ted, 432
Situational imperatives, 197
Smith, Samuel Harrison, 325–327
Snarey, John, 393
Social activism, 279–280
Social identity, formation of, 77, 78
Social roles, 181–218, 487–488
definition of, 182–183
in Erikson's theory, 183–184
examples of, 203
and expectations, 189
ignoring of, as factor in generativity, 185–189
and measures of generativity, 184–185
as processes, 190, 197–201
longitudinal aspects, 201
monitoring–adjusting, 200–201
selecting–managing, 198–200
in quantitative study of generativity, 202–216
future research directions, 211–216
method, 204–206
results, 206–211
structure of, 189–197
and balance of commitments, 191–192

and breadth–diversity, 192–193
and developmental sequences, 196
and interrelationships among roles, 195–196
and quality of experience, 193
and relative importance of roles, 193–195
role-specific approaches, 190–191
Social structural contours of generativity, 227–258. *See also* Social roles
age, 242–249
as coordinate of social structure, 228–230
and education, 228–229, 242–243
mean generativity dimensions, 258
education, 242–256
and age, 228–229, 242–243
as coordinate of social structure, 228–230
mean generativity dimensions, 258
future research directions, 257
gender, 243–249, 253–254, 258
operational definitions, 236–242
generativity, 236–239
social structure, 242
well-being, 239–242
and personal benefits of generativity, 230, 247, 249
and psychological–social well-being, 232–234, 239–242
research findings, 242–253
life quality consequences, 247, 249–253
social structural contours, 243–249
research sample, 234–235
and self, 230–232
Social time, 270–272
Sociohistorical factors, in generativity, 275–276
Spirituality. *See also* Religion
and family generativity, 468–469
and generative counseling, 470–472
Spivey, Ludd Myrl, 417
Spouse role, 203
St. Denis, Ruth, 429, 432
Stages of development, 76–78, 136, 182, 190, 274, 341, 419
Status, 13
Stone, Lawrence, 321
Stravinsky, Igor, 400

Suffering
  and generativity, 490
  sensitivity to, in others, 31
Sullivan, Louis, 401, 411, 412, 418, 420
Survivor syndrome, 337–338
Symbolic immortality, 161–167
Symbolic interactionism, 189

Taliesin Fellowship, 391, 400–407
  motivation for creation of, 401–402
  structure and climate of, 403–405
  teaching in, 405–406
TAT. See Thematic Apperception Test
Technical generativity, 274, 352–353, 368
  and intergenerational buffers, 375–379
Temporality
  and family generativity, 459–460
  and generative counseling, 460–463
Thematic Apperception Test (TAT), 14, 86, 87, 90, 94, 102–109, 111, 114, 122, 126, 336, 346, 350
Time
  cultural conception of, 15–16
  social, 270–272
  working toward goals over, 201
Tobin, Catherine, 397–400
Tolstoy, Leo, 393
Transcendence, 469

University of California, Los Angeles Study, 85
Universal generativity, 354–355
University of Michigan Class of 1967 Study, 86–92
Upward mobility, 59–60
Usonia, 415–418
Utopianism, of Frank Lloyd Wright, 415–418

Vaillant, G. E., 393–394
Virginia, Colonial, 313–315
Virtue, 158
Volunteerism, 35, 193–195

Washington, George, 323

Welfare reform, 181
Well-being, psychological–social, 232–234, 239–242, 247, 249–252
Wentworth, Michael, 321
Willard, Samuel, 320
Winthrop, John, 317
Women, 10. See also Mothering and motherhood
  longitudinal studies of generativity in, 85–89
  multiple case studies of generativity in
    high motivation–high realization, women with, 111–114
    high motivation–low realization, women with, 114–118
    low motivation–high realization, women with, 118–122
    low motivation–low realization, women with, 122–124
  participants, 107–110
  and roles, 204
  self-perception of generativity in, 80–81
Worker role, 203
Worshipper role, 203
Wright, David, 397
Wright, Frank Lloyd, 390, 391–392, 395–425
  as architect, 407–419
    and buildings as extensions of self, 409–411
    and generativity chill, 407–409
    and "truth" in architecture, 411–415
    and utopianism, 415–418
  as father, 396–400
  life chronology, 421–425
  psychobiographic approach to life of, 395–396
  Taliesin Fellowship, 400–407
    motivation for creation of, 401–402
    structure–climate of, 403–405
    teaching in, 405–406
Wright, John Lloyd, 397–399, 405, 406, 408, 414
Wright, Lloyd, 398

Zionism, 354

ABOUT THE EDITORS

Dan P. McAdams is the Charles Deering McCormick Professor of Teaching Excellence and professor of human development and psychology at Northwestern University. He is author of numerous books and articles in the fields of personality psychology and adult development, including his textbook, *The Person: An Introduction to Personality Psychology* (Harcourt Brace, 1994), and the widely heralded *The Stories We Live By: Personal Myths and the Making of the Self* (Guilford Press, 1993). McAdams has pioneered research and theorizing on adult identity and the modern self, developing the life-story model of adult identity, and in the areas of generativity and social responsibility, intimacy motivation, and psychological biography. Winner of the 1989 Henry A. Murray Award from the American Psychological Association, McAdams is a leading spokesperson for the personological tradition in psychology and for the emerging narrative paradigm in the study of lives.

Ed de St. Aubin is assistant professor of human development and psychology at the University of Wisconsin, Green Bay. His research activities and publications lie in the area of life-span developmental psychology, focusing particularly on generativity, life narrative, and the development of personal ideology. De St. Aubin has articulated a new model of personal ideology in the adult years that incorporates the development of personal values, political orientation, religiosity, morality, and assumptions about human nature as embedded in family, schools, culture, and history. He is the recipient of several teaching awards, including selection as a Wisconsin Teaching Fellow and featured faculty member of the University of Wisconsin, Green Bay.